MOGUL INDIA
1653–1708
OR
STORIA DO MOGOR

Frontispiece

MOGUL INDIA
1653–1708
OR
STORIA DO MOGOR

Volume 1

Translated with Introduction and Notes
WILLIAM IRVINE

NICCOLAO MANUCCI

PUBLISHERS & DISTRIBUTORS (P) LTD

7/22, Ansari Road, Darya Ganj, New Delhi
Tel.: +91-11-4077 5252, 2327 3880
E-mail: orders@atlanticbooks.com
Web: www.atlanticbooks.com

Reprint 2022, 2025, 2026

Published by Atlantic Publishers & Distributors (P) Ltd.

Printed & bound in India by Atlantic Print Services

PUBLISHERS' NOTE

This volume is a verbatim reprint of a book, or rather manuscript, which never saw print till the years 1907-9 when it saw the light of day in the excellent four-volume edition published in the Indian Text Series in London.

It gives a vivid eye-witness' account of Mughal India during the reign of Shahjahan (1628-1658), of which period the author draws a rather partial picture of the last six years, and deals fully with the reign of Aurangzeb (1659-80).

Niccolao Manucci was a native of Venice. He was born in 1639 and reached India in 1656. He went to Delhi at a time when the Mughal Court had taken up its residence. During the struggle between Dara on the one hand and Aurangzeb and Morad Bux on the other, he succeeded in obtaining a position of artilleryman in the army of Dara on whose fall he fled to Agra and attached himself in disguise to the army of Aurangzeb. Subsequently he joined the service of Raja Jai Singh (1664 A.D.). He met Shivaji at Aurangabad in 1865. He had a romantic career and occupied various positions of trust and responsibility in the Mughal Court. After resigning his service in the evening of his life he made his way to Bassam, north of Bombay, and stayed for some time in Goa. He was granted late in life by the Governor and Council of Madras household land in perpetuity together with a house in the city where he died in 1717.

Spending as he did a life-time in Mughal India, the record of his reminiscences published here in this volume cannot but be of the highest value. Catrou, the French historian of the Mughal Empire who wrote in 1705 had access to his original MSS. written partially in French, Italian and Portuguese. Like its author, the MSS. wandered from India to France, Italy, Holland, England and finally in Germany where these first came to light in book form.

Needless to add, Manucci played many significant roles in Indian history. He fought in the battle which made Aurangzeb master of the Mughal Empire. He gives herein a succinct, discursive narrative, but all the more interesting and valuable is his work on that account, and as Irvine so aptly puts it, "he supplies us with the necessary correction of life-like detail."

On long and insistent demand from research scholars and the reading public, the first volume is being published, to be followed up by subsequent three volumes in the near future. It is hoped that like the other celebrated travellers' account of the Mughal Empire, this work will be found of great interest and value to students of historical research.

A word now remains to be said about William Irvine (1840-1911), who is responsible for unearthing the Manucci MSS., and bringing to light this valuable historical document in its English version. He joined the Indian Civil Service in 1863. He was Magistrate and Collector N. W. Provinces till 1889 and acted subsequently in various executive and judicial capacities in Bengal. In the 'Journal of the Royal Asiatic Society', Bengal. 1896-1908, he wrote on Mughal history. In a series of articles in the 'Indian Antiquary', 1907, he wrote on Ahmed Shah Abdali and the Indian Wazir 'Imad-ul-Mulk (1756-7). He possessed all those qualities that characterise a historian and translator as will be evident from the perusal of the following pages.

GENERAL INTRODUCTION TO THE INDIAN TEXTS SERIES

When on an archæological tour in India in the cold season of 1899-1900, I obtained the honour of an interview with the Viceroy, and was permitted to lay before him the outline of a scheme for the publication of a series of books of reference on the history of India. Lord Curzon was pleased so far to approve of the idea that he wished to have the scheme laid in fuller detail before him. Accordingly, on my return home, I submitted a draft scheme to the Council of the Royal Asiatic Society. This received the approval of the Council, and the following letter was addressed to the Government of India:

Royal Asiatic Society,
22, Albemarle Street,
London, W.,
June 12, 1900.

Sir,

I am desired by the President and Council of this Society to ask you to be kind enough to lay the following considerations before His Excellency the Viceroy.

The Society venture to ask the Government of India to take into consideration the desirability of publishing a series of historical volumes corresponding to the Rolls Series and the publications of the Historical Manuscripts Commission, published by the English Government.

It is perhaps unnecessary to point out how great have been the results of the publication long ago of two such volumes. The 'Mémoires sur les Contrées Occidentals,' translated by Julien from the Chinese of Hiouen Thsang, and published by the French Government in 1857, have been the foundation of almost all that has been written since on the Archæology of India. And the publication, in 1837, by the Government of Ceylon, of the 'Great Chronicle' of that island has afforded evidence on which many of the main conclusions as to the early history of India depend.

The cost of such a series as is proposed would be very small. It would be desirable only to undertake such works as are both of real importance, and also of such a character that their publication would not pay commercially—conditions also observed in the case of the Rolls Series. The Society could undertake to produce two volumes annually at a cost of £240 per volume (see detailed estimate annexed), and any sums received by the sale of them could be applied towards the cost of future volumes.

The volumes would consist partly of texts, partly of translations, such as the two above mentioned; partly of indices or dictionaries (similar in method to, but smaller in scale than, Smith's well-known dictionaries) of proper names, personal or geographical, of importance for the history of India; and partly of monographs summarizing the historical data scattered through the numerous Oriental texts now accessible to scholars.

The documents in question would have little or no literary merit. They would be materials out of which the history of the development of the social conditions, the industries, and the political relations of the peoples of India could be reconstructed. The texts to be translated or explored would not be histories in our modern sense, even when they purport to be chronicles. In both these respects they would be like the historical documents published in the Rolls Series.

The series might be called the 'Indian Historical Series.' To be a success it would have to be placed under skilled general editorship, and each volume should be entrusted to a scholar so trained in the methods of historical research as to be able, in introduction, notes, and indices, to gather together or elucidate all the historical information obtainable from the document he edits or explores.

For these reasons it would be desirable that, for the present at least, the series should be supervised here; and the authors of the first volume to appear should be European scholars of the first rank. But the editor might be instructed to make use also of native Indian scholarship whenever it should be possible to do so.

No money would be necessary till January, 1902, as at least eighteen months must elapse, after the approval of the scheme, before any payments would be required.

The above estimate of cost is inclusive—that is, it covers the cost of editorship, authorship, printing, binding, insurance, and other miscellaneous charges—and with the gradual increase of the number of volumes on sale the series would in course of time, it may be hoped, become self-supporting.

The publication of such a series is essential to the future progress of the study of Indian History and Archaeology. And considering the smallness of the amount required and the number of precedents that might be quoted in its favour, this Society venture to hope that the proposed scheme will meet with the approval and support of the Government of India.

I have etc.,

T. W. Rhys Davids,

Secretary.

After some correspondence the scheme was finally adopted by the Secretary of State for India, in a letter to the Society, dated November 4, 1902, enclosing the following dispatch from His Excellency the Governor-General in Council:

To the Right Honourable Lord George Francis Hamilton,
His Majesty's Secretary of State for India.

Simla,
July 3, 1902,
No. 191 of 1902.

My Lord,

We have the honour to forward, for Your Lordship's information, a copy of the correspondence noted in the annexed list, on the subject of a suggestion made by the Royal Asiatic Society, London, regarding the publication by the Indian Government of a series of historical volumes corresponding to the Rolls Series and the publications of the Historical Manuscripts Commission.

2. The Society suggest that the volumes should consist partly of texts and partly of translations; and should also include indices or dictionaries of proper names, personal or geographical, of importance for the history of India, and monographs summarizing the historical data scattered through the numerous Oriental texts which are accessible to scholars. The Society are of opinion that, while these documents would have little or no literary merit, they would constitute materials out of which the history of the

development of the social conditions, the industries, and the political relations of the peoples of India could be reconstructed. They suggest that the series might be called the 'Indian Historical Series'; that each volume should be entrusted to a scholar trained in the methods of historical research; that the series should be placed under skilled general editorship in England; and that the editor might be instructed to make use of native Indian scholarship whenever it is possible to do so. The Society offer us their assistance in the matter of publication, and undertake to produce two volumes annually at a cost of £240 per volume.

3. The proposals of the Society meet with our cordial support, and we would make the following suggestions in connection therewith for Your Lordship's approval. We would divide the series into two parts—the one to be called the 'Indian Records Series' and the other the 'Indian Texts Series.' We propose that the 'Indian Records Series' should consist of selections, notes, or compilations from the records of the Indian Governments or of the India Office, supplemented and elucidated where necessary by local inquiry. This series would correspond generally with the English Historical Manuscripts Series, except that the latter deals with private, whereas the former will deal with public records. The greater part of this work would be done in India. But lacunæ in our records might often be supplied from the India Office records, and we are of opinion that the general editing of this portion of the work should be done in England.

4. The 'Indian Texts Series' should consist of annotated editions of or translations or abstracts of or compilations from the works of Indian writers, such as Blochmann's 'Ain-i-Akbari,' Stein's 'Raja Tarangini,' Julien's 'Hwen Tsang,' or Beale's 'Buddhist Pilgrims.' As regards less important authors, little more than brief tables of contents would be needed. At the same time, as suggested by the Royal Asiatic Society, indices, dictionaries, and monographs should not be neglected. The former should aim, not so much at complete information as at complete bibliography. The salient facts being given and sufficient information to identify the man or place, mere references would be sufficient to sources of information which are readily accessible to scholars, though information from sources more difficult of access might be abstracted with some fulness. This series would correspond generally with the Rolls Series,

except that it would deal with times prior to British rule. We think that it should be not only edited, but also for the most part written at home, although we would emphasize the suggestion of the Royal Asiatic Society that the editor should be instructed to make use of Indian scholarship (European or Native) to the fullest extent. The management of the series should, however, be left to the Royal Asiatic Society.

5. The two series would thus be quite distinct as regards authorship and editing. We would propose that two volumes a year in each series should be published, and that the Royal Asiatic Society should be entrusted with the publication of both series if, after a scrutiny of their estimate, which we have no means of making, your lordship considers that their terms are reasonable. With this object we would make a grant of Rs. 15,000 a year for the next five years to meet the expenditure involved in the proposals, which we trust will meet with Your Lordship's approval. In that event, we would ask Your Lordship to inform the Royal Asiatic Society of what has been decided upon. We propose to retain in our own hands the decision as to what books should be published in either series, and in what order.

We have, etc.

As will be noticed, the scheme was, by this decision, not only accepted, but doubled; and shortly afterwards the Government added, to be reckoned as extra volumes in the Indian Texts Series, two volumes of the text, and two of the translation of an Arabic history of Gujarat, then recently discovered by Mr. Denison Ross, Principal of the Calcutta Madrasa. Extra volumes have, in like manner, been added to the Indian Records Series. And besides these additions the Government has, in several cases, made extra grants for special illustrations to be inserted in volumes sanctioned under this scheme.

Under the original scheme the Society undertook the publishing; and the proceeds of the sales, without any deduction for publisher's commissions, were to be applied towards the production of future volumes. In this way it was hoped that the scheme would eventually become self-supporting. Since then it has since been thought advisable to place the publishing arrangements in the hands of Mr. Murray; and the India Office has taken charge of the preparation and production of the Records Series, leaving the Texts Series in the hands of the Royal Asiatic Society.

Having accepted the chair of Comparative Religion at the University of Manchester, I shall only retain official connection with the scheme long enough to wind up work already commenced under the original publishing arrangements. At the moment of assisting at its launch I have, therefore (though glad to obtain leisure urgently needed for other work), with much regret, to bid it farewell. But it is in able hands. And I may be permitted to express the confident hope that a scheme so generously adopted by Government, and so generously enlarged and improved, will continue through the years to provide a succession of just the sort of books that, as tools to a craftsman, will enable the historian of India to trace out the evolution of social institutions, religion, and literature, in the same manner as the provision of the necessary tools has enabled the historians of Europe to do for the West.

The result cannot fail to be of value for the history of humanity as a whole, for what, in the absence of a better word in English, we are compelled to call *Weltgeschichte*. Already, in the history of government, of tribal customs, of land tenure, and of marriage, the Indian evidence has been much used by, and has proved of considerable service to, Western scholars. It will certainly prove more so in proportion as it becomes fuller and more exact. There are many similar questions on which the Indian evidence has not been utilized merely because it is not sufficiently known. And there is action and reaction in all these matters. The more the Indian evidence is used and compared with evidence from other sources, the greater is the light thrown upon the real value and bearing and meaning of the facts recorded in India, the clearer are our views of the order in which they should be arranged, the more suggestive and instructive the study tends to be.

To make a few paths and clearings in the thorny jungle of Indian history is not, therefore, mere useless dry-as-dust work. And there is another consideration. It has long been a matter for regret that the natives of India afford us so small a degree of help in the study of the history of their own country or countries. For one Englishman who can read the ancient literatures with facility there must be scores of natives. Yet how very little of permanent value have they, as yet, accomplished in history. This cannot be for want of intellectual power. As lawyers they show great ability in weighing the value of evidence, and in drawing guarded and reasonable conclusions from complicated documents. And one or two of the native scholars who have devoted their attention to this branch of inquiry have rendered excellent service. Perhaps the methods of the University examinations in India, in which literary fluency counts for so much, and historical criticism for so little, are in some measure answerable for this neglect. But is it too much to hope that, when this series of scholarly handbooks shall have placed in their hands sufficient examples of the right methods in historical research, some of them may be moved by emulation to take up these studies for themselves, and themselves to join, in much larger numbers, in the work? Is it too much even to expect that a more widely diffused knowledge of the history of their own land; of the causes that led to intellectual achievements, and also to long periods of intellectual decay; of the reasons why the social and economic conditions were in some times and places favourable, in others almost disastrous; of the predisposing factors of the rise and fall of governments—is it too much to expect that knowledge of such questions, and of the many similar ones that are included under the name of history, may incidentally also have its due effect in suggesting and strengthening, among the educated youth of India, high ideals of life and policy?

T. W. Rhys Davids.

Harboro Grange,
Ashton-on-Mersey,
August 5, 1906.

CONTENTS

BOOK II—OF THE MOGUL KINGS UP TO THE REIGNING SOVEREIGN, AURANGZEB

217; Shah Shuja', 218; Rajmahal, invasion of snakes, 219; Aurangzeb, 220; Roshan-ara Begam, 220; Aurangzeb's trick on the *faqirs*, 221; Shekh Mir's advice to Aurangzeb, 221; story of Aurangzeb and the Rajput, 221; Aurangzeb in love, 222; Mir Jumlah, 222; Mir Jumlah arrives at Dihli, N. Manucci sees him, 228; preparations for a Qandahar campaign, 228; gift of a great diamond to Shahjahan, 228; Ortenzio Bronzoni, lapidary, 229; Mir Jumlah sent back to the Dakhin, 229; Roshan Ara Begam, 230; Murad Bakhsh, 230; Mihr-un-nissa Begam, 231; illness of Shahjahan (1657), 231; Shah Shuja' takes the field, 232; Sulaiman Shukoh and Jai Singh sent against him, 234; Aurangzeb's attitude, 237; he rebels, 237; persuades Murad Bakhsh to join him, 238; Mir Jumlah's apparent neutrality, 239; the other generals, except one, join Aurangzeb, 242; Aurangzeb offers Murad the throne, 242; Dara's preparations, 245; an imperial army defeated near Mandu, 248; Jaswant Singh, Rathor, story of his wife, 249; Aurangzeb advances on Agrah, 252; Dara entrenches himself on the Chambal, 257; Aurangzeb's flank march, 258; battle near Samugarh (June 8, 1658), N. Manucci present, 259; defeat of Dara, 269; Sulaiman Shukoh, 272; his flight to Garhwal, 274; Dara's retreat to Agrah, 274; thence to Dihli, 274; Aurangzeb occupies Agrah, 276; N. Manucci returns to Agrah, and attempts to follow Dara, 277; Shahjahan invested in Agrah fort, 278; the fort occupied, 282; Aurangzeb and Murad Bakhsh leave Agrah, 284; N. Manucci joins their camp in disguise, 284; seizure of Murad Bakhsh, 286; N. Manucci starts for Lahor, 294; joins Dara at Lahor, 294; Sarup Singh's breach of faith, 296; Dara's march on Multan and Bhakkar, 297; Da,ud Khan Qureshi's fidelity, 302; pursuit by Aurangzeb's army, 302; Bhakkar garrisoned under Basant, eunuch—N. Manucci commands artillery, 303; Shah Shuja' re-appears, 304; Aurangzeb turns back, 305; meets Jai Singh, 305; account of the Panjab and its rivers, 306; imports by caravans, 307; Dara leaves Bhakkar for Sindi and Tattah, 307; Dara in Gujarat, 309; siege of Bhakkar, 309; Aurangzeb's movements, 311; Battle of Kajwah, 311; retreat of Shah Shuja', 315; Jaswant Singh's conduct, 315; Mir Jumlah pursues Shuja' to Bengal, 317; Sultan Muhammad deserts to Shah Shuja', 319;

INTRODUCTION

Through the generosity of the Government of India the elaborate Storia do Mogor,' sent to Europe by Niccolao Manucci more than two hundred years ago, now first reaches the public as he wrote it (allowing for the change from Portuguese and French and Italian into English). It can hardly be said to have earned him the renown for which he laboured so long and so diligently. In his lifetime it was captured and practically suppressed by a Jesuit editor, and the work, as presented to the public by that editor, has ever since borne the brunt of much adverse criticism. Even the true spelling of the author's name has never yet been settled. Beginning with his own form of Manucci, it passed into Manouchi, until, after many variations, it appears as the Manuech of the Madras 'Records and the 'my old acqaintance Senor Monnock' of worthy Jeremiah Peachey, dismissed 'Chief of Mauldah.' An attempt is now made to show the man and his book in their true light, so that in future the shortcomings attributed to the one and the other may be at least their own and not those of somebody else. The inclusion of the work in the present series is due to the initiative of Mr. A. N. Wollaston, C.I.E., of the India Office, following on the paper read by me before the Royal Asiatic Society in June, 1903, and the note subsequently drawn up, which appeared in the *Journal of the Royal Asiatic Society* for October, 1903, pp. 723-733.

II. CATROU'S 'HISTOIRE GENERALE DE L'EMPIRE DU MOGOL,' 1705

Appearance of Book (1705)

In 1705 there appeared at Paris a quarto volume of 272 pages entitled 'Histoire Generale de l'Empire du Mogol depuis sa fondation, sur les Memoires de M. Manouchi, Vénitien, par le Pere François Catrou, de la Compagnie de Jésus.' There is an epistle dedicatory to the Due de Bourgogne (1682-1712), grandson of Louis XIV., and a preface of eight (unnumbered) pages. The subjects treated are Tamberlank, Miracha, Abou Chaid, Sec Omor, Babar, Amahum, Akbar, Jean-Guir, and Cha-Jahan, till the end of the war of succession (1659). The last of these reigns occupies 78 pages. The work concludes with 40 pages of a 'Description de la Cour, des Forces, des Richesses, et du Gouvernement, des Empereurs Mogols.'

WHO AND WHAT WAS CATROU

François Catrou was born at Paris on December 28, 1659, joined the Jesuit Society on October 28, 1678, and died at Paris on October 12, 1737. He was the author of some five separate works, among them a discredited ' History of the Romans' (21 volumes), published in 1721-1737, and translated into English in 1728-1737 (6 volumes, folio). For twelve years, 1701-1712, he edited the literary organ *Journal de Trévoux* and acquired some reputation as a critic, though he displayed singularly little critical acumen in not discarding the earlier for the later and really valuable part of Manucci's historical notices. He was thus a practised and experienced literary man; but on the whole it would not be a libel to style him something of a hack writer, ready to undertake any task, whether he knew anything of the subject or not. Certainly he managed to give the *coup de grace* to the work sent home by Manucci, without establishing any permanent reputation for himself in the process. When he says in his second preface (1715) that the 'Mémoires' were confided to him by Manucci himself, he tells a deliberate lie; for, as we shall see farther on, the unfortunate Italian had vigorously protested nine years before—namely, in 1706—that his manuscript had been communicated to the Jesuits without his knowledge or consent.

CATROU'S ACCOUNT OF HIS ORIGINAL

In his first preface of 1705 Catrou tells us, more truthfully, that he obtained Manucci's manusscript from M. Deslandes, a Pondicherry official, who had brought it to Europe in 1701 or 1702. As to the truth of the earlier historical events, Catrou (Preface, p. 2) relies for proof of authenticity on Manucci's assertion (Text, I. 55) that his facts were taken direct from official chronicles. But in reality, for the period preceding Shahjahan—that is, up to the year 1617—Manucci's history is no more than a tissue of popular stories of no historical value whatever. Thus Catrou, in his volume of 31705, reproduced for the most part what are perhaps the least valuable chapters of Manucci's text. The volume of 1705 ends with the struggle in 1658 between Aurangzeb and his brothers for the imperial throne.

USE OF OTHER SOURCES

Catrou was not content to draw his matter from Manucci alone; he tells us in the *Journal de Trévoux* for 1705, p. 128, and in his first preface (p. 6), that he also had recourse to Maffei, Tossi, Texeira, Pietro della Valle, Thomas Roe, Jean de Laët, Bernier, Tavernier, and D'Herbelot. In the course of another notice on pp. 574-580 of the same volume of the *Journal de Trévoux* he boasts that Manucci is only the *fondement* of his work. He also in his preface acknowledges aid received from another M. Deslandes, connected with Tavernier's works, and still alive in 1705. This is evidently A. Daulier Deslandes, author of 'Les Beautes de la Perse' (1673), who, so far ias I can find out, was never in India at all.[1] Owing to Catrou's giving no indication of which of these sources he is at the moment using, and Manucci himself having hitherto been inaccessible, it has been impossible to know in reading 'L'Histoire' what statements are to be attributed to Manucci and what to other writers.

MENTIONS OF CATROU'S WORK. R. ORME (1728-1801)

Robert Orme, Historiographer to the East India Company, is, so far as I know, the first writer to make use of Catrou's 'Histoire.' After the publication in 1763 of his great work 'The Military Transactions of the British Nation in Indostan from the Year 1745,' Orme began to collect materials for a continuation, his plan including a résumé of Indian history from the year of Aurangzeb's accession (1658). At his death on January 13, 1801, his design was still incomplete; but we have the result of his forty years' labour in his valuable 'Historical Fragments,' the first

1. J. P. Maffeius, 'Historiarum Indicarum,' 1589.
Joannes de Laët, 'De Imperio Magni Mogolis sive India Vera,' 1631.
Pietro de la Valle, 'Les Fameux Voyages,' 4 vols., 4to., 1663, 1664; or in M. Thevenot's collection, 1696.
E. Terry (Sir Thomas Roe's chaplain), 'A Voyage to East India,' 1665; or in Thevenot's 'Divers Voyages,' 1663.
L'Abati Tosi, 'Dell' India Orientale Descrittione,' 1669.
F. Bernier, 'Histoire de la dernière Révolution des Etats du Grand Mogol,' Paris, 1670, 1671.
J. B. Tavernier, 'Les Six Voyages,' 2 vols., Paris, 1676.
P. Teixeira, 'Voyages ' (French translation), 1681.
B. D. d'Herbelot, 'Bibliothèque Orientale,' 1697.

edition published in 1782 (octavo), and the second (quarto) in 1805, after his death. As Orme himself says (p. 169), 'We have taken largely from this work'—*i.e.,* Catrou's. Although Orme knew that Manucci had been at Madras in 1691, he had no access to his manuscripts, and, while admitting the elegance of Catrou's style and the interest of his narrations, comments (pp. 168, 169) on the want of chronological arrangement, and the errors in the few dates given. To this subject of chronology we will recur. In Orme's book there are at least eighteen references to Catrou and Manucci combined.

ANQUETIL DUPERRON (1731-1805)

In 1778 A. H. Anquetil Duperron published at Amsterdam his 'Legislation Orientale' (quarto), and in the index he describes Manouchi as a Venetian physician at the court of the Mogul, whose memoirs he saw in 1763 in the library of the Jesuit Professed House at Paris, this manuscript being the original of Father Catrou's work. Duperron makes over twenty quotations from Catrou in support of his various contentions.

J. BERNOUILLI (1744-1807)

J. Bernouilli in his 'Beschreibung von Hindustan founded on Pere Joseph Tieffenthaler's papers), vol. ii., part ii. (1788), p. 192, has an interesting note on Manucci in reference to Tieffenthaler's criticism (vol. i., p. 29) of the erroneous latitudes and longitudes which appear in Catrou (edition of 1705, pp. 258-261). Tieffenthaler declares Manucci 'a better physician than geographer or astronomer.' If so, Heaven help him, for as a physician his learning was of the crudest. However, the whole of the statements so criticised are absent from Manucci's text, and must have come from some one or other of Catrou's additional sources. Similar instances of misleading interpolations will be referred to farther on. Bernouilli had, however, a most just sense of the need for the original text, for he says: 'This work (Manucci) is worth printing just as the author wrote it, in Portuguese. I invite its learned owner to endow the public with it' ('Recherches sur l'Inde,' 1787, ii., note *a* to p. 284).

J. GRANT-DUFF (1789-1858)

In his 'History of the Maratthas,' first published in 1826, J. Grant-Duff makes more than one reference to Catrou. On p. 88

(Bombay edition of 1873) he uses him to confirm Khafi Khan's account of Shiva Ji's device for getting into Shaistah Khan's quarters at Poonah (see Manucci's text, Part II., 77), and again he quotes him on p. 92 (note) as to a point in Jai Singh's Dakhin campaign. On p. 99 he contests Catrou's assertion that the rebellion of Aurangzeb's son Mu'azzam was collusive (Manucci's text, Part II., p. 122; Catrou, p. 79 of part iii., edition of 1715).

M. ELPHINSTONE (1779-1859)

Next we come to Elphinstone's 'History of India,' published in 1841. In at least one instance, p. 554, fourth edition, he quotes Catrou (or Manucci) for events in the reign of Aurangzeb; and although, in agreement with Grant-Duff's view, he considers the story absurd, it would be easy to show that the objection made by him on chronological grounds is untenable.

M. MULLBAUER

In 1852 Maximilian Müllbauer brought out at Freiburg im Breisgau a most useful work on Catholic missions, 'Geschichte der Katholischen Missionen in Ostindien' (372 pages, 8vo.). He makes some thirteen citations from Catrou. Unfortunately for him, most of these passages are not to be found in Manucci's text, and cannot, therefore, be supported by his authority, whatever it may be worth. I will comment on this more precisely later on.

W. ERSKINE (1773-1852) AND E. THOMAS (1813-1883)

W. Erskine in his 'History of India' (Baber and Humayun), London, 1854, vol. i., pp. 542, 543, quotes with approval the statement of Aurangzeb's revenue given in Catrou, p. 264, 4to. edition of 1705; and Edward Thomas in 'The Chronicles of the Pathan Kings of Delhi' (1871), refers to the same passage, reproducing at the same time Mr. Erskine's misprint of Catron for Catrou. In his appendix (p. 443) he gives the figures in a tabulated form, and on pp. 447-450 inserts the French text of Catrou, pp. 264-267. By a supplementary treatise published the same year (1871) under the title 'The Revenue Resources of the Mughal Empire in India,' E. Thomas returns to the subject, and on pp. 44-48 gives the figures once again, with a further passage of the French text on the miscellaneous heads of revenue. Although rejecting Catrou as a worthless witness in himself,

Mr. Thomas is, on the whole, inclined to accept Manucci's evidence. In fact, he places much more reliance on his figures than I should be prepared to do myself.

H. G. KEENE (1823)

Considerable attention is given to Catrou's work by Mr. H. G. Keene in his 'Turks in India' (1879). On p. 14 of the introduction he quotes Manucci's value for a 'sol,' and on p. 15 he inserts his statements of the Mogul revenues. On p. 116 he notices with approval Manucci's refutation of Bernier's imputations on Jahan Ara Begam, daughter of Shahjahan. His comments upon Catrou's mode of dealing with his materials are excellent and to the point. We cordially agree with Mr. Keene's summing up, p. 118, that 'the Father would have done far better to have left his author to tell his own story.' Many details are given erroneously in Mr. Keene's account, as can be seen from our author's text and the rest of this Introduction. Manucci landed in India in 1656, not 1649; the person to whom he entrusted his manuscript was not Laudes, but Deslandes (Catrou, Preface, 2); the 'favourable mentions' of Catholic missionaries are not Manucci's but mostly inserted by Catrou himself; in 1705 Manucci was certainly alive, but in India, not in Europe; the paintings have *not* disappeared: they are in the Bibliothéque Nationale at Paris, Département des Estampes, and we give reproductions of them; the first edition of Catrou is of 1705, not 1708.

J.T. WHEELER (1824-1897)

The late J. Talboys Wheeler in the introduction to vol. iv, part i., of his 'History of India,' published in 1876, refers to his frequent citations from Catrou, whom he considered as the very best authority for Shahjahan's reign. He had not then seen Catrou's continuation, published in 1715. In 1881, when part ii of his fourth volume appeared, Mr. Wheeler returns to the subject. By that time he had obtained a copy of the volume of 1715, but hazarded the assertion that the original memoirs, written in Portuguese, had not then been discovered.

S. LANE-POOLE (1854-1931)

Another writer who quotes freely from Catrou is Professor S. Lane-Poole, in his 'Aurangzib' (Rulers of India), 1893. His view is that the work is full of errors, savours strongly of the *chronique scandaleuse,* and is the production of a malicious and disappointed backstairs underling. But he adds that Catrou's 'Histoire' would be 'invaluable if there were any means of authenticating it by comparison with Manucci's MS.' An article in the *Quarterly, Review* for April, 1893 (p. 519), couched in the same strain, may probably be attributed to the same writer, since a desire for the production of the Portuguese text is again expressed. Our present volumes, giving a close and faithful rendering of that text, are it is hoped, a sufficient compliance with Professor Lane-Poole's requisition. Until in 1893 Mr. Poole drew my attention to the French edition of 1715, I had read Catrou only in the English version of 1826.

CATROU'S METHOD OF DEALING WITH MANUCCI'S TEXT

It is already abundantly clear that from the first Catrou's mode of editing his text has not met with approval. Anyone dealing who consults the volumes now produced by me will agree, I think, that Catrou, for literary effect, acted wisely. He began ' by throwing overboard all, or almost all, personal narrative, looking on it as so much useless lumber, and then proceeded to dress out the rest according to his notions of what a history should be. While he thus produced a more artistic book, he much diminished, if he did not totally destroy, the authority of Manucci as an original source of history. It might even be doubted, confining one's self to Catrou's pages, whether Manucci ever was in India; or, grating that he did reach India, whether he had ever seen any more of it than a little of the country round Goa, and perhaps the town of Madras. If Manucci's narrative had already been in print, and thus available for reference, Catrou would have been justified in rearranging the material in his own way. But our ideas on the use of original and inedited documents have changed since his time, and unless a man's actual narrative can be consulted we discard him as an original authority. Moreover, it is the personal detail, in which Manucci so abounds, that at once secures our interest in the man, and leads to our believing that he did see or hear or undergo what he tells us. Not only does Catrou omit, but he imports largely from other sources, without affording us any means of distinguishing between such additions and what he drew from Manucci's manuscript.

CONSEQUENCES OF CATROU'S METHOD

Instances of the misleading consequences of Catrou's method can easily be adduced. The chapter on Babar occupies pp. 38-52 of the quarto edition; yet of these fourteen pages almost all that can be assigned to Manucci are the names of Ranguil Das (p. 39, not including the speech), and Amuvi Xa (pp. 46, 47), with the last two paragraphs of pp. 51 and 52. Then, again, Müllbauer on pp. 135-137 of his 'Geschichte,' quoting Catrou in regard to the Jesuit missions to the Mogul Court, believes that he is appealing to the authority of Manucci. Not a word of all these statements is to be found in Manucci's text, as can be readily seen. Quite recently (Bombay, 1903) Mr. Jivanji Jamshedji Modi, B.A., published a most interesting account of 'The Parsees at the Court of Akbar,' where, on p. 26, he gives a table of the arrival and departure of the missions to Akbar, taken from Catrou, 'on the authority of Manouchi'; and again, on p. 80, a detailed account of Akbar's reception of Rudolfo Aquaviva. Mr. Modi will be somewhat surprised to learn that nothing about any of these missions is to be found in the real Manucci text, and the statements made in Catrou obtain no confirmation from an appeal to it.

CATROU'S EDITION OF 1715

In 1715, ten years after his first edition had appeared, Catrou produced a continuation, what he called a Third Part, which deals with the long reign of Aurangzeb and ends with the death of Kam Bakhsh in January, 1709. In the quarto edition this Third Part of 1715 covers 207 pages, and is thus almost equal in size to the earlier publication (272 quarto pages). The narrative, much more valuable than most of the historical matter in the previous work, is almost entirely taken from the Second Part of Manucci's manuscript, and deals with events of which he was a contemporary, and often an eye-witness. But Catrou claimed to have received from India other memoirs, though he admits Manucci to be almost the only writer he has followed in writing the life of Aurangzeb (Preface of 1715, p. 3); and he goes on to say how a person newly arrived from India, to whom he read the manuscript, confirmed whatever it contained. To allay a suspicion that he had tampered with Manucci, he relies upon the manuscript, which he still possessed and could show to anyone expressing such doubts. But, as he goes on to say, he preferred a metaphorical style, like that of the Greek and Roman historians, to the simpler language adopted by Manucci.

DID CATROU USE MANUCCI'S FOURTH AND FIFTH PARTS?

In preparing his volume of 1715, had Catrou access to the fourth and fifth parts of Manucci's work, sent home, one in fourth and 1706 and the other before 1712? I think not. It is true that Catrou carries his narrative beyond 1700, the period at which Manucci's Parts I., II., and III. terminate; but the probabilities are that, for the last twenty to twenty-five pages of his later volume, he relied on those other memoirs from India of which he speaks in his preface.

BIBLIOGRAPHY OF CATROU'S 'HISTOIRE'

I have put together the following list of editions of Catrou from the catalogues of the British Museum and the India Office Library, from Carlos Sommervogel's edition of Backer's 'Bibliographie de la Compagnie de Jeśus,' ii., column 882, *s.v.* Catrou, F., from Lowndes, ed. 1862, vol. i., p. 393, and from the exemplars in my own possession.

In French.

1705, Paris, 4to., 1 vol., pp. 272. (In B. M.)
1705, Paris, 12mo., 2 vols., pp. 403, 434. (Partly in B. M.)
1708, La Haye, 12mo., 3 parts, pp. 380. (Partly in B. M.)
1715, Paris, 4to., reissue of 4to. edition of 1705, pp. 272, plus a third part of 207 pp. (In B. M.)
1715, Paris, small 8vo., 4 vols., pp. 403, 334, 301, 285. (In B. M.)
1715, Paris, 12mo., 3 vols., pp. 301, 285, 207.

In Italian.

1731, Venice, 8vo., 1 vol., pp. 306. (Translated from the edition of 1705, the only additions being a very fanciful portrait of Taimur and a short address from the printer to the reader about the translation. Copies exist in the Biblioteca Nazionale di San Marco and at St. Lazzaro, Venice, and I have recently acquired one.)

In English.

1709, London, 8vo. (Translation of 1705 edition. In I. O. Lib.)

1722, London, 12mo. (Translation of 1705 edition. In I. O. Lib.) [I have compared this edition with that of 1709. It is nothing more than a reissue of the earlier edition with a new title-page, in which F. Catrou is ignored. There is no justification for the statement on this new title-page that it was an Italian text from which this edition, either of 1709 or 1722, was taken].

1826, London, 8vo. (Translation of the Hague edition of 1708. In B. M.)

In Portuguese.

My friend Mr. J. Batalha-Reis, M.V.O., Consul-General for Portugal in London, and Commercial Attache, was under the impression that an edition had been published in Portuguese; but I can find no mention of any such work in Innocencia F. da Silva's 'Diccionario Bibliografico' (fifteen vols., Lisbon, 1858-1862). I therefore come to the conclusion that there was no such edition, and the supposition of its existence may be attributed to an unsupported statement in the 'Nouvelle Biographie Générale' (Didot, Paris, 1860), tome xxxiii., *s.v.* Manucci (Nicholas), an article in which almost every sentence contains an error of fact.

III. THE BERLIN MS., PHILLIPPS NO. 1945.

Its Supposed Disappearance From 1763

Many writers have lamented the disappearance of the manuscript from which Catrou drew his 'Histoire,' beginning with Robert Orme in 1782, and ending with Mr. S. Lane-Poole in 1893. It was in this latter year I first heard that it had found its way to Berlin, and through the intervention of the late Dr. Rost, librarian, was then temporarily at the India Office in London, for the use of Mr. A. Constable, who at that time purposed an edition. During this long period of a century or more the manuscript had never really disappeared; a little search could have found it, and for sixty years or so it was even lying in England, had anybody cared to look for it. Orme himself had a pretty accurate knowledge of where it was when he was writing between 1763 and 1782. Nor was Catrou's text a mere short, mutilated abstract, as J. Bernouilli was led to surmise from the discrepancies between the 'Histoire' and the Venice

Codex (see 'Recherches sur l'Inde,' Berlin, 1787, vol. ii., note *b* to p. 284). The mistake was, under the circumstances, very excusable.

BOUREA-DESLANDES

We know from Catrou's preface (p. 2) that M. Deslandes handed him the manuscript on which he founded his book; while Manucci in various places states that he made over the text of his 'Storia' to that gentleman for conveyance to Europe. Evidently his hope was that it would be published at the expense of Louis XIV.

This M. Deslandes must not be confounded with another gentleman of the same name, André Daulier Deslandes, who went to Persia with Tavernier in 1664, and in 1673 published a book called 'Les Beautés de la Perse.' In 1704 or 1705, according to Catrou (Preface, p. 6), this Daulier Deslandes was still living, but was not the Deslandes who lent him Manucci's manuscript. As to the latter M. Deslandes, known as Boureau Deslandes, he was in the service of the French East India Company at Surat as early 1673; in 1679 he was sent to Siam, where he remained for some time (Jules Sottas, 'Histoire de la Compagnie des Indes,' Paris, 1903, p. 136). He was thus mixed up with the French transactions in Siam during 1680-1683, in which he and Governor François Martin were interested. They were supporters of the Greek adventurer Constantin Phalkon, who rose to be Prime Minister of Siam. There is also a 'Histoire de Constance, Premier Ministre du Roi de Siam' (12mo., 1756), by the younger Deslandes, founded on his father's and the Chevalier Martin's memoirs and letters, the object being to refute Père P. J. d'Orleans' Life of the same man (1690). I have seen the copy of Deslandes' book in the Bibliothéque Nationale (55 pages, small 8vo). A fact or a name might be gleaned from it here and there, but on the whole it adds little to our knowledge of Siam politics, and yields nothing new about the elder Deslandes himself. The most pungent and characteristic passage is on p. 12, where Pére Tachard, S.J., and Mr. l'Abbé de Choisy (both of whom went to Siam and published books on it) are described as 'deux des pius insignes charlatans qu'on puisse lire.' Deslandes married one of Martin's daughters, and was sent to Bengal in charge of the French comptoir of Chandernagore, where he remained until 1701. In 1689 he had a son, André François Boureau-Deslandes (just referred to), who became notorious as a sceptical writer, was the author of many books and pamphléts, and died in 1757 (see 'Biog. Uni.' (Michaud), ii. 195, and 'N. Biog. Gen.'). In 1731 the son brought out a book entitled 'Rémarques Historiques d'un Cosmopolite,' of which the authorship is attributed to his father.[1]

MS. IN PARIS (1705-1763)

The elder Deslandes left India in February, 1701, and on his reaching Paris lent Catrou the MS. Memoirs of Manucci for perusal. Shortly afterwards, on December 28, 1703, Boureau-Deslandes was appointed Commissaire de la Marine in the West Indies, and left France without obtaining a return of Manucci's manuscript. After doing good work for the State, he died at Laogane, in St. Domingo, on February 13, 1706 (Adrien Desalles, 'Histoire Générale des Antilles,' 5 vols., Paris, 1847-1848, vol. ii., pp. 320, 333, 346).[2] Manucci's manuscript remained with Catrou, and when he had done with it he deposited it in the library of the college of his society at Clermont in Paris (now the Lycée Louis-le-Grand, in the Rue St. Jacques, near the Sorbonne). There it remained till the expulsion of the Jesuits from France, and there, in 1763, Anquetil Duperron saw the three volumes.

SALE OF PARIS JESUITS' LIBRARY

In 1763 the Jesuits were expelled from France, and their property sequestrated. Mr. Henri Omont, in his 'Documents, sur la Vente des Manuscripts du Collége de Clermont à Paris,

1. But I think erroneously, for it refers to events long subsequent to the date of the elder Deslandes' death (1706), and makes the writer present at Constantinople and elsewhere, statements quite inconsistent with the known facts of the elder Deslandes' Indian career. The book is a literary medley, and in it may be embedded a fact or two that the son had heard from his father, such as the remarks about faqirs at Surat, and the mention of De Forbin, Des Farges, and others in Siam.
2. As Boureau-Deslandes was an important personage in the history in India of the French Company, and his name has not yet found its way into any biographical dictionary, I place a note on him at the end of this Introduction. Most of the manuscript materials of this note have been collected for me by M. Pierre Bernus, recently a student of the Ecole des Chartes.

1764' (Extrait du 'Bulletin de la Société de l'Histoire de Paris et de l'Isle de France,' 1891, I., xviii., pp. 7-18), gives the *arrét* by the Parliament of July 5, 1763, decreeing the sale of the MSS. Dom Clement, author of 'L'Art de verifier les Dates,' aided for the Oriental MSS,. by de Guignes and Bernard, for the Greek and Latin by Brequigny, produced a catalogue, of which the title-page is: 'Catalogus | manuscriptorum codicum | Collegii Claromontani | quem | excipit Catalogio Mss^{m} | Domus Professæ | Parisiensès | . . . . | Parisiis in Palatio | apud Sugrain subsigno Bonæ Fidei coronatae Leclerc subsigno Prudentiæ | M DCC LXIV.' In it Manucci's 'Storia' appears on p. 324 as No. DCCCLVI.[1] Orme is wrong in asserting it does not appear there, perhaps because he only looked at the catalogue of printed books, which is a separate work. The manuscript is described as written in Portuguese, with several portions of it in French; three volumes in folio, the first of 142, the second of 151, and the third of 132 folios. A notice is inserted that the contents were to be sold on September 1 next (1764) unless bought in bulk, and offers were invited. The king's librarian, Bignon, refused to buy. Baron Gérard Meerman, of the Hague, began negotiations, and a price of 15,000 livres was agreed on for 856 manuscripts, among them being included the three volumes of Manucci. Omont gives an amusing account of the after-attempts to cancel this transaction, and the difficulties surmounted by the purchaser in removing his acquisitions from France. His boxes were stopped at Rouen, and forty-two volumes relating to the history of France were claimed. He gave up thirty-seven works (thirty-nine volumes). The remainder reached the Hague in April, 1765. As a reward for this concession, Louis XV. conferred on Meerman the Order of St. Michael (see 'Histoire générale de Paris—de Cabinet des MSS. de la Bibliothéque Impériale,' by Leopold Deslisle—folio, Paris, 1868—section xix., pp. 434, 435).

BARON GERARD MEERMAN AND COMTE J. MEERMAN

This learned Dutchman, Baron Gérard Meerman, was born at Leiden in 1722, and died at Aix-la-Chapelle on December 15,

1. 'Historia do Mogol, en tre parte de Nicolao Manuchi Veneziano . . . do Reinado de Orangzeb guerra de Golconda e Visapur com varios successos athe a era de 1700'.

1774, leaving an only son, Comte Jean Meerman, who was born at the Hague on November 1, 1753, and died there on August 19, 1815 ('Nouvelle Biog. Générale,' Didot, 1861, vol. xxxiv., p. 74). Some years after the son's death the family library was disposed of. The printed catalogue appeared at the Hague in 1824 in four volumes, 8vo.: 'Bibliotheca Meermanniana sive Catalogus . . . morte dereliquet Joannes Meerman, toparcha in Dalem et Vuren, etc. . . .' There were nineteen sale days fixed, between June 8 and July 3, 1824. I have a copy of vols. i. and ii., but have not been able to procure vols. iii. and iv.; and, so far as I can find, the work is not in the British Museum. The 'Storia do Mogor' must have been entered in vol. iv., 'MSS. Francis, Italiens, Espagnols, Portugais, Hollandois et Allemands, livres Chinois, etc[a],' Nos. 832-1100, pp. 143-182, of which the sale day was Saturday, July 3, 1824.

SIR THOMAS PHILLIPPS, BORN 1792, DIED 1872.

At this sale Sir Thomas Phillipps, the well-known collector of Middle Hill, co. Worcester, was a large buyer. Among other, purchases were the three volumes of Manucci's manuscript 'Storia.' They appear thus in his 'Catalogus Librorum Manuscriptorum in Bibliotheca Medio Montains Dom Thomae Phillipps ab anno 1824 ad 1837,' under 'Codices MSS. ex Bibliotheca Meerman Hagae Comitis olim ex Bibliotheca Collegii Societatis Jesu Claromontanis Parisiis nunc ante D. Bibliotheca Phillippicate,' p. 21, *viz.*:

Codices MSS. Italianici, etc[a].

General Number of Historia de
number, 1945. this collection, 917. Mogol.

THE KONIGLICHE BIBLIOTHEK ACQUIRES MS.

In 1887 the Königliche Bibliothek at Berlin bought the Meerman manuscripts from the heirs of Sir Thomas Phillipps for a sum of 375,000 marks ('Bibliotheque de l'école des Chartes,' 1888, vol. xlix., p. 694). In the twelfth volume of the Berlin catalogues,' 'Verzeichniss der Lateinischen Handschriften,' vol. i., 1893, by Valentin Rose ('Die Meerman Handschriften des Sir Thomas Phillipps'), we are informed that, whereas Baron Meerman secured 349 of the Clermont MSS., there were only 250 left at the sale in 1824, and of these 190 were bought by Sir Thomas Phillipps, and transferred in 1887 to Berlin. Between

1765 and 1824, I59 of the MSS. bought by Meerman had been lost.

THE BERLIN CODEX, PHILLIPPS 1945, DESCRIBDE

The description of the Manucci 4 Storia do Mogor,' acquired by the Royal Library in Berlin, appears in 4 Die I Romanische Meerman Handschriften I des I Sir I Thomas Phillipps I in der Königliche Bibliothek zu Berlin' I beschrieben I von I Alfred Schulze I Berlin I 1892 I, 4to., p. 24, in the following terms as translated by me from the German original:

Codices Phillipici,
Spanish, Italian, and Portuguese Manuscripts,
39 Phill. 1945.

Paper, three folio volumes, of 144, 155, and 135 folios respectively (size 33 to 35 mm. by 21 to 23 mm.) of the eighteenth century.

Leather binding, Meerman No. 917, Coll. Paris. Soc. Jésu, No. 856. The Portuguese text shows the following gaps, which were afterwards filled up in French : Vol. I., leaves 1 to 6; Vol. III., leaves 1 to 34 and 47 to 49. In Vol. II., on leaves 23 to 43, is a French text, giving a translation of the Portuguese on the preceding leaves 1 to 22. Vol. II., leaf 44, and Vol. III., leaves 44 to 46, 70 to 73, 80 to 84, 94, and 125 are blank.

Nicolao Manuchi, 'History of the Mogul Kingdom.'

Vol. I., folio 1[a]: 'Voyage et histoire du Mogol divisé en trois parties par M. Nicholas Manuchi, Venitien. Premiére Partie, contenant le voyage de Nicholas Manuchi, son arrivèe au Mogol, etc[a]. L'histoire des rois Mogols, depuis Tamerlang jusque à l'evènement d'Aurangzeb au trône.'

Vol. II., folio 1[a]: 'Parte seguda da istoria' [*correction* into 'historia' (*sic*)] 'do Mogol de Nicolao Manuchi Veneziano: do reinado de Orangzeb, guerras de Golconda e Vizapur com varios successos athe a era de 1699' [figure struck out, and inserted beneath in another handwriting, ' 1700'].

Vol. III., folio 1[a]: 'Troisiesme partie de l'histoire du Mogol par Nicolas Manouchy Venisien premier médicin du Chaalam fils aisnéd'Aurangzeb, dans laquelle on donne un compte' [struck through and replaced by 'conte'] 'exact des richesses et du grandeur des Mogols et de celles des princes gentils ses voisins, avec plusieurs particularitez curieuses et evenemens remarquables.'

The work of Manouchi has never been printed. On the other hand, founding himself on this production, the Jesuit Father François Catrou published 'Histoiré générale de l'Empire du Mogol depuis sa fondation jusqu'à présent sur les mémoires portugais de M. Manouchi, Venitien.' The first two parts appeared in Paris in 1705 in small octavo,[1] the last two parts much later.[2] As to the different editions, see Backer, 'Biblioth. des Ecriv. de la Comp, de Jésus,' tome i., pp. 1135 *et seq.*; and refer also to J. Talboys Wheeler, 'The History of India from the Earliest Ages (London, 1867), vol. iv., part i., Preface, pp. xii.-xiv. Since the English translations of 1709 and 1826 were both prepared from the re-impression of the French issue published at the Hague in 1708, and end with the accession of Aurangzeb, Wheeler was misled into the statement on his p. xiii that Catrou's work was never completed.[3] Phillips 1945 is with very little doubt the manuscript mentioned by Catrou in his preface (not paged).

REMARKS ON BERLIN CATALOGUE

On the above the only remark I have to make is, that I doubt if the French passages are subsequent additions, catalogue. Manucci, in one of his letters reproduced further on, ascribes the changes from Portuguese to French, or *vice versa,* to the necessity of using a language understood by his amanuensis of the moment. Certainly, as Herr Schulze points out, there is a long passage in vol. ii. where we have two versions, one Portuguese and one French, of exactly the same matter. I may add from a note by my copyist, Herr August Otto, that vol. i. is in four handwritings: (*a*) pp. 1 to 10 (*b*) 11-160 (*c*) 161-208, and (*d*) 209-280. On the margin of folio 2 in all three volumes are the words: 'Paraphé au devis de l'arrest du 5 Juiliet, 1763, Mesnil.'

For the present (translated) edition of Manucci, Parts I., II., and III., I have used the text of the Berlin MS., Phillipps No. 1945, in addition to pp. 417 to 477 of the Venice Codex, XLIV. (Zanetti), as at that point the two texts appear to diverge somewhat widely. I saw and made notes from the original at Berlin

1. Also in 4to. (*see ante*, p. xxvi).
2. In 1715 (see *ante*, p. xxvi). Catrou published only one more part—that is, a Third Part.
3. See, however, Wheeler's introduction to vol. iv., part ii, 1881, by which time he had procured a copy of the whole of Catrou's work.

in June, 1901, and my transcript was made by Herr August Otto, whose services were kindly procured for me by Director-Professor Dr. L. Stern, of the Manuscript Department of the Royal Library.

IV. THE VENICE CODEX, XLIV. (ZANETTI).

N. M.'s Protest and His Latin Letter (1706)

Some time in 1704 or 1705 Manucci received from Catrou an advance copy of his 'Histoire,' or of the preface to it. A perusal of this communication aroused intense indignation in the Italian author, and in January, 1706, he resolved to dispatch to Europe the original draft of his Parts I., II., and III., together with the Part IV. on which he had been engaged since the beginning of 1701, accompanied by a Latin letter to the Venetian Senate, of which the following is a translation, made for me by my friend Mr. James Kennedy:

'Most Serene Princes!

'Love of travel and inborn inclination to visit foreign nations caused the writer, Nicolo Manucci, a client and nursling of the Most Serene Republic, to leave Venice when he was only fourteen, and led him happily to the Empire of the Mogul (Mogol), in which he served divers princes of the blood royal for a period of fifty-four years, as this history shows. There, at the request of certain friends, Frenchmen by race, he began a most extensive account of this despotism, and finished it in 1700. Of which work as soon as the Reverend Fathers of the Society of Jesus residing in India got wind, they left no stone unturned to appropriate it, as if it were their own. But considering my many vigils and the sundry expenses I had to incur, it did not seem to me right that the aforesaid Fathers should transfer to themselves the glory won by another's labour, nor that I should be cheated out of my expectations.

'Wherefore I placed in the hands of a certain friend of mine this work, divided into four parts,[1] in which I treat carefully and accurately of the times from Tamerlane to Aurangzeb, who now holds the scepter, as well as of all his family and of the principal chiefs of the army. With it I handed over to him sixty-four[2] coloured

1. Really only three parts.
2. Should be fifty-six; he is confusing the volume of portraits with that containing the gods and goddesses.

pictures now in Paris. And these' [*i.e.*, the books and pictures] 'ought, according to my directions, to have been forwarded to the Reverend Father Eusebius, a Capuchin of Bourges' [Bituriens, the mediaeval name for that province], 'Apostolic missionary in the East Indies, that he might offer them on my part to the Most Serene Senate to dispose of them as they might think best. But my friend died at Galle' [? Egellia in text], 'and, as I had feared, my said book fell into the hands of the aforesaid Fathers, who wrote to me on this matter. But little gratification did I get from their writings, with selections from my works, for they only set forth what was of comparatively little value in the book, and what was best they kept to themselves.

'Wherefore I earnestly and prayerfully beg and entreat that Your Most Serene Highnesses will deign to order the publication of this little work, which is likely to be of the greatest use to travellers, missionaries, and merchants, etc[a]. asking them to add a short and befitting preface, such as may appear best suited for it. If I could issue it at my own expense, right willingly would I do it; but for such an expenditure my own resources, as well as the resources of my relations living in Venice, are too limited, therefore I have ventured to give this trouble to the Most Serene Senate.

'The original text, which I have always kept by me, I send to Your Most Serene Highnesses by the hands of the said Reverend Father Eusebius (which is a right good opportunity)—namely, the First, Second, and Third Parts already completed. At the same time I send the Fourth Part, written in French, which has always remained with me, and has never heretofore been sent to Europe. In it the life of the Mogul and various events of the government, besides other things omitted in Parts I. and II., are clearly narrated. I am now proceeding indefatigably with the Fifth Part, in which I examine in detail all and every event happening in these last days of King Aurangzeb's life, and I shall willingly give it to the Actor' [who is referred to is not clear] 'if I am alive.

'The said Reverend Father Eusebius [also] takes with him a book containing sixty-six drawings of the false Hindu gods, wherein Hindu marriages and other ceremonies are represented, all of which the Agent (?) will find explained towards the end of the third part. Nor must it be thought strange if various languages appear in the work now sent, for according to the amanuensis whom I chanced upon, did I compose the work sometimes in French, sometimes in Italian, and occasionally in Portuguese. All of which defects, as well as others that may possibly have occurred, I beg the charity of Your Most Serene Highnesses to excuse, whom Almighty God preserve for many years.

'Madraspatanam, the 15th January, 1705 [*i.e.*, 1705/6].
'Your Most Serene Highnesses'
'Most humble and devoted
'Client and Alumnus,
'N. MANUCI.'

N.M.'S SECOND LETTER OF 1706 IN ITALIAN

Inside Codex XLIV. (Zanetti) there lie two loose leaves in Italian, which I imagine to be Zanetti's notes for the articles in his Italian catalogue. But these embody a second letter from Manucci in Italian, which seems to vary somewhat from the one in Latin. I extract any additional facts yielded by this second letter.

He says he began to write to oblige some Frenchmen[1] for the favours they procured him from their king, who in 1699 sent him some medals, one of gold with the image of the king on one side and of the *falfi* (?) on the other, and six others of silver bearing the figure of Victory.[2] In order to show himself grateful for so many favours, he forwarded his history to France in 1700 by one of his faithful friends, a person of consideration, loved and esteemed by all in India. This person on his arrival in France was the object of much honour from the French monarch. But

1. In Part II., 53 (Phillipps), two of these are named—*viz.*, 'Chiefly Monsieur François Martin, Director-General, and Monsieur Deslandes.'
2. I have tried, without much success, to identify these medals in 'Médailles sur les Principaux Evénements du Règne de Louis le Grand,' folio, Paris, 1701, to which Professor E. G. Rapson, of the Coin Department, British Museum, was so kind as to refer me. The first medal mentioned by Manucci might be that struck for the Peace of Ryswick (1697), with the head of Louis on one side, and on the other standing figures of Justice and Valour; and the others, either the medal showing France kneeling at the king's feet, or the one with a standing figure of Peace. Both these also commemorate the same Peace (see pp. 272-274 of above work).

having been sent by his king to the West Indies,[1] he was unable to procure the printing of the three volumes on the Mogul Empire. He was obliged to leave them behind him, and another with sixty-four (fifty-six) portraits. The friend gave these (? the three volumes) for inspection as a curiosity to the Jesuit Father Catrou, a young man of great astuteness, to whom the Jesuits had already written from India requesting him to secure the work if he could, which he thus succeeded in doing. Catrou forwarded to Manucci the preface of the book it was his intention to print. 'I saw that he meant to make the work one to his own glory, and mix me up with the fables told by other authors, thereby usurping the result of my labours and fatigues during so many years, and of such great expenditure, while he would have all the coin and the honour. I therefore requested him to return the work to me. But fearing from what I know of him that this will be of no effect, I have in order to get it back appointed as my attorney the Reverend Father F. Eusebius, of Bourges, a Capuchin and French missionary in this land of India, who is now departing for Europe.'

THE FOURTH PART

Further on Manucci says: 'This' [the Fourth Part] 'the Jesuits have not had, nor had I ever sent it; but now I send it, and I will employ all my diligence to prepare the Fifth Part, if God should grant me life, in order to display my sincerity, and to give ample satisfaction to the inquiring reader.' Again, further on: 'The inquisitive Reverend Fathers above named [*i.e.*, the Jesuits] 'made great exertions to get hold of these two books' [the Fourth Part and the pictures of Gods and Goddesses], 'but my answer to them was "Nescio vos." '

LANGUAGES USED

On the question of language he says: 'The reason is that I have not found in this country any Italian amanuensis.' In conclusion he says: 'Demanding pardon if I have made mistakes

1. Though he is not named, this passage identifies the person meant as M. Deslandes (see *ante*, p. xxvii). Mark also the contradiction between this and the Latin letter, where he says the friend died at 'Egellia' on his way home.

in words or in spelling, for in this land of India I have employed my maternal language only on this occasion, in which I profess myself.

'Venerable Signors,
'NICOLAO MANUCCI.'[1]

THE ITALIAN PRECIS AT VENICE

The maker of this Italian *précis* goes on to abstract from the 'Storia' whatever refers to Manucci's life and travels. He gives the month of leaving Venice as November, thus coinciding substantially with the deduced date of October, arrived at by me independently (see the note on Viscount Bellomont, following Part I, p. 47, of the text). Manucci's age at departure is given as nineteen, whereas it is fourteen in the Berlin text (Phillipps 1945). The abstract ends abruptly with: 'He set out with the prince (Dara) for the war against Aurangzeb.' The writer makes the incorrect statement that part of the 'Storia' is written in *Spanish;* he should have said *Portuguese.*

EUSEBIUS OF BOURGES, CAPUCHIN AND LORENZO TIEPOLO (1673-1742)

I have failed in obtaining much trace of Father F. Eusebius, of Bourges, Capuchin, while in India, and have found nothing at all about him after his return to Europe. Manucci, in Part IV., fol. 193, speaking of 1704, says that a short time before that year Eusebius had arrived at Madras from Surat, on his way to France. He went on to Pondicherry, where the Jesuits spread reports that he had been excommunicated, and thus every door was shut in his face. I do not know what became of him; but we learn from Zanetti that he made over the books to the then ambassador of the Venetian Senate at Paris, Lorenzo Tiepolo (son of Francesco, son of Marco), a man of distinguished ancestry, whose family tree is given in vol. viii. of Count Pompeo Litta's 'Celebri famiglie Italiane' (Milano, n.d.,? 1835). There is a biography of him on p. 162 of vol. xxii. of Gerolamo Baciardo's 'Nuova Enciclopedia Italiana' (Torino, 1887), and in 'II campodoglio

1. In making this last statement, he seems to have quite forgotten the fact that in 1699 and 1700 he,had composed 381 large folio pages of Parts I. and II. in his native tongue. Perhaps those pages were the work of an amanuensis, while the letter of 1706 was his own composition.

Venete' of Girolamo Alessandro Capellan, vol. iv. (of which the manuscript is in the library of San Marco). In the same library, Class VII., Codex DCCCCI., is the manuscript of Tiepolo's 'Relazione della sua ambasciate a Luigi XIV. di Francia.' In the State Archives at I Frari his despatches from Paris are preserved. The first is dated April 4, 1704, and the last April 27, 1708. In none of these sources could I find any mention of Manucci's work, of its arrival in Paris, or its transmission to Venice. The Abbé Morelli, librarian from 1778, says on p. 46 of his 'Della publica Libreria di San Marco' (Venice, 1774), that Tiepolo obtained the Codex in France in 1722, but I do not know what authority he has for this statement. The year seems much too late; but 1712 might be correct.

ZANETTI'S CATALOGUE (1741)

Tiepolo, who is described as a man of vast erudition, became Zanetti's procurator of St. Mark, and in 1736 was appointed librarian. "He died in 1742, at the age of sixty-nine. Under Tiepolo's auspices as librarian, Antonio Maria Zanetti, the younger, drew up a catalogue of the San Marco collection, which appeared under the title of 'Latina et Italica D. Marci Bibleotheca Codicum manuscriptorum per titulos digesta' [&ca], folio, Venice, 1741. On p. 235 we have the following account of the Manucci manuscript:

'Codex XLIV., in folio, paper, ff. 778, of the eighteenth century. "Historical Memoirs of the Mogul Empire," by Niccolo Manuzzi, Veneziano, divided into four parts, written partly in Italian, partly in Portuguese, and partly in French. From the beginning of the fifteenth to about the eighteenth century.'

ZANETTI'S DESCRIPTION OF CODE XLIV

From the first three parts of this work, carried to France by Monsieur Deslandes in 1700, Father Catrou derived his 'Histoire de l'Empire Mogul.,' published at Paris in 1705, two volumes, octavo, and at the Hague, 1708, in 12mo.; translated into Italian in 1731, and printed at Venice. This celebrated literary man, although he had compiled various notices of that kingdom from other authors, nevertheless renders due justice to the labours of our Manuzzi, and he admits him to be the support and foundation of all his statements, wisely dwelling on the character of that author, who was not a simple traveller or merchant (people who are forced either to hurry hither and thither, or to confine themselves solely to cities near the sea), but in truth a medical man, whose profession had detained him at the court for a period of forty or more years, whereby was thrown open to him access to particular information, concealed from every other European, and the means of transcribing the original chronicles themselves. The said Father observes,[1] furthermore, that in the mode of Manuzzi's narration, in spite of the text being in various and obscure languages, there is found a certain ardour of imagination fitted to sustain the historian who works on such materials; to which may be added that at the same time we discover in all these writings a certain air of unstudied simplicity and honest frankness, which still can be detected even when heightened and embellished by a chastened style [*i.e.* Catrou's].

This production of Father Catrou, although much honoured by Manuzzi, had not the fortune to please him when it reached him in India; on the contrary, he was deeply offended that Catrou had inserted the accounts of other people, and had omitted from his book certain statements which Manuzzi considered important. Therefore the author decided to send his own original manuscript to Europe through a Capuchin Father, who gave a pledge that he would hand it over to the first official of the Venetian Republic that he encountered. This monk did as promised, and on reaching Paris delivered it to the Cavaliere Lorenzo Tiepolo, then Venetian ambassador at that court, at present procurator of San Marco, and its illustrious, most meritorious librarian. The gift of Manuzzi was addressed to the Senate with a Latin letter, and these were speedily sent on to Venice by the ambassador. In addition to the above-entered four parts of the 'Historical Memoirs,' there was also a fifth, which went on with the same subject. There was also another volume, with pictures of the gods, priests, and other matters connected with the idolaters who dwell in that country. These pictures are often referred to in the course of the work, and serve to explain the religious beliefs and rites of the ancient inhabitants of Hindustan. But what is more precious for its beauty and its magnificence is a volume containing the portraits of the Mogul emperors, of their families, and other illustrious personages among those idolaters.

1. Preface of 1705, p. 5.

These are painted with incredible labour, and present the most lovely colouring, heightened by much gilding; and although they do not display all the requisites of correct drawing, or of light and shade, yet the figures are not wanting in naturalness, and, if one may infer it from the diversity of idea and from certain details of the faces, the portraits must be very like their originals. Father Catrou, who had seen the pictures, would have liked to reproduce them in his history, but he feared to add to the expense of a first edition. We have felt ourselves constrained to give, at the least, a selection of three, and we have chosen the portraits of our Manuzzi, of Tamerlane, and of Orangzeb; the first as being that of the author of the work, the second as that of the first of the emperors, the third as being that of the ruler under whom the writer lived and dwelt in India.

The portrait, then, of Manuzzi is in the highest degree like him, as is asseverated by more than one person who had personal knowledge of him. He is clothed in Mogul attire, and in the act of feeling the pulse of an Indian patient, giving in this way a sign of his profession.

Tamerlane, or Timur-lenk, a name much spoken of in many histories, was the first among the Tartars who conquered and ruled over Hindustan. He is represented out hunting, in which he greatly delighted, in the act of slaying a lion with an arquebuss. The hunting of these wild beasts the Moguls carry out by throwing down in the path a sheep bound with cords. On seeing it, the wild beast rushes at once to devour it; meanwhile they watch, and can easily kill it. The attire of Tamerlane is noticeable, still more his armour, which consists in a corslet of mail richly adorned with gems. Perhaps this costume was peculiar to the Tartars before that of Hindustan began to prevail among them. The posture of this prince, who is kneeling, is asserted by some as intended to indicate that from birth he was weak in the legs, because the second-half of his name—that is, *lenk*—means in the Tartar language 'The Lame.'

Orangzeb, eleventh emperor, who died in 1707, after a very long reign, left behind him a resounding memory as the man who to gain the summit felled and slew—partly by deceit, partly by force—all his three brothers, and as one who for many a day held his own father a prisoner. Before he became emperor he was of a certain sect of the Mahomedans who style themselves *faqirs*, and maintained throughout his life an assumed exterior of religion. Thus the artist succeeds in taking him to the very life in the act of reading the Quran, in an attitude full of piety and composure, to which there is not wanting any sanctimonious detail.

In many aspects, then, this manuscript of Manuzzi is of value, and the gathering together of all these different books is worthy of high praise. Certainly the public has benefited by a considerable portion of them in the compilation of Father Catrou. All the same, without advertence to the absence of any extracts from the last two parts, it seems that still other chapters from the Memoirs of our author are called for as additions to Catrou's publication. One chapter ought certainly to be on the natural history of Hindustan, which could be gathered so easily from many dispersed passages to be found in Manuzzi's story, and in his notes on his medical practice, where plants, animals, and other rare products are spoken of, not omitting the marvellous properties of the elephant. Another chapter should be on the private habits of the Indians and the Tartars, which could be deduced from particular instances. But let this suffice for a general notice of this Codex, thus deviating no further from our original scheme.

ENGRAVINGS IN ZANETTI

Zanetti's volume includes three fine copper-plate engravings: 1. Orangzeb, XI. (Blochet, 'Inventaire,' No. 13); the emperor is on a white horse, reading, and there are twenty-five other figures round him on foot. 2. Tamur-lang, I. (Blochet, No. 3). A jungle scene, Taimur on one knee, shooting: thirty-one other figures. 3. Portrait of Niccolao Manuzzi, author of the 'History of the Mogul' (Blochet, No. 2). A stout, white-faced, entirely shaven man in Indian costume looking to the left and holding the pulse of a very dark man.

FURTHER DESCRIPTION OF CODEX XLIV (VENICE)

Cardinal Placido Zurla is inaccurate in stating that the Manucci manuscript 'was unfortunately mislaid in the late political troubles,' meaning the days of Napoleon's invasion, his remark, as we shall see presently, applying only to the volume of portraits. Codex XLIV. (Zanetti) is still in its place at Venice, and

I proceed to give further details, such as I was able to glean from an inspection of it in May, 1902.

Codex XLIV, is a large folio of 778 pages, the paper used being of several different sizes; it is bound in calf, and stamped on one side with a lozenge-shaped shield bearing the figure of a winged lion holding in its paw a book, with the letters P E.

T (in other words, it bears the arms of the republic); it is MM lettered on the back, 'Manuzzi, Istoria de' Mogoli.' Lose within it are the two leaves of the Latin letter already quoted, the signature to which appears to be in the hand of a scribe; also four leaves, two written on in Italian, apparently not in the same writing as the Latin letter, but signed on the third line of the second page 'Nicolao Manuci.' A fascimile of this signature is inserted beneath our reproduction of the second portrait of the author. The first two pages (in Italian), 'Notice to the Reader,' are not numbered, and at the end bear the signature 'Nicolao Manuci,' which we have reproduced at the foot of the younger of the two portraits.

The small cramped handwriting of the earlier part might be the same as that of the second letter. The MS. Phillipps 1945, at Berlin, is, on the contrary, in a fair copyist's hand. The first handwriting of Codex XLIV. continues up to p. 366 (in Italian). On pp. 367-406 the hand resembles that of the Berlin MS.; on p. 407 the first hand recommences. Pp. 416-616 are on a smaller (foolscap) paper, and here the third part apparently ends.

The subjects of this third part are as follows—it begins on p. 149; p. 170 (year 1664), p. 212 (year 1666), p. 304, titles of princesses and concubines; p. 305, men's titles; p. 307, palace slaves; p. 320, names of generals; p. 322, *Mansabs*; p. 337, provinces; p. 340, names of peoples. On some unnumbered leaves following p. 366 he explains that 'for want of writers of Italian, I am obliged to continue my work in French.' From p. 368 he goes on in French up to p. 406. On p. 407 Portuguese begins, 'On Elephants,' down to p. 415. P. 416 is blank. On p. 417 he begins (still in Portuguese) about Aduni; p. 419, the royal seal and hand imprint; pp. 421 to 423, blank; pp. 424-427, the Dakhin kings; p. 450, principal Hindu temples; p. 451, temples destroyed by Aurangzeb; p. 455, Joao P. de Faria in Madras; p. 465, St. Thome in 1695; p. 474, Damao in 1681; p. 479, Manuel Macedo at St. Thome; p. 501, one quarter blank; p. 502, blank;

p. 503, begins 'servico' (? a misplaced leaf); p. 511, year 1663; p. 565, year 1678; p. 582, Bassein in 1666; p. 606, year 1694. Page 616 ends with the words: 'Lagrima de sangue emover o modo tao improprio e tao diverco do que antigam[te] obravaon.'

Then on an intermediate size of paper begins in French 'Suite . . . Quatriesme Partie, Preface,' with a new paging, and in a handwriting something like that of the Berlin MS. The history breaks off on p. 122; then pp. 123 and 124 are blank. On p. 125 the author commences to speak of the bad conduct of the Portuguese, and this subject goes on as far as p. 145, attestations from various authorities beginning on p. 140. Between pp. 140 and 141 are bound in four 4to. pages of minute handwriting, apparently the copy of a certificate from the Bishop and Vicar-General of St. Thome, dated January 23, 1705. Pp. 148 to 152 are blank.

Next, with p. 153, comes the large folio paper once more, the writing being that of a copyist, and the language French; mention is made of 1703; and the French text ends with one line on the top of p. 164. On p. 165 there begins in Portuguese an account of Cardinal C. M. de Tournon's stay at Pondicherry. On p. 175 is a date, July 11, 1704. On p. 177 is Manucci's 'Manifesto' to the Friars and Patriarch at Pondicherry, which ends on p. 182, being followed by the Archbishop's letter from Goa, dated September 1, 1704.

On p. 184 the handwriting changes, and the historical narrative is resumed without any heading; on p. 186 is the date, September 9, 1704. On p. 200 we return to more talk about the Portuguese misdeeds, which ends on p. 216. Page 217 is a half-sheet only, apparently intended as the conclusion of Part IV.; and there Manucci promises, if he lives, to go on with a Fifth Part, and the passage is dated Madras, January 5, 1705-I706- At the end is a signature, in a hand differing from the text, 'Nicolas Manuci.' At p. 218 we return to foolscap paper, and the narrative turns again to Aurangzeb. On p. 223 is a date, November 4, 1704, and on p. 226 we have a letter to the author from the Archbishop of Goa, dated January 22,1705. On p. 230 is the Manifesto; on p. 231 a letter from the Bishop of Mailapur (St. Thome). On p. 234, after the fourth line, is scrawled: 'The end of the Fourth Part of Nicolas Manucci, Venetian.'

Then follow four leaves (not numbered) about Aurangzeb and Shah 'Alam; a sheet (also not numbered) with seventeen lines of writing on the upper half of it; one leaf fully written on one side, and with nine and a half lines on the other; two leaves in a different handwriting from the preceding, having three written pages and ten and a quarter lines on the fourth side, referring to Daud Khan and Thomas Pitt. Lastly, there are two large folded sheets, giving the order of battle of Shah 'Alam's and of 'Azam Shah's armies respectively. If these plans of battle accompanied the volume originally from India, and were not sent subsequently with the Fifth Part, then Codex XLIV. could not have left India until after June, 1707, the battle in question having been fought on the eighteenth of that month.

CODEX XLIV. USED AS TEXT FOR PART IV

For Part IV. of my translation I have used the text contained in Codex XLIV. (Zanetti), from the new paging beginning in French 'Suite de l'Histoire du Mogor,' going on to p. 235, and the remaining unnumbered leaves above referred to. I saw this and the other Codices on my visit to Venice in 1902, and, thanks to the good offices of Professor Dr. G. Cóggiola, sub-librarian, who, on this and many other occasions, has been most graciously helpful, I obtained a copy of Part IV., which was made for me by Signor Gilberto Moni.

V. VENICE CODEX XLV (ZANETTI)

Zanetti's Description

This volume is thus described in Zanetti's Catalogue, p. 237: 'Codex XLV., in small folio, on paper, 740 folios, of the eighteenth century. An Italian version of Manuzzi's 'Historical Memoirs of the Moguls,' made by Count Stefano Nivibus Cardeira, Portuguese, the Public Professor of Civil Law in the University of Padua.'

The volume begins with the Third Part (the pages are not numbered); after that another portion begins 'Delli elefanti,' of which the pages are numbered i to 260. Next is the Fourth Part, with Preface, on folios 1 to 197. Lastly is the Fifth Part, with a title-page: 'Parte Quinta | della Storia del Mogol | di | Nicolo Manuci Veneziano | Transportato | dell' Idioma Portoghesi all' Italiano | dal | Co. Diego Cardeira | Portoghese | ,' followed by an Italian letter of February 20, 1712, sending the Fifth Part of the translation, the signature is that of Agostino Gadaldini, then

Secretary to the Venetian Senate, as Dr. Cóggiola informs me. The writer speaks of having made over Part V. to Senhor Cardeira's sons for translation, and states that folios 2 to 90 (of the original) were part in Portuguese and part in French, to which must be added 'eleven detached leaves in one or the other tongue.' Next comes a leaf, written on both sides, and not numbered (probably displaced in binding). Then another title-page: 'Tome Quinto | composito per l'autore | Sinor | Manucci di | Nazione Veneziano in questa | Fortezza di S. Giorgio | di Madrastapattan. On the reverse is the book-plate of the librarian, a winged lion with a sword and book, the year (? of appointment) MDCCXXII., and his name Hieronymo Veniero, Procurator of St. Mark.[1] There is still another title-page: 'Quinta Parte | del raconto della Storia del Mogol | In questo presente anno | 1705 | nel mese di Genaro | di | Nicolo Manucci Veneziano.' | On p. 201, 'Account of Persecutions suffered by the Capuchins' is said to be from the French, and translated by Count Andrea Cardeira. On p. 321 is the death of Aurangzeb, February 24, 1707; on p. 329 Prince Akbar's last letter to his father, with four lines of verse in the middle. On p. 339 we are told that Aurangzeb's final illness began on February 7, 1707. 'Azam Shah's coin inscription is given on p. 341, under the date of March 15, 1707. The work ends on P- 345.

CODEX XLV. USED AS TEXT OF PART V

The only complete and consecutive text of Part V. now extant being the Italian version given in this Codex XLV., I have used it in preparing my translation. There are some repetitions of matter already contained in Codex XLIV., and these I have omitted from Part V., giving merely á reference to the page in that manuscript. I saw the Codex XLV. when at Venice in 1902, and Part V. was copied for me by Signor Carlo Alberto Corti.

HOW THE VENICE CODICES WERE TRACED : CARDINAL PLACIDO ZURLA

It remains to say a word or two of how I got upon the track of these Venice Codices XLIV. and XLV. (Zanetti). For a time I believed I was the first student of Indian history to traced-

1. According to Jacopo Morelli, 'Della pubblica Libreria di San Marco in Venezia' (Venice, 1774, pp. 96, 8vo.), p. 92, Girolamo Veniero was librarian from 1716 to 1736.

unearth them, and that the notice in Zanetti's catalogue of 1741 had gone entirely unnoticed. Misled by the 'Nouvelle Biographie Générale,' I had started in search of a Lisbon edition of Manucci's work, and to that end asked my friend, Mr. J. Batalha-Reis, M.V.O., Consul-General in London, to procure me information from the great libraries of Lisbon. This attempt was infructuous, for I was on the wrong scent; but Mr. Batalha-Reis's attention had been roused, and since, as befits one of his nationality, he is a diligent student of, and deeply versed in, geographical literature, he soon afterwards directed me to a passage he had just seen in the work of Cardinal Placido Zurla (1769-1834): 'Di Marco Polo | e degli altri | Viaggiotori Veneziani | . . .,' 2 vols., folio, Venezia, 1818. In vol. ii., in a chapter headed 'Of Some Learned Travellers,' he says (p. 293, para. 67): 'But more than all is worthy of mention the crown of this chapter, Nicolo Manuzzi, who, resorting to the Mogul (country) towards the end of the seventeenth century, exercised medicine there for over forty years, and by the help of that (p. 294) profession was able to frequent the court, and to inform himself of the history, politics, physical condition, and religion of the country, and inserted most entrancing information about it in his "Historical Memoirs of the Mogul Empire," divided into three books, and written partly in Italian, partly in Portuguese, and partly in French. They begin with the fifteenth and come down to the eighteenth century. These very manuscripts were sent by Manuzzi himself from the Mogol country to the Venetian Senate, and they formed one of the ornaments of the Marciana until in the recent political disturbances they were unfortunately mislaid. Some specimens may be seen in Anton Maria Zanetti's "Latina et Italica D. Marci Bibliotheca," where he reproduces three of the many pictures of that veritably magnificent and priceless codex; and he shows how Father Catrou made use of Manuzzi for his "History of the Mogols." '

LETTER FROM LIBRARIANOF SAN MARCO

Guided by the above passage in Zurla, I discovered and made extracts from Zanetti. Before going to Venice it was necessary to find out if the manuscript had ever been recovered. The questions I drew up were most kindly communicated by Dr. C. H. Hagberg Wright, of the London Library, to the librarian of San Marco. This inquiry produced a full and most interesting reply from the then librarian, Dr. Salomone Morpurgo,[1] under date of March 29, 1899, the opening sentences referring to the volume of portraits which will be dealt with in a succeeding section. The following is a translation of this letter :

'The volume described by you certainly belongs to the Marciana, for it bears our old *ex-libris,* otherwise the lion and sword with the motto *Custos vel ultor*. With equal certainty it once formed part of Codex XLIV., described by Zanetti at p. 235 and following. The said Codex is to this day in the Marciana; but it was in 1797 bereft of this, its most precious part' [quotes Zanetti]. 'A marginal note on our examplar of Zanetti announces that "the book of portraits was made over in 1797 to the Signor Brunet, the French commissary," and it was never subsequently restored. Zurla is inexact enough in his expression when he says the Manuzzi manuscript "was unfortunately mislaid in the late political troubles," for, instead of that, it was *taken* by *force*; but not the whole of it, as he (Zurla) seems to say. You can compare with the originals at Paris the three plates reproduced by Zanetti. Thus, then, the text of the 'Memoirs,' Codex XLIV., remains in the Marciana, also the other volume mentioned by Zanetti, pictures of gods, priests, etc[a]; this is now placed in Classe VI., It. 136. In addition thereto we possess in manuscript (Classe VI., It. 345) descriptions of the portraits in the volume now at Paris, and I send the opening paragraph and the titles referring to each figure. Codex XLV. is still in its proper place on the shelves.'

BERNOUILLI KNEW OF CODEX XLIV

After that letter I was satisfied that my journey would not be fruitless; but it was not till May, 1902, that I was able to codex°XLIV visit Venice, inspect the manuscripts, and arrange to have them copied.

As I have already said, I was convinced for a time that I was the first discoverer of this Venice Codex since Zanetti's and Foscarini's time. But I had not reckoned with the Teutonic genius for research: an eighteenth-century German professor had been before me. There are some rather interesting particulars in J. Bernouilli's note, and as it does not seem to be printed in

1. Now chief librarian of the National Library at Florence.

the more commonly accessible French edition of the 'Récherches sur l'Inde,' I insert it from the German edition, 'Beschreibung von Hindustan,' Band II., Theil II. (1788), pp. 192, 193 :

'Two or three years ago my youngest brother' [Jacques B., born 1759, drowned 1789], 'who is at present an ordinary member of the Russian Imperial Academy of Science at St. Petersburg, stayed some time in Venice. I requested him to inspect this manuscript of Manuzzi, and more especially to give me an idea of the Fourth and Fifth Parts; and I also wanted him to look out for a copyist to transcribe those two parts, or to extract from them all that was valuable. He answered me on February 15, 1786, thus:

' "I went to the library, and unfortunately found the work about as badly divided as it could be in respect of the languages used. The first three books, just those you do not want, are all in Italian, excepting some 100 pages or so in French. The Fourth Part has 122 pages of history, some 20 on the Jesuits and the Inquisition, another 20 of history in French, followed by 20 pages in Portuguese. The Fifth Part has 130 pages of history in Portuguese, and 50 in French on the Jesuit and Capuchin disputes. You must see how difficult it is to find one copyist for all that at any reasonable price, for French is little known here, and Portuguese still less, or even not at all. The latter especially is not of a very easily-read handwriting for anyone not knowing the language, etc[a]."

'At length a capable copyist was found, but at too high a rate, and while negotiations over this were pending my brother was compelled to continue his journey to St. Petersburg. He certainly confided the matter to a German friend in Venice; however, this gentleman died soon afterwards, and since then I gave up the project for the time being, although the Abbate Morelli, custodian of the library' [Jacopo Morelli, 1745-1819, custodian from 1778], 'assured me through another friend in Venice he would willingly produce the manuscript in question, if a diligent copyist could be found as to whose moral character he could entertain no doubts.'

Bernouilli winds up by expressing the hope that these hints will induce some one to follow up the trace and select the most valuable parts of this 'apparently-for-the-greater-part-important manuscript.' The Abbate Morelli's demand for a 'moral' copyist is somewhat diverting.

VI. THE OTHER MANUCCI CODICES AT VENICE.

Codex CXXXVI

Codex CXXXVI., in Class VI., bears the same book-plate as Codex XLV. (Zanetti), the name of the same librarian, Geronimo Veniero, and the same year, MDCCXXII. It is a volume of pictures, all in colours. They represent gods and goddesses, devotees, marriage and funeral ceremonies, Hindu and Mahomedan festivals. There are also plans of the battle between Shah 'Alam and A'zam Shāh, similar to those bound up in Codex XLIV. There are short descriptions of the pictures, some in French and some in Italian.

SUBJECTS PAINTINGS IN SAME

From a transcript of these descriptions (French text) made for me through Dr. Cóggiola, I give the following list of the subjects: (1 a) A representation of Banjāras, or grain-carriers; (1) Brahma; (2) Vishnu; (3) Brahman and his wife, followers of No. 2 (Vishnu); (4) *a* second picture of Vishnu; (5) Brahman (follower of Vishnu No. 4) and his wife; (6) a third picture of Vishnu; (7) Brahman and his wife, followers of the third Vishnu, No. 6; (8) Rudra (Shivā.); (9) priest of Rudra and his wife; (10) Pillaiyaur, son of Rudra; (11) another picture of Rudra; (12) priest of Rudra with his wife; (13) ceremony at the November festival of the goddess 'Culouly' (? Kālī alias Kangālī); (14) first ceremony at a Hindu marriage; (15) second ceremony at a marriage; (16) third ceremony at a marriage; (17) fourth ceremony at a marriage; (18) fifth and last ceremony at a marriage; (19) first ceremony at a Lingāyat funeral; (20) second ceremony at such funeral; (21) third ceremony at the said funeral; (22) funeral of a *grucs* (? *gurū*), or learned doctor of the Hindū religion; (23) burning of a Brahman widow; (24) an eclipse of the moon as pictured by the Hindus; (24*bis*) ritual at eclipse of the sun and moon; (25) burning of the dead; (26) bathing of the widow after her husband's death ; (27) picture of the woman (see Part II, f. 70) who dragged her lover into the pyre; (28) lamentations of a Hindū widow on hearing of her husband's death; (29) sacrifices at the dedication of a Lingāyat temple; (30) representations of a *faqīr's* life; (31) Brahmans branding a man dedicated to their service; (32) ritual against the small-pox; (33) elevation and plan of the temple at Canjivaron [Kanchipuram or Conjeeveram,

'Madras Manual of Ad,,' iii. 210]; (34) elevation and plan of two other temples at Kānchipuram; (35) plans and view of Lanka town, the fairy city of the Hindus; (36) representation of the great temple at Tirupatī [see Part III., f. 201 of text]; (37) Brahmans sacrificing a goat to fire; (38) rejoicings of the Brahmans after sacrificing the goat; (39) flower pavilion erected at temples on great festivals (40) Brahmans blessing water; (41) triumphal car used in processions to bear their idols; (42) a Hindu festival to Lakshmi and Paramal; (43) Hindu devotee with iron chain; (44) Hindu devotee with wooden yoke; (45) Hindu devotee with an iron chain through his lip; (46) a dead Hindu half buried, and a woman begging alms for him; (47) a Hindu asking for alms; (49*bis*) another Hindu mendicant; (48) a Hindu penitent worshipping the sun; (49) another Hindu penitent worshipping the sun; (50) a Hindu penitent in a fixed position; (51) the same, another position; (52) another ascetic in a constrained posture; (53) another of these pemitents; (54) another instance; (55) penitents adoring the Lingam; (56) a Hindu pemtent with a brazier on his head; (57) Hindu strollers attached to temples asking alms and dancing; (5761s) the same again; (58) a Brahman begging; (59) a Hindu on his way to consult a Brahman; (60) a Hindu selling Gangotri water ; (61) a Hindu begging by singing and beating a drum; (62) Mahomedan annual mourning for the death of Hasan and Husain; (63) the idol of 'Manarou Lamy' [? *Mantrālammah*, see 'Madras Manual of Ad.," iii. 530] with worshippers; (64) penitent in a constrained posture; (65) penitent standing and leaning on a rope attached to a tree; (66) a naked penitent with long hair and prodigious nails.

Thus, with double numbers, there are sixty-nine plates in all. Most of them are crowded with figures in action, and are not merely drawings of the gods, goddesses, devotees, and penitents alone.

CODEX CCCXLV., DESCRIPTIONS OF PORTRAITS

Codex CCCXLV., in Class VI., an octavo volume, is the last of the four Manucci manuscripts now in the San Marco library at Venice, and contains Italian descriptions of the pictures in the Bibliothéque Nationale at Paris. With the pictures at Paris are bound up similar descriptions in French.

CODICES OF MANUCCI AND CODEX XLIV.

The 'Marciana Codex of Manucci' is quoted as one of the sources of the notice on him in 'Studii biografici e bibliografici sulla storia della geographia in Italia,' by P. Amat di S. Filippo (second edition, Roma, 1882), vol. i., p. 440, along with Zurla, of whom I have spoken, Legrenzi and Foscarini. Of these last I shall speak when I come to the story of Manucci's life. Some slight errors I have noted in the above work are: *Caton* for *Catrou*, 1707 for 1705, 8° for 4° and 120, 1737 for 1731 (Venice translation). Deslandes did not translate the work into French, but conveyed it to France; for *trasporto in francese*, read in *Francia*. Nor were Parts IV. and V. sent home in 1705, but Part IV. in 1706 and Part V. still later.

THE VOLUME OF PORTRAITS IN THE BIBLIOTHEQUE NATIONALE, PARIS.

Volume of portraits sent with Parts I., II., and III

Manucci, in his Latin letter, mentions that, along with the three volumes of his History sent to Europe through M. Deslandes, he also forwarded a volume of portraits. Catrou (Preface of 1705, p. 4) speaks as if he had control over this volume also, being only deterred by fear of expense from reproducing some of its contents. He may have inspected the volume, but as he did not make it over to the Jesuits' College along with the three volumes of text, we may doubt if he had more than a passing connection with it. I have not been able to discover any trace of the date or the channel of transfer to Venice. That the volume did reach the St. Mark Library at that place we have ample proof. Zanetti catalogued it there in 1741, and reproduced three of the pictures, and, as the present librarian writes, their copy of that catalogue bears the marginal note that the volume of pictures was made over to the French in 1797.

THIS VOLUME TRACED.

In 1898 I came across some articles in the *Gazette des Beaux Arts*, January to June, 1897, p. 281, by Monsieur E. Blochet, on 'Miniatures des MSS. Mussulmanes' and for one of his reproductions, a portrait of Dawar Bakhsh, alias Bulaqi, grandson of Jahangir, he gave as his authority 'Voyage de Manucci.' In March, 1899, being then in Paris, my friend Mr. H. Beveridge kindly made an examination for me, from which there could be no doubt that it was the identical volume that Zurla in 1818 declared had been mislaid, but, to speak more exactly, that had been carried off by the French in 1797 as part of their Italian booty.

INSPECTION VOLUME

I have since seen the book myself. It forms part of the collection in the Cabinet des Estampes at the Bibliothèque Nationale, and it is classed as O.D., No. 45 (reserve). It is now bound in red morocco, impressed with gold imperial eagles at the corners. Evidently it was rebound at Paris after 1797; but the embossed lozenge-shaped stamp of the San Marco Library, cut out of the old calf binding, is inserted in the centre of the new covers. The lining is of pale blue satin with gold edging. It is labelled outside 'Histoire de l'Inde depuis Tamerlank jusqu'a Orangzeb, par Manucci,' and bears the year 1712. Inside is the *ex-libris* of San Marco, bearing the same name (Geronimo Veniero) and the same year (1722) as that in Codex XLIV. (Zanetti) at Venice. Opposite each picture is a description of it in French. Of these an Italian version is found at Venice in Codex Class VI., No, cccxlv.; they are evidently the composition of Manucci. Most of the portraits are very characteristic; those of Aurangzeb and Shiva Jl may be specially noted. Those of Shah 'Alam and the other sons of Aurangzeb, as those of persons known to Manucci, ought to be authentic. The two pictures devoted, one to the kings of Gulkhandah and the other to the kings of Bijapur, strike me as very life-like, and probably also authentic.

MANUCCI'S ACCOUNT OF PORTRAITS.

As an introduction to his descriptions, Manucci says: 'Before I left the Mogul dominions' [that is, before 1686], 'to satisfy my curiosity I caused portraits to be painted of all the kings and princes from Taimur-lang to Aurangzeb, including the sons and grandsons of the last named, together with the portraits of the rulers over Bijapur and Gulkandah, of some of the chief Hindu princes, and of other famous generals. The artist was a friend of mine, Mir Muhammad, an official in the household of the prince, Shāh 'Aīam, and all were copied from originals in the royal palace. So far as I know, no one has yet imparted such portraits to the public; or if any ingenious person has so done, this collection of mine has nothing in common with such, mine being the veritable, which the others cannot be. Meanwhile, to get them I have spared no expense, and have given many presents; and the whole was carried out under great difficulties, it being incumbent on me to observe profound secrecy as to my having the copies. I do not bring forward any portraits of queens and princesses, for it is impossible to see them, thanks to their being always concealed. If anyone has produced such portraits, they should not be accepted, being only likenesses of concubines and dancing- girls, etc., which have been drawn according to the artist's fancy. It should be remarked that all portraits showing a nimbus and an umbrella over the head are those of persons of the blood royal.'

HAND-LIST, BY E. BLOCHET.

In the *Revue des Bibliothèques* for 1898 (vol. viii.), 1899 (vol. ix.), and 1900 (vol. x.), Monsieur Blochet published an 'Inventaire et Description des Miniatures des MSS. Orientaux dans la Bibliothèque Nationale a Paris,' subsequently reproduced in a separate volume (pp. 278, 8vo.; Paris: E. Bouillon, 1900). On pp. 225-229 is a list of the fifty-six paintings in volume O.D., No. 45 (réserve); but this I need not insert, as black and white reproductions of the whole series are incorporated in the present issue of Manucci. The excellent negatives from which they are taken were done by Monsieur P. Sauvanaud, of the Rue Jacob, Paris, who was recommended to me by Monsieur Blochet. The original paintings are, as M. Blochet justly says, 'd'une splendide execution; they lose vastly in effect when stripped of their colouring, at once gorgeous and exquisitely delicate, and I regret that the great expense has made it impossible to attempt their reproduction by some colour process. Apart from their artistic excellence, these pictures have the additional value of forming a collection which has never been disturbed since it was made, while the date of execution and the name of the artist are accurately known. Thus the portraits of men then alive may be accepted as likenesses, so far as the skill of the painter permitted.

PREVIOUS REPRODUCTIONS OF A FEW PICTURES.

Of previous reproductions of these portraits, I have already referred to the three fine copperplate engravings in Zanetti's catalogue of 1741, and Monsieur Blochet's process block of Dāwar Bakhsh, alias Bulāqī (grandson of Jahāngir), in the *Gazette des*

Beaux Arts (1897). In June, 1903, I accidentally took up some lithographs, displayed by Miss Manning at one of her National Indian Association meetings, and to my surprise one of these, a portrait of Aurangzeb, professed to be from 'una miniatura persiana estratta dal MS. di Manucci.' Miss Manning told me she had destroyed the book but kept the illustrations, and she subsequently sent me thirty-three lithographs in all, and of these, a portrait of Akbar was also referred to an original in Manucci's collection. After a good deal of trouble the book was found at Rome. It turns out to be 'Storia delle Indie Orientali,' by Giovanni Flechia, preceded by a 'Geographical Description of India,' by F. C. Marmocchi (2 vols., 4to., Torino, 1862). The geography (262 pages) is good, but the history is a mere compilation from Elphinstone and other easily accessible authorities.

FLECHIA AND MARMOCCHI'S 'STORIA.'

There are forty-seven full-page lithographic illustrations, mostly taken from W. Daniell's 'Oriental Annuals and a few, the most spirited, from originals by Evremont de Bérard (flourished c. 1852-1861). There are five portraits of emperors: (1) Taimur, (2) Akbar, (3) Shāhjahān, (4) Aurangzeb, (5) Bahadur Shah II., all given in gold and colours, very creditably done, that of Shāhjāhan being especially good. Of these, the second, third and fourth profess to be taken from Manucci's volume, but no further indication of its *locale* is given. The one of Shahjahan could hardly be from the Manucci collection, as there is no such portrait of that monarch contained in it.

VIII. MANUCCI'S BIOGRAPHY

Printed Accounts Defective

Although, as Foscarini says, Manucci's life, 'che fu piena d'accidenti curiosi,' can be easily put together from the 'Storia,' the accounts of him in the usual biographical dictionaries are singularly meagre and erroneous. Neither in the old nor the new edition of the 'Biographic Universelle' (Michaud) does his name appear either under Manouchi or Manucci. In the 'Nouvelle Biographie Générale' (Didot), xxxiii. (1860), we certainly have an entry. But, unfortunately, it is one crowded with demonstrable errors. There is no evidence that Manucci died about 1710; on the contrary, his continued existence in 1712 can be proved. That he returned to Europe in 1691 or any other year; that he retired to Portugal; that he published a work which had become very scarce, are all untenable propositions. The entry in Sir Thomas Phillipps's catalogue is of a manuscript, not of a printed book; it is, therefore, hardly to be wondered at if the dictionary contributor (F. D.) had never been able to find a copy. His authority, the 'Mercure Galant' for 1691, I have not been able to consult, as it is not in the British Museum; what his 'documents particuliers' were, we, of course, cannot know now.

FROM BIRTH TO 1656

By the inquiries I instituted at Venice, I was unable to find any trace there of Manucci. I was told that the name was not Patrician. The only other Manuccis that I have come across do not, I fear, shed much lustre on the name; both occur in Casanova de Seingalt's 'Mémoires one was the spy who denounced Casanova as a heretic, and secured his committal to *I Piombi*; the other was a friend met at Barcelona, whose plans Jacopo Casanova inadvertently betrayed.[1] As Manucci nowhere tells us his father's Christian name or the parish of his birth, to search for his birth or baptism was a hopeless task. Nor did the police reports yield any notice of such a boy's disappearance. Further search under the right year and month (November, 1653) has not produced anything, nor any mention of Viscount Bellomont's stay at Venice and departure from it by sea. Thus the only means of reconstituting Manucci's life-story and its chronology is a search through the 'Storia.' This reconstruction I now attempt.

FROM BIRTH TO 1656

In the early part of his book, and up to about the year 1678, there is an almost constant defect of two years in Manucci's dates. From external evidence we know that the eclipse of the sun he saw at Zulfah, in Armenia, took place on August 12, 1654; that he landed in India in January, 1656; that the Battle of Samugarh, near Āgrah, was fought on June 8, 1658.[2] Calculating from these

1. See C. Whibley's article in *Macmillan's Magazine* for February, 1903, p. 273.
2. This mistake of two years in Manucci explains the appearance of 1656 instead of 1658 in Catrou, p. 195, who made here a most uncritical use of his text. He could easily have corrected the error from Bernier.

points as fixed data, we find that Manucci left Venice in November, 1653 (not 1651). He says he was then fourteen, and thus must have been born some time in 1639. He ran away from home, and hid on board a vessel bound for Smyrna; here he encountered Viscount Bellomont (Henry Bard), then on his way to Persia and India. Bellomont had pity on the lad, and took him into his service. From Smyrna they went through Asia Minor to the Persian court at Qazwīn (August, 1654). Thence they moved to Isfahān, where they remained a year (September, 1654 to September, 1655), finally reaching Gombroon (Bandar 'Abbās) *via* Shiraz and Lar. A passage was obtained on the H.E.I. Company's *Seahorse*, in which they reached Sūrat, on the west coast of India, in January, 1656. Leaving that place in April, they travelled by Burhānpur, Hāndiyah, Sironj, Narwar, Gwāliyār and Dholpur to Āgrah; thence they started for the Mogul court at Dihlī. On June 20, 1656, when near Hodal, a place between Mathurā and Dihlī, Bellomont suddenly expired.

1656-1666

Manucci went on to Dihlī, and, through the dispute arising over the late ambassador's affairs, obtained an introduction to Prince Dara Shukoh, eldest son of the emperor Shahjahan. Manucci was enlisted as an artilleryman in Dara's service on rupees 80 a month. In 1658, when the princes Aurangzeb and Murad Bakhsh moved against Agrah, Dara Shukoh marched south to oppose them, Manucci being in his army. A countermarch to Samugarh followed, and there battle was delivered. Manucci was in the field, and after Dara's defeat fled with the rest to Agrah. Subsequently he succeeded in attaching himself in disguise to Aurangzeb's army, and was in it when Murad Bakhsh was seized. From Dihlī Manucci managed to get away and join Dara Shukoh at Lahor. With that prince he marched to Multan and Bhakkar. He was placed at the head of the artillery in the latter fortress, under the command of the eunuch Basant, and the garrison stood a siege, only surrendering after the capture of their prince. Evacuating Bhakkar, the garrison returned to Lahor, and there Manucci escaped with his bare life from an attack in which Basant was killed. Returning with the other European artillery men to Dihli, Manucci refused further service, as he disliked Aurangzeb.

After he had witnessed that monarch's departure from Dihlī for Kashmir (December 8, 1662), Manucci made an expedition eastwards, and, taking boat at Patnah, travelled to Rajmahal and Dhakkah, thence through the Sundarbans to Hugli, returning to Agrah by way of Qasimbazar. At Agrah and Dihli he gradually adopted medicine as a profession, but, obtaining an introduction to Rajah Jai Singh, of Amber, through his second son, Kirat Singh, he was offered by that prince the post of captain of artillery on 10 rupees a day. Jai Singh was appointed Governor of the Dakhin between March and September, 1664. Manucci marched with him for that country, being deputed on the way to negotiate with some petty rajahs north of Bombay. After seven months he rejoined at Aurangabad, where the rajah had united his forces with those of Shah 'Alam. He saw Shiva Ji in the rajah's camp in June or July, 1665. In Jai Singh's further move southwards against Bijapur Manucci also took part.

1666-1677

Apparently tiring of his position, Manucci resigned (II. 108, 109), and made his way via Kaliyani to Bassain, twenty-eight miles north of Bombay; he was there during the Lent of 1667, and narrowly escaped the Inquisition (III. 230). He reached Goa in May, 1667, and after a stay of fifteen months (May 1667 to August 1668) he left it disguised as a Carmelite, and returned to Agrah and Dihli (II. 130). At the latter place he attached himself to Kirat Singh, obtaining from him a horse and rupees 5 a day. After a year's time Kirat Singh was ordered to Kabul, and Manucci resolved to move to Lahor (end of 1670 or early in 1671), and start practice there as a physician. He practised as such for about six or seven years, and, having realized a small competence, decided on removing into territory governed by Enropeans. This must have been in 1676, as he was at Daman, on the west coast, in that year (II. 137, III. 198), and during 1677 (III. 264, 265) he made his home at Bandora, on Salsette Island, nine miles north of Bombay fort.

1678-1682

Having lost his money in a bad speculation, Manucci was obliged to try his fortunes once more at the Mogul court. He returned to Dihli, where, through a court chamberlain, he was called in to attend one of Shah 'Alam's wives, and, having cured her of a gathering in the ear, the lady interested herself in his affairs and procured his appointment by that prince as one of his physicians. This must have been subsequent to January 30, 1678, the date on which Shah 'Alam returned to Dihli from Kabul. On September 28, 1678, Shah 'Alam was made governor of the Dakhin, and Manucci went there in his train. He says once that he was at Agrah in 1679, and possibly the occasion was on this march to the Dakhin. On September 6, 1679, Shah 'Alam's thirty-seventh birthday, they were at Aurangabad; but not long before this (December 18, 1678) Jaswant Singh of Jodhpur had died in Kabul, and Aurangzeb, after failing to seize one of the rajah's infant sons, resolved on the conquent of the Jodhpur state. Shah 'Alam was recalled to take part in the campaign, and the prince (Manucci with him) passed the rains of 1680 at Ujjain (II. 204). In January, 1681, they joined the main army at Ajmer, having seen a comet on their way (December 24, 1680). Prince Akbar had just fled (January 13, 1681), and had raised the standard of revolt. On the 26th Shah 'Alam was sent in pursuit, and remained on this duty until the end of March (1681). Some sort of peace was patched up with the other Rajputs, Akbar escaped to the Mahrattahs in the south, and, in consequence, on September 15, 1681, Aurangzeb began his first march towards the Dakhin, a country from which he was destined never to return.

1682-1684

Finding his position an irksome one, and having some money in the hands of the Theatine Fathers at Goa, Manucci, apparently in 1682 or early in 1683, resolved to get away under the pretext of two months' leave of absence. On reaching Surat he obtained a boat from François Martin,[1] of the French Company, which took him to Daman, and thence to Goa. The then governor of Goa, the Conde de Alvor, had taken charge on September 11, 1681, and at the time of our hero's arrival found himself closely threatened by an army under Sambha Ji, son of Shiva Ji, the Mahrattah. About August, 1683,

1. F. Martin was at Surat from 1680 to 1686 (see J. Sottas, 'Histoire,' 1904, p. 104, and Michaud, 'Biographie Universelle,' new edition of 1860, vol. xxvii., p. 121, article by Pierre Margry).

having unwisely offered battle at Ponda on the mainland, the viceroy was badly defeated. Negotiations were opened, and Manucci was sent to interview Sambha Ji. Nothing resulted, and Santo Estevaoñ, one of the Goa islands, was captured by Sambha Ji during the night of November 25, 1683. Once more Manucci visited the Mahrattah chief, and also went to see Shah 'Alam, who was approaching in a threatening manner. He also took part in a second embassy to Shah 'Alam. For all these services the governor conferred on him a patent of knighthood in the Portuguese Order of St. Iago, this patent being dated January 29, 1684.

1684-1686

On the second visit Shah 'Alam detained Manucci as an absconder from his service. Flight was attempted, but the poor man was brought back much against his will. A difficult march through the Ghats was then made, and the prince rejoined his father at Ahmadnagar. Shortly afterwards Shah 'Alam was sent against the King of Gulkandah. When the camp was at Malkher, Manucci managed to enter into communication with the general on the opposite side, and he was helped to escape to Gulkandah. When Shah 'Alam occupied Gulkandah (1686) Manucci fled further afield to the European settlements at Narsapur and Masulipatam, on the east coast. Soldiers brought him back to Gulkandah, but he was successful in evading delivery to the agents of Shah 'Alam, who had left that place. Once more, with the aid of an Augustinian friar, he managed after two months to get away, and took refuge at the English settlement of Madras or Fort St. George. This was in the second half of 1686.

1686, HIS MARRIAGE

Paying a visit to François Martin at Pondicherry, eighty-six miles south of Madras, Manucci was dissuaded from returning to Europe, and was advised to marry. He was introduced to a Catholic widow, the daughter of Christopher Hartley and Aguida Pereyra. Her first husband, Thomas Clarke, had died on October 6, 1683. Manucci married her on October 28, 1686, and a son was born to them, but the child died in infancy. He resumed his practice as a physician, and much commends a cordial of which he had the secret, while his 'stones,' an imitation of the Goa stones of the Jesuits, had a great vogue.[1]

1686-1700

Almost immediately on his arrival at Madras Manucci's 1686-1700. services were requisitioned by Governor William Gyfford (July 1681 to July 1687). Gyfford wrote to the 'Great Mogull' on February 17, 1686/7, and March 20, 1686/7, sending both letters by Manucci's messengers. Before the answer arrived from the court Gyfford had been superseded by Elihu Yale (July 1687 to October 23, 1692), and on September 16, 1687, the new governor ousted Manucci and made over the negotiation entirely to Khwajah Ibnus, alias Joan de Marke, an Armenian merchant at Gulkandah, with whom the correspondence lasted until July, 1688. During Yale's (1687-1692) and Higginson's (1692-1698) governorships Manucci would appear to have remained out of favour. On the contrary, Thomas Pitt, governor from 1698 to 1709, seems to have liked and trusted Manucci—at any rate, he employed him a good deal.

1700-1703

In 1700 Sir William Norris and Consul John Pitt, who had come out in the interests of the newly-founded rival English company, made overtures to Manucci to join the first-named as interpreter. Manucci declined on the score of age and blindness, but really out of a desire not to offend Governor Pitt.[2]

In O.C., No. 6737 (Masulipatam general letter of September 19, 1699), we have an intimation that a letter was awaited from 'Sen[r] Manuchii,' which was delayed by his absence at Pondicherry, the French settlement, on some business he was transacting for them (the French).

A translation of Manucci's answer to John Pitt is to be found

1. C. Lockyer, 'Account of Trade in India,' 1711, p. 268, and see 'Hobson Jobson,' p. 379, S.V. 'Goa Stones.'
2. Yule, 'Diary of W. Hedges,' ii,, pp. cclxviii, cclxix; iii., p. xlv, where see—
   (a) J. Pitt, Italian letter to N. M. of July 28, 1699 (O.S.) (India Office, O.C., 6685).
   (b) Sir W. Norris to Sir Nicholas Waite, from Masulipatam, January 19, 1699/1700 (O.C., 6836).
   (c) J. Peachey to J. Pitt, from Fort St. George, February 19, 1699/1700 (O.C., 6919).

at the India Office (O.C., vol. lxvi., Part I., No. 6790), and, as Sir Henry Yule does not give it, I insert it in full.

'MOST ILLUSTRIOUS SR. MR. PITT

'I have received the honour of 3 letters, which you have done me the Favour of writing to me, and am infinitely obliged to you, for all the Goodness you show therein; and (as I should be alwayes gladd to serve your Honr.) I would doe it with all my heart, but finding my Selfe Old and Infirme, I am not in a Condition to undertake what You desire of me; If I enjoyed my former health and Strength, it would be a great honour to me, to find soe favourable an opportunity of Serving, his Majesty, his Excellency, and the Noble Company, but my Infirmity and Blindness will not permit me.

'I desire your Honour will assure your selfe, that noe other reason should hinder me from accepting the soe Honourable Offers that you make me with soe much Goodness.

'I have not answered your two former Letters, not having mett with a secure oppertunity; in fine, I offer you my whole heart, and upon all occasions You shall find me punctually ready, as your most humble Servant. God keep your illustrious person.

'Madrastapatan, 1/11 December, 1699.

'Most Illustrious Sr.,

'Your most humble

'NICOLAS MANUCH.

'To the most illustrious'
Signor Mr. Pitt, President of
the Noble Royall Company
of England for the Coast of
Cormandell, Metchlapatan.'

The kingdom of Gulkandah having finally fallen in the Moguls proceeded to invest Jinji, eighty-two miles southwest of Madras, but were unable to reduce it until 1698. From the date of its fall they became very active, and began to interfere throughout the Karnatik. Their deputy-governor, Da'ud Khan, Panni, obeying orders from court, made himself especially disagreeable. In 1702 he invested Madras for many weeks, when Manucci and a Brahmin were sent as joint envoys from Governor Pitt to the besieger (Part IV., 87, 93, 97, 244;

V., 224). The story of these negotiations, from the official point of view, will be found in J. Talboys Wheeler's 'Madras in the Olden Time,' chapter xvi., pp. 195-221. In February and March, 1703, Manucci paid a visit to that Nawab at his house in Kadapah, 137 miles north-west of Madras.

1703-1706 ECCLESIASTICAL DISPUTE

With 1703 begins the active stage of the dispute between the Capuchins and Jesuits, arising chiefly out of the so-called disputes. Malabar Rites or Accommodation Strife,[1] about the supposed concessions of Jesuit missionaries to heathendom. Into this and other ecclesiastical matters Manucci threw himself with great energy. In 1700 he had been the host of some priests who were on their way to China (IV., 231, 232), and at the end of 1701 he wrote to Da'ud Khan about persecutions in Tanjor, being thanked in two letters by the Père Pierre Martin, Jesuit, of that mission (second letter, dated February 6, 1702). With the arrival of Cardinal de Tournon, papal legate, at Pondicherry in November, 1703, ecclesiastical questions took precedence of all others in our author's mind. He devotes many pages to these questions, and in Pére Norbert's 'Mémoires Utiles èt Nécessaires,' Luques (Lucca), 1742, p. 187, under the date of January 10, 1707, we find 'Nicolo Manucci' as one of the four witnesses who attest that a certain request had been presented on September 28, 1706, by Père Michel Angelo, Capuchin, to the Bishop of St. Thome, an ex-Jesuit.

1706-1717 TO HIS DEATH

In 1706 Manucci lost his wife, and at some date between to 'that event and 1712 he moved his home to Pondicherry. In the latter year he proposed to make a journey to the Mogul court at Lahor on the request of Shah 'Alam, who had become emperor five years before. The Madras Council wished to make use of his mediation to clear up certain long-pending difficulties with the Mogul, and secure fresh privileges for their honourable masters. The death of Shah 'Alam put an end to Manucci's plans. But as a reward for previous services during Da'ud Khan's attack, the governor and Council on January 14, 1712,

1. 'Accommodation' in the French sense, as in Molière's 'Il y a avec le ciel des accommodements.'

conceded to him in perpetuity his leasehold house and garden at Madras, situated outside the north-west corner of the then Black Town.

The previous history of this renewal presents one or two points of interest. An order of March 22, 1702/3, directed a renewal for twenty-one years on the levy of a fine of sixty *pagodas*, with the rider: 'It being the general opinion of all that the aforesaid Nicolo Manuch is very poor, and in consideration of his readiness to serve the Company on all occasions, 'tis agreed that upon his payment of the sixty *pagodas* before-mentioned, it be returned to him as a gratuity for his good services' ('Factory Records,' Fort St. George, vol. xiii., fol. 37).

Unfortunately, before the lease was drawn up and executed a Padre at Negapatam sent to the governor (Thomas Pitt) a 'letter full of strange invectives against Sen[r] Manuch,' which, when produced before the Council, led them to suspect he' was not true to the Company's interest.' The lease was stopped and inquiry ordered. It was found that 'the Padre was an infamous and scandalous fellow.' Manucci had detected him in attempts at debaucheries in his family, while the Padres at Madras and other Portuguese of good reputation gave the Padre a very ill character. It was determined on December 18, 1704, to grant the lease on the terms originally sanctioned ('Factory Records' Fort St. George, vol. xiii., fol. 203).

Then follows the lease, dated December 20, 1704. It recites that the first grant for thirty years was made to Thomas Clarke, gent[n], in the year 1671. It consisted of a garden or parcel of ground without the town. Manucci petitioned as heir of Thomas Clarke (having married his widow). The terms were a fine of sixty *pagodas* (remitted as above stated), and a yearly acknowledgment of one *pagoda*.

This house and garden lay to the north of Madras, and just north of it again was a piece of ground known as the Elephant Garden (entry of May 7, 1706). The plot was 657 feet from north to south, and from east to west (at the north end) 353 feet and (at the south end) 482 feet. The boundaries were: North, the garden of Foree Moortepan; south, the Black Town wall; east, Mantangaura's garden and some Pariah houses; west, the highway from Tom Clarke's gate to the Company's old garden. The term granted was for twenty-one years from

March 25, 1703, at a yearly rent of one pagoda (see Madras Consultations, January 15, 1704/5, Range 239, vol. lxxxiii., pp. 19-22, and 69[1]).

The perpetual grant of January 14, 1712, was made under the following circumstances: On November 1, 1711, Mr. Charles Boon, a free merchant, appeared before the Madras Council (Edward Harrison, president) with a petition from Señor Nichola Manuch, 'formerly inhabitant of this place but now in Pondicherry.' The petition recites the lease of ground near Tom Clarke's gate, in which by mistake a piece of ground for which he (Nichola Manuch) held a bill of sale was wrongly included, and he prays for a rectification. On November 6, 1711, H. Davenport, B. Binyon, and W. Warre reported. The terms of the report are not entered, but apparently it was adverse to the application.

But on January 14, 1712, the president revived the matter in council. He informed the Board that a special order had come to Pondicherry calling for Manucci's attendance at Shah 'Alam's court [then at Lahor]. Manucci was about to set out for Arkat to see the *diwan*, who had orders to supply all his necessities and forward him to Dihli. The president reverts to the refusal on November 6, 1711, to admit a higher title than that of leaseholder; and now for the following reasons : (1) As the land is of very small value; (2) as 'the said Manuch during his residence here was very serviceable to the Company's affairs by his perfect knowledge of the Persian language and the customs among the Moors, having been often employ'd between Governor Pitt and Nabob Doud Caun; (3) but yet more in consideration that he may be very usefull in our present circumstances by assisting those that go to court with the Present from Bengal; (4) and likewise representing our quarrel with Surup Sing with advantage on our side' he proposes a new resolution in supersession of the former one. It is

1. I am indebted to the Rev. F. Penny for the information that, up to the beginning of the eighteenth century, the north-west gate of Fort St. George, now called the Choultry Gate, was known as 'Tom Clarke's Gate.' For the Company's garden, marked simply 'Garden,' see the map of 1733, reproduced in Mrs. Penny's 'Fort St. George.' All these houses must have been swept away in 1746, when the French took the place, and formed a *glacis* round the fort.

to the effect that in consideration of the good service done by Señor Nichola Manuch, they confirm to him and his heirs for ever that piece of ground which Thomas Drinkwater bought of Charles and Ann Ryly on September 26, 1674, since sold to Thomas Clarke on April 19, 1675, and by the said Thomas Clarke to Nicholas Manuch.

While on the subject of Manucci's houses, it seems to be tolerably clear that he had a second house or country retreat at Big Mount or St. Thomas's Mount, eight miles from Fort St. George. This property is mentioned distinctly in Part V., folios 101, 102, and elsewhere. It must be the place where Manucci entertained Da,ud Khian. The late Mr. A. T. Pringle objected that in those disturbed times Europeans would not have lived so far away from Madras; and for the same reason doubted Manucci's story about a theft of fruit from the governor's garden at the same place on December 15, 1705 (Part V., folio 55). But the entry of December 1, 1705, ordering the destruction of the Mount House and the building of another there for invalids, shows that Manucci was quite right, and (for once) Mr. Pringle was wrong. There was a governor's house at St. Thomas's Mount in 1705 (Public Consultations, Fort St. George, vol. xxxv., pp. 269, 270).

The first mention of obtaining a *farman* through Zu,lfiqar Khan, the new governor of the Dakhin, is in a letter from Fort St. George of December 16, 1711 (List of Old Records, No. 807); and under date December 1, 1711, the Surat Council speak of their embassy (*idem*, No. 794). The Madras Council anticipated difficulties, owing to their having employed Ziya-ud-din Khan as their go-between, to the displeasure of Zu,lfiqar Khan, whose new office of viceroy made him all-powerful in the Dakhin. However, the emperor Shah 'Alam died at Lahor on February 27, and the report thereof reached Madras in April, 1712; thus, no doubt, Manucci did not start for the court, while the English for the time abandoned their project of an embassy. It was not until some years afterwards that John Surman was sent to Dihli from Calcutta.

I have failed to trace Manucci farther at Madras or Pondicherry, and the only date for his death is a vague intimation in the work 'Della Litteratura Veneziana . . . . .' (4to., Venice, 1854), by the Doge Marco Nicoló Foscarini (b. February, 1695,

d. March, 1763; Librarian of San Marco from 1742 to 1762), which was originally published in one volume, folio, at Padua in 1752. On p. 441 of the 4th edition (1854) it is said that Manucci died in India in 1717 as an octogenarian, 'as he [Foscarini] had heard.' Father Doyle of San Thome informs me that there are no records there previous to 1784, when Tippu's cavalry plundered and burnt everything. I have not been able to search the Pondicherry archives, and some entry may be found there. As would seem, Manucci left an estate of 30,000 *pagodas* (about £10,000), judging by the entry taken from Padre Saverini Capuchin's accounts, as printed in the 'Madras Catholic Directory' for 1867, p. 153. Although 1742, the date of Saverini's appointment as superior (Penny, 'Church in Madras,' p. 240), is rather late for administration to the estate of a man dying in 1717, it is almost impossible of belief that there could have been in that part of the world, in the first half of the eighteenth century, any other 'Mr. Nicholas Manook' than Nicolao Manucci, the author of the 'Storia do Mogor.' The only possible argument against this identification is the fact that twice Manucci made himself out a poor man. Once was when the fine on the renewal of his lease was remitted by the Madras Council; the other instance was the non-payment in 1706 of a death-bed bequest by his wife of two hundred *pagodas* to the Bishop of San Thome. Father Michael Angelo, the Madras chaplain, urged him to pay it. Manucci said he had no money; the Father suggested borrowing, and to that Manucci replied that his debts were already too heavy for him to wish to add to them (V., f. 279).

A search at the India Office in the copies of the Madras Records up to 1719, which are there preserved, has produced nothing bearing upon the question of our author's death or his estate. The reason of this is probably the fact, communicated to me by the Rev. Frank Penny, that for many years the estates of Roman Catholics were left in the hands of the priests for administration, and were not dealt with by the English officials.

SUMMARY OF PLAN AND CONTENTS OF THE 'STORIA.'

Original Plan of 'Storia.'

Manucci started his work on a fixed plan, to which he adhered tolerably closely in the first three parts, though already in the second half of Part III. he becomes discursive. But in Parts IV. and V. it is hardly possible to discover any plan, their contents being so exceedingly heterogeneous—current historical events alternating with personal adventures, stories of long-past years, or even mere fables. In Parts IV. and V. the ecclesiastical element also bulks very largely, the author taking a strongly adverse position to the Jesuits and their missionary methods.

PART I

Part I. consists of two sections—first, a personal narrative of the author's journey from Venice to Dihli, divided into twenty chapters (pp. 1-55); secondly, a short chronicle of the Mogul kings, beginning with Taimur-i-lang, and ending with Aurangzeb's succession and the death of his three brothers: Taimur-i-lang, pp. 57-61; Miran Shah, pp. 61-63 ; Abu Sa'id, pp. 63, 64; 'Umar Shekh, p. 64; Sultan Mahmud, pp. 64-66; Babar, pp. 66-69 (list of thirty-one previous kings of Dihli); Humayun, pp. 69-75; Akbar, pp. 75-98; Excursus on the Chinese in India, pp. 98-100, and on the Baniyas, pp. 100-103; Jahangir, pp. 103-120; Shahjahan, pp. 120-280. Under Shahjahan are set forth the author's personal adventures up to and including the War of Succession (1658-1659).

PART II

In Part II, pp. 1-255, is given the reign of Aurangzeb, Part II. 1658-1700, interspersed with the author's personal history, his journeys and adventures, during the same period.

PART III

Part III is principally a treatise on the Mogul court, with its system of government and statistics of its revenues. Some of the subjects treated are: The royal household, p. 2; names of queens, p. 3; of concubines, p. 4; of harem matrons, p. 4; of chief dancers, p. 5; of women slaves, p. 5; habits of the harem, p. 6; mode of addressing the emperor, p. 11; names of eunuchs, p. 13; of physicians, p. 16; of slaves, p. 17; of swords, p. 17; of shields, p. 18; of horses, p. 18; of elephants, p. 18; of cannon, p. 21; of the nobles, p. 22. Then follows the system of pay and rank, the mode of government and its abuses, p. 29, with a digression on Sir William Norris's (1700) and the Dutch (1688) embassies; the author's work as physician, p. 43; a list of provinces and their revenues, p. 49; descriptions of the provinces, p. 53; the Hindu states, p. 59; routes and distances, p. 67; Mahomedans, p. 72; treatise on the Hindu religion and ceremonial, p. 90; on elephants and other animals, p. 144; Governor Gyfford and the Mogul court, p. 154; origin of Madras, p. 155; empire of Nar Singh, p. 166; the Jesuit Roberto de' Nobili, p. 171; the pearl fishery, p. 171; various stories of Goa, Pondicherry, and San Thome, p. 175; stories of witchcraft and magic, p. 247 to end.

PART IV

Part IV begins by continuing the account of current in the Mogul camp (1701), with earlier reminiscences introduced here and there, pp. 1-33; Sir William Norris's embassy, P- 34; Jesuit missions, pp. 36-49; Tanjor persecutions, pp. 49-60, 62-76; quarrels of Capuchins and Jesuits, pp. 60-62 ; more about the Tanjor persecutions, pp. 76-80; Mogul attacks on Tranquebar, Cuddalur, and Pondicherry, pp. 80-86; Da,ud Khan and Madras, pp. 87-105; Aurangzeb's doings, pp. 105-120; Father Ephraim and the Goa Inquisition in 1649, pp. 124-146; a visit to Da,ud Khan at Kadapah, pp. 147-151; events of 1702-1704, pp. 152-162; Cardinal de Tournon and the Jesuits, pp. 164-197; various events, pp. 197-218; Christian quarrels, pp. 225-230; other events (ends on p. 244).

PART V

In Part V the relation of events is carried on into 1705 and 1706, pp. 1-2371; two Manifestoes by the Capuchins against the Bishop of San Thome and the Jesuits occupy pp. 238-417; then we return to events from 1707 to February, 1709, p. 418 (ending on p. 459). Stories about various earlier years are interspersed—viz. of 1659, I665, 1690, 1699, and so forth.

X. MANUCCI, THE AUTHOR AND THE MAN

Language Used

A work written by an Italian not in his mother-tongue, but in Portuguese, has always presented an interesting problem. We find now, on consulting the Codex at Venice, that about one-third of the whole work was drawn up originally in Italian. I have not used this text much, so I am not able to say fully in what it differs from the final copy of Parts I. to III., prepared in French and in Portuguese for transmission to Europe. But from what I have seen of it, the Italian text is much inferior in arrangement to the Berlin MS.; its only use is to furnish a various reading here and there, and, perhaps, a few extra details worth preserving. The explanation for the choice of language, perhaps not a very sufficient one, as given by Manucci in two or three places, is that he was forced to change the language according to the nationality of the amanuensis available at the time. For instance, what he says (in Italian) on folio 364 of Codex XLIV. (Zanetti) is: 'Owing to the want of an Italian copyist, I have been obliged to continue my work in French, and even in Portuguese. The latter is far from correct, there not being any scribes here who are careful to seek always for the meaning of words; I leave the matter to the goodwill of the learned.' From this point he drops Italian for French, and shortly after changes into Portuguese.

CHARACTERISTICS OF LANGUAGE AND STYLE

The French, as it seems to me, is handled with less freedom and force than the Portuguese. The latter would probably be deemed a patois, but I am not in a position myself to judge it, style-or compare it with more highly-elaborated compositions in that language. As used by Manucci, it has the merits of being simple, direct, and graphic; and it forms an excellent vehicle for his narrative. As a *raconteur* Manucci takes high rank, knowing all the secrets of how to tell a story, precision of place and date, abundance of appropriate and convincing detail. Passages that may be singled out from much that is nearly as good are the death of the eunuch Basant, the author's first surgical case at Lahor, the onset of the Rajput chivalry headed by their red-eyed, opium-maddened bards chanting their battle-songs, the Nathan-like apologue told to Bishop Gaspar Affonço of San Thome, and the scene at the bleeding of Shah 'Alam's wife. Many others might be adduced. His style, though simple and non-literary, is extremely vivacious. He had what Catrou calls 'je ne scai quel feu d'imagination' in his mode of narration; he never fails in interesting and carrying his readers along with him, and reproduces something of the stir of life in Indian cities, and their vividly contrasted splendour and squalor. In an occasional grossness of expression, opposed to our present canons of taste, he is following only the usage of his age and country. On the other hand, he is seldom guilty of pruriency or lubricity.

PLACE AS AN HISTORIAN

An as historian Manucci presents us with a somewhat mingled yarn. His supposed extracts from the Mogul official chronicles 'are for the reigns preceding that of Shahjahan a tissue of absurdities. These fables were, no doubt, current among the people, but they are distortions of the facts, as such folks' talk always is. What is told about Jahangir, whether true or not, is at any rate characteristic, and might be true. With the reign of Shahjahan things alter, and certainly for the later years of that reign and for the fifty years of Aurangzeb Manucci is a writer whose statements cannot be ignored. I will not assert that what he says must always be believed. He was at times misinformed; he was prejudiced; he wrote in the decline of life, thirty to forty years after many of the events had happened. I do not think he was intentionally unveracious; he is, indeed, quite honest and specific, as a rule, about the sources of his information. No doubt he had a penchant for the personal side of history—in fact, he has been called a 'backstairs gossip,' —but I do not think this condemns him as unworthy of credit. Oriental history, as tricked out by venal and fulsome pens, tells us little or nothing of the real character of the actors in it, or of the inner causes of events; and a writer like Manucci supplies us with the necessary corrective of life like, if at times sordid, detail. Merely because they reveal undignified or discreditable actions, I do not hold that his stories should be rejected, while I think they are always true to the spirit of the time and country, and therefore antecedently probable. Governor Pitt's remark that the work was a 'history of Tom Thumb' is absurd, and the less worthy of respect that he had not seen any part of what he was condemning.[1]

One of the principal objects I have had in writing the notes which I have added to the text has been to show that, with rare exceptions, Manucci's statements, where they can be verified, are

1. Governor Pitt to Mr. Wooley, Secretary at the India House, October 19, 1701, in Yule's 'Diary of Sir W. Hedges,' ii., cclxviii, note 3.

historically accurate, and a fair inference is that, where there is no such corroboration, he may equally be accepted as trustworthy.

MANUCCI NOT A PLAGIARIST

In my opinion Manucci has not copied from others, with the partial exception of F. Bernier. Evidently he possessed Bernier's book, and I think that where the two deal with the same events, Manucci took the order of his subjects from Bernier. Even then the topics are used chiefly as suggesting to him his own reminiscences. Another fact which distinguishes Manucci from Bernier is that in the contest for the crown they were on opposite sides, Manucci with Dara and Bernier with Aurangzeb; and we thus obtain the story of the defeated faction, which is frequently suppressed by the victor's eulogists. In one instance Manucci may be convicted of actually copying Bernier. But after 1667, when the French physician left India, no suggestion can be made of any debt due to him by our author. Bernier was, of course, a trained physician and a man of superior education. But Manucci was an equally acute observer, and had an advantage in his very much longer experience of the country. In one or two cases, for instance, that of the siege of Bhakkar, p. 93, Bernier was probably indebted to Manucci himself for his information. If before 1667 Bernier (p. 55, ed. Constable) had the political prescience to see that the Mogul military power was rotten at the core, and could easily be overthrown by a small but well-commanded European brigade, we must not refuse some credit to Manucci for having, thirty years later, equally foretold the course of history. On folio 66 of Part III (written in 1700) he says: 'I assert from what I have seen and tested, all that is required to sweep it away and occupy the whole Empire is a corps of thirty thousand European soldiers led by competent commanders, who would thereby acquire the glory of great conquerors.'

HIS VIEWS GENERALLY

Manucci seems to have had strong likes and dislikes. The chief objects of his dislike are the emperor Aurangzeb, the Portuguese, and the Jesuits. Can anyone assert that in any of these cases he had nothing to justify him? His romantic attachment to Dara Shukoh, his first master, possibly made him unfair to Aurangzeb. But, I ask, can a man who attacks and kills two brothers, imprisons an aged father, and thus 'wades through slaughter to a throne,' be held up as a model of all the virtues? Were the Portuguese, in those days of their decay, not open to the censures passed upon them by Manucci? Were the methods of the Jesuits as missionaries, and their defiance of the Pope, deserving of no reprobation? In all other cases Manucci is usually tolerant, but does occasionally break forth into bitter and bigoted remarks on both Hinduism and Mahomedanism. He also takes a very low view of the Indian character, Hindu and Mahomedan, a view, though far from being the whole truth, which has impressed itself strongly on the majority of Europeans. Strangely enough, he entirely disapproves of and ridicules astrology; yet he is always ready to swallow anything in the nature of witchcraft or sooth-saying. Another of his peculiarities is his readiness to attribute poisoning as the cause of any great man's sudden death. He is constantly making such accusations against Aurangzeb. Possibly there are some grains of truth hidden in this wholesale denunciation; and Manucci's readiness to see poison everywhere may be attributed, perhaps, to his Italian origin, and his knowledge of what had been the case in his own country.

PERIOD OF COMPOSITION

Parts I, II, III were written in 1699 and 1700, Part IV. between 1701 and 1705, Part V. between 1706 and 1709. On p. 21 of Part II. the then date is given as March 9, 1699; when he was writing Part III, p. 241, it was December, 1700. He began the work at the instigation of Françis Martin and Boureau-Deslandes, with whom he was intimate; and the intention evidently was to send it to Europe for presentation to Louis XIV in the hope that he would direct its publication.

MENTION BY OTHER EUROPEAN TRAVELLERS

I can find no reference to Manucci in Tavernier; and Mr. W. Foster informs me that there is no mention of him in the travels of Jean de Thevenot, who in 1666-67 travelled through Gujarat and Gulkandah, visiting Surat and Machhlipatnam. Manucci mentions Tavernier once in passing in rather disparaging terms; but it does not seem that the two men ever met.[1] He speaks of

1. Of Tavernier's six voyages, only two—the fifth and sixth—fall within Manucci's time (see C. Joret, 'J. B. Tavernier, Baron d'Aubonne,' 1886, pp. 143-160). The fifth voyage began in February, 1657, and ended in 1663; he

'Monsu Tavirnier's' presence at Dihli in 1665 (Part V., f. 75), and his recourse to a French doctor (not named, perhaps François de la Palisse),[1] to help him in the sale of his jewels to Aurangzeb, who was far from being so liberal a buyer as Shahjahan. Tavernier holds out a promise to get the doctor a new wife in France, whereupon the man tries to poison his Portuguese consort. In 1666 her sister, the renegade wife of 'Ali Mardan Khan, rescues her, and removes her to Lahor, but afterwards poisons her there herself.

N.M'S ACCOUNT OF A. LEGRENZI

There was, however, another traveller, a fellow-townsman, who encountered Manucci, and is mentioned by him. The year must have been 1679. This man, Angelo Legrenzi, published a book, 'II Pellegrino nell' Asia . . . ,' 240 pp., 12mo., Venetia, 1705. Manucci mentions him (Part V., f. 185) in these terms: 'When I was at the court of Shah 'Alam in Aurangabad, there arrived a Venetian physician called Angello Legrenzi. He had come from Aleppo, having quitted the service of the Most Serene Republic, and at the age of thirty-five had set out to seek his fortune afresh. He was possessed with various ideas, and concealed in his mind many thoughts. He came to see me, and presented to me a recommendatory letter from Father Ivo, Capuchin, of Surat.[2] I received him most courteously, offering him the use of my house, also to his companion, one Signor Protasio, a noble German. I was greatly pleased at his coming, seeing myself thus quit of several patients who came bothering me every day. Forthwith I appointed him my coadjutor, to secure him more respect, and introduced him into the presence of the head physician, Muhammad Muqim, with a view to his

was in Isfahan, 1662. In the sixth voyage Tavernier was at Isfahan in 1664, and at Surat in May of that year (pp. 161-208). Manucci was then at Dihli.

1. Tavernier (edition of 1692, iii. 94) says this surgeon, also known as Saint Jacques, was at the Mogul court in 1666, and married a Portuguese wife. It was through him that the French ambassadors in that year obtained access to Ja'far Khan, the wazir.
2. This is evidently the Père Yves who left France in 1644 with Tavernier and Père Raphael du Mans. Tavernier says the Father died at Surat, and he built him a tomb there.

getting an appointment from the prince and an adequate salary, and thus not being hindered from practising. The worthy "patrician," seeing I treated him so well, was highly pleased, but he would not follow my advice. He displayed great eagerness to enter the prince's service and get a salary.

'To show his ability and that he was not a surgeon but a physician, he wrote a small tract dealing with the four principal kinds of fever, their causes, and the remedies for dispelling them. Seeing that he had no faith in my word, still less in that of other friends, I again took him to the Hakim, to whom he presented the book and explained its contents. Muhammad Muqim was content to let him talk, and by his face seemed to approve of what he was saying. To all appearance Legrenzi was satisfied, believing that he had done a good stroke by presenting the work, and that he would be thereby thought more of at the court.

'However, knowing the contrary, I told him he might be very thankful if he met with any success. When dismissing him, the Hakim said he might renew his visits. I continued to help him with a horse and servants, who every day accompanied him, since the Hakim lived half a league from my house. This going and coming went on for a year without the Hakim ever sending him a single patient, although he still spoke to him, but my "patrician" had no idea what that meant.

'Finally, to disenchant him, Muhammad Muqim one day directed his servant, who acted as interpreter—an Armenian called Giuseppe (Joseph)—to sit down close to him. My "patrician" was aggrieved thereby, and on reaching home told me. I knew not what else to say except that he must have patience. The following day he went back and wasted his time, seated there for over three hours. At last the Hakim asked if he knew what God was. At this question Legrenzi was stunned and said nothing, perceiving that such a demand was equivalent to dismissal; thus was his joy turned into sorrow. Therefore he went back by the road he had come, lamenting his strange fortune, and resuming his old place which he had quitted, where he was well received. Signor Protasio remained with me, as he had no money to meet his journey; a year afterwards he started, I helping him as well as I could, and I never heard of him again.'

It is a mere surmise, but it seems to me very possible that Manucci had seen Legrenzi's book of 1705 before he wrote the above passage taken from Part V., and that it is his retort courteous for Legrenzi's somewhat uncivil depreciation. Or as an Italian writer, P. Amat di S. Filippo ('Studi sulla Storia della Geografia . . . .' I., 440) says: 'This judgment [of Legrenzi on Manucci] is, however, not devoid of prejudice, both being followers of Esculapius'; and again, speaking of the 'Storia,' he says, 'From these [the Memoirs] it can be seen (at least as regards education) that the finding of Legrenzi ought not to be accepted blindly.'

LEGRENZI'S ACCOUNT OF N.M.

Let us turn now to Legrenzi's story in 'II Pellegrino,' Libro Terzo, 192-310 (India), Of the city of Aurangabad, 220-227. On p. 223 the passage begins thus: 'Besides these paid artillerymen the prince entertains several medical men, or rather surgeons, for they practise not only physic but surgery; I do not say in cases of importance—on the contrary, only in more humble operations, such as letting of blood, cupping, blistering and such-like. Among these gentlemen I had the luck to find a fellow-countryman, named Nicolò Manucci, a person with great credit among the nobles, with the handsomest salary I have heard as given in this country—that is, three hundred rupees a month. Such a happy encounter consoled me much, being aware of how rare it is to find' Italians there, much less a Venetian. It is impossible to describe how often we embraced, how lively were our demonstrations of affection, how long our talks and interrogations. For he had been away from home nearly thirty years, and was extremely anxious to learn about his connections, even when not known to me, about the condition of Venice city, and other particulars.

'Our civilities over and the many inquiries ended, he began in a few days to converse seriously with me to find out my plans, and openly asked me if I wanted to enter the prince's service, where he assured me that I should meet with more than ordinary fortune, he meanwhile offering himself for recommendations and good offices with Shah 'Alam. I gave him cordial thanks for his kind feelings in my favour, but answered him that I absolutely refused to engage myself outside my native land, having come to

India to see the country and its chief sights, intending thereafter to return home to my relations and connections.

'Not satisfied with this answer, my friend invited me to reflect on future contingencies at the death of the king; for the prince, as eldest son, would ascend the throne, thereby opening to me the way to benefits not less great than glorious. To sum up, all this made no impression on me, and I answered that I absolutely refused to fetter my liberty, above all with princes, who possess neither sense nor good faith.

'At these remarks my friend was more upset than before, desirous as he was, by whatever means he could, to induce me to rest beside him and supply him with a little light in medicine, devoid as he was of letters, and even any knowledge of the arts. I consoled him, however, on that head by saying that I would remain with him for some months, then take my departure at the decline of the season. Then arose rumours of the prince's departure for Dihli before the end of the rains. I had intended, on leaving Surat, to proceed to Gulkandah, and thence to Goa. But it seemed to me preferable to give up that project, and to embrace the opportunity of staying on and following the route of my friend, so as to see that royal city with all else that might offer itself.'

On p. 230 he says that it was on July 25, 1697, that Shah 'Alam started for the north, which is possibly correct, though the year 1680 is more probable. But the journey is said to have been to Agrah in thirty-four days, and after a stay of four days, on to Dihli in six days. There, as he says, Manucci was greeted by a throng of friends; and after a stay of two months Legrenzi returned to Surat. Then follows an account of Agrah, of Dihli, and other chapters, till the subject of India ends on p. 310. Now, I am convinced that all this journey is fictitious it bears internal evidence, I think, that the man was never either at Agrah or Dihli, and what he knew of them was mere hearsay. Nor did Shah 'Alam, when recalled from the Dakhin for the Rajputanah campaign, go anywhere near Agrah or Dihli. As to the two versions of what happened at Aurangabad, either or both must be embroidered; and, as just shown, Legrenzi is not above a little fiction when necessary. There is a notice of Legrenzi and his book in 'Studii Biografici e Bibliografici sulla Storia della Geografia in India,' by S. Amat de S. Filippo (Roma, 1882), p. 445.

PERSONAL CHARACTER

In Manucci we have obviously a man chiefly self-educated, and not the 'learned traveller' of Cardinal Zurla. There are two portraits of him: the extraordinary attitude—one leg almost in air—of the younger one denotes, I suppose, a lively and mercurial temperament; the older one, in profile, reveals a very long and inquisitive nose. In any case, he must have been full of motherwit, shrewd, and remarkably observant. He boasts himself of his ready tongue, and I infer that a good deal of his success turned on his power of talk, which seldom left him at a loss in any awkward dilemma. This quality made him, I assume, what is called good company, a cheerful companion; perhaps, as professed story-tellers in their old age usually do, becoming slightly a bore, and, like Dogberry, bestowing on his hearers somewhat too abundantly of his 'tediousness.' Though for a time a soldier, I gather that he had more prudence than valour, being thoroughly impressed with the importance of living to fight another day. He describes the great historic battle of Samugarh in June, 1658, as a mere spectator, and we do not hear that he fired there a single shot in his beloved master's cause. Again, outside Lahor in 1659, when his commander, the eunuch Basant, was slain, we do not find Manucci playing a very heroic part.

From his various disputes about money, and his strong dislikes, I infer that he was rather vengeful, and he was certainly pertinacious in pushing a claim. In conduct he seems to have been moral and sober; indeed, in the former respect he paints himself as a very Joseph or St. Anthony, triumphant over all temptations. Even when, as old men use, he follows Falstaff and Master Shallow in letting us know that he, too, has 'heard the chimes at midnight,' he does not seem to have got farther than peeping into the closed litter of a dancing-girl. He was a devout Catholic, and resisted successfully all attempts to make him turn Mahomedan. In his old age he was much preoccupied with ecclesiastical disputes, and had become, I should say, rather bigoted in his faith. I have spoken already of his disliking the Portuguese; the English, among whom he lived for twenty years, he evidently respected, but did not love; his whole affection goes out towards the French, whose praises he sings more than once.

N. M.'S MEDICAL KNOWLEDGE

His medical knowledge must have been limited; but it was evidently sufficient to secure him some professional reputation, perhaps due to the fact that 'among the blind the one-eyed man is king.' His practice evidently consisted chiefly in bleeding, purging, and the actual cautery. He is very proud of the last remedy as a cure for cholera; he refers to it more than once, and, as can be seen in the 'Letters Edifiantes,' he strongly recommended it to Father Martin of the Madura Mission. He also says he introduced the use of the enema, which was unknown to native practice. In selling imitations of the Goa stones he was following an example already set by the Jesuit Fathers; and another source of income was some preparation he calls a 'cordial,' probably intended as an aphrodisiac. But, knowing what we do of the healing art in Italy and France in the seventeenth century, he does not seem to have been so very much behind his European contemporaries.

XI. CONCLUSION.

Having now stated the reasons which have for many years made the question of Manucci and his history a curious literary problem, and having thrown upon it and upon him all the light that ten years of research have produced, I take my leave of him. I know that this book, and still more its translator and editor, are open to adverse criticism; but of one thing I am convinced, that no fair-minded reader ought to say that Manucci is, for many pages together, so dull as to be uninteresting and unreadable.

Here I may state the reasons which have led me to prepare an English translation instead of bringing out the original text. It is obvious, in the first place, that a work in three languages—Italian, French, and Portuguese—would be somewhat of an anomaly. If this be conceded, as I think it must be, it follows that one of the three languages would have to be preferred, and into it the other portions must be translated. Even if Italian, as the author's mother-tongue, be chosen, two-thirds of the book would still be a translation, and we should be as far as ever from a reproduction of the original text. On the other hand, Italian is not so generally known as French or English. But the main reason determining my choice was that the work is one whose interest lies more in its matter than its form. It is not a literary classic, and what it has to tell us can be just as well reproduced in English as in any other language. Then, through an English edition, we address a much larger audience in England and America; and the needs of Indians interested in the history of their country, now an increasing class, are also served much more effectually.

In the course of my task I have received abundant and generous help from many persons, whose names I have endeavoured to record, either in this Introduction, or as occasion arose in the course of the book. I have not willingly overlooked any kindness shown me, but in such an extensive and long-sustained effort, ramifying in so many directions, it may well be that I have omitted some names; and if this be so, I crave those persons' pardon, and so bid all farewell with many thanks.

APPENDIX TO INTRODUCTION.

Note on Boureau-Deslandes

Next to Françis Martin himself, Boureau-Deslandes stands out as the most capable person employed by Colbert's French Company in India in the fifty years of its existence. Yet his name has not hitherto found its way into any biographical dictionary, a fact hardly to be wondered at, perhaps, when we find that it was not until 1860—when the late Mr. Pierre Margry interested himself in the subject—that any adequate, or even tolerably correct, life of F. Martin himself found a place in the 'Biographie Universelle.' I have therefore made some research into the official career and the family history of Martin's son-in-law and colleague, the results of which I here present.

André Boureau-Deslandes, the scion of an ancient and honourable family, was born at Tours probably between 1740 and 1750. I have not been able to procure a copy of his birth or baptismal register, and thus cannot give any more exact date. His early life is not traced, and we first hear of him in India between 1667 and 1672, in the service of the French East India Company, which had been founded in 1665 under the auspices of Louis XIV.'s Minister, Colbert. There being no colonial archives of the *Etat Civil* (births, deaths, and marriages) earlier than 1690, no exact date can be given, but before April 26, 1686, at latest, Deslandes had been married at Surat to Marie Françoise, the daughter of François Martin, then chief of the French factory at that place. In 1694 there were six children issue of the marriage, three sons and three daughters.

The eldest child, a girl, was living at Pondicherry with her grandparents, and the proud grandfather writes in October, 1692: 'La fille que nous avons avec nous, qui est l'ainée, est un petit bijou, une distinction au-dessus de son aage.' In 1693, when the siege by the Dutch began, Madame Martin moved with her granddaughter to San Thome. On the capitulation of Pondicherry they were allowed to rejoin François Martin, and they proceeded with him to Batavia, thence to Huglī, where they joined Deslandes and his wife. The second and third children were sons, and the fourth a daughter (born in 1692).

Their second child and eldest son was André François Boureau-Deslandes, born at Hugh on May 19, 1689, and baptized on May 24 in the church of Notre Dame du Rosaire by the Prior Julian de Gratia, Augustinian, the absent godfather and godmother, F. Martin and Margaret Colinet, being represented by Jean François Cuperly and Gabriel Pellé. This son may be identical with the Francis Boureau, Lord of Chevalrie and Lieutenant of Militia, whose daughter by his wife, Marie Thérése Jaham, was baptized at Martinique on March 10, 1709. In any case, we know that A. F. B. Deslandes was appointed a Commissary of Marine on April 30, 1716, and Commissary-General on May 6, 1736. At the latter date he was serving at Brest, but on January 1, 1738, was transferred to Rochefort. He retired upon pension on December 1, 1746, and died in 1757. He became a well-known light lance in literature, and published many works of a sceptical turn. The best-remembered thing about him is his forming the subject of an epigram by Voltaire:

Erivez français, bourreau!'

Let us turn now to the official career of the elder Boureau-Deslandes. The exact date on which he entered the French Company's service is not known, but it must have been early in his history. Obviously the MS. petition of 1703, applying for letters of nobility, must be in error in assigning 1676 as the year of his arrival in India. We hear of a Boureau at Calicut in 1669, probably our Boureau-Deslandes; and Caron, the first director in India (drowned 1674), is said to have sent him before 1672 to Bālāsor, on the Bengal coast, whence he reached the Hūglī, and then founded (so it is said) Chandarnagar on that river. In January, 1674, there were both a Boureau and a Boureau-Deslandes in the French council at Surat. It is asserted (Weber, 171) that in 1676 Deslandes fortified Chandarnagar, but this may be doubted.

We then hear of him as having been sent from Surat in 1679 in charge of two ships, with orders to re-establish on the Malabar coast the trade which had been broken off by the war. He was instructed to negotiate with the local princes and with the viceroys and governors under the Portuguese crown.

Next we find him on duty in Siam, where he proceeded on board the *Vautour*. He acquired the confidence of the King of Siam, who desired him to remain to conduct the company's trade. The *Vautour*, therefore, left Siam without him on December 1, 1680. On December 26, 1682, he reported from Siam to Baron, the director at Surat. The ambassadors subsequently despatched from France by Louis XIV. were instructed to ask confirmation of the treaties Deslandes had obtained. In 1685 he left Siam on an English vessel. He was bound for Surat, and carried with him commissions to be executed for the King of Siam, amounting to over 200,000 livres. He arrived at Surat at some date prior to October 15, 1685.

François Martin had been transferred from Pondicherry to Surat, where he arrived on August 22, 1681, and upon Baron's death (June 10, 1683) succeeded to the conduct of affairs. It was abount this time (1685-86) that Deslandes married F. Martin's elder daughter. On April 20, 1686, we find Deslandes still at Surat, and we are told that he was preparing for a move to Pondicherry as Second in Council, with the object of being employed on the Choromandel coast and Bengal. F. Martin and his family reached Pondicherry on May 20, 1686, and Deslandes either accompanied them or soon followed them. Before he left Surat he was sent with le Sieur Roques as a deputation to the Mahomedan Governor of Surat to remonstrate at his continual exactions.

On June 15, 1686, Deslandes formed one of a deputation from Pondicherry to Fort St. George (Madras); and an English trader's letter from Mergui (in Tenasserim), dated December 30, 1686, would lead us to believe that he was at Pondicherry at that date. We know he was still there on September 24, 1687. It must, then, have been in the end of 1687 that he revisited Siam at the request of the king; but although the king wished to retain him, he did not remain long, for the French Company required his services to found a trading station in Bengal. On the return journey he and the French ambassador to Siam were off Madras on January 14, 1688, but excused themselves from landing on the plea that business required them to hasten to Pondicherry. We have notices of his presence at Pondicherry on February 2 and 17, 1688.

He now became Director-General of Commerce in Bengal, and left Pondicherry in April, 1688, to take up his new duties. In October, 1689, he was called upon by Martin to send a shipload of food from Bengal to relieve the distress then prevailing in Pondicherry. He remained in Bengal until 1701, as it proved by a whole series of letters.

In 1690 Deslandes had a dispute with the Portuguese Augustinian friars at Hūglī, who had sent their Christians to force their way into the French compound (*loge*). In consequence, Deslandes retired a few miles off to Chandarnagar, and there built another *loge*. This seems the real date for the foundation of the French settlement at Chandarnagar; until this time they had apparently, like the other Europeans, lived in or close to Hūglī town.

The date of the founding of Chandarnagar is somewhat obscure, but some light is thrown upon it by the English records. In a general letter from Hugli, dated October 13, 1686, para. 8, we hear that the French had sent orders to settle factories all over Bengal; to which Fort St. George, September 1, 1688, para. 44, adds the fact that they are endeavouring to procure the Mogul's *farman*. Again, in January, 1689, para. 16, it is said that, 'French trade is increasing by new settlements in . . . Bengal, though no factory had been built, nor any certain terms agreed on.' On January 16, 1692, the Calcutta Council write (para. 17) that 'the French had almost finished a large factory at Chandarnagar.' From Dhakkah, under date May 26, 1690, we hear of a struggle between the Dutch and French, apparently about Chandarnagar. The French had bought a piece of ground 'for which they have a prime writing'; but the Dutch refused to let them build. After taking the dispute before the nawab (the nazim) and the diwan, it was referred to the king. Finally, by the Fort St. George general letter of November 20, 1691 (O.C. 5777) we are told that: 'The Mounseers have been long idle and quiet at Pullicherry . . . tho' their Chief in Bengale is building severall large Factoryes, bigg enough for a mighty trade, but 'tis doubted too large for their Stock.'

From F. Martin's letter of January 22, 1691, we learn that Deslandes then spoke of returning to France. He complained of having been passed over in promotion. Other notices of him at Hugli (for thus he dates his letters) are found in his letters of December 15, 1691, and January 20 and 29, 1693 (? 1694). In the last of these he states that he has just heard of the fall of Pondicherry, and that F. Martin was a prisoner. There are other letters from him to the directors of September 27, 1693, and January 25, 1694.

Pondicherry had surrendered to the Dutch on September 6, 1693 (N.S.) and F. Martin, his family, and the garrison were transported to Batavia. On arrival there he was allowed at his earnest request to return to India, and on February 15, 1694, rejoined his son-in-law Deslandes at the French factory on the Hugll. There he remained until the restoration of Pondicherry to the French under the Peace of Ryswick (1697). We find several letters in that period signed either by F. Martin alone or jointly with Boureau-Deslandes, *viz.*: December 28, 1694; July 10 and 25, November 21, 1696; January 15 and 16, October 19, and December 30, 1697. On January 5, 169!, Martin passed Calcutta in a ship taking him back to Pondicherry (India Office, 'Factory Records,' Calcutta, p. 3). There are passing mentions of Deslandes in the Calcutta records of December 6 and 14, 1690, and June 30, 1698. In February, 1700, he wrote to the governor at Calcutta condoling on the loss of the *East India Merchant*, and sent two sloops to assist in the work of salvage. Boureau-Deslandes remained in charge of Chandarnagar, as is shown by the letters of January 4, February 8, and December 12, 1700, and the list of the company's servants at Hugli, dated January 10, 1700.

From the letter of January 9, 1701, signed by B. Deslandes, Dulivier, and Pelé, we learn that a month before that date

Deslandes had decided to act on the permission he had received to retire on the ground of family cares and poor health. Some *farmans* that had long been desired had just been obtained, and he believed that affairs could now go on without him. He meant to sail by the *Phelypeaux*, and gave overcharge to Dulivier (Pelé and Renault, members of council). On January 10 he embarked for Pondicherry, which he reached on February 3. Manucci, Part IV., fol. 54, also speaks of his being at Pondicherry in February, 1701. He left for France on February 23, and reached that country on August 28, 1701.[1]

In April, 1703, Boureau-Deslandes received from Louis XIV. letters of nobility for himself and his posterity in reward for his services in India. On November 28 of the same year he was nominated Commissary at St. Domingo by the king, also Director-General in America by the Royal Company established for supplying negroes to the Spanish colonies. He died in the West Indies on February 13, 1706.

A treatise by Boureau-Deslandes—'Relations de la France avec le Royaume de Siam'—has been published by Pierre Margry in 'Relations et Mémoires' (Paris: Challamel Ainé, 1867), No. V., pp. 149-184; No. IV., pp. 115-148, in the same volume being a paper by François Martin on 'L'Inde et les Nations Européennes,' dated February 15, 1700.

One point connected with the history of François Martin may be commented on here. Monsieur Weber, in his 'La Compagnie Françoise des Indes' (1904), pp. 181, 182, states that on the capitulation of Pondicherry in September, 1693, F. Martin 'était revenu en France ou le roi l'avait traité avec honneur.' This is evidently an error, probably due to a confusion between *François* Martin, the Director-General, and *Jean Baptiste* Martin, the Second in Council at Pondicherry in 1693.

It is clear from the tenth article of capitulation that François Martin begged to be allowed to remain in India. But this request was refused. His wife and granddaughter with their servants and baggage were recalled from San Thome, where in

1. The statement of Dr. Jules Sottas, 'Histoire de la Compagnie Royale des Indes, 1664-1719,' Paris, 1905, p. 105, note, that Deslandes died off St. Helena of scurvy is due, as that author informs me, to an oversight. It was the commander of the vessel, Captain Le Quentiac, who died.

July, 1693, they had been sent for safety, and they embarked with Martin for Batavia. The Dutch ships from Pondicherry passed Fort St. David on their way to Negapatam on September 15, 1693 (O.S.), and the English write 'we hear Monsieur Martin is in the "Admirall." '

From a resolution of the governor-general and Council at Batavia, dated November 5, 1693, it appears that the French captives had recently arrived there on the *Beurs* and the *Maas*. Among them were Director François Martin and his family, consisting of his wife and the daughter of the French director in Bengal, 'Monsieur de Lande,' by their (the Martins') daughter, one French servant, one Armenian, two slave men, and two slave girls. These were accorded quarters in the governor-general's house, and the Martins were to eat at his table.

On November 9, the governor-general reported that F. Martin earnestly prayed to be spared the long journey to Europe on account of the advanced years of himself and his wife, and begged permission to proceed to Bengal. The matter was deliberated on.

Next day (the tenth) a petition from F. Martin was produced before the Council. It recites the fact that Laurens Pit, governor on the Choromandel coast and commanding the troops at the taking of Pondicherry, had referred the question of Martin's destination to the decision of the Batavia Council. During the negotiations he had asked to be allowed to depart either to Masulipatam or to Bengal, where the French Company had factories. This petition was refused, and in order not to break off negotiations, he withdrew his demand, on being given hope that at Batavia the article would be reconsidered. He appeals to the precedent of San Thome (1674), when Baron, director-general of the French Company, had been allowed to withdraw to Surat by land or water with forty-five to fifty persons. He pleads his own great age and the infirmity of his wife, who was not likely to survive a journey to Europe, and prays for terms similar to those accorded to Monsieur Baron.

After deliberating the Council resolved, on perusal of the conditions allowed to Monsieur Baron, to grant François Martin's request on account of his age, and he was permitted to embark with his family for Bengal via Malacca on the flûte *Walenburg*. We have already referred to his correspondence from Hugli, between 1694 and 1698. He sailed thence for Pondicherry on board the *Gaillard* in January, and arrived on March 8, 1699. On March 21, 1699, the English governor and Council at Fort St. George wrote to the French director-general and Council at Pondicherry, 'congratulating him on his restoration and being in quiet possession of that place once lost in war.'

AUTHORITIES.

Archives Du Ministere Des Colonies, Paris:

C²63. Correspondance Generate, 1676-1691, fols. 8, 62, 63, 67, 80, 82, 90, 138, 141, 173, 174b, 203-217.

C²64, Correspondance Générate, 1692-1698, fols. 102-104, 112-113, 114, 120*b*, 142-145, 145-148, 166*b*, 243, 245-246, 247-250, 252-255, 256-261, 268-278.

C²65, Correspondance Générale, 1699-1700, fols. 49-66, 111-113, 114-122, 138- 139, 170-173, I73*b*-I78b. 179-186.

C²66, Correspondance Générate, 1701-1702, fols. 10*b*-11, 15, 15-35.

Archives Nationales, Paris:

Série T*, 1169, 'Memoires de François Martin, 1664-1694,' 631 fols.' foolscap.

Bibliotheque Nationale, paris:

MS. No. 6,231, 'Mémoires sur la Compagnie des Indes de 1662 a 1720, fols. 15, 18.

MS. Français 31,286, 'Nouveau d'Hozier,' 61; 'Dossier Boureau,' fol. 4.

MS. Français 30,351, 'Correspondance d'Hozier,' No. 122, fols. 239, 240, 241, 242, 243, 244.

MS. Français 27,462, 'Pièces Originates,' No. 978.

India Office Records, London:

Factory Records, Fort St. George, No. 4, 1686.

Factory Records, Fort St. George, No. 21, January, 1687/8.

Original Correspondence, No. 5,549, December 30, 1686.

Factory Records, Fort St. George, No. 31, August 29, 1693 (from Fort St. David).

Factory Records, Fort St. George, No. 22, August 31, 1693 (OS.), September 5, 1693 (O.S.).

Original Correspondence, 5,886, No. 21, July 29, 1693.

Original Correspondence, 5,881, No. 25, September 28, 1693.
Factory Records, Calcutta, No. 9, December 6 and 14, 1690.
Factory Records, Calcutta, No. 3, June 30, 1698.
Factory Records, Calcutta, No. 3, January 5, 1699.
Factory Records, Calcutta, No. 10, February, 1700.

Fort St. George (Madras) Records:

'Letters from Fort St. George,' vol. ix., pp. 30, 31, March 21, 1699.

Dutch Archives (Ms.) at The Hague:

Kolonial Archief, Deel No. 1412, blz. 1037-1044, 'Articles of Capitulation of Pondicherry.'

Kolonial Archief, Deel No. 1412, blz. 1057, 'Expenditure on French Prisoners,' Batavia, December 2, 1693.

'Extracten uit' de Generals Résolutien van Gouverneur-Général en Rade,' Batavia, November 5, 9, and 10, 1693.

Pierre Margry:

Relations et Mémoires inédits pour servir à l'histoire de la France daïs les pays d'outre mer, tireś des Archives du Ministére des Colonies,' Paris. Challamel Ainé, 1867, containing the following papers:

'L'Inde et les Nations Européennes,' par F. Martin, dated February 15, 1700, No. 4, pp. 115-148.

'Rélations de la France avec le Royaume de Siam,' par Deslandes-Boureau, fondateur de la ville de Chandernagore, No. 5, pp. 149-184.

Henry Weber, Docteur En Droit:

'La Compagnie des Indes, 1604-1875' (Paris, 1904, pp. 715), pp. 171, 174, 181, 182, 208, 209, 210, 225.

Dr. Jules Sottas:

'Histoire de la Compagnie Royale des Indes Orientales, 1664-1719 ' (Paris, 1905, pp. 496), pp. 105, 136, 137, 138, 154, 392, 393, 413-415.

ILLUSTRATIONS TO VOL. I.

The photographs are by P. Sauvanaud of Paris and the reproductions[1] *by Messrs. Bemrose and Sons, Limited, London and Derby.*

1. Of the First edition

TRAVELS IN INDIA, AND HISTORY OF THE MOGUL RULERS

Divided into Three Parts

By Mr. Nicolas Manuchi, Venetian

First Part,
Containing the Journey of
Nicolas Manuchi, his Arrival in India,

and

The History of the Mogul Kings from
Tramerlane Until the Accession of
Aurangzeb[1]

1. The Berlin M. S. (Phillipps, 1945) bears at the top of this first page the words: 'Collegii Paris: Societatis Jesu'; and on the margin of the second folio: 'Paraphé au devis de l'arrest du 5 Juillet, 1763.—Mesnil.' Leopold Delisle, 'Le Cabinet des Mss. de la Bibliothèque Impériale' (Paris, 1868), p. 434, reads *desir*, but I make it *devis*, 'inventory, specification.'

NOTICE TO THE READER

As I know that other persons have written their travels, with descriptions of the countries they have passed through, and of the kingdoms where they remained for a time, these descriptions dealing often with the Mogul Empire, I long judged it a vain labour to make public any account of my journey from Venice through Asia, and of my sojourn in the land of the Mogul, where I have passed the better part of my life; but I could not resist the importunities of my friends, who have a great belief in my knowledge of that country, and a conviction that certain persons have written falsehoods in their books (as I myself have observed in several places). Therefore, although already old, I have resolved, with the encouragement of those who know me and who have written to me, to give the reader true information as to what passed there in my time and before it, emphasizing several particulars which could not have come to the knowledge of others.

I shall tell of all that happened to me and of all that I saw, without exaggerating any one thing, for that is abhorrent to me. I shall speak of the kingdom of the Great Mogul, of its politics, and of the conquests made by this eleventh King called Aurangzeb (that is to say, 'Ornament of the Throne '), and of all the kings, his predecessors, whose portraits, with those of the other great lords of this country, I now present to the interested reader, begging him before he leaves Europe for India to read this book, and not to allow himself to be deceived by any less truthful accounts, or by any vain imaginations which may have taken shape in his mind, for I have seen many who bewailed that they had left Europe and come to India, when they found themselves suffering in a strange land; and besides this, all the world cannot meet with such good fortune as that with which it has pleased God to favour me. I warn the reader that, in speaking of certain towns of Turkey and Persia, I speak of them as I saw them and not as they are now. I shall divide my account into three parts, and I shall divide the first into two books. In the first book I shall give an account of what happened to me from the time I left Venice to my arrival at Dihli; in the second a short account of the Mogul Kings until the accession of Aurangzeb to the throne, with the death of his brothers.

In Part II, I shall describe the conquests made by Aurangzeb, his wars and their success. In Part III, I shall say something as to the politics of the Mogul [f. 2] Empire, something of the greatness of the rajahs and other potentates of Hindustan, and of the revenues of that country. I shall speak of several other special matters, and lastly, I shall say a few words as to the religion of the Hindus.

BOOK I
MY JOURNEY TO INDIA

CHAPTER I

OF MY DEPARTURE FROM VENICE

When I was still quite young, I had a passionate desire to see the world, but as my father would not allow me to leave Venice, my native place, I resolved to quit it in some way or another, no matter how. Finding that there was a *tartane*[1] just about to leave, although I did not know its destination, I went on board in 1651,[2] at the age of fourteen. The officers of the vessel, thinking that I was the son of one of the merchants who were going on board, did not ask me who I was, but let me pass without question. We had scarcely left Venice before we ran into the teeth of a gale which lasted twenty-four hours—hours of the greatest misery to me, as I was sea-sick, being unaccustomed to the sea. When twenty-four hours had passed, I was forced by hunger to present myself before the captain, who asked under whose protection I was there. I begged for pardon, saying that, having come on board a short time before he put out to sea, I had fallen asleep, and that, finding myself utterly unprovided for, I had come to him. At this he gave orders for me to be looked after; but fortunately for me I found on board an English gentleman in disguise called Lord Bellomont.[3] He had left England to escape death at the hands of Cromwell, protector of that kingdom, who had condemned him because he belonged to the party of King Charles II., then

1. A small, decked vessel, with one mast and a lateen sail, used in the Mediterranian (Littré).
2. Codex XLIV. (Zanetti) gives the month of November. The true year is 1653.
3. On Lord Bellomont and his history, see Note A at the end of this Book of Part I.

in France. This person showed me much affection, and when he asked me if I would like to go with him, I inquired of him his destination. He then told me that he was going to Turkey, Persia, and India. I was much rejoiced thereat, and answered that I would gladly go with him, when he at once gave me the keys of his wardrobe, and I served him with great affection, seeing he loved me as if I had been his son. We arrived at Raguza, where we stayed several days on account of a contrary wind. Having at last set sail, we coasted along Dalmatia and past several [3] islands, and finally leaving the Archipelago behind, at the end of four months we arrived in the port of Smyrna.

CHAPTER II

OF THE TOWN OF SMYRNA

Smyrna is a Turkish port where we stayed seven days. There is a mingling of many nations there—namely, Italians, French, English, Dutch, and many Armenian merchants, who all live by the borders of the sea. At the time when we were at this port it happened that a Turk gave several blows with a stick to the captain of an English vessel. The Englishman swallowed the affront while he remained in the town waiting to embark, and after he had got a little way out to sea he bombarded the town and fled.

They tell here a story which merits to be recorded at this place by reason of the wit and ingenuity which it displays. At Aleppo, a town of Arabia, dwelt a merchant, a Hebrew by race, the richest of all those in the town. The Bassa (*pasha*) or governor wanted to despoil this Hebrew, and sought an opportunity of so doing without injuring his own reputation. He thought the best, the most refined, and the fairest way would be to send for him to his palace, and in the course of conversation point out to him that there were three different religions—one taught by Moses and accepted by the Jews, one taught by the Messiah and observed by the Christians, and the last promulgated by Mahomed and followed by the Turks. He would then ask the Jew which of the three was the true religion. Because, should the Hebrew reply that the religion of Moses or of Christ was the true one, he thereby decided at the same time, by implication, that the religion of Mahomed was false. If the Jew replied 'Yes, that is so,' then the governor would have him seized, and confiscate all his goods. On the other hand, if the Hebrew, out of respect or through fear, answered that Mahomed's religion was the true one, he would force him either to adopt Mahomedanism or lose his life. In that last case he would become master of all his goods.

The Jew, perceiving the force of the argument, sharpened his wits, and asked permission to tell the story of what had happened some time before. There was a father, said the Hebrew, who had three [4] sons, heirs to the whole of his great riches, and among his jewels there was a precious stone of an unusual size, and therefore greatly valued.[1] The three sons knew that their father had this precious stone; they also knew that it was beyond price, and that it could never be sold for its proper value. Thus each of them hoped to inherit it on his father's death. The latter, knowing his children's thoughts, and desirous of pleasing them all, so that at his death there should be no discord among them nor dispute, sent for a lapidary, and, showing him the stone, gave an order to make two imitation stones of the same size, and the same in every detail as the true one. The lapidary made these two stones so perfectly that when the three were placed together, it was impossible to tell which was the true one.

When he was at the point of death, the father sent for the best-beloved of his children, and made over to him the true stone, enjoining him to preserve secrecy, so that neither his brothers nor the governor of the town should trouble him. He acted in the same way with the other two sons, telling them to keep it a secret, and delivering to each an imitation stone, which he declared to be the true and only one. By this means all three were contented, each being persuaded that he had the true stone which he coveted. In the same manner, said the Hebrew to the Bassa (*pasha*), the Lord our God has sent forth three laws: one to the Jews, one to the Christians, and another to the Turks. Of these one is true, and the others false; but as to which is the true one we know nothing, each believing that it is the one he holds. God alone, who gave them, knows which it is, just as the father, who bestowed the stones, knew which was the true one. The Bassa (*pasha*), seeing the ingenuity with which the Jew had answered, thereby breaking the net in which he had resolved to catch him, praised him for his answer, and abandoned his designs against the goods of that sharp-witted merchant.

1. This story of the three precious stones is found, with variations, in Lessing's 'Nathan der Weise,' in Boccaccio, in the 'Gesta Romanorum,' and in Hebrew literature.

We remained seven days at Smyrna; after that we started with a caravan for the town of Burca (Brusa).[1] On the road we suffered much from cold, owing to the large amount of snow, and we arrived in eight days in good health.

1. The place meant must be Brusa in Anatolia, lat. 40° 27″, long. 28° 58″ (Fullarton's 'Gazetteer of the World,' vol. ii., p. 93). It is about 240 miles north-east of Smyrna.

CHAPTER III

OF THE TOWN OF BURCA

On our arrival at Burca, an ancient town of the Greeks, we were received by an Armenian called Anthoine Cheleby, who acted as governor of the town; and further seeing that we should have to wait a long time before we could meet with a caravan leaving for Persia, we quitted the town and went to live in the country house of the said Anthoine Cheleby. While our clothes were being carried out, under charge of one of our men called Charles, a Frenchman and a great musician, a couly (*quli*) [5] carrying one tin case disappeared. In this box was our money, also the best and the most valuable of what my master possessed. Great efforts were made to recover the things, but all we could find was the empty box, lying outside the town in the middle of some gardens. In this difficulty Anthoine Cheleby gave us whatever we had need of for the expenses of our journey.

During the fifty days that we remained in this town, I noticed the antiquity of the buildings, which in early times the Greeks had built in the form of fortresses—the walls, the bridges, the churches now converted by the Turks into mosques. Outside the town you see statues of stone lying on the ground, and these are defiled by the Turks when on their way to the mosques, which is a great affliction to the faithful. The town is a large one, inhabited by Turks, Armenians, and Greeks; but the Jews are in the greatest numbers, and they are very badly treated. In the middle of the town flows a stream which is used to water the surrounding gardens, and in addition there are several springs of clear water for household use and the seraglios; all this makes the place very healthy. There are hot baths for cleansing the body in the Turkish and Persian fashion. The men resort to them for their bath at five o'clock in the morning, and leave again at six o'clock. When the men have come out, a horn is sounded as a signal that the baths are vacant, and that the women can attend to take their bath. In attendance are barbers to serve and bathe the men, and also there are girls who perform the same duties for the women.

While we were in this town it happened that a young man, disguised as a woman, had been admitted to bathe the women; in the end it was discovered that he was a man, and after being well thrashed, he was taken before the criminal court, where he was condemned to death. Seeing the predicament he was in, he begged the court not to have him executed, but that he might be made a eunuch, that he should be forced to work at the baths, attending on the men and the women all his life without any pay. His request was complied with.

After our departure we learnt that the said Anthoine Cheleby had been called to the court of the Grand Turk to give an account of his government. But he had foreseen a long time before that he would be thus summoned, and he had secretly transmitted all his wealth to Leghorn. In his house were excellent slaves—Poles, Georgians, Muscovites, and Abyssinians; and good horses in his stable, on which to take to flight at the first rumour. A Turkish horseman arrived from Constantinople to summon him, and entered his house immediately, and said to him with threats that he must come forth at once, that the Grand Signor required his attendance. The sharp-witted Armenian, without showing the least fear or astonishment, advanced towards the soldier, and greeting him with a smiling face and all the signs of amity and affection, desired that he would take some repose. In the morning they would set out together. Then, having taken his hand, he made him sit by his side. After a little conversation [6] he ordered several pieces of silk and some jewelled rings to be brought, and told him he had only to choose whatever pleased him. At the same time he directed a serving-boy to carry water to the latrine for ablutions in the Moorish fashion. He then quitted the horseman, and without delay mounted his horse, followed by slaves carrying off all that he had, which was kept ready prepared for this purpose. He took the road to Smyrna, which he reached in twenty-four hours, although usually six days are required. In the harbour was a Dutch vessel, to the captain of which Anthoine Cheleby addressed himself, promising to pay him double what he could gain by remaining anchored, if he would carry him and his men to Leghorn. The captain accepted the proposal, Anthoine Cheleby embarked, and they reached Leghorn. There the captain received in full what had been promised to him by the Armenian. At Leghorn the latter built a bath for his own use, and the perpetuation of his memory among the people.

We pursued our route along with the caravan, which was a very large one. In it were several Armenian merchants, who looked after our food, also our horses, mules, and camels. We put up in their tents, where we were very well treated; but this was not done without an object, for the Armenians are very fond of their own interest. After some days we arrived at Tocat (Tokat).[1]

1. Tokat, in the pashalik of Sivas; it lies in lat. 40° 7′ N. Caravans arrive in twenty days from Smyrna (Fullarton, 'Gazetteer.' vii; 123, 273). It is about 460 miles east of Brusa.

CHAPTER IV

OUR DEPARTURE FROM TOCAT

In this town, which lies among mountains, we remained eight days, after which we started again with the whole caravan, keeping our eyes ever open as we advanced, by reason of the robbers who often on these routes attack caravans. This is the reason why men travel armed, and at night sentinels are set on watch on every side, so that no one can come near the encampment. One day it happened that there was a great alarm, some horsemen having appeared who wanted to rob us. Twenty-two of our mounted men went out against them, and prepared to attack them; but the robbers took to flight. Still, one of them was caught; his horse, being much out of condition, could not gallop like the others. He was made prisoner.

The next day the robbers sent a message praying that their comrade might be released, and 10,000 *pataques*[1] must be sent. If not, they would attack the caravan, and give quarter to no one. This news caused some apprehension in the caravan; but the leader of it, who was a brave man and experienced in these journeys, showed no fear, but, on the contrary, he sent word to them in a rage that he would come out in pursuit and leave not one alive. Thus the negotiations on both sides were confined to threats and defiance; and this went on for three days, during which the robber horseman was always guarded by two of our mounted men. After three days, one night, while the caravan was asleep, the thief escaped, and the quarrel came to an end.

In these journeys one has to be extremely vigilant, taking care never to go any distance from the caravan, for those who do so run a very great risk of falling [7] into the hands of clever thieves, and of losing both goods and life, as has happened to many. If any traveller intends to make this journey, he will do well to arm himself with a great deal of patience, and take good

1. Apparently meant for the *pataca* (see Yule and Burnell, second edition, 683), 'a dollar or piece of eight.' Elsewhere (i. 113) Manucci says it was worth two rupees (about four shillings).

thought of the hardships and disagreeables which he will have to encounter on these roads. For it is not as in Europe, where there are inns in which all the necessities and comforts requisite for life are to be found. When travelling in Turkey, you must sleep on the ground on a piece of carpet, or on the top of some bale of goods, where you suffer from the cold. Then, in the middle of your sleep, you are roused hurriedly to get ready and load up the camels and horses, and start on your way. During the day you are much troubled with the heat of the sun. Often it happens that the Turks seek you out and assail you with much abuse, and subject you to much indignity and shame. In these encounters it is wise to hang your head down like a Capuchin, and not open your mouth. At times it is necessary to bear slaps on the face with humility, and even endure beating with a stick, for fear of worse happening. For if a hand is raised by chance against a Turk such person is forthwith either forced to become a Mahomedan, or he is decapitated. The greatest favour accorded to him would be to let him go free after cutting off his hand. It is requisite to inform all who mean to travel in these regions that they must not wear anything of a green colour. Turks only may wear clothes of that colour. This remark applies to Turkey, for in Persia and in the Mogul Empire Christians can wear any colour they like. But the Turks are very particular about green, it having been liked and approved by the false prophet Mahomed.

No traveller need expect to find wine on the journey, for only water is drunk. In order never to be without water, it is necessary to have a bottle hanging from, or attached to, the beast on which one rides, and thus be able to have recourse to it in case of need. The bottles so used are easily procurable, and are sold ready for use. The merchants who go on these journeys also carry with them nets, with which they catch fresh fish. Many buy a kind of boiled sour milk,[1] called *jugurd*[2] in the language of the country. It is put in a *say* (? sieve), so that the water in it may drain away; and in that way it can be kept several days. We ate it several times mixed with water, putting in it biscuit or dry bread, or it was mixed with *pelos* (? 'pilao'). It is very

1. *Caillé*, milk artificially thickened (Littré).
2. *Jughrat*, 'sour, coagulated milk' (Steingass, 'Persian Dictionary').

palatable. When any dwellings are met with you can get eggs, butter, fowls, goats, and a few kinds of ripe fruit. But it is advisable to carry with you some dried fruit, meat fried in butter and packed in leather vessels; also sausages and puddings of salted beef, for it is at times impossible to obtain any food. And the best advice that I can give is, not to allow your curiosity to carry you so far as to look into the earthen houses of the country, or examine the peasants who dwell in them, for thereby one runs the risk of a thousand mishaps and evil fortunes [8].

CHAPTER V

OUR ARRIVAL AT ERZERUM, AND OUR JOURNEY TO ERIVAN

After having passed over this wearisome road in the midst of dangers and across swamps, we arrived at Erzerum,[1] where are to be found many Armenians, for it is a town with a great trade, lying upon the Turkish frontier. There we remained six days. Good bread and plentiful supplies are found in the town, but the Turks there are dishonest boors ; they examined our baggage with great severity (a common occurrence at this town, one of which all travellers complain). We were able, however, to conceal several presents that we were carrying for the King of Persia. At the end of the six days we left the town and continued our journey. After marching for two days, we came to a fortress built in the rock on the top of high ground; at its foot was a small town called Hassamcala (Hasan-qala'h).[2] When we had passed that place, and on the same day, the men of Erzerum examined our baggage a second time, to see if there were no merchandise hidden by us; and although we had very few things, they insisted on our paying customs dues a second time, finishing up by cursing us as they bade us farewell. However, we had made over to an Armenian the swords that we were taking as a present for the King of Persia; we had also confided to him a box in which were the letters of the embassy. This man had taken another route, and overtook us during the night at a place where we were free from the attempts of such-like people.

Next day we continued our march, and after going on for eight days, we reached a stream called the Aras,[3] over which

1. Erzerum is in lat. 39° 53′ N., long. 41° 18′ E. (Fullarton's 'Gazetteer,' iii. 257).
2. Erzerum is in lat. 39° 53′ N., long. 410 18°′ E. (Fullarton's 'Gazetteer,' iii. 257).
3. The Aras, or Arax (Araxes), flows into the Caspian Sea after an eastward course of 653 miles (Longman and Co.'s 'Gazetteer,' 61). The Armenian town of Zulfah is on the Aras, ninety-seven miles south-east of Erivan,

one has to cross several times. In the end, by slow degrees, we arrived on Persian territory, where we had the consolation of being both freer and more honoured than in the country which we had just left. In due time we came to Erivan,[1] a region which once on a time belonged to the Armenians, and thus there are still a great many of them living there. Erivan is situated just in front of a great mountain called Ararat. They say that it was on this mountain that the ark of Noah rested. At a distance of some ten leagues from the town the mountain looked as if entirely covered with ice on its summit, and when the sun shone on it, its appearance was splendid. There are [9] many brooks at the foot of this mountain, and the ground is covered throughout the year with sweet-smelling flowers. The town is enclosed by very thick and strong walls of earth, so that cannon would not be able to do as much damage as they would on a wall of stone, the reason being that the stones fracture while the earth does not. The country round is fresh, fertile, delicious, abounding in oil and fruit. We halted for ten days.

---

and here there was formerly a bridge mentioned in the history of Taimur's invasion. It is now a mere village with 650 inhabitants (Longman's ' 'Gazetteer,' 651). See Chardin, 'Travels into Persia' (folio, 1691), 347, 348. From a passage a little farther on (Part I., folio 23), we find that the party must have passed Zulfah on August 12, 1654 (N.S.).

1. Erivan, about 160 or 170 miles east of Erzerum. It is in lat. 42° 14′ N., long. 440 57′ E., and since 1827 has been a part of Russian Armenia (Fullarton, 'Gazetteer,' iii. 254). Aravat is about thirty-five miles south-west of Erivan. See also Chardin, 'Travels,' (1691), 332-344, where there is a plate giving a good view of Erivan.

CHAPTER VI

MY LORD BELLOMONT DECLARES HIMSELF TO BE AN AMBASSADOR

We drew up at a spot near Erivan, whence the Armenians who were with us went on to inform the *Cam* (*Khan*), or governor of the place, that an ambassador had come from the King of England, Charles II, son of King Charles I., and was on his way to the King of Persia. On receiving this information, the Khan sent at once to compliment him on his arrival, and invited him to enter the town. On the following day, according to the usage in regard to all ambassadors who come to the King of Persia, we were well received in the greatest pomp by the governor, who gave a banquet, and presented to the ambassador four horses and several pieces of silk. Then he issued orders that every day our wants were to be carefully attended to; we and our animals were to be fed plentifully. We remained in this place ten days, receiving numerous visits and passing our time agreeably, the pleasure being enhanced by seeing ourselves in a land of plenty, and in the midst of a people more polite than those we had just left behind. When we were ready to make a start, the governor sent a horseman and several armed men on foot to accompany us, as it is the habit to do for all ambassadors. These men go on ahead and get ready whatever is required for food and repose in the villages. Thus we were relieved of all trouble and exertion.

CHAPTER VII

OUR ARRIVAL AT THE TOWN OF TAURIS

At the end of five days we arrived with our followers at [10] the town of Tauris (Tabriz).[1] This town is the same as the ancient Ecbatana, built by Arfaxad, King of the Medes, as may be read in the Book of Judith, chapter i. At present it is inhabited by people of various nationalities: there are many Armenian merchants; many carpets are manufactured, and also pieces of silk, velvet, and brocade. Although the governor was not actually present in the town, having gone to one of the provinces, my lord was acknowledged as an ambassador, and treated as is the custom for such. We dwelt for some thirty days in this place, where we equipped ourselves and got ready new clothes to be worn on our arrival at the court of the King of Persia. He was then at Casbin (Qazwin).[2] We were forced to have new clothes, those we had being of Turkish pattern.

Before entering the town, I noticed an open place where stood two pillars which marked the distance that a stick had been thrown by Sultan Morad (Murad),[3] the Grand Signor, when he came to take Tabriz. But it seems almost impossible that a man should be able to throw a stick so far. I noticed also that the town is fairly large, surrounded by gardens which contain fine trees yielding good fruit. There are many mulberry-trees, so that they have much silk, of which they make various kinds of stuff.

At the end of thirty days we started again, accompanied as before, and with the same retinue. As we went along, I saw

1. Tauris, now known as Tabriz. It is described by Chardin, 'Travels' (edition of 1691), pp. 352-370, and there is a plate giving a very fine view of the town. 'In the days of Arphaxad, which reigned over the Medes in Ecbatane' (Judith i. 1). Modern scholars do not identify Tabriz with Ecbatane (see G. Rawlinson, 'Herodotus,' i. 227).
2. Qazwin, about 250 miles south-east of Tabriz. It is described by Chardin, 'Travels' (edition of 1691), pp. 378-383.
3. Probably the fourth Sultan of the name, who reigned 1623-1640. The name is the 'Amurath' of Shakespeare's 'Not Amurath an Amurath succeeds.'

that the land did not produce so many trees, nor was water so plentiful as in Turkey; for in Persia they are forced in many places to bring water from a great distance through underground channels. They make big holes to see if there is running water beneath, and whether it is sufficient. In the open country there are certain dry plants on which the sheep subsist and grow fat. They have very long and broad tails, from which much fat is obtained, and their wool is excellent. The skins of these sheep are very soft, and the wool curly; it is usual to make fur coats from them, and also hats. I have also noticed in Persia that there is no firewood, and in place of it they burn cow-dung, also the droppings of camels, horses, asses, and sheep [11].

CHAPTER VIII[1]

ARRIVAL IN THE CITY OF CASBIN (QAZWIN), AND HOW WE WERE SENT FOR TWICE TO THE ROYAL PALACE

At the end of thirteen days we arrived at the city of Qazwln, where the king, Xaabas [Shah 'Abbas], was.[2] We were conducted to a house made ready for the purpose, and after three days a captain came, accompanied by several cavalry soldiers, to visit the ambassador on behalf of the chief minister of the king. He presented congratulations on our arrival, with many compilments and offers of service. Subsequently the ambassador paid a visit to the chief minister, called Etmadolat ['Azamat-ud-daulah],[3] which means 'Modesty of Wealth,' by whom he was well received with many polite speeches and compliments, in which the Persians are never wanting. Between them there was much conversation in the Turkish language, the chief object of which was directed to finding out what presents we had brought for the King of Persia; secondly, to know the ambassador's rank, so that the proper honours might be paid to his person. Hearing from the Armenians that he (Bellomont) was of a great family, 'Azamat-ud-daulah sent to Smyrna to obtain information whether or not he were of the great family that he claimed to be. Meanwhile, after eight days from our arrival, we were sent for the royal palace, into which we went through numerous gates, ending in a large courtyard, in the midst of which stood two beautiful trees full of shade. Beneath them were two lions fastened with heavy

1. At this point the original ceases to be in French, and is continued in Portuguese.
2. Shah 'Abbas II, succeeded 1642, died 1667. The presence of the court at Qazwin is confirmed by the news in a letter from Aleppo, dated March 19, 1654/1655, printed in the *Mercurius Politicus*, No. 265, July 5 to 12, 1655, pp. 5466, 5467. The Shah arrived there on the 10th Rajab, 1064 H. (May 27, 1654), *Qisas-ul-khaqan* of *Wali Quli, Shamlu*, British Museum, Additional MS. 7,656, fol. 131*b*.
3. The true meaning is 'Pomp of the State.' Schefer, 'Estat de la Perse,' 41 (Paris, 1890), transliterates it as 'I'timad-ud-daulah' (Trusted One of the State), which may be the true reading.

golden chains; before each lion was a large golden basin full of water. Also below each tree stood a well-dressed man with long moustachios reaching to his shoulders, in his hand a short spear all of gold, with his face turned towards the royal seat. We went on our way, and next came to an open hall which had twenty beautiful gilt pillars, ornamented with many kinds of floral designs and many-coloured enamels. Here we seated ourselves in the expectation that the King would come out.

An hour afterwards the King arrived in great state, whereupon all rose to their feet, and crossed their hands on their breasts, and made a bow with lowered heads. This, too, was done by the ambassador, seeing that this was the custom of that court. Then, approaching the king, he delivered to him the letter, which the king took with his own hand and placed in that of the chief minister, who stood at his side.

The king seated himself in his place, and the master of ceremonies, who was close to the ambassador, pointed out to him his place, which was the fifth on the right hand [12]. He was to sit there. On taking his seat, he presented a breast-plate, a head-piece (*morion*), and sword-mountings, all of fine work made at Paris. All these were accepted by the king, who looked at the ambassador with a pleased face, saying to him that he was delighted at his coming. All this was spoken through an interpreter, an Armenian, who was in our employ. Then he asked after the health of the King of England, inquiring if he had any brothers, if he were married, how old he was, and whether he was loved by his people. To all these questions the ambassador replied, and after the lapse of one hour the king rose, saying to the ambassador that he should take rest and recover from his fatigues. Meanwhile he forwarded to Espahao (Isfahan) the letter brought by the ambassador in order to have it translated by a Capuchin friar named Frey Raphael Dumans,[1] well acquainted with the Turkish and Persian languages, a priest of great virtuts, loved by the king and all the court.

The letter having been translated, the king sent to the ambassador an invitation to come to court, where he gave him a banquet at his own table. It was given in the hall already described,

1. The Père Raphael du Mans (Jacques Dutertre), Capuchin, born in 1613, went to Persia in 1644, and died at Isfahan on April 1, 1696. He is the author of 'Estat de la Perse en 1660,' edited by Ch. Schefer (Paris, 1890).

which was decorated with rich carpets, and seats covered with rich brocade, and handsome cushions. In the assembly was the king seated in the midst of ten persons. That is to say, on his right hand 'Azamat-ud-daulah, then three of the great officials, and in the fifth place the ambassador, and on his left hand other five men, who were the chief generals then actually present at court. Of all these, the first was 'Azamat-ud-daulah, which means Great Minister of State; the second was Sepacalar (*Sipah-salar*), who is the commander-in-chief; the third Corchy-Bassi (*Qurchi-bashi*), the general of infantry; the fourth Couler Agassi (*Qular-aqasi*), who commands the king's slaves. All these are noblemen. The fifth was Nazer (*Nazir*), who is the major-domo of the royal household; the sixth Divan Begui (*Diwan-begi*), who is chief justice over the nobles of the kingdom; the seventh was Topchy Bassi (*Topchi-bashi*), who is the commander of the artillery; the eighth Cachiq Agasi Bassi (*Qashiq-aqasi-bashi*),[1] who is captain of the royal guard and master of the ceremonies; the ninth Cedar (Sadr), who is the judge in all cases of the law; the tenth, Vaquia-navis (*Waqi'ah-navis*), who is the Chief Secretary of State. Below the royal seat, which was raised the height of a foot, there were on each side thirty persons, all men of rank and position.

They placed in front of the king twelve large basins of gold filled with polas (*pulao*) of various kinds, and four dishes of different roast meats, six porcelain vessels holding various other meats, and several boxes having their covers ornamented with all sorts of precious stones. Each of those who were on the two sides of the king had the half of what the king himself had placed before him; and the sixty who were further down, away from the king's side, had each of them four basins of *pulao*. At this banquet wine was absent [13], and although the king knew how to drink a drop or two, on this occasion he refrained as a matter of dignity. When the first course was finished, the second was brought, consisting of much fruit and numerous sweet dishes.

The reader will be pleased to learn what *pulao* means. *Pulao* is rice cooked with many spices, cloves, cinnamon, mace, pimento, cardamoms, ginger, saffron, raisins, and almonds, to

1. Query meant for 'Ishaq-aqasi' (lord chamberlain) (see 'Estat de la Perse,' p. 20).

which is added the flesh of sheep, or fowls, or goats, and the whole dressed with plenty of butter. They make these *pulaos* of many sorts and of different flavours.

When the feast had ended, the king rose and said to the ambassador that he might start for the city of Isfahan,[1] for which he himself would set out, in a few days. This sending off of milord was because they were waiting for the answer from Smyrna, whether it was true that he had been sent as an ambassador by the King of England, Charles II, and whether he was of the rank that he claimed. At the end of six months the answer came, as I shall mention presently. Meanwhile we had spent fifty days in this city of Qazwin, and every day there came to us food in abundance for everyone of our people, with sufficient wine, and whatever was necessary for our animals.

The city of Qazwin stands in the midst of several mountains; it has sufficient water, many gardens, and much fruit, a fitting place for the holiday resort of a king, however great he may be, where he can go out after game, with which the country is well supplied.

1. This relegation of the ambassador's business to Isfahan is borne out by the letter in the *Mercurius Politicus* already referred to.

CHAPTER IX

WE QUIT QAZWIN AND ARRIVE AT ISFAHAN

We came out of Qazwin to start for Isfahan, and neither at the time of leaving nor during the journey were the accustomed supplies delivered to us. None the less, we managed to make our journey in sufficient comfort, and in twelve days we reached Isfahan, where there was made over to us as a dwelling a large house with a lovely garden. It was the property of the general of the king's artillery, who was then in Qazwin. There we fed ourselves at our own expense.

Finally, at the end of three months, when winter had passed, the king arrived at Isfahan,[1] and we were obliged to leave that house where the general lived, and they made over to us another. After a few days the ambassador sent a message to 'Azamat-ud-daulah that he desired to pay him a visit, but the answer returned was that in these days, the king being newly arrived, he was very much occupied, and he (the ambassador) must have a little patience, and that notice [14] would be given of the time when they could meet.

Thus matters were kept in suspense till the answer from Smyrna should arrive. Finally, they learnt that, without any doubt, the Belmont (Lord Bellomont) had been sent as ambassador, and that he was of the rank he asserted. Three months after the king's arrival at Isfahan 'Azamat-ud-daulah sent for the ambassador, and held with him a long conversation. I was present the whole time, quite close to the ambassador, who put me forward as his son.

In the speech he made he (the ambassador) told how the king, Charles I., was unjustly beheaded by his subjects, who into his place had raised a man of low origin, banishing King Charles II. and his brother James from the kingdom and per-

---

1. The Shah passed the *Nauroz*, or Vernal Festival (March 21, 1655), at Qum, and reached the capital on the 9th Rajab, 1065 H. (May 15, 1655). See *Qisas-ul-khaqan* of Wall Quli, Shamlu, British Museum, Additional MS. 7,656, fol. 132*a*, 132*b*.

secuting them. He had, therefore, come to His Majesty of Persia to ask for help, in accordance with the friendship which had always existed between the crowns of England and of Persia.

'Azamat-ud-daulah asked in what way could his king give aid such as he required. Then the ambassador replied that he should call to mind the word given long ago by the King of Persia to afford held to the King of Great Britain, should occasion arise. That also he still owed for the expenses incurred by the King of England when he sent a fleet to take the fortress of Orumus (Ormuz) from the hands of the Portuguese, and made it over to Persia. It was also most desirable that he should assist King Charles II at this conjuncture, by expelling from his dominions all the English who were partisans of the rebellion, and compel them to abandon their trade. By thus doing the praise of the generous acts of the famous Persian king would go through all the world. 'Azamat-ud-daulah, having listened to this reasoning with a solemn countenance, replied with a smile that he would report to the king all that had been said, and would give an answer afterwards. With this ended the interview.

CHAPTER X

HOW WE WENT A THIRD TIME TO COURT

When eight days had elapsed from the visit to the wazir, the ambassador was invited to a grand banquet in a beautiful palace that the King had recently completed. At its gateway stood the large and handsome cannon which were captured at Ormuz. They were near a large reservoir of nice appearance and very pleasant. At this second feast [15] which the king gave him, the ambassador was treated with great honours in deference to his embassy, 'Azamat-ud-daulah and a number of officers proceeding to the gates of the palace to meet him, and continuing in his suite until he arrived before the king. The latter caused his guest to be seated in the second place—that is to say, 'Azamat-ud-daulah came first, then the ambassador, then three of the king's officers; there being on the left hand five other persons, the greatest of the generals. The seat was larger than in Qazwin, with greater richness, and the room more beautiful. In it were sundry officials and captains, who stood.

There was not much conversation. The king only asked the ambassador whether the climate of Persia suited him; to which the ambassador replied that after all the climate of Persia had much resemblance to that of England, by reason of the frosts and snow that it had. I was standing behind the ambassador, and the king asked who I was. The ambassador answered that he looked upon me as his son. The king said to him that if he chose to make me over to him he would treat me very well, and thus there would be a memorial of him left at the court. The ambassador said that if I were in reality his son he would make me over to his majesty; but as my parents had placed me in his care, he could not part with me.

This was the conversation that we had until, after one hour had passed, the table was laid; it was much more imposing and more highly adorned than the one at Qazwin. The place where the king was seated was larger, and the carpets of greater value and more beautiful. The king's whole table vessels were of gold with covers, having handles ornamented with precious stones. In the lower seats were on each side fifty men, all nobles, including a few men of learning. Among these the king ordered me to take my seat. Each person had four plates full of *pulao*, also various dishes of roast and fried meat, and some of pickles. I noticed that all these men were of large frame, tall, and well made, with huge moustachios, which some of them had twisted round their ears, so that they might not fall on their shoulders. All were well clad in rich stuffs, and wore enormous turbans. Many of them ate voraciously.

The first course being finished, they set before us the second, consisting of a great quantity of fruit, which in Isfahan is very plentiful. This course lasted two hours, and at the end of it the king rose and entered the female apartments. 'Azamat-ud-daulah conducted the ambassador to the end of the room, holding him by the hand, saying that nothing should be wanting on his part to do him service, with many amicable speeches, in which this kind of people are never deficient.

CHAPTER X

[16] OF THE PRESENT THAT THE KING SENT TO THE AMBASSADOR, AND OF THE FOURTH TIME OF OUR BEING AT COURT

Some days elapsed after the above invitation, when 'Azamat-ud-daulah sent to the ambassador from the king fifty pieces of gold and silver brocade, velvet, and various-coloured silk, four pairs of handsome carpets, and 2,000 *patacas*,[1] the which arrived just at the right time; for the ambassador had run into debt with certain Armenian merchants, and with this money he paid his debt. After a very few days the ambassador went to the house of 'Azamat-ud-daulah, where he remained a long time in consultation, the subject being the following.

The ambassador demanded a favourable reply, saying that it was necessary for him to leave. 'Azamat-ud-daulah made use of many friendly expressions, but was not desirous of answering the proposition laid before him. By putting questions he feigned an eagerness to know whether England was a large kingdom, how many men it could place in the field, if there were a route to it by land. He appeared to be much amazed that all the Kings of Europe, being themselves Christian, did not afford succour to the King of England.

The ambassador replied to all this, but chiefly to this last question. He said if the King of Persia would pay the money that he owed, the King of England could then, without other assistance, obtain possession of his kingdom, and seize his enemies. Seeing the stiff answer of the ambassador, 'Azamat-ud-daulah succeeded in sending him away with pleasant words.

During the time the ambassador was in Isfahan, the king decided to have a parade of his armed force, and make a display of his power. For this affair he sent an invitation to the ambassador. We repaired to the very large royal hall, containing forty pillars, which has an outlook on the great square. In this hall the king

1. Yule, 683, the dollar or piece of eight. Elsewhere Manucci makes this equal to two rupees in India, or about four shillings.

takes his seat but rarely, and only when he has a review of his cavalry. These reviews are held twice a year; each time they last three days.

We went one day only. We saw the cavalry enter at one side of the plain and march out at the other. The soldiers, forty thousand in number, were mostly clothed in mail, and bore maces; some squadrons had lances, others bows and arrows, others matchlocks. All were mounted on good and swift horses, and they carried standards bearing devices. At the end of the review we saw two Persians bound each on a camel, with their bowels protruding. Their offence was causing a disturbance after they had drunk too much wine. These men were conducted thus through the city until they died.

CHAPTER XII

REPLY OF 'AZAMAT-UD-DAULAH TO THE AMBASSADOR ON THE PART OF THE KING

The ambassador, although somewhat doubtful of obtaining an answer such as he desired, never desisted from importuning 'Azamat-ud-daulah, reminding him that it was close upon a year that he had been in Isfahan without making the smallest advance in the negotiations, for which he had come so far. 'Azamat-ud-daulah put him off from day-to-day. At length, tired out by so many remonstrances, he made up his mind to give an answer. With this view he sent a message to the ambassador, requesting him to be good enough to come to his house, as he wanted to speak to him.

We repaired to the house of 'Azamat-ud-daulah, who received the ambassador with many gracious words and much politeness. Seating themselves, they began a long conversation to the following effect: 'Azamat-ud-daulah began a very long way off by remarking that the King of Persia was a great friend of the King of England, and cherished for him the same amity that he had felt towards the former kings, his ancestors; he greatly desired to assist that king, chiefly owing to the great necessity of the case. This was the reason that he had postponed his reply, while he searched for and considered ways in which he could give assistance. But he could find no manner of so doing. The Persian cavalry and the rest of their troops could not be sent, by reason of the great distance, by the land route. On the road were many kingdoms through which they must pass. Thus it was impossible to be of any use by sending an armed force. Then he had sought for some means of helping him by way of the sea; but to send a great fleet he saw was extremely difficult. In Persia they had no ships, and, should they attempt to construct them, they had not sufficient materials for the purpose.

Another reason for the long delay in giving an answer was this: They had used the interval to find out from the nations of Europe—the Portuguese, the Dutch, and even the English themselves—whether they could purchase any ships in which to send reinforcements to the king. But, in spite of all the offers they had made, they could not obtain what they wanted. The ambassador knew well that this was all a pretence, but he kept his temper, although showing signs of impatience at all this long-winded and superfluous talk.

When 'Azamat-ud-daulah had finished this long speech, the ambassador began as follows: First of all, he expressed his thanks for the great efforts that the King of Persia and 'Azamat-ud-daulah had taken to assist the King of England. Then, half making fun of 'Azamat-ud-daulah's many words, he said to him that he himself had a [18] much easier method of remedying all this, without giving trouble to the Persian monarch, and without fatiguing the Persian soldiers, so famous throughout Europe. His plan was that the King of Persia should pay, cash down, the money due on the bill owing to the King of England. He had not come all that long journey in search of cavalry, nor a fleet, nor ships, but of a debt in arrears. If he would excuse him, he would say a word or two frankly. To this 'Azamat-ud-daulah replied that he might speak as freely as he liked.

Upon this the ambassador continued that all that had been said by him showed that his king had no intention of paying the debt. 'Azamat-ud-daulah, in a deceptive manner and smiling, said that his king wished to pay, but, seeing that the amount demanded was very large, it would require a great number of beasts of burden, that it would be necessary to pass through other kingdoms, that possibly he might be robbed on his way. Nor was the difficulty met by saying that he could carry the amount by sea, for all the world knew what risks were run at sea, both of being attacked and of being wrecked, whereby the whole amount would be lost.

The ambassador's answer was that, if they gave him the money, he knew quite well how to take care of it and remove it in safety. If they paid over to him a sufficient sum, the King of England, his master, would have no other demand to make. He would hold himself satisfied, according to the orders he had received, as set forth in the letters that he had presented. This he said with a certain show of emotion, for by this time he saw that their object was to pay him in words.

'Azamat-ud-daulah hung his head down and affected a mild expression of countenance, then said in a low voice: 'Necessity is not the most perfect of judges.' He added that, as to banishing from the Persian realm the English traders, that could not be. For the king had allowed them willingly to enter his territory—the land of Persia was free to all—and the king declined to turn out anyone unless he had been guilty of an offence. All the same, they would grant him (Bellomont) leave to eject them from the kingdom himself by his own forces. The king would back up neither one side nor the other.

Finally, being wearied out, the ambassador said, with a certain amount of passion, that he had not looked for such an answer from a king of such fame in the world, especially after the Persian kingdom had received aid from the King of England, at great cost to the latter. 'Azamat-ud-daulah did not change countenance, but endeavoured to pacify the ambassador, saying that such events were sent from above, that never was all that we asked of God granted us, that in due time God would bring to mind his king. Encouraging him and consoling him with kind and soft words, he added that if he were in any difficulty for expenses, he could send to his interpreter [19], who would help him.

Hearing this, the ambassador said not a single word, but rose hastily, came forth, and returned home. When he had arrived there, he by-and-by gave an order for the sale of some pieces of cloth and some carpets which still remained to provide for our road expenses. The above conversation was in Turkish, which I could already speak and understand sufficiently. Listening to everything with the greatest attention, I admired the way in which 'Azamat-ud-daulah was able to evade the aggressive answers of the ambassador without betraying any sign of ill-humour.

CHAPTER XIII

HOW THE KING OF PERSIA MADE OVER TO THE AMBASSADOR A LETTER FOR THE KING OF ENGLAND

The firm words of the ambassador were the cause of their giving him his leave to depart after a brief delay. With this intent, eight days after the above-mentioned conversation, he was sent for to court on behalf of the king, when we were given another feast like the one which I have described, and in the same place. At the end of the banquet, 'Azamat-ud-daulah took the ambassador by the hand and led him in front of the royal seat at a distance of two or three paces, and with his face towards the king. The ambassador was on the left side of 'Azamat-ud-daulah. The latter put his hand into his pocket and drew forth a bag of gold brocade, in which was a letter. Lifting this bag with both hands, he placed it on his head, making a profound reverence to the king, bowing his head most deeply. Then he handed the said bag to the ambassador, saying that his king sent that letter to the King of England. He was directed to make obeisance as he had seen the other do. During this short speech 'Azamat-ud-daulah held half of the bag in his hand, while the other half was in that of the ambassador. As soon as the brief speech was ended, the ambassador drew the bag from the hands of 'Azamat-ud-daulah, and quickly turned his back, and without any sort of bow, held it out contemptuously to the interpreter. This man at once hastened up to receive the letter with both hands; for the motion made by the ambassador showed that if he did not hurry near, the ambassador would throw the bag at him.

Then, without any civility, or any sort of bow, he left 'Azamat-ud-daulah standing where he was and went out, his head high, while the king sat with cast-down eyes as if [20] he saw nothing of what was passing. All those present remained in silent wonder at such boldness. I was quite close to the ambassador, and came out, notwithstanding, with some amount of dread, anticipating that the king would send out some order to have us killed. But we were not interfered with.

On arriving home, we took measures to prepare ourselves without delay for continuing our journey. In fact, we did so at the end of nine days, and the ambassador not being provided with sufficient funds for our expenses, he applied to the head of the English factory at Isfahan, who was called Mestre Jhon (Mr. Young),[1] a very short man, but most generous and very liberal, as I made note of from the feasts and offerings which several times he had given to the said ambassador.

1. 'Mestre Jhon' is identified by Mr. W. Foster as Henry Young, who was at Isfahan in 1655. He left it on September 26 for Gombroon (Bandar 'Abbas), and sailed for Surat on November 20 in the *Diamond*.

CHAPTER XIV

OF THE CITY OF ISFAHAN, AND OF CERTAIN EVENTS WHICH HAPPENED THERE

The city of Isfahan is very large, situated in a great plain at the foot of some low hills. It has four canals of water, which flow through the midst of it, and these serve for irrigating the gardens. These canals issue from a river which flows between Julpha (Zulfah) and Isfahan; its name is Senderuth (Zindah-rud); over it are four bridges somewhat distant from each other. Of the four, two are especially handsome—namely, the one on the road from Isfahan to Julpha (Zulfah). You approach it by a long and wide raised way, adorned on both sides with the great and beautiful walled gardens of the king, and with high trees, called in Persian chenar (*chanar*), and in European languages, planes. In the midst thereof flows one of the aforesaid canals of water, which fills various reservoirs for the use of the said gardens, and goes on its course until it reaches again the river from which it was taken. Horses are ridden on the raised way. There are many seats where the Persians imbide tobacco from crystal 'guriguris,'[1] called by them 'caliao' (*qualiyan*), which are long and narrow-necked circular flasks filled with water, having a vessel of tinned copper or of silver in the shape of an open flower of the water-lily[2] stuck into its (the flask's) mouth, and filled with tobacco. With this they sit, telling stories until late, sometimes, without exaggeration, as many as five or six [21] thousand of them.

The second bridge, which is the finest of them all, is called the bridge of Xiras (Shiraz), thus named because when going from Isfahan to Shiraz you cross over it. This bridge consists of three stories, besides the chief one, which is in the middle. The king goes there sometimes with his harem, and he can

1. Probably from *gurgur*, a whisper, in allusion to the sound made by the water-pipe. The Indian form of *gurguri*.
2. The text has *nolifero aberto,* which I take to be the Persian word *nilufar*, a water-lily.

descend to the water without being seen. By all these stories you can cross from one side of the river to the other. The water runs over dressed stones, made artificially high or low, so as to produce waves pleasing to behold.[1]

I noticed that the houses of Isfahan and those throughout Persia, seen from the front, are not pleasing, being all made of clay; but they are lovely inside, and highly decorated..hey have both large and small gardens, with good fruit-trees—that is to say, pears, apples, peaches, apricots, mulberries, sweet and sour quinces, like the apples of Europe, vines of Boas Vuas, and vineyards of Vuas,[2] grapes without stones, which are called "quiximis" (*kishmish*), many kinds of plums—and all the varieties of flowers that grow in Europe; for the Armenians are very fond of growing European flowers, and present them to the Persian nobles. The Persians, as also the Moguls, are fond of flowers and perfumes.

In front of the royal palace is a large plain, where throughout the year stand fruit-sellers' booths, and a large quantity of exquisite melons. Here they drink coffee and smoke tobacco; the place is always full of people going and coming. Here are to be seen dancers, wrestlers, and other performers. In one corner of this open square is a palace where musical instruments are played; and there stands the clock found by them in the fortress of Ormuz, which they preserve as a memorial of their victory over the Portuguese. The city was always clean, due to the energy of the gardeners, because with what was removed from the streets they manured their gardens. They collect most industriously the sewage from the houses for the same purpose. This is a great help to keeping the air pure, by not allowing dirt to accumulate in the city. There are also many baths where the body may be washed. The soul also profits (as they believe), for when they wash themselves they imagine themselves to be absolved from their sins. Ablution serves among the Mahomedans—and speaking always with due reverence—like confession and absolution among us Catholics.

During the time we were at Isfahan rumours were current to the effect that the Great Mogul meant to come against the

1. There is a good description and two views of these bridges in Chardin's 'Voyages on Perse' (Amsterdam, 1711, ten volumes, 12mo.), vol. viii, p. 220, and Plates XLVII, XLVIII.
2. 'Boal Vua,' a kind of grape?

fortress of Candar (Qandahar), which is held by the King of Persia in defiance of the Mogul. For this reason they began to prepare to march out to encounter him; then the spies brought them the news that this year the Great Mogul would not come.

It happened in those days that the son of an officer, being twenty-two [22] years of age, was in attendance on the court. He fell in love with a lady in the palace and sent her several presents. When the king was told of this, he ordered the man to be beheaded. As the young man was actually at court, he got word of the king's order, and returned home with all the haste he could. There, with his own hands, he totally castrated himself, and without delay sent the severed member in a covered golden vessel to the King, with a request that he would chastise that which had committed the offence. The king, with regard to this deliberate act of his, pardoned his life, and gave him the title of the "Valiant Eunuch."

In the city are two factories, one of the English, the other of the Dutch. There are also four churches, one of the Portuguese Augustinians, which the present king caused to be entirely gilded at his own expense, and he went there several times to see our ceremonial. Another church belongs to the barefooted Carmelites, another to the Jesuits, another to the Capuchins.

There are also in the city many mosques, among them a dome with two tombs, which are much venerated. The door of this dome is opened only once a year, on the occasion of a great festival, to which flock people from different provinces on the appointed day. One tomb they assert to be that of 'Ali, the other they state to be that of his sons Assen (Hasan) and Ossen (Husian), who are revered as martyrs. Others declare they are tombs of the companions of Muhammad, although he had no Court or courtiers.

Once during the night, when the king, Shah Abbas, was lying asleep, he woke all of a sudden, having dreamt that he had seen a vision. Calling to the captain of his guard, he gave him an order to open at once the door of the dome and both the tombs, and after looking with great care at what was in them, make a detailed report of his inspection. The captain of the guard caused both the tombs to be opened, and found in them two dead Capuchin priests, with their clothes and their bodies equally intact. The captain stood in amazement, and ordered the tombs and the dome to be closed up as before. He reported at once to the king what he had seen. Listening attentively to the story, the king pronounced these words: 'None can know the secrets of God, unless He Himself'. This event remained a secret, and the same veneration was continued as before.

At the distance of a league or a little less from Isfahan is an inhabited place called Julpha (Zulpha), where great numbers of Armenians live, all merchants, with their churches. These people dwelt long ago in ancient Zulfah, upon the banks of the river Aras, three days' journey before you come to Tabriz. It was there that I saw an eclipse of the sun in the middle of the day [23], beholding the stars as in a dark night.[1] They left that place with the permission of Shah 'Abbas, coming with their families and all their belongings to found this new Zulfah on the farther bank of the river Zindah-rud, and there they dwell in complete liberty, having sufficient facilities in the way of houses, gardens full of fruit, and water with which to irrigate them. This water flows in canals through the middle of the streets, which are adorned on both sides with great trees.

1. I am indebted to Dr. A. M. W. Downing, of the Nautical Almanac Office, for the information that a total eclipse of the sun occurred in 1654, August 12 (New Style). The central line crossed the east shore of the Black Sea at about lat. 45°, and the west shore of the Caspian Sea at about lat. 40°. It would, therefore, have been visible as a considerable partial eclipse in the region indicated (*i.e.*, Zulfah in Armenia).

CHAPTER XV

OF THE GOVERNMENT OF THE PERSIAN KINGDOM, AND OF SOME STRANGE EVENTS

The kingdom of Persia was very well governed, having no rebellions or treasons, neither robbers nor highwaymen on the roads, as there are in some kingdoms, chiefly those of the Turks. For Shah 'Abbas took the greatest care that the land was well governed, and allowed no wrong to be done. This king was much loved and esteemed by his people; not only did they love him, they adored him as a saint. The reason was that his family was descended from 'Ali, who was married to the daughter of Muhammad. The Persians say (though the Turks and the Moguls decline to concede this) that 'Ali succeeded Muhammad as prophet. But this was not the sole cause that he was esteemed and venerated as a holy man; it was also his singular qualities which made him venerable.

The king was a man of good stature, well nourished, broad in the shoulders, slender in the waist, a fine horseman, of a bright countenance, strong in his resolves, and a lover of wine. With reference to this, I may recount how he employed a golden vessel called Azarpexa (*Hazar-peshah*), which means 'a thousand kinds.' It would hold two *canadas*[1] and a half of wine. When the king wanted to have a joke with anyone, or impose on him a slight punishment, he would force him to drink in his presence the measure of wine contained in the said vessel.

This he did on several occasions to the French goldsmiths who were in his service, when they did not make the enamel work, rings, jewels, and clocks to please him. He would threaten them that if they did not execute the work as perfectly as he wanted it, he would have to double their punishment. For this reason the goldsmiths, before finishing off the work made over to them, carried it many times into the king's presence to see

1. *Canada* is a measure of liquid holding three English pints. The quantity was thus seven and a half pints, nearly a gallon. Tavernier also mentions *Hazar-peshah*.

if it met with his approval or not. For it is no joke to drink at once so much wine.

In my time there were six French goldsmiths, and the king showed to them great love and affection, giving [24] to each of them 150 *patacas*[1] every year in addition to food, of which they had abundance, and also presents, which he gave them when he was pleased with the work that they did. Many a time when he was happy he would send for them and make them sit in his presence, and, drinking wine himself, he made them drink too, though not out of the 'thousand kinds.' Conversing with them, he would ask as to the state of things among the kings of Europe—how they fought battles, and many different questions. He took delight in hearing the doings of the King of France, and the mode in which he carried on war; he also liked to hear from the mouths of these goldsmiths witty sayings, and showed singular affection to Europeans.

For this reason it is, I believe, that in Persia there is liberty, if you so choose, to put and reply to questions on matters of the Christian religion between Christians and Persians, without fear of being interfered with on that account. The reader should understand that among the laws of the Mahomedans is one, that to all questions about religion put to them by Christians they should answer by the sword. This rule is followed most rigorously in Turkey, Arabia, in the realm of the Mogul, also in Balq (Balkh), Bocara (Bukhara), among the Osbeques (Uzbaks) and Patanis (Pathans). Thus it is impossible for anyone to utter a word there against the Mahomedan superstition without the chance of losing his head. But in Persia you may use arguments, make inquiry, and give answer in matters of religion without the least danger.

The men of Persia are big, very strong, and fairly good-looking, most subtle in mind, and lovers of music, scents, and flowers. They are of a generous disposition and quick-witted, nor do they fail in becoming good soldiers, intrepid and crafty. With all this, they hold their king in such great esteem that no one makes so bold as to speak against him, or to evade obeying his orders. When he sends an order to behead any grandee, no one raises the least opposition or utters the least contradiction. The orders of the king are considered to be the orders of God; and thus, when a report arrives that the king has sent

1. This would be about £ 30.

for the head of any governor or other official, the culprit issues forth to meet the executioner of the royal orders, and offering himself for the stroke, requests him to carry his head into the presence of his king, which he gives as a sacrifice to the royal commands.

It happened about this time, when he was in Isfahan, that Shah 'Abbas received a report that Xaabascan (Shabash Khan), governor of Tabriz, a man of great stature and much strength, commanding twelve thousand horsemen, had been guilty of an omission of some consequence. The king issued an order that a soldier should be sent to cut off his head. When the emissary arrived the governor was giving public audience; the man laid hold of his sword, and called out that the king demanded his head. Shabash Khan, without any remonstrance, presented his body, and putting down his head, told the soldier to cut it off. The man struck [25] a blow, but Shabash Khan, being of a large build, it did not go very far, and only wounded him. In a rage, the governor raised his hand and gave the man a heavy backstroke, by which several of his teeth were knocked out, exclaiming that the king had ordered him to cut off his head, but not to torture him. Holding down his head anew, he directed the man to deliver a proper cut, and then with two more blows his head was severed. It was carried to the king's presence, where orders issued, as was the custom, that it should be shown for three days in the public square as an example and warning for others. Now I will recount some other events, which will give to the reader some idea of the strict justice done by Shah 'Abbas, and the quickness of his mind in unmasking impostors.

There happened during the time that I was in Isfahan another remarkable instance by which you can gauge the attention which Shah 'Abbas devoted to deciding justly. There were two rich men, one of whom had, during many months, run up an account with the other, there having been no opportunity of a settlement between them. One of them was called Mahomed Raza (Muhammad Riza), and he owed a large sum of money to the other, who passed as an upright man, and his name was Miza Esmail (Mirza Isma'il). Seeing that they could not come to an agreement, they decided that each should write down his argument and his version of the account. Folding up the papers, each man was to write his name on his own documents; then they were to be enclosed together in a bag sealed with each man's seal and those of several witnesses. So said, so done. The good Mirza Isma'il, not suspecting the deceit of his debtor. Muhammad Riza, left the bag in his hands, with the understanding that when Shah 'Abbas returned from the chase, the said bag should be made over to the king, praying him to give orders for judging the cause. The agreement was that after the judge nominated by the king had given his finding, not another word should be said.

Muhammad Riza had time, before the king returned from hunting, to cut open the bag; and withdrawing the papers of Mirza Isma'il, in which were weighty and convincing reasons, he substituted for those writings and accounts other papers bearing his creditor's name. Then, sending for a workman, the bag was resewn with such neatness that no one could believe it had been cut.

The king returned from his hunting, when both men appeared in his presence and delivered to him the bag, with the prayer that he would graciously order a speedy decision to be given. The king, being eager that justice should be done, as will be seen further from a case that I will mention later on, sent at once for one of his ministers [26] named Fazel Beg (Fazil Beg)—that is to say, 'Learned Person,' of whom he had a high opinion as being a disinterested and very truthful man. To him the bag was delivered.

Coming forth in company of the two petitioners' Fazil Beg repaired to his house. Then, showing the bag to the two litigants, and to the witnesses called in for the purpose, he asked them if it was exactly the same as when they saw it before. All of them answered that there was no difference, that it was the same, with the same seals and the same arrangement. He then sent them away, and they returned to their homes.

Mirza Isma'il expected that Fazil beg would send for him and decide in his favour, therefore he took no further steps; but the cunning Muhammad Riza did not allow a day to pass without importuning the judge to end the history and the suit; because, as he asserted, the case was very clear that, so far from his being the debtor of Mirza Isma'il, the latter owed him (M. Riza) a large sum of money. Thus he went on every day, until at last Fazil Beg, having well studied the papers, arrived at the finding that Mirza Isma'il was the debtor. He therefore sent for him.

On his arrival, he (Fazil Beg) told him he was much astonished that a man held to be truthful and just could have made an unjust demand, and, being himself the debtor, should have claimed to be the creditor of Muhammad Riza for a large sum. Mirza Isma'il stood astonished at these words of the judge, and requested, as all he desired, that he would refer to his papers, which would clearly demonstrate that Muhammad Riza was in his debt. The judge satisfied him by giving him a sight of the papers. Hardly had Mirza Isma'il glanced at them than he said, surprised and confused, that these were not his papers nor his accounts. As they were forged, a decision should not be given, and he hoped time would be allowed.

Fazil Beg replied that he had the king's orders to decide according to the papers enclosed in the bag, and according to them there was nothing else for it but to decide in favour of Muhammad Riza. Mirza Isma'il, seeing that there was no hope of getting anything out of him, had recourse secretly to the king, and falling at his feet, assured him that in the transaction there was some deception, done either by Fazil Beg or through some trick played with the bag.

The king had no suspicions about the judge, for he had already tested him several times, and still less would Fazil Beg risk such a thing, for it would be sure to cost him his life. Nor could he suspect Mirza Isma'il of any imposition, he being known as an upright and truthful man, against whom none could make any accusation, for he was a just man with a good conscience. For these reasons the king said to Mirza Isma'il that he must be patient for a little while until he could get at the truth.

Among other things, the king reflected that the bag had been in [27] the hands of Muhammad Riza, that he could have cut it open and then closed it. Therefore he decided to put his suspicions to the test. Thus do princes act who desire to have justice done in their realms! He resolved to burn a piece of the carpet on which he sat, a piece of rich stuff excellently woven, and so much prized that he seldom used it to sit upon. Secretly he burnt a hole in the said carpet, and said nothing about it. The employee who had charge of it, discovering the burn, was in great fear lest the king might order his hand to be cut off, or otherwise punish him for taking so little care of such a precious article. Taking possession of the carpet, he removed it in secret to his own house, and diligently searched for a workman who could darn it so perfectly that no one could see that it had been repaired. Through God's will it so happened that he got hold of the workman who had sewn up the bag.

After some days the king asked where his favourite carpet was. When they had brought it and spread it out, the king took his seat upon it, and, without attracting attention, searched for anything in the nature of a darn. In spite of its having been repaired, he could not find the place. Thereupon the king ordered the employee to produce in his presence the workman who had darned the burnt place. The man, being frightened by this sudden question, could not deny, and went off to bring the workman. Both returned to the king's presence, when he asked with a serious look, as if he already knew, 'How much did you get for mending this bag?' showing him the one that he had sewn up. The workman replied that they had given him a goodish sum; for the said bag had a hole, which (as they said) had been gnawed by the rats. It was of great importance to his good name, the owner said, that it should be darned at once and with skill. The king asked if he knew the man who gave him the job, and he answered 'Yes.' At once orders were given that a number of officials and servants should attend in the presence, with Mirza Isma'il and Muhammad Riza in their midst. When they had all arrived, the king asked the workman which was the man that had given him the bag to be darned. Then the workman pointed out Muhammad Riza, adding that he had done the work in his house and in his presence, stating the day, the hour, the house, and the place in the house where he had carried out the work. These statements having been verified, the king ordained that Muhammad Riza should be cut into four pieces, which, being attached to the tails of four camels, should be dragged through the city, preceded by a drummer and a man shouting: 'This is the justice that the king has ordered to be done.' The house of this Muhammad Riza was cleared of its contents, and the whole given to Mirza Isma'il. Thus was justice done, and impostors were kept in order; thus should act all princes if they would not be instruments of oppression, if they are desirous of cutting short the career of knavery [28].

The story I am now to tell will prove that Shah 'Abbas loved to do justice. He who related it to me told me how the king allowed no Christian to be ill-treated. Nevertheless, the

Armenians are not held in much esteem in Persia, this very king having several times taken from them their wives and daughters, picking from among them the best-looking. All the same, he would not permit them to be oppressed by anyone else.

It happened that a Persian soldier, considered brave but very arrogant, a tall man with huge moustachios, went daily and seated himself at the shop of an Armenian trader who sold all sorts of drugs. This trader had a daughter eighteen years of age who looked after the shop. The soldier passed his day in conversation with this girl, whence it came to pass that the Armenian was unable to sell his goods. The customers were frightened at the terrible appearance of the soldier, and would not venture to approach the shop.

Thus the frightened trader was obliged, after much hesitation, to say to the soldier most humbly that he would feel obliged by his doing him the favour of not coming so often to his shop, seeing that no one dared while he was seated there to come up to it to buy anything; that thus he suffered greatly in his business. He must beg to be excused for making this petition, but it was necessity alone that compelled him to make the request; for if things went on as they were, he would be unable to exist himself or maintain his family. Hardly had the Armenian finished his humble speech than the soldier seized his sword, and with one blow severed the man's head from his body, and, jumping on his horse, rode off to hide in a place set aside by the king as a sanctuary for offenders, whence not even the law itself could withdraw him.

The Armenians were informed of this deed. Assembling themselves, they proceeded to lay their complaint before Mirza Cuchuc (Mirza Kuchak), which means 'Little Noble,' who was the chief justice. This man was so inimical to the Christians, that when he had succeeded in catching the murderer, the sentence he passed was that a small wound should be inflicted on the little finger of the man's left hand, from which only three drops of blood flowed, and that he should pay in cash a fine of ten *patacas*.[1] This sentence showed that he valued the Armenians as worthless and people of no account. The Armenians,

---

1. *Pataca,* Yule and Burnell, second edition, 683, 'a dollar or piece of eight.' From *Abu-taqah,* Arabic, 'Father of the Window,' a coin with a scutcheon on the reverse, taken by the Arabs for a window, N. M., i., 113, makes one *pataca* equal to two rupees.

upon the issue of this unjust sentence, made all possible haste to inform the king of the circumstances. He admitted them to an audience, and verified their account of what had happened. He told them to be patient, that he would not forget the case, and justice should be done to them. After the lapse of some days, Mirza Kuchak appeared before the king to report to him on various matters, but made no mention of the Armenian's death. The king dissembled. After a little conversation, he asked what would be the necessary sentence on a Christian who had slain a Mahomedan [29]. Mirza Kuchak replied that first of all he must be forced to pay three thousand patacas, and after many tortures his head must be cut off, as punishment for his great audacity in raising his hand upon one of the faithful friends of God and a follower of 'All. All this he delivered in a loud voice, as if he were pronouncing an admirable decision. The king pretended he approved the answer, but this was a mere subterfuge; and he went on to ask him, If by chance a Mahomedan wrongfully killed a Christian, what would have to be done? Mirza Kuchak, who supposed that his first reply had been pleasing to the king, and glorying so much the more in exalting Mahomedans as he depressed Christians, answered that the Mahomedan murderer must receive a small wound in the little finger of the left hand, from which three drops of blood could flow, and not more, paying, in addition, ten *patacas* to the relations of the deceased. Thereupon the king said: 'Why make such a difference between Mahomedans and Christians? It does not appear fair to favour the Mahomedans so greatly and show such harshness to the Christians.

Mirza Kuchak began to give the rein to his eloquence, exalting the Mahomedans and depreciating the Christians. Among other arguments, he said that the Mahomedans of Persia were faithful to God, that they adored the great 'All, that there was a great difference between Mahomedans and Christians, both in this world and in the next, for Christians could never get to heaven, being infidels. To preach sound doctrine and afford a good example in this world, it was necessary to decide cases as he had stated, nor were Christians worthy of anything better.

Shah 'Abbas changed colour, and with an angry voice told him to be silent. He declined to hear such arguments; he had only to look into the books of Moses and see the rightful verdict:

'Who slays shall himself be slain.'[1] If he (the chief justice) had not been a descendant of Muhammad, he should have been forced to order him to be torn in pieces by lions, on account of the unjust sentence that he had given in the case where a soldier slew an Armenian. The king ordered him never to appear in his presence again, and the false accusers were expelled from the court.

The king ordered the soldiers of his guard to go and claim the soldier who had committed the murder, bring him out from wherever he was hiding, and cut him to pieces. They told the king that the place was a sanctuary, a place of safety that the king had granted to misdoers. The king answered: 'He who granted the sanctuary can withdraw it.' Thus in this king's time there is no longer any place of refuge. The soldier was quartered and the pieces dragged through the city of Isfahan, and Mirza Kuchak quitted Persia. Subsequently I encountered him in the empire of the Great Mogul, in the city of Laor (Lahor), and in the proper place (Part II, 198) I will recount what happened to him [30].

The events of which I have spoken caused the subjects of Shah 'Abbas to talk much about his many virtues. Hearing all this, an English gentleman lately arrived in Persia conceived a great desire of seeing so renowned a monarch.[2] He therefore hastened on to Isfahan, and during a stay there of some days he became familiar and friendly with the king's goldsmiths, particularly with one of them called Clodio.[3] This man was specially favoured by Shah 'Abbas, he being somewhat of a jester, and the king frequently delighted in listening to him.

The gentleman, learning the inclination that the king had to the said Clodio, begged and entreated him to arrange some

1. 'Whose sheddeth man's blood, by man shall his blood be shed' (Gen. ix, 6).
2. This story is also told by J. B. Tavernier (French edition of 1692), i. 2, chap. x. (Fifth Voyage, leaving Paris February, 1657), pp. 267, 268, 272. He makes the hero one De Reville, a Norman gentleman, whom he met at Smyrna. De Reville was put up by the English in their factory at Isfahan, and they sent their interpreter with him when he saw the king. Tavernier, who says he was there, introduces the name of the Frenchman Claude; but the details and date do not accord with Manucci. Between them, who shall decide?
3. 'Claude Musin, armourer,' according to Tavernier (i. 267, edition 1692); or, as in vol. iii, p. 108, 'C. Muzin, arquebusier du roi.'

way in which he could have an audience. He said that it was for this that he had come so far, and that he would go back to Europe satisfied if able to declare that he had seen and spoken to the King of Persia. Clodio inquired of him whether he had any business about which he could speak. The gentleman replied that he had none; it was solely for his own satisfaction and out of curiosity that he desired to see and speak to the king. To this Clodio said that as to seeing him, that was very easy; but in regard to speaking to him, it was against rule when there was no special business. The gentleman persisted that he had an ardent desire to speak to the king, and for that reason begged him to do this favour, which he would never forget as long as he lived; thus he must continue to search for some mode of accomplishing his desire.

As Clodio was quite willing to do this kindness to a gentleman of good family, he told him he must wait for some days, and then without fail he would carry him into the presence of the king. It so happened that a few days afterwards the king sent for Clodio. After a little conversation the latter reported to the king how there had come an English gentleman with many European recommendations, a great soldier, and of high family. This gentleman greatly desired to have the honour of being allowed to appear before the royal presence. He did not want to quit Persia for Europe without having accomplished this his purpose.

The king asked if the gentleman had come on any business. Clodio replied that he had none; his only business was to be able to boast of having spoken to the most renowned king in the world. The merits of his majesty were apparent to all, but chiefly to those of Europe. The king asked if the gentleman was of as high rank as the ambassador (Bellomont) who had already left. He was told that there was little difference. Upon this the king gave him permission to bring the gentleman the next day.

Clodio left the court and went straight to see the gentleman, who was waiting for him with great and impatient longing. Hardly had he appeared when the gentleman asked him if he brought good news. Clodio answered 'Yes'; next day he would have to go to the palace, and therefore [31] he must make ready for the anxiously desired visit. The gentleman was very pleased, and in high delight embraced Clodio, declaring that his whole life long he would be ready to serve his interest in any way he wished. Clodio bade him good-bye. The gentleman was busy all the night, without once stopping, in arranging his hair and attaching various ribbons to his clothes. His hat bore curled feathers of various kinds; his shirt and clothes he rubbed with different kinds of scent. When all this was completed, he passed the rest of the night composing sentences and searching for the choicest Turkish words to use. Next, he began to picture to himself how he must present himself before the king, the arguments and answers that he would have to give to the royal questions, which last he invented himself. From one thing to another, he finished by staring out of the window for the approach of dawn. Day had hardly broken when he issued forth hurriedly in search of Clodio, who pointed out to him that it was not yet time; when the hour arrived, he would fetch him. This he did, bringing with him Mestre Pit (? Mr. Pitt),[1] who had also quitted Europe to see the world, and for the time being was to pass as the gentleman's servant.

They arrived at the palace, the gentleman highly delighted at being so near the satisfying of his curiosity. He was as one very weary and very thirsty who reaches a crystal spring, not knowing how dear his curiosity would cost him. Announcement of their arrival was made to the king, he being at the time in his garden taking a walk. Permission having been accorded, all three went in—that is to say, Clodio and the gentleman and Mestre Pit (Mr. Pitt), who passed as a servant. Arriving within sight of the king, the gentleman raised his hat and made his bow in the European manner with great politeness. Drawing still nearer, he dropped on his knee, as Clodio had instructed him, and began to speak thus: 'The greatness and the renown of your majesty's royal person are spread throughout the world, and the name of such a dread sovereign stands higher than that of the greatest monarchs. The whole of Europe is lost in admiration on learning that in Persia is a sun illuminating with its rays the whole of the Arctic and Antarctic regions. Thus have I come this immense distance to acquire the honour of beholding and of speaking to such a great king.'

All this he said in the Turkish language. Shah 'Abbas motioned with his hand for him to rise, and with a pleased

1. Mr. W. Foster was good enough to make a search for this 'Mr. Pitt' in the India Office Records, but without success.

expression requested him to come nearer. Then he asked his name, of what country he was, through what lands he had passed, and many other questions. After this he inquired how he supported himself in his own country. The gentleman replied that he owned land which yielded him a sufficient income [32], adding that he was a captain in the King of England's cavalry.

Shah 'Abbas replied: 'Can you tell me how it happened that his own subjects came to behead him, a thing I am unable to believe, seeing that it would be the greatest piece of disloyalty and audacity that could ever enter the heads of reasoning beings? I trust you will tell me the truth without any concealment.' The gentleman said: 'I will tell your majesty the truth: it took place with great barbarity, in public, upon a staging, a great crowd being assembled to look on at this event; among them I myself was quite close, and out of the deep affection which I had to my king, I have managed to preserve a handkerchief dipped in his blood.' Hearing these words, the king, Shah 'Abbas, placed both hands on his sides, and, changing colour, exclaimed in an angry voice: 'Oh, traitor! you were in his service and his subject; how could you be such a coward as to allow your king to be beheaded, being present yourself at this barbarous deed, without forthwith giving up your life for him?'

At these words, which issued from the king's mouth with the sound of a lion's roar, the gentleman stood dismayed, speechless, giving himself up as lost. The king, turning to his suite, said, in the same severe tone: 'Take away this coward and traitor, unworthy to remain in the world, and shut him up in a prison-house apart, and thus let the world know that Shah 'Abbas cannot suffer in his presence a man who, calling himself a gentleman and a valorous captain, could be present at the beheadal of his king without attempting the slightest effort in defence of his liege lord.'

Hardly had the king ended this speech when the men who were on guard fell upon the English gentleman, disarranging his feathers, hair, and garments, which had cost him a whole night's labour, and binding him, they dragged him off to a dark dungeon, where the poor gentleman expected every moment to be put to death, lamenting that his own curiosity had been the cause of this great peril. Meanwhile Clodio and Mestre Pit (Mr. Pitt) returned sadly to their homes, in shame, with hanging heads. Shah 'Abbas' object was to give a lesson to his own nobles as to the manner in which they should serve their king and the fidelity they ought to display, when the occasion arose, in defence of their monarch.

After a few days Clodio went to the king and petitioned for the gentleman's pardon, and that his release might be graciously ordered. But the king still showed severity, and replied that such a fellow had no right to live. However, Clodio did not lose heart, knowing the favour in which he stood. He uttered some witty remark which chanced to take the king's fancy, and, laughing, he said he would grant the man's liberty if he (Clodio) would give his dog its liberty to remain all its life with the monarch of Persia. This dog was very clever [33], and several times the king had asked Clodio for it, but had always met with a refusal for one reason or another. Now, finding himself under an obligation to get the gentleman released, Clodio was forced to present to the king the dog he loved so well. Then the gentleman was set free, who that same day, in the greatest haste, left Isfahan, apprehending some further misadventure. When seeing him off, Clodio said to him that when he had reached Europe he should impart to his friends the honour that had been done him, and tell them that the kings of Asia were not devoid of sense.

CHAPTER XVI

OF OUR DEPARTURE FROM ISFAHAN AND ARRIVAL AT THE PORT OF BANDARABASSI (BANDAR 'ABBAS)

We were now to continue our journey, wherefore we begged the help of Mestre Jonh (Henry Young), who gave to the ambassador the assistance he required. We wished to leave Isfahan in company of the said Mestre Jonh (Henry Young), but we could not conclude our business in time. He left several days before we did, and we left at the end of September of one thousand six hundred and fifty-two (1652).[1]

During our journey to the town of Xiras (Shiraz) we obtained good supplies of food, but the road is somewhat difficult, owing to the mountain ranges which must be crossed, where horses are fatigued not a little in trying to keep their feet. But I must allow there is also some fine open country, notwithstanding there are some very difficult swamps. The mountains are like all those in Persia—that is to say, generally bare of trees, though not wanting in fodder for sheep and goats, which in some places produce the stone called *b'azar* (*bezoar*).[2] Of these stones I will speak when I come to write of the kingdom of Gulkhandah (III. 59), where there is an abundance of them.

The sheep of Persia are very prolific; they bring forth young twice a year, by the help of a grain called *chicharos*,[3] on which they are fed at a certain time of the year; and their wool is of the sort already described (I. 9).

Finally, at the end of fifteen days' travel, we arrived at the town of Xjras (Shiraz), where we stayed for thirty days, the ambassador having fallen ill. He received many visits from a

1. The correct year is 1655. Henry Young left Isfahan on September 26, 1655.
2. Yule and Burnell, p. 90, *bezoar*, from Persian *padzahr*, 'poison stone,' a hard concretion found in the stomach of a wild goat in the Persian province of Lar.
3. Evidently the *Cicer arietinum* or *Pois chiche*, in Persian nakhud (Schlimmer, 'Terminologie,' p. 136, Tahran, 1874); or the Indian *channa*, which Anglo-Indians call '*gram*' (from Portuguese grao, 'grain').

barefooted Carmelite friar, a missionary to the Armenians who dwell here. The air of this town is very fresh; there are many gardens with good fruit, and the country round produces a quantity of grapes; consequently they make a great deal of wine, which is exported to all parts of India. Although the law of the Mahomedans forbids the drinking of wine, still the King of Persia permits the English to make it [34]; but they only produce enough for the company, and not to sell to others. In this region there is no deficiency of food produced, of oranges, of lemons, nor, above all, of roses, which they distil, and the rose-water is forwarded in boxes to all parts.

One of the wonderful things round Shiraz is a famous building standing at a distance approximately of two leagues, where dwelt, as they declare, the great Darius, King of Persia, who was defeated in battle by Alexander the Great. There is also a mountain in which is a cave where drips a liquid called by the Persians *mumihay* (*mumiyai*).[1] This liquid belongs to the king exclusively, and thus the cave is closed by doors and guarded by vigilant sentinels. It is the business of these men to collect the liquid (which drips in minute quantities) and then forward it to the king. When he wishes to make a gift to anyone, he gives them a little of this liquid. This is on account of the admirable results it produces—that is, for all bruises, fractures of bones, and sores.

If what they say is true, though I have not made the experiment, should the leg of a cock or other animal be broken and you take of the above liquid ten to fifteen drops and give it to the animal to drink, at the same time anointing the wounded place with it, then, if it is a true story, in twenty-four hours the bones will unite. I possessed a little, given me by one of the king's eunuchs. He had effected wonderful cures with it. The principal case was the recovery of a stonemason who fell from a great height and lay with his bones broken, blood pouring from his mouth, nostrils, and ears, the man having entirely lost

1. *Mumiyai* is bitumen, or Jew's pitch. It exudes from crevices in the mountains of the Fars province, in which Shiraz lies. J. L. Schlimmer, 'Terminologie . . . francaise-persane' (Tahran, 1874), p. 60, says the Persians attribute to it miraculous powers; but, like Manucci, he never saw any of the miracles. Mr. A. G. Ellis tells me the word is a transfer from 'mummy,' the lower-class mummies being preserved in pitch. Morier's 'Haji Baba' descants on the virtues of 'momai.'

his senses and being without hope of life. In two days he was perfectly well. There is also a pond (*pauso*) where on the top of the water floats a ready-made gum which is sold by the natives as the royal liquid, thus cheating a few simpletons. It is not devoid of virtues, but they are nothing like so great as those of the royal liquid.

When the ambassador began to recover his health, we quitted Shiraz, and in nine days we were at the fort of Lar, which they say was formerly much larger, with a great enclosed space. But in the Middle Ages it was quite small, inhabited by many Hindus, who bought there the goods brought by traders from Isfahan and other places, and then exported them to many countries, principally from the ports of Congo[1] and Bandar 'Abbas.

During our journey from Shiraz as far as Lar, we were in excellent health, but were in some concern lest we should not find water for drinking; for on the roads the water which is used is that collected during the rainy season in great cisterns. The earth being salt, the water which flows over it acquires the same property, and therefore is not potable. For this reason they preserve water in cisterns, in which there are all kinds of filth, and it is only out of absolute necessity that one feels inclined to drink.

In spite of this defect of water the country was sufficiently humid, and many places had their gardens of oranges [35], of palm-trees, and date-trees, bearing dates. In Lar we obtained sufficient food-supplies, but water only of the quality already described. There was water below ground in channels, as is the custom over almost the whole of Persia. The fort of Lar is placed upon a small hill standing in the midst of four other hills of the same size. Thus the fort in time of war is in want of protection from good walls and dependent edifices, for any enemy who occupied the aforesaid hills could easily attack the fort.

After a day's rest we left Lar and journeyed through open and agreeable country, coming to different 'sarays' (*saraes*), where we obtained grapes and melons for our consumption. We moved between hills of salt; we crossed several streams, whose crystal clearness invited us to drink, but their waters were

1. Yule and Burnell, 246, a port formerly of some trade, about 100 miles west of Gombroon (Bandar 'Abbas).

so salt that no one could even pass them over his tongue. Among the rest is a stream called Ryo Salgado (the river of salt), over which was a great bridge of more than thirty arches. In nine days, after sufferings enough, we arrived at Gomoram (Gombroon), of which the other name is Bandarabassi (Bandar 'Abbasi), meaning 'Harbour of Shah 'Abbas'; for, being a port on the sea, it is called 'Bander' (*bandar*), and having been established by the Great Shah 'Abbas,[1] they have added 'abassi,' and have come to call it Bandarabassi. This harbour was made by Shah 'Abbas, after having recovered from the hands of the Portuguese, with the aid of the English, the famous island and fort of Orumus (Hormuz).

HORMUZ ISLAND

This island was formerly the greatest and most frequented port on the ocean, where dwelt traders to every region in India—men of great wealth—so that a merchant possessing more than a million of *patacas* [about £100,000] was not a man of very great account. Shah 'Abbas considered that by making himself master of Hormuz, and transferring the port to the mainland, lying not over a league from the island, he would be able to draw all this wealth into Persia. But he was frustrated in his object because the traders were afraid of his interference. The island has many hills of salt, and the climate is therefore prejudicial to life. Notwithstanding this, the Persians are so jealous about the island that they do not wish a single European to set foot in it.

After we had been in Bandar 'Abbas three days the ambassador ordered me to go to the English factory to speak to the chief, requesting him to send [36] a trustworthy person to discuss certain negotiations of great importance. The chief sent to him Mestre Pit (Mr. Pitt), who had acted as page to the English gentleman desirous of speaking to Shah 'Abbas. With him there was a full hour's discussion. Next day the chief himself came with the officials of the factory to visit the ambassador. Offers were made to him to serve him in every way they could. At the time there was an English vessel belonging to a private owner, about to sail for the port of Surrati (Surat). They asked the ambassador to embark in her, as she would be the last vessel to leave Bandar 'Abbas in that monsoon. Then we ate

1. Shah 'Abbas I, reigned 1587-1629.

mutton which came from Hormuz, also good and cheap fish caught in the harbour.

The water at Bandar 'Abbas is either rain-water or brackish, and of such bad quality that it disorders the bodily humours, and generates worms as long as your arm, which appear on the hands, jaws, and legs. When they begin to show themselves, you must lay hold of them by the head, and pull at them daily, winding them round a *hide* (? twig)[1] or cloth very slowly. For if they break they turn inwards, causing great pain, and becoming very difficult to cure. For this reason everybody who can do it sends to fetch water by camels from inland, three leagues off, at a place called Hixin. The climate of this port is most noxious by reason of the salt ridges, and of certain hot winds, and the noise of the sea. I noted that many of the inhabitants had defective sight and teeth, and I was informed that on this coast, as far as Arabia and Mecca, they suffered from these ailments by reason of the many dates that they eat; for the larger number of the inhabitants live upon that fruit in addition to fish.

1. I have failed to trace this word *hide* (or, as in Part III., 187, *yde*), but 'twig' will satisfy the meaning in both passages. Mr. D. Ferguson writes: 'In Sinhalese *iratta* is the central fibre of the cocoanut or palmyra-leaf, and brooms are made of these. Perhaps *hide* or yde represents a Malayalam word with above meaning.'

CHAPTER XVII

OF OUR ARRIVAL IN THE PORT OF SINDY AND DEPARTURE FOR SURRATI

Two days after the visit that the Englishmen had paid to the ambassador—that is to say, on the fifteenth of December of one thousand six hundred and fifty-two (1652) [should be 1655]—we went on board the said vessel. During the whole of our voyage the captain treated us with great politeness and civility. Setting sail, we arrived in twelve days, having favourable winds, at a port in the Great Mogul's territory called Sindi.[1] There the vessel anchored, and we travelled upstream by the river for a whole night to an inhabited place, which stood twelve hours' journey from the sea. This river is a very large one, it being formed of seven rivers which flow down from the interior of the country, as I will relate hereafter (I. 222). Here we saw many Arabian and Persian vessels which [37] import great quantities of dates, horses, seed-pearls,[2] pearls, incense, gum-mastic, senna-leaves, and Jew's stones,[3] which come from Mecca. In return they load up with white and black sugar, butter, olive oil, and *cocos*, which medical men call *nos Indica* (Indian nut).[4] Of this product and its virtues I will make mention farther on (III. 232). They also export many kinds of white linen [? cotton cloth] and printed goods, which are manufactured in the same region.

In the town were three small factories, one English, another Dutch, and another Portuguese. A barefooted Carmelite father

---

1. Probably identical with Lari-bandar in Sind (see Yule, 320, 507, 837).
2. *Algofres*, Yule and Burnell, 12, 203. *Aljofar*, 'seed pearls,' said to be from Arabian aljauhar.
3. The *lapis Judaicus*, or *hajar-ul-yahud*, is considered by the Persians to be diuretic, and a dissolvent of stones in the bladder (see J. L. Schlimmer, 'Terminologie' (1874), P. 339.
4. For 'Indian nut' (*Cocos nucifera*), see Yule, 228, and the quotation there given for 545, 1292, 1328, 1340, 1350, 1598, 1610, 1690 A.D.

also dwelt there in his little hermitage,[1] but nowadays [1698-1699] there are none of these Europeans there. The principal city of the country of Sind was at a distance of twelve leagues from this town, further in the interior; it is called Tata (Tattah), and is the residence of a governor or viceroy, who rules over this country. When the business was finished that our captain had to do at this place, we left it, and returned to the vessel. Setting sail, we arrived in a few days at the port of Surat on the twelfth of January of one thousand six hundred and fifty-three (1653) [correctly 1655/6].

As soon as we had anchored milord went ashore secretly, following the advice given to him by our captain and by a private trader to seek a refuge in the town. For the English were going to seize him and put him by force on board one or other of the English vessels, then in harbour and about to sail for England.[2] It produced great astonishment in me to see how milord landed without breathing a word to me. But I heard the reason afterwards when I reached Surat, bringing all the baggage which was in my charge. There we found Mestre Jonh (Henry Young), who had left Persia a short time before us; and my master announced that he had come as an ambassador from the king to the Great Mogul.

When the governor of Surat heard of the ambassador's arrival, he ordered his secretary to pay him a visit. The message thus brought was that rumour said he had come as ambassador, therefore he was requested to state whether this was true or not. It was necessary for him (the governor) to send a report to the emperor Xaaiahan (Shahjahan), then ruling over the empire of the Great Mogul. The ambassador replied that it was correct, that he could write in all confidence and

1. The Cermelite Mission in Sind was founded in 1615 by Pere Johannes a *Jesu Maria*, who sent there Père Lud vicus Franciscus *a Matre Dei*. The mission was abandoned at some date previous to 1712, when the Portuguese were ejected and trade had decayed. . . . Müllbauer, 'Geschichte,' p. 344.
2. See Note A on Lord Bellomont, where it will be seen that the directors of the East India Company had given orders of this description. Henry Young sailed for Surat on November 20, 1655, in the *Diamond*. The *Seahorse*, with Lord Bellomont on board, reached Swally January 5 (15), 1655/1656.

announce his arrival. Before I say anything of our stay, I will state something about this port [38].

SURAT

Three times have I visited the port of Surat. It lies on the banks of a large river at a distance of nine leagues from the sea. The first time I was there Surat was very populous, but not encircled by walls, its only defence being then a fort on the bank of the river. On the second and third occasions that I visited the port the town had a good wall, made by Orangzeb (Aurangzeb) on the occasion of the war with Xevagi (Shiva Ji), as I shall state in its proper place.[1]

On my first arrival I was much pleased to see such a large river of sweet water full of ships. These latter were not very large, for such only as were of moderate size could come up it unless unloaded; therefore, they send the cargo in boats as far as the sea and load there, and from the sea they also send the cargo inland by boats. It is a great delight to take a seat on the bank of the river and behold the numerous boats which shoot to and fro like arrows. It is the largest port in India and the best river. Thus, it is resorted to by a great number of ships from different parts of Europe, Persia, Arabia, Mecca, Bassora, the coasts of Malabar and Choramandal, Massulapatao (Masulipatam or Machhlipatanam), Bengal, Siam, Acheen, Queddah, the Maldives, Malacca, Batavia, Manilla, China, and many other parts of the world.

Whenever a loaded vessel arrives, the Hindu traders go aboard, and ask if the captain wishes to sell the whole cargo of the ship. If so, they pay for it in money, or furnish goods for the return cargo, whichever is preferred. This is all done without delays, and merchants can thus acquire whatever merchandise they are in search of, and for which they have left home. On this river are built very fine lofty ships in a very short time, everything necessary being found, principally excellent timber; for which reason these ships last much longer than those made in Europe.

1. In ii. 89 the building of walls round Aurangabad and Burhanpur is mentioned. I cannot find the entry about the Surat wall. Grant Duff (89, note), referring to the India Home Records and Thevenot, says the work was in active progress early in 1666.

On my first visit to the port I found there no more than two factories, one English and one Dutch, and a little church belonging to the French Capuchin fathers, whose superior was the famous priest Brother Ambrozio. Afterwards the French came and built a handsome factory. Thus Surat, which was inhabited by rich traders, Mahomedan, Hindu, English, Dutch, became still more populous by the arrival of the French. Upon the sea-shore, on the other side of the river, the Europeans have their gardens, to which they can retire [39] should at any time the Mahomedans attempt to attack them. For there, with the assistance of the ships, they would be able to defend themselves.

I was much amused when I landed to see the greater number of the inhabitants dressed in white clothes, also the many different kinds of people, as well men as women. The latter, mostly Hindus, do not conceal the face as in Persia and Turkey, where women go about with their faces hidden. It is true that the Mahomedan women do not allow their faces to be seen by anyone, it being contrary to their law to allow themselves to be seen with an uncovered face.

But among other things I was much surprised to see that almost everybody was spitting something red as blood. I imagined it must be due to some complaint of the country, or that their teeth had become broken. I asked an English lady what was the matter, and whether it was the practice in this country for the inhabitants to have their teeth extracted. When she understood my question, she answered that it was not any disease, but [due to] a certain aromatic leaf called in the language of the country pan, or in Portuguese betele. She ordered some leaves to be brought, ate some herself, and gave me some to eat. Having taken them, my head swam to such an extent that I feared I was dying. It caused me to fall down; I lost my colour, and endured agonies; but she poured into my mouth a little salt, and brought me to my senses. The lady assured me that everyone who ate it for the first time felt the same effects.

Betel, or *pan,* is a leaf similar to the ivy-leaf, but the betel leaf is longer; it is very medicinal, and eaten by everybody in India. They chew it along with 'arrecas' (*areca*), which physicians call *Avelans Indicas* (Indian filberts), and a little *catto* (*kath or kattha*),[1] which is the dried juice of a certain plant that grows in India. Smearing the *betel* leaf with a little of the *kath*, they chew them together, which makes the lips scarlet and gives a pleasant scent. It happens with the eaters of *betel*, as to those accustomed to take tobacco, that they are unable to refrain from taking it many times a day. Thus the women of India, whose principal business it is to tell stories and eat *betel*, are unable to remain many minutes without having it in their mouths.

It is an exceedingly common practice in India to offer betel leaf by way of politeness, chiefly among the great men, who, when anyone pays them a visit, offer *betel* at the time of leaving as a mark of goodwill, and of the estimation in which they hold the person who is visiting them. It would be a great piece of rudeness to refuse it.

THE PARSIS AT SURAT.

In Surat there is a class of men called Parsis, worshippers of fire, who in former days were inhabitants of Persia. But when first the Mahomedan religion got into Persia, the king tried to force them to become Mahomedans. For this reason they sent an embassy to the Hindu prince of Surat, asking him to grant them permission to emigrate into that country with their families, where they would become his permanent subjects. The Hindu prince received the embassy and allowed them to come, on condition that they should neither slaughter cows nor eat cows' flesh. He promised them the same rights as his other subjects. They came to Surat, where unto this day there are numbers of them, as also in different villages, and in the Portuguese territory adjacent to Damao (Daman).

Their religious belief is such that, if through misadventure anyone's house takes fire, on no account will he allow the fire to be interfered with or extinguished, it being, according to them, the greatest good luck and cause of rejoicing that he could have, he believing that his gods have conferred on him an especial gift and favour, in return for the adorations he has paid to them. And if ever, through negligence, the fire goes out in any of their houses, a fire that all of them maintain with especial care, there is great lamentation, much more than they would make if their nearest relation had died. After such a

1. The juice of *Mimosa catechu*, or the *khair* tree.

mishap the owner has recourse to his priest, begging his pardon for the crime he has committed in allowing the extinguishment of his household fire. The usual penance imposed is that the culprit must invite a number of families of the highest position among them. When these have all collected, well-washed and well-clad, they go off to the priest's house, and he, in their presence, makes a speech to the house-holder, and at the end of it delivers fire from his own house. This they carry, with a grand array of trumpets and drums, and arriving at the sinner's house, he is obliged to give them all a feast. These people have made a vow never to go upon the sea, in order not to defile it, since the sea unfailingly induces vomiting; and in gratitude for the benefits it has done to them they hold it in this great respect.

It happened at the time when I was in Surat that Shah-jahan, King of the Great Mogul, sent a severe reprimand to the governor because he had not acquired a lovely pearl of great value and forwarded it to the court. The reader should know that the governors sent by the king to Surat are persons of rank, men highly thought of and favoured by the king. These men have orders [41] to buy all things that are most beautiful, precious, and rare, and send them to the king. Yet this pearl passed through without the knowledge of the governor, and reached the king, who bought it at a fair price. Then he issued the aforesaid reprimand once more, enjoining on the governor to take special care to buy all the best things that came to that port, more especially pearls and horses, which come from Arabia and Persia. For all these things are used by the king as gifts to the princes and the court officials. Therefore he searches with great exactness through all merchandise to find out if there is anything rare or valuable.

We remained for seventy-five days in that port—*i.e.*, Surat—the revenues of which had been given by Shah Jahan to his daughter, Begom Saeb (Begam Sahib), to meet her expenditure on *betel*. During this time we were making our preparations for going on to the court of the Great Mogul. I was much gratified at seeing such plenty in this place, for I had never had such a satisfaction since [I left] my Venice, and felt proud at staying some days in this port, especially after the arrival of the French. During the time we remained the English never ceased to offer a thousand civilities to milord, the ambassador.

But his true friends told him not to trust them, for all they did was in order to get hold of him and carry him off to England. They did their very best once to persuade the ambassador to go on board of an English vessel, then about to depart for England, under the pretext of offering him a banquet with all the state befitting his dignity. But the truth was that they wanted to confine him in the ship, and he most politely made excuses. Then we began to get together our baggage, for which purpose the ambassador was in want of funds. Mestre Jonh (Henry Young) secretly offered to supply all that was required, whether in money or in different sorts of goods, among the latter some fine broadcloth, a handsome clock, an Arab horse for a present to the king, with swords, pistols, matchlocks, and numerous European playthings. We started from Surat, bearing a passport given us by the governor, and in fifteen days we reached the town of Brampur (Burhanpur), where was the court of the prince Aurangzeb, with whom we had much to discuss. We did not meet with him, by reason of his being at that time in Orangabad (Aurangabad) [42].

CHAPTER XVIII

OF THE TOWN OF BRAMPUR (BURHANPUR), AND OF OUR ARRIVAL IN AGRA (AGRAH), AND DEATH OF THE AMBASSADOR

We found Brampur (Burhanpur) a town of medium size, and without a wall. Aurangzeb, in the year one thousand six hundred and seventy-six, being then absolute king, caused it to be enclosed by a bulwark and wall along the bank of the river which flows beneath it. This river is not very large, but its waters are very clear and good. The town is much frequented by Persian and Armenian traders, on account of the many kinds of excellent cloth manufactured there, chiefly various sorts of women's headdresses (*touca*) *and* cloth for veils (*beatilha*), scarlet and white, of exceeding fineness;[1] also for the quantity of iron to be procured there.

In this town there is plenty of fruit, such as *amb* (*ambah*) or mangas (mango)—the best fruit to be found in India—oranges, limes, citrons,[2] and grapes in abundance. There is also in this town, as throughout the kingdom of the Mogul, a large supply of vegetables of various sorts. On the road to this town we found every day different streams and brooks with good water, also villages, shady and pleasant woods, peopled with many varieties of animals of the chase, such as harts, stags, gazelles, wild oxen (*ores*), peacocks, cooing doves, partridges, quail (*cordernizes*), blackbirds (*tordo*), geese (*patto*), ducks (ades), widgeon (marecas), and many sorts of birds. I would warn the reader never to stray far from his companions, because he might come across robbers in these woods. When they find any person apart from his company they rob him. I was very near falling into their hands, for, having gone some distance from the rest of the caravan, I had got off my horse. I was

1. As to these goods, see Tavernier (Ball's edition), i. 51.
2. The text has *sioras*, which Mr. D. Ferguson proposes to read *sidras* = *cidras* ='citrons.' He has many instances he can adduce where in Portuguese works *limoens* (limes or lemons) and *cidras* (citrons) follow each other in such lists of tropical fruits. I have adopted his emendation.

about to shoot at a peacock with my matchlock, when all of a sudden there came out towards me two men with bows and arrows, who with signs and calls invited me to approach them. But I, apprehending what they wanted, went on my way in the direction the rest of the company had gone, never ceasing to have an eye upon those men. These, seeing me choose a different direction, placed arrows in their bows, and, hastening their pace, came after me, trying to overtake me. Seeing that otherwise I could never escape them, I stopped and put my matchlock to my cheek as if I meant to fire. Frightened at my firmness, they placed their hands on their heads as a sign of politeness, and, turning their backs, fled with even more agility than they had followed me. I continued on my way in dread of a similar [43] encounter, and thus I learnt never more to leave the rest of the travellers, and I put off my longing to go out shooting until we should reach some place or village. Then I went out to shoot, and without hindrance killed whatever I wished, there being no scarcity of things to kill.

We delayed eight days in Burhanpur, then, resuming our journey, we came in six days to a river called the Narbada, where there was a town called Andia (Handiyah); there was also on the bank of the above-named river a little fort situated at the crossing-place. This river is of great breadth, and full of large stones. Its waters divide the lands of the Dacan (Dakhin) from those of Industan (Hindustan), which word means 'Hindudom ' (*gentilidade*, place of the heathen).

We crossed the river, and after going eight days through jungle, we arrived at a large town called Seronge (Sironj), which in old days was founded by a Hindu prince, but at present the overlord thereof is the Grand Mogul. This town lies in the midst of the territories of several Hindu princes of the Rajput tribe. Of these the nearest and the most powerful is the Rajah Champet Bondela (Champat Rae, Bundelah), whose country extends to twenty leagues from Agra (Agrah), and he has command over fifteen thousand horsemen and three hundred thousand infantry.

In this town is made much cloth, both white and printed; Armenian traders dwell there, who buy the cloth and send it to various parts. Sometimes European traders come there to do business in this cloth.

It happened that more than once the said Champet Bondela (Champat Rae, Bundelah) came to plunder this town, on account of certain dissensions between him and the Mogul king. For this reason it was always garrisoned by a considerable force of Mogul cavalry under a general. In spite of this the fighting was not put an end to; there were many battles, in which on many occasions the Moguls had the worst of it. By reason of these Hindu princes, these routes are very dangerous for travellers. For the use of wayfarers there are throughout the realms of the Mogul on every route many 'sarais' (*sarae*).[1] They are like fortified places with their bastions and strong gates; most of them are built of stone or of brick. In every one is an official whose duty it is to close the gates at the going down of the sun. After he has shut the gates, he calls out that everyone must look after his belongings, picket his horses by their fore and hind legs; above all, that he must look out for dogs, for the dogs of Hindustan are very cunning and great thieves. I may find a good opportunity [44] to speak of the cunning of these dogs (III., 152).

At six o'clock in the morning, before opening the gates, the watchman gives three warnings to the travellers, crying in a loud voice that everyone must look after his own things. After these warnings, if anyone suspects that any of his property is missing, the doors are not opened until the lost thing is found. By this means they make sure of having the thief, and he is strung up opposite the *sarae*. Thus the thieves, when they hear a complaint made, drop the goods somewhere, so as not to be discovered.

These *saraes* are only intended for travellers (soldiers do not go into them). Each one of them might hold, more or less, from 800 to 1,000 persons, with their horses, camels, carriages; and some of them are even larger. They contain different rooms, halls, and verandas, with trees inside the courtyard, and many provision shops; also separate abodes for the women and men who arrange the rooms and the beds for travellers. I will speak hereafter of the deceits of all these, when I come [I., 71] to talk of the sultan Amayum (Humayun).

We halted four days in Sironj, and then went on our way across inaccessible mountains, with numerous beautiful trees,

1. See also i. 71 for an account of *saraes*.

and traversed by crystal streams whose waters are most wholesome, 'doing no harm to those who drink them fasting; rather are they beneficial and most palatable. In six days we reached the town of Narvar (Narwar),[1] which lies at the foot of a great range of hills six leagues in circumference. On the very highest point of these hills is a fortress, which occupies all the level ground on the summit, with a circumference of two miles—a little more or less—with many houses and rooms, a work made long ago by the Hindus. But in the course of years, and by the inclemency of the weather, the walls are crumbling away, through the negligence of the Mogul king. His object is to destroy all the strong places of the Hindus of which he can get possession, so that their conquered princes may not rebel against him. His only anxiety is to fortify and supply the forts that are on the frontiers of his kingdom.

We did not halt at this place (Narwar), but pressed onwards. In five days we arrived at the well-known fortress of Gualior (Gwaliyar), where it is usual for the Mogul to keep as prisoners princes and men of rank. This fortress is on the top of a great mountain having a circuit of three leagues. It is in the middle of a fertile plain, and thus there is no other high ground from which it could be attacked. There is only a single road to ascend it, walled in on both sides, and having many gates to bar the way, each having its guard and sentinels. The rest of the [45] hills is of rock, perpendicular as a wall, though made by Nature. All around this mountain are to be seen many balconies, lanterns (? kiosks), rooms, and verandas, in different styles of architecture, with Hindu sculptures, all of this making the view most agreeable and pleasant to the visitor.

On the crest of the mountain is a great plain, on which are sumptuous palaces with many balconies and windows of various kinds of stone, and delightful gardens irrigated from many crystal springs, where cypress and other lovely trees raise their heads aloft, so as to be visible from a distance. Within this fortress is manufactured much oil of jasmine, the best to be found in the kingdom, the whole of the level ground on the summit being covered with that shrub. There are also in this

1. See Tieffenthaler's description of Narwar (where he lived many years) in Bernouilli's 'Beschreibung,' vol. i., p. 116, and the plan No. 4 in the appendix thereto.

district many iron-mines, of which numerous articles are made and sent to the principal cities in the Mogul country.

In the town, which lies at the foot of the hill, there dwell many musicians, who gain a livelihood with their instruments; and many persons maintain that it was on this mountain that the god Apollo first started Hindu music.

Continuing our route, we came in three days to the river called the Chambal, at which is the town named Dolpur (Dholpur), where Aurangzeb gave battle against his brother Dara (Dara Shukoh), in the year one thousand six hundred and fifty-six [correctly, 1658], at which I was present, and to which, further on, I shall refer [I. 182-184]. Thence, in four days, we arrived at the city of Agrah, having ended by doing four hundred and sixty leagues, for such is the number reckoned from Surat as far as Agrah. At this place the governor assigned to us a handsome house to stay in.

We remained in this city, of which I will speak on a future occasion (I. 83), and, a few days after our arrival, the Englishmen who at that time were present at their factory came to visit the ambassador, showing themselves desirous of being useful to him, making him frequent and handsome offers. But these the ambassador would in no way accept. After several visits they invited him to their house, where they gave him a splendid feast, with dressed meats and beverages after their style. The ambassador complained very much of the great heat that has to be endured in that country, and the English offered him a powder, declaring that if he mixed it and drank it he would experience great relief and coolness.

When a few days had passed we resumed [46] our route for Dely (Dihli), where at that moment the king, Shahjahan, was living. Then, after three days from our leaving Agrah, towards the evening, when in sight of the place where we meant to halt for that night, the ambassador called out to me in great pain, asking me for water. Then he expired without allowing me time to give it to him, those being the last words that he uttered. He died on the twentieth of June of one thousand six hundred and fifty-three [correctly, 1656], at five o'clock in the evening. We carried the body at once to a sarae called Orel (Hodal), between Agrah and Dihli, and, it being already late, we did not bury him that night. The official at the *sare* sent notice to the local judicial officer, who hastened to the spot, and, putting his seal on all the baggage, laid an embargo upon it. I asked him why he seized and sealed up those goods. He answered me that it was the custom of that realm, and that he could not release the things until an order came from court, they being the property of an ambassador.

After seven hours of the night had passed, we removed the body of the defunct from the palanquin in order to enshroud it, and, as day began to dawn, we proceeded to lay him in the grave. Taking him by the arms, I tried to lift him, but, while in my hands, a blister burst from which exhaled such a fetid odour that all those standing by nearly fainted and fell down. We were forced to cease to lift him, and await the day. When day arose we somehow or other put him into a coffin, with all the haste that the odour compelled, and interred him on the bank of a reservoir which adjoined the town, marking the spot so that his bones might be transported elsewhere, as accorded with the rank of such a person. And as a fact they removed the remains after fifteen months to the city of Agra (Agrah).

Having interred the ambassador, the servants all disappeared, and I was left alone, sad and anxious, having nothing to console me, nor anywhere to turn in order to recover my things, which had been sealed up by the official along with the ambassador's, although all the keys were in my possession [47].

HENRY BARD, VISCOUNT BELLOMONT

Manucci's Lord Bellomont is an historical personage, a Cavalier whose biography will be found under his name (Henry Bard) in the 'Dictionary of National Biography,' vol. iii., p. 175. That account, in spite of its giving much interesting information, cannot be called satisfactory, being in many places not only deficient, but incorrect. The most important points are: (1) Erroneous year of birth; (2) omission of Bard's doings in Persia and India; (3) erroneous place and year of death.

First, then, as to the year of Bard's birth.

He was born at Staines, Middlesex, where his father, the Rev. George Bard, was Vicar (died 1616); but I am informed by the present Vicar, the Rev. S. Theodore Wood, that the earliest parish records date from 1644; nor is there any register at Eton College of a date early enough to show when H. Bard entered and left that school. Fortunately, through the kindness of

Mr. W. H. Macaulay, M.A., of King's College, Cambridge, I have obtained a valuable note drawn up by Mr. J. C. Clarke, the bursar's clerk. From this it appears that Bard was admitted a scholar on August 23, 1632, at the age of sixteen; thus the year of birth must have been 1615 or 1616, and not 1604, as in the 'Dictionary of National Biography.' On August 24, 1635, he was admitted a Fellow, took his degree of B.A. in 1636, and ceased to be a Fellow at Michaelmas, 1645 (no doubt owing to his marriage). There is no record of his proceeding M.A.

In a MS. Catalogue of the Provosts, Fellows, etc., by John Hall (who came to King's College in 1645), is the following: 'Henry Bard travelled on foot (what possibly might be so passed) in France, Germany, Italy, Turkey, Palestine, Arabia, Egypt, etc. When he came home he gave to the college a fair Alcoran in Arabic, which he had to that end purchased in Egypt. He came home a little before the time that King Charles set up his standard at Nottingham [1642]. He went into the King's army, where for his worth he was soon made a Colonel. He was a man of very personable body, and of a stout and undaunted courage. He was made prisoner at Ailsford fight, in Hampshire, near Winchester, being very much wounded; he there lost the use of one of his arms. But he was soon released, and at his coming to Oxford, the King's headquarters, he had the command of a brigade committed to him, and was made Knight Baronet, October 8, 1644, and soon after Viscount Bellomont,[1] still continuing Fellow of this college until he married. He was sent by His Majesty the King of Scots from Bruges in landers Ambassador to the Great Mogul, in which embassy he died (1656).'[2]

The Quran is still preserved in the college library, and the following description is taken from Dr. M. R. James's 'Catalogue of King's College MSS.' (1895): 'No. 29, A Koran of cent. xvi., xvii. On paper $7\frac{1}{2}$ + $4\frac{1}{2}$, with two illuminated pages at the beginning, and the following inscription:

'"Henricus Bard, Eques Auratus et Baronettus [postea Vicomes Bellomontanus], Collegii Regalis Socius, postquam Collegiali commeatu impetrato Europam Asiam et Africam maxima ex parte perlustrassit, hunc librum Ægypte allatum amoris simul et peregrinationis monumentum Collegio Regali dedicavit, May 28, 1644."'

In the life of Charles Mason (1616-1677), 'Dictionary of

1. Created, on July 18, 1645, Baron Bard of Dromboy, Co. Meath, and Viscount Bellomont of Co. Dublin.
2. John Hall, born at Windsor; M.A. in 1653, appointed to a college living in Hampshire, 1661; died about 1673 (see British Museum MS., No. 5816, W. Cole's 'Miscellaneous Collections for Cambridge,' vol. xv., p. 189).

National Biography,' xxxvi., 416, and in Thomas Harwood's 'Alumni Etonensis,' p. 233 (under date A.D. 1632, Car. I., 8), it is said that H. Bard entrusted Mason with the manuscript account of his early travels. I have not been able to trace this manuscript; it is not at King's College.

Next, as to the embassy to Persia and India. Miss Eva Scott, in her recent work. 'The King in Exile' (1905), p. 285, speaks of Bard's appointment as Ambassador to Persia and Morocco; beyond that fact she has no information. A rough draft of his instructions, undated, is to be found at the Bodleian, in the Carte MSS., vol. cxxx., fol. 144, and Miss Scott assigns this document to 1650. The terms of this draft are as follows:

'INSTRUCTIONS FOR OUR RIGHT TRUSTY AND WELLBELOVED VISCOUNT BELLAMONT NOW BY US EMPLOYED AS OUR EXTRAORDINARY AMBASSADOUR TO THE EMPEROURS OF PERSIA AND MOROCCOS.

'1. You shall beginne your journey with what speed you may, and shall repaire first to eyther of those princes as shall be most commodious for you.

'2. When you come to the Emperour of Persia you shall at your first audience deliver our letters to him, and shall as you have occasion acquaint him particularly with the circumstances of the King our late royal father's murther, and with the proceeding of the rebells since, and that the grounds upon which they proceede are such as are destructive to all Monarchy, and ayme only to sett up the power of the people, that accordingly they endeavour to exclude us from the right of our succession, have seised our revenew, palaces, jewells, plate, and royal ornaments, together with our fleete, castles, forts, and forces within our Kingdome of England, of all which they now make use to invade and disturbe our right in our other Kingdomes, and that though we have considerable forces under our present command yet the Kingdome of England being by much the greatest, richest, and most populous of our dominions, we are much distressed for want of money to pay our armies and supply our other important occasions.

'3. You shall therefore propose to the Emperour to fournish vs with some considerable summe of present money for our assistance in this great exigence of our affaires, and to pay it unto you for our vse to be returned or conveyed to vs, and we leave it to you to particularise the summe according to ye hopes you shall have of obteyning the same when you are vpon the place.

'4. You shall engage our royall worde for the repayment of the same at Ormuz or elsewhere within the Emperour's dominions as soone as we shall be settled in just rights of our kingdom of England.

'5. We authorise you in like manner to negotiate with the Emperor of Maroccos (*sic*) and to procure what money you can from him for our assistance (the like with the Prince of Georgia).

'6. You shall advise with Mr. John Webster[1] of Amsterdam how money may be returned from eyther of those places to Amsterdam or other part for our service, or how you may dispose of any commodities you shall receyve to our use.

'7. You shall not pay any of the money you shall receyve but by spetiall order from ourselfe under our hands except it be for your owne charges and for necessary disbursements in the service, and you shall keepe very secret from the knowledge of all persons except those that are trusted with this negociation what money you shall procure for vs in this employment.

'8. You shall keepe constant correspondence with our secretary Robert Long, esq.,[2] and shall from tyme to tyme signify your proceedings and success to him who will give vs an account thereof when you cannot immediately send to ourselfe.

The like instructions you are to observe in the rest of the kingdomes you goe into.'

Endorsement. 'Instructions for Lord Bard. Mr. Mason drew the other, whereof I have noe copy.'

I infer that these instructions were drawn up in 1651, and not in 1650, for the following reasons. In the same volume of the Carte MSS., fol. 238, there is another draft letter of a similar character, addressed to 'Mulay Mahomett Chee, Kinge of Maroccos, Fez, Sus, and Ginie.'[3] It has no day or month affixed, but professes to have been prepared in the 'third yeare of our Reigne,' and to be given 'at the head of our Army in our Kingdome of Scotland.' Now, the third year began in January, 1651, and Charles crossed the Border into England early in August, 1651 (E. Scott, 'King in Exile,' pp. 201, 202); therefore the draft was written between January and August, 1651, and I presume it is the 'other' referred to in the endorsement to the Persia instructions, and thus both would be of about the same date. It is possible that these letters were in

1. This John Webster appears in E. Scott's 'King in Exile,' p. 390, being asked (1652) to try and revictual Dunottar Castle. He is also mentioned in connection with Amsterdam in C. J. Lyon's 'Personal History,' p. 26 (June, 1650).
2. See 'Dictionary of National Biography,' xxxiv. 107. Made a Baronet September 1, 1660; died in 1673; fell out of favour early in 1652; dismissed in 1653 ; restored to favour in 1654.
3. Muhammad III., of the Hasani Sharif line, who reigned 1635-1654 (S.I., Poole, 'Mohammadan Dynasties', 61).

existence in about June, 1651, for, as Mr. W. Foster has kindly informed me, at a court held on June 20, 1651, the committee of the then East India Company resolved: 'The Court having intelligence that there was a designe of sending some person by the King of Scotland or the late Queene of England to Persia to obstruct the Company's trade, and they considering how prejudicial it might prove unto them, if effected, They ordered Mr. Sambrooke to write a letter to their President and Councell at Suratt requiring them in case any Englishman or other shall arrive there with any letter or commission either from the King of Scotts or his mother with a purpose to interrupt the Company's trade, that they should seize upon him as a prisoner and return him for England with the first opportunity.'

The germ of this insane attempt to obtain money from Persia is probably to be traced to a letter in French (undated) from one Hogia Pedre (Khwajah Petrus), son of Sefer (Safar), a Persian Christian (Carte MSS., vol. cxxx., fol. 145). It was probably addressed to the Queen Mother, Henrietta, and is a proposal to intercept the Customs dues of Hormuz, half of which had been received since the Treaty of 1622 by the East India Company's agents, who are held up as rebels and embezzlers. Petrus offers to collect the dues on the King's behalf, and remit two-thirds of the proceeds to Amsterdam or Paris; or, in the alternative, proposes that someone be sent to Persia with him to receive there two-thirds of the proceeds on His Majesty's behalf.

We have no record of the reasons for abandoning the projected visits to Morocco and to Georgia, nor have we any trace of Bard's appointment as Ambassador to the Great Mogul. Originally, as it would appear, that employment was assigned to Sir Andrew Cogan (who died 1660), the founder of Madras. At the Louvre, on April 11, 1652, Charles II. appointed Sir Charles (*sic;* should be 'Andrew') Cogan, Knight and Baronet, as 'Ambassador Extraordinary to China, the Mogul, Japan, the Kings of Golcondes, Pegu, and Siam, and the Princes and Potentates of the East Indies.' The authority quoted is Drake's 'Hundred of Blackheath,' p. 79, note 8 (a work I cannot find). This entry was communicated by Sir George Musgrave, Baronet, of Edenhall, Cumberland (a descendant of A. Cogan), to Mr. J. Livingstone Jay, treasurer of Greenwich Hospital, by him to Mr. W. Duncombe Pink, of Lowton, Newton-le-Willows, and by Mr. Pink to me. The year 1654 in the 'Complete Baronetage' of Mr. G. E. Cokayne, vol. iii., p. 304, which rests on the same authorities, should be 1652. In any case, Andrew Cogan never returned to the East; he was at Venice on February 7, 1653 (Calender of Clarendon State Papers, vol. ii., p. 176, No. 979, (3); and Hyde, writing to Nicholls on April 11, 1653 (ibid., vol. ii., p. 192, No. 1068) says: 'Sir A. Cogan is not an excellent ambassador.' Presumably, this is an allusion to his selection as Ambassador to India and the Farther East, and probably led to the substitution of Henry Bard, Viscount Bellomont.

If Bellomont's Letters of Appointment were drawn up in June, 1651, how came it to pass that no start was made till late in 1653? I guess that the cause was want of funds. I have not met with any direct evidence of the date on which Bard sailed; it can only be inferred approximately from other dates. Several statements are found that Charles II. was at Bruges when Bellomont was dispatched. Now, as far as I can make out from C. J. Lyon, 'Personal History of King Charles the Second' (1851), and O. Airy's 'Charles II.' (1904), Charles landed in France on October 16, 1651 (Airy, p. 106), and did not leave it again until July 8, 1654 (ibid., p. iii). He did not settle at Bruges until April 22, 1656 (*ibid.*, p. 130), and this is too late to allow of that place being his residence when he gave authority to Bellomont. It is noticeable that Manucci says Charles II. was 'in France' when Bellomont started from Venice.

We learn from the Aleppo letter quoted below that Bellomont carried with him recommendatory letters from the States General of Holland to their agents at Isfahan. The Commonwealth was then at war with Holland, hostilities beginning in April, 1652, and peace being made in May, 1654 (see S. R. Gardiner's ' History of Commonwealth,' vol. ii., pp. 116,370. I have not been able to procure any confirmation from the Dutch archives that any such letters were issued; but, assuming the fact, they must have been anterior to the peace of May, 1654. Professor C. H. Firth has been kind enough to furnish me with a copy of a letter written from Aleppo on March 19, 1654-55 (*Mercurius Politicus*, No. 265, July 5 to 12, 1655, pp. 5466, 5467). Nine days before its date the East India Company's agent at Aleppo had received letters from Persia in which it was stated that 'a pretended ambassador from the late King of Scots at Cullen is come to the Persian Court with purpose to disturb the Companies affairs there, and to obtain the rights of Ormus Customs from them, having recommendatory letters (which if true were doubtless obtained in the time of the war) from the States of Holland to the Dutch in these parts to assist him therein, unto whom he hath written to Spatan (Isfahan) from Khazbien (Qazwin)—where the Emperor then kept his Court—to that purpose. . . .'

Manucci's date in the text, 1651, is hopelessly wrong, and the same chronological error recurs in his 'Storia' for many years up to about 1680. But by calculating backwards from several unimpeachable dates, it is possible to arrive approximately at the period when the journey from Venice commenced, *viz.*, late in 1653.

In a general letter from Isfahan (India Office, O.C. 2420), dated October 14, 1654, we find that they had just heard there of Bellomont's arrival at Tabriz. Manucci's text (i. 33) fixes September as the month of arrival at Qazwin, and elsewhere (i. 23) he states that on the journey he saw an eclipse of the sun at Zulfah in Armenia. Dr. Downing, of the Nautical Almanac Office, has been kind enough to verify this, and fixes it as an eclipse of August 12, 1654, which would have been visible at that place. Assuming that they reached Qazwin on September 1, 1654, I calculate from Manucci's entries of halts and journeys that,206 days were occupied (say six months and twenty days) from their landing at Smyrna until their arrival at Qazwln. Deducting this number of days, we get February 11, 1654, as the date of arrival at Smyrna, and since the voyage to Smyrna had occupied four months, we obtain October 11, 1653, as the approximate date of setting sail from Venice. This corresponds fairly well, as to the month, with Manucci, who says it was November. I have not been able to secure any verification on this subject from the Venetian archives.

As to Bellomont's proceedings in Persia, Manucci's text must be referred to as the only full account which has come down to us. Some additional facts are disclosed in the East India Company's records, now at the India Office, and these sufficiently confirm Manucci's story. An extract from John Spiller's and Henry Young's letter from Isfahan of October 14, 1654, is as follows:

'. . . The premenconed were no sooner sealed, but by advises from Tabreeze &^c^ we were informed that there was an English embassador arrived in those parts by way of Turkey, haveing 3 English men more in his comp^y^ and was rec^d^ by all the Kings Governo^s^ wi^th^ greate respect; wch also a letter to ye cheife of ye Carmelite Order heere in this place confirmes and sayes the Embassador goes by the name of my Lord Belamont, and so much does some frenchmens Lres averr that were sent from Khazbien where this King still keeps his Court, but at those advises date he had not spoken wi^th^ the King, whoe for some reasons defered awhile to admitt him unto his presents, one we are told is to inquire out exactly the quallitie of the person, and import of his message, that he may receive respect accordingly; for when wee heard of him first, wch was from Aierwan (Erivan), we were informed that hee was one of the Palsgraves brothers, and so went for currant awhile, but afterwards to be as above menconed, but there are so many reports raised of him that we cannot now say what he is; though we have wrytten and made muche inquirie to finde it out; nor beleive shall not justly, until our Linguist-wrytes us, whoe is gone to Court about our Customes and some other businesses, of which the embassador is none of the least, though in or petition to the Atamaam Dowlatt, we have not in ye least made mention of him.

'The 24th last month [September 1654] we rec^{d} by the Pashaw of Buszorahs servts advises from that place dated the 18 August and with them letters from the Consull of Alleppo of the 12th June in wch we were given to understand that the beginning of Aprill last a peace was concluded betwixt us and the Hollanders; so we cannot thinke lesse but that the Eagle or such Shipps as you intend forth for these parts, will bring out the Articles thereof, and that we shall have shipps in Band^{r} suddainely. Wherefore Mr. Young is now journying thither, with what estate wee have of yo^{rs} ready in cash; and John Spiller intends to follow as soone as he receives some newes from Court, of the aforemenconed Embassadors proceedings.

'One thing by all the information that we have yet rec^{d} is that he seekes for yor right of Customes of Gumbroon; and for his assistance therein, hath brought recomendatory letters from the States of Holland, wch we are perswaded to give credence to; being to our knowledge hee hath wrytten to the Cheife of the Dutch heere; therefore wee may easily iudg that he is not on our side, but against us; but we hope y^{t} he will doe yor affaires little hurt; espetially now the premenconed peace wth the Dutch is concluded; wch by our severall letters to Court the next day after we rec^{d} the newes, we have spread abroad wth divers other particulars, as we rec^{d} them from Alleppo. . . .' [O.C. 2420.]

Search in the Dutch Archives at the Hague has produced no trace of the suggested recommendatory letters from the States General; but there is on record a Dutch translation of an Italian letter from Bellomont to Philips Angel, the Dutch company's chief merchant and agent in Isfahan. It is dated Qazwīn, September 23, 1654, N.S. The original was received in Isfahān on October 22, and the translation was sent from Gombroon to Amsterdam on November 16, 1655; it is to the following effect:

'QAZBĪN,

'*This 23rd September, New Style*, 1654.

'SIR AND FRIEND,

'I am sending you the accompanying [letter] from Mr. Edward Blijdenberck, along with these two or three lines by way of salutation, and thereto I add that you must not accord credit to what is said here, that peace has been made with the unnatural monsters. The Devil is capable of much, and if this peace was made by him it cannot endure, as will soon be discovered.

'Moreover, having heard of your goodness of heart combined with much prudence, I greatly rejoice to have found a person of such great consideration in these regions with whom I can take counsel; and assuredly, as soon as possible, I shall transfer myself to Isfahan in order to procure that high honour.

Here we have entered a little into business, but have been able to conclude nothing, until I know things better, and in this, by God's grace, Your Honour's advice will be of great benefit to the king.

'In his (the king's) letter I am styled "cousin," and he states, for his Persian Majesty's information, all my titles. As one reason of non-success is the fact that 1 present myself here with 8 to 10 followers only, while not many days ago the Mosbych (?) envoy left this attended by two to three hundred men. The second reason is that in regard to money, when giving a morsel to one, the other is opening his mouth. [The passage is obscure.] But this difficulty can be understood by those coming through Turkey. I carefully sought opportunity to make it known that for many years we have suffered, and our means are exhausted. Where can we find [money] to uphold our position? Finally, they have been satisfied here with this explanation.

'Whenever anything is paid to me I shall try not to give to the Wāiqi'ah-navīs [treasurer ?] a "casbegi" (?) of the coin I am soliciting for my king, but the same shall be placed in your hands in order to be transferred to those of the king. Then, I should return again by way of Aleppo, after y leave-taking. Here they are my good friends and treat me right royally. But as soon as I am through with a purge that I have taken for a cold which has troubled me continuously for eight months, I shall start from here [Qazwīn]. Finally I beg of you to keep the English in ignorance. I am &c.

[Undersigned]
'Your Honour's affectionate Servant,
'HARRIGO DE BELLEMONTE.'

[*Postscript.*]

'Will you kindly get your servant to find a house for me for a month or six weeks.'

To THE CHIEF MERCHANT AND AGENT,
PHILIPS ANGEL,
AT ISFAHAN.

The Dutch agents at Gombroon wrote on the 1st January, 1655, that the English envoy was in favour at Court, and his negociations were so secret that neither they nor the English had heard anything. The latter were much concerned, as it was presumed that the affair was meant "to stick a needle into their Company here." The English had sent their interpreter to Qazwīn to find out. The last notice to be traced is in a letter, also from Gombroon, of the 23rd October, 1655, where the Dutch say that, after a year's stay at Isfahān, Henrico Bellemonte had left it a month before, having received from the king on his leave-taking a sum of 100 *tūmān*, equivalent to 4,000 *gulden*. The result of his negociations had remained secret, but they would enquire further.

The story is carried on [O.C. 2426] in the transcript of a letter from J. Spiller and Anthony Daniell to the President and Council in Sūrat, dated from Isfahān November 2, 1654:

'By coppie of o^{r} last letter unto ye Comp^{a} yo^{u} may please to perceive the reasons that John Spiller went not to Band when Mr Young journied thither; being about some Court business from whence lately we have rec^{d} a letter from o^{r} Linguist in wch he advises, that as yet he hath not delivered or Petition to the Atamaam Dowlatt by reason of his being abroad wth ye king a hunting; from which sport returning both king & nobles kept their houses for 3 or 4 dayes; and for ye English Embassadore his cheife businesse is such as we alwayes heard it to bee, to witte, for yor right of Gumbroo Customes, but what successe he hath had therin we have not yet heard, he haveing ben but once wth the king when our Servant wrote his letter; other advises we dayly & howerly expect; wch so soon as rec^{d} we intend to make our repaire to Bander; as we shall wthout them, if they be long acomeing, that as nigh as possible we may comply wth your commands. . . . '

Next there is a Surat letter in O.C. 2455, dated Swally Maryne, March 15, 1654-55, and signed by Edward Pearce, John Spiller, and Henry Gary. It says. Mr. Spiller from Psia hath not failed you in his Advices Overland, wherein wee finde hee hath not been wanting to give you the best informacon hee could concerning yor Affaires in those parts, you will reade that my Lord Bella-mount, the pretended Embassadore from wee know not whome, and supposed Brother to one Mr Bard Silkman in Paternoster Row[1] was lodged 4 daies before he left Spahaun, since wch time wee reade from our Broker that hee hath shut up his doores and takes physick, we are perswaded hee will never prejudice yor Affaires now wee have Peace wth the Dutch, but had the Warrs continud by theire Assistance hee might have troubled you much in your Customes at Gombroone, which as wee hear is ye only thing hee aymes at.'

On December 3, 1655 (with a postscript of the 4th), William Weale, Daniel Otgher, and Anth° Daniell wrote from Gombroon to the President and Council in Surat as follows:

[O.C. 2508]: '. . . . The 30th (being Sunday at night) ye pretended English Embassador, whoe goeth under ye stile of ye Lord Bellamount, arrived heere from Asphahanne; whoe pretendeth he is bound for India after a moneth or toos stay heere; but his

1. This is, of course, Maximilian Bard, the elder brother, afterwards of Caversfield, Bucks.

Linguist who was formerly a Jessuitt saith, he hath a Phirmaan from ye King of Persia for ye Comp[as] Customes; and that hee stayeth here in expectacon of 10 Sayle of Shipps, that should come from we cannot imagine whence; also y[e] kings officers heere say that y[e] kings commaund is on them, that in case he will accept of y[e] Customes they should turn us out; and settle them on him; if not continue them as they are to vs; but there are soe many reports in towne and soe little appearance of his acting anything therein, that we cannot believe anything thereof; however thought it good to acquaint you what we heare. . . .'

Postscript

'. . . In a former clause we acquainted yo[u] of y[e] Lord Bellamount's arrival here; whoe to shew that he hath noe intent to injure the Comp[a] or trouble thier Servants heere, hath desired his passage on y[e] *Seahorse* for Surratt; w[ch] we y[e] willinger granted that his presents heere might not raise any more rumours, for of a certayne y[e] Atamaam Dowlatt would faine have him accepted of ye customes a while; thereby to have an occasion to turne vs out; as he would alsoe him in a very short time afterwards; soe y[t] we hope you will not take it ill that we gave him his passage; Mr. Young can acquaint you more fully how much hee protested never to endeavour to injure y[e] Company in Spahaune or any place, to whose relation please to be referred. . .'

The *Seahorse* reached Swalley on January 6, 1655-56 [O.C. 2525, Swally Marine, January 19, 1655-56], and we have one more notice in a letter from Surat, dated January 29, 1655-1656, and signed by John Spiller, Henry Gary, Thomas Reynardson, and Ant[y] Smith. '. . . The L. Bellamont is in Surat where he hath taken a house, so it should seem y[t] hee intends to remain there for some time, wee wish y[t] his remove from Persia may be a meanes to free yo[u] from all trouble aboutt y[e] Customes and allso cause of a greater annuall inlargemt. . . .' [O.C. 2534.] At this point the Company's records become defective, so that we have no further official evidence of Lord Bellomont's proceedings in India. But Manucci's account of their stay in Surat and journey via Burhanpur and Agrah towards Dihli may be accepted with some confidence.

Something is to be found, however, in the Dutch archives. On February 6, 1656, H. van Gent (and others) wrote to Joan Maatsuycker (Maatzuiker), Governor-General and Council at Batavia, that the envoy from the young King of England, named Henrico de Bellemonte, had arrived. He had been to the Persian Court about a share in the Customs, but had failed. He had fallen ill (in Surat), and had asked for aid from the Honorable (Dutch) Company's surgeon. He had a cancerous sore in his cheek, but he could not trust himself to the English there for any help. The request was willingly accepted, but they feared it would be a difficult business to heal him, as the cheekbone was exposed. 'The said lord seems a very well-informed, modest, and courteous man, who is very afflicted over this accident that has happened to him.' Maatzuiker was Governor-General from 1653 to 1678.

Nor are there any reasons for declining to accept Manucci's statement that his Lordship died at Hodal on June 20 (1656). I have tried, but without success, through my friend, Mr. H. W. W. Reynolds, Commissioner of Agrah, to obtain from the Roman Catholic Bishop there a copy of any entry in the burial registers. As Bellomont had turned Catholic several years before his death, he must have been buried in their cemetery, which was, indeed, the only one at that period. Possibly there may be duplicate registers somewhere in Rome, but I have not been able to institute a search. A curious mention of Bellomont, which must refer to his stay in Agrah, is to be found on fol. 26 of B.M. Sloan MS., No. 811. John Campbell, speaking of placing the King of England's arms on some cannon he cast, says: 'I had one of his Maties great seales from my Ld Bellmount by wch I cast his armes.'

The 'Dictionary of National Biography' places Bellomont's death in 1660, and Manucci in 1653. For these years I would substitute 1656, confirmed as it is by John Hall's memorandum at King's College, Cambridge, and the India Office records. Where the writer in the 'Dictionary of National Biography' got 'Arabia' as the place of death I know not; his own authorities say 'Persia.' But both statements must be wrong in the face of the official evidence that Bellomont left Persia and landed safely in India, from which he never returned.

His arms are delineated in W. Coles' 'Cambridge Collections,' vol. xv., p. 137 (British Museum Manuscript, No. 5816). As to his children, there is some difference in various authorities. The 'Complete Baronetage,' by Mr. G. E. Cokayne, ii., p. 228, gives him three daughters, but denies (in note *b*) that I. he left a son who survived until 1686. On this point I think the author must be wrong. Bellomont's widow in her petitions to the King in 1660 (Calendar of State Papers, Domestic, Charles II., vol. xvii., No. 98, p. 300), when speaking of her children, says, 'one your Majesty's godsonne'; and in her second petition (*ibid.*, vol. xx., No. 3, p. 331) is the expression, 'having 4 children.' Mr. W. Duncombe Pink (on the authority of Maddison's 'Lincolnshire Pedigrees,' i. 78; Harleian Society, vols. 50, 51, 1902), gave me particulars which, if accepted, overrule Mr. Cokayne's suggestion of a confusion with Charles, Earl of Bellomont, d. 1683, of a totally different family (Van der Kirkhove). The year of Charles Bard's death was 1665, and not 1685. The result is as follows:

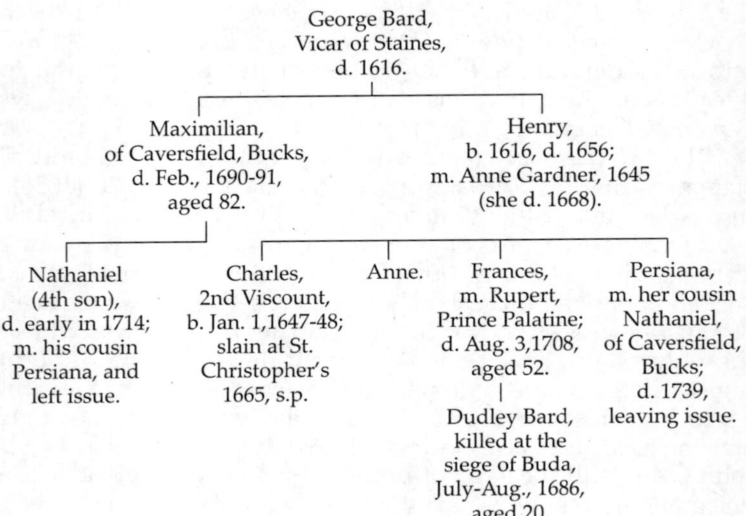

Anne was a spinster in 1668, when she took the oath as heir and administratrix to her mother's estate (Probate Office, Administrations, July 13, 1668, p. 105). The year of Frances' death is given in an inscription quoted by Miss E. Scott in her article in the *Eng. Hist. Review*, vol. xv., p. 760 (October, 1900), though I have not been able to verify it myself from the authority she quotes, *viz.*, 'L'Histoire du Peuple de Dieu.' This is a work by I. J. Berruyer, S.J. (1681-1758), the first edition being of 1728 (Paris). It is a history of the people of Israel, in many volumes, and seems to have no possible connection with an inscription on Frances Bard's tomb. There is some error somewhere. If the lady was fifty-two in 1708, she was born in 1656, more than two years after her father left Europe; and if her son was twenty in 1686, he must have been born in 1666. Therefore, she had a son when she was ten years of age, and the marriage certificate being dated July 30, 1664, she was only eight when married. Everything points to an understatement of her age at death; more probably she was sixty instead of fifty-two. Mr. J. F. Chance thinks she must have been the eldest child, and born some time in 1646. The exact date of her death, which took place in the Elector of Hanover's camp at Muhlburg, close to Karlsruhe in Baden, is obtained from 'Briefe des Herzogs Ernst August zu Braunschweig Luneburg an Johann Franz Diedrich von Wendt,' edited by Erich, Graf Kielmansegg (Hannover, 1902), p. 162.

The date of Persiana's husband's death is from Mr. J. F. Chance's paper in the *Eng. Hist. Review*, vol. xi. (1896), p. 527. There is no evidence at King's College, Cambridge, that Anne, Lady Bellomont, applied there for pecuniary relief, or was ever granted any, as stated by some writers.

Maximilian Bard seems to have been about seven years his brother's senior; he is said to have helped Henry with money, and had a great admiration for him. Maximilian must have made money by his trade of silkman or mercer, for on June 20, 1653, the manor of Caversfield, in Buckinghamshire, was conveyed to him and another. At his death it passed to Nathaniel as son and heir, who was followed by his son Thomas. He, with his two sons, Thomas and George, conveyed the estate on February 3,1704, to William Vaux, an attorney, who held it till 1735, and so on (Lipscombe, 'History of Buckinghamshire,' 4 vols., 4to., 1847, vol. ii., pp. 594, 595). There is some discrepancy between Lipscombe's date for Nathaniel's death and that given in the table; the latter is taken from Mr. J. F. Chance's article already quoted.

CHAPTER XIX

TWO ENGLISHMEN SEIZE THE AMBASSADOR'S PROPERTY, I APPEAR IN THE KING'S PRESENCE, AND THE ENGLISHMEN ARE MADE PRISONERS

After we had buried the ambassador I wrote to the English factory at Agrah informing them of his death and the embargo imposed by the local official on his property as well as mine, wherefore I prayed them to send me the necessary recommendatory letters. I received no answer; but eight days afterwards two Englishmen appeared, one called Thomas Roch (? T. Roach)[1] and the other Raben Simitt (? Reuben Smith), dressed after the fashion and in the costume of the country, men in the service of the king Shahjahan, and captains of the bombardiers in the royal artillery.

They came to visit me, and when I saw them I asked what they had come about. They informed me that they had come under the king's orders to carry away the property of the ambassador, which lapsed to the crown. To that I retorted by asking if they bore any order, whereupon they laughed, and asked who I might be. I told them I was the servant of the ambassador, that the property in question had been made over to me, that I did not mean to let it go without their delivering

1. Thanks to Mr. W. Foster, of the India Office, I have been able to refer to Sloane MS., No. 811, in the British Museum, 'Travels of Richard Bell, Gunfounder to Shah Jahan and Aurangzeb, 1654-1668'. The Indian portion (fols. 1-22) seems to be a narrative by J. Cambell (Campbell), taken down by R. Bell. It is a wild romance, utterly unchronological, at the side of which Manucci's wildest flight reads like sense and soberness. Still, there are some grains of fact. On Vol. 5 Thomas Roach, Robert Smith, and John White are named as being with Aurangzeb, while Campbell was with Dara (?) [or Murad Bakhsh ?]. Thomas Roach, chief gunner to the Mogul, appears in the Surat Records in 1667 and 1672; and in 1704 his son, Thomas, then sixty years of age, received charitable aid there. 'Surat Factory Records', Miscellaneous, vol. ii. (May 26, 1667), 'Factory Records', vol. cv. (Roach's letter from Agrah, May 8, 1671), vol. ii. Miscellaneous (November 20, 1672), and vol. xii. (September 25, 1704).

to me my belongings—that is, two muskets, four pistols, clothes, and other trinkets, which had been set apart. Their answer was that the whole belonged to the king; and without another word they went to find those who had put on the seals, and obtaining their consent, made themselves masters of everything, arranging to remove the whole to the city of Dihli.

I did not mean to abandon the property, and resolved to set out in their company. On the road they showed me not the least little sign of civility, such as Europeans, even of different nations, are accustomed to display in all parts of Asia when they come across each other. Many a time did I entreat them for God's sake to make over to me what was mine; but as they saw I was only a youth, they scoffed at me, and said: 'Shut your mouth; if you say a word we will take your horse and your arms away.' Seeing there was no other way out of it, I dissembled for the time being, but never despaired of getting back what belonged to me.

After three days' journey we arrived at Dihli, where the Englishmen deposited the property in a sarae, put seals on the room doors, and told me to go about my business. Then I began to make request that they would be so good as to separate my property from that of the ambassador and make it over to me, for it did not belong to the king. They burst out laughing and mocked at me, giving me the customary answer. As I took my leave I prayed them to do me the favour of telling me their names, so that if any one called me to account about that property I should be able to defend myself by pointing out the persons who had taken possession of it. I expressed my astonishment that they should lock up in a *sarae* room property that they said belonged to the king. I asked them angrily whether the king had no other place in which to store [48] the goods that he owned; but they knew quite well that the property did not belong to them, and that they were taking the king's name in vain, solely in order that they might get hold of other people's goods. They replied that there was no need to know their names. As for my second remark, they only set to laughing, and thus went away in apparent triumph, not foreseeing what was to happen to them.

I retired to a room in the same *sarae,* not far from the one where the property was. Then I found out the names of those two Englishmen, so as to be able to take my own measures. Being anxious to know what was going on, there turned up on a visit to me a Frenchman called Clodio Malier,[1] a founder employed in the artillery of Dara, first-born son of Shahjahan. With him I talked over what had happened to me with those two Englishmen; and said again that it did not seem to me possible that so great a monarch as the Mogul king should possess no other place to store the goods that belonged to him than a mere sarae, where travellers took up their quarters. The Frenchman assured me that the Englishmen had not seized the goods by order of the king, but that Thomas Roach, learning of the ambassador's death, had sent in a petition to the prince Dara, by whom he was favoured, in the following terms: 'A man of my country, a relation of mine, came from Europe, his purpose being to obtain the honour of serving under your highness, but his good fortune was of such little duration and so scanty that he was unable to attain his desire, being overtaken by death on reaching the *sarae* of Hodal, whereupon those who govern in that place laid an embargo upon his goods. Therefore I pray as a favour that your highness be pleased to issue orders for their delivery to me.'

The prince dealt with this petition as Thomas Roach hoped; but Raben Semitt (Reuben Smith), getting word of what Thomas Roach was about, held it not to be right that he should acquire the whole of the ambassador's property, that it must be divided between the two of them. Thus he (R. Smith) accompanied him (T. Roach) as far as Hodal. Should he not consent to a division, he (R. Smith) threatened to tell the whole story to the king. Thomas Roach accepted the situation, so as not to lose the whole. 'This was the story told me by Clodio Malier, who bade me adieu with much civility and many offers of service. Being thus informed of what was going on, and confiding in my knowledge of the Turkish, but more especially of the Persian language, which is that chiefly used and the most current at the court of the

1. This Clodio Malier is probably identical with Claude Maille, of Bourges, in Tavernier's 'Travels', i. 116, 117 (December, 1665, surgeon at Allahabad), 286, 289 (September, 1652, gunner in the Karnatik). In part iii., f. 223, Manucci speaks of meeting Clodio Menolhao, a French merchant, at Goa in 1666-67, and, as he calls him an old friend, it was probably the same man.

Mogul, I resolved to go to the secretary of the king, whose name was Vizircan (Wazir Khan)[1] to lodge a complaint. For this purpose I went to his house, and obtaining permission to enter, I reported to him what was going on. He directed me to sit down opposite to him, alongside one of his sons, who was of my age [49].

The secretary asked me whether I knew the accustomed mode of making obeisance before the king by those who enter his presence. I answered that I did. As he displayed a desire to see me do this, I arose, stood quite erect, and bending my body very low until my head was quite close to the ground, I placed my right hand with its back to the ground, then raising it, put it on my head, and stood up straight. This ceremonial I repeated three times, and this is done to the king only. The secretary was delighted to see a foreigner, young in years and newly arrived in the city, make his obeisances so confidently. I was dressed like a Turk, with a turban of red velvet bound with a blue ribbon, and dressed in satin of the same colour, also a waist-cloth of a gold-flowered pattern with a red ground. He was amused to see me got up like this, and asked the reason for adopting such a costume, and why I did not adopt the Mogul fashions, whereupon I acquainted him of the journey that I had made and the countries through which I had passed.

During this time a notice reached him that the king had decided to hold an audience that morning. Then, rising at once, he took me with him to the palace, telling me that it was requisite for me to go with him before the king. He warned me that, when I came into the king's presence, I must perform the same obeisances that I had practised before him. When we got to the palace the king had already taken his seat on the throne. The secretary directed two men to present me to the king, while he (the secretary) should be talking to him. Accordingly they did present me, ordering me to appear in front of the king at a

1. Manucci must mean here not the King's *wazir*, but Wazir Khan, the head official or Diwan to Prince Dara Shukoh. This man, Muhammad Salih (Wazir Khan), was killed at the Battle of Samugarh in June, 1658, *Tarikh-i-Muhammadi* (1068 H.). The only other Wazir Khan then alive was serving in Malwah, and the office duties of Shahjahan's wazlr were then carried on by Rae Raghunath, Sa'dullah Khan having been dead two or three months.

distance of fifty paces, waiting until he should take notice of me before I made my obeisances.

I had noticed that when the secretary reached the place where is the railing, he made one bow, such as I had done in his house, then, when close to the throne, he made three bows, and approaching still nearer, he began to speak to the king. After a few words he raised his hand towards where I was, as if pointing me out. The king raised his eyes towards me, then the courtiers with me told me to make my obeisances, which I did. The secretary went on with his conversation, which I could not overhear by reason of the distance at which I was. All those who were present before the king were standing; only one man was seated at the side of the throne, but his seat was lower, and this was the prince Dara, the king's son.

I noted that the throne on which the king, Shahjahan, was seated stood in front of and near to the palace of the women, so that as soon as he came out of its door he reached the throne. It is like a table, adorned with all sorts of precious stones and flowers in enamel and gold. There are three cushions, a large one, five [50] spans in diameter, and circular, which serves as a support to the back, and two other square ones, one on each side, also a most lovely mattress. For in Turkey, and throughout the whole of Hindustan, they do not sit upon chairs, but upon carpets or mattresses, with their legs crossed. Around the throne, at the distance of one pace, are railings of gold of the height of one cubit, within which no one enters except the king's sons. Before they enter they come and, facing the king, go through their obeisance, then enter the palace and come out by the same door from which the king issued. Arriving there, they again make obeisance, and upon a sign from the king they take their seat in the same enclosure, but at the foot of and on one side of the throne. Thereupon the pages appear with the umbrella, parasol, betel, spittoon, sword, and flybrusher.

Below the throne, several feet lower than it, a space is left, sufficient for the secretary (? *wazli*) and the greatest officials of the court. This space is surrounded by a silver railing. Near it stand 'grusberdares' (*gurz-bardar*)—that is to say, the bearers of golden maces, whose duty it is to carry orders from the court to princes of the blood royal. After a descent of a few more steps there is another space of greater size, where are the captains and other officials, also the 'grusberdares' (gurzbardars) with silver maces, who convey the orders of the court to the governors, generals, and other princes. These are placed with their backs to a railing of wood painted vermilion, which surrounds the space.

The hall in which stood the royal seat is adorned with twenty highly-decorated pillars, which support the roof. This roof stretches far enough to cover the spaces enclosed within the silver railing, and is hidden half-way by an awning of brocade. Further, a canopy over the king's throne is upheld by four golden pillars.

Outside the wooden railing is a great square, where, close to the railing, stand nine horses on one side and nine on the other, all saddled and equipped. Near to the pillars are brought certain elephants on everyday that the king gives audience, and there they make their obeisance, as I shall describe when I speak of the elephants (ii. 5). Behind the horses already spoken of were four handsomely-adorned elephants, and in the square a considerable number of soldiers stand on guard. At the end was a great hall, where were stationed the players on instruments, and these, upon the king's appearing to give audience, played very loudly, to give notice that the king was already in the audience hall.

The silence preserved was astonishing, and the order devoid of confusion. For this purpose there are officials, whose business it is to see that the people are placed in proper order. Some of these officials held gold sticks in their hand, and these came within the silver railing. The others carried silver sticks, and they took great heed that throughout the court nothing was done which could displease the king [51].

After I had received my permission to go, I left in the company of the two courtiers, and returned to the *sarae*. There I showed them where I had put up, and the room in which was the property. Thereupon they broke the seals and brought out all the things and carried them away.

The next day, about nine o'clock in the morning, there came two servants of the secretary (*wazir*) to fetch me. They took me to his palace, where I found him seated in the same hall where I had spoken to him the day before. As I came in I observed that the ambassador's property was lying there.

I made the usual obeisances to the secretary (*wazir*). Then, with a pleasant look on his face, he asked me if I identified the two thieves, pointing with his hand to one corner of the hall. Noticing this, I turned my face that way and saw the two English impostors, loaded with iron, fetters on their feet and shackles on their necks, and very much ashamed, being afraid they would be decapitated.

Turning again to the secretary, I craved leave to speak to them, and going near to them, I said: 'It would have been more honest to let me have the little that was mine, but then you wanted to acquire more than was yours; you suffer through your excess of greed, and in your desire to embrace all, you are left with nothing. You laughed, you scoffed, and had no tenderness for me, and now I sorrow for love of you, and feel compassion for the miserable condition in which I see you. You may make certain that I shall not fail to deal towards you with more charity and consideration than you showed to me on the road from Hodal.'

Returning to the secretary (*wazir*), he told me to look at the things and inform him whether any article was missing, for the prisoners would have to pay for anything deficient. I examined the property in his presence, and ascertained that it was complete. Since my things had been separated and were kept apart, I prayed him as a favour to issue orders that they should be returned to me. In addition, most of the ambassador's goods belonged to an English trader, named Mestre Jonh (Mr. Young), dwelling in Surat, from whom the ambassador had obtained them, promising to repay him afterwards.

The secretary (*wazir*) told me to sit down beside his son who was in front of him; he said he would give me many things, and making me great promises, said to me, that if I consented to remain in his house he would treat me like a son. In case I did not agree, he did not mean to give me anything. My answer was that I could not live in his house, that I cared very little about the loss of my own things, but should grieve a very great deal if he did not give to Mestre Jonh (Mr. Young) those that were his.

Upon this the secretary (*wazir*) asked me minutely which were the ambassador's and which Mestre Jonh's (Mr. Young's) things. I pointed them all out in detail, one of the secretary's clerks taking the whole down in writing. I told him that besides these goods Mestre Jonh (Mr. Young) had lent the ambassador the sum of four thousand *patacas* [about £800] and an Arab horse (already in the secretary's (*wazir's*) possession). Finally, I begged [52] leave to return to my abode, and he, in sending me off, directed me to return in two days to speak to him in the same place.

Accordingly this I did, and he said to me then that he had spoken to the king, who ordered that the property should be sent to the Governor of Surat for the purpose of being made over to Mestre Jonh (Mr. Young), with the exception of the Arab horse, which the king kept for himself, giving an order to pay to the said Jonh (Young) one thousand *patacas*, the price at which it had been valued. He took nothing else but the litter which was destined for him.

After this I made a fresh application to the secretary (*wazir*) that he would order my property to be given to me; but his answer was that the whole must go to Surat and be made over to Mestre Jonh (Mr. Young), who, if he liked, might give them to me. Thus he was unable to dispose in any way of this property. But if I consented to live with him, he would give me a great deal more, and repeated that he would cherish me as his son, and many other promises. For all these words and the kindness he had displayed I gave him thanks over and over again; but as for living with him, that could never be. It was not right for me to do so, being a Christian. The secretary (*wazir*) cut short my speech, and, losing his temper, said angrily: 'You do not know that you are the king's slave.'

Hearing these words, I rose to my feet, and answered that Europeans were not, and never would be, slaves of anyone; and in great haste I left the hall, resolved to give my life rather than live in his house. Coming out at the door, I vaulted lightly on to my horse, and took my way somewhat hurriedly, dreading lest the secretary (*wazir*) might send some one after me to attack me. Then my groom warned me that two foot soldiers were hurrying after us, trying to overtake us. Then I turned my horse round, and, putting my hand on my cutlass, set off to face them. I asked what they wanted. They made me a bow, and answered that the secretary (*wazir*) sent me ten gold rupees for the purchase of *betel*. I took them and went on my way. I was determined to return to Surat that I might find myself among Europeans.

At this time I met Clodio Malier, who carried me off to his house, and there I told him of my resolve. He did not approve. Then by his arguments he succeeded in persuading me. Having got as far as the court, what was the good of leaving it again without first seeing what there was there, so that I might report on the riches and greatness of the kings of the Mogul, exceeding the riches of other kings, as may be seen in the course of this my book?

As I was a youth, carried away by curiosity, but still more by the friendship shown to me by Clodio, and reflecting that I had already in him one friend who could do me some good in this kingdom, and be of help to me in some affair, I determined to remain where I was [53].

CHAPTER XX

OF THE WAY I WAS SENT FOR TO THE COURT OF PRINCE DARA

After three days had elapsed, Clodio Malier was sent for to the palace of Prince Dara, who inquired if he knew of the arrival of a European youth who had come with the ambassador of England, and a few days before had appeared in the king's presence to make a complaint of injuries done by a captain of artillery and other Englishmen. Clodio answered that he knew me well, that, seeing me unprotected, he had taken me into his house, adding that I was a youth of quality. He wished that, before allowing me to leave the Mogul kingdom, I should see something of the king's and the princes' riches, so that on my return to Europe I might declare the wealth and grandeur of the Moguls.

Thereupon the prince said to him that he wanted to speak to me, and thus he must not fail to find a way to bring me to his presence. When Clodio Malier came home, he said to me at once, with a joyous countenance, that I had already captured good fortune, for the eldest prince, a generous man and friendly to Europeans, had shown himself interested about me and wanted to speak to me. I rejoiced at this good news, knowing that the Europeans who served this prince had a good life of it, and received adequate pay. Thus I, too, was desirous of obtaining some employment at his court. I made up my mind, for that reason, not to put off my visit, and I asked Clodio if we should have to wait long before complying with the prince's desire. My friendly shelterer replied to me that it was not wise to delay, otherwise we might lose the favourable opportunity. For the resolves of the great were like. birds: if the bird-lime stuck to them, they were easily caught; but if they once flew away, it was very hard to lay hold of them a second time.

For these reasons we started the very same day, and repaired to the court of the above-named prince. As soon as he was informed of our arrival, he gave the order to allow us to enter. When I reached his presence, and had made the usual obeisances, he asked me if I could speak Persian, and put some other questions with a pleased and friendly expression on his face. He was delighted at seeing a youth of not more than eighteen years and a foreigner, with such quick-wittedness that he had learned to make the proper obeisance without any shyness. Then I answered the questions, showing myself acquainted with Turkey and Persia and other important matters. The whole of my replies were in Persian, by which I proved to the prince that I could [54] speak sufficiently well the language about which he had asked me.

At the conclusion of the above talk he directed that the ambassador's letter be given to me. It had already been opened; and I was directed to translate it into Persian. The letter was in Latin, written in letters of gold, and it differed but little from the letter presented to the King of Persia. Being thus already acquainted with the business, I had little difficulty in translating it. Next the prince asked what the letter was written on, for it seemed to him like a skin, and not paper. I answered that it was of vellum skin, and it was the usage for European kings, when forwarding letters to far-off kingdoms, to have the more important matters written on vellum skin, in order that they might be better protected against the inclemencies of the weather and of the journey than they would be if they were on paper.

At the end of this conversation Dara asked me if I wished to remain for a time in the Mogul country, to which I replied affirmatively. He said to me, with a smile on his face: 'Would you like to enter my service?' As this was the very question, and none other, that I was hoping for, I replied that I should have put to very good use the wearinesses and fatigues of my journey if I had the good fortune to serve under so famous a prince.

He then directed that every month they should give me eighty rupees of pay, a sum equal to forty *patacas*.[1] He ordered them to deliver to me at once, in his presence, a serpao (*sarapa*)[2] and thirty rupees and a good horse. He put me in the charge of one of his trusted eunuchs called Coja Mosquis

1. This passage proves that the *pataca* is to be taken as worth two rupees.
2. A *sarapa* (literally, 'head to foot') is a complete set of vestments.

(Khwajah Miskin), with instructions to look after the little European and see that he was well trained and educated. I returned thanks to the prince, and seeing how well Dara was inclined towards me, I prayed for leave to entreat another favour—that is to say, the liberty of the two English prisoners; and through the mediation of the prince, they were released in a few days by order of the king.

I came out from the prince's presence. Although Dara desired that Khwajah Miskin should teach me the court ceremonial in order to turn me into a courtier, I took means to prevent my being made into a Mahomedan. So I did not go to seek out the said Khwajah Miskin, but kept in the company of the Europeans. Some of these were surgeons, but the greater number artillerymen in the Mogul service, an honourable employment. For European artillerymen who took service in that branch had only to take aim; as for all the rest—the fatigue of raising, lowering, loading, and firing—this was the business of artificers [55] or labourers kept for the purpose. However, when Aurangzeb came to the throne, he, seeing the insolent behaviour and the drunkenness of such-like men, deprived them of all their privileges, except that of distilling spirits, and forced them to do sentry duty like other soldiers, thus leaving them with no estimation or reputation in the army. But the old plan continued in force up to the evacuation of the fortress of Bacar (Bhakkar) and the beheadal of Prince Dara, as further on I shall relate (I., 254, 258).

For some time I dwelt in the house of Clodio, and when I had acquired the means, I hired a separate house. Then came a man to me and said that he would put me in the way of gaining money. I inquired from him what it was he wanted. He told me that he wanted nothing beyond permission to distil spirits under my protection and close to my house. He would give me ten rupees every day; thus I should be put to no expense: all I had to do was to assert that he was my servant. I agreed to the bargain, and out of regard for me no one said a word to him, for the Europeans in the service of Dara had this privilege of distilling spirits and selling them without hindrance.

Finding myself with sufficient pay, and in good condition, I wrote to Mestre Jonh (Henry Young) at Surat, giving him notice of the king's orders—how he had ordered all the ambassador's property to be placed in the hands of the governor of Surat with directions to make it over to him. After some months he replied that he had then received delivery of everything.

When I left Venice I already knew sufficiently how to speak the Italian language, and in addition a little French. During this journey I learnt the Turkish and Persian languages. Finding myself established in India, I now set to work to learn the Indian tongue. Furthermore, as I was desirous of knowing about matters in the Mogul kingdom, I found an aged man of letters, who offered to read to me the 'Royal Chronicles of the Mogul kings and princes.'[1] Therefore, I am of opinion that the reader will be glad to listen to me, seeing that I have special information. I will speak of all the Mogul kings in my Second Book, which will close with the death of Aurangzeb's brothers, and therein will be seen what happened to me.[2]

1. Manucci's aged man of letters proved only a broken reed, for, until the reign of Shahjahan is reached, his 'Royal Chronicles' yield nothing more than a farrago of the wildest and most improbable legend.
2. In the text folio 56 is blank.

I. Taimur-i-Lang

Vol. I *To face page 97*

[57] BOOK II

OF THE MOGUL KINGS UP TO THE REIGNING SOVEREIGN, AURANGZEB[1]

I Wished to divide this book into chapters to make easier to the reader the succession of the events I write about; but since the authors of the Chronicles, and the historians of the wars, do not divide their books into chapters, it would be impossible to arrange under special headings a history so full of varied occurrences. Therefore the reader must be satisfied if I conform to their practice, simply dividing the work under headings for each particular king.

OF TEMURLANG (TAIMUR-I-LANG) THE GREAT

Much might be written about this great conqueror. But as so many have described the exploits of Taimur-i-lang, I will content myself with giving a simple mention of this great king. His father [? grandfather] was of the Tartar race, of the Chagata (Chaghata) family, and a Mahomedan. He was the lord over several villages, owner of many flocks, camels and horses, and a man of great authority in that province, He had an only daughter of great beauty, who was sought in marriage by many potentates, including even the King of Tartary himself. But her father would not accord her to any of them.

It came to pass one day when she had reached a sufficient age that she became with child, whereby her father was much enraged, and sought to slay her. Questioning her, he asked why she had thus dishonoured her family. Her answer was

1. The following shows the true names and order of succession in juxtaposition with our author's statement:

Manucci's List.	S. Lane Poole's List.
1. Taimur.	1. Taimur, died 807 H.
2. Miran Shah.	2. Miran Shah (third son), died 810.
3. Abu Sa'id.	3. [Muhammad]
4. Sekh 'Umar.	4. Abu Sa'id, died 873.
5. Mahmud.	5. 'Umar Shekh (fifth son), died 899 ruler of Farghanah.
6. Babar.	6. Babar, died 937.

that it was no dishonour, because if he wished to know the father of the child she bore, he need only go into her room at early morn, and he would know all that had happened. Without fail the father went the next morning to his daughter's room, and saw that a ray of the sun came through a chink in the window and played upon her, then, turning into an animal, went out by the same window with a cry. The father, fully satisfied, declared that she was pregnant by the sun. Thus is it written in the Chronicle of Taimur-i-lang.[1] I also was told that if this were so, then Taimur-i-lang must have been engendered by some evil spirit. All the same, he called himself Child of the Sun, and for such he is accounted. Thus all the Mogul kings and princes bear a sun as the device [58] upon their standards, and nobody else may use it. As he was born with a crown of hair longer than usual in the centre of his scalp, the astrologers prognosticated that he would be a great man, lord of many crowns. On this account he wore the whole of his hair, and his descendants, as they are not born thus equipped, shave their heads.

Taimur-i-lang was slightly lame in one leg, which is indicated by his name, for *temur* signifies 'separated,'[2] and *lang* means 'lame.' This cripple devoted himself from his youth up to arms, and early showed that he had come into the world to govern it. Thus many a time he would play with his boy companions at government, always making himself the king. When he had grown up a little, he said to his playmates that he wanted to start a new game. This was the appointment of the boys to different posts of authority; he divided the neighbouring villages among them, and constituted himself king and judge. They came and reported how a camel had fallen into a pond: would he decide what was to be done? His decision was that if the pond was unprotected, the owner of it must take out the camel alive, or would have to pay; if there were a hedge, he was not under that obligation. They came with another complaint—that a wolf had carried off a lamb;

---

1. This story of miraculous conception is transferred, apparently, from the daughter of Juina Bahadur, Qiyat, Barlas, who gave birth at one time to three sons, one of whom was the ancestor, in the fourteenth degree, of Taimur-i-lang (see *Akbarnamah*, translated by H. Beveridge, i. 178-183).
2. According to the dictionaries, *taimur* is Turkish for ' iron.'

his answer was that this was due to the shepherd's neglect, and he deserved a beating. Finally, they came to say they had captured a thief. He ordered him to be hanged, which was done accordingly. In carrying out the jest the boy died in sober truth, the terrified lads taking flight each to his own home.

The relations of the boy who had been hanged, who belonged to another village, took up arms against Taimur-i-lang. The latter, helped by his servants and shepherds, defended himself and routed his enemies. Thus little by little war extended, Taimur-i-lang always coming out the conqueror, so that he soon acquired the adjoining villages. Seeing his strength so much increased, he resolved to obtain the territories of a powerful prince called Sultan Mahamud (Sultan Muhammad). Suddenly he entered the land and took the largest village that the other had, which was situated in the middle of his province. Still, things did not happen to Taimur's liking; in the end he was totally defeated, and forced to disguise himself as a poor traveller in order to get back to his country, begging alms as he went.

Arriving at a certain village, he prayed an old woman to give him something to eat. The old woman gave him a dish filled quite full, and he, being very hungry, thrust his hand into the very middle of the platter, thereby burning himself. Blowing on his hand [59], and shaking it about, he said the dish was very hot. The old woman laughed heartily, and at the same time taught him a good lesson, saying: 'You are like Taimur-i-lang, who did not know how to take this country, for he came right into the middle of it, and had to go out again defeated. If he had begun by attacking the confines, he could in time have made himself master of the whole. It is the same with you, who have just tried to begin in the middle, while if you had travelled round the edge, you could have eaten the whole without once burning yourself.'

Listening to her, Taimur-i-lang profited by the good lesson, and when he reached his own country, he gathered together a new force and renewed the war. He followed the old woman's advice and became master of all his adversary's country, but he could not capture the king himself; therefore he issued a proclamation that whoever caught him should receive a reward. When he heard this, the prince disguised himself and fled, hiding himself in a tower. It happened that a herdsman, searching for a cow he had lost, entered the tower. He was a man whom the prince recognised; supposing that he had come to search for him, he drew forth some jewels and gave them to the herdsman, praying him not to say a word to anyone. The herdsman went off with the jewels to the abode of Taimur-i-lang in the hope of selling them and then buying another cow. On his arrival he was brought before Taimur-i-lang, who asked where he had got these jewels. The herdsman answered: 'You take the jewels and give me a cow.' They bound him until he confessed where he had obtained the jewels. He admitted that a man in a tower not far off had given them to him. They presented the herdsman with two cows, and by Taimur-i-lang's orders started for the said tower, where they laid hold of the fugitive prince and threw him down from the wall. Taimur-i-lang remained the master, and began to increase in strength.

Desirous of continuing his successes, he attacked the King of Kabul. After many adventures and struggles, and the murder of the Kabul king, he became ruler of that rich country. Issuing thence, he crossed the river Indo (Indus), and rushing from one place to another, began to interfere with the Patani (Pathan) princes, more especially he of Dihli, so that the said princes might submit to him and pay him tribute; for Taimur-i-lang, having been victorious from his earliest youth, had formed the design of becoming a still greater conqueror, not resting content with one principality or one kingdom. With this idea he proceeded to claim tribute and homage.

Following up his victories, he next wished to compel the Rana, a Hindu king dwelling in the middle of Hindustan,[1] to pay him tribute and obey his orders [60]. The Hindu king refused to comply. As soon as he heard that Taimur-i-lang had with him a large army, he took the field against him at the head of one hundred thousand horsemen, all of them Rajputs. These are the most warlike people in all Hindustan. When the Rana saw that Taimur-i-lang had no more than twelve thousand horse, he decided that it was not expedient to

1. This campaign against the Rana is, of course, quite mythical, Taimur never having penetrated as far as that territory. It may be a garbled version of Babar's contest with Rana Sanga in 1527 (Elphinstone, 375).

lead the attack in person, and it would suffice to send his generals to annihilate the invader.

Tamur-i-lang on his side was afraid at seeing come against him so great an army of such valiant warriors; he therefore held a council of war. His generals were of opinion that he should give up the undertaking. When this decision became known to one of Taimur-i-lang's mule-drivers, he sought at once to speak with him; but the guards would not allow him to enter, so he took his turban and threw it into the tent of Taimur-i-lang, crying aloud that he had urgent need of speaking to his lord.

On hearing the voice, Taimur-i-lang called him in and gave him leave to speak. The man spoke thus: 'You, my lord, have been victorious unto this day, and all the princes against whom you have made war have been subdued and rendered submissive to your orders. But now a rumour is heard that you mean to retreat for fear of the Rajput soldiers. If that is true, it will lead to the rebellion against you of all those you have conquered. Thus, both you and us, we shall lose our lives ingloriously. Better were it to die sword in hand like heroes than like cowards to retreat, even a single step.'

This speech of the muleteer was the cause of Taimur-i-lang's deciding not to retreat. On learning that the Hindu king did not mean to command in person, he gave orders that two thousand horsemen should march by another route to a place where they could attack the tent occupied by the king. When a force had been detached from that huge Hindu army with the intention of sweeping away the Mahomedans, apparently so few in number, he would give the agreed-on signal.

The two thousand men started, and at dawn the Rajputs came out into the field of battle against Taimur-i-lang. The latter, pretending to take to flight, allowed the enemy to pursue him. Meanwhile the two thousand Mahomedans attacked the Rana's tents, which became the scene of a great uproar, and it was with great difficulty that the Rana escaped with his life. When this news came to the ears of the Rajputs pursuing Taimur-i-lang, they turned round at once to aid their king. Taimur-i-lang's soldiers, recovering heart and courage, pursued their pursuers and won the battle. Thus Taimur-i-lang forced the Rana, or Hindu king, to make a peace and concede great advantages. In consequence of this defeat, the Rana made a vow never to attack the Moguls, but to be content with defending himself; and this vow he transmitted as an ordinance to his descendants, who observe it to this day.

After this victory Taimur-i-lang returned to Kabul. Finding himself [61] master of great wealth, with great experience in warfare, he made up his mind to march against the great Bayazet (Bayazid) the Second.[1] Passing through Persia he appeared preoccupied. His generals asked the reason, assuming that he was in doubt of succeeding well. They said to him that there was no occasion for depression; he was already accustomed to conquer, and had with him valiant and veteran soldiers under invincible commanders. Taimur-i-lang replied with the greatest calmness that he had never had any anxiety about victory over the Persians, but what he was in search of was a suitable governor to place over Turkey instead of Bayazid. He assumed that he had already got the latter in the cage.

I shall not write here the doings of Taimur-i-lang against Bayazid, many authors having written about them. All I will say is that after so many and such great victories, he became desirous of invading Hindustan, and taking possession of all these realms; he marched through his kingdoms, and a little time after his arrival died at Kabul.

The cause of his death was his own son, Sultan Miraxa (Sultan Miran Shah), the sole heir of so famous a father. There was a fixed order that the soldiers must see that their horses did not fight with each other, and if such fighting occurred, Tamur-i-lang at once ordered the owner of the horse to be decapitated. It so happened that his son's horses fought, and thus it became necessary that the universally promulgated sentence should be executed upon Sultan Mir Shah, and dearly as he loved his son, he did not like to give a bad example. But at the thought of losing him he fell into such grief and became so cast down, that in a few hours he died himself.

No one could recount properly the courage or the vigour or the wealth of this conqueror, who paid his soldiers and generals at one time for eight years in advance, relying on the fidelity of his vassals. Then, after having reigned twenty and

1. Should be Bayazid I., 1389-1402. Bayazid II. reigned 1481-1512, whereas Taimur died in 1405. Bayazid I. was made prisoner in 1402 (see S. L. Poole, 'Mohammadan Dynasties,' 195, 268).

II. Miran Shah

four years, nine months and two days, his courage and his enterprises came to an end in the year one thousand four hundred and one, and he was buried at the city of Kabul.

OF THE KING SULTAN MLRAN SHAH, THE SECOND [KING] OF THIS FAMILY

Sultan Miran Shah wished to be heir of the conquests and valour of his father as he was of his wealth, but Fortune did not design to accord to him the favour she displayed to Taimur-i-lang. This king, like his father, made irruptions into Hindu-stan, plundering it in one direction or another, but usually he was compelled to flee defeated into his own territories. His chief efforts were directed against the King of Cascar (Kash-ghar), his neighbour, but he could never secure the victory over this king [62]; nay, he was seven times defeated and a prisoner of that same king. But that king was so generous that each time he captured him (Miran Shah) he released him after a few days. Scoffing at him, he would tell him to go back once more to his own country; he should go there and make ready a new army and more valiant warriors. He would then take the field in the hope of meeting him, and capture him once more. For it was a delight to fight against him, and to see the persistence in warfare which he had inherited from his father.

Fortune never long favours the same persons, and she allowed this king during one battle to fall into the hands of Sultan Miran Shah. This latter took advantage of this piece of good luck, never once remembering the favours received from this very king. Forthwith he ordered his eyes to be removed, and placed him in very harsh confinement. Thus, did he repay the liberty given to him seven times by this king. But neither in this way did Miran Shah increase his fortunes, and he met his death from those same hands that so many times had freed him.

The interested reader should know that most of the Mahomedan great men pride themselves much upon their good shooting with bow and arrow. For this reason they practise many times a day in shooting at the target. One day Miran Shah was at this exercise, when his nobles said to him that the king, then his prisoner, could shoot so well with the bow that, even in his then condition, devoid of sight, and without aiming at the target, he could make no mistake in his shot. It sufficed to strike the mark with your foot, and on hearing the sound, he would shoot straight at it. Miran Shah, being anxious to see such a feat, gave an order to place in his hands a bow and arrow, causing him to be told that he should draw when he heard the sound. He excused himself, saying that no one could direct him to shoot when the king was present but the king himself. This message was brought to Miran Shah, who assented, not knowing the trick that the prisoner meant to play him. When he said 'Shoot,' the prisoner, having beforehand his arrow in readiness in his bow, let it off straight it the place whence came the king's voice, and with such dexterity that it penetrated his chest and killed him on the spot. This king, Sultan Miran Shah, reigned nineteen years, three months, and five days, and came to the end of his misfortunes, leaving in his place his firstborn son, Abuxaid (Abu Sa'id) [63].[1]

OF THE THIRD KING OF TAIMUR-I-LANG'S FAMILY, SULTAN ABUXAID (ABU SA'ID)

This king did not yield to his people the love and affection that his two predecessors had done. On the contrary, he was a great tyrant, and did much injury to his vassals, chastising them most rigorously and unjustly. This was the reason that, seeing themselves so oppressed, they resolved upon slaying their king and delivering themselves from such an encumbrance. Abu Sa'id learnt that not only the people, but also the nobles of the court, were resolved to kill him. He therefore decided to absent himself. Disguising himself in the garb of a mendicant, and taking with him two servants, he would beg alms in foreign lands, and thus escape with his life.

He fled, and the nobles placed upon the throne his brother, expecting to secure better treatment from the second son of Miran Shah than they had obtained from the elder brother. But they were treated according to the proverb, 'Whoever flees from the lesser evil often finishes with falling into greater.' For this second son, without right or reason, ordered the beheadal of high and low, rich and poor, lords and serving men,

1. Really, Miran Shah only survived his father three years, Abu Sa'id was not his son, but his grandson.

III. Abu Sa'id

To face page 104

making no distinctions. Not content with robbing them of wealth and honour, he wanted in addition to drink the blood of the innocent.

Therefore they decided to go in search of Abu Sa'id, and request him to be good enough once more to take on himself the care of governing the kingdom. After much exertion they found him, and raised him to the throne. In place of giving thanks to his brother for the vengeance he had taken upon the rebels, and for the life which he had conceded to him, he (Abu Sa'id) was a cruel fratricide. For, forgetting the favours that he had received from God, he sent a tyrannical order to have his brother beheaded. Thus began the evil custom still followed in the Mogul realm, that on the death of their father one brother seeks the means of killing all his brethren, never failing in this if he finds a chance, as can be seen further on in my story.

The two servants who had accompanied Abu Sa'id in his misfortunes, seeing him once more king, looked forward to great rewards for the fidelity they had displayed. But the king overlooked their great love and affection. At length, receiving nothing at all, they decided to go in person to the king, praying him to be so good as to give them some office as a recompense for the fatigues, hardships, and pains that they had endured on his account. On hearing the request of these faithful servants, in which they set forth the burdens that they had borne on his account, and prayed for some reward, Abu Sa'id frowned, and in a harsh and menacing voice told them to go away and never come again into his presence. They were astonished at this kind of talk, and made petition most humbly that they desired to know the offences for which he was angry with them. For they were as faithful in his misfortunes as in his greatness [64], while others turned him out and persecuted him to the death. He answered that from this very cause he detested the sight of them, for beholding them brought to mind his sufferings, whereby he was made sad. Therefore they must depart. He did them a great favour in not ordering their heads to be cut off. But he warned them not to remain in his territories, for it would not be very long before he executed that design, which had been in his mind for a long time.

Besides hearing it from the chronicles, this story was frequently related to me by Mirza Ad,[1] who was manager of the estate of the queen, wife of Aurangzeb and mother of Shah 'Alam, when I complained that Shah 'Alam did not carry out the promises he had made to me on the occasions when I was indispensable to him for the treatment of his women. I was then, as will be seen in my second part, physician to his house-hold. This man (Mirza Ad), who was a very great friend of mine, and a person without private interests to serve (a thing to be remarked on, as being so rare among Mahomedans), said to me that the Mogul kings were the descendants of the above king (Abu Sa'id). They bestow gifts on anyone when they require him, but the gifts and the memory of the benefits received cease directly the time of necessity has passed. This puts me in mind of the Italian proverb: *Passato il ponto, gabato il fato* ('The bridge crossed, Fate is mocked').

This king in his time did nothing of any value. He loved to be always at peace, and take his ease at home amidst the endearments of his women. Thus, after a reign of eight years, one month, and twelve days, he died, leaving behind him two evil precedents for the Moguls. The first was the assassination of brothers; and the second one, shared by almost all their great men, the speaking of fair words, and backing them by oaths upon the Alcorao (the Quran), when they are pressed by necessity, and declining to be bound by those promises when the necessity no longer exists.

OF SULTAN SECOMOR (SHEKH 'UMAR), FOURTH KING OF THE FAMILY OF TAIMUR-I-LANG

When Sultan Abu Sa'id died, he left his eldest son, named Sultan Secomor (Shekh 'Umar), heir to his kingdom, but not to his great wickedness. Thus the son was much esteemed and loved by his people, feared and respected by all the neighbouring kings. These latter, recollecting the conquests of Taimur-i-lang, dreaded that he (Shekh 'Umar) might be inheritor and imitator of his great-grandfather—he who had conquered many kingdoms with such ease. But he was satisfied with what

1. Perhaps meant for Mir Hadi. There was such a person, but I have no evidence that he held the office referred to.

IV. Shekh 'Umar

V. Mahmud

Vol. I

To face page 107

he had inherited and acquired, and desired to live in peace, having found that everyone respected him.

The Mahomedans are very keen on breeding pigeons in large numbers; they make them fly all together, calling out, whistling, and waving with a cloth fastened at the end of [65] a stick, running and making signals from the terraced roofs, with a view of encouraging the pigeons to attack the flock of someone else. In this way the flocks are so trained that they fight in the air. Then, when the owners whistle and make the signs above described, the pigeons assemble and fly away to their homes, except a few, who, losing their way in the confusion, allow themselves in their innocence to be carried off along with their adversaries. It is for this end that they fly these flocks, and over and over again they send them out and win more pigeons. Every owner is overjoyed at seeing his own pigeons the most dexterous in misleading their opponents.

Sultan Shekh 'Umar was much enamoured of this game. At last, on one occasion, he was running from one end to the other of his roof with the stick in his hand, making signs and whistling, when he fell by accident to the foot of the palace wall, and was dashed to pieces, leaving an example to his descendants to be more careful, and to erect a defence on their roofs to prevent such a fall. For this reason they make fences of large ornamented pillars. This king reigned twenty and five years, two months, and seven days, leaving his eldest son as heir to the kingdom.

OF THE FIFTH KING, SULTAN MAHAMED (MAHAMUD)[1]

He was a strict observer of the Mahomedan faith, an enemy of idols, and consequently of the Hindus. He made war against them many times, and defeated many petty Hindu kings, rendering them tributaries of his crown. This king never failed to read the Quran many times a day, and thus covered his iniquity, for he was very ambitious and covetous. He never failed to draw profit from any opening for the acquisition of territory or the defeat of a neighbouring prince.

1. The person intended is, I suppose, Sultan Mahmud, died 900 H., second son of Abu Sa'id, and therefore brother, instead of son, of 'Umar Shekh, uncle, instead of father, of Babar.

Once it happened that he gained a great victory over a Patani (Pathan) king in the open field, not far from the mountains of those Pathans. After the battle he rode out, towards the evening, puffed up with the spectacle of the numerous deaths that his army had caused among the enemy. He was full of vain-glory at seeing so many dead bodies, and, unable to contain himself for joy, made various demonstrations, and made up his mind to continue this career of victory. But a Pathan—I know not whether out of fright or for some other cause—had hidden among the corpses. Seeing the king unprotected and on horseback, he let fly an arrow, with which he ended the vain-glory, the victories, and the projects of Sultan Mahmud. After a reign of eight years, one month, and fourteen days, he left his immense treasures to his firstborn son, Sultan Babar [66].

SULTAN BABAR, THE SIXTH KING

Although Sultan Babar had inherited so much wealth from his father, Sultan Mahmud, he was not thereby induced to be content with the countries conquered by his predecessors. But instigated by their victories, he, too, was anxious to give like proof of his valour. For this reason he warred against divers petty princes of Hindustan, until at length he came against the King of Dihli, of Pathan race, Sultan Amavixa.[1] A sanguinary battle ensued, and after the war had taken various turns, he (Babar) succeeded in killing the said Sultan Ibrahim Shah. Thus the victorious Babar took the city of Dihli, and there set up the throne, which is still occupied by the kings, his descendants.

This city was founded by a powerful Hindu king called Biguer Magid (Bikramajit), by whom the name of Dihli was given to it. The meaning is 'steadfast.'[2] It was here that he established his court; furthermore, he believed that no one could ever capture the city. But the Sultan Alaudin ('Ala-ud-din), a Pathan king, came down and conquered the Hindu king, and

1. 'Amavi Xa' is, I presume, intended for Ibrahim Shah (1517-1526).
2. Platts suggests, on the contrary, that the name is from a word *dahal*, 'trembling, shaking,' the soil being so loose that a tent-peg would not hold in it.

VI. Babar

began to reign at the selfsame capital in the year one thousand and ninety-five or thereabouts. The Pathans continued to govern Hindustan for four hundred and twenty-four years, a little less or more, until Sultan Babar of the Mogul race conquered Sultan Ibrahim Shah in the year one thousand five hundred and nineteen.[1]

NAMES OF THE PATHAN KINGS.

After this mention of the Pathan kings I give their number, with the name of each and the number of years he reigned.

	LENGTH OF REIGN.		
	Years.	Months	Days.
1. Sultan Alaudin (Fire of the Faith), 'Ala-ud-din ...	57	7	11
2. Sultan Xabudin (Crown of the Faith), Shahab-ud-din	22	7	7
3. Sultan Maxudin goris (Soldier of the Faith), Mu'izz-ud-din, Ghori	19	4	12
4. In default of a male heir, the daughter of Sultan Maxudin, Gori, succeeded, called Bibi Rage (Bib! Riziyah)—that is, 'Prosperous Queen' [67]	7	7	11
5. Sultan Nassuridin, her son (Victorious in the Faith), Nasir-ud-din	12	3	11
6. Sultan Jaiodin (Voice in the Faith), Ghiyas-ud-din	30	1	12
7. Sultan Gelaludin (Impassioned in the Faith), Jalal-ud-din	5	6	7
8. Sultan Cotabdin Assen (North in the Faith), Qutb-ud-din	14	5	8
9. Sultan Tocluc (Standard of the Faith), Muhammad Tughlak	9	0	9
10. Sultan Mahamed Adel (Thanks to God), Muhammad 'Adil'	22	3	3
11. Sultan Ferusxa (Of Lucky Day), Firuz Shah ...	47	5	12
12. Sultan Peroxa (Royal Saint), Piru Shah	10	3	11
13. Sultan Fatexa (Victorious King), Fath Shah	5	6	8
14. Sultan Babar (The Lion), Babar	7	0	5
15. Sultan Amanetcan (The Entrusted), Amanat Khan	1	7	7
16. Sultan Gueseria (The Pious), Khizr Khan? ...	11	1	7
17. Sultan Mobarec (May it be lucky), Mubarik ...	9	8	5
18. Sultan Mahamed (Praise to God), Muhammad	7	5	10

1. The chronology here and the successions in the list that follows are so hopelessly wrong that it is useless to spend time in correcting them. Manucci's translations of the names are also most of them quite wrong. I give them without alteration.

	LENGTH OF REIGN. Years.	Months.	Days.
19. Sultan Jacodin Lodi (Voice in the Faith), Ghiyas-ud-din ?	5	5	8
20. Sultan Caxoro Calan (Lucky Day), Khusru kalan? ...	3	6	8
21. Sultan Alaudin (Faith of the Fire), 'Ala-ud-din ...	1	6	10
22. Sultan Belol can (Powerful among the Strong), Bahlol Khan	40	8	6
23. Sultan Secunda Lodi (Alexander), Sikandar, Lodi ...	29	5	7
24. Sultan Ebraim (Admiration), Ibrahim	8	8	3
25. Sultan Babar Calandar (The Poor Lion), Babar, Kalantar	5	4	9
26. Sultan Amayunt Gori (Regal Grandeur), Humayun, Ghori	1	1	3
27. Sultan Shams (The Sun), Sher Shah ?	8	8	3
28. Sultan Salemxa (Welfare of the Laws), Salim Shah ...	5	10	8
29. Sultan Ferroxa (Brave Warrior), Firuz Shah?	0	0	15
30. Sultan Mahamed Adil (Doer of Justice), Muhammad 'Adil	1	4	1
31. Sultan Amuvixa (Light of Peace), Ibrahim Shah? ...	2	6	0

This was the last of the kings of Pathan race [68]. I will not note what I have seen in the chronicles, a task for which I should require many years. It is impossible to describe all the different events of their rule—the conquests that they made, or their political acts. All I shall say is that they were barbarous, avaricious, and harsh. They were the first Mahomedans to descend from the western frontier into Hindustan, their abode being up to the present day between the river Indus and Kabul.

Babar was much loved by his people, who saw he possessed good qualities, was a conqueror full of liberality and generosity, and fond of making large presents. Above all, they found that he observed the greatest care in seeing that strict justice was done. When a people is well ruled, the king must be very energetic. Still, the chief cause of the realm being in such good order was a highly-placed official at the court called Ranguildas (? Rangi Das).[1] He was so wise that his mere word was as

1. This name and the story connected with the man are quite impossible. Mr. H. Beveridge, the greatest living authority on the period, can only suggest a distant resemblance to Baqi Chaghaniani's advice to Babar (see the ' Habib-us-siyar,' Bombay edition, ii. 318; Babar's 'Memoirs,' (Pavet de Courteille), i. 274; W. Erskine's ' History of India,' i. 209, and 'Khafi Khan,' i. 34).

an oracle to the government, and of such good judgment that his counsels were ever most accurate. But as courts are usually productive of envy, there were never wanting those who were envious of this great man. These backbiters told so many idle tales about him that the king made up his mind to seize him and take his life. This principal official did not foresee that as the reward of his faithful service he should undergo such misfortunes, in order to satisfy the ill-will of his rivals. He was taken, and while the king was still hesitating whether he should be executed or not, he managed to escape from prison. Disguising himself, he took refuge in a little village, where, being content to pass his life in poverty, he was unlikely to be discovered.

It happened that after the removal of this great counsellor the people began to find that things did not continue as before, nor was the accustomed justice done. They began to speak against their king; they plotted treason, and he became very unpopular. Babar was astonished at this change, for he did not know the reason why such a quiet and submissive population should begin to plot a rebellion. Inquiring into the matter, he found out that the administration was not in good order, for his ministers were not acting with the justice that had been customary. He thus became anxious to find once more his faithful Ranguildas. He made every possible effort, but could not discover where he had gone. Being aware that the fugitive was a man of judgment, Babar came to the resolve to issue an order throughout his empire that all inhabitants of the villages should repair to Dihli. In this way he expected to discover the whereabouts of that great administrator of Hindustan, for the villagers would without fail search out the cleverest men to put forward objections against an impossibility. Thus through their excuses he might be able to attain his desire.

Thus it came to pass that the inhabitants of the village where dwelt Ranguildas, by reason of their experience [69] of the clever and appropriate advice he had already given them, laid before him the command and will of the king. They could not think of what excuse to bring forward at court, for how could the whole population go ? Ranguildas answered that they should go at once to court, and say to the king that his people had already decided to come to Dihli, but not knowing their way there, the inhabitants of that city must come forth to be their guides. When the king heard this excuse, he asked who was the inventor of such an answer. As they did not know the man's name, the king ordered them to produce him at court, and thus he recovered his counsellor, who in a brief space restored the kingdom to order. If only kings could know how all-important it is to find good counsellors, they would be more careful in the selection of their ministers, and more suspicious about crediting the slander which abounds in royal palaces.

This king, with the help of such a minister, continued to look after his people, and finding himself in Hindustan, and the possessor of great wealth and of an extensive empire, he paid little heed to his ancient country, from which Taimur-i-lang had sprung. Thus he left an opening for the descendants of the King of Cascar (Kashghar) to revolt, and crowning themselves kings of the territories they had lost, they soon made themselves masters of the villages originally owned by Taimur-i-lang. Nor up to this day do the Mogul kings take the trouble of acquiring again the lands referred to, which are very remote, and yield little revenue. This king, Babar, after governing for nineteen years, three months, and twelve days, came to the end of his life, leaving behind him to his descendants in Hindustan great renown as a conqueror and a just ruler, above all to his eldest-born son the Sultan Amayum (Humayun).

OF SULTAN HUMAYUN, SEVENTH KING OF THE FAMILY OF TAIMUR-I-LANG

As is taught by experience, and is recounted by historians, the strength derived from the power to tame tigers and lions serves oftentimes to make men lose their human qualities and change into wild beasts. Thus it happened to Xira (Shera), of Pathan race—that is to say, 'Lion's Cub.' This man was transformed into a great lion, for such was the name he took when he became a king—that is, Xirxa (Sher Shah), which means 'Royal Lion.' This man, from being one of his retinue, was made by Sultan Humayun a general; yet, after so many and so great benefits, the king having raised him above all others, he revolted and turned his weapons against his lord. The latter was forced to order out against him a' powerful

VII. Humayun

army. But the evil fortune of Humayun decided that Xira (Shera) [70] should come out victorious over and over again. At length the king found it necessary to take the field in person. But as the course of war is uncertain, it came to pass that Humayun too was defeated, and was obliged to take to flight in disguise in order to save his life. After he had reigned eleven years he fled and took refuge in Persia, obtaining the armed assistance of the king of that country, and then returned to tempt Fortune.

What happened to this king during his flight was a very curious thing. It was on this wise : Once at noon he had dismounted for a rest. An eagle with outspread wings hovered in the air over his face until Humayun awoke. It thus prevented the rays of the sun from interrupting the sleep of the fugitive king. The few people who had followed the king in his flight were amazed at this occurrence. When the king awoke, his courtiers told him with great delight not to be cast down, that he was destined to be once more King of Hindustan, thus foretelling what was actually to happen.

After arrival in Persia, the first meeting with the king took place in a garden. There the Persian king received him, being seated on a stool of small size, whereon two persons could not take their place. One of the followers of Humayun saw at once that the object of the King of Persia was to behold a King of Hindustan either standing on foot in his presence, or seated on the bare ground. Forthwith the man cut open the covering of his quiver and spread it out in front of the royal seat. On this cloth Humayun at once sat down.[1]

The King of Persia was lost in admiration at the readiness with which this official, a companion of Humayun's misfortunes, extricated his master from the embarrassment in which he found himself, being obliged, although King of Hindustan, either to sit down on the ground or to remain standing in the presence of another king. The Persian king asked King Humayun how he could lose his kingdom when he had such attentive and well-affected servants. Humayun answered that he lost his kingdom because he raised to greatness men who were ungrateful. After a little talk the sixth successor of the

1. This incident is historical; it occurred in 1544, and the hero of it was Haji Muhammad, Kushkah (see W. Erskine's 'History of India,' ii. 294, and Stewart's 'Jouher,' p. 73).

famous Taimur-i-lang took his leave and went to a palace, where the King of Persia sent the necessary supplies until the opportunity arose of aiding him to recover his kingdom.

Shera was such a just man, that after he had made himself master of the kingdom, he had compassion upon Humayun and sent him his wife, who had been left behind in Hindustan. At that time she was with child. Sher Shah sent him (Humayun), a letter, in which he swore by the Quran that her honour had in no way suffered, for she had done her husband no injury during their quarrel, not even in thought, adding that he was wrong to conceive such a shameful idea of his wife, a woman respected, well-behaved, and virtuous. When this letter reached Humayun, he decided to take back his wife and live with her; after this he quitted Persia, as I shall tell hereafter.

[71] I know that some authors, notably the author Faria, the Portuguese,[1] write otherwise about the way that the queen was obtained. But he was not well informed, and wrote what the common people told him. He did not know that the inhabitants of India are very loquacious, taking no care, either grandees or poor people, whether they are speaking truth or falsehood. Many authors write down what they hear without making the inquiries they ought to make. It would be much better if, before they wrote, they dwelt for some time in the Mogul realm and learnt the language of the country, and consorted with the officials of the court; in that way they could easily get hold of the truth. I am one who has had time enough; I lived with the men best informed of any; I had long converse with them, and they told me the truth. In addition to what I have seen in the chronicles, it was no little profit to me in writing these pages that I dwelt within the Mogul realm for thirty and four years, and that I was physician to Xaalam (Shah 'Alam), the eldest son of Aurangzeb.

Shera, when he became lord over the kingdom, changed his name, and to impose fear upon his enemies called himself Sher Shah. When he became undisputed king, he never forgot to treat his subjects with great equity and kindness. For this end, he sent out orders through all the land to build, at

1. The only passage I can find in Faria y Souza's history, edition of 1666, is in i. 344, and it seems to agree, and not conflict, with what Manucci has said.

a distance of twelve leagues from each other, *saraes* where travellers could take shelter. To provide attendants at these *saraes*, he bought a number of married slaves, and appointed them and their wives to look after travellers—to prepare their food, to provide cool water for them to drink, and warm water for washing their bodies, a bedstead to rest upon furnished with mattresses and sheets; and they were to wait on travellers just as if they were their own private servants, and provide food for wayfarers on foot at the cost of the king. Of these *saraes* I spoke before in the eighteenth chapter (I. 43).

Since the time of Humayun many more *saraes* have been built upon the royal highways throughout the realm, from one end of it to the other. Nor are there ever wanting charitable persons who every day are building new ones, with gardens, reservoirs, and ponds to perpetuate their own names. In these *saraes* travellers are pestered by dealers, who offer for sale different kinds of cloth, not only white, but coloured; also by musicians, dancing-boys, women dancers, barbers, tailors, washermen, farriers with horse-shoes, endless cheating physicians, and many sellers of grass and straw for the horses. All these things are cheap; but there are no longer dainty morsels for the foot-travellers, to be eaten at the cost of the king, or any supply of bedsteads with mattresses and sheets. Still there is never any dearth of women of pleasure.

In the time of this king, Sher Shah, weights and scales were introduced into Hindustan, for before then everything was bought by inspection. It was then also that there were first introduced yard-measures with the royal seal; previously everything was measured by spans and cubits. The king was so generous and liberal that those [72] who wished to go to Mecca were granted passages both ways and the necessary means of support. Finding himself undisputed master of Hindustan, and loved by his people, he made war against the Rana, a Hindu king, assuming command of the army in person. But he was repulsed in such a fashion that if the Hindu king had pursued he would have become the lord of the whole country. However, the Rana contented himself with winning the battle and delivering his kingdom. During the retreat Sher Shah admitted that it was his own fault, and said to his confidants that for a few fields of millet he had run the risk of losing his kingdom. This he said because the territories of the Rana yield great quantities of millet.[1]

Sher Shah was much interested in directing the use of cannon, often discharging them himself; and at the end of his reign, not far from the territories of Bengal, after he had governed for twelve years, he fired off a cannon the recoil of which killed him. He was buried in the middle of a great reservoir, not far from a place called Samchergao (Sasseram), where I was several times, but it is not worth while to speak of that.[2]

The king, Sher Shah, being dead, Hindustan fell into confusion, for there were many who tried to become king and govern it. Thereupon a holy mendicant (*faqir*) named Xadaulah (Shah Dulah),[3] sent off in great haste one of his faithful disciples with boots and a whip as a present to the king, Humayun, and a message to the effect that Effort was the Mother of Good Luck. Humayun understood what Shah Dulah meant. With great skill he asked help from the King of Persia, promising to show him gratitude, and should he win back Hindustan, to give him the country from the confines of Candar (Qandahar) as far as the town of Serend (Sihrind), which lies at a distance of eighty-four leagues from the city of Dihli. The king sent to him twelve thousand selected horse-men, and advised him to make use of the Rajput princes in attacking and defeating the powerful Pathan tribe.

Thus he (Humayun) left Persia with his son who was born there, and went off to tempt Fortune anew, and try to get back his throne. He entered his former territories, and continuously added to his army from the men of Cabal (Kabul), the Baloche (Biloch), Gaqueres (Ghakkars), and Rajputs. He was uninterruptedly victorious over the forces of his enemies. Anticipat-

1. This was in 1544 (compare Elphinstone, 'History,' 396, where the story is given; see also the *Ain-i-Akbari*, Jarrett, ii. 271).
2. In spite of this assertion, it is doubtful whether Manucci could ever have been at Sasseram (in Behar).
3. Shah Dulah, Gujarati, Panjabi, is the person intended. There is, however, a clear anachronism; for, at the earliest, that holy man was born *circa* 1567-1568, while Humayun recovered Dihli in 1555, and died in 1556. The saint's shrine is in Gujarat town (see Khazinat-ul-asfiyah, ii. 102, and S. Mahomed Latif in *Journal* of the Royal *Asiatic Society*, July, 1896, p. 574).

ing that it would be difficult to capture the city of Laor (Lahor), he had recourse before he reached it to the following deception. He chose five hundred valiant men of high spirit and recklessness, who dressed themselves like hermits in tattered raiment, and went barefooted with chaplets of beads in their hands. They represented themselves as specially holy men, and gave out [73] that they were on their way to Mecca. They entered the city, and assembled below the palace of the governor, called Aziscan ('Aziz Khan), of the Pathan tribe, and demanded alms for themselves, so that they might be able to go on their road. 'Aziz Khan compassionately sent and called them within the fortress, in order to give them food and some help in money, thereby hoping for a reward to his own soul. They came into his presence most devoutly, but resolute to carry out their trick. On drawing near to the governor, they began to pray God to grant him great reward for the alms he had given them. Then, drawing their swords from beneath their cloaks, they cut him to pieces, and gaining possession of the fortress, slew all that were found there.[1] The result of the trick was notified to Humayun, who, marching on without delay, made himself master of Lahor. After a short time he left it, in order to capture the city of Dihli. He fought several battles, the principal one in the neighbourhood of Panipat, three days' journey before arriving at Delhi. There he fought a very stiff battle, and in it the Pathan who called himself king having been killed, Humayun became once more lord of Hindustan, and brought the Pathans under subjection.

First of all Humayun remembered the holy mendicant Shah Dulah, to whom he gave villages and an income sufficient for him and his descendants, also many privileges, of which they have the enjoyment to this day. This faqir is venerated as a saint, the Mogul kings and princes having much respect for the village which contains his tomb. This village is not far from the town of Little Guzurate (Gujarat), forty leagues from Lahor. His descendants are much favoured and receive many presents from the Mogul princes. But he (Humayun) did not know that he had to die so soon, and his death came to pass in the following manner.

1. There is nothing about this in the *Akbarnamah,* nor any mention of an 'Aziz Khan (see H. Beveridge's translation, i. 624).

Humayun knew full well that after the years of our life all men, great and small, king and subject, are bound to quit this world. He therefore took steps to prepare a mausoleum where his body should repose. He issued orders for the preparation of the materials, and he had already selected the site. This was at the approach to Dihli, close to a long bridge of twelve arches.[1] While the building was being erected he was anxious to inspect it, and mounted to the highest point, not foreseeing that he was going to his destruction. Leaning his breast upon his staff, he admired the beauty and nobility of the structure. His staff slipped, and he fell to the bottom, breaking his bones. He was buried in the building, which stands in the midst of a [74] great garden. It is adorned inside with many paintings and stones of various kinds, and the roof of the dome is gilded. At this mausoleum, as well as in those of all the kings, there is placed an official of position, having a good salary, who looks after the building and distributes abundant alms to the poor, for which purpose there is a special income. It is his duty to enter the vault once every day, to sweep it out, to place over the tomb a coverlet made of rich brocade, and upon this again a quantity of flowers—such as roses, jasmine, and other sweet-smelling blossoms. At the sides of this covering are placed the arms of the dead king—that is to say, his quiver full of arrows, his bow, his sword, dagger or poignard, lance, musket—all of them weapons of the greatest price. Once I obtained entrance to this mausoleum through the favour of one of my friends, as I will relate when speaking of Akbar's tomb (I., 90).

Humayun died two years, nine months, and fourteen days after he had recovered his kingdom, leaving an only son called Akebar (Akbar).

OF AKBAR, THIRD KING OF HINDUSTAN AND EIGHTH OF THE FAMILY OF TAIMUR-I-LANG

If any of the Mogul kings inherited the valour and judgment of Taimur-i-lang, it was, without contradiction, the king Akbar,

1. This is the Barahpalah (twelve-arched) bridge, built in 1612. The tomb is about half a mile to the north of it (see Carr-Stephen, 'Archaeology of Delhi,' 202, 209).

VIII. Akbar

who was born in Persia[1] at the time when his father, Humayun, was living there, as I have already stated above (I., 72). This king, adopting the advice given to his father by the King of Persia, allied himself to several Rajput princes, thus bringing them over to his side. With their aid he conquered the greater part of Hindustan, routing the remaining Pathans in different battles and bringing them into subjection to his orders. So great was the dread in which Akbar was held by the Hindu princes that they came to offer their services, paying him tribute and voluntarily giving him their daughters. He received them all with open arms; but he forced them to fight against the other Hindu princes, aiding them with his own army. In this way he destroyed many of them in those days. Still, in spite of all this, the Hindus are up to this day more numerous than the Mahomedans. But they can do nothing against the Moguls, for from of old time it has been the fashion of the Rajputs to dispute among themselves. If they were only of one mind they would be able to thrust out every other tribe and race [75]. Although the conquests of Akbar were many, I will recount only some of the principal; still, in this king's time some special events have happened, and I will take leave to give to my readers some notion thereof, at which they will rejoice not a little.

In the first place it is fitting to speak of the conquest that he made of the kingdom of Guzurate (Gujarat) from the king Sultan Bahader (Bahadur). It was from him at the same period that the Portuguese took the fortress of Dio (Diu), which is in the vicinity of Surat and Cambaya (Kambayat). At his death he (Bahadur) left his sons captives in the hands of Akbar, and there they remained until the end of their lives. Akbar well demonstrated on this occasion how important it is for a king to be present himself during an enterprise of importance, for his forces being in battle array opposite those of Sultan Bahadur, his captains began to talk of avoiding an action for fear of being beaten, since Bahadur's army was much the more powerful. When Akbar learnt this, he hurried in person to the spot, although at a distance of four days' journey from the army, and thus so completely restored the courage of his troops that they gained a victory and routed the foe.

Secondly, it is necessary to speak of Akbar's conquest of the Decan (Dakhin), of which the principal places are Brampur

1. As is well known, Akbar was born in Sind, not in Persia.

(Burhanpur), Acer (Asirgarh), Amadanagar (Ahmadnagar), and Doltabad (Daulatabad). The two first named belonged to Melec Mostafa (Malik Mustafa), a Mahomedan. Amadanagar (Ahmadnagar) belonged to the princess Chande Bibi (Chand Bibi), and Doltabad (Daulatabad) to Meleque Ambar (Malik 'Ambar).[1]

The events connected with the conquest of Asirgarh are worthy of notice. At Asir dwelt Malik Mustafa, lord of forty thousand horsemen. Akbar strictly invested the said fortress, and a scarcity of water arose. Malik Mustafa resolved on flight, but while leaving the place he was captured by the sentries. Concealing that he intended to escape, he asked to be taken into the presence of Akbar, having something to say to him. They took him to the king, and as soon as he arrived Akbar asked: 'Who are you, and what do you want?' He answered: 'I am the king Malik Mustafa, and come to seek your advice.' Obtaining leave to speak, he said: 'I have no water in the fortress, only enough for this one night; what advice do you give me?' Akbar's answer was: 'Go your way; if God means to leave you the fortress, He will equally give you water.'

The following night so much rain fell that much damage was done in Akbar's camp. Repenting of having given liberty to one whom he had already in his hands, Akbar raised the investment. Some time afterwards he returned to invest the fortress and took it, as also Brampur (Burhanpur).

Subsequently he (Akbar) went against the Princess Chande Biby (Chand Bibi)—that is, 'Lady Moon'; she also was a Mahomedan. She defended herself with great vigour, but was obliged to surrender the fortress for want of provisions. This princess was so grieved at seeing herself despoiled of her dignities that she made up her mind not to allow her wealth to fall into the [76] hands of Akbar. With this idea she gave orders that all the gold she had should be melted and made into cannon-balls. Upon these she had words engraved to the effect that the ball belonged to anyone who found it, that no one had the right to take it by force from the finder, adding other words of malediction against him who acted otherwise. The cannon were loaded with these balls, and they were discharged in all directions. After the fortress was taken King Akbar fell in love with her

1. I do not know who is meant by Malik Mustafa; the other two names are well known.

for her beauty, and transferred her to his own palace. In my time it happened that near the said fortress a grass-cutter found one of the said balls, which weighed eight pounds and was of gold. When the general Bader Can (Bahadur Khan) heard this fact, he ordered the ball to be brought before him, and directed that the inscribed letters should be deciphered. Their meaning was that the ball should be left with the finder. He (Bahadur Khan) took it for himself, saying he had complied with the wishes of Chand Bibi, and that he had not fallen into any sin. After this conquest, Akbar marched against Malik 'Ambar, lord of fifty thousand horse, and overcoming him, took from him Daulatabad. Thus those who knew not how to aid each other were all defeated, and Akbar remained master of the whole Decan (Dakhin).

In the third place we must put the conquest of the kingdom of Caxemir (Kashmir). For this realm was not taken by force of arms, but solely because the King of Kashmir was greatly frightened by Akbar's victories, and made an offer to him of the kingdom rather than go to war. Akbar saw the feebleness of heart of this king, for with a few men he could have defended himself, Kashmir being a country which cannot be entered by force owing to the great height at which it lies—on very high mountains, with steep paths so few and so narrow that one man could stop a whole army. Akbar therefore issued orders that men of that country should not be recruited as soldiers, that they were unworthy to carry arms. In effect, he allowed not one of them to serve as a soldier. They are employed only as tailors—being good at needlework—as barbers, and they are excellent cooks. Many of them are dealers in the very fine wollen materials made in the said kingdom. The people of Kashmir are very good-looking, of a light complexion, with black hair and eyes and high noses. Thus there is little difference between them and the Jews, either in physiognomy or character, being deceitful and without stability.

In the fourth place we come to the war he (Akbar) waged against the Rana, a Hindu king whose lands were twelve days' journey distant from Dihli. The first thing he (Akbar) did was to surround the fortress called Chitor, the which I have seen many a time. This fortress was on a hill [77] of no very great height, but its sides are quite smooth like walls; it lies in the midst of a wide, open plain. This plain is a league and a half long and half a league wide. At the foot [of the hill] is a stream called Nag—that is to say, 'Snake.' In this fortress are fine springs of sweet water, and during a time of siege supplies are collected enough to support the people in it; it cannot be taken by force of arms, as will be seen from this my narrative.

Before Akbar came to invest this fortress, he dispatched an ambassador to the rajah who was governor, directing him to forward his wife. If he did not agree to send her, he would come himself to fetch her. For he had been told that she was of great beauty, and so perfect that in all the world there was none other like her. Since, also, there was in the world no other king of greater valour or of greater wealth than himself (Akbar), therefore the most beautiful of women was his by right. If she were not delivered to him he would harry the whole kingdom with fire and sword in order to accomplish his desire. Therefore it were well if the rajah agreed to send him the lovely Padmany (Padamawati),[1] as she was called, meaning 'the woman perfect in everything.' The Portuguese writer Faria mentions her many times.

The rajah replied to Akbar that he need not trouble himself to come, because rather than give up his wife he would lose a hundred thousand lives, and in case he resolved to come he would encounter a veritable Rajput. Akbar was angered at this answer, believing that there could not be in the world anyone who would dare to resist his demands or risk himself against his valour. He began his march to the fortress. When he heard of this movement, the rajah, who was called Jamel (? Jai Mall), which means 'Well-born,' with his brother called Fata (Fath)—that is to say, 'Victory'—came out against Akbar at the head of his cavalry, all of Hindu race and of the Rajput tribe. There followed many encounters in the open plain. For Akbar was anxious to demonstrate his bravery, his strength, and the wealth he possessed, and at the same time to

1. *Padmini* is the first and highest of the four classes into which women are divided by Hindus. Padmawati, a heroine of romance, is, I think, meant. So far as she is historical, she lived about 1303, and was taken by 'Ala-ud-din when he conqured Chitor. There are four poems in which she figures. Manucci's tale seems constructed out of three elements: (1) The 'Ala-ud-din story; (2) the attack on Chitor by Bahadur Shah of Gujarat in 1533 (E. C. Bayley, 'History of Gujarat,' 370), (3) Akbar's siege of Chitor in 1568.

prove that he was able to punish those who resisted him. He had taken with him a very large army, against which the brothers were unable to hold their own. They were therefore forced to take shelter in their fortress, where they endured an investment of twelve years. Akbar was astonished at such great persistence, and began to understand that there might be found in the world a fortress which could resist his victorious arms. Seeing that he was able to do nothing against this fortress, he made up his mind to continue his conquests [elsewhere], and leave this fortress in the hands of its owner, or, to speak more correctly, he feigned so to do, in order to acquire by means of treason what he had not been able to take by force of arms.

For this end he sent an ambassador to Rajah Jai Mall, informing [78] him of his intention to depart. Before starting, however, he would like to meet him, a feast by way of farewell. His reason was that he wished the pleasure of seeing such a valiant man; should he not wish to quit the fortress, he (Akbar) would go himself to say farewell, if permission were granted. The rajah, who would not venture to come out for fear of some treachery, and having no idea of what Akbar was about to do, replied with the greatest openness that, should he (Akbar) wish to come into the fortress, he would be thoroughly welcome. If the fortress had been closed against the great hero, it was only because he had tried to enter it as a conqueror; but when he wanted to enter in a friendly manner, its gates would be thrown open. The only condition was that there should not be more than five hundred persons in his suite. No offence ought to be taken at this condition; for, as a faithful vassal of the Rana, he was under an obligation to take the precautions usual in time of war.

Akbar accepted the proposal. He entered the fortress with his five hundred, where he was well received, and great honours were paid him. The rajah gave him a great feast, and laid before him many presents of valuable jewels. Akbar received all this with signs of friendship, and as a return for this good feeling, he gave to the rajah several elephants and caparisoned horses, also a sword accompanied by a shield ornamented with valuable stones, and other rarities. In the conversation that they had Akbar praised greatly the rajah's courage and that of his officers, but above all displayed his admiration of the fortress, declaring it to be impregnable.

With this talk he succeeded in gaining the affection of the rajah, and taking his leave, said to him that from that day henceforth he would always look on him as a friend. With these demonstrations of friendliness and such-like talk Akbar took his leave, the rajah escorting him as far as the gate. When the false friend and great conqueror Akbar found himself there, he raised his hand to his neck and took off a string of pearls of inestimable value, saying to the rajah: I offer you this string of pearls in remembrance of me, and as a mark of how much I like you.' So saying, he put the necklace round the rajah's neck. Then he (Akbar) embraced the rajah with both arms in such a manner that all of a sudden he dragged him out of the fort gateway. The five hundred men in Akbar's retinue placed their hands on their swords, and began to strike out right and left; and men held ready for the purpose ran up and carried off the rajah to the army before his soldiers could come to his assistance.

Great were the astonishment and upraor in the fortress; with equal expedition they closed the gates and stood to arms. They suspected that the enemy by treachery had made himself master of that invincible fortress. All the commanders hastened to their posts. It was only the chief of them all that was wanting—the rajah! Not knowing what to decide upon, they carried the sad news to lovely Padmini. She bravely replied that they should not lose [79] their accustomed courage, that they must consider the rajah as already dead, and that she had assumed his place in the defence of the stronghold. Thus the treacherous Akbar would not be able to triumph through his deceptions, if they on their side resolved not to falter. Inspiring the officers with fresh courage, she forthwith mounted a horse and seized a lance; and thus equipped, followed by all the officers, she went the rounds, giving new orders, saying that not only need they not fear the strength of Akbar, but she was certain and assured in her mind that they were able to resist the armies of the whole world, and she could never lose the fortress while backed up by such troops.

Akbar imagined that, having taken Jai Mall prisoner, the fortress was already in his hands, and that he was already in enjoyment of Padmini's beauty. He therefore wrote a letter to pretty Padmini requesting her to surrender the stronghold, adding that if she did not make it over to him, he would cut off the head of her beloved rajah, Jai Mall. The courageous

Amazon replied that so far as she was concerned Rajah Jai Mall was already dead, while to take his place there were within the fort other braver and stronger warriors. They counted this as the day on which the siege had commenced, and were determined to fight on while life endured. Never would they yield.

Akbar, seeing them so resolute, and knowing how stiff-necked the Rajputs are, raised the siege. But he left all the carpets spread in his tents as a sign that he would shortly return, and had not given up the hope of taking the place. He marched away and repaired to the town of Fatepur (Fathpur Sikri), which he had founded in remembrance of a great victory won over the Pathans. Here he placed Rajah Jai Mall in solitary confinement. Meanwhile he still solicited the famous Padmini with a thousand promises, letters, and valuable presents. He sent a message to her that if she would accede to the desires of a renowned king and conqueror, he pledged his word to make of her the greatest queen in his palaces. But Padmini would not consent, neither through messages, nor presents, nor soft words of intermediaries. She remained faithful to her husband.

Still, in order to deceive the deceiver, she pretended to have been won by Akbar's love. After much carrying of messages to and fro, she sent word to him that, overcome by his persistence, she had made up her mind to join him. There was, however, one condition: before she appeared in his presence she wished to say farewell to her husband, in order to be absolved from the oath of fidelity that she had given him. When that was done, she would without hesitation place herself at the king's disposal. King Akbar conceded everything that the lovely Padmini demanded, flattering himself that his pains of martyrdom were on the way to be soon assuaged.

She set to work to make the necessary preparations for her journey with great [80] pomp and majesty. She prepared a handsome palanquin, well closed up, collected many eunuchs and foot-runners to surround it, giving them orders not to allow anyone to come close to it. Then, pretending she had relinquished the fortress into the hands of Fath, she caused the closed palanquin to be sent out, accompanied by three thousand Rajput horse, all men of valour; following it were many other well-closed palanquins, as if each held a lady of her suite. The start was so conducted that everybody understood Padmini had gone (all except those who had been charged with carrying out the matter), and lamentation arose at the loss of such a princess.

When this cavalcade set out, a message was dispatched to Akbar, saying that the princess was now on her way, full of longing to take up her abode with him; but she sent a warning not to forget the promise that he had given her, to allow her to take leave of her former husband. If the slightest hesitation arose about this promise, she was resolved to kill herself, having brought with her for this purpose a large, well-sharpened poignard. The whole of this story was make-believe, for in the palanquins there was no one, while the horsemen were intended for the rescue of Rajah Jai Mall from prison.

Akbar, who thought that the princess in her letter was speaking the truth, sent to her many times messages with presents of fruit and flowers, displaying his anxiety to behold her for whom he had such ardent longing. On the arrival of the messengers, the clever eunuchs received the gifts, and, approaching the palanquin, pretended to deliver the message and receive the reply, which they invented themselves and sent back to the king. Once they returned an answer to the king that he must relieve her from such constant gifts, for was she not already assured of his affection and goodwill? The only thing yet to be done was to say goodbye to her husband, when she would be at his disposal. So great was the anxiety of Akbar to see the beloved Padmini delivered into his hands that he feared she might take her life with her own hands, believing that she spoke the truth, and he was anxious that nothing should be done to displease her. He sent back word that she might advance in all confidence, that he gave her the liberty of going wherever she pleased.

On the day that she was to enter the town the king sent out a lovely litter for her to ride in after she had said goodbye to her husband, also a number of palanquins and carriages full of ladies, a great many eunuchs, and all the state retinue of a queen. But the men on guard over the princess, having well learnt their lesson, allowed no one to draw near to the palanquin. They made straight for the prison where Rajah Jai Mall was kept, taking with them the palanquin, into which they put two men to cut off the fetters of the prisoner. On reaching the place he was freed at once. In a very little time three men came out of the prison, one being the rajah, who mounted a good horse, kept ready at hand for the purpose. He placed himself in the midst of his Rajputs, who were waiting for him and gave him hearty salutations; then, without delay, spurring [81] their horses, they rode off, leaving behind the empty palanquins and the astonished eunuchs and ladies who had come out to escort the princess to Akbar.

Akbar was waiting in a garden, where he intended to receive the princess. A messenger arrived in the greatest haste to acquaint him with what had happened. On seeing him, the king with a cheerful face asked him if the long-desired Padmini had arrived. The messenger hesitated, not liking to speak for fear the king might in a passion order his head to be cut off on hearing a report of the deception practised and the flight of the rajah. But upon Akbar repeating the question, he answered that the rajah had fled, and recounted the events. Akbar stood amazed at such a report, and pressing his head with both hands, said in a loud, heart-rending voice: 'I am deceived by those I had deceived!' Then he gave orders that the rajah should be pursued and seized. But before the order could be carried out the rajah had gone a long way, there being on the road many changes of horses. In a short space of time he arrived at the fortress of Chitor, where he was received with great rejoicing by all, more especially by the faithful Padmini, to whom was accorded the praise of being a clever, prudent, and experienced woman, who had known how with such finesse to regain her husband and deceive the man who imagined himself the astutest person in all the world.

When the rajah found himself again within his fortress, he sent a letter to Akbar, wherein he at one and the same time denounced his treachery, and intimated that, since women could do so well against him, he had no fear in challenging him to come once more to attack the fortress. He ordered the erection at the highest point in the Chitor fort of a pillar, on which were inscribed words to the effect that no faith should ever be placed in the treacherous Moguls. Angered and aggrieved, Akbar marched a second time against the fortress of Chitor, resolved either to lose his life or to take the place. It was invested, and at the cost of much bloodshed he raised a wall with a tower (*cavaleyro*, a cavalier, or tower upon a wall), and fought on for a long time without doing any harm to the fortress, although on both sides many men were killed.

It happened one day that Akbar was upon the tower (or cavalier), whence he saw a man appear in the fortress near the walls to make an inspection. He fired with his matchlock and killed the man. The following day he heard that the man he had killed was the Rajah Jai Mall, who, following the Rajput custom, was burned lying in the arms of the renowned Padmini.

This custom was introduced by a law of the great king Biguer-Majid (Bikramajit), founder of the city of Dihli, by reason of Rajput wives murdering their husbands by poison. By this glorious end was taken from the world the most beautiful woman of Hindustan, about whom there had been so many and such prolonged wars [82]. Thus Akbar with all his tricks could not achieve his designs, and her death put an end to the vain hopes of the enamoured king. He continued to invest the fortress, and the Rajputs defended it with the same valour as before.

The Hindu king, the Rana, seeing that Akbar did not mean to raise the siege, while on his side he had no intention of surrendering the place to him, sent out to sue for peace on the condition that the fortress should belong to neither him nor to Akbar. Akbar accepted the offer, and as a memorial of so many wars a tablet was placed above the gate with an inscription to this effect: 'Neither yours nor mine for ever.'[1] I have seen this stone several times, and up to this day it is in the same place; but the fortress was a mere night-shelter for herdsmen until Aurangzeb ordered it to be repaired, as I shall recount hereafter (II., 189).

Although King Akbar found that his conquering star did not seem willing to accord him the mastery over Chitor, not in the least did he on that account desist from attempting other enterprises. He took from the hands of the Pathans and of the Hindus the kingdoms of Bengalla (Bengal), and of Tata (Tatthah) or Sindi (Sind). In the latter is the fortress called Bacar (Bhakkar), of which I shall speak further on, in connection with the war of Prince Aurangzeb against his brother Dara, the heir-apparent (I., 225, 251).

It happened to Akbar, as it usually happens to conquerors, that he saw himself several times in peril of losing both his

1. Catrou, 82, renders it 'Ne vous fiez jamais aux Mogols qui vous ont trahis,' and attributes the placing of the tablet to the Rana. The text says 'was placed,' and the words are 'Nem eu nem vos pera sempre.'

conquests and his freedom. But the fidelity of his soldiers prevented ill-luck from overwhelming him. Among other risks he ran, one of the chief was when some of his captains put it into the head of his only son Janguir (Jahangir) to rebel. Jahangir assigned as reason that he was already of an age that made him fit to govern, and he did not approve of waiting longer; he meant to demonstrate his ability as a governor, and adduced other reasons equally devoid of validity. Jahangir, then a youth,[1] allowed himself, in spite of his natural goodness, to be led astray by the soft words of traitors, and rose against his father, hoping that Fortune, abandoning Akbar, would transfer herself to his side. But it was not so. Akbar was able to make such efforts that in a short time Jahangir was taken a prisoner. The love which Akbar had to his only son held him back from the severity with which he ought to have chastised him; still, he did not omit to give him somewhat of a lesson. Some days afterwards, when both were going out together to the chase, Jahangir saw on the roadside the impaled bodies of the rebellious captains. Akbar said to him: 'Thus are rebels dealt with; you knew well that I had no other son than you, and that you must inherit the whole of my conquests. Therefore, you set a very bad example [83], and historians will not fail to record you as the first of the great Taimur-i-lang's race who rebelled against his father. It may well be that the crime was not really yours, but that of those men there who gave you bad advice, for which they have received their reward. It very nearly happened that, as you had shared in the crime, so likewise you should have shared the penalty. But the love and affection that I have for you would not permit me to vent on you my just indignation.'

Since the killing of these captains induced perturbation in the army, Akbar decided on taking a rest for a time, to give opportunity for the remembrance of their impalement to be effaced. He resolved to found a city as a memorial of his victories, and gave to it the name of Fateabad (Fathabad)—that is to say, 'Peopled by victory.'[2] In this city he lived for some time. Then, for certain reasons, chiefly in order to reduce some rebellious

1. This revolt occurred late in 1600, when Jahangir was about thirty-two.
2. Evidently Fathpur Sikri, south of Agrah, is intended.

Rajput villagers, who objected to pay tribute until they had been overcome by force of arms, he (Akbar) decided to leave Fathabad and found another city twelve leagues off, on the bank of the river Jamana (Jamnah). For this purpose he selected the village called Agrah in the year one thousand five hundred and sixty-three. After the foundation of the city, it was renamed Akbarabad—that is to say, 'Built by Akbar.' Thus Fathabad became uninhabited. In spite of this, the rebellious villagers did not desist from their risings, chiefly round about the town of Matora (Mathura, Muttra), to which Aurangzeb gave the title of Essalamabad (Islamabad)—that is to say, 'Peopled by the Faithful.' Mathura is twenty leagues from Agrah in the direction of Dihli, and on the same side of the river Jamnah. The chief cause of these risings is their not wishing to pay the customary tribute.

When Akbar decided to build the city of Akbarabad, he gave an order that his palaces should be made of copper (*bronze*). But they represented to him that this could not be done. Enough metal could not be procured to erect lofty palaces such as the king desired. Another reason was that they would not be habitable in the hot season on account of the high temperature, or in the winter, from the great cold. Thus he abandoned this project, and built his palace and the fortress of red hewn stones of great size.

The city is situated in a great open plain on the bank of the river Jamnah, which, as it were, divides it into two halves on the eastern side. The city is a large one, with a circumference of twelve leagues, and is surrounded by many gardens. It is not walled, but nevertheless has great gateways in the principal streets. The fortress is placed on the bank of the river, with a ditch which can be filled [84] with water from the river. On both sides the fortress is adorned with beautiful palaces for the princes of the blood-royal and the grandees. Opposite these palaces, on the other side of the river, is a large garden and a village, and many tombs, of which I shall speak hereafter.

During the time that the said city was being brought to perfection the king's amusement was to mount on a mad elephant, simply to make it combat with another one. This is a very dangerous affair, for many elephant-drivers (*cornacas*) lose their lives in this amusement, and thus their wives, when drivers mount their elephants for a combat, break their bracelets and take off their jewels as a sign that they are widows. I shall speak of these elephant fights in another place (III. 20); the only object of what I now say is to let you know the courage of this king (Akbar), of which I now relate the following instance :

It happened that the villagers, of whom I have spoken before (*ante*, f. 83), raised such a great rebellion that Akbar was obliged to go against them in person. He surrounded a fort into which many of them had retired, a place that it was impossible to escalade. Therefore orders were given that the most courageous of the elephants should be sent to batter in the gate. He (Akbar) disguised himself, and at dawn appeared near the gate, and, mounting upon a very bold elephant, attacked the gate. In the first assault the animal was not able to knock it down; it was driven to the assault once more, the gate fell, and the fortress was taken. The driver of the elephant asked the pretended elephant-driver what his name was, as he was anxious to report his bravery to the king and announce that he was the cause of the victory. Akbar replied that before giving his name he wanted to know that of the elephant. The driver said the elephant was called the 'Active'; thereupon Akbar said that his name was 'Breaker-in of Gateways.' The following day, when the elephants were paraded before him, he gave to 'Active' the title of 'Active, Breaker-in of Gateways,' and made him captain of all the elephants, with an increase of pay. He rewarded the elephant-river by a serpao (*sarapa*), whereby the man learnt that the 'Breaker-in of Gateways' was the very king himself.

He had a great deal of trouble with these rebels, and after returning home victorious he was forced to order his captains to go against them several times. These officers, on reaching the rebel villages, carried out their orders to slay and behead (the only remedies he applied, and after him the other Mogol kings did the same). In order to defend themselves these villagers hid in the thorny scrub or retired behind the slight walls surrounding their villages. The women stood behind their husbands with spears and arrows. When the husband had shot off his matchlock, his wife handed him the lance, while she reloaded the matchlock. Thus did they defend themselves until they were no longer able to continue [85]. When reduced to extremity, they cut their wives' and daughters' throats, then in desperation they threw themselves against the enemy's ranks, and several times they succeeded in gaining the day by mere reckless courage.

Every time that a general won a victory the heads of the villagers were sent as booty to the city of Agrah to be displayed in the royal square before all the people as a proof of their success. After twenty-four hours the heads were removed to the imperial highway, where they were hung from the trees or deposited in holes on pillars built for this purpose. Each pillar could accommodate one hundred heads. Many a time have I seen in the city piles of these villagers' heads. Once I saw ten thousand of them; they could be recognised by their being shaven, with huge moustaches, mostly reddish in colour. In the thirty-four years that I dwelt in this Mogul kingdom I travelled often from Agrah to Dihli, and every time there was a number of fresh heads on the roadside and many bodies of thieves hanging from the trees, who were punished thus for robbing on the highway. Thus passers-by are forced to hold their noses on account of the odour from the dead, and hasten their steps out of apprehension of the living. The villagers were not able to take vengeance on their first enemy, Akbar, in his lifetime, but how they avenged themselves on his bones after his death I shall tell hereafter (I. 91).

Some astrologers assert that the planet Mars dominates this country (India), for even the animals are bold and resolute, and men who travel there, through drinking its water, acquire a great eagerness to fight. Thus it happened to an Armenian acquaintance of mine called Alaberdy. He had come to this country to sell some merchandise. After seven days had passed he felt an itching to quarrel, every moment laying hold of his sword as if making ready for combat. He began to reflect that he was a trader, and had come to sell his goods; it was not proper for him to risk the loss of his capital. He managed to suppress this impulse, chiefly from not being a man of much courage. There was no reason for his being so restless, but in spite of his reasonings he continued to feel these desires. Thus it is only fair to assert what I did just now as to [the cause of] this inclination. I noted with special interest as I travelled about in this country that all the oxen and cows of these provinces have their horns turned to the front and very sharp, and it is recognised throughout the Mogul realm that while only of small stature, and not very bulky, they are very savage.

On the occasion which was lately spoken of (*ante*, f. 84), when Akbar engaged in the great feat of knocking [85] down the gates of a fortress, a powerful Hindu prince said to him that he wished to give him a piece of advice if he would deign to listen to him. Akbar replied that he might speak openly. The prince told him that it was not a good thing to get upon an elephant by placing one foot upon its tusk, as Akbar and the grandees usually did in those days, the elephant being seated, for in that way they ran great danger of the elephant, when savage, killing the man who was trying to mount, a thing very easy for it to accomplish. It were better to mount at the side with the aid of a ladder. The king was pleased with the prince's advice, and put it into practice. To show himself grateful, he said to the prince that he was desirous of giving him, too, a piece of good advice; it was that he should return to his own territory. If perchance he (Akbar) or any of his descendants invited him to visit the court, he should send excuses, for a great man never had much benefit from a stay in the court of another great man, as the great never had much love or affection for others of their own rank.

He said this because he was aware of the way in which he himself treated the princes who attended his court—that is, he sought some method of giving them with civility some affront. This he did to another prince, to whom he had promised many honours. On arrival at the court the noble found that Akbar did not carry out his promises. On this account the prince was much distressed. To make fun of him, Akbar said to him that if it were his desire to leave for his own country permission would be given to him. This speech allowed the prince an opening for displaying by his very disgusted face how he felt the affront of such words, but he spoke not a syllable in reply. Noticing this silence, Akbar flew into a rage, and said to him that liberty to go home should never be accorded him until he had spoken in his (Akbar's) presence. The prince persisted in not speaking; he would not say even a single word. Thereupon the king issued an order that every time he sat in audience the prince must appear. It would be seen whether he would speak without being asked. Akbar was anxious that the prince should speak, so that he might give him leave to go. But he found that after coming for many days to audience, the prince could not be made to speak. Then he (Akbar) invented this trick to make the man speak without any question being put to him. He ordered them to find out what the prince was most interested in, and they ascertained that he was very skilful in the chase, and well acquainted with the points of animals. Orders were given that every day when the prince was present they should introduce talk about the virtues and properties of the above-named, but saying always the contrary to the facts. One day the king asked one of his intimates a number of questions about the nature and the age of animals. To these he answered the exact contrary of what is the case, when His Majesty displayed his admiration, and seemed perfectly satisfied with the reply [87], while the Hindu prince rubbed his hands, bit his lips, and changed colour, displaying every sign of wishing to speak and instruct them as to the truth. But, on account of his vow, he did not dare to speak unless spoken to by the king.

Finally Akbar asked how you could distinguish an old lion from a young one. They answered that the lion when old stuck his claws into the ground, and raising himself on his paws, gave forth roars that made the hills to tremble. This time the prince was unable to suppress his desire to speak. With an agitated countenance he said to the courtiers that he was much astonished at their temerity in telling so many falsehoods to such a famous king. He wondered much that, having no knowledge of such things, they should attempt to give descriptions as if they were past-masters in the subject. The other lies he would allow to pass, but must protest that when the lion sticks his claws into the ground, and lifting himself on his paws, roars aloud, it is a sign that he is young and is calling to his lioness. When he walks with the pads of his feet on the ground and his claws sticking up when he roars, it shows that he is old and is not in health. Akbar was very pleased at seeing himself at quits with this prince, who had refused to speak. He bestowed on him a string of pearls, an elephant, and a 'erpao' (*sarapa*, a set of robes), and gave him leave to depart for his own country. But before he left, Akbar demanded of him his tents, which were of scarlet colour and embroidered, sending him in their place others of a different colour. He imposed on the prince the command that he should never again use scarlet tents, and made it a law that only the Mogul kings and princes of the blood-royal should be allowed either to possess or to use tents of scarlet colour.

Although Akbar took rest several times for short periods, he was ever possessed with a craving for the conquest of new territory. Such was his anxiety that even in his sleep he was unable to refrain from giving hints of his designs. Once upon a time it happened that while asleep he rose to a sitting posture in his bed, made signs with his hand towards the territory of a Hindu prince, and laid hold of his chin with the other hand, as if defying him; for he shaved off his beard as do the Rajputs, with the idea of thereby winning them over with greater ease. These movements were noticed by a water-carrier of the royal household, who thereupon disclosed the king's intentions, saying the king meant to march against Raja Carn (Karan).[1] Off went several officials to tell the king that in the city there was much talk of his wishing to march against Rajah Karan. At this the king was much amazed, because he had wished to carry out this project without letting anyone know. He gave orders that they should [88] search diligently for the first publisher of this his purpose. On finding out that the water-carrier was the first spreader of the report, the king asked him if he had heard this piece of news from anyone. The water-carrier replied that one day His Majesty had made the gestures above described, and in this manner he had guessed his intentions, and in order to be ready for a march, he had begun to make the necessary preparations. Thereupon the king said: 'The fault is mine and not yours, for you show yourself rather a man of understanding than a culprit, and Rajah Karan is under great obligation to you.' Thenceforth he confided to the man a more honourable office.

Nevertheless he determined to attempt another enterprise. This was to make war against the Pathan tribe, which dwells on the other side of the Indus River, to the west, up to the boundary of the Kabul kingdom. There are in these regions several princes, all of whom dwell in the midst of mountains. They are a very ferocious people, of fair complexion, and all adherents of the Mahomedan faith. One of these princes alone can collect three hundred thousand lance-men, all barbarous, uncouth, and unruly, for they do not make much use of cavalry. Against them Akbar sent a force of eighty thousand cavalry, in order to force them at the least to submit themselves and pay tribute, imagining that the mere fame of his conquests, which had

1. Probably Rae Lonkaran, Kachhwahah, Shekhawat, of Sambhar, is intended (see Ma, *asir-ul-umara,* ii. 116).

subdued many princes and impelled them to offer relinquishment of their territories and payment of tribute, would equally impose on these Pathans the necessity of submitting.

Thus, the eighty thousand horsemen passed into the hills, but no one knew what happened to them, seeing that not one living creature of them all came out to convey the news of their fate. The rumour is that the guides conducted the army by certain difficult routes, and when they were once within the passes the inhabitants closed the exits, so that all died without effecting anything.

During the conquests that this king made in Hindustan, he acquired much artillery made by the Chinese, who in ancient times were lords of the whole of Hindustan, as I shall state hereafter under this same heading (I., 98). Although he had seen artillery fired off many times in battles, he was yet most anxious to see practice at a target. But finding that his gunners were no use at taking aim, and knowing Europeans to be most expert, he forwarded an order to the governor of the port of Surat to send him a good gunner.

There was at the time in Surat a very skillful Englishman (they say that the English were the first European merchants to arrive in the said port). With the permission of the chief of the English he was sent to the king, who assigned to him as pay the sum of five hundred rupees a month. However, the English race [89], like other Europeans, being fond of drinking wine, a thing they cannot procure in Hindustan owing to its prohibition under the Mahomedan law, the gunner, in spite of all those rupees, was most unhappy. One day Akbar directed the Englishman to fire at the target, for which purpose a great sheet had been erected in front of the palace on the bank of the river. The gunner intentionally fired the ball into the air, so that it disappeared. On this account the king was much put out, thinking that the gunner had no skill in aiming. He asked the man the reason of such a great error in his aim, when he had such repute in the art of discharging cannon. The Englishman replied that the mistake arose from his not being able to see; if he had drunk wine he could aim straight at the target. The king commanded that they should bring him spirits (of which there was no want in the royal household, where it is made for giving to the elephants to increase their courage).

When he saw the spirits, the Englishman was highly delighted; he seized the bottle, putting it to his mouth with the same eagerness that a thirsting stag rushes to a crystal spring. At one go he drank the whole, and then licked his moustaches. The king was amazed and astounded to see the great pleasure that the Englishman had in drinking spirits. Purposely the Englishman made all sorts of gestures to show his satisfaction; then, turning towards the target, he rubbed his eyes, and asked them to take away the sheet and replace it by a pot stuck upon a stick. So said, so done. He discharged the piece and knocked the pot to bits. At this the king and all the courtiers were lost in amazement at such a good shot. It was on account of this fact that Akbar conceded to Europeans the permission to distil spirits for their own consumption, and would not allow anyone to interfere with them. He said that as the European people must have been created at the same time as spirits, and if deprived of them were like fish out of their element, unless they had drink they could not see plain. Thus it is recorded in the chronicles of Akbar, and until this day the Farangis retain the privilege that he granted to them.

This affair was also the cause of Akbar's fondness for Europeans, and the reason why he ordered that a great number should be taken into his service, such as lapidaries, enamellers, goldsmiths, surgeons, and gunners of various nations. Among them there being many Catholics, they petitioned the king that either he would allow them to depart for their homes or permit the religious orders to settle in Agrah, for the fact was that without priests they could not exist. Akbar sent envoys to the city of Goa to obtain priests, whereupon the Jesuit fathers came. For them he ordered the construction of a church in Agrah, and thus first of all Europeans became servants of the Mogul kings.

Finding himself conqueror of almost the whole of Hindustan, Akbar followed [90] the example of his father. Although he made little account of his soul, he took care to prepare a resting-place for his body with extreme magnificence. For the site he chose a garden on the road to Dihli, at three leagues' distance from Agrah on the west, to which he gave the name of Secandara (Sikandrah)—that is to say, 'Alexandria.'

This mausoleum is a very large dome (vaulted roof) of great height, made all of marble adorned with many kinds of precious stones, the roof all gilded and enamelled in many pleasing colours. The garden is very large and pleasant, walled in on all sides, with various seats inside. There were drawings of human figures. Over these the king Aurangzeb ordered a coat of whitewash to be applied, so that the drawings might not be seen. He said such things were prohibited by the Mahomedan religion. I obtained entrance to this garden several times to inspect the mausoleum, being anxious to see the above-named figures before Aurangzeb should order them to be covered over.

The figures in the principal gateway of the garden were a crucifix, the Virgin Mary, and Saint Ignatius. I had a great desire to obtain entrance into the great dome I have spoken of, and at last one of the officials at the mausoleum, who was a friend of mine, and also wanted to make use of me, believing I was a physician, took me with him. The condition was that I should make a bow such as he made, with great reverence and punctiliousness, just as if the king were still alive. He opened the door, and I joined with him in making a very low bow in total silence, then barefooted I went round and saw everything. As I have already said, there was a holy crucifix delineated on the wall, on the right hand of the crucifix the image of Our Lady with the infant Jesus in her arms, while on the left was Saint Ignatius, the whole delineated.[1] In the ceiling of the dome were great angels and cherubim and many other painted figures. There were also many censers which were lighted every day. The hall is paved all over with stones of different colours.

Outside the mausoleum, in the garden, were many Molas (*Mulla*)—that is to say, learned men—reading the Quran. On the dome outside, on the very highest point, was a ball, and upon it a pyramid, the whole gilt. Most curious of all is the reason for having these paintings; it was only because they were a novelty in those days; it was not on account of religion. During the time that Aurangzeb was actively at war with Shiva Ji,[2] the villagers, of whom [91] I spoke before (I., 84), broke into the mausoleum in the year one thousand six hundred and ninety-

1. Compare all this with Catrou, 114, who reproduces *capa di calzo* as a *piece de brocard d'or*, and turns the wall-paintings into a crucifix in relief and two *statues*. Nor does Manucci say that he received any permission from Aurangzeb to visit the tomb.
2. Note that here, as often elsewhere, Shiva Ji is used generically for the Mahrattahs. Rajah Shiva Ji having died in 1681, Aurangzeb could not be fighting him in 1691.

one (1691),[1] and after stealing all the stones and all the gold work to be found, extracted the king's bones and had the temerity to throw them on a fire and burn them. Aurangzeb was much put out at the boldness and unruliness of these villagers, and ordered against them his valiant Bader can (Bahadur Khan), of which I will speak in its proper place (II., 252).

Akbar had been anxious for a long time to satisfy two subjects of curiosity, which he kept in his heart. The first was to know what language a child would speak who had not the use of speech or any master to teach it.[2] The second was to find the source of the famous river Ganges. For the first of these inquiries he ordered the erection of a house with many rooms at a distance of six leagues from the city of Agrah, and directed them to place in it twelve children, who should be retained there till the age of twelve years. An injunction was laid on everyone that, under pain of death, no one should speak a word to them or allow them to communicate with each other. This was done, because one set of men asserted that they would speak the natural language, that which was the language of our first parents. Others held that they would speak the Hebrew language; others that they would not speak anything but Chaldean; while the Hindu philosophers and mathematicians asserted that they must infallibly speak the Samskript (Sanskrit) language, which is their Latin. However, the twelve years having passed, they produced the twelve children before the king. Interpreters for the various languages were called in to help. Each one put questions to the children, and they answered just nothing at all. On the contrary, they were timid, frightened, and fearful, and such they continued to be for the rest of their lives.

For the second inquiry he selected persons of good judgment and provided them with everything necessary—servants, conveyances, and sufficient money. They were on their travels for several months, and at the end of the time they returned

1. For this desecration of Akbar's tomb, see ii. 252, and the note there given.
2. For Akbar's own account, see H. Beveridge's 'Father Jerome Xavier,' *Journal of the Asiatic Society* (Bengal), vol. lvii., 1888. Part I., p. 38. See also 'Akbarnamah' (twenty-seventh year of the reign), 'Bibliotheca Indica 'edition, iii. 393; Lakhnau edition, iii. 241, line 6; and 'Muntakhab' (Budauni), Lowe's translation, vol. ii., p. 296.

and repaired to the king. He asked them what they had seen and where they had been. After all, the only thing they could say was that they had climbed many mountains, keeping always to the course of the stream, which each day grew smaller. After much marching, they arrived at mountains covered with forest. Here they had hard work to get through. When they had traversed these woods, they encountered a very high and large mountain having at its foot a great cow's head sculptured out of the very rock. From the mouth in this head issued a stream of water with such force that no one could keep his feet in front of it. They exerted themselves to ascend the great mountain, to see whether there was any river on beyond. But it was not possible to reach the top. Therefore, they turned back and reported what they had seen. I am unable to affirm whether this was verily [92] the river Ganges or not. For it would require one to exhaust one's purse, and perhaps lose one's life, if another attempt were made.[1]

There happened to this king several things which will either be of use as a guide to his descendants or will serve to divert the reader. The first of these that I wish to recount is what happened to Akbar with a *baniani* (*baniya*).

The reader ought to know that the *baniyas*, of whom I will speak after the death of Akbar, under a separate heading (I., 100), are very chary of giving a direct answer. Akbar was desirous of satisfying his curiosity by an experiment on this great reluctance to answer. He gave an order that the chief of the *baniyas* should be sent for. This threw the whole of them into a great state of mind, and they assembled in much dread and tribulation beneath the fort to see what was going to happen. The chief of the *baniyas* entered the royal palace all of a tremble, surmising that some misfortune was about to befall him. On reaching the presence of Akbar, who was taking a walk in a

1. On this question of the source of the Ganges and the cow's mouth carved in the rock, see Bernouilli, 'Researches sur l'Inde,' 1788, ii, 282, where, in a treatise on Tieffenthaler's map, Anquetil Duperron quotes F. Catrou, 'Histoire,' i. 162, 264 (101, 102 of 4to. edition). Anquetil also refers to a statement by Terri (E. Terry), printed in Melchizidec Thevenot's 'Recueil,' i. 10, and to Petis de la Croix's translation of 'Sharaf-ud-din,' iii. 131,139 (English edition of 1723, ii. 78), or the Persian text, 'Bibliotheca Indica' edition, ii. 145, or Elliot, 'Historians of India,' iii. 478.

garden on the banks of a stream, Akbar asked him where that water went to. The *baniya,* confused and frightened, shook his head without saying a word. The king showed himself angry at this delay, and directed him to reply without any fear. The *baniyd* answered tremblingly that, if His Majesty pleased, would he allow him the space of thirteen days in which to reflect over such an important piece of business ? The *baniya* left the garden, much puzzled over such a question, while Akbar smiled to himself. Seeing that the king knew where the said water ran to, the *baniya* argued that the question must conceal some mystery.

Hardly had the man left the fortress, when all the other *baniyas* ran up to find out from their headman the reason of his being sent for. He replied in great dejection that he invited the oldest of them to his house, where he would disclose the royal questions. On arriving there he told them the whole matter, stating that he had not had the temerity to reply, since the king knew very well which way the said water ran; and as the king made himself out so simple, they ought to look out for some mishap. They were all amazed, not knowing what to think; they all anticipated ruin, and remained silent. Only one man got on his feet and said that if they would agree to give him something for his trouble, he would offer himself as able to satisfy the king without doing harm to anyone.

When the thirteen days had elapsed, men came from the king to summon the headman. He pretended he was very ill, and sent back [93] excuses to the king, and said that he would send some one in his place. When his reply came back, and along with it the substitute, this fresh *baniya* was called in, and Akbar asked him where the water went to. The wary and astute *baniya* pretended to be plunged in thought, as if he had no anticipation of such a question. After a few moments he asked for leave to tell a story. The king gave permission. It was about how he had married, and the sum of money that his father-in-law had promised him. After the marriage the promise was not kept. On his demanding payment of the debt, his father-in-law gave him a box on the ears. As he talked he moved his hands about, and when he said that his father-in-law hit him on the head, he struck his own hand on his turban, causing it to fall into the channel. Turning round, he looked on in amazement at seeing his turban moving along with the current of water. Then he turned to Akbar and said, as if astonished: 'Your Majesty saw whither the water carried off my turban?' In this mode he pointed out where the water of the channel went. The king laughed heartily at seeing the *baniyas* so crafty in their affairs. He gave this baniya a serpao (*sarapa*) and made him head of them all, he being a man of some estimation in his tribe.

If the case of the *baniya* is a curious one, none the less curious is that which befell Akbar with the poor man. You must know first that in the Mogul kingdom there are different kinds of poor, otherwise called *faquires* (*faqir*), who ask alms. The more important among these are the *bequedes* (*be-qaid*)—that is to say, 'liberated'; while others are *beters* (*be-tars*)—that is to say, 'fearless.'

The first are very rude in manner, using great liberty in speech, fearing no one and paying no one respect, whatever his rank, using much abusive language and scandalous words, or polite sayings, just as it pleases them. These men often enter boldly into the houses of great men, and if the doorkeepers stop them from going in, they apply to the whole family much abusive language, sparing neither master nor mistress, nor sons, nor grandchildren, nor ancestors, coupling their names with the coarsest abuse. In spite of this the people of the house show no anger, but secure their departure by soft words, giving them some alms and begging their pardon. If the *faqirs* are allowed entrance, they march straight to where the master is and seat themselves close to him, although dirty, their feet all over mud, and clad in filthy rags. Without any deference or civility of speech, they take the tobacco-pipe out of the master's mouth and place it in their own. With much respect the master returns thanks for this honour, and secures [94] the man's departure by some money. They are so contumacious and insolent that sometimes they are not satisfied with what they get, and it is necessary to give them all they demand. Never do they beg you to give for the love of God, imagining they would anger God by asking alms in His name, alms being such a petty thing in comparison with the greatness of God. Everyone tries to find a means of satisfying them without showing any hesitation, for fear of some curse. In addition, the people of Hindustan are very kindly and compassionate.

The beters (*be-tars*) are faqirs who ask for alms with a sharp knife in their hand. They place themselves in front of a shop, and begin to shout for alms to be given them, pointing at what they want. When the shopkeeper refuses to give a man what he asks for, he wounds himself on the arms or on the head or on the legs, and, taking the blood, throws it into the shop as a sign of his curse. Ordinarily these faqirs ask for alms at the shops of the baniyas, who are very timid, and rather than see such wounds, give them what they ask, usually some money.

Akbar having noticed this class of *faqirs,* who cut their own bodies, concluded that such men would be sure to fight with great spirit and courage. He selected four thousand as armed horsemen with good pay, and he sent them against the villagers of Matora (Mathura). At the very first advance, without waiting for the fighting to begin, all of them turned tail, and fled as hard as they could go. On hearing of this cowardly flight, Akbar ordered them to be summoned, and asked them the cause; they had not even waited for the enemy, and yet had such courage that they inflicted wounds on themselves. Their reply was in very few words, and they made Akbar understand that their making cuts on themselves was not courage but deceit. They said: 'When we cut our own flesh, we avoid veins, nerves, and bones; but an enemy wounds without mercy, and it does not suit us to have our bodies cut about by the hands of others.' The king on hearing these words thrust them forth, being satisfied at having unveiled the cowardice and the deceit of this sort of faqir, of whom in the Mogul country there are to this day a great number.

I will now write of two cases which led to Akbar's leaving behind him regulations for his descendants. The first case was when at one stroke he raised one of his servants of low rank to the position of a great lord. This man, finding himself so suddenly wealthy, fell into anxiety about his manner of living, his behaviour to others, and the regulation of his expenditure. Thus by the next day he was mad. On hearing what had happened, Akbar fixed as a rule for his [95] descendants that they should not make any man a grandee all at once, but only little by little, and as a fact the royal house observes this rule to this day.

This rule was good, but the following one was nothing more than a piece of diabolical policy. It happened that Akbar had married his daughter to a noble. After a time this son-in-law rose in rebellion with the idea of obtaining the throne, but fortune did not favour him in this enterprise, for he was captured through treachery and beheaded. Thus Akbar bequeathed to his descendants the rule not to give their daughters in marriage. This rule remained in force up to the time of Aurangzeb, who gave his daughters in marriage upon their insisting, as I shall recount hereafter (II., 41). However, although not married, the princesses nevertheless were not without their hidden pastimes. Recollecting what Shera—*i.e.*, Sher Shah— had done to his father, Humayun—that is, he rebelled because he found himself very wealthy—Akbar left it as a law to his descendants that the Pathans should never receive higher pay than four hundred thousand rupees a year, that they were not to be appointed governors, and should only be employed as soldiers.

The grandeur he had attained and the conquests he had made rendered Akbar so proud that by his ordinance no one was allowed to sit down before him, except those of the blood royal. Unto this day this regulation is observed at the court of the Great Mogul. Everybody stands, only ambassadors receiving permission to be seated in the royal presence. Nor was he content with this, but ever grew in pride, as we read in the Holy Scriptures: 'The pride of the enemies of God grows ever more and more' (*Superbia eorum qui te oderunt ascendit semper*). He attempted to found a new sect, a mixture of the faith of the Jews, the Christians, and the Mahomedans, with much taken from the Hindus, adding certain matters invented by himself. His ambition was to display himself as a new founder of the faith, and therefore he entitled himself 'Xa Gelaludim Akebar' (Shah Jalal-ud-din Akbar), which means 'King powerful in the sovereign faith.' But God did not accord him time to accomplish his intention, for, coming to an end of his ill deeds, he procured his own death when trying to kill others by poison, as I now recount to you.

Akbar was a great warrior and also a great hunter. When he sought relaxation after any victory, or when awaiting an enemy, his usual diversion was to march hither and thither, enduring great fatigues, in search of something to kill. Since he was very bold, he went into the woods and wastes and mountains without [96] any protection. Once it happened that, with the greatest eagerness, he went into the hills to kill a tiger, having failed in getting a shot at it. Separated from his men and weary, he sat himself down beneath a shady tree. While reflecting on what it was best for him to do, there came towards him a hairy creeping thing of scarlet colour. Akbar took an arrow from his quiver and slew the creeping thing or worm (*verme*), the arrow falling on the ground before him. Hardly had the creeping thing or 'worm died when a deer passed in front of him. Taking up the same arrow with which he had slain the serpent, he fixed it in his bow and shot at the deer, which forth with fell dead, without having been wounded in a mortal place. Akbar was amazed at seeing the fallen deer lying quite motionless. He was still considering what could be the reason of such a sudden death when the huntsmen arrived, who were in pursuit of the same deer that the king had killed. On their appearing, he gave orders for the deer to be dragged before him. The huntsmen laid hold of the deer, when it fell to pieces, one portion here, another there, the whole being rotten. The king was astonished and amazed, and suspected that someone had done him a trick and placed poison on the arrows. He asked what could be the cause of this thing. The huntsmen answered that the deer had died of some subtile poison. Thereupon the king said that before shooting at the deer, with the same arrow he had killed a worm, to which he pointed. The huntsmen examined the snake and then begged the king to leave the spot at once, for that worm was the very essence of poison, its smell alone was sufficient to cause death. If it had done him no harm it was because he had sat to the windward, and thus the smell could not reach his royal person.

The king ordered that the said snake should be kept and put in a glass phial; and he confided to an official the duty of preserving poisons so that they could be produced when he gave the order. This practice has been passed on to all the Mogul kings, it being one of the bad examples that Akbar bequeathed to his descendants. The official has the care of various poisons, and when the king desires to take the life secretly of any grandee, he orders the poison to be applied on the hood and the cuffs of the *cabayas* (*qaba*, Persian, 'a long gown') which are given at his audiences to those present at court; or to those who are not there he sends a messenger with this kind of robe (serpao =

sarapa),[1] and thus, under the cloak of honour, abridges their lives. In this manner Akbar killed many princes, who either, afraid of his power, came voluntarily to offer their submission and pay him tribute, or, overcome in battle and warfare, were forced to submit themselves [97].

The policy of thus getting rid of these great men he bequeathed to his descendants, who unto this day follow it with great exactitude. The practice consists in never showing any irritation, whatever be the offence committed by these princes or rajahs. On the contrary, at such junctures he made a show of being well-inclined towards them, gave them promotion to higher rank, and, if away from court, sent them friendly letters. Having thus put them off their guard, he took their life by poison, which was put upon the gowns or other presents.

He employed another method at court, whereby he finally met with his own death. The reader should know that the greatest honour that can be done by a Mogul king to a favoured person is to give him with his own hands a folded betel-leaf. Akbar did this honour to various persons at different times; but many, having been thus honoured, died shortly afterwards. This king had a box to hold betel with three divisions: in the first were the leaves; in the second, the restorative pills which he ate; in the third, other pills, poisoned but quite similar to the restorative ones. When the king was pleased to confer a very great honour, he gave a betel-leaf and then one of his restoratives. But when he meant to kill anyone, after offering the betel, he handed him one of the imitated pills, whereby without fail the man's life was sacrificed.

It happened one day that the king wished to kill one of the grandees, and took by oversight one of the poisoned pills and ate it, taking it for one of the restoratives, with the object of giving confidence to the other man. After a little time he recognised the mistake he had made; but there was no remedy, and thus, through his own death, was disclosed the way that he had killed others. This was the well-earned chastisement of his crimes, and he received the measure that he had meted out to so many others.

Leaving an only son, Janguir (Jahangir), he was buried in the tomb that he had himself prepared, as I have already said

1. *Sarapa*, literally 'head to foot,' a complete set of robes of honour.

(I., 90), after having governed Hindustan for forty-nine years, seven months, and three days. There is no doubt that this king was the first who brought Hindustan into subjection, and was the most successful in war. He transmitted to his descendants several precepts of policy which, although not suitable for a mortal man with an immortal soul, who knows that he must give account before God for all his deeds, and there obtain their merited reward or punishment, were still in accordance with the faith of Muhammad. They demonstrated that Akbar was a man of good judgment, if we are to speak of him as a whole.

With regard to Akbar's possession of artillery in Hindustan, and also in connection with the affair he had with the *baniya*, the opportunity is given me to speak first of the Chinese, secondly of the *baniyas*. I judge it appropriate to place here what I have to say on these two points, in order to afford the reader clearer and more distinct information as to how very probable it is that the Chinese were once the lords of Hindustan, and also to paint in accurate colours the astuteness of the *baniyda* [98].

PROBABILITY OF THE CHINESE HAVING BEEN IN HINDUSTAN

I opine that this little account will be of some satisfaction to the reader, more especially at a time when so many write about the Chinese, their empire and their conquests. Although I do not affirm that the Chinese were in ancient times masters of any other countries besides China, nevertheless it appears to me very probable that, in addition to the lands they now occupy, they might once have had a much more extensive empire. I could adduce many reasons for this assumption of mine, but as I have decided not to write on any other subject than the Mogul Empire, I leave it to other inquiring minds to deal with this question. All I will say is that there is a good foundation for asserting that the Chinese were once lords of Hindustan, and that they were ejected by the Pathans, seeing that they were opposed to the entrance of foreigners into the empire of China, and put to death those whose evil fortune impelled them to enter the Chinese territory.[1] On the whole, it

1. The second half of this sentence is obscure, but it reads so in the text.

appears to me the strongest reasons for affirming that the Chinese were once in Hindustan are the things I have seen there; of which I will give a brief account to the reader, leaving it to him to decide whether they ever were or not in the lands of which we are speaking.

During the time that I dwelt in Hindustan I saw various ancient buildings with many Chinese images and letters cut on the stones and other such works, all of which give rise to the idea that the Chinese had dwelt here. Two leagues from the city of Dilhi there is an ancient city called Cojacotobdim (Khwajah Qutb-ud-din), so named from an ancient tomb, still existing, whose builders have vanished. At this place I have seen several times a very ancient hall built of great stones. In front of the said hall there is a pillar of bronze[1] buried in the rock; it is two arms' length in height and nine palms in circumference. On this pillar there are some engraved letters, and to this day no one has been able to recognise what letters they are, although many inquirers have done their best to find out what they are meant to denote. The inhabitants say that the letters are Chinese.

Signs of the presence of the Chinese are not wanting in Hindustan. These are found chiefly in the country of the Dacan (Dakhin), where there is a hill called Alura[2] (Ilurah, Ellora), twenty-four leagues distant from Aurangabad, towards the west. At that place there are several caves dug out by pickaxes, forming lovely open courts, halls, rooms, cells, having corner-stones ornamented with various Chinese figures, and some reservoirs of natural water provided with many steps. In one of these halls there are thirteen statues, sculptured out of the live rock. Each one has its own special form. The principal statue is one with a wound on the finger and a comical expression of face; it is

1. As to this pillar, which is of iron, see Carr-Stephen, 'Archaeology of Delhi,' pp. 16-24, and A. Harcourt, 'Guide,' p. 115. The inscription, in an ancient form of Nagari script, was first deciphered by James Princep, and, of course, has no connection with the Chinese language or people.
2. Ellora is about fifteen miles north-west of Aurangabad (see Willmott and Syed Hossain, 'Sketch of Nizam's Dominions,' ii. 440, who quote, on pp. 442-448, Jean Thevenot's description of his visit in 1667). Mr. Burgess has published a full account in his 'Rock Temples of Elura' (1877).

breathing on the wound and writhing its body. The others behold this figure with wonder and amaze [99]. One bites his lips, another puts his finger in his mouth, another holds his head with both hands, another twists his nostrils, another seems to be weeping; the eyes of another are starting from his head with fear; one has his mouth open, another bites his tongue; one has his hands folded, another is in the act of striking the ground with his foot, one has his hand placed over his mouth, and another is holding his heard. These works of art are in an open place. As they are so cleverly done, and their appearance somewhat Chinese, many say that they were executed by the ancient Chinese. Besides these statues, there is in the same place a fallen building which seems to have been a tower. At the foot of it are many stone figures resembling the Chinese.

I also visited the island of Salcete (Salset),[1] owned by the Portuguese, and not far from the town of Bassaim (Bassein). In the middle of this island there is a mountain having many sculptured figures and many dwellings. You go into a very deep cave which is quite dark. When you have got well in you hear a great noise of waters. An inquiring Portuguese of some boldness went in with a light until he reached a deep cavern, whence issued the noise of running water. He threw in a bundle of straw, which came out in the river six leagues from the said cave, near a village called Thana, which is situated in the same island, near the mainland. The inhabitants of the island, and the most experienced old men, say that this labyrinth is extremely ancient, made in the time when the Chinese were lords over India; that they cut through a tongue of land to allow of the passage of the river, and thus formed the island. It can be plainly perceived that this is the work of man's hand, for if you cross the river at its narrowest part you can see (and I have seen) the severed rocks.[2]

1. Salsette (Sashti) is an island to the north of Bombay Island, with which it is now connected by a bridge and causeway. It is eighteen miles long by ten broad. The hill in its centre is called Kaneri (Kanheri). Thana is about three miles east of that hill ('Bombay Gazetteer,' xiv., Thana,' pp. 121-190).
2. As Dr. Codrington points out, this is a mere fancy. The island of Salsette is formed by the Bassein creek joining the Thana creek at Thana, the junction not being artificial or through any high or severed rocks; it is a tidal way of a not unusual kind.

On the coast of Choramandal, near the sea, there is also a rock called Mavelivarao (Mahaballipuram),[1] distant four leagues from a place called Sadrasta patao (Sadrasta-patanam, or Sadras), where there are many sculptured figures resembling Chinese.

There is also on that coast a town called Negapatao (Negapatanam),[2] and outside the town on the sea-beach is a large temple (*pagode*) known as the China Pagoda. In the year one thousand six hundred ninety and two there was a war between the Dutch and the owner of that territory. Lourenco Piter,[3] who at that time was governor of Negapatanam and of all the Choromandal coast, ordered this pagoda to be destroyed; and he converted it into a battery, on which he mounted eight pieces [100] of artillery. More than half of the pagoda was knocked down after the greatest exertions. They discovered in the pagoda, between the walls, many images of a metal which looked like gold, and up to this day no one knows of what kind this metal is. The images were Chinese.

I reserved for this place what I have to say about the artillery that Akbar possessed in Hindustan, because the statement I am about to make may be held a novelty in Europe—that is to say, the idea that the first inventors of artillery were the Chinese. For the most experienced historians of our Europe write that artillery was invented in the year one thousand three hundred and eighty by Bertoldo Nigro, a German, whereas the artillery owned by Akbar was much older. I have seen many large cannon of excellent metal, with the breach made plain just like a drum. The imperfection of the work proved that these were the earliest; nor can the credit for such work be given to any other nation than the Chinese, who of all peoples are noted as the most ingenious. Thus it becomes proved, as the most

1. Maha-bali-puram, or Seven Pagodas, thirty-three miles south of Madras 'Madras Manual of Administration,' iii. 806). Sadras is a town on the coast, seven miles south of Seven Pagodas (*ibid.*, 775).
2. A town on the sea coast, in the Tanjur district, 160 miles from Madras. An ancient brick tower, 70 feet high, of supposed Jain or Buddhist origin, is known as the China tower (' Madras Manual of Ad.,' iii. 581).
3. This is Laurens Pit, the younger, who was Dutch chief at Negapatanam in 1690, 1691 (see Dubois, 'Vies des Gouverneurs generaux,' pp. 247, 263). He also conducted the correspondence with Johannes Bachurus, an envoy sent to the Mogul's Court in the Dakhin.

probable opinion, that the Chinese were once in ancient times the masters of Hindustan.

ABOUT THE BANIYAS

Events give rise to the writing by historians of many things they would not otherwise record. Although I meant to write elsewhere about these *baniyas,* of whom there are many in the Mogul kingdom, I apprehend it to be appropriate to write about them here, seizing the occasion of what happened to Akbar.

The *baniyas* are a certain class of Hindus who eat neither flesh nor fish, and only consume grain, vegetables, milk, and a great deal of butter. They are very desirous of owning a cow, from the worship that they pay to this animal. They are so devoted to the cow, in whom rests their entire hope of salvation, that in the agony of death they take hold of a cow's tail and die with it in their hand. By this act they imagine they are absolved from all their sins; they think that the cow carries them aloft into the sky without their touching those flames of fire that they have merited for their sinful deeds. It is amazing to see the foolishness of this ill-placed devotion [101] paid by them to cows, for when perchance the animal urinates on the dying man while holding its tail in his hand, far from trying to keep him out of the way, they say that he has been made holy, and perform great rejoicings at great expense in gratitude for such a favour.

The reader must understand that it is not only the *baniyas* who thus reverence the cow, but also the whole of the Hindus, of whatever station in life. But the *baniyas* are the most superstitious on this subject. So much is this the case that when anyone commits a great sin—that is to say, either against the idols, or by forsaking his religion—if he consents to cleanse himself of such sin, he goes to the Brahmans, who are their priests. They give him cow-dung dissolved in its urine, adding a little butter, some sweet and some sour milk. On drinking this he is absolved, and some penance is added. I have seen one of these men with a padlock hanging from his lips, and he went about with it for some days as a penance.

By nature these *baniyas* are very timid, and object to carry arms. This is why they do not keep any weapons in their houses, neither a knife nor other implement by which injury can be inflicted. They are very careful about the answers they give to questions, as can be seen from the affair which I recounted a little time ago (I., 92), and, according to popular sayings, it is their habit to dissemble even when someone asks them what day it is (they are, however, much more ready to answer if you talk about business). They give a useless answer; but if the questioner insists on a reply, they say first of all that they do not know. After that, if he still demands a direct answer, they say (for example): 'Do you not know that yesterday it was Thursday?' If the other returns to the charge, they say: 'Do you not know that to-morrow is Saturday?' And if the inquirer persists, they answer with hesitation: 'Everybody says that to-day is Friday.'

On the contrary, if the talk is of business, they give a ready answer, and are such strong arithmeticians that in the shortest time they can make any sort of calculation, never making a mistake of a single figure. They hold it as a great sin to kill any animal. Therefore, if they find on their bodies any louse, bug, flea, ant, or other kind of vermin, they lay hold of it gently with the tips of their fingers, and carry it away to a distance into a place of security. In their houses they have different receptacles full of these animals, whose sustenance is provided in the following manner: They search for some necessitous wretch, and paying him money, leave him for the whole night bound upon the receptacle or the bed, and in this way the animals referred to are fed; for these *baniyas* are of a character more full of charity for animals than for men. Thus they make for animals niches in the walls of their houses, where all sorts of birds assemble to build their nests. To these they give food [102], and never do them any harm.

In the kingdom of Guzurate (Gujarat) there is a town near the sea called Cambaya (Khambayat, Cambay); there these *baniyas* have a hospital for sick birds, and reward a surgeon for treating them. Once they got an injured falcon, and it was put among the other birds, whereupon it began to kill and devour its fellows. Upon seeing this, they turned it out, saying that it must be of Farangi race.

These *baniyas* have great veneration for the river Ganges. They say that by bathing your body in it you attain redemption and become delivered from your sins. The same end is gained for those whose ashes are thrown into that river. For this reason,

IX. Jahangir

Vol. I *To face page 153*

after burning the dead man's body, as is the custom, the ashes of great nobles are carried from great distances followed by a great concourse, with much ceremonial and expenditure, to be thrown into the said river.

The *baniyas* carry this Ganges water in brass vessels through the kingdom far and near for delivery to their devotees, from whom they receive their reward. Many Hindu princes hold it a religious duty to drink such water. To this intent they send camels, who daily go and come, even if it be a two or three months' journey. There is another piece of foolishness they have—that is to say, when a man is near death they carry him to the bank of the said river, and finish off by killing him by dint of its waters. It happens often that out of devotion men die on the banks of this river, as I have seen, and the Hindus who pass by throw the body into it. This will suffice for an account of a people who do not deserve the name of man, who are to be found in great numbers in the Mogul kingdom.

OF JANGUIR (JAHANGIR), FOURTH KING OF HINDUSTAN, NINTH OF THE RACE OF TAIMUR-I-LANG

It is a truth tested by experience that sons dissipate what their fathers gained in the sweat of their brow; nor do all sons imitate the good qualities of their ancestors. Thus it was in Hindustan, for, after having seen one king who was a great soldier and a great conqueror, such as Akbar was, it had for king his only son, Jahangir, a man with no desire to undertake the labour of further conquest, one who contented himself with enjoying the fruit of his father's labours.

This king was fond of feasts, dancing, and music. Just as much as he was a friend of and devoted to these amusements was he inimical to the Mahomedan religion. For this reason he did many [103] things against it, chiefly in not observing the fast customary among the Mahomedans, in drinking wine, in eating pig's flesh, and other such things. In these actions he sought a means of scoffing at the Mahomedans, which I will recount as I proceed.

Once he sent for the Jesuit fathers and asked them what pork tasted like. They replied that it had a special taste and a most extraordinary flavour. He was desirous of eating of this flesh, and visited the house of the said fathers. There he ate pork and drank wine, and acquired such a liking for such food and drink that subsequently he ate it and drank wine publicly many a time. The learned in the Mahomedan law gave him to understand repeatedly that wine and pork were prohibited in the Quran. Enraged at so many warnings, he sent out orders one day to assemble all the learned men. He inquired from them the religions in which it was allowable to drink wine and at the same time eat of pork. They replied that only the Christians had that liberty. He (Jahangir) then said publicly that he meant to become a Christian. To this end he forthwith ordered that tailors be summoned to cut out clothes after the European fashion, and that search should be made for hats. The learned men were in amazement, and taking counsel together, said that the king might eat and drink whatever he liked. I have met persons who were present at the time.

Jahangir, finding these men so easy to deal with, seized every occasion to aggravate them. To this end he ordered the casting of several figures of pigs in solid gold, which he kept in his palaces; and when he awoke from sleep, on seeing these images, he used to say he would rather see the figure of a pig than the face of a Mahomedan. These figures remained until his death, when his son Xaaiahan (Shahjahan), who then became king, ordered them to be buried in front of the royal seat in the fortress of Lahor, where Jahangir usually lived. Many a time I sat there with the governor of the fortress. He used to say to me that if he had the wealth then beneath his body he would be a very rich man. This governor's name was Amanatcan (Amanat Khan),[1] an old man belonging to the times of that king (Jahangir), a great friend of mine and of all Christians; he delighted to listen to talk about the Gospel. It was in this hall that King Jahangir gave audience; it was three hundred paces long and two hundred and fifty wide.

Among the other things done by Jahangir to annoy the Mahomedans was refusing to fast as they do every year for a whole

1. Apparently the man meant is Mirak Mu'in-ud-din Ahmad of Khwaf, made Amanat Khan in the early years of 'Alamgir's reign. His first entry into the imperial service was in 1050 H. (1640-1641), and he died in 1095 H. (1683-1684). He was grandfather of Shah Nawaz Khan, author of the 'Ma, asir-ul-umara' (see that work, i. 258-268) In 'Khafi Khan,' ii. 261, Amanat Khan is named as a former Diwan of Lahor. He appears again in Part V., f. 26.

month. During the daytime they eat and drink nothing; it is only at night they eat what is then made ready; during the day they retire [104] and go to sleep. At night they are jovial, taking their meal and conversing with their house fully lighted up. This king (Jahangir) did the exact contrary. Not a day passed without his giving audience, as he did near the middle of the day for about two hours or more, so as to incommode the people about his court. He ate and drank in front of them all, giving portions to those who seemed to him the most bigoted, with a view to make them break the fast. They ate for fear of an order being given to throw them to the lions. There beasts were kept in his presence, and were used to put to death whomsoever he pleased. Besides this, he had a small tray in which there were some very sharp lancets. When any soldier came into his presence with a courageous look or with his turban cocked, he called him near, and with one of the said lancets pierced his nose. If the soldier showed that it hurt him, he ordered the man to be ejected from the court with cuffs and buffeting, saying that a soldier who was afraid of such a little piece of iron as that would never in war-time endure lance-thrusts and sword-cuts. On the contrary, if the soldier made believe to meet the lancet without fear, he would double the man's pay, and his estimation rose at court. The king would say such men deserved the name of soldiers—they were veritable men of war.

It happened that a soldier killed a tiger, and making the skin into a coat, came to court with great pride. On seeing him, Jahangir fired his gun at him, and the bullet went through the man's leg, so that he fell where he stood. The king said: ' If I had not killed that tiger my lion would have got enraged.'

If there was any youth too lively and too fond of women, he would order him to be shut up with a woman of low caste, dirty, malodorous, and covered all over with filth. Thus he would leave the youth for several days, punishing in this manner the riotousness of youth.

He never forgave his physician, a very religious man, who came to court once when the king had already several cups in his head. Jahangir called for a bow and arrow wherewith to slay the physician. The queen, who was behind a screen, humanely ordered them to produce arrows of cane, so that the king might not kill him. Thus, when the physician arrived, he shot at him with the said arrows. In spite of this attack the physician behaved in a very dutiful manner, though the king never desisted from shooting at him. At length the courtiers, by order of the queen, made a sign to him that he should fall to the ground. He fell as one dead, and Jahangir said that he deserved death, having by his pretences taken the life of many a one. All this he did by reason of the displeasure he had against Mahomedans.

Some assert that Jahangir was willing to become a Christian, and this is why [105] he mocked so much at the Mahomedans. Many times he ordered the learned men to dispute with the Jesuit fathers over the Faith in his presence, and the fathers always came out the victors. Once the learned men, not having any other answer to give, replied: 'What can we reply? Those with any knowledge are aware that our reasons are the stronger'—that is to say, that the Gospel was falsified. Of the givers of this answer, among the rest was the *Qazi*. The father retorted instantly with some animation: 'On this very spot I can prove to your majesty and the whole court that the Gospel which I hold in my hand has not been falsified, but is the Truth. If you will order a stack of straw to be brought into your majesty's presence, I, with my book in my hand, will seat myself on the straw, and there shall also be seated with me the *Qazi* holding his *quran*. When we have seated ourselves in this manner, let them set the straw alight, and thus will be seen which faith is the true one.'[1]

The *Qazi* was in great fright at this speech; and knowing that Jahangir was just the man to make the experiment, he dropped his head, the colour left his face, and trembling, he defiled himself, filling the whole court with the odour, but answering never a word. When the smell reached Jahangir, he held his nose, as also did the courtiers.' Then he spoke briefly: 'I see that the padre is ready to prove the truth of his faith, but the *Qazi* is already in a fright, and has made one mistake.' He said

1. Catrou (i. 119) says this story is attributed in Europe to P. Rodolfo Aquaviva in the time of Akbar. See E. D. Maclagan's article on 'Jesuit Missions to the Emperor Akbar,' *Journal of the Asiatic Society of Bengal*, 1896, Part I, pp. 41, 51, quoting 'Budaoni,' ii. 299 ('Bibliotheca Indica'). Bernier has the story of Pere 'Atash,' with slightly different details ('Travels,' edition Constable, p. 288). H. G. Keene ('Turks in India,' 1879, p. 255) says Joseph de Castro died at Agrah in 1646. His tomb is among those in the Padre Sântus Cemetery there (see Father Symphorien's article in the *Transactions of the Archeological Society of Agrah* about 1874).

to the padre: 'Your name shall be from this day forth "Padri Atax" (Atash)—that is to say, 'Father Fire.' The name of the padre in question was Joseph da Costa, a Portuguese by race, but after this he was always called Padre Atash.

Jahangir, being at his palace within the city of Lahor, which he had built upon a river called the Ravy (Ravi), saw a covered boat pass with its curtains down. When it arrived near the royal seat, he saw that in the boat was a beautiful woman. He fell so violently in love with her that he had no sleep nor rest; but the woman replied firmly to all the solicitations made to her on behalf of the king, that she was the wife of a soldier of position named Xir Afgam (Sher Afgan)—that is to say, 'Tearer of Tigers'—nor would she hear a word from any other man so long as her husband remained alive. The king, who was deeply in love with her, sent an order to the governor of the city of Patana (Patnah) that as soon as Sher Afgan should arrive there with a letter he must be slain. This was done, but the valorous soldier, although taken unawares, killed five persons in defending himself. Sher Afgan being dead, Jahangir took the woman [106] into his palace. The condition made was that she should be principal queen, and her father be made *wazir*, with absolute power throughout the empire, her brothers and nearest relations to be grandees at the court. All of these things were conceded by the king; he made a grand feast which lasted for eight days, and many gifts were conferred on all the men at court. The queen thus obtained, to whom Jahangir gave the title of Nur Jahan—that is to say, 'Dawn of the World'—governed the kingdom, and did everything that she pleased. She was a woman of great judgment and, of a verity, worthy to be a queen. They struck coin in her name, which had for symbol the twelve signs of the zodiac, and in her time these were current money.

Nur Jahan succeeded in making the king drink less than he had done formerly, and after many entreaties he agreed that he would not drink more than nine cupfuls. Every time he drank it must be offered by her hand. If on any account he should ask for more, he was to be satisfied to allow her to put him off by excuses. Many days had not passed when the king, being engaged in listening to the singing of his musicians, began to drink joyously. In a short time he had come to the end of his nine cupfuls. As the music went on he asked for more, but the queen would not give it, saying that he had already had his nine cupfuls, and she did not mean to give him any more. Jahangir went on asking for just one cup more. When he saw that the queen would not give ear to his words, he fell into a passion, laid hold of the queen and scratched her, she doing the same on her side, grappling with the king, biting and scratching him, and no one dared to separate them.

The musicians, hearing the noise going on in the room, began to call out and weep, tearing their garments, and beating with their hands and feet, as if someone were doing them an injury. Thereupon out came the king and queen, who had been struggling together, to find out the reason of all these cries. Seeing that it was a feigned plot of the musicians, they fell a-laughing, and the fight ended. The king was highly delighted with the trick played by the musicians, to whom he gave a handsome reward.

But the queen, after the custom of petted women, showed herself more angry and offended than before. She would neither take his gifts, nor listen to the excuses he made to her. In the end, through a third person, she gave Jahangir to understand that the only way of being pardoned for the affront was to throw himself at her feet. The king, who could not live without Nur Jahan, was willing to carry out her wishes, but he feared to be blamed for such an act, which would give rise to a great deal of talk among his people; therefore he took counsel with an old woman. At once she got him out of his difficulty by advising him that, when the queen was walking in the garden, and the sun was shining on her, he should place himself before her in such a way that the shadow of his body should reach [107] the queen's feet; then he could beseech his loved one as if he were at her feet. The old woman got the queen into the garden by beguilements, and thus the king approached until his shadow was at the feet of the queen. Then he said to her, 'Behold, my soul is at your feet!' and thus peace was made.

The queen, to show that her heart was won by so much love, invited the king to a sumptuous banquet, lasting eight days. She ordered all the reservoirs, both in the garden and in the palace, to be filled with rose-water, prohibiting anyone from washing his hands in these reservoirs. It happened that she went to sleep near one of the tanks. At early dawn she rose, and as she was anxious that no one should foul the water in these tanks, she went at once to see if there had been any defilement. She noticed on the top of the water a film of oil. At this she flew into a passion, suspecting someone had thrown fat into this tank. She was curious to know what it could be that had dirtied the water, so she ordered someone to pass a hand over the oil referred to. Smelling it, she found it had a very sweet smell. Two or three times she smelt it, and each time was aware of the same smell; hence she concluded that the said oil had formed from the rose-water like dew. Very much pleased at having acquired such an excellent perfume; she quickly rubbed some on her clothes, and went off to embrace the king. He was asleep, but on being roused he was lost in admiration at such a fine perfume, while Nur Jahan recounted to him the story. It was thus that the secret of essence of roses was discovered in Hindustan; and in those days a hundred rupees were paid for one rupee's weight of the said essence. Nowadays it is to be got for fifteen rupees, owing to the great quantity of roses grown in the empire.[1]

I was anxious to find out the descent of this queen, and I came to know for a certainty that she was the daughter of a Persian who arrived from Persia as a camel-driver in the service of some Armenian merchants. He brought with him his wife, who was *enceinte*. On the way, near the fortress of Candar (Qandahar), she was delivered of a child, and one of the merchants lent him an ass on which to convey the woman in that state of distress. The child that was born in this miserable plight came to be this most famous queen (Nur Jahan). Through her influence the court of the Great Mogul was filled with great nobles from Persia [108].

This king was very fond of carrying out works for the benefit of the public and the adornment of his kingdom. To this intent he issued orders to have trees planted on the royal highways from one end of the country to the other, commencing at the city of Moltan (Multan), and going as far as the city of Ilavas (Allahabad)—that is, for five hundred and thirteen leagues. At the distance of one league apart are to be seen something like pyramids, and by these the traveller can reckon the distance he has traversed. Near to every such pillar there is a village for the refreshment of those passing by. On these roads are found *saraes*, reservoirs, gardens, and villages.

1. This story of the discover of essence of roses is to be found in the Indian histories. The place assigned is the Shalimar Garden, just outside Lahor.

The king came out to inspect this work of his, and went from Lahor as far as Agrah. One night, being in his tent drinking his liquor, he heard the jackals call. These are a breed of small wolves which exist also in Persia, and in India there are a great number. The king asked why these animals were not quiet. The courtiers answered that, knowing of the arrival of His Majesty, they craved some protection against the cold. Jahangir there and then ordered that they should be presented with 'serpaos' (sarapa, or complete suits) and shawls to wear. The order was carried out. No one failed to approve this regal generosity.

The night following, once more the king heard the cry of the jackals. He inquired if his order had been carried out. On receiving an affirmative reply, he wanted to know why they repeated their calls. The courtiers answered that this time they had not come to complain, but to render thanks to His Majesty for the alms given them by him on the preceding night. The king was highly pleased at this answer, for the Moguls are very avid of praise. So much is this the case that flattery, which to European princes would appear mere mockery, would by the Mogul king and grandees be accepted as sincere laudation. Though they are quite aware of their falseness, they are pleased nevertheless to hear such words, and swallow them at their superficial valuation.

I will recount here some ridiculous instances, and I am telling the truth without the least exaggeration. If a Mogul king or prince sees an elephant or a horse not of very much account, and should say that it is a fine elephant or a powerful horse, then the courtiers begin to praise the elephant, saying that there is not in the world another as large or its equal in strength and staunchness; that once it fought against five or six other elephants clad in armour while it was unprotected, yet it routed them all; that, being present in such and such a war, it threw the enemy's army into confusion and disarray; that its trunk could carry more than would go on the backs of five or six other elephants, and other things like this, which, if I were to state, the reader would think me fooling him.

In the case of a horse, they would at once say that it is of such mettle that it would pass through hills of fire. If they discharged a whole battery of artillery at once in front of it, it would not, owing to its high courage [109] and temper, stir more than if it were made of brass; of such cleverness that you need only move the rein a little to get it to carry out the order that the rider had in his head; and that on the occasion of a battle it could jump at one leap a river as wide as the length of a musket-shot.

I beg the reader to believe that it is impossible to set forth completely the flatteries used by the courtiers; they exaggerate everything excessively in order to find favour with the great. On the other hand, if a great man, on seeing a handsome elephant of great height and well-proportioned body, or a well-made horse, says something depreciatory as to these animals, those present begin at once to express all the ill that can be said of an animal, calling it wretched, miserable, timid, out of condition, of no use. With all this the great men are delighted, for two reasons: first, to see others adopt their opinions out of mere submissiveness; secondly, because these flatteries divert their minds from the cares they have.

What I have mentioned about animals may equally be said about men. For to have the repute of valour, it suffices that a noble praise a man; and to be scouted, even if a valiant soldier, it is enough for a great man to say a little word in dispraise. It is the same thing also about women. A woman may be really foul and fetid, but a great man need only say a word in her favour, and she becomes a Venus descended upon earth; while a woman may be really lovely, and if a noble for his own ends runs her down, all who are there make her out to be so repulsive that never in the world was seen such a coarse creature. This will be enough to put the reader in possession of the extent to which the Moguls are flatterers, each one working for his own ends in every matter.

Although this king was of a kind disposition, seeking methods, as I will tell hereafter, of doing good to all except the Mahomedans, there was, in spite of this, a Rajput prince, master of twenty-five thousand horse, who considered himself aggrieved because the king would not give him what he asked. One day he had the temerity to come with his cavalry to the city of Lahor, beating his drums, a thing that no one may do except the king, and posted his army on the bank of the river at a little distance from the royal palace.

Jahangir was amazed at such temerity, and wanted to take vengeance on him for this affront. But he did not judge it in accordance with his own greatness to send out an army against such a petty prince. He decided to send for a cavalry soldier named Mahobet (Mahabat Khan).[1] One day Jahangir had gone out shooting, and getting separated from the rest of his companions, became tired out and hungry. Mahabat was the only man with him. Making some cakes, he got a light by firing his musket; he then roasted two of them on a little spit, and sprinkling salt and pepper [110] on them, gave them to the king to eat. This made Jehangir anxious to reward this cavalry soldier; he therefore sent for him and asked him in secret if he would undertake to kill the Rajput prince. Mahabat replied: 'It is for your majesty to order and me to obey.' To carry out the project he requested that he might have a pearl necklace, a jewel ornament for the breast, and a set of robes of honour (*sarapa*), and, in addition, as his companion, one of the king's scribes who was his special friend, also his majesty's boat with energetic rowers. All this was agreed to by Jahangir.

Mahabat with the above-named preparations left the city at eight o'clock at night. On drawing near to the Rajput camp, the sentinels challenged and asked who he was. He answered that he was an envoy from the king who came to speak to the rajah. Mahabat instructed his companion to remain with the door-keepers, and when these men should be heavily asleep warn him by coughing at intervals.

Mahabat went in and accosted the rajah with a most cheerful face, and, full of confidence, said that he had come from the king to inform him how much his majesty loved him and cherished him to a high degree. To show that these were not mere words or inventions, he had sent as marks of the favour he held him in this string of pearls, this jewel, and this rich set of vestments. He was considered at court to be a brave and valiant captain, worthy of the most honourable employments; thus the king was anxious to employ him in some extensive enterprise, and to reward him as far as was in his power.

The rajah, puffed up at this news and proud of the present the king had sent him, conversed pleasantly with Mahabat. With delusive words the latter said to the rajah softly that the course he had followed was excellent, for if they did not act like that the Rajputs would never be esteemed. With such talk he kept

1. Mahabat Khan, Khan Khanan, Sipahsalar, Zamanah Beg, son of Ghyur Beg, Kabuli (see 'M-ul-U,' iii. 385-409). He died in 1044 H. (1634-35).

the rajah up till beyond midnight. The Rajputs who were in his company, heavy with sleep and full of opium, of which they are accustomed to take largely, went out a few at a time, and the rajah was left alone intoxicated with praises and flatteries.

Seeing that the rajah was now alone, and his companions at the door coughing at intervals, Mahabat decided that it was time to make the *coup* he had designed. Thus continuing the conversation, he said: 'The king is so well inclined towards you that he enjoined on me to seek every mode of smoothing away your grievance. He is therefore very desirous of favouring you, nor does he wish that you should be any more offended. As a mark of this desire he gave me these orders, whereby you are made viceroy of the kingdom of Bengal.'[1]

Saying this, he drew out a bag of gold brocade, and placing it on his two hands, presented it with great deference [111]. Then suddenly he struck the rajah through the heart and down as far as the bowels with a sharpened knife hidden in the bag. He issued from the hall silently, leaving the unfortunate prince dead, and passing through the door, took with him his companion. They got into the boat and hastened back to court, where the king was waiting for him impatiently to know what had happened. He was so much on the *qui vive* that he heard the sound of the oars, and with a shout he cried in a loud voice: 'What news, Mahabat?' The valiant soldier replied: 'My lord, the rajah is already dead.' At this the king was much contented, and made Mahabat a great man in his court, transgressing the rule bequeathed to him by his father that no one should be promoted to great station all at once. He gave the man the title of Mahobet Can (Mahabat Khan)—that is to say, 'great affection.'[2] In this manner this man became in a short time the greatest general at the court of the King Jahangir. He treated the Rajput princes with great friendliness, and succeeded with great skill in attaching them to his interests.

1. Mahabat Khan (Zamanah Beg), while still a boy, was in Jahangir's service from before his accession. The accepted story of this assassination is given in 'Ma,asir-ul-Umara,' iii. 386, and the victim was the Ujjainyah Rajah of Parganah Bhojpur in Bahar (represented now by the Dumraon Rajah in the Shahabad district). Jahangir had called for some volunteer to deliver him from this *ganwar* (rustic).
2. This is a wrong etymology, the word being from *haib*, 'fear,' and it means 'august, majestic.' *Mahabat*, 'loving,' is from a different root.

Although the kings of this world hold it as part of their glory to exalt their courtiers, they are not always rejoiced to see them powerful. Often the loyalty of a grandee is in their eyes treason. Thus happened it to Mahabat Khan. Although faithful to his sovereign and grateful for the benefits conferred, and seeking every mode of showing his fidelity, he was nevertheless an object of envy, not only to the other courtiers, whose nature it is to be envious, but to the *wazir*, Ascef Can (Asaf Khan),[1] the king's father-in-law, and to the queen, who sought for a way to have him assassinated. To this intent they placed ten thousand armed horsemen on the roads, hoping to get him killed. But on learning of this treachery, he (Mahabat Khan) went to the palace and entered, unheeding the protests of the door-keepers. Reaching the king's presence, he advanced closer than allowed by etiquette. The king was amazed at so much boldness, and dreaded his doing some violence. He asked Mahabat Khan what he wanted.

The valiant general replied: 'I desire that your majesty do me the honour of coming to my house, for it is most necessary.' Saying these words, he seized the king's hand, who, observing his determined manner, made no resistance, although in great trepidation. He came out of his palace followed by some soldiers who had entered with Mahabat Khan into the royal presence.

No sooner had they reached the gate of the fortress than Mahabat Khan gave orders for the king to mount his elephant, and behind him was placed one of the Khan's Rajput soldiers, blind of one eye, with a drawn sword in his hand. After they had gone a few yards the king complained that the soldier had a foxy smell, and wanted him removed. Mahabat Khan replied: 'It is very obvious that if your majesty [112] had any general as brave as these soldiers of mine, I should not have ventured to carry you off to my house, as I am doing.'

They passed through the roads where were posted the armed horsemen sent to slay Mahabat Khan; but no one attempted to use force for fear the Rajput might decapitate the king. Thus the king entered into his general's house. The queen and the court expected that Mahabat Khan, having killed Jahangir, would crown himself king, and all the city was in great confusion. But

1. I'timad-ud-daulah Mirza Ghyas Beg, Tahrani, was the father of Nur Jahan. He died 1031 H. (1621-22) (see 'M-ul-U,' i. 127). Asaf Khan was her brother.

Mahabat Khan had other intentions. Therefore on arrival at the house he made his king take a seat in the best place in his mansion, while he himself stood humbly and respectfully, waiting on him and offering him various fruits and perfumes.

The king showed great desire for wine, and wanted the queen. But Mahabat Khan said wine-drinking was not good, and as for the queen, she would come, but for the present he should take repose. The night passed without his getting any wine. Everyone expected that Mahabat Khan would declare himself king, but when the morning came this loyal subject had a long talk with the king. He demonstrated to him that, to deliver himself from death and save his own life, he was forced to make use of this means and attempt more than he designed. He had made use of his majesty's person as a refuge from the hands of traitors. He complained much about his mode of government, telling him that it was indecorous to let a woman govern the empire. He gave him other reproofs, and declared himself a loyal vassal; after saying this he drew his sword, presented it to the king, and, placing himself on his knees, said that if the king held him culpable in any degree, or was himself to the slightest extent offended, he could order his head to be cut off with the very sword which had been dedicated to the defence of his royal person.

Jahangir, finding him so submissive, took him to his arms and said he need not be afraid, no one should harm him; he gave his word and swore on the Quran to hold him ever as his most loyal servant. He would therefore defend him against everybody, and declared himself much obliged for the good advice he had received. As further confirmation of his love, Jahangir ordered the queen to come to his place of detention. Mahabat Khan prepared a magnificent banquet, which lasted for three days. The queen presented him with many gifts, swearing to hold him always in favour and acknowledge him for the most loyal vassal in the whole kingdom. The king increased the rank of Mahabat Khan, and until this day this family still exists at the Mogul Court in considerable dignity. I had a great friendship with the son of this Mahabat Khan, who also had the same title. He was a general much esteemed by the king, Shahjahan, but further on I will say something more about him (I., 212) [113].[1]

Jahangir was by nature very generous and grandiose; the least sum he ever ordered to be given to anyone was one hundred thousand rupees; nor was it seldom that he made this present; he did so many times, just as if it were of no account, while it is a large amount. The king ordered one hundred thousand rupees to be laid on the ground so that he might see what height it had. This was done. The *wazir* believed that on seeing its bulk he would be more chary of ordering the giving of so much coin. It was the contrary that happened, for he said he had thought one hundred thousand rupees would take up more space; and thus, from this time, when he made a gift, he ordered the double to be given of what he had given before. The wazir repented of having thought he could thereby check the king's extravagance.

It happened that a French trader called Monsieur Bravet brought from Europe some bric-a-brac, which, although curious, was of little money value, hoping to sell it to the king. Jahangir, who was well inclined to Europeans, directed that the whole of the things should be bought, and whatever the sum the owner asked should be paid to him. This was done accordingly, and they paid him thirty thousand rupees, which are equal to fifteen thousand patacas.[2] Afterwards all the things were laid before the king, who was much delighted with such a set of curiosities. Among the other trinkets was a very tiny padlock, which Jahangir took in his hands, and admiring it, said such a padlock was not the work of human hands, but of angels. He added that no one but the King of Hindustan could pay the price of it, and after many exaggerated words he directed them to give the merchant thirty thousand rupees more, for the padlock alone was worth the whole of the money. To get presents or rewards from this king it sufficed to say some witty thing, whereupon he would give elephants and a number of rupees.

1. Mirza Lahrasab, Mahabat Khan II., Governor of Kabul, eldest son of Zamanah Beg, Mahabat Khan I., died at Amanabad in the Panjab in 1085 H. (1674-75), aged sixty-two years (' M-ul-U,' iii. 590). Two sons survived him.
2. As before (I., 6), the *pataca* is here shown as worth two rupees. Yule (683) says *pataca* was a name for a dollar, or piece of eight.

While Jahangir was a liberal giver, neither was he reluctant to allow any and everyone to approach his person. It seemed as if this king was born to be a contrast to the pride of his father, who never spoke to anyone but the grandees. On the contrary, this king often walked about alone and in disguise. It happened one evening that he went into a tavern, where he found a man singing and already merry from the wine he had drunk. The king was pleased at seeing so much mirth, and seating himself near the man, made himself his friend and drank along with him. After several drinks the king asked his new friend what he was called. He answered that his name was Alexandre (Alexander or Sikandar), the weaver, and gave him directions as to where he lived. After complimentary speeches on one side and the other [114] the king demanded food and more wine. The weaver, in gratitude to such an excellent comrade, invited him to come next day to his house, as he wished to regale him. Thus they took leave of each other with many civilities.

The following day the king rode out on his elephant to find the rendezvous. He ordered them to pass through the street where the weaver lived. At the time the royal cavalcade and the elephants were passing Sikandar was busy attending to his preparations for the day's work, with a hammer in his hand, knocking into the ground the pegs to which his ropes were to be fastened. The messengers asked him where Sikandar the weaver lived; the king had come in search of him to dine with him. Recognising that, without a doubt, the man who had eaten with him the day before must be the king, he fell into perplexity. He pretended that he had not heard. The king had now come close, while the messengers insisted on his answering and telling them where Sikandar lived. Without lifting his eyes, and as if he did not know what they wanted, he exclaimed in a loud voice: 'Anyone relying on a drunken man deserves a severe blow with this hammer.' The king laughed heartily at this response, and ordered them to give him a reward, which was so great that he ceased to work as a weaver.

A similar case occurred with a drunkard who, meeting the king on his elephant, began afar off to shout out, asking whether he wanted to sell his elephant. Jahangir gave an order that the drunkard be detained and brought the next day into his presence. When the man was produced, he was asked if he wanted to buy the elephant. The reply was that 'the purchaser was outside; he was nothing more than the broker.' The king was pleased with the answer, and rewarded him with an elephant.

It was not only this once that the king showed himself capable of making light of regal pomp, for many times he did similar things, in scorn of the pride and imperturbability of the great nobles. Sometimes he passed through the city upon his elephant, followed by many elephants, on which meat was being cooked, or wine and drinking-cups, bread, a supply of pickles, and small boxes of fruit, were carried. Others bore musicians, instruments, and drums, making a great noise. Jahangir sat eating and drinking.

One day he came with this array into the royal square, where there was a crowd of mendicants called 'Bequed' (*Be-qaid*, 'emancipated'). When they beheld the king, they cried with loud voices: 'Oh! you eat by yourself and drink without sharing with us.' On hearing this, the king descended from his elephant and sat himself down in the midst of them, eating and drinking, accompanied by music and mirth. The faqirs, who had already been drinking, began to give every one of them his criticism on the manner in which he ought to govern. Having listened patiently until they had finished talking, he fell a-weeping, and sent them on their way [115].

Weeping came easily to Jahangir, for without any reason at all he would burst into tears. It was enough for the queen to deny him a drink of wine to drive him to tears, and to dry them you had only to present him a glass well filled with liquor. Anything and everything made him cry, just as any sort of gift sufficed to pacify him.

Although of such a soft disposition, he was still very watchful that real justice should be done; and if he was loved by the people, he was feared by his officials. These were compelled to walk in the right way, since, if they went wrong in any matter of justice or in any important business, he ordered them to be thrown to the lions, which were always present in his hall of audience.

It happened one day that he was on the banks of the river and saw a pot carried down by the stream. He ordered that this pot should be produced before him. It was found to contain a dead body cut into pieces. Orders were given for the officers of justice to discover the culprit, with the warning that if they did not find him, all of their heads would be cut off. Among the other expedients they resorted to, one was to order every potter to deliver one pot, and by examining the marks on these, they hoped to trace the vendor of the pot in question. It is customary in the Mogul country for every potter to put his own special mark on his pots. It was thus that they caught the culprit.

Another time, returning from the chase, he saw the officers of justice carrying away a Rajput to be hung. The king asked what offence he had been guilty of. They replied that he had forced a Mahomedan woman, then present and demanding his execution. The king called the woman before him and asked her if the Rajput's body was hairless, like he was in the face. 'Yes,' answered the woman. She supposed that as it is the fashion of the Rajputs to shave their beards, they must also be accustomed to remove the hair from all the rest of their body. The king ordered an examination. It turned out that the woman had raised a false complaint; whereupon he ordered that the woman should die and the Rajput be released. He also fined the officials for their negligence.

Among the other fancies that he had was a particular affection for the Jesuit fathers. He gave them a house and a church in Lahor. In that reign Europeans had much freedom in regard to hearing about Christianity; and the said fathers instructed the king's sons, one of whom, by reason of some affront received from the fathers, after he had become king, sent an order to burn the church and carry off the bell at Agrah, as I shall state hereafter (I., 137). It is now time to speak of his sons.

Jahangir [116] had no son by his beloved queen Nur Jahan, but there were two by other mothers. The heir-apparent was Sultan Bolaqui (Bulaqi),[1] and the name of the other son was Sultan Corram (Khurram). Bulaqi had two sons, of whom I will speak farther on (I., 120); Sultan Khurram, besides two sons, Dara (Dara) and Xaxuja (Shah Shuja') had a pregnant wife with the most extravagant fancies and complaints. Jahangir gave the order that when this princess was delivered he should be informed in

1. *Bulaqi,* a pet name from *bulaq,* an ornament worn by women; it hangs from the cartilage of the nose. His real name was Dawar Bakhsh, and he was the *grandson,* not the son, of Jahangir. His father, Jahangir's eldest son, was Khusru. and as he died in his father's lifetime, 1031 H. (1622), aged thirty-six years. Dawar Bakhsh, according to Mahomedan law, was excluded from inheritance, and had no rights to the throne.

whatever place he might happen to be, and if asleep they were to awake him.

The princess brought forth a male child, and at once they went to report to the king, who at that moment happened to be relieving himself. Jahangir said that if that prince survived to be king, he was destined to conquer the whole of Hindustan. Nor in this did he deceive himself, as we shall see hereafter, this child being that same Orangzeb (Aurangzeb) who now reigns.

Sultan Khurram, who was the second son, perceiving that his father Jahangir favoured the sons of Sultan Bulaqui, and intended their exaltation, went into rebellion. He took up arms against his father, but was defeated several times. After his last defeat he passed near to Ugolin (Hugli), in the territory of Bengalla (Bengal), a village that the king Jahangir had given to the Portuguese in order that they might frequent the said port. Some Portuguese sallied forth and seized two beloved female slaves of the princess Taigemahal (Taj Mahal, a corruption of *Mumtaz-mahal*, 'chosen one of the harem'). This lady sent word to them that it would be better for them to help a prince then seeking refuge in flight than to attempt to rob him. Therefore she urgently prayed them to send her the two slave girls. But the Portuguese paid no heed to her request, an act which cost them dear, as I shall explain hereafter (I., 120, 121).

Meanwhile Sultan Corram (Khurram), pursued by the forces of his father, finally took refuge in the territories of the King of Vizapur (Bijapur). He lived in a town called Juner, distant thirty leagues from the city of Bassaim[1] (Bassein), which belongs to the Portuguese. The King of Bijapur ordered that one of his own houses should be given to the prince to dwell in, with a garden full of vine-trees, where I have been myself. Thus was Jahangir delivered from the attacks of one son, who left behind him nevertheless this bad example to a new generation of revolt against his father. He had learnt it from Jahangir, who rebelled against his father, Akbar.

Jahangir followed his father's example, and gave orders for his tomb to be erected opposite the royal palace at the city of

1. Bassein, a town twenty-eight miles north of Bombay; Juner, a town in the Puna district, seventy miles east by north of Bombay. The two towns are about seventy miles apart. Khurram did live for a time at Juner (see 'Ma,asir-ul-Umara,' i. 163, article on 'Islam Khan').

Lahor. In preparing this mausoleum he went to great expense, building a dome adorned with many precious stones. These were removed by orders of King Aurangzeb, only allowing stones of small value to remain, such as agate, amethyst, turquoise, and such-like [117]. These stones were cut into the shapes of various flowers.

Some years before the death of Jahangir it happened that the secretary (*wazir*) presented to him a Persian, exaggerating greatly about him, and saying that he was known to everyone in Persia, and even to the king himself, who ate salt in his house. As the king heard this about him he made him a great noble, and gave him the title of Cassam Can (Qasim Khan). Persians are famed for favouring their own nation in the Mogul Empire, and the larger number of the nobles are Persians. But in addition to this, the wazir was indebted in some small way to this vendor of salt, and desired to favour him on this occasion, so that he might share his (the *wazir's*) own good fortune. Others told the king that this so-called Qasim Khan had been a seller of salt in Persia, and Jahangir asked the *wazir* why he had uttered such encomiums of a man who sold salt. The *wazir* replied: 'Let your majesty fully understand that he sold salt in Persia, for I said that even the king ate the salt of his house, for he held a farm of all the salt in that kingdom.' For this reason Jahangir styled him Cassam Can Namaquin (Qasim Khan Namakin, from *namak*, 'salt')— that is to say, 'distributor of salt,'[1] and his title of nobility was left with him. I dwelt seven years in his house in the city of Lahor. It had been given me by the governor to live in, he (Qasim Khan) being then dead. It was one of Jahangir's laws that the crown was heir to the wealth and houses of his servants when they died, also to those of his vassals who had no sons.

Favours often serve for the downfall of those who receive them, seeing that they do not know how to control themselves afterwards. Thus it was with the English who dwelt in Hindustan. Relying on the kindness that Jahangir always showed to Europeans, when they had a difference at the port of Surat with the governor, in order to take their satisfaction they laid an embargo

1. See 'Ma,asir-ul-Umara,' iii. 741, for quite a different and more reasonable derivation of the epithet 'Namakin' given to this Qasim Khan. Compare also Blochman, 'Ain,' vol. i. pp. 414 (note), 470, No. 199.

on the ships that the king and the *wazir* destined for Mecca, and also on those of many merchants, obstructing them in their voyages. Jahangir observed what was going on, and forwarded an order to adjust the dispute without incensing the English. At various times many different complaints about them were laid before the king, until, displeased at hearing so many complaints, he ordered the English to be seized. As they resisted the execution of the royal orders, he sentenced them all to be beheaded. Hence was brought about the death of those who were in the territories of Agrah and Surat. This event happened in the year one thousand six hundred and twenty-two,[1] two years before his death [118], which came about as follows:

This king was, as can be seen by the above account, somewhat over-jovial. In the hot season he went away for recreation to Kashmir, and returning in the cold weather, he came to live in the city of Lahor. He happened to fall ill while coming from that country, and before he could reach Lahor he died of disease, after having reigned twenty-two years seven months and eleven days. His corpse was carried to the mausoleum of which I have spoken (I., 116).

OF SULTAN BALLAQUI (BULAQL), ELDEST SON OF JAHANGIR

When Jahangir died, Sultan Bulaqi, his eldest son,[2] took possession of the kingdom without opposition. He looked on himself as absolute sovereign, and believed that no one could oppose him except his brother, who had been banished, as I have already said (I., 116), to the territories of Bijapur, and to him the usurper paid no attention. Thus he followed in the footsteps of his father, and occupied himself with dances, music, and other pastimes. Nevertheless, he sent off an envoy to the King of Bijapur, warning him against according any favour to his brother, or permitting him to leave his then abode. If the king disobeyed

1. These events at Surat seem to be the same as those assigned by Hunter to 1623 ('History,' ii. 55). Jahangir did not die till 1627.

2. Bulaqi (Dawar Bakhsh) was Jahangir's grandson (see *ante*, note to fol. 116). He was put on the throne by Asaf Khan at Lahor in opposition to Shahryar, the fifth son, who was Nur Jahan's candidate (see Elphinstone, 592). Native historians state that, on being deposed, Dawar Bakhsh was killed, but some Europeans say they saw him in Persia in 1633 (Elphinstone, quoting Olearius, p. 190; and see forward, fol. 120, where Manucci says much the same).

X. Dawar Bakhsh *alias* Bulaqi, Grandson of Jahangir

Vol. I *To face page 172*

this direction, war would be declared, and his whole kingdom devastated. The King of Bijapur, frightened by these menaces, kept his eyes open, and meant to prevent Sultan Khurram leaving, and thus avoid drawing upon himself the wrath of Sultan Bulaqi.

Sultan Khurram was a prisoner with all his family—that is to say, his wives, four sons, Darā (Dārä), Xaxuja (Shah Shuja'), Oranazeb (Aurangzeb), and Moradbaex (Murad Bakhsh), and three daughters—namely, Begom Saeb (Begam Sahib), Gonorara Begom (Jahanara Begam), and Roxonara Begom (Roshanara Begam). There was also a wife who was enceinte, who longed to eat apples, a thing difficult to procure thereabouts, nor was it the right season for them. He (Khurram) was vexed at his inability to gratify the princess, and went forth from his house much cast down.

On his way he met a faqir, who offered him two apples. Highly delighted, he (Khurram) carried them off at once to the princess, and told the poor man to wait, as he had something to say. Going inside, he delivered the apples to the princess, then came back humbly and reverently to the faqir, and said to him: 'I suspect that you are some holy man, since you have succoured me in the time of trouble. May it please you to do me the favour of telling me if that is so.' The man [119] replied that it was. They had a long conversation, and the faqir told him many things.

Among other things he said that he (Khurram) would fall ill, but on those occasions he must smell his hands. So long as they had the scent of apples, his illness would be neither dangerous nor mortal. When they ceased to smell of apples, it would be a warning that he had reached his term of life. In the end the prince asked him which of his sons would be the destroyer of his race. The faqir answered that it would be Aurangzeb, who in those days was quite a child.[1] This was the reason that Sultan Khurram never had any love for Aurangzeb. From this time he (Khurram) began to scoff at him (Aurangzeb), calling him the White Snake, he being fairer than all his brothers. Sometimes he resolved to kill him, but his elder sister, called Roshanara Begam, always preserved him, and God reserved him to be the chastisement of his father.

1. Aurangzeb was born in 1618, and if this conversation was in 1627, he would be about nine.

Meanwhile the prince Khurram had abandoned all hope of ever leaving the territory of Bijapur. There now came to him a letter from his father-in-law, Acet Can (Asaf Khan), the wazir, father of Jahangir's beloved queen and of Sultan Khurram's wife, but by different mothers.[1] The contents were that he (Khurram) must leave his place of refuge by whatever method he could devise, and procure a secret meeting with Mahabat Khan, then actually governor at the city of Brampur (Burhanpur). If he (Khurram) would come to court he should be made king, and everything was in readiness.

The prince, finding that the King of Bijapur would neither consent to assist him nor even grant him his liberty, resorted to the following trick. He feigned for some time that he was ill, until the news spreading abroad everywhere, the King of Bijapur sent his people to see him and find out the truth. Sultan Khurram was informed of the men's arrival, and sent secretly to order the slaughter of a goat, the blood of which he drank. After this he ordered the envoys to be introduced. When they came in he shammed being overcome with nausea, and vomited blood, making himself out to be at the point of death.

On coming out, the envoys forthwith reported to their king how the Mogul prince was at the last gasp, and could not survive in any case. Finally, Khurram's household set up cries and lamentations, calling out that he was dead. Putting on mourning, they went to the court of the king to ask permission to quit his territory, and carry the corpse of the deceased prince to the sepulchre of his ancestors. The king gave them leave, and they carried him (Khurram) off, placed in a bier covered with all the trappings of woe, and followed by all his people weeping and lamenting as they went.

This news reached the court of Sultan Bulaqi, who was very pleased, saying: 'Now am I delivered from a great enemy, and become absolute monarch.' They travelled [120] through the city of Burhanpur, and Mahabat Khan came out to follow the bier until they arrived at the suburbs of Agrah city. When the bier had arrived so far, Asaf Khan, father-in-law of the fictitious

---

1. This is an error. Arjumand Bana Begam, Mumtaz Mahal, wife of Shah jahan, was the daughter of Asaf Khan, who was the *brother*, and not the *father*, of Nur Jahan. Thus, Mumtaz Mahal was her niece, and not her half-sister.

defunct, requested leave from Bulaqi to go himself at the head of a large cavalry force to meet the bier, pleading that such was the custom. Sultan Bulaqi, who had no suspicion of the fraud, but, on the contrary, in his joy regaled himself with music, dancing, and wine, gave the permission to go and make whatever preparations he might please. He had no idea that he had only a few moments more to reign.

Asaf Khan left the city, and coming to the bier, found the prince Khurram alive and well, and put him on an elephant kept ready for the purpose. Thus they entered into the city with all their cavalry, raising a rebellion against Bulaqi, beating the royal drums, marching with drawn swords in their hands, and shouting: 'Long live King Shahjahan!' It was thus that he entitled himself from this time forth—it means 'King of the World.' Bulaqi was amazed at the prince's thus returning to life, and all of a sudden becoming master of his (Bulaqi's) forces. Since there remained no other method of saving his life, he took to flight, and thus escaped from his brother's wrath.

OF THE KING SHAHJAHAN, FIFTH KING OF HINDUSTAN AND TENTH OF THE RACE OF TAIMUR-I-LANG

The first thing undertaken by Shahjahan was, by the utmost efforts, to attempt the capture of his fugitive brother, Bulaqi. But, in spite of all he did, he could not overtake him: he (Bulaqi) fled until he entered the kingdom of Persia, where he ended his life in destitution.[1] This is why he was not included in the number of the kings, nor was he ever accorded that title. Finding that he could not seize his brother Bulaqi, Shahjahan sent out another force to the city of Lahor, where there were two sons of that prince. Express orders were given that where-ever they were found they should be walled up forthwith. They were in the hall where King Jahangir gave audience, and were busy writing. Without showing them any mercy, Shah Jahan's emissaries built up the door, leaving them inside, and up to this day it remains bricked up. It is a custom with these kings and lords that after their death the chamber where they die is walled up and never opened any more.

Finding himself undisputed King of Hindustan, Shahjahan was compelled to make war against the Portuguese of Hugll,

1. See *ante*, note to fol. 118, for the contrary statement of native historians.

for this was demanded by Taj Mahal, from whom the Portuguese [121] had carried off two slave girls (*ante*, I., 116). He sent against them the general Qasim Khan,[1] who, when he arrived close to Hugli, made an arrangement with the Portuguese. These paid a large sum of money, whereupon he (Qasim Khan) retired the distance of a day's journey, but again advanced towards Hugli, with the excuse that the king had ordered him to take the place.

They defended themselves as long as they could, but, unable to continue longer, they surrendered. Qasim Khan seized by lot five thousand souls, among them some Augustinian and Jesuit fathers. It seemed as if God desired to chastise the Portuguese of Hugli, seeing that they were unable to escape with their ships by way of the river Ganges, on the banks of which the town referred to stands.

The water in the river had fallen, and the boats lay stranded, a thing that had never happened before or since. I have no desire to record in this place the arrogance displayed by these same Portuguese, of whom I will write somewhat elsewhere (III., 192). Qasim Khan carried off the prisoners to court, and God willed that before they arrived there the queen, Taj Mahal should die.[2] Shahjahan gave orders for the construction of her mausoleum opposite the royal palace at Agrah with great expenditure. It is in two stories, in the lower being deposited the body of his beloved wife. No one may see this sepulchre, for it is in the charge of women and eunuchs.

There cannot be the least doubt that if the Portuguese had reached the court in the life-time of Taj Mahal she would have

1. This Qasim Khan was the son of Mir Murad, Juwaini, and died in Rabi' I., 1042 H. (the middle of that month corresponds to October 1, 1632). Thus, as he died three days after the taking of Hugli, that event must have happened about the end of September, 1632. Elphinstone (519) assigns the siege to 1631; Danvers (ii. 247) says it was from June 6 to September 29, 1633; Beale and the 'Maasir-ul-Umara' (iii. 78) have 1631. Compare the 'Padshahnamah' of 'Abd-ul-hamid ('Bibliotheca Indica'), vol. i., part i., pp. 433-439, and Elliot and Dowson, vii. 30-34, where it is placed under the fifth year, and the capture is fixed on the 14th Rabi' I., 1042 H. (September 30, 1632, N.S.). The best European account is in Sebastian Manrique (Augustinian), 'Itinerario de las Missiones qui hizo el padre Fray S. M. . . . , Roma, 1649, 476 pp., 4to. (pp. 419-445). He is partly quoted by H. G. Keene in 'Turks in India,' p. 255.
2. Taj Mahal died on July 6, 1632, N.S.

ordered the whole of them to be cut into pieces after great tortures, for thus had she sworn when they did her the injury. All the same they did not escape a sufficient amount of suffering; some abjured their faith, either from fear of torture and of death or through the desire of recovering their wives, who had been distributed by Shahjahan among his officers. Others, the most beautiful among them, were kept for the royal palace. Of some of these I shall have something to say further on (II., 24).

The fathers were more tenacious in holding to the Christian faith, saying that they adored a Master who could preserve them, nor for anything that Shahjahan might do would they become renegades. There were also a few others—laymen—who held fast to their faith, but were released through the petitions of some persons at court, chiefly of an Armenian, who was a great favourite, or through the money paid by a Venetian, my compatriot, called Hieronomo Veroneo, a man ransomed by the Portuguese. These released prisoners lived in the city of Agrah, and until this day there are some of their descendants.

After the death of his beloved queen Taj Mahal, Shahjahan selected in Hindustan the city of Dihli in order to build there a new city as his capital, and thereby perpetuate his memory, the climate at that spot being healthy. He used the ruins of ancient Dihli and Toquilabad (Tughlaqabad) for building this new Dihli, to which [122] he gave the name of Shahjahanabad—that is to say, 'Built by Shahjahan.'

He expended large sums in the construction of this city, and in the foundations he ordered several decapitated criminals to be placed as a sign of sacrifice. The said city is on the bank of the river Jamnah, in a large plain of great circumference, and it is in the shape of an imperfect half-moon. It has twelve gates, and ancient Dihli forms a suburb, as also do several other villages.

The walls of the city are built one half of brick and the rest of stone. At every hundred paces is a strengthening bastion, but on these there is no artillery. The chief gates are the one leading to Agrah and the one leading to Lahor. Within the city are large and well-built *bazars*, where are sold things of every kind. The chief *bazars* are those that correspond with the streets leading to the fortress, and end with the two above named gates. There are also in Dihli fine palaces for the nobles; a great number of the other houses have thatched roofs, but are highly decorated and commodious inside. The city on the eastern side, along which the river Jamnah flows, has no wall. In one corner of the city, on the northern side, is the royal fortress, facing to the east. In front of it, between it and the river, is left a sufficient space for the elephant fights. The king sits at a window to look on, as likewise the women, but they are behind gratings. Thence also the king beholds the parades held on the same space, of the omaraos (*umard*, grandees), rajahs, and nobles. Beneath the royal balconies there is, night and day, a mad elephant kept, out of ostentation.

The fortress is encircled by walls of large red stones, and it has a bridge of some twelve arches, by which access is obtained to the fortress of Sellemguer (Salimgarh), situated on an island made by the river Jahnah. It was built by the king Selem Xa Patany (Salim Shah, Pathan). The royal fortress has two gates leading into the city, there being a large open space in the midst. Shahjahan planted two large gardens, one on the north side, the other on the south side, and for the reason that the river Jamnah does not rise high enough to permit of its irrigating these gardens, Shahjahan, at great expense and labour, constructed a deep canal from a river adjacent to the city of Serend (Sihrind), one hundred leagues from Dihli. This canal flows into the fortress and fills the water-channels, into which Shahjahan ordered some beautiful fish to be thrown with gold rings in their heads, each ring having one ruby and two seed-pearls. This watercourse circulates through [123] all the fortress, except the side towards the river Jamnah. Opposite to the fortress, on the west side, is the royal mosque, where the king goes once every week to say his prayers.

Shahjahan fancied that just as he had easily taken the town of Hugli from the Portuguese, so in like manner he would be able to take from them everything they had in Hindustan. Therefore he ordered his son Aurangzeb, then fourteen or fifteen years of age,[1] to march against Damao (Daman) and take it

1. This statement as to Aurangzeb's age places the events in 1632 or 1633, but I can find no confirmation in Danvers or Elphinstone. Danvers (i. 522) speaks of one Luis de Mello, Governor of Daman, but that was in 1560-61, in the reign of Akbar. The man's son Diogo is referred to by Manucci (part ii., 78).

from the Portuguese. But these fought valiantly, and since the fortress possessed good walls, Aurangzeb could not reduce it. After an investment of three months he (Aurangzeb) was forced to retire after losing a considerable number of men. Finding that the Portuguese defended themselves bravely, and that he could do nothing against them, Aurangzeb sent a message to Luis de Mello de Sampayo, known as 'The Snorer,' who was then governor of the fortress, that it was easy for everybody to snore behind walls. Angered by this message, Luis de Mello sent back word that on the next day but one, about noon-time, he would come forth into the open field, and as a sign that he was there in person he would lift his hat. He issued from the fort, and Aurangzeb's men charged him and killed him. The Portuguese returned to the fortress to defend it.

Shahjahan sent this son against Daman because he knew him to be brave and fearless. It was for this reason that he afterwards ordered him to go against the kingdom of Balq (Balkh). Aurangzeb invaded the territories of the said realm until he encountered the enemy's army in the field. These being the stronger gained the battle, and Aurangzeb was very nearly taken prisoner. Without fail would this have happened had not Mir Baba, his foster-brother, come speedily to his assistance.[1] Still, although this prince (Aurangzeb) was held to be bold and valiant, he was capable of great dissimulation and hypocrisy; pretending to be an ascetic, he slept while in the field on a mat of straw that he had himself woven. He stitched caps with his own hands and sent them out for sale, saying that he lived upon what he made by them. He ate food that cost little, such as radishes, lentils, barley, and such-like vegetables and cereals; he gave alms publicly, and also let it be known that he underwent severe penances and fasting; he allowed himself to be found in prayer or reading the Quran; went out frequently with his chaplet in his hand; and on all occasions called on the name of God as if he made no account of the things of this world. All the same, under cover of these pretenses, he led in secret a jolly life of it, and his intercourse was with certain holy men [124] addicted to sorcery, who instructed him how to dissimulate and to bring over to his side as many friends as he could with witchcraft and soft speeches.

1. This campaign in Balkh belongs to 1647 (Elphinstone, 511).

One day Shahjahan marched on a campaign to recover the fortress of Candar (Qandahar), which Alimerda Can ('Ali Mardan Khan), the Persian, had voluntarily surrendered, when he rebelled against his own king. Xaabas (Shah 'Abbas) retook it in the following way: A goat had escaped from its herd, and the goat-herd pursued in order to catch it. The goat, by one leap after another, got upon a high hill, and thence, following a route full of rocks, arrived inside the fortress. The goat-herd also entered it by the same way, and came out again without anyone knowing of his being there. When he got back, he went off to make a report at the court of Shah 'Abbas. With the goat-herd as guide, a sufficient number of soldiers started for Qandahar, and taking the hidden path above referred to, they made a secret entrance into the place; during the night they decapitated the sentries, and got possession of the fortress. Although Shahjahan made three attempts to retake this fortress, he was not able to do anything.

One day, on the march already referred to, a mendicant came up to him (Shahjahan), and the king intended to give him something; but Aurangzeb told him not to do so, because the mendicant had a considerable sum of money tied round his waist, and in this Aurangzeb showed himself to be a true prophet.

The king ordered the mendicant to be searched, and in his girdle they found forty rupees of gold. He (Shahjahan) said to his son: 'If what you did and said was not a plot, you are a saint.' Aurangzeb, seeing that his father had begun to place faith in his pretenses, made believe to intensify his abstinence, simply to deceive his father, so that his rank might be increased. It was found out afterwards that the mendicant had been tutored by him (Aurangzeb); in spite of this, all the simple-minded people took him for a saint. But his father, who knew well the nature of this son, and also recollected the words of the faqir with the apples, gave little credit to all this show of holiness. It was for this reason that he did not increase the low rank that he had first given him. To his other sons he gave many tokens of paternal affection—above all, to the eldest son, Dara. Envious of this preference, Aurangzeb sought means of injuring his brother Dara, to whom he had a great antipathy.

Shahjahan was anxious to prevent the occurrence of any trouble at court. He therefore ordered that only one prince should come each day to his presence. But Aurangzeb, pricked by envy and the desire of injuring his brother Dara, rode out on horseback, lance in hand. He waited until Dara should come out of the fortress. Then he spurred his horse in such a way that it struck his (Dara's) palanquin with its hindquarters, so that the litter nearly fell to the ground. Dara, thus insulted, made bitter complaints to his father [125].

The father, seeing this want of harmony among his sons, and fearing some misfortune, separated them. He knew that Aurangzeb was in treaty with his brother Xaxuja (Shah Shuja') for the marriage of his son, Sultan Mahamud (Muhammad), with the latter's daughter when she arrived at a proper age. He therefore sent the prince Shah Shuja' to be lord over the kingdom of Bemgalla (Bengal), and Prince Aurangzeb to the city of Moltan (Multan), and Prince Moradbacx (Murad Bakhsh) to the kingdom of Guzurab (Gujarat); while he kept with himself the prince Dara, his eldest son, as being the most esteemed and loved.

Aurangzeb knew that his father put no faith in him, and did not love him. He therefore wrote to him (Shahjahan) letters in most humble terms, also making use, with great foresight, of his brother Dara. To the latter he wrote many letters, begging a thousand pardons for the affronts he had committed; he said he had done them as one having no sense. He offered him the services of his family and of himself, if he would only have compassion upon him and his sons; adding that he looked on him (Dara) as a father. Dara, who was of a genial character and compassionate nature, sent loving letters in reply. Then Aurangzeb, seeing matters well arranged, wrote to his eldest brother a letter in which he entreated him to obtain from their father leave to quit the city of Multan, where the climate did not agree with him and he was always ailing, and asked that he might be transferred to the Dacan (Dakhin).

The cunning man made this request because he saw that in the Dakhin he could establish his fortunes through the continual activity of the armies there, owing to the existence of the kingdoms of Vizapur (Bijapur) and Golconda (Gulkandah), and because the lands of the Dakhin are very productive, abounding in supplies of food and various sorts of cloth, and contain many minerals. The petitions that Dara made to his father were so insistent that this favour was granted Aurangzeb; he was withdrawn from Multan and ordered to the Dakhin. Shahjahan was unwilling to concede these requests; still, from Dara's importunities he granted what was asked. But he said to Dara: 'You are acting on behalf of a venomous snake, and you will have to suffer from its poison.'

Aurangzeb went to the Dakhin, where his strength began to increase. Near to Doltabad (Daulatabad) he built a city that he called Aurangabad—that is to say, 'Built by Aurangzeb.' There he began to weave the web of his rebellion, including the destruction of his father and his brothers.

Before speaking of the wars waged by Shahjahan and of his downfall, it is necessary to say something of his disposition. Although warlike, as he showed [126] by his rising against his father, he was at the same time fond of music and dancing to the same degree, more or less, as his father Jahangir. His usual diversion was to listen to various instruments, to verses and poetry; and he was very fond of musicians, especially of one who was not only a graceful poet, but also a buffoon.

This musician was worried by the palace gate-keepers, who are exceedingly rude to anyone who requires entrance to court. They will not permit anyone's entrance or exit without some douceur, excepting the officials, to whom they can say nothing for fear of a beating. Every time that this musician came to court the gate-keepers made him wait a long time, until he either gave them or promised them something. Anxious to rid himself of such hindrances, he composed some verses, and arrived to recite them in the presence of the king. The gate-keepers did not fail to display their accustomed insolence, detaining him until he had promised to give them all that was bestowed on him this time by the king. He went in and recited in such fine style and with such graceful behaviour that the king was much delighted, and ordered for him a reward of one thousand rupees. The singer transmuted his joy into tears, raising his hands to heaven, weeping and beating his breast to show his sorrow at such a present. He said to the king with many bows that he prayed him as a favour to order him in place of the thousand rupees to receive one thousand stripes. Shahjahan smiled, and asked why he made such a request.

He replied that he had promised to the gate-keepers all that he should acquire, or his majesty should make a gift of to him during the day. Thus, since they were rude, not allowing him to enter or go out without his taking out his purse and giving something, he was willing to transfer to them the thousand stripes, or even more if the king so wished. The king laughed heartily, and to satisfy him sent an order to serve out the thousand stripes to the twenty-five gate-keepers then on duty. The gate-keepers complained; but the poet made his excuses, saying he had only kept his promise. The gate-keepers got the thousand blows, while he carried off the thousand rupees, and, in addition, a horse of which the king made him a gift.

The horse they gave him was gone in the loins. He tied a bundle round the neck of this horse, and when the king came out he mounted it, and showed off its paces before him. The king asked him why he had tied on the bundle; it hindered the horse in his paces. He answered that it was there to equalize the weights, thus giving a hint that the horse was gone in the back. Shahjahan was delighted, and ordered them [127] to give him another horse. From that day forth the gate-keepers were very respectful to this musician, so that they might not get any more beatings.

Another thing happened to one of these gate-keepers. Shahjahan, who thought highly of the man, ordered him on a campaign, after having by gifts and favours raised him to the position of a great noble. This favourite met with great success, and was sent for to court to receive further rewards. All the nobles went out to meet him except the physician, who would neither go out to greet him nor visit him afterwards. The officer was aggrieved, and went in person to see the physician. The latter, making no account of the other's person, sent out word that he might come in. The physician remained seated, and appeared to be writing. The general entered, and the physician in a soft voice said he might take a seat, but showed him no other mark of civility, and pretended to go on writing.

The newly-risen great man waited to see whether the physician would show him any sign of politeness, this being the only object for which he had paid this visit; but finding that the physician never stirred, neither paid any heed to him, he begged leave to depart. The physician, in the same soft tones, continuing his occupation, gave him permission to go away without any token of kindness.

The general went off at once to complain to Shahjahan, exaggerating the slight done to him by the physician, and the latter fell under the king's displeasure through the disrespect he had shown to the general. The physician replied: 'Your majesty may create many generals of that sort, but you cannot make any man similar to me, for it has cost me forty years to acquire the knowledge that I possess, and there is a great difference between us.' The reason of this affront became known afterwards. It was that when the general was a door-keeper he put many difficulties in the way of the physician. Thus was the proverb verified: 'What you do you get' [Tit for tat].

Not only was Shahjahan fond of music; he was also eager to have at his court all sorts of wrestlers. These are men of great strength, who frequently contended in his presence. And he also ordered boxing matches. But his ordinary amusement was tiger-hunting, for which he kept ferocious buffaloes with very long horns. These fought with each other or with tigers; they are very [128] brave animals, and skillful in the sport above referred to.

When the king desires to go out hunting, the huntsmen are warned.[1] These men see to the finding of the tigers, and send out into the jungle asses, cows, sheep, and goats to prevent the tigers changing their haunts. The king goes out on his tallest elephant, and the other princes likewise on elephants acquainted with the requirements of this sort of fight. They sit in uncovered howdahs, each one with his matchlock. Then they encircle the jungle with high nets, leaving only one opening, through which the king and the huntsmen enter. Around the net, on the outside, stand a number of soldiers, who cannot wound the tiger when it comes near the net, nor can the tiger injure them, for in no manner can it break the net and get out.

The order in which the king moves is as follows: In front go the buffaloes, sometimes more than one hundred in number, all in a row. On each one is mounted a man with his legs guarded by leather, and having a broadsword in one hand and holding with the other the reins, which are passed through the

1. This account is very imperfectly reproduced by Catrou (159, 160).

XI. Elephant Fight

Vol. I *To face page 185*

buffalo's nostrils. Behind them comes the king on an elephant, and after the king the princes and the men in highest favour.

When they get into the jungle where the tigers are, the buffaloes advance slowly in the formation of a half-moon, until the tigers are in sight. After locating the tigers by sight and smell a circle is formed, leaving them in the centre. In this way the tigers, finding themselves caught, search for an exit. Unable to get away, each one makes its spring in the direction that it sees best. When this spring takes place the man who is mounted on top jumps off with agility, and the buffaloes seize the tigers on their horns with great dexterity, and, shaking their heads tear them to pieces. If any one of the tigers escapes the horns, or refuses to stir from its place, the king fires his gun and kills it, or gives an order to kill it.

Sometimes they go out to these hunts without taking any buffaloes, but riding on elephants, as I have before said. This way of hunting has much more risk for the hunters. Once it happened to King Shahjahan that a badly wounded tiger bounded up and hung on with its claws fixed in the elephant's head. The elephant-driver fell to the ground from fright. The king, seeing himself in this urgent danger, clubbed his matchlock and hit the tiger with it on the head. But the tiger did not let go, and the elephant, finding he could not make use of his trunk, ran furiously till he found a tree, against which he crushed the tiger. It was on this account that Shahjahan gave orders for the head of the elephants to be protected in future down to the end of the trunk with a covering of thick leather, studded with sharp nails. In addition to the huntsmen, there is always an official present whose business it is to take possession of the tiger's whiskers; and therefore, as soon as the tiger is dead, they put on his head a leather bag, coming down as far as the neck. Having tied the bag, the official attaches to it [129] his seal. After this the tiger is carried in front of the entrance to the royal tents, when the official appears who has charge of the poisons, and removes the whiskers, which are employed as a venom.[1]

1. Bernier also describes these hunts (pp. 182, 183, 378, 379, edition Constable). He mentions the nets, but not the buffaloes, and his description is not so precise a Manucci's. I find nothing in the text here to justify Catrou's 'lames d'epees assez larges et fort pointues,' which he says were attached to the buffalo's horns (p. 159).

All the world knows that the Mahomedans, following the example of their master, Muhammad, are very licentious; wherefore there are men among them, some more and some less, chiefly the nobles and the kings, who do not content themselves with a few wives, but seek for every method of gratifying themselves in this particular. It may be asserted that Shahjahan was not superior to others in this respect, for, not contenting himself with the women that he had in his palaces, he forfeited the respect of the nobles at his court by intrigues with their wives, whereby he came to his ruin and his death.

The chief of these women, one that he thought a great deal of, was the wife of Jafarcan (Ja'far Khan),[1] and from the love he bore her he wished to take her husband's life, but she saved him by praying that he might be sent as governor to Patana (Patnah), as was done. In the same way he had an acquaintance with the wife of Calican (Khalil Khan)[2] for some time, and this man took his revenge in the battle fought by Dara against Aurangzeb, as I shall relate further on (I. 192).

Here it seems appropriate to state how the spies reported to Shahjahan that the wife of Khalillullah Khan wore shoes worth three millions of rupees, owing to the numerous precious stones with which the said shoes were garnished. When Khalilullah Khan came to audience, the angry king scolded him, saying that if his wife wore shoes of such great value, it was a sign that he had great wealth, the greater part of it got by theft, and therefore the first thing was for him to render an account of what he had embezzled. He (Khalilullah Khan) stood speechless, and could make no answer. But one of his friends who was present obtained permission from the king to reply on behalf of Khalillullah Khan. He said there was nothing for his majesty to

1. Ja'far Khan was son of Asaf Khan's sister, and was married to that noble's daughter, Farzanah Begam (Bibi Jiu). Thus, if that wife is alluded to, she was Shahjahan's sister-in-law, and the story is almost incredible. Ja'far Khan became *wazir*, and died in 1081 H. (1670-71), ('M,ul-U.,' i. 531).
2. Khalilullah Khan was the younger son of Mir Miran, Yazdi, and his wife was Asaf Khan's grand-daughter. She was thus Shahjahan's niece by marriage. Khalilullah Khan died on the 2nd Rajab, 1072 H. (February 21, 1662). His elder brother was Asalat Khan, Mir Bakhshi (died 1057 H.).

complain of, for the whole wealth of Khal-llullah Khan was in those shoes, because his wife was in the habit every day of shoe-beating him on the face, and gave him thus all the riches that she had. On hearing this Shahjahan sank his head, and laughing to himself, said: 'It is a sufficient punishment to have in your house an angry wife.' All those who were present also began to smile at such an act of friendship. Khalilullah Khan left the audience in shame, quarrelling with his friend about the affront done to him in the king's presence by giving such an answer. His friend retorted that he had [130] no room for complaint, rather was he under a heavy obligation, for if he had not come to his aid the king would have ordered his execution. Khalilullah Khan let the matter pass, and he lived the rest of his life under this disrepute.

Some authors[1] assert that Khalilullah Khan was beaten with shoes in the audience of Dara. I know of a certainty that this is not so, because never again would Khalilullah Khan have left his house, nor would anyone have had respect for him, nor would he have been captain-general of the king's cavalry, as he was. If they write thus, they record tales got from the common people, and not from those at court.

Shahjahan did not spare the wife of his brother-in-law, Xaahish Can (Shaistah Khan), though it was by a trick, for she would not consent. The procuress in this affair was Begom Saeb (Begam Sahib), the daughter of Shahjahan, who, in complaisance to her father, invited the said woman to a feast, at the end of which Shahjahan violated her. This lady was so much affected that, going to her house, she would neither eat nor change her clothes, and in this manner ended her life in grief. Shaistah Khan dissembled, hoping to have his revenge in due time, as will be seen farther on (I. 176).

The intimacy of Shahjahan with the wives of Ja'far Khan and Khalilullah Khan was so notorious that when they went to court the mendicants called out in loud voices to Ja'far Khan's wife: 'O Breakfast of Shahjahan! remember us!' And when the wife of Khalilullah Khan went by they shouted: 'O Luncheon of Shahjahan ! succour us!' The women heard, and, without taking it as an insult, ordered alms to be given.

1. This is a hit at Bernier (see 'Travels,' p. 53, edition Constable, and Mr. Constable's reference to Tavernier, edition Ball, i. 143).

For the greater satisfaction of his lusts Shahjahan ordered the erection of a large hall, twenty cubits long and eight cubits wide, adorned throughout with great mirrors. The gold alone cost fifteen millions of rupees, not including the enamel work and precious stones, of which no account was kept. On the ceiling of the said hall, between one mirror and another, were strips of gold richly ornamented with jewels. At the corners of the mirrors hung great clusters of pearls, and the walls were of jasper stone. All this expenditure was made so that he might obscenely observe himself and his favourite women.

It would seem as if the only thing Shahjahan cared for was the search for women to serve his pleasures. For this end he established a fair at his court, which lasted eight days every year.[1] No one was allowed to enter except women [131] of all ranks—that is to say, great and small, rich and poor, but all handsome. Each one brought what merchandise she could. But the best piece of goods she could produce was her own body. Their only object was that the king might fall in love with them; thus honourable women would not go to the place. In those eight days the king visited the stalls twice every day, seated on a small throne carried by several Tartar women, surrounded by several matrons, who walked with their sticks of enamelled gold in their hands, and many eunuchs, all brokers for the subsequent bargaining; there were also a set of women musicians.

Shahjahan moves past with his attention fixed, and seeing any seller that attracted his fancy, he goes up to the stall, and making a polite speech, selects some of the things, and orders whatever she asks for them to be paid to her. Then the king gives an agreed-on-signal, and having passed on, the matrons, well versed in these matters, take care that they get her; and in due time she is produced in the royal presence. Many of them come out of the palace very rich and satisfied, while others continue to dwell there with the dignity of concubines. These eight days were observed in the palace with great festivity, dancing, music, acting, and other amusements. The fortress remained shut, with no man inside but the king. Once out of curiosity the women were counted as they came out, and there were more than thirty thousand.

---

1. Compare Bernier (272, edition Constable). These fairs were instituted by Akbar (Blochmann, 'A,in-i-Akbari,' i. 276).

It is impossible to explain satisfactorily the passion that Shahjahan had in this direction. Not satisfied with so many inventions for his inordinate desires, he also permitted great liberty to public women, of whom the greater number were dancers and singers. All of them paid taxes to the king.

Among them is one caste called Cancheny (*Kanchani*), who were under obligation to attend twice a week at court, for which they received pay, and to perform at a special place which the king had assigned to them. This class is more esteemed than others, by reason of their great beauty. When they go to court, to the number of more than five hundred, they all ride in highly embellished vehicles, and are clothed in rich raiment. All of them appear and dance in the royal presence.

Once the king fell in love with one of them, retained her in his palace, and gave her the title of concubine. Some of the nobles said to the king that a woman of that rank was unworthy of being placed in the royal palace. Xaaiahan (Shahjahan) replied: 'Matei nec her ducan que baxat'—that is to say, 'A good article may be [132] from any shop.'[1] One time when these women (the *Kanchanis*) were at the court, Khalilullah Khan, who was the officer on guard, attempted to dally with one of them. Upon this account the king flew into a rage and wanted to issue an order for his execution for having had the temerity to forget his respect to the royal abode. But on the petition of Ja'far Khan's wife, the culprit was pardoned. Ordinarily the dancing women dance in the principal open places in the city, beginning at six o'clock in the evening and going on till nine, lighted by many torches, and from this dancing they earn a good deal of money.

Although Shahjahan delighted in well-made women, he also required them to have good sense. Therefore, at different times, by different questions, he tested the understanding of every one of them. But it was a strange thing that happened to him with four servant women in his palace, who bore the names of the four quarters of the world. He rose at midnight to try the good judgment of these four, and going into the room of each one, asked her if dawn were near. The first replied 'No,' giving as her reason

1. *Mithai nek har dukan kih bashad*—'Sweetmeats are good, whatever shop they come from.'

that she still had the taste of betel in her mouth. The second also gave a negative answer, because the light of the candle in her room was still bright, whereas when dawn was approaching it no longer burnt so clearly. The third said that it was still a long time to daybreak, the reason being that when daylight was coming on the pearls that she wore felt cold, whereas at that hour this was not so. The fourth, a woman from the kingdom of Kashmir, where it is the habit of the women to speak freely, told Shahjahan that the day would not be here so very soon, for when it was near she felt the call to relieve her necessities, and at that moment her bowels gave her no such warning. With these answers Shahjahan retired, and when the next day arose, he gave to the first the office of looking after the betel that he ate; to the second charge of the royal lamps; to the third the care of the pearls and jewels; to the fourth, the supervision of the cleanliness of the royal retiring place.

The lasciviousness of Shahjahan did not interfere with his care to govern his kingdom most perfectly. He upheld the maxim of his father [133] that true justice must be enforced, rewarding the meritorious and punishing the guilty. He kept his eye on his officials, punishing them rigorously when they fell short in their duty. This was the reason that he kept at his court an official with several baskets full of poisonous snakes. He would order that in his presence they should be made to bite any official who had failed to administer justice, leaving the culprit lying in his presence till the breath left him.

Thus he did, as I saw, to the cotual (Kotwal) called Mahomed Said (Muhammad Sa'id), who is the magistrate. This man did not decide uprightly, and took bribes. Therefore an order was given that he should be bitten in one hand in his (Shahjahan's) presence by a *cobra capello*, the most poisonous snake on earth. The official in charge of the snakes was asked how long the man could live. The official replied that he could not live more than an hour. The king remained seated until the *Kotwal expired*. He then ordered that the body should lie two days in front of his court-house. Others who had deserved death were ordered to be thrown to mad elephants, who tore them to pieces.

Fear of this punishment was the cause of a cazi's (*qazi's*) action. A youth who had demanded justice against a relation paid to this *qazi* twenty thousand rupees for a favourable decision of his claim. The relation had been entrusted by the plaintiff's father with all his wealth, his son being then an infant. The defendant in turn paid thirty thousand rupees to obtain an unjust decree. The *qazi* went off to the king and reported that he had been paid thirty thousand rupees to give an unjust decree. The king, having been informed of the truth, forced the relation to pay to the youth the whole sum claimed, and ordered the thirty thousand rupees to be placed in the royal treasury. The *qazi* appropriated the twenty thousand rupees, and retained at the same time the reputation of a just judge.

If perchance any commander fled from battle, or did not do his duty, he was severely punished, both in his own person and that of his wives and daughters, the king directing rats to be placed in the latter's trousers, simply to disgrace and frighten them, and as a warning to other officials to do their duty with care.[1]

Before Shahjahan sent his son Moradbux (Murad Bakhsh) to be Viceroy of Guzurate (Gujarat), the previous governor was Nacir Can (Nasir Khan).[2] This man tyrannized over the people greatly, collecting extraordinary contributions and behaving harshly. As the merchants of that region were unable to obtain access to the king's audience to make their complaints, they bribed secretly some actors to represent their grievances in [134] detail before the king. Among the actors were mingled also some of the traders, who were to appear in the play and make petition to the court to be given redress, on showing that they had brought sufficient money.

They reported to the king that some strange actors had arrived, and wished to give a representation of a novel kind. Being a lover of such amusements, he gave permission for their entry. Then they played a piece which showed the misgovernment existing in the kingdom of Gujarat. The king was in astonishment at

1. A threat to cause mice to be put into his women's trousers was used by the Emperor Farrukhsiyar to his *wazir*, Qutb-ul-Mulk, in 1719 (see *Journal of the Asiatic Society of Bengal*, vol. lxxiii., part i., 1904, p. 340).
2. Possibly this is intended for Hafiz Muhammad Nasir, *diwan* of the province under Dara Shukoh, 1648-52. He was sent in 1653 to take charge of Surat ('Bombay Gazetteer,' vol. i., part i., 1896, pp. 280, 281, from the 'Tarikhi-i-Ahmadi').

the wrongs represented, and said: 'Can there be a man in the world to do such wrongful acts?' All the veritable merchants, but pretended actors, prostrated themselves on the ground before the king, and said to him: 'Let it be known to your majesty that everything we represented for your amusement is actually done by the governor. Disbursing our money, we tried in vain to lay before your majesty our complaints, therefore we have invented this device.' The king made inquiries, and finding that everything was true, he issued orders that the governor should be carried a prisoner to the fortress called Rotasgar (Ruhtas-garh), which is near Patana (Patnah), in the region of Bemgalla (Bengal), there to remain for the rest of his life. It is a rule that he who enters the said fortress ends his life there in misery on insufficient food. The king ordered all the governor's goods to be confiscated, whereby he was deprived of much ill-gotten wealth.

But still more terrible was the penalty inflicted on two forgers in the year[1] one thousand six hundred and fifty-four (correctly 1656), I being then at the court of Dara. It happened that a youth wanted to marry a certain woman. She refused; where upon he had recourse to a lawsuit. He said that after the woman had promised to marry him, and he had consumed with her all that he had, she refused to keep her word. The judge ordered inquiry to be made from the woman. She replied that the whole was false; neither had she given him her word, nor did she wish to marry. The judge asked the youth if he had any witnesses to the promise. He answered that his witnesses were the marks she bore on her body, the whole of which he described. He had learnt these marks from an old woman who was on familiar terms with the defendant, braiding her hair and bathing her body. Eunuchs and women were sent in order to examine the body of the women, and the conclusion was that the youth had detailed the marks with accuracy. Thereupon the judge decreed that the woman must marry the complainant.

The woman petitioned the judge [135] for a delay of several months, after which she would marry the youth; and the latter agreed to this proposal. The woman knew that no one except the old woman could give information of the marks on her body, for

1. The correct year must be 1656 or 1657, as Manucci did not arrive at Dihli before the middle of 1656 (see Introduction, p. lvii).

she was a chaste woman, living a retired life. After the lapse of a month, more or less, she issued from her house, followed by two sturdy slave-girls, and made for the dwelling of the youth. The latter was then ill. Entering the house, she seized him by the throat and shouted that now she had caught the thief who had robbed her. Thus saying, she carried him off by force to the judge and accused him of theft. Her story was that the night before, when sleeping with her, he had stolen a valuable bracelet like the one then on her arm. The youth swore it was not true, never had he known such a woman; and it being a total falsehood, he demanded justice for the false accusation.

Then the woman asked for justice to be done her in respect of the false claim the man had made a month before. At that time, expressing a desire to marry her, he had sworn that he had lived a long time in her house, and that she had promised to marry him. As a proof of his truthfulness he had called in eunuchs and women to examine her body, and had thus dishonoured her. The eunuchs and the women were summoned, and they testified that she was the very woman to whom they had gone to examine the marks on her body. She appeared before the king and made her complaint. The youth was asked by what channel he had learnt the marks on this woman's body. He then gave the name of the old woman, who had suggested to him this method of effecting his purpose. Shahjahan praised the astuteness of the woman, and gave orders for the old woman and the youth to be buried in the ground up to the waist, after which they were shot to death by arrows, and their dead bodies left lying there for twenty-four hours.

Another case occurred in the kingdom of Kabul, when Mahabat Khan was governor. It was that of a woman of that kingdom called Dariacatu (Daryae Khatun), who dwelt in the city, and had slave-women who solicited the travelling merchants of Osbeque (Uzbak) race. As Mahomedans are very facile about entering into marriage, and seeing this woman was very rich and had much goods, they would agree to marry her. There were nineteen men who had thus become her husbands. After a little time had passed, she used to take the husband to her villages to collect the rents. The man, delighted at the thought of acquiring more wealth, left the city with a light heart. She took them all into the lands of the Pathans, where she sold them to her acquaintances. The muscles near the heel were severed, so that they could not run away. She then returned to the city.

When they reported [136] the matter to the governor, she was seized. The governor, when fully informed of the facts, thought the case such an extraordinary one that he submitted it to the king. He ordered the woman to be torn to pieces by the dogs, which in that region are very handsome and savage. The Pathans keep them to protect their herds from wolves.

Not only did Shahjahan do justice against those guilty of great crimes: he also dealt with the nobles whenever he found an opportunity, in order to terrorize the rest. His object was to make the governing of his kingdom easier, so that he might pass his time with his women and be free of vexations. Thus, it happened that one day, going out to hunt, there came before him a servant complaining that for months his master had not paid him, and he was in great distress. On hearing the complaint, the king, without advancing a single step, ordered the man's master to be brought, whereupon he presented himself. He acknowledged the wrong done to the servant. The king ordered the gentleman to dismount, and the servant to get upon the horse of his master, while the master should remain running in front, in the servant's place, where he (Shahjahan) could see him. This continued until the master, unable to run any longer, fell to the ground, whereupon the king said to him: 'I do not fail to pay you, because you serve me; it is equally just that you should pay those who serve you.'

Equally terrifying was the sentence passed on one of his slaves. For just as he was liberal in giving rewards, he was equally exacting of obedience. Shahjahan had among his slaves one that he was very fond of, called Saadet Can (Saadat Khan)—that is to say, 'Efficacious.' He had an income of fifty thousand rupees, and was lord over two thousand horse. He was in charge of the betel consumed by the king, and to him was given one of the Portuguese women who had been taken prisoners at Ugulim (Hugli). The king saw several times that Saadat Khan gave away betel to the nobles at court. Shahjahan enjoined him not to give betel to anyone, and to remember this order. Saadat Khan, paying little heed to such an order, and relying on the love the king bore him, distributed the betel secretly. One day it so happened, unluckily for him, that the king saw him give betel to a noble [137] of the court. But he dissembled. At the end of the audience Shahjahan went into the garden, and without compunction ordered him to be beaten to death in his own presence. He said: 'This is what those deserve who do not obey the king's orders,' whereat the nobles trembled, and served him in fear.

The king handed over the whole of Sa'adat Khan's wealth to his wife, in spite of the rule made by Akbar that the king should confiscate all the goods left by anyone in his service. This Shahjahan did in order not to let it be hinted that he killed his slave to get possession of his wealth. This wife was a Christian, though she lived as a Moor (Mahomedan). When I was in the city of Agrah in the year one thousand six hundred and seventy-nine, I was sent for by the *qazi,* a great friend of mine, who told me privately that for love of me he did not interfere with the Jesuit fathers, then actually dwelling in the city. For he knew of a certainty that the said woman resorted in secret to the house of the Jesuits. Such a thing was strictly prohibited. He earnestly entreated me that so long as he was in power the woman should never go there again. If she did he might suffer great damage. I gave him my thanks, and advised the said woman, and the fathers were under an obligation to me. For Aurangzeb was very inimical to those who interfered with his religion. This was chiefly because Shahjahan had given an order to knock down the bell-tower of the fathers' church, out of the ill-will he bore them; still, for some reason or other, he accorded permission for the building of a smaller church, one without tower or bells.

To make still more clear how Shahjahan was anxious that justice should be administered in his realm, there are other interesting cases to be described. The first is that of a soldier who took wrongfully the slave-girl of a Hindu clerk. The latter brought a complaint before the courts. The soldier said the slavegirl was his, and so likewise said the girl herself, as she wanted to live with the soldier. The charge was transferred to the king's tribunal, and he ordered the slave-girl to be placed in his palace. When he wanted to write he directed the girl to pour a little water into the inkstand, and this she did most dexterously. This proved to the king that she was the slave of the scribe, and not of the soldier; thus he decreed that the girl should be made over to the scribe, from whom she had learnt how to pour water into an inkpot. The soldier was expelled from the service and banished the country.

Another very interesting case happened at Dihli.[1] At that place dwelt four merchants, who owned equal shares in the goods stored in a shop. The agreement was that each of them should attend there in turn for one day, and on his day each should provide the oil [138] required for the lamp and the food for a cat kept at the shop. He would also have to buy another cat if the old one happened to die. It came to pass that the cat broke its leg. The three other partners were called upon to pay their share of the expenses of the cure incurred by the one whose day it was when the cat's leg was broken. They refused to pay anything, contending that they were under no obligation to pay for curing the cat. While the cat was still under treatment with a rag tied round its leg, it was scratching itself near the lamp when the rag caught fire. The cat, finding itself in this danger, ran beneath the goods, whereby the total contents of the shop were burnt.

The three other merchants threw the blame upon the one that was doctoring the cat, and asserted that he was under an obligation to pay them for the whole of the damage caused. The case was taken into court, and the decree given was that he who was responsible for curing the cat must pay the losses of the others. The king was informed of the dispute, and reversed the decree, deciding that the three merchants should pay him who was responsible for the cure of the cat. He said that the broken leg could not walk, and that the three legs belonging to the three traders were those that had caused the fire; therefore, they were bound to pay the man who was in charge of the cat. Reluctance through avarice to meet a small expense is many a time the cause of total ruin.

If Shahjahan was opposed to injustice, he also followed up thieves in a particularly rigorous manner, and never pardoned them. If their offence was a small one, for which they did not deserve death, he ordered them to be transferred to the other side of the river Indus, and exchanged for Pathan dogs. If it chanced

1. A mere folk's tale (see Story No. 18 on p. 9 of R. B. Swinton's 'An Indian Tale or Two,' Blackheath, no date). There is also a Japanese version in the *Pall Mall Magazine* for September, 1905, p. 395.

that the thieves could not be caught, he forced the officials to pay. Thus did it happen in the year one thousand six hundred and forty-five at the port of Surat, when thieves robbed the Dutch factory at night. Although the loss was not great, the Dutch complained to the governor. He paid no attention to their complaint. They removed the best of what they had in their factory, loaded it on their ships, and blockaded the entrance to the river, allowing no one access or exit. They demanded from the governor a heavy penalty for having allowed them to be robbed within his jurisdiction. Shahjahan got notice of this affair, and he issued an order that the Dutch should be indemnified from his treasury, while the governor should be pestered and worried until he paid. On this occasion the Dutch made a profit of a thousand per cent., and up to this day it is the practice that whoever is in authority has to pay for loss by robbery.

[139] Although the king was so feared by all, still there were a few who defied him when they had reason to be angry. I have already stated above (I. 95) that Akbar made a rule that no one was to sit in the presence of persons of the blood royal. It happened that a commander had failed in his duty, and Shahjahan called him into his presence, and after a severe talking to, turned him out of the service. The officer, regardless of his life, sat himself down boldly on the ground in the king's presence, saying: 'Now that I am no longer your vassal nor your servant, I can sit down.'[1] Shahjahan was astonished at the officer's resoluteness, and restored him to his pay and position. Then the captain rose to his feet, as before, and he was sent to Jagarnate (Jagarnath) to fight certain rebels.

Something similar happened with the ambassador of the King of Golconda (Gulkandah). He appeared to Shahjahan to be a man of great wisdom, and he resolved to try an experiment upon him at the public audience. He asked him if the King of Gulkandah, his master, was the same height as one of his slaves, then actually present and brushing away the flies. The ambassador, understanding what was meant, lifted his eyes and looked at the slave, then spoke boldly to the king: 'My king is four fingers taller than your majesty.' The reply pleased Shahjahan

1. This story is repeated in the case of Muhammad Khan, Bangash, of Farrukhabad, in the eighteenth century.

very much, and he praised the ambassador as a loyal vassal aud true subject of his king. He remitted three years' payment of the tribute received from the King of Gulkandah. This tribute amounted to nine hundred thousand rupees. He also gave the ambassador a rich *sepao* (*sarapa*) and a handsome horse. I was actually present in the court when this conversation took place.

I have already stated that the Mogul kings were the heirs of the men in their service, taking all the wealth left at their death. A commander who was assumed to be very rich because of his lavish expenditure (which was done by him deliberately, so that he might leave behind him nothing for the king) was found on his death to have nine great and well-constructed boxes, with locks and nails of gold, sealed with his seal, and labelled to the effect that these boxes were to be made over to the king. At his death they were carried off to court, everybody supposing that the king had inherited a large amount. Shahjahan joyfully ordered the boxes to be opened, and praised the loyalty of the commander. The boxes were found to be full of horns and old shoes! By this he intended [140] to declare that if he (Shahjahan) dishonoured his own officials, he would in turn be dealt with in the same way, and the wealth that he gave away to women would lead to his having to wear old shoes—a fact that was well verified, as we shall see a little farther on (II. 54). Seeing this result, the king ordered that the property left by the said leader should be put into his tomb. He added that he did not care for any such bequest, for the general's father must have been some butcher or other, and his mother a shoemaker; and thus he left behind him only what his parents had bequeathed to him.

These goods were not sent by Shahjahan into his treasure-houses. Of these, in addition to the old ones, he constructed for himself two—one for gold and another for silver. The one for gold was called Zaura (? *zakhirah*)—that is to say, 'Treasure' and that for silver, Baura[1] (*bhaunra*)—that is to say, 'Horn beetle.' These receptacles were two square cisterns seventy feet long and thirty feet high, with two handsome marble pillars in the middle.

1. From his explanation of *bizouro* (Portuguese for a flying beetle), N. M. evidently thought the Indian word was bhaunra, a large black bee. But it must be a word spelt just the same. . .bhaunra, 'a vault,' 'a cellar (see Platts, 'Dictionary,' 197). For *zaura*, all I can suggest is *zakhirah* 'a treasure.

The treasuries were closed by trap-doors; and above these cisterns were large halls, also used as special treasuries for the money to be expended. In the treasury for gold there were current coins worth each seven *patacas*.[1] There were other coins, which were not current, of the value of seven hundred, of three thousand five hundred, and of seven thousand *patacas*. These were very beautiful, and the king gave them as presents to his ladies. When I was attending as physician on one of these, she made me a present of one of these coins. While Aurangzeb was king, the whole of these treasures, and the treasures of Queen Nurjahan, were expended,[2] owing to the falling off in the revenue.

Out of policy Shahjahan refrained from disgracing one great plunderer, making use of an excellent proverb. He often left the fortress (palace) early in the morning, and as a recreation would gather fruit in the garden in company of his favourite pages. Among these was one called Fedai Can (Ficda,e Khan), brother of Bader Can (Bahadur Khan),[3] foster-brother of Aurangzeb, a man who at one time was a very great friend of mine. This Fida,e Khan was an enemy of the Wazir Vizir Can (Wazir Khan), and was in wait for an opportunity of calling the king's attention to the bribes taken by that official. Gathering the best of the fruit, Shahjahan placed them in the hands of Fida,e Khan, and when about to enter the door of the harem, he asked for them [141]. Fida,e Khan made excuses, and said that his majesty had given nothing to him. Shahjahan was displeased, and said to him: 'I

1. Therefore worth fourteen rupees each, he having told us elsewhere that the *pataca* was equal to two rupees. The other beautiful large gold coins referred to have been several times described (see S. Lane Poole, 'Coins of Moghul Emperors,' (lxxxvii.). Five-and-thirty years ago (1869) a banker at Benares owned one, which I have seen.
2. The statement is not literally exact, for both Bahadur Shah in 1707 and the Sayyid brothers in 1719 disinterred large hoards within Agrah Fort.
3. These two brothers were Mir Muzaffar Husain, Khwafi, entitled Fida, e Khan, and afterwards A'zam Khan, Kokah (died 1678-79), and Mir Malik Husain, Khwafi, entitled Bahadur Khan up to the sixteenth year of Aurangzeb, and then Khan Jahan, Bahadur, Zafar Jang, Kokaltash (died 1697-98) (see 'Ma,asir-ul-Umara,' i. 247, 798). Wazir Khan is, no doubt, the Wazir Khan, Muhammad Salih, *diwan* to Prince Dara Shukoh; he was killed at Samugarh in 1658, *Tarikh-i-Muhammadi* (year 1068 H.).

gave you the fruit, and you have the temerity to deny it?' Thereupon Fida,e Khan produced the fruit, and gave it to the king, saying: 'Your majesty observes the petty theft I committed, and overlooks the large amount of more than thirty thousand rupees that every day is robbed by the wazir?' Shahjahan replied quietly: 'I know it well, and much do I desire to punish him, abhorring as I do all thieves, but sometimes it is necessary to dissemble in order to be well served.'

At the court of Shahjahan was a great Hindu prince, called Amarsin (Amar Singh)—that is to say, 'Lion-minded.' For several weeks he had failed to attend the court. It is the practice for the Hindu princes and the commanders to encamp with their tents for twenty-four hours every week below the royal fortress. The above rajah after a time came to court and entered the royal presence, and the wazir (Wazir Khan), who was very fond of him, went up quietly to him, and asked him why he had not come to court and performed his duties. Amar Singh, with his face all aflame, made no answer; there upon the wazir said to him some words which are offensive among the Rajputs—that is to say, 'May you be, you villain!'

Hardly had Wazir Khan pronounced the words, when Amar Singh, laying hold of his dagger, plunged it into the wazir's breast, and he fell dead in the royal presence. There stood Amar Singh, with the dagger still in his hand, looking at the king. All were in consternation at such an act, but Shahjahan dissembled, and rising, retired into the privacy of his harem without uttering a word. But he made a sign for them to kill Amar Singh, as was done. The officers then present leapt upon him, and with his dagger he wounded six of them. The cavalry and infantry of Amar Singh,[1] who were outside the fortress, on learning the death of their lord, made use of their weapons, killing and decapitating whomsoever they encountered, getting away in safety. King Shahjahan afterwards granted the dignities of Amar Singh to his younger brother, named Jacont Sing (Jaswant Singh), whom he

1. Rao Amar Singh, eldest son of Rajah Gaj Singh, Rathor, of Marwar (Jodhpur), killed Salabat Khan, Roshan Zamir, Bakhshi, in *darbar* on the last day of Jamada I., 1054 H. (August 5, 1644), and was himself slain (see 'Ma,asir-ul- Umara,' ii. 230, 732). For Jaswant Singh (died 6th Zu,l Qa'dah, 1089 H.—December 19, 1878, N.S.), see 'M.-ul-U.,' iii. 599.

XI. *bis*. Elephant Fight as No. XI. (outline only)

Vol. I *To face page 200*

liked much; and as to him, I will relate farther on what he did in the days of Aurangzeb.

Once Shahjahan was much incensed against a Pathan officer, whom he suspected of treachery, and he meant to order the man's execution. The officer got word of this and fled, with the whole of his troops. When the king learnt of this flight, he inquired wrathfully [142] from those present which of them would undertake to lay before him the head of that rebel. The son of the fugitive offered to produce it. Shahjahan gave him an army, and marching off, he overtook his father near the fortress of Gualior (Gwaliyar), where a great contest took place. The fugitive was defeated, and worn quite out, he took refuge under a tree. There the son came up to him, but having compassion upon his father, offered him horses to continue his flight. He said he would make excuses to the king. The father would not consent; on the contrary, he requested that his head might be cut off, whereby the son might obtain reward at court and continue their race, for he knew well he could never escape. Listening to this advice, the son cut off his father's head, and carried it into the presence of the king. Thus he displayed more loyalty to Shahjahan than love to his father. Their descendants still exist in the Mogul country.

There happened in the reign of Shahjahan an event which will with difficulty be credited in our Europe, being a thing that may never have been heard of in that part of the world. It was this: The governor of Sindi (Sind) wrote a letter to the king offering congratulations on the prosperity of his kingdom, which he ruled with such care; nor had it ever been heard that any other king did so much to keep his realm in peace. Every day he (the governor) ordered proclamation by beat of drum that if anyone had a complaint he should present his plea in the royal presence. Months passed without a single complaint being heard of. But the midwives informed him that a girl only nine years of age had given birth to a male infant. Shahjahan ordered that the child should be forwarded to court, and gave him the name of *Avalvast*[1]—that is to say, 'Before Time.' He was the son of an oilman. When he had reached a proper age he received charge

1. Possibly a compound of *avval* (Arabic, 'first'), and vast (Hindi, 'thing,' 'substance').

of the lamp department at the royal court. Although it may be a very improbable thing, this [early child-bearing] was, nevertheless, not impossible, more especially in India, where the climate is so hot.[1] There even the nobles are forced to go about with a simple *cabaya* (*qaba*, a long loose shirt), and nothing more; and they sleep uncovered in the dew, or on the damp ground upon a simple mat.

A Hindu prince called Champet Bondela (Champat Bundelah)[2] rebelled against Shahjahan, and collecting sixty thousand Rajput horsemen, raised a disturbance in the king's territories, plundering in all directions, committing a thousand insolent acts, and refusing to pay tribute. The king intended to order out a large army against the rebel, while he himself remained among his women. But seeing that his officers were more or less afraid of Champat, Shahjahan asked [143] his astrologer, a Hindu, whether he ought or not to march in person to put down this rebellion.

The astrologer replied that, if he wished to have any good result, he must go in person, otherwise the Rajputs would defeat his majesty's army. Having heard the words of the astrologer, the king left the capital at the head of a great army, resolved to attack Champat without delay. But finding the rajah showed a bold front, he halted, and had recourse to the tricks of policy, as counselled by his renowned wazir, Sadulacan (Sa'dullah Khan),[3] a man of great wisdom, one of whose retorts I will relate a little farther on (I. 144). This wazir pledged himself to defeat the rebel without any battle. With this intent he opened a secret correspondence with Champat by friendly letters, sent him some presents, offering to serve him and to act towards him as a friend.

Champat placed confidence in him, assuming that things would be settled in a manner favourable to himself. The wazir

1. *Sic* in text, but there is obviously some break in continuity here or omission.
2. Champat Bundelah is spoken of again at I. 185 and III. 61.
3. Sa'dullah Khan, a Shekhzadah from Jhanwat in the Punjab, became wazir in the seventeenth year (1644-45). He died 23rd Jamada IX., 1066 H. (April 19, 1656), at Shahjahanabad, aged sixty-seven. In rank he was 7,000, 5,000 horse, *duaspah*. Chronograms of his death are *Sa'dullah Khan mard* and *Jami'-ul-faza,il* (see 'Ma,asir-ul-Umara,' ii. 441, and 'Tarikh-i-Muhammadi' under 1066).

wrote to him that the anger of the king against him being by this time abated, it would suffice if he retreated for one league. Champat answered that, the king having come in search of him, he could not retreat unless first of all the king retreated. Sa'dullah Khan replied that, as he was a feudatory of Shahjahan, it did not accord with the king's dignity to withdraw. But if he would retire, he pledged his word that the king also would move back and would forgive him his tribute-money.

Champat drew back his forces, but the king marched forward. Champat complained of this deception; but the wazir wrote to him that he must continue his retirement leisurely, that the king would retire without fail. If he had advanced for a time as he had done, it was only that his army might not murmur against him. Champat once more believed what he was told, and retreated again. This caused his soldiers to take fright, seeing that the king continued to follow, without the rajah ever daring to attack. Thus most of the Hindu army dispersed, in such a manner that Champat was forced to take refuge in the jungle. The king's army invaded the territories of the prince and plundered them. Champat complained to Sa'dullah Khan about having been misled, but Sa'dullah Khan replied that the king had also broken his word to him. Thus was the Bundelah left in the extensive forests and the mountains with a considerable force, where the king was unable to get at him. In the end he was obliged to enter the king's service [144] in person with three thousand horse and accept pay from him; and until this day there are descendants of his who always assume the name of Champat Bundelah, and serve, as he did, under the Mogul flag.

With reference to Sa'dullah Khan, I beg to inform the reader that the lord Dom Matheus, of Canarese race, was Bishop of Bichulim.[1] He went into the Mogul realm to carry on a mission, and, desirous of obtaining a permit from the king, he came to court and prayed an audience, stating that he was a man who had come from a very distant country to make a proposition to the king. When he reached the royal presence Shahjahan recognised

1. Bicholim, in Portuguese territory, lies eight miles north of Goa in lat. 24° 55, long. 92° 42' (Thornton, 'Gazetteer,' 119). Müllbauer ('Geschichte,' 368) speaks of a Matthä us, a Christian of St. Thomas, Bishop of Chrysopolis in *partibus*, who may be the person intended by Manucci.

that he was a learned man of ascetic life. He therefore sent for all the most learned Mahomedan doctors; and when they had arrived the king gave permission to the bishop to speak. Thereupon Dom Matheus announced this proposition: 'A traveller in a foreign country met two persons, one of whom was sleeping and the other was awake. I ask your majesty, from which of them ought he to ask his way?' He put forward this proposition because the Mahomedans say that the Messiah is alive and awake, while Muhammad is sleeping until the Day of Judgment.

They were all perplexed by this question, but Shahjahan ordered them to answer. Sa'dullah Khan, who was the most learned of all, seeing their silence, and fearing some reply which would open the field for Lord Dom Matheus to preach the true faith of Jesus Christ, craved leave from the king to give the answer. He said: 'It was necessary to wait until he who was sleeping should awake, because the very man who was awake was himself waiting to ask from the sleeper which was the right way.' By this he meant to suggest that the Messiah had lost his way, and was waiting for Muhammad to awake to ask him the road. No delay was allowed for Lord Dom Matheus to open his mouth, but the king gave him the signal to take his leave; and Sa'dullah Khan remained a proud victor, receiving the congratulations of all the bystanders.

The astrologer who had advised Shahjahan to march in person (*ante,* I. 143) said one day to the king, as a proof of acquaintance with the courses of the stars, that it was advisable for his majority [145] to quit the fortress, because there was a planet then dominant which prognosticated the death of the greatest person dwelling therein. He was of opinion that for governor he should select the *kotwal* (chief police officer). This plan was adopted, and the king went out to hunt. After the lapse of two months Shahjahan received news that the *kotwal* was dead. He returned to the fortress, and made a great deal of the astrologer, and conferred on him very great rewards.

But it seems to me that it was the astrologer's artfulness, for he had a very great friend in the physician who attended the *kotwal.* It may be that they took counsel together, and he may have had him killed to prove the truth of his reading of the stars. For I have seen many similar cases, and these Hindus, without fear of God and devoid of scruple, do many such-like things out of desire for money. Nevertheless, there is not a great man who has not in his house an astrologer, if it be only to know the right hour for leaving his house on any business, even down to when to put on a new cloak (*cabaxa*). Of this astrologer tribe there are great numbers in the Mogul kingdom; even the *bazars* swarm with these folk, and by this means they find out all that passes in the houses. Both Moguls and Hindus are so credulous that they put faith in all that these men choose to tell them.

During the march made by Shahjahan against Champat Bundelah there died a great captain called Camcana (Khan Khakan).[1] Out of carelessness the king did not appoint anyone in his place. There was then present at the court a general whose ancestors had fought in the wars of Taimur-i-lang. The king made use of his advice, he being a man of excellent judgment. One day he appeared in the royal presence anxious and pensive. Shahjahan asked him what was the cause of his anxieties. He answered that a kingdom was like a palace built upon pillars: when one of them was missing, if no remedy was applied, it was bound to fall. Just as in the case of that palace without the pillar there was wanting a good officer in the kingdim; and if another were not put in his place, it was inevitable that the kingdom would go to ruin. The king was pleased with the advice, and directed him to select someone at court who was fitted to occupy that post. In a short time this order was carried out.

The said general's name was Said can Bahadar (Sa'id Khan Bahadur);[2] he had neither sons nor daughters. The king was desirous that he should have [146] issue. He therefore ordered his physician to refer to a receipt in the 'Chronicles of Taimur-i-lang,' which was composed of eleven ingredients. I have tested it several times, and always with good results. Sa'id Khan Bahadur swallowed the medicine, and at the end of four years he had a number of sons by various wives, concubines, and

1. I cannot tell who is meant, unless it be 'Abd-ur-rahim, Khan Khanan (son of Bairam Khan), who died in the last year of Jahangir's reign. The Bundelah troubles began almost immediately after Shahjahan's accession.
2. Sa'id Khan, Bahadur, Zafar Jang, a Chaghatae by race (see the 'M.-ul-U.,' ii. 429). He died in 1062 H. (1651-52), leaving twenty-two sons.

slave-girls that he possessed. After this interval Shahjahan asked him how many sons he had, to which he replied that next day he would give him an answer. He then found that he had sixty male children, without counting the female. He expressed his gratitude for the gift made to him by his majesty, adding that all of those children were ready to be offered up a sacrifice to the royal orders. The king gave them all the epithet of Canazat (*Khanahzad*)—that is to say, 'Born in the House,' by which they were mostly known, and all drew good pay.

Not only was Shahjahan liberal in rewarding and prompt in chastising the great; he was equally grateful in every matter, even the smallest. It happened that one day on his way to hunt he became separated from his men. Worn out and very thirsty, he went into a village lying on the king's highway from Agrah to Dihli, and arrived at a hamlet where as a charity a Brahman was giving water to the wayfarers. The king came up to him, and requested him to give him water. The Brahman, seeing that Shahjahan was drinking greedily owing to his great thirst, threw into the vessel a little grass, thereby forcing him to drink slowly. The king in anger asked him why he had put in the grass. The Brahman, not knowing to whom he was speaking, said: 'It is what I do to my asses when they are tired, so that they may not get colic pains.' The king took a rest at the edge of the village, beneath a tree. His retinue arrived, when the Brahman in a fright, recognising that it was the king, prostrated himself on the spot and asked for pardon. But Shahjahan rewarded him with a gift of the said village, which at this day is known as the 'Brahman's village.'

The same thing that happened to his grandfather Akbar also happened to Shahjahan, when he had made up his mind to make war upon the Rana, a Hindu king. He sent for his wazir, Sa'dullah Khan, to come to the palace at an unusual hour, and directed him to prepare the army secretly for a campaign against the said Rana. Coming out of the fortress, Sa'dullah Khan heard [147] a Ragateira[1] woman, who cried out to her husband, calling him a lazy, idle fellow; he must get up at once and go to buy whatever was required before starting against the Rana,

1. All I can suggest for this is 'Rajput.' *Raga* (= *raja*) + *teira,* the usual Portuguese ending.

whose territories the king intended to invade. Hearing this, the wazir returned to court and related to Shahjahan all that he had heard. At once the king sent out spies to discover what was being said. These men came back and reported that the common people in the city said openly that the king would march against the Rana. This report caused the king to abandon his intention, and the Rana made terms with him, ceding some territory and paying a considerable sum of money. The Ragateira woman arrived at her opinion because the wazir had been sent for to the palace during the night, and since the people of Industan (Hindustan) are great gossips, as I have said earlier (I. 87), they sometimes get hold of the truth.

The purpose that Shahjahan had of fighting with the Rana was diverted to a campaign against the Hindu prince of Scrinaguer (Srinagar), which is in the midst of lofty mountains in the north, covered all the year with snow. But it did not happen to him as he had hoped. To effect his purpose he despatched a general at the head of thirty thousand horsemen besides infantry. The prince allowed his enemy to penetrate into the mountains, retiring as they advanced. When the soldiers of Shahjahan had got a certain distance he closed the roads, so that they could neither advance any farther nor retreat, and there was no way of deliverance for them. Finding himself in this danger, the general sent proposals for peace negotiations, but the Hindu prince returned the answer that his resolve to treat was too late. Already the commander had a deficiency of supplies, and all his camp was in great confusion. He therefore requested from the prince permission to withdraw, and although the rajah could have destroyed them every one, he did not wish to do so. He sent to say that he would grant them their lives, but his soldiers required all their noses as a memorial of having given them a gift of their lives. Shahjahan's soldiers finding themselves in such dreadful straits, rather than lose their lives were content to lose their noses. They abandoned their arms, throwing them down where they stood, and issued one by one, leaving their noses behind them on the spot. From this Shahjahan out of shame never again attempted to make war against the rajah, and he gave an order that ever afterwards this prince should be spoken of as the Nactirany (Nak-kati-rani)—that is to say, 'Cut-nose'—and until this day he is known by this name. The general, who could not endure coming back with his nose cut off, took poison, and put an end to his life before [148] he got back to the plains. Of this rajah I shall have to say something in the reign of Aurangzeb (I. 274).[1]

It is now time to speak of the sons of Shahjahan; but first of all it is requisite to state that Shahjahan only preserved four sons and four daughters, and whenever it seemed likely that the number would be exceeded, he did not allow his wives to come to delivery, but directed medicine to be administered to cause abortion. He left behind him this evil practice, of which Aurangzeb made use, and also his sons.

The first daughter whom he had was Begom Saeb (Begam Sahib), the eldest of all, whom her father loved to an extra ordinary degree, as most lovely, discreet, loving, generous, openminded, and charitable. She was loved by all, and lived in state and magnificence. This princess had an annual income of three millions of rupees, in addition to the revenues of the port of Surat, assigned for her expenditure on betel. She had in addition many precious stones and jewels that had been given to her by her father. She favoured the interests of her brother Dara, securing thus that the nobles at the court adopted the same side, and did not join that of his adversaries. She exerted herself a great deal to secure the crown to her brother Dara; this was due to her eagerness to marry, Dara having promised to give his consent as soon as he was crowned. With this end in view, she employed all her cleverness and energy to satisfy her father; she served him with the greatest love and diligence in order that Shahjahan should accede to her petitions. It was from this cause that the common people hinted that she had intercourse with her father, and this has given occasion to Monsieur Bernier to write many things about this princess,

1. *Srinagar.*—This story is probably an imperfect version of Mirza Shuja', Najabat Khan, Badakhshi's campaign in Srinagar (Garhwal) in Shahjahan's ninth year, 1045 H. (1635-36). The story is told differently in 'Ma,asir-ul-Umara,' iii., pp. 822-824. The widow of the ruler of Garhwal was previously known as Nak-kati Rani, from her habit of cutting off rebellious subjects' noses. But though Najabat Khan escaped alone to Sambal, supporting life on the leaves of trees, nothing is said about his losing his nose. He did not die till 'Alamgir's seventh year, 1074-75 H. (March 29, 1664, to March 18, 1665).

founded entirely on the talk of low people.[1] Therefore it is incumbent on me, begging his pardon, to say that what he writes is untrue.

He says that Shahjahan, learning that this princess had a lover in her palace, forthwith went to seize him. The princess had hidden the man in a stove, and the king caused it to be lighted, and thus secured his death. I leave the reader to judge if a father, who loved so much this princess, would do such an infamous act to his daughter at such a great court, where there were so many ambassadors. Although he might know that his daughter had her hidden diversions, he always dissembled, holding the princess equal to her mother, of whom it might be said she governed the kingdom.[2]

One day, owing to his love for her, he had complained to her, saying [149] that his vassals no longer obeyed him with the accustomed promptitude, this being a sign that he was getting near the end of his reign. The daughter, imagining that she would be able to remedy this by lengthening the days of the old man, gave largely in alms and liberated many slaves, male and female. First of all the latter were made to circumambulate her father three times, and then sent out of the harem, as if they carried away with them the royal infirmity outside. She also distributed many elephants and horses. This custom is very common in Hindustan, and this superstition being very widespread, everyone distributes, according to his ability, alms of food and other things.

Dara wished, and petitioned his father accordingly, that the princess should be married to the chief general at the court,

1. Constable's edition, pp. 11, 12, and note.
2. Anand Ram, Mukhlis, in his 'Chamanistan,' p. 25, gives a short account of Jahanara Begam, known as Begam Sahib. He says she was the author of one or two religious treatises. She died in 1093 H. (1682), and was buried in the courtyard of Nizam-ud-din Auliya's shrine at Dihli. The inscription is given in 'Asar-us-sanadid,' p. 45, No. 44, and part iii., p. 73; also in Carr-Stephen's 'Archaeology,' 108. On her gold bedstead were the Hindi words: '*Begam Sahib ka palang sone ka*' (*sone ka*, 'of gold,' or 'for sleeping on'; *sona* (noun), 'gold,' or *v.* 'to sleep').

whose name was Nezabet Can (Najabat Khan),[1] a man descended from the royal family of Balq (Balkh). He was brave and well-proportioned; but Shaistah Khan, brother-in-law of Shahjahan, becoming aware of this proposal, said to him (Shahjahan) that it was not advisable to make such a marriage, because when married to the said princess the husband would necessarily have to be placed in the same rank as any other prince. Najabat Khan was related to the King of Balkh, against whom his majesty must sometime make war. Furthermore, he ought to bear in remembrance the regulation of Akbar that daughters should not be given husbands.

This was the reason why Shahjahan did not give his daughter in marriage, although from his fondness for her he would have liked to find her a husband. All the same, this princess did not desist from waiting on her father with great affection, contenting herself with the pleasure she had with her lovers. The principal one was a vigorous youth of goodly presence, the son of the chief dancer in her employ, who was her mistress of music. This person was brought to the harem when he was quite small, and he sang with such charm before the princess that she gave him the epithet of 'Born in the House.' Under cover of this title these princesses and many great ladies gratify their desires.

When he began to get a little bigger, she gave him the name of Dulera—that is to say, 'Always a Bridegroom'—and he received rank like any other commander, with a number of cavalry and infantry and gorgeous standards, and his name was great, in the city. One day it happened that this man was going to the court of the princess, her mansion being outside the fortress. On the way he encountered Mahabat Khan, who was proceeding to the royal audience-hall. When passing each other in the street, their respective retinues had a slight dispute. As Mahabat khan recognised the standards as those of Dulera, he ordered his own to be furled, and went on to court without them. Information of this was given to Shahjahan, and he asked him for what reason he had come to court without his usual insignia. Mahabat Khan

1. This Najabat Khan is identical with the general who commanded in the campaign against Garhwal (*ante*, fol. 148). He was the third son of Mirza Shah Rukh, ruler of Badakhshan. Abu Talib, Shaistah Khan, Khan Khanan. Amir-ul-umara, was Shahjahan's brother-in-law. He died at Agrah in 1105 H. (end of 1693) at a great age.

responded most humbly [150] that his time had passed by now that musicians had begun to carry standards. The king investigated the matter, and sent orders for the flags of Dulera the musician to be destroyed. Mahabat Khan did this on purpose, not being on good terms with Prince Dara, and hoped by what he had done to vex the princess, knowing that he would at the same time annoy Dara.

This princess treated herself to many entertainments, such as music, dancing, and other pastimes. It happened one night while engaged in such-like dances that the thin rainment steeped in perfumed oils of the princess's favourite dancing-woman caught fire, and from the great love she bore to her, the princess came to her aid, and thus was burnt herself on the chest. From this arose great disturbance in the court, but what caused the greatest sorrow to the princess was that the dancing-woman died.[1] In addition to these amusements the princess was also found of drinking wine, which was imported for her from Persia, Kabul, and Kashmir. But the best liquor she drank was distilled in her own house. It was a most delicious spirit, made from wine and rose-water, flavoured with many costly spices and aromatic drugs. Many a time she did me the favour of ordering some bottles of it to be sent to my house, in sign of her gratitude for my curing people in her harem. This liquor profited me greatly. The lady's drinking was at night, when various delightful pranks, music, dancing, and acting were going on around her. Things arrived at such a pass that sometimes she was unable to stand, and they had to carry her to bed.

I say this because I was admitted on familiar terms to this house, and I was deep in the confidence of the principal ladies and eunuchs in her service. I have no wish to state all that went on. But I am very surprised at what Monsieur Bernier has

---

1. Stewart, 'History of Bengal,' p. 251, places this incident in 1636 (1046 H.), connecting it with the visit to Agra of Gabriel Boughton, the English surgeon. But Yule, 'Diary of W. Hedges,' iii. 159, thinks this is not proved, and places Boughton's visits in 1645 (iii. 182). Khafi Khan (i. 598) assigns the Begam's accident to the year 1053 H. (1643-44), which is certainly rather near Yule's date. See also the 'Badshahnamah, ii. 363, which gives the exact date, 27th Muharram, 1054 H. (February 4, 1644, N.S.). The Court seems to have been at Dihli at the time, and not in the Dakhin.

written—namely, that the nazir, or chief eunuch, of the princess would not allow any desired person to enter the palace of the princess, and for this reason she caused the nazir to be put to death by poison. On the contrary, the man obeyed her, and sought every mode of gratifying her, seeing the great interest he had not to work against her.

When Begam Sahib leaves her palace to go to court, she proceeds in great pomp, with much cavalry and infantry and many eunuchs. The last named, who surround her closely, push on one side everyone they find in front of them, shouting out, pushing and assaulting everyone without the least respect of persons. The same is done by all the princesses of the blood- royal when they come out. Thus it is that, perceiving the approach of these princesses, everybody forthwith hastens out of the way. They proceed very [151] slowly, men in front sprinkling water on the roadway to lay the dust. They are placed in a palanquin which has over it a rich cloth or net of gold, sometimes ornamented with precious stones or pieces of looking-glass. The eunuchs surround the palanquin, driving away the flies with peacock-feathers stuck into handles of enamelled gold-work or adorned with precious stones. The men-servants hold sticks of gold or silver in their hands, and call out, 'Out of the way! Out of the way!' Near the palanquin they carry various perfumes. The wife of Ja'far Khan, being the mistress of Shahjahan, moves about with the same dignity.

If perchance any noble with his retinue is met on the road, he, being anxious to acquire such protectors at court, persons through whose hands pass the most important affairs, with-draws from the road by way of respect and reverence. He dismounts and stands with his hands crossed at a distance of two hundred paces, less or more. There he waits until the lady has come close, when he makes a low bow, showing his expectation of some honour. When these princesses wish to do honour to the noble, they send him several parcels of betel in a gold-brocade bag ornamented with precious stones. If they do not accept the civility, they order him to receive a shower of blows, which makes him run. Among all of these ladies the most esteemed and respected was Begam Sahib, because she obtained from her father whatever she asked.

This princess, to preserve her memory, gave orders for the construction of a *sarae* in the square which is between the fortress and the city.[1] This is the most beautiful *sarae* in Hindustan, with upper chambers adorned with many paintings, and it has a lovely garden, in which are ornamental reservoirs. In this *sarae* there put up none but great Mogul and Persian merchants. The king went to view the work that had been done for his beloved Begom Saeb (Begam Sahib), and he praised her energy and liberality. Sadulacan (Sa'dullah Khan), who never allowed an occasion to escape without the customary flattery, said: 'Aguer ferdus berrui zimin as, aminas, aminas' (*Agar fardus bar rue zamin as, hamin ast, hamin ast*)—that is to say, 'If the terrestrial paradise is on earth, it is here, it is here.'[2]

The first-born son of King Shahjahan was the prince Dara, a man of dignified manners, of a comely countenance, joyous [152] and polite in conversation, ready and gracious of speech, of most extraordinary liberality, kindly and compassionate, but over-confident in his opinion of himself, considering himself competent in all things and having no need of advisers. He despised those who gave him counsel. Thus it was that his dearest friends never ventured to inform him of the most essential things. Still, it was very easy to discover his intentions. He assumed that fortune would invariably favour him, and imagined that everybody loved him. He was very fond of music and dancing, and once fell in love with a public dancing-girl named Ranadel (Ra'na-dil). His love was so violent that when his father refused his consent to a marriage with her, the prince began to pine to death. Seeing this state of things, Shahjahan was obliged to accord permission for the marriage, and she was granted the same dignities as the other princesses. This Ra'na-dil displayed afterwards her love and fidelity to Dara, as may be seen further on (I. 261).

Among other pastimes indulged in by Dara was that of listening to buffoons, who invented many things to amuse him. At times, well dressed and followed by a number of servants,

1. See Bernier, 280, 281, for a description of this *sarae* at Dihli, and Carr-Stephen, 'Archaeology,' p. 247, under the name of 'Sarai of Jahan Ara Begam.' The site is now occupied by the Queen's Gardens (H. C. Fanshawe, 'Delhi,' 52).
2. Native writers also attribute the lines to Sa'dullah Khan. The correct text is—

   'Agar fardaus bar rue zamin ast,
   Hamin ast, wa hamin ast, wa hamin ast!'

See 'Asar-us-sanadid,' p. 42.

they would attend the prince's court. When they saw anyone come in search of employment as a soldier, they would seat themselves and order him to be called before them. They would ask him what he wanted. Having ascertained the status of the unhappy man, they would praise up their prince by all sorts of talk, and thus induce the victim to present himself before Dara on all-fours. They would assert that by appearing in this fashion he would be given double pay. They found some men so foolish as to do this before the whole court, whereby Dara was much delighted.

But the best joke of these buffoons was the following: Making the acquaintance of some other soldiers of equally low intelligence, they began to talk about how they meant to advance these men's interests. In this conversation one of them said he was physician to the prince, and began to ask the soldier what he was suffering from. The soldier turned pale at such a question, and said that he had no disease of any sort. On this the buffoon became still more emphatic, and said he had a very severe complaint, and if he did not come to his aid, he would soon lose his sight. At such an assertion the soldier trembled, supposing that the case was serious. Thereupon the buffoon made use of this opening to feign great affection for him, asserting that he meant to cure him in a few moments [153] with a certain smoke. Thus he caused the soldier to be taken by his servants to a room, where he was mounted, with sword, shield, and quiver full of arrows, into a large pot to be fumigated. Once inside he was shut in, and they began to apply the smoke, inducing him to stay where he was. Then, thus shut up, they had him carried by two *culles* (*qulis*) into the presence of Dara during his time of audience. When they took off the cover of the pot, the poor soldier came out of it fully armed, and was quite terrified at finding himself in such a magnificent court, grander than any he had ever seen before. Everybody began to laugh at him, whereat he was ashamed, and began to run. The prince was much amused; but men of judgment were in consternation at finding a prince who hoped to inherit a kingdom, and already forty years of age, amuse himself with such childishness.

Dara was very fond of Europeans. Added to this, as everyone knew, he held to no religion. When with Mahomedans, he praised the tenets of Muhammad; when with Jews, the Jewish religion; in the same way, when with Hindus, he praised Hinduism.

This is why Aurangzeb styled him *Cafar* (*Kafir*)—that is to say, 'The Infidel.' At the same time he had great delight in talking to the Jesuit fathers on religion, and making them dispute with his learned Mahomedans, or with a Hebrew called Cermad (Sarmad), an atheist much liked by the prince. This man went always naked, except when he appeared in the presence of the prince, when he contented himself with a piece of cloth at his waist. He (Dara) much delighted in hearing the fathers overcome everyone with their arguments: in my time the fathers who were at the court of the prince Dara were three. The first was named Father Estanilas Malpica, a Neapolitan;[1] the second, Father Pedro Juzarte, a Portuguese; and the third, Father Henriques Buzeo, a Flamand. The last was much loved by the prince, and every time he went to court he received fifty rupees and two shawls.[2] Of this father, who was much cherished and esteemed by all the nobles, I shall have to speak again (I. 259, II. 117). On some occasions Dara drank with the fathers, for this prince was fond of wine-drinking, but did it discreetly.

Dara was also possessed with the craze of putting faith in astrologers, of whom he entertained a considerable number. The chief of them [154] was called Bavani Das (Bhawani Das), who had a great liking and affection for me, because he enjoyed drinking my wine. This man had placed his head in danger by a paper, in which he declared that without the slightest doubt the said prince would become king. I asked him in familiar conversation how he could have had the audacity to sign such a paper, and what excuse he had ready to produce if it did not happen accordingly. The astrologer laughed long and heartily at my question, and said to me that if the said prince should come to be king, he would accord to him the greatest credit; if not, the prince would be sufficiently busied in saving his own life, and not likely to have time to seek that of an astrologer.

This prince (Dara) had two sons, the elder called Sultan Suliman Xacu (Sultan (prince) Sulaiman Shukoh)—that is to say, 'King Solomon'—and the younger called Sultan Super Xacu (Sipihr

1. Malpica is mentioned again on fol. 1. 277. Busée's name will appear again several times.
2. The non-appearance in this enumeration of Heinrich Roth's name must be accounted for by his absence in Europe when Manucci was at Agran, 1656-58. He is named by our author in 1662-63 (II. 58).

Shukoh)—that is to say, 'High as the Stars'. These were the children of the principal wife, who was of the blood-royal.

When Shahjahan assigned to each prince a separate establishment, he kept Dara by his side, and made him lord of the kingdoms of Kashmir, of Lahor, and of Kabul. Out of the great love he bore him he granted him several privileges, such as to cause elephants to fight together whenever he pleased, and to display in his presence gold and silver maces, a thing otherwise allowed to the king only. To demonstrate still more his affection, he ordered a small throne to be placed near his own, and on this the prince was to take his seat. It must be added that out of the great respect he had for his father Dara would never consent to sit on this throne. He (Shahjahan) gave an order that all the nobles of his court should go first to make their morning bow in the presence of the heir-apparent, Sultan Dara, and then come to his (Shahjahan's) daily audience. He declared on various occasions that this son (Dara) was the successor that he desired, and he would do all in his power to get him made king; but the matter was according to the will of the Paraverdigar (*Parwardagar*)—that is to say, of the Creator, from whom he besought the gift of such a happy event.

By reason of these things the haughty Dara scorned the nobles, both in word and deed, making no account of them. It happened that one of Mahabat Khan's soldiers killed one of his (Dara's) men. Falling into a rage, and without any inquiry into the matter, he (Dara) ordered his troops to be collected, with orders to drag [155] Mahabat Khan before him. On hearing of this, the noble made ready to defend himself in his mansion. Shahjahan heard of these preparations, whereupon he ordered his son Dara to be sent for, and administered a severe reproof for what he had intended to do. He said that if soldiers had disputes among themselves, that was no reason for interfering with their commanders. After this incident Mahabat Khan bore a grudge against him (Dara), and failed him at his time of need, as I shall recount further on (I. 212).

It was also a rumour that Dara likewise took the life through poison of that able noble Sa'dullah Khan,[1] a man esteemed by

1. See *ante*, I., folio 143, and the note there, for the date of Sa'dullah Khan's death.

the king and the whole court. He was a partisan of Prince Aurangzeb. Dara also insulted Rajah Jasing (Jai Singh),[1] a very powerful Hindu prince, lord of forty thousand horsemen and one hundred and fifty thousand infantry. He said that Jai Singh looked like a musician, an occupation much despised in Hindustan, because all such men act the part of buffoons. Apparently the rajah submitted to the insult received from Dara, but he only dissembled, and postponed the taking of vengeance to the time when Dara would need him. This he accomplished, and I will relate it hereafter (I. 169).

Not content with having affronted so many, he must needs ridicule the great soldier Mirzamula (Mir Jumlah),[2] when he arrived at his father's court. He ordered the noble's sword, that he was wearing at his waist, to be stolen as soon as he entered the royal palace by active fellows, of whom he kept a number for the execution of such-like tricks. In addition, he ordered his buffoons several times to imitate the gait and the gestures of the said Mir Jumlah, making mock of him.

Not contenting himself with these affronts to a commander who, for the benefit of the prince's father, Shahjahan, revolted against the King of Golconda (Gulkandah), as I shall tell hereafter (I. 162), Dara, three days before the said Mir Jumlah left for the Dacan (Dakhin) to conquer the territories of Gulkandah, deprived him by bribery of the eighty European artillerymen he (Mir Jumlah) had in his service. Mir Jumlah knew of all these things, and granting that he was capable of some dissimulation, he was not able to ignore this last piece of treachery, and racking his head, he tried to find some course to take, so that the artillerymen might continue under his orders. This in effect happened, because Aurangzeb afterwards made him (Mir Jumlah) the royal captain-general [156] for the conquest of Axami (Assam), and thus the artillerymen came under his command, as I shall relate hereafter (II. 72).

But one of the chief generals of Shahjahan was suspected by Dara of being unfriendly. This man was found in his bed with

1. Jai Singh (Mirza Rajah), Kachhwahah, of Amber, born about 1605, succeeded in 1617, and died in 1667.
2. Mir Muhammad Sa'id, a Sayyid from Ardistan, entitled Mir Jumlah, and afterwards Mu'azzam Khan, Khan Khanan, Sipah Salar. He died in Bengal on the 2nd Ramazan, 1073 H. (April 10, 1663). See 'Ma,asir-ul-Umara,' iii. 530.

his throat cut, and the populace whispered that he (Dara) had ordered the assassination. To sum up, he (Dara) depreciated all the nobles at the court, above all the generals and commanders. In order to insult them still more, he gave exaggerated praise to Barcandas Can (Barqandaz Khan)[1]—that is to say, 'Grand Thunderer'—who, being a soldier of repute, was made by Dara head of his artillery. The appointment was due to his having killed an owl which had taken up its place upon the room where the prince was sleeping. He said this man was the bravest in the whole empire; that he by himself would suffice for the destruction of any prince who was his (Dara's) enemy; that all the commanders and generals put together could not reach the hundredth part of that man's valour. At this praise the other commanders showed themselves aggrieved and disgusted. All these things united were the chief causes of Dara's ruin and death. He might have been King of Hindustan if he had known how to control himself.

The second son of King Shahjahan was called Xaxujo (Shah Shuja')—that is to say, 'Valiant King.' He was arrogant, and reputed to be courageous, steadfast, and prudent in his undertakings. He knew how to acquire friends likely to aid him in his important and seasonable affairs. At the court of his father he had many agents, especially when he was in Bengal. These persons were able to seduce from the court of his brother Dara the best soldiers, artillerymen, and engineers by money grants and promises of doubling their pay. Besides this, he maintained a great friendship with Rajah Jasont Sing (Jaswant Singh' Rathor), an ally of Prince Dara; and in the harem he had his sister Genorara Begom,[2] who acted for him, and reported to him all that went on. I have nothing to write about that princess, and may be

---

1. Barqandaz Khan (name, Ja'far) was general of artillery to Dara Shukoh. In Shahjahan's twenty-seventh year (1653-54), he obtained a *mansab* and the above title. In the first year of Aurangzeb he was confirmed in his rank; in the seventh and thirteenth years of the reign he was on duty in the Dakhin. Nothing further is known of him (Kewal Ram, 'Tazkirat-ul-umara,' British Museum Additional MS., 16,703, fol. 21*b*). He is also named as having been at the Battle of Samugarh in 'Ma,asir-ul-Umara,' i. 592. Manucci speaks of him again (I. 240, II. 134).
2. I am in doubt as to this name; it is meant for the youngest daughter, but the name does not correspond, even approximately. The four daughters were: (1) Parhez Bano Begam, (2) Jahan Ara Begam (Begam Sahib), (3) Roshan Ara Begam, (4) Suraiya Begam.

excused from taking that trouble. I will only state that she was proud, very passionate, fancied herself clever, was envious, not generous, and, furthermore, not good-looking.

Shah Shuja' followed the habits of his father, being a lover of songs, dances, and women, among whom he spent days without giving [157] audience, drinking wine to excess, and spending a great deal of money on dancing women, to whom he gave valuable jewels and handsome clothes, conferring on them increased pay, as the fancy took him, without any regard to merit. He had such a high idea of himself that he supposed his valour could conquer everybody. From this cause he despised his opponents, and was at times negligent in important things. He was the first to revolt against his father, as I shall tell hereafter (I. 166). Some assert that he followed the sect of Aly ('Ali), venerated by the Persians as a prophet; whereas in the Mogul realm, Balq (Balkh), Bocara (Bukhara), Badacxam (Badakhshan), Samarcand (Samarqand), and Cascar (Kashghar), they do not recognise 'Ali as a prophet, but follow the religion of Turkey and Arabia.

During the time that this prince governed the kingdom of Bengalla (Bengal), where he held his principal court in the city of Ragemal (Rajmahal), there happened, a few years before the rebellion in the Mogul kingdom, an extraordinary case, about which he wrote to King Shahjahan. At eight o'clock in the day there appeared near the said city, in a plain a league and a half broad, a great number of cobra snakes, large and small. They covered the field and moved from west to east until four o'clock in the afternoon; they looked like ripples in the ocean. In the greatest fright, the inhabitants of the villages climbed upon the tops of their houses and upon trees. They beheld moving in the midst of the said cobras one of great size, which carried on its head another smaller one, entirely white. They pursued their way without harming anyone, many remaining behind in the suburbs of the city and in the villages, and through losing their companions they died. Hearing of this event, Shahjahan asked his astrologers what it meant. They replied that the wickedness of the empire was taking its departure, and that he would survive for many prosperous years.

The prince Shah Shuja' also consulted his astrologers, and they told him that before much time had passed [158] there would arise a rebellion in the empire, and that he would become emperor.

The little cobra carried upon the head of the large one was, they said, the king of the cobras, who had come to the end of his reign, and was thus compelled to leave his old abode. This event caused considerable fear to all people, and it was spoken of in many directions. Both Mahomedans and Christians assured me that it was as the astrologers had divined, and that it must happen as they had said. But in saying that Shah Shuja' must become king they went too far. All the same, this may have been the reason for Shah Shuja' rising in rebellion against his father.

The third son of King Shahjahan was the prince Aurangzeb, the present King of Hindustan. This prince was very different from the others, being in character very secretive and serious, carrying on his affairs in a hidden way, but most energetically. He was of a melancholy temperament, always busy at something or another, wishing to execute justice and arrive at appropriate decisions. He was extremely anxious to be recognised by the world as a man of wisdom, clever, and a lover of the truth. He was moderately liberal, distributing rewards and conferring gifts wherever suitable. But above all, for a long time he pretended to be a faquir (*faqir*), a holy mendicant, by which he renounced the world, gave up all claim to the crown, and was content to pass his life in prayers and mortifications.

Still, being then in the Dakhin, he never refrained from urging his claims at court by the mediation of his sister, Roxonara Begom (Roshan-ara Begam). All was done in great secrecy, with much craft, so that his brothers could neither know nor suspect anything. He was aware that his father was not fond of him, and being afraid that he might be removed from charge of the Dakhin, he sought by his pretences to secure some of his affection. However, Shahjahan recollected every day the faqir and the apples (I. 118), and thus gave no credit to the make-believe of Aurangzeb. In addition, Dara said several times to his father that he was not afraid of any of his brothers except the bigot and prayer-monger.

With this cloak of renunciation he deceived many, and secured intimacy [159] with the poor mendicants, many of whom were devoted to him, and the greater number of them were used as spies, to give him news of the many things that occurred. He was so subtle as to deceive the quickest-witted people, among whom are these *faqirs*.[1] For, having been told that many of these people had considerable sums hidden in their patched coats, he issued an order at the city of Brampur (Burhanpur) that all the mendicants should be collected at an entertainment, where he meant to distribute alms. In addition to the banquet, he intended as a sacrifice for his sins to give to each of them a new coat.

A great number of the mendicants assembled, for none could refuse this chance of filling his belly and covering his nakedness with a new garment. After having dined, the new clothes were given to them as they left, taking from them the old ones that they had on their bodies. Finding themselves thus cornered and knowing the loss they must suffer, they became anxious, and shouted that they could not give up their clothes by reason of their great holiness, and many said that they had vowed they would be buried in those clothes, which they had carried about on their bodies for so many days. Their objections were of no avail, and they were sent away, carrying the new raiment.

Aurangzeb ordered the said clothes to be piled up, and after they had been searched he acquired a large number of golden coins. With these he wished to purchase a string of lovely pearls. He asked his teacher, Secmir (Shekh Mir),[2] a man of great wisdom, whether the pearls were worth a hundred thousand rupees, which the owner demanded. The teacher, without inspecting them, and keeping his eyes cast on the ground, said to him: 'If your highness does not mean to acquire greater pearls, you can buy these; but my advice is that with the said money you raise soldiers, and by them you will become master of larger pearls and greater riches.' Aurangzeb followed this advice, and praised the judgment of Shekh Mir.

Not content with pretending to be a *faiqir*, Aurangzeb went further, and acted the mola (*mulla*, man learned in theology), catechizing this one and the other. When at the city of Orangabad (Aurangabad), where he held his court, he had in his following a Rajput prince, whom he began to catechize in the hope of

1. Captain Symson, 'Voyage to East India' (London, 1715), p. 24, has this story, which he picked up at Surat in 1701.
2. Shekh Mir, Khwafi, was killed at Ajmer in 1069 H. (1659), in the battle against Dara. He was the son of Mir Muhammad Khan Khafi, and was one of 'Alamgir's great nobles (see 'Ma,asir-ul-umara,' ii. 668, and the 'Tarikh-i-Muhammadi' under 1069 H.).

making him a Mahomedan. But finding the prince remained fixed in his religion, he said to him that if the Hindu faith was the true one, he would be able to hold of a red-hot iron with his hand without being injured. If he remained uninjured, then he (Aurangzeb), too, would follow the same religion.

The Rajput accepted the offer [160]; the red-hot iron was put into his hands, but, not able to retain it, he threw it forthwith on to a tent of Aurangzeb's close by, which took fire and was burnt. The rajah, who was injured by the fire, said:

'It seems to me that we both of us live in error—I because I burnt myself, and your highness because your tent was burnt.' In spite of this Aurangzeb did not desist from his habit of catechizing both Hindus and Christians, turning some of them into Mahomedans, and of these some only agreed in order to acquire promotion, and others in order to obtain employment in his court, or to earn some rupees [161].

Aurangzeb grew very fond of one of the dancing-women in his harem, and through the great love he bore to her he neglected for some time his prayers and his austerities, filling up his days with music and dances; and going even farther, he enlivened himself with wine, which he drank at the instance of the said dancing-girl. The dancer died, and Aurangzeb made a vow never to drink wine again nor to listen to music. In after-days he was accustomed to say that God had been very gracious to him by putting an end to that dancing-girl's life, by reason of whom he had committed so many iniquities, and had run the risk of never reigning through being occupied in vicious practices.

During the time that Aurangzeb was in the Dakhin a man called Mirzamula (Mir-Jumlah),[1] who was a Persian by birth, was the wazir of the Gulkandah king and general of his army. Mir Jumlah came to the kingdom of Gulkandah in the service of a Persian merchant, and was in charge of some horses that the trader had brought from Persia for sale to the King of Gulkandah. Mir Jumlah went through the streets from door to door selling shoes; but fortune resolved to favour him, and little by little he rose to be a great merchant of much fame in the kingdom. Owing to his being very rich, with ships at sea, also

1. For his biography, see 'Ma,asir-ul-Umara,' iii. 530-555. His name was Mir Muhammad Sa'id, and he came from Ardistan (see 'Tarikh-i-Muhammadi' under 1073 H.; also see *ante*, note to fol. 155).

a man of much wisdom and very generous, he gained for himself many friends about the court, who looked after his interest at the king's audiences.

Anxious to rise in life, Mir Jumlah made a present to the King of Gulkandah of some fine elephants and various cloths of Europe and of China. In this way he was well received, and obtained an appointment with good pay. He filled various honourable offices, and in all of them gave a good account of himself, and the king thought so highly of him that he made him governor of the Carnatte (Karnatik) province. There he was on terms of familiarity with and much esteemed by the great; and above all, he kept up a great friendship with Dom Phelipe Mascarenha, Viceroy of Goa.[1] They sent each other presents. Dom Phelipe sent him several kinds of brocade and porcelain from China, accompanied by many curiosities from Japan. Besides these, he sent him some armes blanches—a breast-plate, a morion, and a sword. All of these were much prized by Mir Jumlah, and he made use of them on necessary occasions in battle. He replied to these gifts by sending a number of jewels and diamonds, which he extracted from the mines that are in the said province of Karnatik. During the time of his government in the Karnatik, Mir Jumlah gathered together the great treasures which then existed in that province in the ancient temples of the Hindu idols. Besides these, others were discovered by his exertions in the said province, for which (*i.e.*, precious stones) it is very famous.

He had a separate army of his own, with efficient artillery, and many European artillerymen, besides the soldiers in the service of the King of Gulkandah. This was the reason that many at the court became envious of him, and these men succeeded in making the king disgrace him. Already the king had become somewhat suspicious of him, and had thought of dispossessing him gently, so as to obtain possession of his riches. But, above all, he felt resentment at the report they made to him that Mir Jumlah had been too familiar with his best-loved and most beautiful queen. Although he awaited the return of Mir Jumlah to court in order

1. Dom Filippe Mascarenhas, nominated Viceroy on April 10, 1644; assumed charge at Ceylon September 16, 1644: arrived at Goa, and was installed December 30, 1645; handed over the government on May 31, 1651 (Danvers, ii. 287, 302).

to obtain satisfaction, he could not refrain from expressing himself in strong language and menaces against him (Mir Jumlah).

Mir Jumlah was informed of the king's intentions by the said queen, and by his son Mahamedemi Can (Muhammad Amin Khan)[1] and other relations, who held the principal offices at the court. He then wrote to his son that he should seek some way of escape, so that [162] they might unite forces; but although Muhammad Amin Khan remained on the alert, he could not get away, as the king kept him constantly near to him.

Finding that his son was unable to escape, Mir Jumlah decided to destroy both the life of the king and the kingdom of Gulkandah. With this object he wrote to the prince Aurangzeb, who at that time was at Aurangabad, fifteen days' journey distant from Gulkandah. He informed the prince that the King of Gulkandah was trying to ruin him and his whole family, and he claimed the protection of his highness, so that he might avenge himself for the injury that the king wished to inflict on him, forgetful of the services he (Mir Jumlah) had done to the crown, as known to all the world. If he (Aurangzeb) would listen to his advice and confide in him, he would inevitably arrange events in such a way that the king and realm of Gulkandah should fall with ease into his hands. Forty thousand chosen horsemen from his army would suffice. But they must advance on Gulkandah with the greatest expedition by forced marches. On the road they should give out that it was an ambassador from King Shahjahan, proceeding for negotiations of great importance with the King of Gulkandah and his *dabir* (secretary), who was his chief minister and a relation of Mir Jumlah, on whom he could rely.

It was sufficient for his highness to arrange to come with all haste, that he (Mir Jumlah) would manage things so that no one should know of his approach until he arrived at the gates of the Baganagar (Bhagnagar)[2] fortress. When the king came out to receive the letter, as was usual, he could be captured without any difficulty, and as a consequence the whole of his family would fall into their hands. He (Mir Jumlah) added that he himself would provide the sum of fifty thousand rupees for every day's march.

1. See the 'M.-ul-U.,' iii. 613. Muhammad Amin Khan died at Ahmadabad on the 8th Jamadi II., 1093 H. (June 14, 1682) (*ibid.*, p. 619).
2. Bhagnagar, the old name of Haidarabad in the Dakhin.

Prince Aurangzeb, who sought an occasion for displaying his fidelity to his father and enlarging his dominions, replied to Mir Jumlah that without fail he would start at once from Aurangabad, and would follow in every point the instructions contained in his letter. Then he began his march.

The King of Gulkandah, finding that Mir Jumlah did not mean to obey the repeated orders issued for his return to court, directed the arrest of Muhammad Amin Khan. The latter, when he came to know the royal order, fortified himself in his mansion, and resolved to defend it. He fought three days against the soldiers of the king, when Aurangzeb arrived at Bhagnagar, without anything being known, except that he was an ambassador from King Shahjahan.

The arrival of this disguised prince was announced to the king, and at once he went forth to meet him and receive the letter at a garden, as is the custom. While on his way to the rendezvous, a spy told him he had heard there was treachery afoot, that Prince Aurangzeb himself had come to seize him. On obtaining the information the king did not continue on his way, but putting his horse to the gallop, sought safety in the fortress, which lies at one league from the city.

Monsieur Bernier writes[1] that the king reached the presence of Aurangzeb, and it was here that a spy warned him that the ambassador was none other than Aurangzeb himself. Thereupon he fled. But it was not so. If he had got as far as that he could not have escaped from the hands of Aurangzeb, for the relations of Mir Jumlah and the agents of the prince would have laid hold of him.

Aurangzeb thereupon made himself master of the royal palace and all the wealth therein, stripping bare the tombs of the ancient kings of Gulkandah, whence he derived great treasures. At the same time he left at liberty, and did no injury to the women, who went off in search of their sovereign master. This practice is followed in India.

He (Aurangzeb) then invested the fortress most closely for a period [163] of two months, aided by Muhammad Amin Khan and his men. During this time Mir Jumlah arrived, burning to

1. Constable's Bernier, p. 20.

take vengeance upon the king. When Shahjahan heard of this uprising, he issued orders for the siege to be raised, and for the retirement of Aurangzeb to the city of Aurangabad. These orders were obeyed by the prince. But before he would raise the siege Prince Aurangzeb obtained payment for all his expenses, and for much more than he had disbursed. Besides this, he forced the King of Gulkandah to give his daughter in marriage to his (Aurangzeb's) son Sultan Mahamed (Sultan Muhammad),[1] handing over with her as dower the revenues and the district of Ramguir (Ramgir). He also made the promise that on his death Sultan Muhammad should be his successor, and he agreed that on one side his coin should bear the impress of King Shahjahan. Then he (Aurangzeb) carried off in his train Mir Jumlah, with all his family and wealth, making the King of Gulkandah undertake that no one should interfere with the palaces or the property of the said family, and that they should enjoy the same privileges as before.

The reason for raising the siege of the fortress and liberating the King of Gulkandah was that Begam Sahib and Dara were unwilling that the King of Gulkandah should fall into the hands of Aurangzeb. By acquiring possession of Gulkandah he would become more powerful than before, thus making it easier for him to lay claim to the throne of Hindustan.

When Shahjahan sent his order to Aurangzeb to raise the siege of the fortress occupied by the King of Gulkandah, he also directed that on his way back to Aurangabad he should visit a place belonging to the King of Vizapur (Bijapur) called Beder (Bidar), a fortress of some importance. It was not sufficient for him that early in his reign he had compelled without justification the same king to make over to him the

1. Sultan Muhammad was the eldest son; he was born December 29, 1639, and died in 1677-78. The campaign occurred 1066. (January, 1656) (Elphinstone, 515). As to the marriage of 'Abdullah Qutb Shah's daughter to the prince, see Khafi Khan, i. 746, 749, where that author speaks of the marriage gift of '*Sarkar* Ramgir, adjoining the borders of Barar and Bidar.' For its position, see Constable's 'Hand Atlas,' Map 32, Ab, Yelgandal District.

fortresses of Juner, Calliani (Kaliyani), and Beomdi (Bhiwandi), with their lands.[1]

Without fail the two generals—that is to say, Aurangzeb and Mir Jumlah—executed the orders of Shahjahan. But the principal object of Aurangzeb was to gain Mir Jumlah by soft words, promises, and offers, recognising that he was a brave leader and a wealthy man. He was thoroughly convinced that this noble would be of use to him in carrying out his intention of seizing the kingdom of Hindustan. In the course of conversation Aurangzeb acquired a knowledge of Mir Jumlah's disposition, and began to complain to him of his father. His phrase was that Shahjahan was the father of Dara, while he, on his side, could never find a kinder father than he (Mir Jumlah), that he built his hopes upon him, and accepted him as his protector. He prayed him as a favour to have compassion upon him and his family. He pledged his word that if he ever reigned he would make him (Mir Jumlah) the greatest man at his court, and his son, Muhammad Amin Khan, the second, giving them all the privileges of princes. This conversation was kept absolutely secret, and he ended it with very earnestly entreating him not to enter into relations with Dara, or give him any sign of encouragement. Mir Jumlah, seeing how he (Aurangzeb) relied upon him, became very friendly to that prince, and gave him his word, binding himself to support him with his entire strength and his life, when the occasion arose. From that hour they began to plan the important undertaking of getting the kingdom into the hands of Aurangzeb, both men being masters of the requisite prudence and power of concealment.

When Shahjahan was informed of the valour shown by Mir Jumlah at the taking of Beder (Bidar),[2] he wrote him several friendly letters, inviting him to court, where he would

1. This refers to the Treaty of Zi,l Hijjah, 1045 H. (April, 1636), mentioned by Khafi Khan, i. 534. Bidar, lat. 17° 54′, long. 77° 34′, is now in the Nizam's territories. Juner is, apparently, the place in the Poona district, lat. 19° 14′, long. 73° 65′, and Kaliyan that in the Thanah district, lat. 19° 14′, long. 73° 12′. Beondi is probably Bhiwandi, a little to the north-west of Kaliyan, and also in the Thanah district.
2. Syed Hoosain and C. Willmott, 'Historical Sketch,' ii. 377, say that Bidar was taken by Aurangzeb and Mir Jumlah in 1656.

appoint him absolute secretary.[1] He acted thus because he wished to make use of [164] him and of his valour to recover the fortress of Candar (Qandahar). Mir Jumlah started for Dihli, and wherever he passed the governors of the places came out to greet him, doing him great honour and giving him presents, all by order of the king. Upon his arrival close to Dihli the greatest commanders were sent out to greet and escort him. Orders were given that all along his route the streets and shops should be decorated in the same manner as done for the king's passing.

At the time I was at Dihli[2] he was received with great pomp, and given the highest place in the royal audience. Shahjahan accorded him the title of Vizir Azam (Wazir-i-a'zam)—that is to say, 'Great Secretary,' and the name of Mazamcan (Mu'azzam Khan)—that is to say, 'Greatest of the Great.' After a short time he was ordered to make ready an army for a march without delay against the King of Persia, from whom he (Shahjahan) was pledged to take the fortress of Qandahar. With this intent he had already made ready his artillery and a certain number of cavalry.

Mir Jumlah, or the newly-made Mu'azzam Khan, gave a present to Shahjahan of a large uncut diamond which weighed three hundred and sixty carats.[3] He added that if Qandahar produced such precious stones, his majesty might undertake the labour of going there, or could despatch some loyal vassal to take it. But to his mind, his majesty had better send some trusty person to conquer the lands where, of a verity, such stones were to be found. These were the kingdoms of Bizapur (Bijapur) and

---

1. These words possibly are intended to represent *wakil-i-mutlaq*, or vicegerent.
2. Mir Jumlah reached Dihli on the 25th Ramazan of the thirtieth year, 1067 H. (July 8, 1657) ('Ma,asir-ul-Umara,' iii. 535).
3. The 'M.-ul-U.,' iii. 535, gives the weight of this diamond as 216 *surkh*, or 9 tank, and values it at 216,000 rupees (about £21,600). Ball says Tavernier (ii. 439) weighed it after it was cut by Hortensio Bronzoni, and it was then Florentine carats (319½ ratis). The *surkh* is said to be the same as the Hindi *ratti*, the red seea of the *Abrus precatorius*, L. (see Ain-i-Akbari,' translation by Blochmann and Jarrett, i. 16, ii. 354, and iii. 123). But Tavernier (Ball, ii. 89) took the *ratti* as $\frac{7}{8}$ carat, or 3½ grains (Yule, 'Hobson-Jobson, 777). This diamond is held by Ball (p. 441) to be identical with the 'Kohinur,' now in the possession of the English Crown.

Golconda (Gulkhandah), and the island of Ceilao (Ceylon). Having spoken thus, he once more held forth his hand full of diamonds, already cut, of considerable size, though not so large as the first one.

He then undertook that he would himself deliver to Shahjahan after a short time the kingdoms referred to, and make him lord of all the coast of Choromandal and of Gerzelim (Ginjili).[1] Shahjahan was delighted at this speech, and at once ordered that the artillery should turn back from its march to Qandahar. He made a present to Mu'azzam Khan of the splendid mansion of the famous Sa'dullah Khan,[2] which stood opposite the royal palace.

The large diamond was returned to him to have it cut by an expert, and for this purpose they sent to him a Venetian lapidary named Ortencio Bronzoni.[3] I saw this diamond many a time; it was as large as a nut.

After the lapse of some months, King Shahjahan decided to despatch a powerful army to the Dakhin country, appointing Mu'azzam Khan to the command thereof. Dara was much aggrieved by this resolve of his father, and did his best to hinder the undertaking. He was afraid that Aurangzeb would be assisted by this army. But the extreme eagerness of Shahjahan to possess himself of the diamond-mines weighed more than the petitions of Dara and of Begam Sahib. In addition to other famous leaders, there were sent with Mu'azzam Khan Najabat Khan (*ante*, I. 147), Mahabat Khan, son of the great Mahabat Khan, of whom I have already spoken (*ante*, I. 112), and Salabetcan (Salabat Khan).[4] The condition was imposed that Prince Aurangzeb should remain at the city of Aurangabad as governor,

---

1. The Choromandal coast began at Negapatam, and extended as far north as the mouth of the Godavari, and the Ginjili coast began at the Godavari River, and ended at the pagoda of Jagarnath on the Orissa coast. See Temple's 'T. Bowrey' (Hakluyt Society, series ii., vol. xii.), pp. 2, 3, 120, 121; also Yule, 257, 258 ('Choromandal'), and 375 ('Ginjili').
2. Sa'dullah Khan died on April 19, 1656, new style. The mansion, now destroyed, stood between the end of the Faiz Bazar and the Dihli Gate of the Fort (palace).
3. This man is called Hortensio Borgio by Tavernier (i. 396). He reappears in Part III., 256, as the hero of a story at Agrah.
4. This Salabat Khan is possibly Khwajah Mir, Khwafi (see 'Ma,asir-ul-Umara,' ii. 742). That noble died in 1103 or 1104 H. (1692 or 1693).

and should not enter the lists of war; while Mu'azzam Khan was forced to leave at court as hostages his son Muhammad Amin Khan and the rest of his family. Marching rapidly for the Dakhin, he passed close to the city of Aurangabad, and invading the territory of Bijapur, he surrounded a place called Caliany (Kaliyan).[1]

At court Aurangzeb's interests were attended to by his sister, called Royonara Begom (Roshanara Begam). She was not very good-looking, but very clever, capable of dissimulation [165], bright, mirthful, fond of jokes and amusement, much more so than her sister Begam Sahib. But she was not of equal rank with the latter. She was generous, and drank wine when she could get it. On the whole she had not the same liberty, and was not so much confided in as Begam Sahib, nor had she the same powers, seeing that she lived within her father's harem. In spite of her power of concealment, she could not hide the fact that she was the declared enemy of Dara and of Begam Sahib. As she lived in the palace, she never was at a loss for finding out matters of importance, and of these she sent secret intelligence to her brother Aurangzeb, who thereupon took remedial measures.

The fourth son of King Shahjahan was Morad Bacx (Murad Bakhsh), the youngest of all the brothers. He was a man of little wisdom, who could not plan anything beyond his amusements, drinking, singing, and dancing. He was very bold and valorous, for ever practising himself in the use of arms, and perfect in the use of bow and arrow. He was a constant and energetic hunter, risking his life by spearing wolves and boars with his own hands, a thing none of his brothers did. He delighted in listening to talk about war, and through his over confidence he felt contempt for all that was done at courts; relying solely on his own right hand and on his sword, he thought other men of no account.

While he was governor of Gujarat, a man who was disaffected to his minister told him that this official was a traitor. Without any further inquiry he gave the minister a spear-thrust that passed right through him, whereupon he died.[2] Murad Bakhsh was a concealed adherent to the sect of Aly ('Ali).

---

1. Evidently the place already referred to (*ante*, I. 163), now in the Thanah district.
2. The person thus killed by Murad Bakhsh was Mir 'Ali Naqi, the *diwan* of Gujarat (see Muhammad Salih, Kambu's, "Amal-i-Salih,' thirty-second year of Shahjahan).

The fourth daughter of King Shahjahan was called Merniza Begom (Mihr-un-nissa Begam). She took the side of her brother, Sultan Murad Bakhsh. She was young, and always occupied with her toys and games, and was rather pretty. I have nothing to tell about her, for being so young she did not trouble her head about affairs of State, and during the disturbance in the kingdom lived on in the harem.

At the time when Mu'azzam Khan was investing Kaliyani Shahjahan fell suddenly ill. It was in the year one thousand six hundred and fifty-four,[1] on the 17th November, when the court was at Dihli. I was then in the service of the prince Dara. Shahjahan brought this illness on himself, for being already an old man of sixty-one,[2] he wanted still to enjoy himself like a youth, and with this intent took different stimulating drugs. These brought on a retention of urine for three days, and he was almost at death's door. This illness produced great confusion in the city of Dihll and throughout the empire. When the king saw himself in this plight, he ordered all the gates of the fortress (palace) to be closed up, leaving only two wickets open. Placing no reliance on the Mahomedan commanders, he ordered Rajah Jaswant Singh (Rathor) to post himself at one gate with his men, and the other he made over to Rajah Ram Sing Rotella[3] (Ram Singh). These officers guarded the fortress on all sides with thirty thousand soldiers, all of them Rajputs. Their orders were that only Prince Dara might enter twice a day with a retinue of ten persons. But he was not allowed to sleep within the fortress. Begam Sahib decided to stay inside to look after her father's food; but both she and the other persons left in the fortress were made to swear on the Quran to be faithful to him. He was afraid of being given poison.

Imagining that the king, his father, had but a few days to live, Prince Dara [166] set to work to raise as great a force as

1. Bernier (Constable's edition, 25, note 1) has September, 1657. Manucci's year is wrong, as usual, but the month may be correct.
2. As Shahjahan was born on January 15, 1592, he was sixty-five in 1657.
3. This man was Ram Singh, son of Karmsi, Rathor (see 'M.-ul-U.,' ii. 266). He is mentioned further on (I. 177, 191, and also in Part III.). In those passages he can be fully identified. Thus, *Rotella* must be either a popular form for Rathor, or one of their subdivisions. He was Rajah of Kishngarh, just north of Ajmer. Possibly the correct etymology is *Rawat* plus *ela*.

he could. Orders were sent to enlist men at the cities of Lahor, Agrah, and Dihli, which are the chief towns in the empire. His chief reason was his anticipation that when Shahjahan should fall ill, everybody would fly to arms for the defence of their houses from the robberies and assaults that would take place.

This confusion lasted in the city for three days and three nights, the shops remaining shut, and there being a scarcity of supplies. The agents (*procuradores* = *wakils*) wrote, each of them, in haste to the princes about the king's illness, whereupon every one of the sons began to plan and prepare his army. The 'sarrafos' (sarraf, a banker or money-lender), who are the men who issue bills of exchange, wrote to their correspondents in metaphors that they should guard themselves, as follows: 'Let it be known to your worship that the vessel of butter was filled to overflowing, and the butter in it was lost.' By this they wished it to be understood that the king was already dead, and they wrote as above, not daring to write any plainer, for these men are very cautious in conducting themselves. Many letters were received in which it was distinctly stated that the king was already dead. These were founded on the non-appearance of the king, as is the custom. Shahjahan was very much concerned at being unable to appear, he being in great pain, and he feared some disturbance.

When the above news reached Prince Shah Shuja', he arranged to take the field with a large force and a quantity of treasure, collected by him in the realm of Bengal, a very productive country, a treasure to which he had added by plundering several Hindu princes. He started with forty thousand horsemen and a great many infantry. Of the latter no count was taken, because in Hindustan such troops are not esteemed. He also placed a fleet on the river Ganges; it was commanded by Portuguese in his service. Having come to this resolution and ended his preparations, he mounted his horse, with this exclamation: 'Hia thech, hia tabut!' (*Ayo takht, ya tabut*)—that is to say, 'Either throne or tomb,' a proverb current among princes laying claim to a crown.

This prince marched along with the greatest confidence, relying on his bravery and on certain favoured captains of his who were at the court of Shahjahan, of whom the greater number had left (for the Dakhin) in the suite of Mu'azzam Khan. He chose the route past the city of Agrah, giving out that King

Shahjahan was already dead through poison given by his son Dara. For this reason, as he announced, he was on his way against Dara, and meant to avenge himself for the death of his father.

King Shahjahan was already somewhat recovered, although still weak, when he heard of the revolt of this son. He wrote him a letter telling him not to advance any nearer, and assured him that his complaint was not vital, and he was already much better. He might return to the place whence he had come. Prince Dara to whom it was of the greatest importance that the letters should be delivered [167], for he feared no one except Shah Shuja', was most energetic in getting these letters written. But Prince Shas Shuja's friends at the court wrote him to the contrary, asserting that his father's illness was mortal. Shah Shuja' received the letter of Shahjahan, but, concealing the fact, he moved ever on, announcing either that his father was dead; or, that if he should be living, on arrival at Agrah he (Shah Shuja') would ask his forgiveness, and submit himself to his authority.

It was reported to Shahjahan that Shah Shuja' had not obeyed his orders. He was thus forced, ailing and weak as he was, to leave the city of Dihli, and start for the city of Agrah, a distance of sixty-six leagues. His object was that all the people should hear, and that word should run throughout the empire that he was alive. Thus would he intimidate his sons and any traitors. But all was of no avail. Shah Shuja', now that he had taken the field, meant to seize the kingdom; and thus he continued his march. By this conduct, Shahjahan was forced unavoidably to send against him Sultan Suliman Xacu (Sulaiman Shukoh), eldest son of Prince Dara, then at the age of twenty-five years.[1] He was a well-grown young man, generous, of good judgment, loved by everybody, above all by his grandfather, Shahjahan, who conferred on him great wealth at the time of his marriage, which took place one year before the rebellion.

1. Sulaiman Shukoh was born in April, 1635, and thus, in 1658, was twenty-three solar or twenty-four lunar years of age (Beale, 390). He was married to the niece of Ja'far Khan on the 19th Muharram, 1067 H. (November 7, 1656) ('Amal-i-Salih,' thirtieth year). He died in prison at Gwaliyar in Shawwal, 1072 H. (May to June, 1662) ('Tarikh-i-Muhammadi').

This prince (Sulaiman Shukoh) was appointed general of the army sent against his uncle, Shah Shuja'. They sent with him the famous general called Rajah Ja Sing (Jai Singh),[1] who was a partisan of this prince, a man of great power and riches, renowned throughout Hindustan, and of so great capacity that there was not his like in the kingdom. They also gave him the great leader Dalil Can (Dilel, or Diler Khan)[2] of the Pathan tribe, and a force of selected troops. To these leaders the king (Shahjahan) gave secret orders that on no account were they to give battle unless compelled. They were to do all they possibly could to make Prince Shah Shuja' withdraw to Bengal.

Shah Shuja' heard that this army had started against him, and he made up his mind to fight if he came in contact with the enemy. Equally Prince Sulaiman Shukoh wanted to earn a name for valour, and determined to attack Prince Shah Shuja', his uncle, if he came up with him. But this was not the view of Rajah Jai Singh. Therefore, every day during the advance he sent off letters to Shah Shuja', and did all he could to prevent the two forces encountering each other. But, in spite of all his exertions, he found it impossible to make Shah Shuja' agree to give way. When the armies arrived within sight of each other, Prince Shah Shuja menaced his adversaries with his artillery. Rajah Jai Singh, who had the direction of Sulaiman Shukoh's army, took no notice, and prudently gave no other answer to the artillery fire than the following letter:

'Mighty Prince—Shah Shuja'!—News was received by the emperor Shahjahan, your highness's father and my sovereign, that your highness had come from your province with valiant soldiers and captains to wreak vengeance on someone for putting your father to death, as was asserted. But the report is false, for Shahjahan still lives and enjoys perfect health. As an intimate friend of your highness, I can assure you that he continues alive and well. Thus you can turn back to your province. As an addition to it, Shahjahan makes you a grant of the city of [168] Patana (Patnah), with its territory, in recognition of the love you have displayed to him at this time. It was an excellent decision,

1. Jai Singh, Kachhwahah, of Amber, known as Mirza Rajah, died 1667 (see note to fol. 155).
2. Jalal Khan, Da,udzai, entitled Daler Khan, son of Darya Khan, the founder of Shahjahanpur in Rohilkhand, died at Aurangabad in 1096 H. (1682-83) (see 'Ma,asir-ul-Umara,' ii. 42-56).

on the receipt of such news, to take the field, whereby your highness proved yourself a valorous prince and leader. But it would be a still better resolve if you were now to retreat, when you find that your father lives. You will thereby avoid causing him to suspect you of rebellion, and forcing him to send against you a still greater army for your destruction. I hope that your highness will listen to my advice, and withdraw without delay. I make promise of assisting you when the need arises.'

The prince Shah Shuja', having received this letter, appeared to be satisfied, and seemed to desire nothing more, giving out that he intended to retrace his steps. But he had a cunning mind, and had resolved to mislead Rajah Jai Singh, whom he dreaded, knowing him to be an experienced commander. With this intent he answered him as follows:

'Valorous Captain, Rajah Jai Singh!—The reason of my coming from the territory of Bengal is notorious throughout Hindustan, and the news received of the death of my father constrained me to collect what forces I had and take the road for Dihli. But now that you assure me my father is alive and in good health, I am satisfied to withdraw once more into my government. But it is imperative that you, being a vassal, retire the first, as befits the honour of a royal prince, such as I am; and I give my word that I will retreat, praying you meanwhile to retain your affection towards me.'

Rajah Jai Singh fathomed the intention of Shah Shuja' to fall upon him during his retirement, and made as if he accepted the proposal to withdraw first. He issued orders for the next morning that they should load the elephants, horses, and carts, and the rest of the baggage; he also gave the signal for a march, thus misleading the spies of Shah Shuja'. But secretly he directed that when the drums should beat for the march, his cavalry should remain on the alert. When Shah Shuja' learnt that the drums were beating for the march in Sulaiman Shukoh's army, he ordered his men to make ready for a rear attack on his nephew. But he did not find the opportunity, because Rajah Jai Singh at break of day fell all of a sudden on the army he had prepared, and many lives were taken. He did not allow Shah Shuja' a chance of rallying his troops, routed him, and took some of his artillery, some elephants, and a number of prisoners. Of the latter, forty were sent to the city of Agrah for production before the king as an attestation of the victory. Prince Dara did not deal with these prisoners as a valorous soldier should, but, by a most unjust sentence, ordered each to have a hand cut off. He imagined that this victory was the beginning of his reign.

Prince Sulaiman Shukoh continued the pursuit [169], contrary to the opinion of Rajah Jai Singh, being anxious to seize his uncle and complete his destruction. But Rajah Jai Singh so controlled matters that he (Shah Shuja') was allowed to retreat and save himself. He (the rajah) could have taken him, but did not wish to do so, for three reasons: the first was that Shahjahan still lived, and would release him, thus he (the rajah) would only gain one enemy the more at court; the second was the orders of the king requiring him to avoid a battle; the third was his grievance against Prince Dara, as already spoken of, when he called him (the rajah) a musician (I. 155). If he preferred to rout him (Shah Shuja') by the exercise of finesse, that was for two reasons: the first was that he would lose reputation if he attempted an attack on the prince's rear, a movement in which there was much risk of his being defeated; the second was not to leave an opening for Prince Shah Shuja' to act with still greater boldness, and thereby create more disorder at court.

Rajah Jai Singh wanted to let Shah Shuja' get away; he therefore said to Sulaiman Shukoh that it was better for him to return to court, since other matters were still pending there, and thus be on the alert in case of any other rising. But the prince replied to him that his father Dara could in that event gather together a new army, and send the general Barqandaz Khan against the new rebels. Thus he would not consent to desist; but Rajah Jai Singh continued to give Shah Shuja' the opportunity of retreat, and thus they followed him until he had almost arrived at the Bengal boundary.

The report of his father's illness having reached Aurangzeb at Aurangabad, he began secretly the necessary preparations for taking the field. But he conducted himself more prudently than did Murad Bakhsh. The latter, assembling such small army as was in his power, took the field, declaring himself a rebel, and proclaiming that he was on his way to Dihli to rescue the king [folio 170 is blank].

[171] King Shahjahan and Prince Dara believed that they were already freed from danger, seeing that Prince Shah Shuja'

had retired in the manner just described, and they attached no importance to Prince Murad Bakhsh's rising. They supposed that, through some present or other and letters they would send him, he would assuredly return to obedience. They did not foresee what was going to happen. For this reason Shahjahan ordered all his baggage to proceed to the city of Dihli. He announced that he would leave Agrah shortly, and that he was already recovered from his illness. In pursuance of this resolve, the greater part of the army had already reached the city of Dihli, and the roads were crowded with those who were still marching there day and night.

Meanwhile, in silence, a greater rebellion was in preparation. For Aurangzeb, who had for a long time been eager to make himself king, although covering up his ambition by his subterfuges, now availed himself of the outbreaks of the other princes. He wrote a letter to a rebel of Bijapur named Sevagi (Shiva Ji) to gain him to his cause, in case he met, perchance, with any failure in the purpose he was aiming at. He sent Shiva Ji presents, together with a golden tablet, by which he granted to him the collection of a fourth part of the revenues of some provinces of the Dakhin province, then held by the said Aurangzeb. This grant was to be perpetual; all the same, the time came when he broke his word, according to his habit, as will be seen hereafter (II. 117).

Being assured of the neutrality of Shiva Ji, he (Aurangzeb) declared himself against his father. The latter was on the point of mounting his horse and starting on the aforesaid journey,[1] when they delivered to him a sad letter, in which he was told that the Prince Aurangzeb had rebelled. This threw the court into confusion and the Prince Dara into great anxiety. All the people came back to the city of Agrah—in fact, I was already in Dihli, and now returned.

King Shahjahan wrote a letter to Aurangzeb repeating the protest that he had written to Prince Shah Shuja'. Prince Dara also wrote, but his letter was full of threats. But Prince Aurangzeb

1. *I.e.*, the return journey from Agrah to Dihli. Shahjahan quitted Agrah on the 18th Rajab (April 21, 1658), and hearing on the 2nd Sha'ban (May 5), at Bilochpur, about eighty miles north-west of Agrah, of Jaswant Singh's disastrous battle, fought on the 20th Rajab (April 23), he turned back and reached Agrah again on the 9th Sha'ban (May 12) (see 'Alamgiramah,' pp., 81 82).

dissembled and gave the same answer as Shah Shuja'. Finding himself with only a small force, and Murad Bakhsh being also in the field, Aurangzeb decided to write this letter to him:

'Be it known to the mighty Prince Murad Bakhsh that I have received word that Prince Dara has killed our father by poison, and has taken possession of the government, meaning to assume the title of emperor. From this cause Prince Shah Shuja' marched with a powerful army, intending to secure the throne and avenge himself on Prince Dara. This fact has forced me to write this letter, to let you know that there is no one, no other prince except you, worthy to be emperor of the Mogul Empire. Dara is an infidel and idolater, a destroyer of the Mahomedan faith; Prince Shah Shuja is a heretic, following the sect of 'Ali, and thus opposed to our faith; while my zeal for the Quran requires me to devote all my strength to making you emperor of the whole empire. For, as everybody knows, it is a long time since I renounced the world and made a solemn vow to end my days at Mecca. All that I ask of you is [172] a sincere statement, supported by an oath on the Quran, that after I have, relying on the strength of Allah, seated you on the throne and made you absolute sovereign, you will be pleased to take compassion on my family, and cherish them in memory of me with paternal love. If you give me your word with an oath on the Quran thus to act, I promise to use all my strength, devices, and ingenuity, and make every possible effort to seat you on the throne of Dihli. As a guarantee of what I say here, I send you one hundred thousand rupees, in order to establish between us a firm and perpetual union and friendship, being brothers, as we are, of one father and of one faith, and both defenders of the Quran. Therewith I conclude, awaiting your arrival.—Your faithful brother, Aurangzeb.'

Prince Murad Bakhsh, on receipt of this letter, in which he believed, was highly delighted, and showed it to all men in his army, in order to raise their spirits and encourage the adhesion of more leaders. He also used it to induce the great merchants to lend with a better grace the money he wanted from them, and thus obviate the use of force. His spirits rose, he looked on himself as already king, and he made great promises to everyone. By these means he raised a large force for the campaign. He replied as follows to his brother Aurangzeb:

Most prudent and most faithful brother Aurangzeb, Champion of the Quran!—Upon the receipt of your letter I was much gratified at the goodwill you enounce towards me, still more to find you so zealous for the Quran, and so ready to save our religion from the destruction that threatens it, should either of our two brothers become emperor. As I wish to prove myself grateful for the many kindnesses you show me, I accept the proposal that you make to me, and give you my word, attested by an oath on the Quran, to maintain your family in their rank as princes, and, above all, treating your own person in conformity with your directions, shall always hold you in respect and *in loco parenties*. As a mark of the great affection with which I accept your exhibition [of love], I employ the hundred thousand rupees on soldiers, whom I am sending to take the castle of Surat. I am making ready for the junction of our two armies, to carry out what Allah the Most High shall inspire. Awaiting further news, and believing that their can be no doubt of what you have promised me, your faithful brother, MURAD BAKHSH.'

Murad Bakhsh selected three thousand horsemen, and placed them under his loyal eunuch called Xaabas (Shahbaz),[1] a very brave man, and sent them to take the castle of Surat.

During this interval Prince Aurangzeb sent his son Sultan Muhammad, who was married to a daughter of the King of Gulkandah, as I have already stated (*ante*, I. 163), to bring back Mir Jumlah, then busy at the fortress of Kaliyani. Mir Jumlah was to rejoin him (Aurangzeb) at the city of Aurangabad. The prince sent a message that there were affairs of great importance on which he must consult him. Mir Jumlah, though it was all a pretence, made excuses, saying in a loud voice that he was the officer of the King Shahjahan, and not of Aurangzeb, nor was he under the latter's orders: for the king was alive, and not dead [173] as was asserted; that there was trustworthy news of the fact; that all his family was at the court in Agrah in the hands of Prince Dara. In no way could he accede to the proposals, or adopt the side of Aurangzeb. In this way Sultan Muhammad went back to the city of Aurangabad, and pretended to be very much put out with Mir Jumlah for not having carried out the business wanted of him.

---

1. The correct name of this eunuch, Shahbaz, is got from a passage in the 'Ma,asir-ul-Umara,' i. 298. He held the rank of 5,000.

The second time Prince Aurangzeb sent his second son, Sultan Mahazan (Sultan Mu'azzam), to show him (Mir Jumlah) the letters written by his father (Shahjahan). These were forgeries. They were in very cordial terms. They showed him to be so affectionate and friendly that Mir Jumlah declared it impossible to refuse to go. He then arranged terms with the garrison of Kaliyani, and hastened with his army to join that of Sultan Mu'azzam, and they marched together for the city of Aurangabad. Upon Mir Jumlah's arrival, Prince Aurangzeb made a false display of affection, using to him phrases of the greatest possible endearment, styling him 'baba' (*baba*) and 'babagi' (*baba Ji*)—that is to say, 'father' and 'lord father'—and embracing him repeatedly. He prayed him most earnestly to come with him to take part in his enterprise and to adopt his cause. Mir Jumlah appeared to be much incensed, and said that he was a most loyal subject of King Shahjahan. In public he reprehended him (Aurangzeb); all this being a comedy, to the end that the spies might write to King Shahjahan and Prince Dara of his apparent loyalty.

Foreseeing what might happen, and wishing to show his zeal in the prince's service, Mir Jumlah, in order to be able to succour Prince Aurangzeb if he failed in his first attempts, allowed by consent the fortress of Doltabad (Daulatabad) to be occupied [by Aurangzeb]. His reflection was that in case Prince Aurangzeb lost the battle that he had resolved to fight against Prince Dara and was routed, it was probable that King Shahjahan would send him (Mir Jumlah) in pursuit to wreak vengeance for the affront done to him. If so, he could once more be of some assistance to Aurangzeb.

The latter took possession of all his (Mir Jumlah's) treasure, cavalry, and artillery. Mir Jumlah had given secret orders to the generals and officers of his army to dissemble and make boastful demonstrations, without injuring anyone. These orders were executed. Both sides had recourse to their arms; many matchlocks were discharged, but nobody was hurt. To every one of the generals of King Shahjahan, who lay at half a league's distance from the force of Mir Jumlah, Aurangzeb sent an envoy saying that King Shahjahan being dead, if they would adopt his (Aurangzeb's) side, he promised them higher rank than they already held. As otherwise they would now come into the service of Dara, they ought to prefer to serve him (Aurangzeb), who was also a son of King Shahjahan. It was not fitting for such high-minded captains to serve an infidel prince, an enemy of the Mahomedan faith, of which he (Aurangzeb) was a true observer.

Mahabat Khan would have nothing to do with such arguments, but thereupon beat his drums for a march, and took the road for Agrah. Aurangzeb used considerable efforts to make him come back, sending him several messages with presents. But Mahabat Khan, holding faithfully to the cause of King Shahjahan, continued his march, and on his arrival at Agrah the king at once made him governor of the kingdom of Kabul [174][1]

The other generals expressed doubts, and said there was no certain news of the death of King Shahjahan, and that it was not for them to take the prince's side until they knew the truth. If the king were dead, they would come over to his side. They asked for fifty days' time, so that they might send their spies and learn what was going on. If no answer arrived within that limit of time, they pledged their word to adopt his cause. To make sure of their promises, Aurangzeb took from them an oath on the Quran.

In this interval, knowing well that the king was alive, he (Aurangzeb) resorted to some of his devices, and sent an order to a trusty captain called Mirza Abdulha ('Abdullah), who was in charge of the castle on the Narbada, the river which divides the lands of the Dakhin from Hindustan. This is an obligatory point for crossing, a place where no one can come or go without being examined. The orders were that everybody returning to the Dakhin should be searched. If he captured any letters saying that King Shahjahan still lived, he must forthwith burn them, and behead those who carried them.

In this way the generals were prevented from receiving their answer within the appointed time, and all of them transferred themselves to the side of Prince Aurangzeb. The latter lost no time in completing his preparations, writing to his friends whatever suited himself. Having taken the field with all his troops, he ordered everyone to kneel on the ground, as he did, and ask God with great earnestness to give them the victory. At the time of his mounting to start he raised his hands to heaven and

1. According to the "Amal-i-Salih,' this appointment was made on the 11th Jamada I., 1068 H. (February 14, 1658).

said: 'Hia ser deem, hia setanem' (*Aya sar diham ya sitanam*), by which he meant: 'I will lose my own, or take my adversary's head. These are the very words spoken by Alexander the Great when he marched against King Darius.

After making several marches there came news to him how the castle of Surat had surrendered to Shahbaz, the general of Prince Murad Bakhsh, but, not finding in it the cash that had been expected, it was sacked. All that was found in it was carried off to Prince Murad Bakhsh. The latter was requested by Prince Aurangzeb to join him with all his forces. He marched off to find him (Aurangzeb), so that they might unite and pursue their road to Agrah together. When he mounted his horse to set out on this journey, he said: 'Aguer talle daram, ech parua naderam' (*Agar tali' daram, hech parwa na daram*), that is to say: 'If I hold Fortune, I need no one.' The eunuch Shahbaz, having no faith in the word of Aurangzeb, advised his master, Murad Bakhsh, on no account to quit the kingdom of Gujarat, nor even leave the city of Amadabad (Ahmadabad), the chief place of that province. He (Shahbaz) would make him master of all the fortified places, adding greatly to his treasures; he should place no faith in the soft and misleading words of Prince Aurangzeb, but should refrain from going where that prince wished; and time would show what they ought to do.

Aurangzeb continued his march towards Murad Bakhsh. Apprehensive that he might send no answer, Aurangzeb redoubled his sweetly-worded letters, which were most subtle. He reaffirmed that he would make him (Murad Bakhsh) King of Dihli, as he had already promised; that his purpose was confined to making him king and entrusting to him his sons, whom he (Murad Bakhsh) should deal with as with any other men in his service. He (Aurangzeb) kept a number of secret agents at Murad Bakhsh's court, and these men persuaded that prince that these overtures were made solely to place his (Aurangzeb's) family and his own person in safety beneath his (Murad Bakhsh's) protection. On becoming king he was at liberty to grant Aurangzeb something by way of alms for his journey to Mecca, and to provide him a dwelling there, where he would pass the remaining days of his life, as he had vowed to God.

Murad Bakhsh declined to listen to the counsels of the eunuch Shahbaz, ambition to reign misleading his judgment. Then he made ready and started, meeting Aurangzeb, who awaited him near the mountains and woods [175] of Manddo (Mandu). Aurangzeb advanced to greet him, bringing with him his son, Sultan Muhammad; he was received with great respect, addressed as king by Aurangzeb, who stood before him with crossed hands. All the grand promises were renewed. Aurangzeb assured him he made not the slightest pretension to the crown; his only object was to help him (Murad Bakhsh) against Prince Dara, his enemy, and place him upon the throne. To this he had pledged himself solely with a view to retaining his friendship.

The two armies marched by equal stages. During this time Aurangzeb repeated continually his promises of friendship. He showed Murad Bakhsh the greatest respect, and always, in public and in private, referred to him and spoke to him as king and sovereign. Aurangzeb let him understand that if he had had any wish to be a king, the affair at Gulkandah would have sufficed; if he had any esteem for things of this world, he would be already king of Gulkandah. Murad Bakhsh believed that he was his true friend, that he would perform what he promised, that he sincerely loved him. In return, Murad Bakhsh made him the most magnificent promises.

Once, at ten o'clock at night, after Aurangzeb had arrived at the woods of Mandu, he being in his tent reading the Quran, there appeared at his right hand a hideous snake, which advanced towards him. Without being perturbed or losing his head, he drew with the greatest calm a little sword that he always carried about with him. By one sudden blow he separated the snake's head from its body, and, seated as he was, the blood splashed all over him. Getting to his feet, he shouted for his servants, and they finished off the snake, for they struck it all over its body. After it was dead he ordered it to be weighed. They made out a weight of sixty pounds (*arates*).[1] He declared that this was a sign that God would give him the victory, for the Mahomedans are very superstitious.

Some critical persons will ask how there could be a snake of that size, and being so large, how it could get into the tent of Prince Aurangzeb. Leaving on one side what other authors have

1. See Yule, 770, under 'Rottle,' for the Arabic *rati*, adopted into Portuguese as *arratel*, pl. *arrates*.

written, I say that I have seen them of much greater size. As for its getting into the tent, let the reader recollect that the said tent was in a wood full of rocks, where the ground could not be levelled. The whole army was scattered about in the same way, for in default of level ground the greater part of the army rests beneath trees, or among rocks, as I have seen on several occasions.

These two armies when joined together formed a powerful force. The court of Shahjahan was now thrown into confusion, fear, and anxiety, which were shared by the king and the prince Dara, for they already perceived the strength their adversaries possessed, and the persistence with which they were marching on; also the ability of Aurangzeb, coupled with the great courage of Murad Bakhsh.

Clearly did they see that a fire had been lighted, which it would be very difficult to quench. By means of many letters and protests sent to the two princes, Shahjahan told them to return each to his own government. He pledged them his word that in no way would he take notice of their rebellion. Nothing he could say was of any avail. But Aurangzeb continued ever to pretend, and told Murad Bakhsh that such letters were forged by Dara, that Shahjahan was of a truth dead. Even if he were not, it was right to deliver him from the hands of Dara, by whom he had been seized, for he never appeared in public. If their father [176] were alive, they would beseech him to pardon them, disculpating themselves by saying that they wanted to deliver him from the hands of Dara, and then go back each to his own government.

The whole of this was falsehood, for have I not seen with my own eyes that one day he (Shahjahan) gave audience, ailing as he was, for more than half an hour in his royal apartments, seated at a window looking towards the river. There were present a very great number of men from the army and the common people, all of whom heard and saw. But the greater part of them said that it was not Shahjahan, but a made-up figure prepared by Prince Dara for that purpose. That could not be truly said by those who were present.

There were many traitors at the court friendly to Aurangzeb. They wrote to him that he should arrange to reach Agrah before the arrival of Prince Sulaiman Shukoh from Bengal. This prince had been ordered by Dara to rejoin at headquarters. They also wrote that the illness of Shahjahan was mortal. Letters of this sort which had been despatched by Xastecan (Shaistah Khan)[1] and Muhammad Amin Khan, son of Mir Jumlah, were seized by Prince Dara. Thereupon he (Dara) arrested those two nobles and confined them in a room of his palace. The whole court supposed that without a doubt he would order them to be beheaded, and the whole of that day I waited on in the court solely to learn the end of the business. At seven o'clock at night they were liberated on the prayer of Roshanara Begam and other princesses, who persuaded the king that the captured letters were forgeries. Dara had afterwards to repent that he had not then and there ordered their decapitation.

The unhappy king, Shahjahan, saw that his sons had lost all respect for him, neither paid they any obedience to his orders. They marched on by long daily journeys, fully resolved and determined to give battle to Dara; and even if King Shahjahan went out in person to resist them, they were not likely to desist from an attack, the greater part of the advancing host being traitors and asserting that the king was dead (whereas he was very much alive, only with little strength left). Shahjahan told Prince Dara that the best thing was, in any case, for him (the king) to be present in the battle, even in such feeble condition as he was; by his going forth it might happen that the traitors would be held in more subjection. With this arrangement Dara seemed satisfied.

Having heard of this plan, the traitors objected to it, chiefly Callilcan[2] (Khalilullah Khan), who said to Dara: 'It is not right for your highness, whatever happens, to allow the king to be present and to fight this battle, because I give you my word that the victory will be with your highness, and if, perchance, the king take part, the name and the fame thereof must inevitably be his.'

The good old man (Shahjahan), believing that his appearance in the field might be of some use, began resolutely his preparations, ill as he was, to share in the battle. Spurred by honour and by the advice of the traitors, Dara in the end said to his father that if he went out to give battle, he (Dara) would take his own

1. Shaistah Khan, brother of Queen Mumtaz Mahal, and therefore maternal uncle of Shahjahan's children.
2. For Khalilullah Khan, see note, *ante*, I. 129. The statement that Shahjahan wanted to take the head of the army in person will be found also in the 'Ma,asir-ul-Umara,' iii. 827, line 14, *s.v.* Najabat Khan.

life with his dagger in his father's presence. The disconsolate old man, with tears in his eyes, said: 'I abandon to you all my authority, and God aid you!' Dara was very elated, believing that he would be the victor, owing to his reliance upon the traitors, and exclaimed: 'With my bowstring will I without fail bring in my enemies bound.' He (Dara) made ready with all imaginable energy to give [177] battle and wreak vengeance upon his brothers.

Meanwhile the poor king was in great affliction, finding himself thus persecuted and oppressed in the evening of his days, forced to divest himself of his treasures and confide them to the descretion of Dara. Then he sent for Chatarsal (Chhatarsal)[1] and Ra Ramsing Rotella (Rao Ram Singh Rawatela),[2] and placed them over the other generals at court, some of whom were not well affected to Dara. He gave these men orders to fight on his behalf against his own sons. In spite of all this, the king never ceased to feel the very greatest concern at the disorder existing in the empire, and the peril he was in of seeing himself soon destroyed. The larger number of his descendants would, he felt sure, be beheaded; and he never forgot what the faqir had told him, the man with the two apples (I. 118).

Dara sent off fresh orders in all haste to Sulaiman Shukoh, his son, to give up the campaign against Shah Shuja', and come promptly with his commanders to join forces with him (Dara), and deliver battle against Aurangzeb and Murad Bakhsh, who were then advancing by forced marches. Imperative injunctions were given not to make any delay, seeing how very important it was for their forces to unite before the battle. The decision thus arrived at was very good, but it was too late, and it was impossible (owing to Dara's unlucky star) for Sultan Sulaiman Shukoh to arrive in time. If his force could have joined, it would be almost impossible to conceive Aurangzeb and Murad Bakhsh having the audacity and temerity to attack as they did, the sides becoming then very unequal.

---

1. Rao Sattarsal (or Chhatarsal), Hada, grandson of Rao Ratn of Bondi (see 'M.-ul-U.,' ii. 260).
2. Ram Singh, son of Karm Si, Rathor, and nephew through his mother of Rana Jagat Singh of Udepur (see 'M.-ul-U.,' ii. 266, also mentioned in Part I., fols. 165, 191, and again in Part III.). *Rawatela*, 'of the Rawat branch-line' (?).

XII. Murad Bakhsh, son of Shahjahan

Vol. I *To face page 247*

In this interval of preparation for the army to take the field, there arrived news at the court of Agrah that Aurangzeb and Murad Bakhsh had crossed the river at Brampur (Burhanpur), and traversed by a very narrow passage the difficult, hilly, and wooded country of Mandu.[1] I have passed through these defiles many times myself. Dara had hoped to block their exit; now the above news only augmented the confusion at court. King Shahjahan thereupon sent for two famous leaders—the first, Raia Jacont Singh (Rajah Jaswant Singh, Rathor), the king's loyal subject; the second, Cacamcan (Qasim Khan),[2] a man not well affected to Dara, and enjoined them to proceed against Aurangzeb and Murad Bakhsh. His orders to them were to take every possible step to induce the two princes to retire. If they declined to listen, they were to be stopped by force.

To please Shahjahan, Qasim Khan joined Rajah Jaswant Singh, but he had little inclination to undertake the campaign or withdraw from the king's court. At the farewell audience Dara gave splendid presents to Jaswant Singh, and also to Qasim Khan. He presented them with several elephants and horses with their trappings, and some costly arms. He behaved in a most friendly manner to them, and thus they were sent off.

During the march they sent letters to Aurangzeb and Murad Bakhsh, telling them they ought to withdraw to their governments. But all these requests were in vain, for no replies were sent, nor did the men who carried them appear again. The princes marched with such expedition that before Shahjahan's generals expected to meet them, they were espied on some high ground not very far from the river at Ugen (Ujjain). It was during the time of the great heats at the end of April, and there was little water in the river. Thus on the instant the generals of Shahjahan made ready for battle; but Aurangzeb took no notice of the movement. Neither had his whole force arrived, nor was his army in battle

---

1. As to the campaign in Malwah, compare Bernier, pp. 36-41. The wording of some passages suggests that here Manucci, more or less, copied from Bernier.
2. Muhammad Qasim, entitled firstly Mu'tamad Khan, then Qasim Khan, son of Hashim Khan, son of Qasim Khan, Mir Balhr, was killed on the way to Mathura by his wife's brother towards the end of the year 1070 H. (July or August, 1661) (see 'Tarikh-i-Muhammadi,' year 1070; the 'Ma,asir-ul-Umara,' iii. 95, has 1071 H.).

array; he therefore ordered some of his pieces of artillery to be discharged to hinder the enemy from coming [178] too near to the river. The object was to allow time for the remainder of his army to arrive, and for his men to get some rest, they being worn out by the march and depressed by the great heat. He also wanted to secure a position with better air. All these things were managed by him. For if the rajah had attacked at that very moment, in the condition he (Aurangzeb) then was he must have been defeated without making much resistance. At this time I was at the court in Agrah, and I was not present in this first battle. All the same I am able to describe it, because I was on very familiar terms with the higher officers who took a part in it, and in addition thereto I obtained good information from some Europeans of different nations who directed the artillery of Aurangzeb. All of these set forth the facts in one and the same fashion. But Rajah Jaswant Singh contented himself with holding a position on the bank of the river to bar its passage in accordance with the orders that he had received.[1]

After Aurangzeb had given his army a rest and had delayed the enemy, he made dispositions for crossing the river. He ordered the whole of his artillery to be discharged, and directed that, under cover of this fire, Murad Bakhsh with his whole force should plunge into the river, the banks of which are very difficult of descent and ascent, being encumbered with many stones of all sizes, though the bed is not of any great breadth (I have crossed it myself many times). Qasim Khan, on his part, likewise ordered his guns to be fired, making a show of fighting the enemy and disputing the passage with him. But he had come to a secret understanding with Aurangzeb, and had already on the previous night hidden away the powder and shot, leaving only enough to let off three volleys. At the beginning the fighting was very fierce and severe, and the crossing was well defended by the men of Jaswant Singh. But in the end Murad Bakhsh plunged into the river with such valiant spirit that the rajah could not resist him,

1. For this river, see Thornton, 'Gazetteer,' 868, under 'Seepra,' where the position and character of the various crossings, with the width and depth of the stream, are given and the steepness of the banks is described. Aurangzeb's camp was at the village of Dharmatpur, seven *kos* from Ujjain, and that of Rajah Jaswant Singh immediately opposite (see "Alamgirnamah,' p. 56, top line).

Qasim Khan having already withdrawn. But the rajah never ceased to fight most desperately, until at length he saw himself left with only the smallest remnant of his force.

When Aurangzeb's troops reached the other side of the river, Rajah Jaswant Singh was advised, owing to his reduced numbers, to beat a retreat. If he survived, he could gather together many armies and fight many battles. Listening to these counsels, he retreated against his will in the best way he could, followed by five hundred horsemen, and started for his own country, which was at a distance of seventy leagues from the scene of the defeat. He did not wish to return to Agrah, owing to the great loss of some ten thousand Rajputs, who had followed him and were all his subjects. Aurangzeb gave orders to put up on the site a same and plant a garden, calling it Fatepur (Fathpur)[1]—that is to say, 'Filled with Victory.' Here he made himself master of all the artillery and baggage, with which he strengthened his army, digging up the powder and shot that Qasim Khan had buried.

Rajah Jaswant Singh arrived in his country with only fifteen horsemen, all the rest from various accidents having quitted him. His wife, the daughter of the Rana, a Hindu king, was named Ranagi (Rani Ji). She had been informed of his defeat, of what had passed in the battle—with what valour he had fought, and how with the few men remaining he was unable to resist [179] the enemy any longer. But instead of sending a message to meet him and console him in his discomfiture, she at once ordered the gates of the fortress to be closed. This was at Udepor (Udepur),[2] the chief town. He was not to be allowed to enter; and she added the contemptuous words: 'From this day he is no longer my husband, and I never want to see his face again. As a descendant of the great Rana, his soul should not have been thus vile; he ought to have recollected his connection with our illustrious house. His business was to gain the battle or die on the spot; then should I have acquired one of two glorious things

1. Perhaps this may be identical with the Fathabad, twelve miles south-west of Ujjain (see Thornton, 'Gazetteer,' 315). Note Manucci's wrong etymology, *pur* (Persian), 'full,' instead of *pur, pura* (Hindi), 'a town.' Fathpur is 'Victory-town.'
2. This story also appears in Bernier, 40, 41, but without the introduction of Udepur (the Rana's capital, and not Jaswant Singh's), which seems to be Manucci's own contribution.

—the renown of being a hero's wife, or an honoured widow's death by burning.' Her rage and passion were so extreme that she knew not what she was inventing or saying. She had conceived an idea that her husband had been killed in the battle, and that all they were telling her was only meant to prevent her burning herself [as a *sati*]. She issued orders for the preparation of the necessary materials for her death by fire, announcing that her husband was dead, for how could it be otherwise?

On being assured once again that her husband was really alive, she suddenly flew into a greater rage; turning pale, she had a fit, and fell to the ground. On recovering her senses, she exclaimed passionately: 'Better were it that I had not been born, or had died before I saw this day; or at the least had not been born into this family, or else married to a man of honour though of low degree, and not to this coward.' Worn out by all this grief, she said in the end that all her life long she would never look on the face of such a white-livered soldier. She would lead a life of renunciation.

Then came her mother to her, and with every effort sought a means of consoling her. It was promised to her that in a few days they would furnish to the rajah another army, with which to renew the attack on Aurangzeb. Thus in one way or another his honour could be vindicated by them, they sparing neither their wealth nor any of their treasures. In spite of all this she would not allow herself to be comforted. She would not on any terms permit her husband to enter the fortress, nor would she receive his messages; she ordered that no one should mention his name in her presence. Things remained thus for some years, until Aurangzeb, who had then become king, offered himself as a mediator to restore friendship between them. He sent several women from his palace and eunuchs on various occasions. As a mark of respect to the king's requests, she reluctantly consented. Nevertheless, she never forebore from showing the rajah a wry face as a token of her disapproval, which she persisted in with much rancour. Once the rajah wanted to eat a melon, and along with it the serving-maid presented a knife. Thereupon Rani Ji suddenly fell upon the maid and seized her by the hair, beating and thumping her, saying: 'Knowest thou not the courage of this runaway, that when he sees a bit of iron of any sort he swoons?' This was her behaviour for the rest of her life.

When Shahjahan heard of this unfortunate defeat, he raised his hands and his eyes to heaven, saying, 'Ala ham di lillah!' [*Al hamdu il'llah*!]—that is to say, 'Praise be to God!' 'Already I knew that the time of my rule was nearing its end, but not that there would fall upon me this calamity, so that, filled with anguish thereby, I cry, "Hia Ala teri raza" [*Ya Allah! teri raza*!]—that is to say, "O God! thy will be done"—'it is my sins that chastise me, and I deserve it all, "mere Ala!" [*mere Allah*!]), "my God!"

When Dara received the report that the river passage at Ujjain had been forced, he was greatly enraged, and in a passion stamped on the ground, [180] and, wringing his hands, cursed Qasim Khan. If he had him there, he would without fail order him to be cut into pieces. With the same passion he let himself loose upon and railed against Mir Jumlah. He said to his father that he (Shahjahan) was the chief cause of the mishap. If his majesty had not confided an army to Mir Jumlah, he could not have transferred it to the rebel Aurangzeb. 'But this day our own arms are turned against us. If your majesty had only listened to my advice in the first instance, we should never have arrived at this plight.' He joined in his accusation the names of Muhammad Amin Khan and Shaistah Khan, saying they also were traitors. He wanted to have them beheaded, and their families sent to a house of ill-fame. And without a doubt he would have done so, through the great excitement he was in; but Shahjahan, whose affliction was added to by Dara's disordered condition and his wild words, employed all his wisdom and mildness in assuaging the violence of his son. He impressed on him that all this was merely the wiliness and plotting of Aurangzeb to secure Mir Jumlah and seize his goods, having discovered that Muhammad Amin Khan and Shaistah Khan had no intention of exposing themselves to his severities. Dara listened to these arguments, and although he disagreed, he dissembled, and busied himself with the preparation of his entire army.

Aurangzeb and Murad Bakhsh, finding themselves victors through the good results attained in this first fight, became emboldened and thought themselves invincible, and assumed that no army existed in the world able to oppose them. Thus all the soldiers in the army boasted that after they were masters of the empire, they would without fail press on into Persia and Turkey, uttering unending rodomontade. To raise the spirits of his troops,

Aurangzeb announced (very truly, as I saw when the time came) that in the army of Dara there were thirty thousand Moguls ready to come under his standards.

The eunuch Shahbaz, seeing clearly that Aurangzeb was deceiving his master, Murad Bakhsh, and that certainly he would lose his life by such deceits, made up his mind after the victory to commit a terrible act. When Aurangzeb came to see his brother Murad Bakhsh, as he often did, accompanied by his son, Sultan Muhammad, he (Shahbaz) resolved to take his life as he was issuing from the tents. When all three princes were in conversation, the eunuch said meaningly to his prince that, if he gave permission, he would order some 'cloth' to be cut. Murad Bakhsh's star being unpropitious, he replied that it was not necessary. He was aware of the intention of the eunuch; thus, if he said 'Yes,' he knew the man to be quite prepared and resolved to kill the two visitors by violence, and for this purpose he had placed men in hiding beforehand. These were the 'cloth' that the eunuch asked permission to 'cut,' for 'to cut out cloth' has two meanings; ordinarily, it is to cut out cloth for garments. The eunuch acted the simpleton, trying to get assent for carrying out the project, as I have already said, and after the deed meant to disculpate himself. Even should he lose his life, he would die content, having put to death those who meant to kill his master. He clearly perceived that Aurangzeb would never leave his master in life, such not being the custom among the descendants of the Moguls. On hearing the conversation, Aurangzeb knew at once that his life was in danger; in his mind [181] he was disturbed, but externally betrayed no sign, and thenceforth never again went to the tents of Murad Bakhsh, sending his son Sultan Muhammad instead, making the excuse that the heavy work he had to get through allowed him no time to go in person to visit his brother.

Prince Murad Bakhsh was anxious to continue their victories without allowing time to Sultan Sulaiman Shukoh to join his father Dara; and the second day after the battle he wanted to resume the march, without giving the army an interval of rest. He therefore raised the pay of his soldiers, and started again in great pomp on the third day. Aurangzeb neglected no efforts that appeared to him suitable, sending his spies to his friends with letters containing many promises. He desired to know from them the arrangements and conditions at the court, so as to adopt means to carry out his projects with greater security. The traitors replied unanimously that he might advance without the slightest hesitation; and all of them assured him that other battles would be won with even greater ease.

Perceiving clearly the boldness and resolution of the two princes Aurangzeb and Murad Bakhsh, and recognising finally that there was now no hope of making them return to their governments, Shahjahan was so embarrassed that he was at a loss what to decide upon, and foresaw great misfortunes. He made great efforts to emerge from this position, but the fates would not permit it to be otherwise. Finding himself in bodily weakness, and desirous of pleasing Dara, he transferred [to him] all his powers and dignities, and ordered everyone to yield him obedience. He wanted to try if, by this means, he could relieve himself of all the ills from which he suffered, including the danger in which he stood of being captured by Aurangzeb and dispossessed of his authority.

Some authors, recording what they have been told, say that Dara seized his father and divested him of power by force; but I assert this to be a great untruth, for I know, and have tested, that Dara was quite submissive. He did nothing without communicating it to his father. I might produce several proofs of what I say; but I will ask the reader to do me the favour of recollecting what I have said as to the letters written by Muhammad Amin Khan and Shaistah Khan. On account of these Dara wanted to have them decapitated, yet they were liberated by the order of Shahjahan. If Dara had, as others write, taken possession of his father and of his authority, he would have exercised this absolute power to order their heads to be cut off, as justice required.

Another case I will bring forward in proof of what I say. A few days before we took the field against Aurangzeb the police seized a Genoese youth for having in his possession a bottle of wine, a thing not prohibited for Europeans. In order to petition for his release, I went off to the magistrate, who at once placed me alongside the youth. I made a sign to my servant, who rushed off to tell my friends, artillerymen in Prince Dara's service. These men came in a body [182], all of them armed, and, breaking down the doors of the prison, liberated us. The soldiers ran from the police-office, leaving the magistrate by himself in a state of astonishment at what was going on. Being aggrieved as I was, I thereupon went up to the magistrate and put a pistor to his breast; I did not slay him, but took compassion upon him on his humbling of himself. This affair was brought before Shahjahan, who complained to Dara of what his artillerymen had done. To satisfy the king, Dara ordered the captain of the artillery to administer a reproof to the Genoese. We all went in a body to the captain to lodge a complaint against the magistrate for the disgrace done to us, the king having accorded us the right to drink wine. Now, if Dara had been as others say, no one would have had the audacity to displease his employees, nor to complain of them to Shahjahan.

On finding the king Shahjahan had delivered himself with all his authority and his army into the hands of Prince Dara, everybody seized their weapons, there was great uproar, each man acting on his own inclination. More than one hundred thousand horsemen assembled and more than twenty thousand infantry. There were one hundred pieces of field artillery, every one of them carrying shot of from eight to twelve pounds; in addition there was a twenty-pounder culverin, and over two hundred European artillerymen. There was no want of subordinates, of shopkeepers who furnish supplies for the sustenance of the whole realm and army, a large number of sarrafos (*sarraf*) who provide the cash required by the whole army, many majestic and well-armoured elephants, and five hundred camels. On each of the latter was a man seated atop with a swivel-gun, carrying a ball of from three to four ounces, which he loaded and fired without dismounting. There were also five hundred elephants with their howdahs, and in these sat two men with two guns like those upon the camels.

After all these preparations we issued from the city of Agrah on the 14th May in one thousand six hundred and fifty-six.[1] When on the march we covered the ground as far as the horizon, making a brave and splendid show. What disconcerted me was that no one would say that Dara was sure of gaining the battle with all this grand array. Furthermore, I remembered the answer given me by Father Buzeo, a man of much wisdom, when I asked him if he entertained any doubt of Dara's being emperor, seeing that he had under him that great army and so much treasure. The father replied to me, with the great kindness and trust he had ever bestowed on me, that he was much afraid that Dara would never

1. The correct year is 1658; the day of the month is probably correct.

become emperor, pointing out to me that the people of Hindustan were very malicious, that such a race required to be ruled by a more malignant king, and not by a good-nature man like Dara.

The reasons why no one declared that Dara must win in the struggle appear to me to be the following: Because Shahjahan meddled a great deal with the wives of the nobles, who awaited such a good opening as this to take their revenge for the insults they had received, by handing him over to Aurangzeb, his deadly enemy; that if Dara had a failing [183], it was not to conciliate the great nobles and win them over to be his friends. The chief reason of all for his misfortunes was, however, that Sulaiman Shukoh would not listen to the advice of Rajah Jai Singh, but increased his distance from the court, and was thus unable to rejoin at headquarters in time. Thereby the best men that Dara had among his troops were lost to him.

The greater number of the soldiers that Dara had newly enlisted were not very warlike; they were butchers, barbers, blacksmiths, carpenters, tailors, and such-like. It is true that on their horses and with their arms, they looked well at a review; but they had no heart and knew nothing of war. If only Sulaiman Shukoh had arrived in time, there would have been no need of men like these, nor of Khalilullah Khan. The wife of the latter had warned Dara to put no reliance on her husband nor trust his soft speeches, for she knew him well, and given the occasion, he would inevitably engineer some treachery. Nor should he rely upon the thirty thousand Mogul troopers in his father's service.

Shahjahan earnestly desired that Dara should not offer battle until Sulaiman Shukoh had arrived. But Dara's two brothers and enemies came on with such haste that they left him no chance of delaying. I have been assured that Aurangzeb professed such determination as to say that if Taimur-i-lang and all his descendants came against him, on no account would it be fitting for him to retreat. He was resolved to give battle, putting his faith in the traitors to be found in Dara's camp.

When placed in the field our army was so well distributed that it looked like a lovely city adorned with beautiful tents, flying innumerable flags of all colours and different shapes, each tent having its own flag and device so that it might be recognised. The prince Dara went to take leave of the king, his father, and of Begam Sahib, his sister, who at that time were living in the fort of Agrah. On beholding the son and brother so well beloved, they melted into floods of tears. The king began to speak, and thus addressed Dara: 'My loved and cherished son! I have always been well inclined towards you as being my firstborn son and full of good qualities, above all of the quality of obedience, which you have always displayed to me. Your father hoped to see you become king peacefully, but none can fathom the secrets of the Lord Most High. My desire was to leave you in this fortress, and go forth myself against those rebels Aurangzeb and Murad Bakhsh, unworthy of the name of my sons or of your brothers. I had hoped to chastise the rebels and traitors who take the side of my enemies; but you have had compassion on my years and infirmity, and mean to expose your life for the peace of the kingdom, the freedom and the safety of your father. Not to dishearten you. I consent to your doing as you wish; but entreat you, my beloved son, to avoid a battle until the arrival of Sultan Sulaiman Shukoh your son. You will thus increase your chance of victory. I beg of you to curb your ardour. Being incapable of doing more, I pray that your life may be spared and that you may survive to become emperor of all Hindustan, and [184] that our enemies may be slain. I place you in the hands of God, in whom we trust to give us the victory and make us triumph over rebels and traitors.'

Having bade farewell to his father, Dara soon appeared in the army; but the march could not be undertaken that day. Some of the war *materiel* was still wanting, nor did the astrologers judge the hour auspicious for a start. On the third day[1] this huge army began its march. When Dara was about to mount his magnificent elephant Fatejang (Fath Jang)—that is to say, 'Victor in War'—he said these words: 'Guerrib maf, magrur marg' (*Gharib mu'af, maghrur marg*)—that is to say, 'To the humble, pardon; to the haughty, death.' The generals then present replied simultaneously, 'Hixa Alla' (*Inshallah*)—that is to say, 'By the favour of God.'

We began the march in such great order that it seemed as if sea and land were united. Prince Dara amidst his squadron appeared like a crystal tower, resplendent as a sun shining over all the land. Around him rode many squadrons of Rajput cavalry whose armour glittered from afar, and their lance-heads with a

1. Presumably May 17 is meant.

tremulous motion sent forth rays of light. There were other squardrons of cavalry armed with lances, in front of whom went many ferocious elephants clad in shining steel with chains on their trunks, their tusks encrusted with gold and silver, and broad cutlasses affixed thereto by rings. In advance was one with a handsome flag, and the driver, who guided the elephant, was armed with *armes blanches* (sword and shield).

A marvellous thing was it to behold the march, which moved over the heights and through the vales like the waves of a stormy sea. Thus we held on our way for four days[1] until we reached the bank of the river Chambal, where was a village called Dolpur (Dholpur). Our powerful army took up position on this ground, and entrenched the crossing, placing its pieces of artillery to cover the most exposed points.

We awaited the enemy, who was already near; he appeared afar off after three days.[2] Being fully prepared, and in every way desirous of finding ourselves engaged in battle, we begged for leave to attack the enemy. But Dara, for two reasons, would not consent: the first was that he was waiting for Sultan Sulaiman Shukoh and his force, who could not be very long in coming; even if they were delayed, he was sure that the enemy would never risk a crossing at this place, which was well occupied and fortified. The second reason was the inadvisability of attacking the enemy in a situation full of hollows and rocks, and altogether a dangerous place.

All this time Aurangzeb persisted in his usual stratagems and intrigues. After having encamped his army on the farther side, not far from the river, he called together his generals. He said to them that they must be prepared to deliver battle, and be every one ready with his force of cavalry. In making haste lay their chance of victory, and full of confidence in their courage, he hoped [185] in a brief space to be victorious. They could not postpone the battle, seeing the danger of Sultan Sulaiman Shukoh's arrival.

1. Counting from the 17th, four days brings us to May 21. Dholpur is thirty-seven miles south of Agrah, and situated about a mile from the left bank of the Chambal.
2. This would be on May 24.

A report of the above speech reached the army of Dara, and was received with pleasure. Everybody made his preparations with the greatest eagerness, and expected every day that the enemy would come to attack us.

But Aurangzeb's secret plan was to win over Rajah Champet (Champat),[1] to whom he sent valuable presents, proposing for him high rewards and making him liberal offers. He asked the rajah to allow him to pass through his territories in order to get across the river by another unknown ford, situated twelve leagues from us. These demands were conceded by Rajah Champat, hoping to avenge himself on Shahjahan for the acts I have already told you of (I. 142-144). Gained over by entreaties, and all unwitting of the misfortune that he had to undergo, the rajah

---

1. Here we may compare Manucci with the official narrative in the "Alamgirnamah,' pp. 79, 85. Dara Shukoh, with his younger son Sipihr Shukoh, left Agrah on the 25th Sha'ban (May 28, 1658, new style), having previously, on the 16th Sha'ban (May 19), deputed Khalilullah Khan, Ram Singh, Rathor, and others, to seize the Dholpur ferry, and watch all fords or suspected crossings. Meanwhile, Aurangzeb had arrived at Gwaliyar, and learnt there that the ferry at Dholpur was defended, while all known crossings had been blocked by the erection of batteries. Inquiries were made from local zamindars, who informed him of a crossing in the Bhadauriyah territory, east of Agrah, some forty miles off, the place being fordable and not guarded. Khan Jahan and other commanders were detached by Aurangzeb. They reached the place on the Chambal the next day (the last of Sha'ban, June 1). Aurangzeb left Gwaliyar the same day (May 31), and in two marches reached the spot, crossing the river on the 1st Ramazan (June 2).

   More light is thrown by Bhim Sen, an adherent of the Datiya Rajahs, in his 'Nuskha i-dilkusha,' British Museum, Oriental, 23, fol. 15*b*, upon the mode in which Aurangzeb got his information. After he had reached the Chambal and encamped opposite to Dholpur, Subhkaran Singh, Bundelah, Rajah of Datiya, produced Champat, Bundelah, 'who all his life had learnt nothing but robbery, and having no abode, wandered like a stray pigeon through every hill and plain. Great promises of reward were made to him; he was tamed by specious devices, and made a Panj *Hazcari*. He reported that Dholpur ferry was strongly defended. But within an easy distance, at a place called Gorakhtah, there was a ford which could be reached in one day.' A night march was ordered, and by noon next day the army was in battle array at Samugarh. Dara was unable to remove his guns from the batteries at the Chambal, while heat and thirst killed many of his men. In the battle Subkharan was wounded, and Aurangzeb ordered a grove to be planted and a sarae erected on the site of the battle (Fathabad?).

accompanied Aurangzeb. The route was so difficult, the march so impeded by jungle and uneven ground, that Aurangzeb was unable to take with him the whole of his forces. He left his tents standing, and some of his men behind, by way of formality, in order to conceal his design the more effectually. He crossed the river (as I was told) with over eight thousand horsemen, and though they were all much fatigued, he made himself master of the crossing on the 30th of May, 1656 (*i.e.*,1658).

This day was as full of joy for Aurangzeb as it was full of sadness for Dara. The latter, receiving a report of the carrying out of the above design, fell into a great rage with Champat, who had given his word that in no case would he allow Aurangzeb to cross, and it was for this reason that Dara had not blocked the ford in question. When the news came that Aurangzeb had actually crossed Dara was desirous of moving personally in pursuit of him.

He was, however, well advised by the general Hebraim Can (Ibrahim Khan),[1] son of Alimerda Can ('Ali Mardan Khan), to send instead, with the greatest expedition, twelve thousand horsemen to fall suddenly upon Aurangzeb and his soldiers, who were much fatigued, very scattered, and lying about on the river bank. But the traitor Khalilullah Khan, having heard that Dara had decided upon making this attempt, came to him and said that it was inadvisable; it would not add to his credit or reputation. For, of a certainty, the name and fame of any victory would accrue to the commander, and not to his highness. He ought not to listen to the advice of these boys, quite inexperienced in war; and it was a mistake to detach those twelve thousand cavalry from his division, for by so doing the victory which was now a certainty would become doubtful. The following day we marched in pursuit of Aurangzeb, but it was already too late. For during the night, and very early on the following morning, almost the whole remaining army of Aurangzeb came up, and quitting the river, we arrived in an extensive plain.

---

1. Ibrahim Khan died at the end of Safar or early in Rabi 'I., 1122 H. (*circa* April 30, 1710), while Governor of Kashmir, aged eighty years. He was the son of 'Ali Mardan Khan, Amir-ul-Umara, who died at Machhiwarah (Panjab) in 1067 H., 12 Rajab (April 27, 1657, N.S.) (see 'Ma,asir-ul-Umara,' i. 295, ii. 795). In 1658 Ibrahim Khan must have been about twenty-six years of age.

It was the 1st of June of one thousand six hundred and fifty-six.[1] We made use with great labour of the water in the ponds in the open fields, and the heat was stifling. Between the two armies there was not more than a league and a half's distance. During the time we were taking up ground for our army the rest of Aurangzeb's force continued to join his ranks, but the whole of his artillery and baggage had not arrived. Having detailed information of everything in Aurangzeb's force, and knowing his men were exhausted, Dara wanted to commence [186] the action. But the traitors intervened on astrological grounds by saying that neither the day nor the hour was favourable. He must postpone the battle. He was already sure of the victory, because he had a good army, with valiant and high-spirited soldiers quite sufficiently numerous for the destruction of Aurangzeb, who in comparison with him was an invisible speck on this earth. All this they did solely that Aurangzeb might have time to take rest, to refresh his people, and secure the arrival of his guns.

The traitors had made an agreement with Aurangzeb that when he was ready to give battle he should warn them by three discharges of cannon, and thereupon they would make dispositions for delivering Dara into his hands. Meanwhile Aurangzeb gave proof of how he understood recompensing those who helped him in his unjust undertaking. He caused his friend Champat to be sent for, who waiting not far from his tents, in expectation of the many favours and presents promised to him. When he reached the presence, having no anticipation of what was about to happen to him, Aurangzeb instantly caused him to be bound and carried to the route along which he designed to advance next morning to give battle; there he was to be offered up a sacrificial victim, and beheaded. This command was executed.[2]

1. As usual, the date is wrong by two years; it ought to be 1658.
2. From a passage in Part III., 198, it would appear, that this Champat's son was Dalpat Rao, Bundelah (died June, 1707, at Jajau). This is wrong; Dalpat's father was Subhkaran (died 1683). The difficulty is explained by the passage already quoted from Bhim Sen. Subhkaran (father of Rao Dalpat) and Champat (father of the more celebrated Chhatarsal), both Bundelahs, were both concerned in the matter, and Manucci confounds them. Neither of them, however, was executed in 1658. Subhkaran died in 1683, and Champat Rae was hunted down and killed in October or November, 1661 ("Alamgirnamah,' p. 630, fourth year of Aurangzeb).

On the 2nd of June (1658) Dara received a letter from his father Shahjahan, directing his retreat to Agrah, there to entrench himself until the arrival of Sulaiman Shukoh. This could not be done, because if Dara retreated, the enemy would without fail resume his advance with still greater spirit, while our troops would lose all confidence in the valour of their prince and commander. They would imagine if he retired that he had not the courage to attack. The greater part of our army directly they saw such a movement would inevitably transfer themselves to the enemy's side.

So far was Dara from following the advice of his father that he had, on the contrary, made up his mind to deliver battle. In reply to his father, he wrote that he ought to take his ease and keep in good heart. He promised him that within three days he would drag Aurangzeb and Murad Bakhsh bound into his presence, when he might punish them as he saw fit. The truth is that he (Dara) wished to fight on the 3rd of June, a Saturday. But the traitors, taking advantage of a shower of rain which fell in our camp, said it was not a good time to attack, for already the skies wept over his defeat as soon as they heard he meant to fight. It would be much better to delay until the next day, which was known to be the first day, when God created light—a very suspicious day, on which without any doubt he would be victorious. All this they said, because if Dara had attacked the enemy on that day he would have gained a certain victory. For Aurangzeb had not then his ranks in proper order, nor had the agreed-on signal been given.

The presumption that I discovered in Dara afflicted me, seeing him give credit to the words of traitors. But I consoled myself a good deal, being so young, with the hope of getting some experience of war. On the whole I did not feel [187] satisfied, finding that Dara was not making the exertions required for the good ordering of such a huge army. He had no sufficient experience in matters of war, having been brought up among the dancing-women and buffoons of his father, and gave undue credit to the words of the traitors.

On the 3rd of June,[1] at midnight, the enemy fired three pieces of artillery, the signal agreed upon with the traitors, showing

---

1. For Bernier's account of the Battle of Samugarh (Fathabad), see pp. 49-54 (Constable's edition). He gives no date. The "Alamgirnamah,'

them that Aurangzeb had now made his dispositions for giving battle at daybreak. We replied with other three shots. After one hour had elapsed Dara emerged from the camp through the midst of our artillery, for which it was necessary to take down my tent to allow a passage for his exit with the few cavalry in his retinue.

A short time afterwards I mounted my horse and went forth out of curiosity to know what was going on, this being the first battle that I had been able to see. Trusting to my good horse, I went on, and halted on a height adjoining an uninhabited village; thence I saw, though it was still dark, many horsemen leave our army for that of Aurangzeb, and never return.

Almost at daybreak there came forth from the army of Aurangzeb several camels laden with bombs, escorted by some horsemen and many men on foot, who halted in the village and distributed themselves at considerable distances. As the light grew clearer I saw that Aurangzeb was advancing very leisurely with his whole army. It was formed into five divisions of cavalry.

In the first division, placed in the middle, was the strong and valiant Aurangzeb seated on a large elephant, accompanied by fifteen thousand horsemen, well armed with lances, bows and arrows, and matchlocks. At his right hand he had his son Sultan Muhammad, and Mirbaba (Mir Baba), his fosterbrother, to whom on this occasion he gave the title of Badercan (Bahadur Khan),[1] at the head of another fifteen thousand horsemen. The third division, on the right hand of Sultan Muhammad, had also fifteen thousand horse under the command of Nezebetcan (Najabat Khan)[2] and other generals. The fourth division was composed of another fifteen thousand well-armed cavalry, with whom was

p. 94, assigns the battle to the 7th Ramazan (June 8, 1658, N.S.; May 29, O.S.). The date adopted by Elphinstone, p. 522, fourth edition, is the 8th Ramazan.

1. Mir Malik Husain, son of Abul Mu'alla, Khwafi; he died in 1109 H. (1697-98). The title of Bahadur Khan was given on the march from the Dakhin; he commanded Aurangzeb's right wing. He was afterwards made Khan Jahan, Bahadur, Kokaltash (see 'Ma,asir-ul-Umara,' i. 798, 799).
2. This Najabat Khan was probably the Mi'rza Shuja' already twice referred to. He survived to the seventh year of Aurangzeb. He was son of the ruler of Badakhshan, and a descendant of Taimur (see 'Ma,asir-ul-Umara,' iii. 821).

Prince Murad Bakhsh, seated on a lofty elephant, which rose like a tower in the midst of his squadrons. With him sat his little son.[1]

The remainder of Aurangzeb's army consisted of one division of problematical value, made up of low-class men of unwarlike habits, in addition to baggage, carts, camels, and unloaded oxen; these had their place on the left of Murad Bakhsh. Behind followed all the artillery. As this army continued its advance in tranquillity, so I in the same manner retired until I saw that they had arrived close to the deserted village. Then the artillery was ordered to the front, behind them the musketeers, behind them again some camels carrying swivel-guns (*trihoens*). In their rear was the army, as I have above described. I answer for all this with confidence [188].

I awaited the approach of our army, in order to take my place. But seeing from afar that it did not stir, I went back close to it, where there were several scattered horsemen. There I halted to look at it, and consider our great army and its disposition. I noticed that while I had been away to look at the army of Aurangzeb, Dara had arrayed his forces in the following order: The artillery was all in one row, and each carriage bore two scarlet pennons. This row of guns served as a wall to protect the musketeers behind it, to the number of twenty-five thousand men. These were supported by five hundred camels with swivel-guns (*trilhoens*); to their rear stood the armour-clad elephants, and then the cavalry, twenty-eight thousand horsemen. Last of all was Dara on his magnificent elephant, followed by numerous elephants carrying drums, trumpets, and all manner of music, forming his retinue.

In the division to the right of Dara was Ramsing Rotella (Ram Singh, Rathor) with his fifteen thousand Rajputs, all well-armed men of war. On their right was Khalilullah Khan with thirty thousand Moguls, whose orders were to encounter the miscellaneous division of which I spoke, this being his (Khalilullah Khan's) own pretext. On the left hand of Dara was posted the valorous general Rustomcan Dacanj (Rustam Khan, Dakhini)[2] with fifteen

1. 'His little son.' Other instances of this practice of taking little children into battle could be adduced.
2. Rustam Khan, Dakhini, was by race a Charkas from Northern Persia. He first served the Nizam Shahl kings, and then went over to Shahjahan's side. At Samugarh he was in the right wing commanded by Sipihr Shukoh ('Ma,asir-ul-Umara,' ii. 270-276). His death is mentioned by N. M. a little farther on (fol. 191).

thousand horse in all; at his left Raja Chartersilara (Chhatarsal Rae)[1] with fifteen thousand horsemen, the greater part of them Rajputs. All this array made a lovely sight, both by the beauty of the arms and by the number of standards and pennons of so many colours.

Be it known to the reader that these two armies were not ordered in the disposition obtaining in Europe. But one division was close to another as the trees of a pinewood, in the order that I have described.

I remained where I was in safety, there being no firing from either side. It was already eight o'clock of the day, when there came an order from our army that all the scattered horsemen must retire, because they wanted to discharge the artillery. Thereupon everyone withdrew into the army, and a poor Mogul cavalier riding behind me, not getting back in time, fell at the first fire of our artillery. Repeated orders poured in to keep up a continuous artillery fire, although the shot did no damage. They fell short of Aurangzeb's men, who were at a great distance from us. I was much amazed at their making us work thus for nothing. During the time that we were making this deafening din with our guns, the enemy saluted us with nothing but a few bombs with tails, after the style of rockets.

After the first discharge Aurangzeb ordered one of his pieces of artillery to be fired in continuation of the signal to the traitors. After we had fired again several times he let off two pieces together. When we had fired ten [189] times he replied with three pieces at once. This was the desired signal by which he was to let the traitors know that he was prepared to receive an attack where he was, without moving towards Dara. Then, leaving his division, Khalilullah Khan came in search of Dara. On reaching his presence he greeted him as victor, speaking thus: 'May the victory be auspicious to the invincible Dara! Without losing any of his men, solely by use of his artillery, he has destroyed the greater part of the enemy, and little effort remains to gain a complete victory. It is not desirable to continue artillery fire, but we must now advance and lay hold of the enemy.'

1. Chhatarsal, Hada (see 'Ma,asir-ul-Umara,' ii. 260). He, too, was killed.

Orders were given not to discharge the artillery any more, and the well-reputed general, Rustam Khan, was sent for in order to hear what he advised. When the latter heard the views of Khalilullah Khan, he replied that it would be better to await the enemy and leave him to attack us, for he had come a great distance to seek us, and, according to usage, he could not avoid being the attacker. When he came on, we could receive him with the fury and valour befitting the advantage that we had over him.

This advice was most prudent, but the cunning Khalilullah Khan turned it into disparagement of Rustam Khan, saying: 'I am greatly amazed that a captain so famous should tell us at such a juncture to show ourselves such cowards and of so little courage, that after we have almost destroyed the enemy, we should yet be afraid to take the offensive.' Dara, without listening to other arguments, adopted the counsels of Khalilullah Khan, and set his elephant in motion in order to attack the enemy with his heavy divisions. Orders were given to Rustam Khan to return to his division, and give evidence of his well-known valour. The artillery was ordered to be unchained to allow the troops to pass through the line.[1]

Khalilullah Khan, pleased at having accomplished his purpose of exposing Dara to the risk of death, went with him halfway, and then returned to his own command, the enemy being still at some distance. On this side, when Dara started with his division against the enemy, everything fell into confusion. The barbers, butchers, and the rest, turned right-about face, abandoning the artillerymen and the guns. Many made for the baggage-train to plunder it, which they did, breaking open the chests of gold and silver, and carrying off what they could lay hands on. This resulted in many men being murdered while trying to rob their companions.

Dara pursued his route courageously, making signs with his hands from the top of his elephant that all should hasten to take a part in the victory. To this intent he ordered his drums to beat. I admired Dara's high spirit, and I noticed that the enemy did not stir, contenting himself with a discharge of shells until Dara had come quite close. Then, all of a sudden, the enemy discharged

1. By the rules of Indian fighting, the cannon were bound together by chains (*zanjir-bandi*) to prevent the enemy's horse from riding between them and slaughtering the gunners.

his cannon, musketry, and swivel-pieces, which struck us and frightened numbers of our men, who scattered this way and that. Finding himself in imminent peril, Dara ordered the guns to be dragged forward and the musket-men to advance; the *franquis* [190] (Europeans) were also to join in the movement. But it was no longer time, for all his men were in disarray, and everyone had taken his own road.

In spite of all this he (Dara) did not lose heart, but waving his hands, made signs to continue the advance. Then Rustam Khan and Chhatar Sal Rae, although they had suffered by the first discharge from the enemy, came up and collected as many fresh men as they could. Dara did the same. Then with such vigour, courage, wrath, and violence did he attack his opponents that he broke through the guns and penetrated to their camp, putting to the rout camels, infantry, and everything that was to be found in that direction.

Seeing the boldness of Dara, the enemy then sent as reinforcement a large division led by Secmir (Shekh Mir),[1] teacher of Aurangzeb, and other famous captains. This body made all haste, and at this point arose the hottest of the fighting on both sides. At length, coming to closer quarters, they took to their swords with the greatest vigour. Dara continued to hold his ground, seated on his elephant, shouting and making signs with his hands. He advanced always with the greatest composure, until, unable to bear up against this stout resistance, the enemy was forced to retire.

I saw in this action, as in so many others where I was afterwards present, that the only soldiers who fought were those well to the front. Of those more to the rear, although holding their bared swords in their hands, the Moguls did nothing but shout 'Boquox, boquox!' (*Ba-kush! ba-kush!*), and the Indians 'Mar! mar!' (*Mar! mar!*)—that is to say, 'Kill! kill!' If those in the front advanced, those behind followed the example, and if the former retired the others fled, a custom of Hindustan quite contrary to that of Europe; and if they begin to take to flight, by no method is it possible to stop them.

---

1. Shekh Mir, a Khwafi was killed in the Battle of Ajmer on the 29th Jamada II., 1069 H. (March 13, 1659, O.S.) (see Beale, 'Oriental Biography,' 371).

Owing to the great disorder of his people, caused by the valour of Dara, Aurangzeb, who was not very far away, ran great risk of being taken. But he disregarded the danger, and ordered a large division of his best cavalry, which was close at hand, to take up the resistance to Dara's advance. He tried to raise the courage of the few soldiers left to him by calling to the principal men, each by his name, saying, 'Mardaney delavaram bahader vactas' (*Mardani, dilawaran-i-bahadur! waqt ast*)—that is to say, 'Men of power, valour, and courage! now is the time!' Then, raising his hands to heaven, he exclaimed: 'Hia Coda, hia Coda!' (*Ya Khuda! Ya Khuda*!)—'O God! O God! In you is my trust! I will sooner die on this spot than give way.' Placing his hands upon his morion, he ordered them to attach iron chains to the feet of his elephant as an attestation of his resolve. He pricked his elephant a little onward to reanimate the leaders who had gathered round him, all pledging him their word that they would yield their lives in his sight, rather than recede one single step [191].

Dara's design was to continue his advance until he had closed with Aurangzeb, and could attack him in person. But owing to the difficulties of the ground, and to the fatigue that overcame him, he made a short halt. This hindered his winning the day; for if he had kept his original rate of progress and maintained the vigour of his onslaught, the victory was his. Aurangzeb could have made no resistance with the small force left round him, for with a few men it was not possible to repel his enemy's victorious fighters, full of bravery and strength.

But Aurangzeb's lucky star worked in his favour, for while Dara was still halted, news came to him that Chhatar Sal Rae had been routed and killed by Najabat Khan's force. Subsequently another still more unhappy report reached him (Dara). Rustam Khan, who fought against Sultan Muhammad and Bahadur Khan, was also dead, and his division in disorder. These leaders were killed by the traitors in their ranks, it being the more easy to kill them that they were riding on high elephants.

Learning that the troops of the two deceased generals were still fighting valorously, he (Dara) turned off to reinforce those divisions, doing his work so effectually that he routed Sultan Muhammad and Najabat Khan, and failed not at all in that which is expected of a valiant general. If that coward traitor Khalilullah Khan had made the slightest effort in support of his Prince

Dara, there can be no doubt that this day would have seen the destruction of the rebels, and have become a consolation to Shahjahan, a glory to Dara, and a day of peace for all Hindustan. For Shah Shuja', although a valiant soldier, had not a large army, nor had he much sense, and it would have been possible to defeat him quickly, of which we will speak hereafter (I. 226).

But it seems as if God meant to punish the sins and lasciviousness of Shahjahan and the overweening pride of Hindustan. For there came once more to Dara a piece of news still more overwhelming—that is, the death of Ram Singh, Rathor. This rajah attacked with such energy the prince Murad Bakhsh that he penetrated the enemy's ranks, and gave them much to do. He dispersed their vanguard, captured their artillery, and coming close up to Murad Bakhsh with his brave Rajputs, stuck his elephant and its howdah full of arrows, and killed the *cornac*, or man who guides the elephant. Finally they planted three arrows in the face of Murad Bakhsh. He had as much as he could do to defend his life, to guide his elephant, and look after his restless infant son. The boy was so anxious to see what was going on that his father was forced to cover him with his shield and place one foot over his head.

There was no one else on Aurangzeb's side who fought so well as this prince. Raging at this resistance, and finding it impossible to slay him, Ram Singh, Rathor, and some of his Rajputs dismounted, and, like ravening dogs, leapt [192] on the elephant, hoping to sever the girths by sword-cuts and lance-thrusts, and thus bring Murad Bakhsh to the ground. The latter, seizing the occasion, saw that he could make a good shot, and planted an arrow in the breast of Ram Singh, Rathor, who forthwith fell to the ground. The elephant turned and seized him with its trunk, and, throwing him beneath its feet, finished him off. Thereupon the Rajputs, seeing their beloved captain was dead, increased in rage and fury, and battled more violently than ever.

Already a victor in three encounters, Dara, when he heard this report, hastened with greater courage than ever to the reinforcement of the Rajputs against Murad Bakhsh. He felt certain that if this brother were put to death, he could easily gain his purpose. But his evil fate would not concede to him the effecting of this, however great and glorious he held himself to be. There now came to pass a treason that had never been looked for, such as none had ever seen, none could ever have imagined. It was the cause of Dara's total loss and ruin, although this did not appear at the time.

What happened was that the astute traitor Khalilullah Khan, using the pretext of a good chance of seizing Aurangzeb, came to Dara and acclaimed him as victor, and spoke to him thus: 'I know well that I have been in many battles and campaigns, and beheld the mighty deeds of renowned warriors, yet never have I heard of a prince like your highness, who, appearing for the first time in the battlefield, accomplished such valiant acts. One thing alone remains to display to the world your qualities—that is, the capture of Aurangzeb. I feel compassion for the fatigues your highness has already undergone, but it would be wrong to lose such a good opportunity. Yonder stands Aurangzeb with a scanty following; let us go at once and seize him, as can be done without any difficulty. Let your highness be pleased to descend from your elephant and mount your horse, and ride at the head of your own cavalry and the squadrons committed to my charge. We will go together to the attack. It was for this alone that I saved my division, seeing that up to now there was no necessity for my engaging.'

Poor Dara! without fully considering what he was doing, and what would follow when he was no longer to be seen on his elephant, towards which all turned their gaze; but relying on the soft words of the traitor Khalilullah Khan, by which he allowed himself to be persuaded and deceived, he took the advice, as it appeared to him that what had been said was very true. He alighted from his elephant, and this was as if he had quitted victory; for the soldiers and commanders, who in the midst of the battle kept an eye on Dara, not seeing him on his elephant, assumed that he must be already dead. For this reason they were thrown into great confusion.

I myself was in astonishment and in great dismay, not knowing what to imagine, finding all in confusion and Dara no longer visible on his elephant; meanwhile the whole army was fleeing to the rear, like dark clouds blown by a high wind, seeking safety for their lives in the belief [193] that Aurangzeb, although still at a good distance, was already upon us. Dara, on beholding this great confusion and flight, fell into deep thought and saw now the mistake he had made and the plot laid for him by Khalilullah Khan. He repented him of the fault, but it was too late. Full of wrath and raging, he asked where was the traitor

Khalilullah Khan. Let him be sought for and brought, for he meant to slay him. But the traitor was already far off. His lord having dismounted from his elephant and mounted his horse, he (Khalilullah Khan) rejoined his division, with the object of transferring himself and his soldiers to the side of Aurangzeb. The soldiers who followed him did not exceed five thousand horsemen; the rest of those under his command were soldiers of King Shahjahan. But these latter fell into disorder like the others, finding themselves without a leader to direct them, owing to the treachery that had occurred.

These events of the battle which I have related occupied some three hours. The affair beginning at nine o'clock in the morning, it was near midday the rout took place. A great many men and a still greater number of horses and other animals were killed. The reason of this was that our horses were much out of condition, and not used to the heavy work of a battle; while, on the contrary, Aurangzeb's horses were not overfed and were used to work. Other causes were the great heat prevailing, the want of water, and the excessive dust. It seemed to me more died in this way than by injury from weapons.

Leaving, then, the flight of Dara and my retirement from the field to be spoken of afterwards, let us tell now how Aurangzeb, seeing that Dara's army was in flight, took possession of the tents and baggage of that army. Already we have mentioned how Khalilullah Khan deserted to Aurangzeb's side with his five thousand horsemen. But great was the finesse with which he was received by Aurangzeb, now that he found his victory was assured. When this traitor appeared, Aurangzeb struck up his drums in sign of victory. All the soldiers collected and placed themselves under the orders of Aurangzeb, including Murad Bakhsh and his troops. A few words of congratulation were exchanged between them. Aurangzeb praised the valour of Murad Bakhsh, attributing to him the victory. He then presented to him that traitor Khalilullah Khan, and said he was the king's most faithful friend. It was as 'king' that he addressed Murad Bakhsh whenever he had to speak to him. Khalilullah khan, he said, was the most loyal subject to be found in his realm; that he could be employed in the most difficult matters; that he knew well the high qualities and generosity of his king, Murad Bakhsh, and the fealty with which he must be served. He added words of praise for both Murad Bakhsh and Khalilullah Khan.

After all this, they set themselves in array and marched for the tents and camp of Dara. Aurangzeb and Murad Bakhsh advanced tranquilly, and when they were near, they ordered out some horsemen and infantry to reconnoitre the tents and dig up the ground round them to see if there were no powder-mines laid. They feared there might be treachery.

Assured [194] that there was no treachery, they both advanced to the tents of Dara, and, alighting from their elephants, entered. Aurangzeb remarked to Murad Bakhsh that it was the first day of his reign, renewed his congratulations on the victory, and behaved to him as to his sovereign and master. He offered him exaggerated respect in the presence of Khalilullah khian and others then present. He went through a thousand bows and submissive gestures, just as if he were any insignificant servant. Here once more Murad Bakhsh received the traitor Khalilullah Khan with soft words and many promises. Leaving Murad Bakhsh at Dara's tents, everybody else withdrew.

Most people fathomed the purpose of Aurangzeb. While professing himself adverse to reigning and anxious to follow for ever the observances of a holy mendicant, all he did was out of refined policy, and only to arrive at being emperor. When the opportunity arose, Murad Bakhsh would certainly be destroyed. For this end he worked hard, writing day and night, and sending letters in all directions to every viceroy and governor in the empire. He took counsel with his maternal uncle, Shaistah Khan, a man of great sense, the greatest *omarao* (*umara*, noble) that there was in the country. This man was related to the greater number of the nobles, and was the oldest, best known, and best liked of them all. Aurangzeb asked him to write to all his friends in his (Aurangzeb's) favour, and to pursue Dara as persistently as he could. He (Aurangzeb) knew that Shaistah Khan would not fail to aid him, for he hated Shahjahan, and did not love Dara, but acted in every way as Aurangzeb desired.

Among other letters one was written by Aurangzeb to Rajah Jai Singh, also one to Daler Khan; these were the chief commanders under Sultan Sulaiman Shukoh and servants of Shahjahan. They were given to understand that henceforth there was nothing to be looked for in the way of benefits from Dara. He had already lost the battle, the last hope and only chance he had of reigning. The whole army of Dara had submitted to him (Aurangzeb), and was now at his orders; Dara was in solitary flight, but could never escape. He must fall into his (Aurangzeb's) hands, orders having issued throughout the empire to send him back a captive. They need not refer to Shahjahan, who was already very ill, and there was not the slightest hope of his surviving. They could plainly see, as men of good judgment, what course they had to adopt. If they desired to be well treated and be among his friends, they should listen to his advice and should bind Sultan Sulaiman Shukoh and produce him before him.

On getting this letter, Rajah Jai Singh found himself much embarrassed, and it troubled him greatly to decide what to do in the circumstances. He feared for the lives of Shahjahan and of Dara, and still more he disliked laying hands upon one of royal blood. He dreaded that, sooner or later, there might happen to him some great discomfiture, either from the old king, from Prince Dara, or from Aurangzeb himself. The latter, as I have seen, took the life of everyone who laid hands on one of the blood-royal, as I will tell you farther on. In addition to all this, Rajah Jai Singh well foresaw that Sultan Sulaiman Shukoh had too great courage to allow of his being taken quietly; that he would sooner die defending himself than fall into his enemies' hands.

He (Jai Singh) took counsel with his great [195] friend, Daler Khan, as to what should be done. They resolved that Rajah Jai Singh should go at once to the tents of Sulaiman Shukoh, where he was awaited with great impatience. The prince had already heard the news of the defeat of his father, Dara. At the interview Jai Singh disclosed to him clearly all that was going on, and showed him the letter received from Aurangzeb. He veiled under this letter and the orders of Aurangzeb the revenge he wanted to obtain on Dara for having called him a 'musician.' He (Jai Singh) pointed out the danger Sulaiman Shukoh was in; that there was no remedy; that he could not rely on the larger number of his officers, for nearly all were traitors. He (Jai Singh) gave the advice that, with all expedition, he should flee into the mountains of Sirinagar (Srinagar), of which I have spoken earlier (I. 147). This was the best and safest place for him to select, being a very secure refuge. There the rajah would receive him willingly, and thence he could watch the course of events without fear of Aurangzeb.

After this speech, Sulaiman Shukoh saw that he could rely neither on the rajah nor on Daler Khan, the rajah's friend. He then consulted his general, Dautcan (Da,ud Khan), as to what could be done in this extremity. This man proposed that, on the pretext of bidding them farewell and imparting to them some secret, they should be sent for together. As soon as they arrived in the tent, they should be then and there slain, and their troops taken over. With their united force they might then march resolutely against Aurangzeb, and wreak vengeance on him for what he had done to Sulaiman Shukoh's father, Dara. If this were done, Aurangzeb could not so easily carry out his purpose.

The advice was sagacious, but it was not kept sufficiently secret. The rajah learnt of it through the prince's surgeon, an Armenian by race, called Sikandar Beg, all of which I was told by this very rajah himself (Jai Singh). To carry out the above intent Sulaiman Shukoh, his mind made up and all things ready, ordered the rajah and Daler Khan to be sent for with the accustomed ceremony. But having been warned, they sent him a private and straightforward message that their first answer and the advice then given were enough. It were well that, with all haste, he took the road the rajah had told him of. He must not wait for them, for their coming would be of no use to him.

With this reply Sulaiman Shukoh lost all hope. Fearing they might arrest him, he issued orders to load up the best of what he had. He took the road to the mountains, accompanied by some men who loved him, such as eunuchs, slaves, and a few real soldiers. With them went the Armenian who had betrayed the secret. He stuck to the prince by reason of the great profits he made and in the hope of increasing them. I encountered this fellow at the court two years afterwards, and by him I was told in detail the excessive hardships which the prince endured, as I will acquaint you later (I. 276).

The remainder of the soldiers and officers either took the road to their homes or enlisted under the rajah and Daler Khan. Although these men were such great captains, powerful and well reputed, they committed at this juncture a signal act of baseness—they sent men to fall upon the baggage of the fugitive prince. They robbed him of one elephant loaded [196] with precious stones and one loaded with golden rupees, also of several camels bearing the greater part of the wealth that the poor prince possessed to meet his necessities. This act caused great confusion among and inconvenience to the small body that had adhered to Sulaiman Shukoh. From this moment many abandoned him.

Wherever he passed, on every route, the villagers assassinated or stripped his people. One or two at a time, his followers continued to disappear, and when he reached the hills there remained with him under forty persons besides his family. There the Rajah of Srinagar received him with all possible honour and civility, assuring him of succour to the full extent of his strength, saying that he would be as safe there as if himself ruler of the country.

The miserable and unfortunate Dara, by a hurried flight, reached the gates of the Agrah fortress at nine o'clock at night, and sought some repose. But he did not want to enter, fearing that Aurangzeb might invest it and thus prevent his exit, when he would fall a prisoner and be abandoned by everyone. At the same time he was greatly ashamed at appearing before his father. He remembered that Shahjahan had wished to be present in the battle, but he had withheld consent, whereat he was now exceedingly sorry. So far had he lost his wits that he knew not what he said or did.

He sent this message to Shahjahan, his father, and his well beloved sister, Begam Sahib: 'What has now happened to me is what you foretold.' He grieved them much, but as they loved him, in place of repining at his evil fate and in spite of all differences, the good old man, his father, sent to him a faithful eunuch called Faim (Fahim), to console him (Dara) and assure him that he still cherished for him, and would forever cherish, the same love and strong friendship that he had always had for him; he felt deeply the misfortune that had befallen him. But he must not despair. There was still the other great army under Sulaiman Shukoh; with it he could renew the attack on the rebels, and routing them, inflict vengeance on them for their temerity.

At the same time, Shahjahan ordered to be sent to Dara mules laden with gold coin. He suggested his proceeding to the city of Dihli, and taking all the horses and elephants in the royal stables. Orders were sent to the governor of Dihli to open the gates to Dara, and to deliver to him the fortress, with all the treasures and other things within it. He was to be received with the same ceremonial and deference as if it were he (Shahjahan) *in propria persona*. For the execution of these orders trusty and well-known persons were sent in his suite, carrying letters to the above effect. He was advised to remain in Dihli, and not proceed farther. He (Shahjahan) gave his word of honour that he would do all he could to seize and chastise Aurangzeb. He would keep him (Dara) informed of everything that happened.

The eunuch delivered this speech, but Dara was to such an extent confused, enfeebled, and cast down, with his thoughts wandering and his mind full of tribulation, that he was unable to utter a word, and lay writhing on the ground. The eunuch tried all he could to console him, on seeing him in this deep affliction, but he could not extract a single sensible word.

His sister, Begam Sahib, sent another faithful eunuch to him with some valuable jewels. She expressed her deep grief, telling him that she was even more discomfited than he [197]; but she had not lost all hope of some day seeing him reign peacefully—that ever would she petition God in her prayers to look favourably on him. After this talk Dara repaired hurriedly to his mansion, and ordered the removal of all the precious stones that could be carried off. At midnight he made a start, taking with him his three wives, his daughter Jani Begom (Jani Begam), his little son Super Xacu (Sipihr Shukoh), and some chosen slave-girls. On his departure for the city of Dihli he was followed by some five hundred soldiers, for the most part slaves of his household. It was a great affliction to see such a down-come.

On arriving at the city of Dihli he sent at once the orders of his father to the governor, requiring him to make over the fortrces. But the governor, already averted by the letters of Aurangzeb, to whom he was well affected, declined to comply with Shahjahan's orders. Thus the unhappy Dara was forced, after seizing what horses there were in the royal stables, to resume his march and make for Lahor.

Seeing our total defeat, I made in haste for the city of Agrah, where I arrived at ten o'clock at night. The whole city was in an uproar, for a Portuguese called Antonio de Azevedo, who early in the battle had witnessed the plunder of the baggage, rode off at full speed. On arriving at the city of Agrah at two o'clock in the afternoon, his horse fell dead at his door. Thus the news began to spread that Dara had lost the battle, and the confusion was increased by Dara's own arrival. The curiosity of everyone was aroused to know how the defeat had happened, and men asked each passer-by about the safety of his master. This happened to me. An old woman asked me what had become of Khalilullah Khan. Owing to the rage I was in at his treachery, I replied at once that I was present when he was torn to pieces. The old woman was very disconsolate, and hastening her steps, went off to give this news at his house. Much weeping and lamenting was caused thereby, they supposing it to be the truth, for I had entered into some details on purpose.

On learning that Dara was resuming his journey and making for Dihli, I decided that very instant upon rejoining him. But my steed was so worn out that he could hardly stand, just as were those of everyone who reached the city that night. I decided to take a rest for twenty-four hours, and after that to start and go in search of Dara.

Aurangzeb showed no want of promptitude in carrying out his designs. Within twenty-four hours he despatched Bahadur Khan with several troops of cavalry to occupy the road to and from Agrah on the west. This was to hinder anyone following Dara. As a result, the first men to take to the road before the day dawned, among them several Europeans, found free passage; but the rest, not knowing that Bahadur san was already in position, started on the journey, only to be plundered of all they carried and sent away with a good beating, coming back to the city.

Without knowing these facts, at nine o'clock in the morning I made a start, riding my horse, followed by a loaded camel and some servants. Issuing from the city, I saw several squadrons dispersed in the plain. As I imagined these to be our men, I decided to join them. Then I saw that a body of some five hundred horsemen with its commander was bearing down upon me. On its drawing near, the leader advanced from it, attended by two horsemen. When quite close [198] he asked me lovingly where I was going. I replied without subterfuge that I was on my way to find my master, Dara. He took compassion on my youth and innocence, and said to me that if I followed his advice, I should return home, for if I proceeded farther I ran great risk of losing my life. This captain was so generous that, to protect me, he escorted me safely to my house.

If he had not done this, there can be little doubt I should have been plundered by others posted on the road, or even by his own soldiers, who betrayed every desire to plunder me had he not prevented them. Seeing me into my house unharmed, he advised me not to leave it again. The government had already changed hands, and Aurangzeb was victor. For that time I had escaped, and I looked out for a safer opportunity to start in search of Dara, for whom I had a great affection. If Aurangzeb had not barred the way, all Dara's people would have gone on to rejoin him. But they could not then do it, as I have told you, for they came in tired out by their flight, and their horses quite exhausted.

I remained in the city of Agrah, and observed the way in which Aurangzeb forwarded his designs. For on the eighth of the month of June, one thousand six hundred and fifty-six (correctly, 1658), four days after the battle, Aurangzeb and Murad Bakhsh arrived at Agrah. They posted their army close to a garden called Zafarabad (Ja'farabad or Zafarabad)[1] near the city, at a distance of two miles. Thence Aurangzeb sent his eunuch, called Fahlm, an able, astute, and loyal person, to visit his father, carrying a thousand beautiful protestations of love and submission. He professed to be much affected by what had passed, his excuse being that the ambitions and evil thoughts of Dara had forced him into resorting to all these extremities. As for the rest, he was highly elated at the good news of his (Shahjahan's) better health. He was now at the capital, ready to receive and obey his orders.

The eunuch Fahim made no stint, either of obeisances or of soft and humble speeches. He dwelt on the goodwill and excellent intentions of Aurangzeb. Nor, on the other hand, was Shahjahan wanting in a plentiful display of loving satisfaction. Desirous of keeping on the throne, he resorted to wiles, for he knew the character and hidden malice of Aurangzeb. He never forgot the words said to him by the faqir, that he must not put trust in Aurangzeb, nor in his soft words.

Therefore he devoted himself to searching for a plan to remedy his present evil case. He thought first of coming out and passing through the city, to find out whether his generals mean to succour him. But he saw perfectly that it was already too late: all of them had gone over to Aurangzeb. Even if the city residents were willing to join him, he saw clearly that nothing could be effected through them. If the citizens were like those of Europe, there can be not the least doubt that they could have at that time given Aurangzeb plenty of occupation.

1. The "Alamgirnamah,' page 112, line 3, says the camp was at the garden (*bagh*) known as Nur Manzil. The site of it is included in the present cantonment.

Finally, Shahjahan came to the determination to play a game of finesse with Aurangzeb, a supreme master in that line. To this end he sent a eunuch called Almes (Almas) with a statement that he knew well enough the evil condition and small capacity of Dara. He was delighted at the arrival of his son Aurangzeb, and out of the special love he bore to him, he had granted him the vast territories of the Dakhin. He had a great longing to converse with him in person, and communicate to him several plans that must be carried out to repress the disorders in the empire [199], and he was awaiting his appearance, having the greatest longing to embrace him.

All this was said to draw Aurangzeb into the fortress; and without a shadow of doubt he meant to murder him if he went there. He had previously made all preparations in secret. There were many strong-limbed Tartara (Tatar), Calmaca (Qalmaq), and Osbeca (Uzbak) women in his guard, all skilled in the use of arms. These would have slain Aurangzeb with their matchlocks, arrows, and swords. But the wily Aurangzeb, the very quintessence of deceit, quite foresaw that he ought not to trust in the words of Shahjahan, and knew thoroughly that Begam Sahib, very fond of Dara, and always present with her father, would never cease exerting herself in every possible way for his (Dara's) cause as against him (Aurangzeb). He had no need of listening to words; what he had to do was to obtain mastery over the realm without delay. Thus he declined to risk himself.

All the same, he never ceased to spread the rumour, one day after another, that he was going to see Shahjahan. When the appointed day arrived, there arose some excuse to put it off to another date. In this way he went on from day to day postponing the date of the visit. Meanwhile, he continued in secret to seduce by soft words the greater nobles at the court. In the end, having everything thoroughly ready in secret, he was in a position to carry out what he had planned. When everybody was looking for the visit to be paid, Aurangzeb ordered his son Sultan Muhammad to assume command in his (Aurangzeb's) name at the office of the cotual (*kotwal*), who is the chief magistrate ruling over the whole city. Under cover of this movement, he was to rush on and encircle the fortress, and allow no one to enter.

Shahjahan was thrown into dismay at finding himself all of a sudden invested—above all, when he found that Aurangzeb and all his men were posted opposite the fortress, near the tomb of Taia-mahal (Taj Mahal or Mumtaz Mahal), the wife of Shahjahan, of which place I have already spoken (I. 121). When Aurangzeb had arrived here, Shaistah Khan and Muhammad Amin Khan, son of Mir Jumlah, with many others then in the city, went forth to receive him. They offered him costly presents, and congratulated him on his great success, all of them in high spirits at seeing what they had so keenly desired. I do not know that among the men of any standing there were more than two not included in the ranks of the traitors. These were Danijbad can (Danishmand Khan),[1] the greatest scholar in the empire, and Mecoromcan (Mukarram Khan), physician of Shahjahan, natives of Persia, who both stopped at home and declared their neutrality.

Poor Shahjahan found himself in the fort with no one except Assetcan (Asad Khan), of whom I will say more presently (I. 201). He came forth from his palace and went the rounds in the fort, and gave orders to equip such fighting men as there were, and get ready his artillery. On noticing that Aurangzeb's men were closing in, he ordered them to be fired on; he had by this time given up all hope of the interview for which he had been waiting. But Aurangzeb paid no heed to these shots, and went on with his advance, taking possession of the whole city. He posted his forces beneath the walls of the fort, under cover of the rows of houses that surrounded it.

Although already caught as in a cage, Shahjahan never desisted from firing his guns and his musketry to hold back the investing force from nearer approach. But no damage was done, the enemy being safely under cover, and without need to return

1. Mulla Shafi'a,i, Yazdi, Danishmand Khan, came to India to practise medicine, and was taken into Shahjahan's service in the twenty-fourth year (*circa* 1650). In the thirty-first year he had risen to be Mir Bakhshi, with the rank of 3,000 (800 horse). He died on the 10th Rabi' I., 1081 H. (July 28, 1670) ('Ma,asir-ul-Umara,' ii. 30). He was Bernier's patron (see 'Travels,' p. 4). For 'Mukarram' (referred to again in Part II, fol. 44), we should probably read 'Taqarrub' Khan (Hakim Da,ud). He was physician to Shahjahan at Agrah, and died early in 1073 H., which began on August 15, 1662 ('Ma,asir-ul-Umara,'i. 490). There are also details of Hakim Da,ud's career in Kewal Ram's 'Tazkirat-ul-Umara,' British Museum Additional MS., 16,703, fol. 25b. It is there said that he resigned his offices in the first year of Aurangzeb: he had come from Iran in the seventeenth year of Shahjahan (*circa* 1643).

the fire. The guns were loaded and discharged for three days and three nights, making a great noise. At the end of that time the artillerymen, at whose head was the man called Rabin Simitt (? Reuben Smith) [200], an Englishman, commenced to escape, descending the walls by ropes. They had been bribed by Aurangzeb, who communicated with them by letting fly an arrow into the fort. The remainder of the garrison, when they saw the departure of the artillerymen, lost heart, and began also to plan the means of flight.

At this time Aurangzeb sent in a petition to Shahjahan, making excuses for the delay there had been in coming to pay his visit. He made use of the pretext that he had been ill, that he was unable to come, and that meanwhile, against his will, his restless soldiers had taken the initiative. Now he begged leave to send his son Sultan Muhammad to visit him, and pay to him his most humble respects. Then, restored to health, as would soon be the case, he would be able to perform this duty in person.

Shahjahan agreed to this proposal, in the hope of still executing his project. To this intent he made ready many lengths of valuable cloth to be presented to Sultan Muhammad, who was to be received with great pomp. He wanted to see if by this method he could draw Aurangzeb. But that Machiavelli was very far from having that sort of feeling. His orders to Sultan Muhammad were, on the contrary, that on reaching the gate of the fort, he should enter promptly, and secure the entrance. Then he should bring in all his men, killing anyone that resisted. These instructions were carried out by his son, without omitting a single point.

Shahjahan was greatly amazed at this treachery, being then in his palace amid his women, over two thousand in number, all resolved to die in defence of their lord. From this cause Aurangzeb did not push matters farther, fearing that there might happen to him some misfortune in carrying to the end his design. He knew the proverb: 'Quern todo quer, todo lo perde' ['He who wants everything loses everything'—or the French: 'Qui trop embrasse, mal étrain.'] He sent word to his father that he should take his ease in his harem, that he was no longer in a state to rule, that he should enjoy himself with his ladies and abandon all anxiety. For he (Aurangzeb) took the whole weight of the empire on himself. When Aurangzeb effected this project Shahjahan was sixty-one years of age, and had reigned thirty-two years and three months.[1]

Finding that by this time it was no longer in his power to do anything likely to secure his liberty, Shahjahan invented a plot which, if successful, would have been the overthrow of Aurangzeb. Thus was necessity a subtle counsellor. His device was to send for Sultan Muhammad to his presence, on the pretext that, finding him so able, he intended to make him king. The prince would never fail with such a bait to come to the palace without an hour's delay, and would never neglect this excellent chance of getting the crown from the hands of his grandfather, coupling with it a deed pleasing to God and the whole world by setting free one unjustly oppressed. But Sultan Muhammad, a man of sense, was not carried away by the words of his grandfather. He knew certainly that all his own leaders and the majority of men in the city were well affected to Aurangzeb, his father, since they had invited [201] him to come. If he attempted what his grandfather proposed, he would fall into the same condition as the old man. Thus, he declined to listen to or accept the proposal, nor did he set foot within the palace. He sent instead a rough answer that he had no orders from his father either to visit or to listen to him. He had injunctions not to return without bringing the keys of all the gates of the fortress.

Shahjahan did not lose his wits, but replied that his grandson could come freely and in all security into the palace. He longed to embrace him, and into his hands he would deliver the keys, not only of the fortress but of all the empire, making over the crown to him. But Sultan Muhammad persisted in his resolve, and replied that those words were mere vanity; it was no longer the time to talk thus. Let him send the keys, unless he wanted to be reduced to a worse state. Finding him thus resolute, Shahjahan made up his mind to send the keys. For he observed the great activity of Sultan Muhammad and the people under him. They allowed no food-supplies to pass. The people inside

1. Shahjahan was born on the 1st Rabi' II., 1000 H. (January 16, 1592, N.S.), and succeeded his father on the 8th Jamada II., 1037 H. (February 14,1628, N.S.). He was deposed, according to Elphinstone, on the 17th Ramazan, 1068 H. (June 18, 1658, N.S.). Thus, he was sixty-eight and a half lunar, and sixty-six and a half solar, years of age, and had reigned thirty-one years three months nine days (or thirty years four months four days), at the time of his deposition.

suffered hunger and thirst, and little by little they were forced to abandon the post they occupied near the private apartments, which is called the 'Am chai' (? 'Am-Khas), where Shahjahan gave audience.

Finding himself in this plight and without any security for his person, he sent the keys. His determination was that if the enemy advanced farther, he would elect to die by force, with the women, eunuchs, and Asad Khan. The latter declined to leave his king, and kept the door to the harem, just as if he were a humble servitor. This he did out of the great affection and loyalty that he had for Shahjahan.

When he sent the keys, Shahjahan forwarded a message for Aurangzeb that he must come to see him at once: he had business of very great importance to consult him upon. He hoped thus to get him into the harem and assassinate him. But Aurangzeb, sagacious, able, and quick-witted, only laughed at such words. He sent instead a trusty eunuch that Shahjahan had given him long before, called Atbarcan (I'tibar Khan). This man now succeeded in shutting up Shahjahan in his harem with Begam Sahib and the rest of the women, removing Roshan-ara Begam, the beloved sister of Aurangzeb, who was dispatched with great pomp.

Then I'tibar Khan caused many gates and wickets to be built up, posting here and there harsh women guardians in such a way that Shahjahan could neither speak nor write to any stranger, nor come out from the door of his harem to enjoy a stroll in his garden without the eunuch's leave. Even here Aurangzeb's astuteness did not end. As justification for his acts, and to turn away the people from Shahjahan, he prepared a forged letter in his (Shahjahan's) name. It was addressed to Dara, and advised him not to go very far away from Agrah; for already the time was near when he would see his rebellious and inimical brothers slain by the very hands of him whose misfortune it was to be their father, those monsters filled with the basest barbarities. Soon Aurangzeb and Murad Bakhsh would come to visit him; they would enter alive, but never come out on their own feet. They would be carried out by the hands of others bearing them to burial. Then if he (Dara), his faithful and only son, would come to Agrah, he could enjoy and rule over the empire.

This forged letter was brought to Aurangzeb when he was giving audience, and many people were present at court. It was opened [202] by Shaistah Khan. On hearing its contents, Aurangzeb feigned consternation, and his face blanched; he began striking the ground with his feet and beating his pillows with his open hand; he made display of the greatest terror, as at some most displeasing news, and betrayed all the signs of having learnt of some great treachery. He held his head down in thought, and then directed the letter to be read aloud, and after that told them to give it to anyone who wanted to read it for himself. By these actions everybody was greatly terrified. Then, resuming his wiles, Aurangzeb expressed his desire to see his father, and said the letter might be a forgery. Thereupon the great men in attendance urged that his highness should not run any such risk. But he, multiplying his devices, would not be appeased.

He (Aurangzeb) directed the votes of all at court to be taken whether it was advisable or not for him to pay this visit. All with one consent replied that it was undesirable, nor would they ever consent to it. At this answer he pretended to be very hurt and aggrieved, though inwardly rejoicing. He decided to write a note to his father, which he caused to be read out to the whole court before he sealed it. Among other arguments this note stated that he knew of a certainty that, in spite of all the great protestations of esteem made to him, and the displeasure declared against Dara, and all the warm affection said to be retained for him (Aurangzeb), he (Shahjahan) had nevertheless made over to Dara on his leave-taking mule-loads of gold coin, simply to pay a new force to oppose him (Aurangzeb). But, all the same, he (Aurangzeb) would never desist until he had captured Dara, the cause of all these troubles. After this design was achieved, on that very same day, he would undoubtedly visit Shahjahan, and submit to him like an obedient son. Furthermore, he besought him to pardon him, and not to persist in his anger. When he had crushed the power and overcome the ill designs of Dara, he would himself throw open the doors and make him lord and master, as before.

At one time I knew some women left to serve Shahjahan and Begam Sahib, whose business it was to receive and reply to letters and notes arriving from outside. They assured me that such a letter never reached the court of Shahjahan. Aurangzeb started these stories solely to the end of conciliating the people and excusing his deceptions. He wanted to place the culpability upon Shahjahan and Dara, and to prove that all the tyranny employed against his father was amply justifiable.

At this time there happened a ridiculous occurrence, known to everybody. Begam Sahib's musician, called Dulera, seeing that Shahjahan and Begam Sahib were prisoners, and there was no hope of getting the accustomed presents planned the acquisition of new friends. He went to see several of Murad Bakhsh's commanders, and was well received, for he could sing to perfection. Being in merry mood, the wine began to go round. Dulera, already heated, ran down the wine they gave him. He ordered his servants to fetch some more exquisite wine, such as he always drank.

The officers noticed the grand ways of the musician; and when the wine arrived, they found it was in bottles of gold and enamel, adorned [203] with precious stones, such as the officers themselves did not possess. Dulera exalted himself a good deal in his talk, assuming to be the equal of the officers. Seeing so much impudence and assumption, and also moved by the envy and resentment they felt towards Begam Sahib, they had him bound, and stripping him of his trousers, forced a lighted nightlamp into his anus, leaving it to burn until the musician begged pardon for his transgressions. They sent him off with blows and kicks. This occurrence made him lower the lofty ideas that he had, and retiring to his house he stayed there until his death, and never appeared again.

Finding himself already practically with control over all the nobles at court, and Shahjahan securely lodged in prison, Aurangzeb appointed his maternal uncle, Shaistah Khan, governor of the city of Agrah. Taking out of the treasury whatever money he wanted, he and Murad Bakhsh started in pursuit of Dara. The latter was already in Lahor raising a new army, having lost all hope of aid from Sulaiman Shukoh.

On the day that the two armies quitted Agrah, which was in the beginning of June, I disguised myself as a holy mendicant and joined their train, meaning to stick to the service of Dara. The eunuch Shahbaz and the more intimate friends of Murad Bakhsh advised him to allow Aurangzeb to go after Dara by himself, while he should conduct an investment of Agrah and Dihli with his army, which was already far larger than before.

But, not perceiving the finessing and wiliness of Aurangzeb, he relied on the promises and oaths of fidelity which had been made to him upon the Alcorao (the *Quran*). He neglected to listen to these faithful men, and allowed himself to be played with by that fabricator and deceiver.

The two armies took the route for Dihli, the one at a distance from the other of a short mile or so. They marched along the bank of the river Jamnah until they were near to an ancient Hindu town called Matora (Mathura), distant eighteen leagues from Agrah, where there is an imposing temple. During the march a great number of Dara's men came in, and several of the defeated officers. These sought service with Murad Bakhsh, and he granted them high pay. Daler Khan also arrived, he who had deserted Sulaiman Shukoh. He visited Aurangzeb, who paid him a thousand civilities, and gave him many presents with an increase of pay. Jai Singh departed for his own territories.

On the way Aurangzeb omitted nothing in pretended deference and consideration for Murad Bakhsh. He sent him several times during the day men with quantities of fruit and choice flowers, repeating that he must prepare himself; for, in a few days' time, he meant to crown him (Murad Bakhsh) king. To this intent he ordered to be made ready a number of new tents, raiment, jewels, caparisoned elephants and horses. He also ostentatiously began to collect food to be cooked in his kitchen, sweetmeats, several kinds of scent, and flowers. Orders were given to all the dancing-women and musicians to prepare and hold themselves in readiness.

I noticed that in Aurangzeb's army there was a great deal of secret confabulation with nods and metaphors (a habit very common in Hindustan), such as 'The tiger big with young will soon bring forth,' or, as others said, 'The sick man can never recover.' Thus the intention of Aurangzeb was sufficiently obvious to his people. But in the army of Murad Bakhsh there was nothing but music, dancing, wine-bibbing, and revelry. Still, many friends of Murad Bakhsh, and above all, the eunuch Shahbaz, pressed on him that Aurangzeb had evil designs; that without a doubt there would be some trickery; they had information from several sources that Aurangzeb was setting some trap for him. But he (Murad Bakhsh), infatuated [204] with the lying words of his brother, and intoxicated with power, paid no heed to such advice, holding the erroneous opinion that his brother's oaths were sincere, and his soft words the daughters of truth.

Before reaching Mathura, Aurangzeb selected a place called Coliquigat (Koli-ki-ghat).[1] It was spacious, open, and every way suited for such a joyful day as a coronation, both by the loveliness of the country and the charms of the river. The latter seemed by the murmurs of its waters either to rejoice at the good luck of Aurangzeb, now almost arrived at the accomplishment of his purpose, or to weep over the disenchantment of Murad Bakhsh. When he was looking forward to being crowned, surrounded by the nobles and generals in his service and subjection, Murad Bakhsh found himself instead in the hands of the soldiers of retributory justice, and was made to pay the penalty of his obstinacy. For he would not listen to his faithful advisers, who said they were certain of Aurangzeb's evil designs.

On the 15th of June, after a halt of four days at the above place,[2] Aurangzeb sent his son Sultan Muhammad and all the great captains to invite Murad Bakhsh to visit his camp, where his desire would be fulfilled, and the pledge given him redeemed by his being crowned as king. The said day was pronounced by the astrologers to be propitious. Then Murad Bakhsh arranged to start, never imagining that a prison awaited him. But the faithful Shahbaz and other officers entreated him to send an excuse for that day, informing Aurangzeb that he had a slight ailment, and that another day must be fixed. In the interval he could make more certain of what Aurangzeb was working for. Several of Aurangzeb's officers continued their visits, and through them he could find out the truth. But he would not listen to them any more, and the advice was thrown away, for Prince

1. Through the kindness of Mr. H. C. Ferard, collector of Mathura, I have obtained a most interesting identification of this place by S. M. Abdul Hadi, the senior Government pleader there. The Koli *ghat* or crossing, lies six miles south of Mathura, and a little over a mile from the modern Aurangabad on the Agrah road, where the stables erected by Aurangzeb still exist. The inhabitants say that Aurangabad was the site of the camp, and that the Emperor erected a mosque, and gave the village its present name.
2. Bernier gives no day, but the ' 'Alamgirnamah,' p. 138, top line, has the 4th Shawwal, 1068 H. (July 5, 1658). The 'Tarikh-i-Muhammadi.' year 1071 H., says on hearsay authority that Murad Bakhsh was killed at Gwaliyar, by Aurangzeb's order, on Wednesday, the 21st Rabi' II., 1071 H. (December 25, 1660). He was thirty-eight.

Murad Bakhsh had no distrust of Aurangzeb. More fixed than ever in his purpose, and relying on the oath of his brother, he mounted his horse, and set out for the tents of Aurangzeb, attended by Shahbaz and other officers.

At a short distance from his tents he was met by an officer, Ibrahim Khan.[1] This was the man who advised Dara, after the river passage had been forced, to send off twelve thousand cavalry against Aurangzeb, as I have related (I. 185). After a salutation he approached, and laying hold of the prince's reins, asked in a low voice, with a perturbed face, where he was going. Murad Bakhsh replied very quietly that he was on his way to declare himself absolue monarch. The officer replied: 'I rejoice greatly; but what is the necessity for your highness to go to another's house, when with greater security you can carry it out in your own?' Saying this, he gently turned Murad Bakhsh's horse round. But he in a rage resumed his course, and the officer, seeing the deliberate resolve and determination of the prince, said aloud. 'Your majesty is on your way to prison.' Hearing this, Shahbaz would not lose this occasion, and drawing up to his master, prayed him for the love of God and the great Muhammad to be pleased to accept the advice of the officer. But Murad Bakhsh laid his hand on his sword, and exclaimed: 'Asman que si bahader nis' (*Az man kase bahadur nist*)—that is to say, 'None is braver than I am.'

He went on until he reached the entrance to the tent of Aurangzeb. At this moment the qazi came out, and while making a lowly reverence, whispered: 'With your feet you have come,' meaning thereby that when he came out it would be against his will. But he, bewitched by the friendliness of Aurangzeb, did not pause to reflect, but went within. Aurangzeb now multiplied his wiles, and came out to greet him, along with Sec Mir (Shekh Mir)[2] and his brother, Amircan (Amir Khan), and other officers, his intimates and devoted followers, handsomely attired, and with beaming faces. Embracing him, he (Aurangzeb) expressed the abundant love he had for him, cajoling him [205] with obsequious bows and many expressions of civility. Leading him to a great and handsome seat, he prayed him to be seated, and drove away

1. Ibrahim Khan, son of 'Ali Mardan Khan, as the passage on fol. 185 shows.
2. For Shekh Mir, see footnote to I., fol. 241.

the flies by agitating a handkerchief gently before his face, wiping away the sweat and the dust, and treating him throughout as king and lord.

Then there appeared men and women musicians, and during their singing flowers were scattered and rose-water sprinkled everywhere; also many scents and perfumes were employed. Outside the tents different instruments struck up, and within were the dances of the ballet girls. At all this Murad Bakhsh was elated and pleased, as if already in enjoyment of the first-fruits of his glory. Three hours after his arrival, when it may have been two o'clock in the afternoon, they began the feast. Aurangzeb had beforehand ordered his officers to invite those of Murad Bakhsh to their tents, and the whole night was spent in mirth. Word of all this passed through the camp, and Murad Bakhsh's soldiers, seeing that their officers had settled down to a night of festivity, on their side made plans to go out in search of supplies and forage for their horses.

Murad Bakhsh was left with no one but his eunuch, Shahbaz, who all the time he was dining stood at his back fully armed. Then they began to eat and drink. All Aurangzeb's officers stood serving and pouring out wine for Murad Bakhsh, while Aurangzeb offered him different dishes and acted as his table servant. All this was done with much dissimulation and great efforts to please. The meal lasted for two hours. At the end of it Aurangzeb said to his brother that he must take a rest, while he (Aurangzeb) made ready the throne, and ascertained from the mathematicians (astrologers) the exact moment for taking his seat thereon, when he would come in person to awake him.

The hapless prince retired to another room to take some repose, and found there a beautiful woman, with whom he wanted to toy; but the eunuch, Shahbaz, forbade him, and turned the woman out. Sleep soon fell upon him, for he was heavy with wine, and Shahbaz, seating himself, kneaded his master's feet, and kept an eye fixed on the door. In a short time he saw Aurangzeb come out alone from another door opposite, in white shirt and drawers and a plain cap. With head bent and smiling, he advanced very deliberately, pulling at his beard, just as if he wanted to ask Shahbaz something. When at a little distance from the door, he halted, and raising his head, made a sign with his hand to the eunuch for him to approach, as if he wanted to get his opinion on some point. Poor Shahbaz hastened to obey, hut hardly had he put his head outside the door, when four men seized him by the shoulders and lifted him off his feet, so that he could neither shout nor use his weapons. Then forthwith strangling him, they buried him without a sound.

Oppressed by wine, Murad Bakhsh went on sleeping. But Aurangzeb was wide awake. His brother having been deprived of his faithful eunuch, he felt sure of his plan succeeding. Still, to make assurance doubly sure, he sent for his son, Sultan A'zam, then six or seven years of age,[1] and living in the harem. When the boy appeared, he showed him quietly a lovely ornament, and told him if he would carry off his sleeping uncle's sword without rousing him, he should receive the jewel. This was done so that if Murad Bakhsh should wake, he would see that he who had roused him was an innocent child, and would suspect no evil.

The boy, to gain the reward, went cautiously into his uncle's room and silently drew away the sword from his [206] side, and made it over to his father. Again he showed the boy another jewel, and said he should get it if he went once more and took away the dagger also. Highly delighted, the child went in as he had done before, and carried off the dagger also. Poor Murad Bakhsh was now unarmed, and without a defender. Pleased at finding himself master of the arms, of the army, and of the person of Murad Bakhsh, Aurangzeb drew a deep breath of joy and relief at the finish of his labours, cunning plots, and anxieties.

Then he called in the men hidden for the purpose, and ordered them to bring in the fetters already lying ready for use. Some, on the other hand, want to make out that these fetters were of silver, intended by Aurangzeb to terrify his son Sultan Muhammad if he were disobedient. Six men went into the room where Murad Bakhsh was, and, laying hold of his feet forcibly and disrespectfully, began to place on them the fetters. This was very different from what the eunuch Shahbaz used to do: he used to waken him by gentle pressure on the feet. Turning his body hastily, and not seeing his eunuch, but unknown men with fetters in their hands and angry faces, Murad Bakhsh reached out hastily to the place where his weapons had been. But, finding himself deprived

1. Muhammad A'zam was born on the 12th Sha'ban, 1063 H. (October 17, 1653, N.S.), and therefore his age was four years seven months and twenty-eight days on June 15, 1658.

of all resource, he lost heart, and, becoming aware from that moment of his treacherous betrayal, he allowed his feet to be held, and made no movement while they put on the fetters. Then with bent head he muttered: 'This is the word and oath sworn to me on the Quran.' Some men have asserted to me that, if Aurangzeb had failed in this plan, he had resolved and determined to take his brother's life by violence that very day.

The project had been kept so secret that no one had an idea of what was passing. To mislead everyone still further, Aurangzeb ordered the instruments to strike up anew, both within and without. The whole army, hearing once more those strains of gladness, supposed that the festivities had been renewed and would last all night, as is commonly the practice in Hindustan. Thus the soldiers took upon themselves to seek such diversions as they pleased, and dispersed in all directions. All this was done by Aurangzeb with the object that, having scattered and sought repose, the soldiers should be prevented from suspecting what he had on hand. He was a little afraid that Murad Bakhsh's soldiers, on hearing of the treachery, might not break out into mutiny. He also, for the same reason, strengthened the guards round his own tent.

When it was six o'clock in the evening, there appeared all of a sudden two elephants with covered howdahs, such as are used for harem women, with an escort of four thousand cavalry armed with sword and lance, under the command of Daler Khan, who had lately joined. There were other four thousand horsemen, armed in the same way, under the command of Bahadur Khan, foster-brother of Aurangzeb. Entering the tent enclosures, one body from the east and the other from the west, Murad Bakhsh was fastened upon the elephant brought in on the east under the orders of Daler Khan. After a brief delay there issued from the enclosure [207] the closed howdahs, one towards Dihli and the other towards Agrah. Each was escorted by one of the squadrons already alluded to, and they travelled with celerity.

This invention was to leave everyone in doubt, so that they could not decide upon which elephant Murad Bakhsh was mounted, should they intend any outbreak. The whole business was carried out with the greatest secrecy. The hour of night was also chosen, in order that if anyone attempted a rising it could not easily be carried out; the time of feasting was chosen because

Murad Bakhsh's officers were at the tents of others, separated from their soldiers. Therefore, if any officer well affected to Murad Bakhsh should attempt anything in defence of his master, he would be stopped by his (Aurangzeb's) adherents, to whom he had promised many and valuable presents if they allowed no one to issue from their tents.

On the departure of those two elephants from the camp, the soldiers suspected some treachery, and there arose a great confusion, as they knew not what mystery lay hidden under the sending-off of those two elephants escorted by the troops of cavalry. Then there came out several horsemen and some men on foot, shouting loudly: 'Long live King Aurangzeb!' adding that all those in the service of Shahjahan, of Dara, and of Murad Bakhsh who were willing to enlist under King Aurangzeb would obtain double pay. Murad Bakhsh's officers, who were feasting, were disturbed in mind and tried to get away, but Aurangzeb's officers laid hold of their hands and advised them not to expose themselves to any risk, but to accept the pay promised by Aurangzeb. They should not, they told them, go in search of death for a cause already beyond their help, for so had Murad Bakhsh decreed.

The officers and soldiers spent that night in great anxiety, knowing not what course to pursue. By the time morning dawned they accepted the proposals of Aurangzeb. The latter took possession of all the wealth and forces of Murad Bakhsh. All his wives, sons, and daughters, and all his dependents were sent to the fortress of Dihli. The orders given to Daler Khan, who went in charge of Murad Bakhsh, were that, on getting near to Dihli, he should uncover the howdah, and in that condition enter into the city. The prince was to be carried to the stronghold of Selimguer (selimgarh), built long ago by King Selim Xa (Salim Shah) of the Pathan race. This place is in the middle of the river Jamnah, close to the Royal Fortress newly reconstructed by Shahjahan, and called Xaaianabet (Shahjahanabad). You cross to it (Salimgarh) by a great bridge, which stands between the one fortress and the other.

It was very pitiful to see poor Murad Bakhsh make this miserable entry into Dihli visible to all, his face dejected, wearing a blue turban ill put on; behind him an executioner with a naked sword in his hand, ready upon any attempt at rescue to cut off his head. Daler Khan followed at the rear of Murad Bakhsh upon another elephant, an arrow ready in his bow. Thus, too, rode the troopers of his squadrons, and it seemed as if some criminal were being borne to the scaffold. Thus was this unfortunate prince taken into the fortress aforesaid with great precautions, and it was ordered that poppy water be given him to drink to deprive him of his senses.

At this juncture Aurangzeb disclosed his motive for asserting himself to be and pretending to be a poor mendicant [208]; it was only to secure an easier access to the emperor's seat, and mislead everyone. For, hardly had Murad Bakhsh fallen into his hands, Dara and Sulaiman Shukoh been defeated, and his father imprisoned, than he proclaimed himself emperor. He conferred many distinctions and gifts on the men of Shahjahan, Dara, Murad Bakhsh, and Sulaiman Shukoh who came over to his side, thereby the more easily to gain their adherence and attach them more strongly to his interests. Thus he became at once master of a great army.

Beholding all this, and hearing that Dara had decided to raise a fresh army in the province of Lahor, I started as a humble mendicant for the city of Dihli. There I remained some fifteen days, awaiting the assembling of more travellers. For the villagers and thieves were plundering on the highways, and created a good deal of tribulation to travellers, robbing and slaying them. They were forced to do their stages with arms ready in their hands, while pursuing their way. Each night we took shelter in the *saraes*, where we were able to take rest in some security. Every day we halted at noon to feed and rest the animals; and at two in the afternoon we resumed our march, until we reached another *sarae* somewhere before sunset. Once on this journey we were resting at midday near a town called Panipat distant from Dihli four days' journey. When the time came to start again, my cart-man could not be found, and the convoy set out. I knew not what to do, for after a good deal of effort I was unable to get hold of my cart-driver. By this trouble I was much put out, for I found the oxen would not obey me; nor could I travel on foot, for fear of being attacked. The men of the place surrounded me and wanted to rob me, which they did not do, only because I had nothing. I was much perplexed. They advised me to continue my route, for during the night (as they assumed) someone would be able to kill me [209].

Meanwhile my cart-driver turned up; he came running in great haste from the halting-place. As soon as he got near me I fell upon him in a great rage and gave him a sound beating. I knew not the favour that had been accorded me by Divine Providence, which 'in sui dispositions non falitur,' and even does us the most benefit when it seems the most against us. I started on my road, and the cart-man wanted to hurry, fancying that he could catch up the rest of the party, who were two hours ahead of us, and thereby enter into my good graces again. But I assured him we could never overtake them, anyhow, could not reach the sarae. He had better drive on at a moderate pace. Still displeased with the cart-man, I inquired why he had been so heedless, knowing the perils existing on the road. He replied that, overcome by his necessities, he had gone some distance from the town, and then there had come on him heavy sleep, so that he had been unable to wake sooner; this was the cause of his delay.

During this conversation we had entered into a wood, through which we had to pass. When within it, I beheld with terror the greater number of our party heaped together, either decapitated or wounded, and all plundered and ruined; the few who survived were stripped naked, The cart-man, frightened to death at the spectacle, wanted to drive off with his cart across the jungle without attending the dead and wounded lying on the road. I told him to go slowly, that there was nothing to be afraid of, for the danger had passed (although I was a good deal frightened myself). I found one poor creature lying in the middle of the road with a spear thrust through him, who raising his hands to heaven, prayed me to help him. Taking compassion on him, I stretched forth my hand to lift him into my cart, whereupon the driver picked up his bullocks, and did not give me the chance of doing this deed of charity.

We went on our way, and coming forth from the wood, I noticed that the inhabitants of the village where we were to put up appeared before us. Aware of the great mishap that had occurred, when, in spite of all that, they saw a cart appear quietly from such a perilous spot, they were in the greatest amazement, and questioned me as to how I had saved my life. Then I replied that God knew how to deliver poor men from the hands of scoundrels.

I continued my journey, always in fear of thieves, until I reached the river called Bear (Biyas or Biah), where I found an officer, Dautcan (Da,ud Khan),[1] who quitting Sulaiman Shukoh, had come to join Dara through jungle and desert by a very difficult route, where he had been in fear of his life. This he did for the love he bore him (Dara). The latter had entrusted him with sufficient artillery, cavalry, and infantry to bar the passage of the river to Aurangzeb.

I presented myself to him (Da,ud Khan), and as he recognised me, he treated me with much honour and granted me a passport for my onward journey. Without such no one could go on to the city of Lahor. There I arrived at four o'clock in the afternoon, when Prince Dara was actually seated giving audience. Quitting the cart, I threw my small wallet across my shoulder, and taking in my hands my bow and seven arrows, I entered the palace. When my commander Barcandas Can (Barqandaz Khan) saw me, he advanced to greet me, and after embracing me with great affection, he led me joyfully to the presence [210] of the prince, just as I was. There I performed the usual obeisances, and he (Dara) with exceeding gladness exclaimed in a loud voice: 'Xabas! xabas!' (*Shabash! shabash!*)—that is to say, 'Bravo! bravo!' His eyes brimming over with tears, he turned to his officers and said in a troubled tone: 'See, you others, the fidelity of this European Farangi lad, who, although neither of my religion nor of my race, nor for long an eater of my salt, having only entered my service when these wars began, came after me with such loyalty through the midst of such dangers; while those maintained by me for so long, and getting immense payments, with base ingratitude and utter disloyalty abandoned me when I had need of them, just as you others have seen.'

After this speech Dara asked if other European Farangis accompanied me. To this I answered that the hardships of the road hindered many from coming, but as they found a chance they would come. Dara ordered a horse to be given to me, which was at once brought. Not liking the look of it, he directed them

1. Da,ud Khan, Qureshi, Shekhzadah of Hisar Firuzah, left Dara at Bhakkar, and returned to his home via Jaisulmer. He was afterwards Governor of Patnah (1659-65) on behalf of Aurangzeb. In 1081 H. (1670-71) he was Governor of Allahabad (see 'Ma,asir-ul-Umara,' ii. 30).

to give me another and better one. He increased my pay, making it in place of eighty rupees one hundred and fifty rupees every month. An order issued for a present to me of five hundred rupees with a 'serpao' (*sarapa*). I put up at a house where several of my European friends were staying; they had got away from Agrah before it was invested, and with them I dwelt.

Prince Dara wasted no time, but with extreme energy enlisted fresh men to form a good army and resist Aurangzeb, whose acts he knew of. He had already some thirty thousand horsemen of various races, Mongolis (Mughals), Saheides (Sayyids), and Patanis (Pathans). While these preparations were going on there came Raja Sarupsing (Rajah Sarup Singh)[1]—that is to say, 'Beauty of the Lion'—who had been sent for by Dara. He brought four thousand horse and ten thousand infantry. The territory of this rajah adjoins the mountains in the kingdom of Kashmir, and he has an army of fifteen thousand cavalry and three hundred thousand infantry, all of them Rajputs. Dara with great entreaty had begged him to be so good as to do him the favour of coming at this time to join him with all his men. He would never forget it, when the time came to reward and recompense him. To gain him more securely to his side, he (Dara) allowed his wife to send for the rajah to her harem, where with soft words the princess once more begged for his aid and gave him many presents, the chief being a string of [211] pearls of great value that she threw over his neck. She addressed him as her son, and said she looked on him as in the place of her son Sulaiman Shukoh. Then she did a thing never done before in the Mogul's empire—that is say, she offered him water to drink with which she had washed her breasts, not having milk in them, as a confirmation of her words. He drank with the greatest acceptance and swore he would be ever true, and never fail in the duties of a son. But he needed some money for expenses, so as to enlist all the men he could, in addition to those he had already brought.

Dara believed in him, and at once ordered them to give him a million of rupees (1,000,000 = ten lakhs!). He left for his own

1. In Part III, this man is called Rup Singh. The correct name seems to be Rajrup; he was the son of Rajah Jagat Singh, son of Rajah Basu, of Mau and Pathan in the Bari Du,abah (see 'Ma,asir-ul-Umara,' ii. 277). Pathan is, I fancy, the same as Pathankot, fourteen miles east of Nurpur, on the road into Kashmir, lat. 32° 18', long. 75° 42'.

country, promising to return very soon, equipped in every way. When Aurangzeb learnt what the rajah had done, he wrote him a letter, which sufficed to make him disappoint Dara. The latter, being informed that Aurangzeb was marching onwards, wrote letter after letter to Rajrup Singh urging him to come and make no more delay, for the time when his aid was wanted was now drawing near. But he never answered, and remained in his own country with the money he had received, and the poor prince beheld the hopes he had in this man disappear. Aurangzeb was aware that Dara did not want for loyal officers, among them the great Da,ud Khan being the most faithful of all. Seeking a method for taking this man away from the prince his brother, and attracting him into his own service, he sent messengers to the crossing upon the river, where this officer was posted, to inquire of his intentions. Would he agree to become one of his (Aurangzeb's) officers? But Da,ud Khan, ever firm, fixed, and faithful to Dara's interests, replied that he had already given as a sacrifice his life and goods for the service of Dara, and he would accept no other's proposals.

This matter gave an opening for Aurangzeb to sharpen his wits, never being at a loss for some trick. In order to throw Da,ud Khan out of favour with Dara, he caused a forged letter to be written as in the name of Da,ud Khan, making him say as follows: 'Your majesty may rest assured that at the first opportunity I will do what I promised, and never be false to my word.' Aurangzeb so managed that this letter fell into the hands of Dara. Thereby Dara began to suspect not only Da,ud Khan, but all his officers, as it appeared they had already [212] fallen under the influence of Aurangzeb. He ceased to treat Da,ud Khan on the same familiar terms as formerly. Da,ud Khan felt that the prince entertained some suspicion of him. He therefore, decided to fall on his knees in Dara's presence (as he did); then taking off his sword, he laid it on the ground and said: 'If your majesty has any doubt of my fidelity, order me to go and loyally offer my life in the defence of your person and family.' On hearing this speech, Dara took compassion on him and began to have an idea that the letter was forged.

But many days had not passed before Aurangzeb wrote another letter to Da,ud Khan in which he asked why he delayed so long in fulfilling his promise to lay before him in a short time the head of Dara. He could not fathom the reason of such delay.

This letter fell, as was intended by Aurangzeb, into the hands of Dara. The sight of it totally destroyed his confidence in Da,ud Khan. Word was sent to him not to appear again at court; his appointment was taken from him, and everybody fell under suspicion.

Finding himself in this great extremity, and Aurangzeb still continuing his march by forced stages, Dara made up his mind to remove to the kingdom of Kabul, and thence implore succour from the King of Persia. He therefore despatched an envoy to Mahabat Khan, who was governor of the Kabul kingdom, and to the Pathans of the hill-country, requesting them to give him free passage on his way to Persia. But his object was not to pass through, it was to obtain possession of, that kingdom, and thereby increase his strength. Mahabat Khan remembered their former disputes, of which I have spoken (I. 155), and sent him the reply that it would be better to choose another road, because no reliance could be placed upon the Pathans in the hills, thus throwing upon others the blame for his own disinclination.

Dara penetrated sufficiently the object of Mahabat Khan, and, adopting a new idea, now gave orders that all the artillery and munitions of war got ready by Shahjahan for taking the fortress of Qandahar should be embarked on boats. To these were added all the treasures that he had carried with him, and at that time present in Lahor. Other appliances for strengthening the fortress of Bacar (Bhakkar) were added. Aware that Aurangzeb was drawing nearer and nearer, and distrusting his officers, having a force insufficient [213] for resistance, Dara sent an order to withdraw the few men and guns posted at the river crossing. He directed his powder-magazine to be blown up, which was speedily done. He then left Lahor in the end of October one thousand six hundred and fifty-six (correctly 1658).[1] He took with him the whole of his family, and at the head of eight thousand horsemen started for the city of Moltan (Multan), which lies on the bank of the river Ravi, the same river as at Lahor. The distance of that city (Multan) from Lahor is ten days' journey.

I made up my mind not to march along with Dara, owing to some business, but to leave on the third day. During the

1. According to the ''Alamgirnamah,' 186, top line, Dara left Lahor on the 29th Zi Qa'dah,' 1068 H. (August 28, 1658).

second day I passed before the door of the officer second in command of the artillery, a Turk by race, called Rumican (Rumi Khan), who was busy in preparations and the enlistment of men; he had also some field-pieces, which he meant to take with him. As soon as he saw me he called me, and as I got near, ordered me to dismount at once. He asked me where I was off to, and I answered that I was on my way to make preparations to start for the army. He told me to sit down, and said he also was starting that day; he would send to fetch my baggage, and I could go with him. I was suspicious, believing that he distrusted me, and I concluded that it would not suit me to march with him; for then it could be said that he had brought me by force, which would be to my discredit. So I answered him by praying his leave to go to my house to collect some cash and pay my debts, and to put together my things; after that I would come back and join him. But the obstinate Turk would not listen to me nor give me leave, so it came to my deciding absolutely to kill him, if he would not allow me to go. For it was not right for me to be made to march by force. I was in Dara's service, had a good reputation, and wished to rejoin without the slightest delay. Thus I told him plainly that the favours I had received from Dara left me under such obligation that I would sooner lose my life than miss an occasion to prove my gratitude to my king. For Dara I would sacrifice my person; and if he did not believe me, let him send twenty horsemen with me to my house, which was close by [214]. I would then come back with them. Thus I spoke to him, having absolutely the intention of killing him, although I should lose my own life, if he refused. But God was good to me! For the Turk accepted this my ultimatum, and sent with me twenty horsemen with express orders to bring me back to his presence.

I got on my horse highly delighted, and went on faster and faster, paying no heed to their telling me to go slowly. They urged on their horses to overtake me. This irritated me, so I turned in my seat with an angry face, and, laying hold of my sword, so threatened them that they were afraid and drew back. They contented themselves by following me at a distance until I went in with a rush into the house of a friend, leaving the escort at the door. Directly I had got inside, I seized a musket that was standing in a corner, and then went for them, discharging the piece to frighten them. Next, laying hold of my sword, I shouted, 'Strike,

strike!' though without much hope of success. But they, supposing there were a number of us, scattered in all directions.

After the flight of these horsemen, I told my friend to get upon his hours and come along with me. For, when the news should reach that officer, he would send a great many more soldiers and capture us if we stayed. He would not listen, and, leaving him in his house, I mounted on horseback, and went outside the city until night came on. Then I came home peacefully. My poor friend had been carried off against his will, as I had prophesied. Next morning I removed such chattels as I could not carry with me to the house of another friend. When I was about to bind my bundle on my horse's back, meaning to start on my journey to rejoin the army and Prince Dara, there appeared one of the officers set over the *kotwal's pioens* (policemen), who was very drunk. This man had complete control over that officer of justice (the *kotwal*). He began to abuse me, and with harsh words ran down Dara's followers. I dissembled and made use of all my patience, which conquers everything, chiefly because I saw there would soon be a change in the government of the city through the departure of Dara.

Rendered still more impertinent by my apparent quietude and patience, the officer went on with his insolence. In time he exhausted my patience, and in a rage I picked up a stone, and, hurling it with the greatest force, hit him in the mouth, cutting his lips and sending two teeth down his throat. He fell to the ground and spoke no more. I resumed the tying on of my bundle, and before I mounted I gave the fellow several kicks, owing to the rage I was in. Taking to my horse, I set out on my way, unaware that the man's servant had gone to tell his [215] men. Having gone only a few paces, I perceived some thirty foot-soldiers, all armed, coming hastily in search of me to take vengeance for the affront done to their officer. I wanted to turn back, simply that I might rid myself of them. Then I reflected that I should only light upon others lying in wait for me. Fixing my turban more firmly, angry and resolute, sword in hand, I spurred my horse, on which I relied a good deal. I flung myself into their midst, and they, seeing my anger and resolve, were not bold enough to attack me, only having enough presence of mind to salute me and leave me a free passage. They followed me afar off, relying upon others who had been sent in my pursuit. To these it happened as to the first lot, and they all followed me up to my issuing from the city. I then got rid of them and went on my way.

After three days I arrived in the army of Dara, where I found the officer who had tried to carry me off by force from Lahor. I told him I had come to lay a complaint against him before Dara. He had been the cause of other Europeans not accompanying me, who subsequently had decided to remain where they were owing to the bad way he had treated me. The Turk, on hearing this, embraced me with the greatest submissiveness, and begged me to suppress my grievance for the sake of his good name.

We continued our marches till the early days of November, when we arrived at Multan, an ancient city where in old days, before the Portuguese were masters of the Eastern seas, there came many *cafillas* (*qafilah*) of merchandise and spices and drugs of India. With us marched the great Da,ud Khan who, spurred by the loyalty and affection that he had to Dara, would not abandon him, offering through others to serve him faithfully, as he had done for many years. But Dara did not trust him, led astray by the forged letters that Aurangzeb continued to write.

To impose on the people of Multan, Dara made believe that he intended to stop in that city and enlist troops. He began to repair the houses in which [216] formerly Aurangzeb lived when he governed that territory. He ordered them to send for the relations of a false prophet, then deceased, called Coia Bahaudim (Khwajah Baha-ud-din)[1]—that is to say, 'Price of the Law'—one greatly venerated by the Mahomedans, who is buried in the middle of the city in a great dome covered with blue tiles, an ancient building. He earnestly entreated them to intercede for him with Muhammad that he might favour him and give him the victory over Aurangzeb. They gave him their word that without fail they would supplicate Muhammad; he might rest assured that his petitions would be considered, being as they were so just. During the following night they would so arrange that they should precede everyone and be the first to receive audience from Muhammad, and thus comply with his highness's desire.

1. This must be Shekh Baha-ud-din Zakariya, son of Qutb-ud-din, son of Kamal-ud-din, a saint of Multan, born 1170 A.D., died 1266. His son Sadr-ud-din died in 1309 (Beale, 'Oriental Biography,' 97).

The following day very early Dara took care to have them called, so as to know the result of their prayers. They appeared, as this sort of knave knows so well how to do, with downcast faces, and told him that all night long they had been in the presence of Muhammad, but were unable to speak to him, because Aurangzeb was in conversation with him. But without fail they would the following night find an opening for his petitions. In order to gratify them, and bind them still more to his interests, Dara made them a present of twenty-five thousand rupees and a covering of costly stuff to be spread on the tomb of the false prophet (*i.e.*, of Baha-ud-din). But on their being sent for again the next morning, they came with the same answer, and it was the same on the third day.

When Dara was informed that Aurangzeb had left Lahor in pursuit, he lost faith in his prophets, and held it best to withdraw from Multan. For this purpose he gave orders that all the boats, five hundred and seven in number, should be made ready for a voyage towards the fortress of Bhakkar. They were loaded with supplies of food requisite for a beleaguered citadel; they also put on board eight cannon carrying shot of from sixty to one hundred and twenty pounds' weight, besides light artillery, ammunition, and the necessary *matériel* of war. Each boat carried, more or less, a hundred tons of cargo.

While Dara was thus preparing to resume his march, Aurangzeb was coming after him by long marches, moving on day and night without halting at the head of the finest part of his army [217]. These were enough to overcome the small force still attached to Dara. Aurangzeb had left behind the rest of his army with orders to follow. Finding that he was pursued, Dara was compelled to move. He ordered the boats to be started down the river, putting in command of them a valiant eunuch, Coia Vacent (Khwajah Basant)—that is to say, 'Springtime.'[1] The prince left by the land route at the head of five thousand horsemen and five thousand infantry. Dara's favoured general, Barqandaz Khan, went with him; most of the others deserted,

1. The eunuch Basant is named in the "Alamgirnamah,' p. 274. In the rest of his narrative, Manucci styles this man 'Primavera.' According to the 'Ma,asir-i-'Alamgiri,' p. 16, Dara left Bhakkar on the last of Muharram, 1069 H. (October 28, 1658). The pursuers, under Shekh Mir and Safshikan Khan, arrived at Sakkar and Bhakkar respectively on the 5th and 6th Safar (November 2 and 3).

as did those that he had taken on at Multan, carrying off the large sums of pay that he had disbursed to them.

Much to be marvelled at was the obstinate fidelity of Da,ud Khan. Keeping at a little distance from our troops, he continued to follow. He sent a clear message to Dara that he might trust in him; he wanted to accompany him whenever the occasion arose, and with his blood would seal the testimony of his loyalty. The prince should accept his advice, and not believe in the forged letters that had fallen into his hands. But Dara, more and more suspicious, sent word to him that if he were true to him, let him cease to follow him and go his own way. By this time Da,ud Khan saw that it was of no use to try and remain with his well-beloved prince, and sent an answer that he would obey orders on the condition that his dismissal was by writing.

It was not long before Dara made over to him a paper in which it was stated: 'I, Dara, discharge Da,ud Khan, and command him to withdraw from my army, and accord him liberty to serve whom he pleases.' What things may not be worked by a falsehood when accepted as true by a prince! Without reflecting on the evil that might accrue to him, the prince persisted in the unjust impression made upon him. Da,ud khan received this writing at the city of Vehu (or Ochu, perhaps Uchh).[1] Weeping like a child, so that it was pitiful to see him, he exclaimed: 'It seems to me as if evil fortune dogged the steps of Dara,' and therewith he departed.

Learning the news, Aurangzeb, when he arrived at the city of Multan, detached a force in pursuit of Dara, with orders to capture him if they could; they were to pursue him wherever he went. Then he sent off an affectionate letter to Da,ud Khan, tempting him with very high pay, an offer which was accepted on condition that he should not be ordered to take up [218] arms against Dara. This Aurangzeb accorded, and treated him with great consideration, and in that reign he held high appointments.

We continued our marches, suffering somewhat from failure of supplies, and several times from want of water. We passed through several rough woods, and arrived opposite the fortress of Bhakkar in the middle of the treacherous river of Sind, thus

1. Dara was at Uchh for three days about the 8th Muharram, 1069 H. (October 4, 1658), and the departure of Da,ud Khan is mentioned (see "Alamgirnamah,' 272, 274).

called after the union at this place, distant one hundred and thirty leagues from Multan city, of seven large rivers, which further on I will tell you about (I. 222). There we found the valiant eunuch, Primavera, occupied in the disembarkation of the big guns and the other munitions for the said fortress. At this time Dara received word that Aurangzeb's troops, commanded by Bahadur Khan, sent in pursuit of us, had already arrived quite near. He saw that he could not resist such a strong force; he therefore ordered with all possible haste two thousand selected men—Pathans, Sayyids, Mughals, Rajputs—twenty-two Europeans of different nationalities, and other servants to occupy the said fortress. The command was given to the eunuch Primavera. The remainder of the army was ordered to cross with the same haste to the other side of the river and seize all the boats to be found there, in order to hinder the enemy's crossing at that point.

When I knew of this order I presented myself before Dara and urgently besought him to take me along with him. With words of exceeding love and tenderness, he replied that he longed to take every one of us with him. But it was of the greatest importance to him to make sure of the said stronghold, and for this reason he left us in it, having such great reliance upon our valour and fidelity. I renewed my application, with protestations and entreaties added to tears, indications of the grief I felt at our separation, asking him to leave all the rest behind, but take me along with him. Dara, with a pleased face, repeated that it was desirable that we should all remain in the fortress, seeing that the place was of the greatest use to him against his enemies, that in it were goods which he held as dear as his own person [219]; and, using other words of much affection, he sent me off.

I was overcome with tears and sighs at this parting; and seeing the downcast state in which I was quitting the presence, he had me called back. He then made me captain of the Europeans, and ordered them to give me five thousand rupees to divide among my men, and doubled my pay. It had been one hundred and fifty, and he made it three hundred rupees. He gave me his word that if God made him king he would create me a noble of his court, and reward my men, in whose loyalty he had much confidence. He added the present of a 'serpao' (*sarapa*), and directed that I should receive a boat-load of Persian and Kabul wine. He recommended me earnestly to Primavera, the eunuch, and told him to look well after me and my men.

After shedding more tears, I left and went into the fortress with the eunuch, while Dara departed thence, taking all the boats. Hardly had he gone when we heard the drums of the enemy, and the report came in how Aurangzeb had left Multan for the Agrah direction in the greatest haste, in the fear that Sulaiman Shukoh might come down from the mountains of Srinagar.

This alone was not the cause of Aurangzeb's leaving Multan; it was due still more to his having received advices that Prince Shah Shuja' with a great army was marching from Bengal against the city of Agrah. So great was the terror of Aurangzeb lest Shah Shuja' might arrive first at Agrah city with his army, that he went on in advance of his army two or three leagues, followed by very few men, sometimes quite alone. His object was to make his men follow with greater quickness. He rested beneath some trees, his head supported on his shield, until [220] some men overtook him and formed a retinue. In this way Aurangzeb moved on with extreme haste, and passing by Lahor, he left there as viceroy the traitor Khalilullah Khan, and, without delaying, continued his route to Agrah, taking the whole of his army.

Going on one day in advance, with only five horsemen, he was passing through a grove of trees in a wood, when all of a sudden there appeared from the opposite direction Rajah Jai Singh, who had come to seek him through the wilds of the Laqui Janguel (Lakhi Jungle).[1] With him were three thousand well-armed horsemen, all Rajputs.

Be it known to the reader that, as I have already said, Aurangzeb never lost an opening for getting officials, officers, and soldiers to desert their masters and transfer themselves to him. He acted on this principle with Rajah Jai Singh, managing so that he left Prince Sulaiman Shukoh, as we have related. When it was known that Jai Singh had abandoned the said prince, he wrote him a friendly letter, declaring his anxiety to see him, as he had important business to communicate to him. But he fixed no place for a meeting, and after the evil deed he had been induced to do the rajah came in search of Aurangzeb, and met him at the above-named place at a time when he had left his army behind.

---

1. The Lakhi Jungle was a name for the region south of the Sutlaj, having its eastern limits at Ludhianah and Sunam; to the south of it lay the Bhati desert (see the map in Francklin's 'Shah Aulum,' 1798).

Aurangzeb was much alarmed when he saw the rajah, he himself having only an escort of five horsemen, for he knew the rajah had great affection for King Shahjahan, and was much troubled, as one can imagine, at the danger of losing his life. And, as a fact, the officers round the rajah, when they saw Aurangzeb in this unprotected state, advised him to kill him, or allow them to do so. They said his name would be renowned in the world through the release and liberation of Shahjahan. But the rajah would not listen to such advice, although the occasion was excellent and the accomplishment easy. As it seems to me, he refrained from acting because he was on bad terms with Dara, and while succeeding in doing good to Shahjahan, he could not have helped favouring [221] Dara. But to the latter he wished all possible evil, for the reasons stated by me earlier.

Suppressing all agitation and keeping on his way, Aurangzeb went straight to meet the rajah, and, while still at a distance, signed with his hand that he should approach, calling out, 'Raiagi! Raiagi!' (*Rajah Ji! Rajah Ji*!)—that is to say, 'Mr. Rajah! Mr. Rajah!' When the rajah was close to him, Aurangzeb spoke to him thus: 'I am waiting with great anxiety to see you, as I have already stated in my letter to you. I have great regard for your person, because I can find no other friend with sense and judgment like you, so full of experience and natural ability, who can help me in the great enterprise which it has pleased God to lay upon me. Already is Dara lost and without an army, and I have sent after the fugitive Bahadur Khan, who cannot fail in a brief space to bring him before me in chains. Thus, helped by your wisdom and prudence, I shall easily be able to complete what God has purposed.'

During this speech Aurangzeb took from his neck a valuable necklace of pearls and placed it in the rajah's hands, and said: 'This is a token of the love and affection I bear you, and of the obligation imposed on me by what you did in quitting Sulaiman Shukoh and coming to find me. I make you governor of Dihli city, and grant you the province of Sambar (Sambhar). Proceed there without delay, for it is of importance to me.' He got rid of the rajah with high delight, because he dreaded that he, out of his love and gratitude to Shahjahan, might play some trick upon him, as he could easily have done, owing to his (Aurangzeb's) small retinue. The prince continued his journey for Agrah city with all haste,' in order to attack Shah Shuja'. The province of Sambhar, of which Aurangzeb made a gift to the rajah, brought in to the Crown a million and more of rupees, the price of the salt that comes out of the lake, which is [222] adjacent to the province of Asmiar (Ajmer).

It is now time to speak of the defeat that befell Dara, but before we talk of that I will give the reader an account of the country, so that afterwards we may the more clearly continue our story. It should be known that close to Bhakkar seven rivers unite—namely, five issuing from the kingdom of Lahor, which have their sources in the mountains of Srinagar and Kashmir, and reach the province of Lahor by five openings. This is why the kingdom of Lahor is called Panjab—that is to say, 'Five Waters.' The names of the rivers are, firstly, Satleg (Sutlaj), on which there is a large town called Lodiana (Ludhianah). From it to the second river, called Biat (Biyas), is a distance of thirty-five leagues, and on this second river is a large town called Gonduval (Govindwal). From the second to the third river it is also thirty-five leagues; this river is called the Ravi, which flows below Lahor. The fourth river, called the Chenau (Chinab), is distant twenty-five leagues from Lahor. This river also has on it a large and fine town called Vizirabad (Wazirabad). From this place it is twenty-eight leagues to the fifth river, called the Biat (Behat), which, too, has its town called Jelem (Jihlam).

These five rivers, which are all navigable by large boats, and the towns named, which serve as harbours, belong to the province of Lahor. The sixth river and the chief one is called Ateke (Atak), or otherwise Indo (Indus), because it separates the lands of India from the lands of the Pathans, from Persia and the province of Kabul. On the western bank of this river Atak is a town named Zafarabad,[1] and on the eastern a castle called

1. Zafarabad must be, I think, another name for Atak, although that place is on the east bank of the Indus. There is a castle, Khairagarh, on the opposite (western) bank. Mr. M. L. Dames is inclined to the same opinion. Zafarabad might be Kalabagh, with Mari opposite; but this could never have been a crossing-place for *kafilas*, like Atak was. There is no evidence that Atak was ever renamed Zafarabad; but there is an obscure, insufficiently identified mint town of that name, which is usually placed at Zafarabad in the Jaunpur district, though I suggested long ago Zafarabad Bidar in the Dakhin. Mr. Dames says the shape of the letters on the coins suggests rather a northern than a Dakhini origin. If Atak was also called Zafarabad, a gap is filled; for Atak, as a mint town,

by the same name, where all the caravans halt from Persia, Tartary, Balque (Balkh), Samarqand, Bukhara, Cascar (Kashghar), Kabul, and many other kingdoms. Thence come every year one hundred and fifty thousand horses, more or less, besides many camels. Most of these are loaded with various kinds of fruit—melons, pears, apples, pomegranates, quinces, grapes, and other dried fruit; three kinds of raisin, almonds, filberts (avelans), and nuts, [223] and pine-nuts (pinhoens). All these are brought across the river to be sold in Hindustan, from which the Mogul king derives a great revenue.

Across this swift and treacherous river, on the farther side, there are the lofty mountains of the Pathans, thirty leagues off, with a walled city at their foot, named Pexor (Peshawar). People from India who pass the river (Indus) lose the rights and privileges which they imagine they enjoy in their own land. This river is at a distance of one hundred and fifty leagues from the river Biat (Behat), and eight leagues from the seventh, called Nilab, whose waters are blue in colour. Close to the fortress of Bhakkar these seven rivers join to form the wide and famous river Sindi (Sind, or Indus), and thence it flows with great force until it falls into the sea, on the shore of the Sind province, thus called from the river running through it.

After he had sent us away, Dara set out for the port of Sindi by land,[1] ordering all the boats to assemble at that place for his departure. Having reached the vicinity of that port, he used all the boats found there to cross the river to the town of Sindi. When he had got over, he ordered all the boats that could be found to be collected, so that by this means he might hinder the passage of the enemy then in his pursuit. Next he and his army began to march for the city of Tata (Tattah), twelve leagues off, as I related in my journey from Persia. Entering that city, he

---

disappears between Akbar's reign (1556-1605) and that of Muhammad Shah (1719-1748), while Zafarabad appears in the interval (coins of Shah Jahan, 1627-1658; Aurangzeb, 1658-1707; and Bahadur Shah, 1707-1712).

1. Dara reached Bhakkar on the 25th, and left it again on the last day of Muharram, 1069 H. (October 23 and 28, 1658). At first he set out for Qandahar; then, turning off, he reached Tattah upon the Indus on the 26th Safar (November 23, 1658) ("Alamgirnamah,' 273-275, 281).

rested a few days, and enlisted as many more men as he could find, offering very high pay. During the time of his stay in this city, he inquired if there were any Farangi European priest to be found. There happened to be there a barefooted Carmelite monk, Frei Petro de Santa Terza (Teresa) by name, Flemish by race, whom I had met in the city of Espao (Isfahan).[1] He was a man of much virtue and learning, well acquainted with the Arabic, Persian, and Indian languages. Hearing about this man, Dara sent for him, and had divers conversations with him on the Gospel and the articles of our faith. After listening to his arguments, he became for a time thoughtful, then, raising his hands to heaven, he said: 'If [224] there is any true faith in the world, I believe it to be that of the Catholics, for many a time I have talked about it to different Roman *padres* from different countries, and it always came out the same without the slightest difference. This is not so with other religions, such as those of the Hebrews, Hindus, and Mahomedans, in which I have found many variations.'

Turning towards the friar, he said to him: 'Father, I pray Jesus, who is the Messiah, to make me king, and I give you my word, I will issue orders for the erection in Agrah city of a temple (church) to Her Majesty (*Hazrat*) Bibi Mariam'—that is to say, the Holy Lady Mary—'and, furthermore, I will permit the fathers to build churches and preach the Gospel freely throughout my empire.'

After a few days had elapsed Dara resumed his route, followed by some six thousand horsemen, carrying with him sufficient gold and silver and his family. He passed through the country of the Rajah of Cachanagara[2] with great energy on his way to the province of Guzurate (Gujarat). When Aurangzeb was told of this, and found that Dara, leaving the road to Persia,

1. The Carmelite mission at Tattah was founded from Persia in 1613 (see p. 364 of R. P. Berthold Ignace de Sainte Anne's 'Mission de Perse,' Bruxelles, 1885). Müllbauer (347) gives the year as 1615, and the first missionary as Ludovicus Franciscus a Matre Dei. I cannot trace Frei Petro.
2. This must be intended for Kachh (Cutch), plus *nagara*, 'a town.' According to the "Alamgirnamah,' p. 283, Dara reached the *Chul* Desert, or Rann of Cutch, on the 11th Rabi' I., 1069 H. (December 6, 1658). He went on to Kachh (*ibid*, p. 296).

had come into the Gujarat province to raise a new army, he tried to mislead him by the following stratagem:

He sent a letter to his second son Sultan Mu'azzam, nowadays known as Xaalam (Shah 'Alam), then living at the city of Aurangabad. He ordered him to feign rebellion, enlist new troops, and announce that he meant to protect and deliver his grandfather, Shahjahan. To this intent he should write to Dara, inviting him to rally to his side against Aurangzeb. When Dara should appear, he (Mu'azzam) must make every effort to seize him, dead or alive. But Dara, who after all was not devoid of sense and judgment, being now guided by experience, detected the plots and while of Aurangzeb, and made a joke of the offer [225] from Sultan Mu'azzam.

He (Dara) entered the province of Gujarat, and took possession of the chief city, called Amadabad (Ahmadabad), which had been wrested from its king, Sultan Bahader (Sultan Bahadur), by King Akbar, as I have already stated (I. 75). The governor of the city at this time was Xanevascan (Shah Nawaz Khan),[1] father-in-law of Aurangzeb. Without making the least resistance against the small force led by Dara, he handed over the town to his opponent, not from want of courage, but because it was not correct that he, a vassal, while his king was still alive, should oppose a royal prince, heir to the empire.

Shah Nawaz Khan was a descendant of the ancient princes of Maxad (Mashhad) in Persia, and was satisfied with passing his life in feasting and pleasure. He issued from the fortress to meet and receive Dara with all possible honours, promising to serve him faithfully. As I shall recount farther on, he did, as a fact, lose his life for love of Dara in the province of Asmir (Ajmer), although some author[2] says he was an enemy of that prince.

While Dara was renewing his strength in the province of Gujarat, the enemy began a most rigorous investment of Bhakkar fort, where we were shut up along with the loyal and valiant

1. Mirza Badi'-uz-zaman, Safawi, entitled Shah Nawaz Khan. His daughter was married to Aurangzeb in the tenth year of Shahjahan (1637-38). He was killed in the Battle of Ajmer on the 29th Jamada II., 1069 H. (March 24, 1659) (' Ma,asir-ul-Umara,' ii. 670).
2. The allusion is, I suppose, to Bernier (see p. 87 of Constable's edition).

eunuch Primavera. No one could get out, no one could enter. This fortress[1] is in the middle of the mighty river Sind! (Indus), founded upon the live rock, stones from which could be used as flints for muskets. The fortress was nine hundred and seventy-five paces long and five hundred and fifty-three broad. In the middle was a 'cavalier' (tower) overlooking both banks of the river. On the east was a large town called Xaquer (Sakkar), and on the west another called Rori; at a short distance from the fort towards the north was a little island known as Coia Quitan (Khwajah Khidr), where is a tomb held in great veneration by the Moors (*i.e.*, Mahomedans).

We were very well fortified, provided with plenty of artillery and munitions of war, and had a considerable store of gold and silver, precious stones, and a great deal of baggage. In addition to this, Dara left some ladies who had accompanied him, one wife of Sulaiman Shukoh, and two young sons much cherished by Dara as being his grandsons. His plan was that if he did not succeed in the province of Gujarat and suffered defeat, this fortress of Bhakkar would serve as a base to help him again.[2]

After a few days of investment, the enemy [226] prepared two batteries mounted with large cannon, left behind by Dara in the foundry at Lahor, he not being able to move them owing to the hurry with which we started, and the enemy leaving us no chance of putting them on the boats. With these they did us a good deal of damage. Be it known to the reader that those seven

1. Bhakkar is an island 800 yards long and 300 yards wide, and the fort almost entirely covers it. Sakkar is a town on the west or right bank, and Rori (or Lohari) is on the opposite or left bank. At Rori there are four rocky islands, the largest of which is Bhakkar (Thornton, 'Gazetteer,' 150, 425, 838, 939). Manucci reverses the true positions of Sakkar and Rori. Mr. M. Longworth Dames informs me 'that Burnes, in his "Bokhara," iii. 72, edition 1834, says: "There are several other islets near it, on one of which stands the shrine of Khwajah Khizr, a holy Mahomedan, under a dome which contributes to the beauty of the scene." Khwajah Khizr, or Khwajah Khidr, the ancient river-god of the Indus, now identified with the Mahomedan saint Khidr or Elijah. He plays a great part in local legends, and is represented as an old man with a long beard, clothed in green. He is, in fact, the Indus personified, a sort of Father Tiber. One of my Balochi ballads speaks of the river as the "Khwajah." '
2. For the siege of Bhakkar, see Bernier, 93-104. Manucci was, no doubt, one of the Europeans from whom he got his information.

rivers of whose junction I spoke did not touch the sides of the fortress for more than a pistol-shot on the west and two musket-shots on the east, because they flowed between rocks and hills. Thus the enemy gave us trouble enough; nor did we desist from doing our duty with our guns, dismounting his artillery, damaging the towns, and killing a number of men. Several times we made sallies under cover of our artillery, swarming into their trenches, killing and destroying all we found there. Once we captured Four field-pieces and a quantity of baggage lying close by them. Thus the traitor Khalilullah Khan, at whose cost the investment was conducted, was forced to send more men against us. Regardless of these reinforcements, the commandant, Primavera, sent off before daybreak some boats with musketeers, who delivered attacks at various points and alarmed the enemy. They went on increasing the investing force until the place was evacuated, as further on I shall relate.

When Aurangzeb received the news that Dara was busy raising a new army in the province of Gujarat, he did not turn aside to attack him. It was more urgent to hinder Shah Shuja' from reaching Agrah. But he was much concerned on learning that Sulaiman Shukoh, by favour of the Rajah of Srinagar, was making ready to descend from the mountains; and aided by the said Rajah, at the head of a considerable force, hoped to avenge himself for what had happened to his father (Dara) and himself. Aurangzeb, therefore, wrote a letter, giving many promises to the said Rajah, and also caused others to be written by different rajahs, chief among them being Rajah Jai Singh [227], asking the Srinagar rajah to dissemble, and suggesting that by the use of certain arguments he should force the poor prince to remain quiet in those mountains.

Meanwhile Aurangzeb drew nearer to Shah Shuja', who was in strength at a little village called Coiva (Kajwah),[1] which is pleasingly situated near a number of palm-trees, as I have more than once seen. He had taken possession of a large artificial lake (*tanque*) in a great plain, having crossed the river Ganges. The place is one hundred leagues from Agrah. Aurangzeb came

1. Khawah is in the Fathpur district, lat. 26° 3', long. 8o° 35' (Thornton, 531). See also Bernier, 75, and Constable's note there and on p. 77. The passage from Tieffenthaler is on p. 167 of the 'Beschreibung von Hindustan,' vol. i.

up, leaving his baggage on the other side of a little stream, and delivered his attack on Prince Shah Shuja'. The latter was well entrenched, and had efficient and well-posted artillery, commanded by Mirzaiany (Mirza Jari), many of the gunners being Europeans. They resisted valorously the fierce attack of Aurangzeb, and in spite of his superior strength in men he was unable to win the day; he could not even make the other side quit their ground, as he had hoped. He was forced to retire several times in disorder. He was so much perplexed that he could not hit upon any course to take, the more so that Shah Shuja 'declined to come out and venture himself in the open; nor would he evacuate his position. All he attempted was to defend himself. Aurangzeb was aware that he could not make any long delay by reason of the great heat then prevailing,[1] and he knew that of a certainty he would be forced to retire and seek shelter in Agrah to save his army from severe hardships. Then Shah Shuja' would certainly pursue.

Aurangzeb saw his evil case very clearly, and thus was more urgent than ever, giving Shah Shuja' not a moment's rest. Propitious Fate decreed that at this time the long-looked-for Mir Jumlah should arrive from the fortress of Doltabad (Daulat abad), whereby he greatly served him on this most critical occasion of which I speak. One day Aurangzeb came forth from his tent seated in his sedan-chair, and took his way to the battlefield to renew the attack on Shah-Shuja'. Then came Rajah Jaswant Singh from his tent and met him, and after the usual obeisances, came close and took hold of the chair [228] with one hand, and with a disturbed face walked alongside Aurangzeb for some steps, making inquiries about the post appointed for him to occupy on that day.

Aurangzeb, who was delighted to remove the rajah to some distance, not liking the action he had adopted, and suspecting him of some treachery, ordered him to take charge of the rearguard. Thereupon the rajah mounted his horse and went off energetically. Aurangzeb remarked: 'Great are the courage and boldness of this rajah; I like him not.' Then came trustworthy reports of how the rajah was colluding with Shah Shuja', and, having attacked the rear-guard, was plundering the baggage

1. Here Manucci's memory fails him. The fighting was in January, when the heat is *not* great (see Elphinstone, 530).

and all the treasure kept there. This report caused great dismay to Aurangzeb, and furthermore he feared that the army, suspecting that letters had passed [between Shah Shuja' and Jai Singh], should lose heart and disband. As a fact, many did take to flight, and scattered in all directions. Aurangzeb continued to conceal his opinion, hoping to find out the exact intentions of the rajah, and whether he would content himself with the plunder.

Then they came to tell him that the rajah had taken to flight towards Agrah, carrying with him all the treasure and anything else he could seize. Mir Jumlah, who that same day had arrived, counselled Aurangzeb at this juncture to reanimate his men by ordering them to slay and plunder all the Hindus to be found. This was carried out. The slaughter lasted for an hour or more, and it put his men into heart, not a soul having resisted them. Mir Jumlah also advised the writing forthwith of a short letter to Alaberdican (Allahwirdi Khan),[1] then the chief adviser of Shah Shuja', in which it was written: 'Allahwirdi Khan!—If this day you wish to make me King of Hindustan, it suffices to induce Shah Shuja' to get down from his elephant during the battle, and I pledge you my word to reward you and all your family, who are on my side. I have the strongest hope that you will not fail me.—Aurangzeb.' [229]

Noticing the disorder in the ranks of Aurangzeb when the rajah fell upon his rear-guard, Shah Shuja', without giving a chance for re-forming or collecting the scattered people, although it was getting late for an onset, felt that he was master of the situation, and moved out against Aurangzeb in order to seize this favourable moment. Displaying great energy and valour, he speedily routed the vanguard, which he threw into a state of terror, and advancing, attacked Aurangzeb himself, who stood fast seated on his elephant. The elephant-driver was killed by an arrow, thus forcing Aurangzeb to assume himself the control of the elephant. The arrows fell like rain upon the elephant, which, finding itself encircled and in pain, beat a retreat. Aurangzeb was all this time a target for Shah Shuja''s arrows.

1. Allahwirdi Khan, a descendant of the Saljuqs, rose to favour under Jahangir. He and one son, Saifullah Khan, were killed at Akbarnagar (Rajmahal), by Shah Shuja''s orders, in the middle of Rajab, 1069 H. (*circa* April 8, 1659) (see 'Ma,asir-ul-Umara,' i. 207; 'Ma,asir-i-'Alamgiri,' p. 26; 'Tarikh-i-Muhammadi,' year 1069 H.; and Bernier, 77).

Owing to this great extremity, it came to the point of his putting one foot out of the howdah, as if he wished to get down, and yet was unable to decide what was best to do in the midst of all that confusion and uproar. He hardly seemed to know where he was. Mir Jumlah, who was quite near, doing his duty as a good leader (and from him nothing else could be expected), when he noticed Aurangzeb's movement, shouted in a loud voice: 'Kaem! kaem!' (*Qa,im! qa,im!*)[1]—that is to say, 'Stand fast! stand fast!' Dara lost the empire by getting off his elephant. He called out: 'Kaem! kaem!' (*Qa,im! qa,im!*) in reliance on the note sent to Allahwirdi Khan.

Already Aurangzeb was in the last extremity, abandoned by all, fearful of capture, and Fortune seemed to have deserted him. He thought he could never escape from his enemy's hands. But such was his lucky star, that he stopped upon his elephant and endured the severe assault. He remembered the battle he had fought against Dara at Samugarh, and believed that by sitting patiently on his elephant he would conquer.

Allahwirdi Khan, when he received the note from Aurangzeb, went off to Shah Shuja' [230] and resorted to the same tactics as Khalilullah Khan used with Dara, calling out to him: 'Congratulations to my sovereign on the victory the Most High has given your majesty! All that is left to do is to take the coward Aurangzeb before he can escape. Why do we delay thus? Let us advance with more speed; and to do this, let your majesty descend from your elephant and mount on horseback, and in a single charge we can seize our prey.' Here we can see how eagerly Fortune favoured Aurangzeb. For by this time the prince Shah Shuja' had won the day, and Aurangzeb was without hope and utterly lost. She changed the hands they held, so that Aurangzeb came out the winner, and Shah Shuja' the loser.

All this came to pass, notwithstanding Shah Shuja' knew what had happened to his brother Dara, who by quitting his elephant became a lost man. In spite of this, he followed the advice of Allahwirdi Khan, left his elephant, got upon his horse, and started for an attack on Aurangzeb. But the evil-minded traitor, Allahwirdi Khan, in place of going on with his prince, turned back, and, displaying great terror, began to ask everybody

---

1. This appears in Bernier, 76, as 'Decankon,' which Constable reads as 'Dakhin kahan' ('Where is the Deccan?').

anxiously what had become of Shah Shuja'; he could not be seen on his elephant. All the army looked in that direction, and not perceiving him, fell into confusion and dismay. They imagined that he must be dead, and they began to take to flight—above all, the division of Shah Shuja'; this was just as it had happened to Dara. Thus Sha Shuja', finding that there was no longer any hope, was forced hurriedly to join the fugitives. Meanwhile Aurangzeb sat unmoved on his elephant, with no more than five hundred horsemen round him. Perceiving that Sultan Shah Shuja' was no longer on [231] his elephant, he advanced with vigour to the attack, beating his drums to make it appear as if the victory was already his. By this manoeuvre he increased the hesitation of Shah Shuja''s army, which, losing hope entirely, took to flight.

Shah Shuja' retreated upon the city of Ilavas (Allahabad). On the day that he arrived at his quarters, he took measures against Allahwirdi Khan. The latter with the greatest assurance, as if he had done some great deed or benefit on his prince's behalf, stayed with the defeated army. He was put in chains and brought into the presence of Shah Shuja'. Recognising too late the treason committed, in great anger and without putting a single question, Shah Shuja' deprived him of life by a spear-thrust from his own hand (a chastisement well earned by this ungrateful traitor). God purposed, by taking the life of this clever traitor, to give to vassals a lesson of fidelity.

Jaswant Singh had assumed that Shah Shuja' would come out the victor; he therefore made for Agrah, where he halted for some days. Then came the unexpected news that Shah Shuja' had lost, to the great relief of Shaistah Khan, at that time governor of Agrah city; and the rajah started for his own country. For previously a rumour had been current that Aurangzeb had lost the battle and had been taken prisoner along with Mir Jumlah, and that Shah Shuja' had carried them off in chains. Thus, Shaistah Khan, aware of the treachery he had committed, already held his life as lost, and had resolved to swallow poison and kill himself. He had the goblet ready before him, and commending himself to Muhammad, expected as a certainty that Jaswant Singh would come into the city to seize him. If Jaswant Singh had only entered the city, he could without a doubt, by the slightest pressure or threat, have caused the commandant of the fortress, called

Mortuzacan (Murtaza Khan),[1] a very old man who had under him the fighting men, to open the gates, and Shahjahan would have been delivered from prison; for, seeing the agitation [232] into which his men were thrown by the news brought in by the men of Aurangzeb's army who had fled at the beginning of the battle, the said commandant was already in a tremor. But as Fortune favoured Aurangzeb, she hindered Jaswant Singh from even this small effort. For twenty-four hours the city of Agrah was transported at the news of Aurangzeb's defeat, and everyone hoped that the rajah would enter and deliver Shahjahan. But the rajah having exact knowledge of what had passed, it was inconvenient for him to make any such effort. While we admit that he was not wanting in a wish to release Shahjahan, he judged that in existing circumstances it was impossible, there being no one to take his side. By himself he could not oppose the army of the victorious Aurangzeb. For these reasons he arranged for a speedy retirement to his home country.

Fearing that Jaswant Singh might undertake something in favour of Shahjahan, Aurangzeb turned and hastened in person to Agrah. He thought it sufficed to leave Mir Jumlah with a large force to pursue Shah Shuja'. He was nominated generalissimo of the army and perpetual viceroy of the whole province of Bengal, the appointment to pass on his death to his son. But from reasons of State he left behind in his (Mir Jumlah's) company his own first-born son, Sultan Muhammad, who was to make the campaign under the orders of Mir Jumlah, but without a command. At this arrangement Sultan Muhammad was much put out, but he kept this grievance within his breast, waiting until an occasion arose to wreak vengeance.

At this time Shah Shuja' had fortified himself in the city and fortress of Allahabad, without much reduction of his numbers [233]. He made use of the Hindu princes who live on the right and left banks of the river Ganges, and gathered together in a short time a huge force, through the reputation he had with everybody of being wealthy and liberal. In this way he became extremely strong at

1. Possibly Murtaza Khan. Sayyid Shah Muhammad (see 'Ma,asir-ul-Umara,' iii. 597); but there is no mention of his being put in charge of Agrah fort. Moreover, as this man survived for twenty years, he could not have been so *very old* in 1659.

that important and famous fortress, which forms the first gate into Bengal. Recognising the valour and strength of Shah Shuja', Mir Jumlah did not venture to attack him by force of arms. It sufficed to send him valuable presents and many letters with misleading promises. In another direction he set to work to raise against Shah Shuja' certain Hindu princes living about Benares and Patnah. They had an old quarrel with the prince, and now rose against him; they hindered his supplies, while they gave Mir Jumlah free passage. The latter lost no time in sending his troops and closing the routes. On receiving this melancholy news Shah Shuja' beat a retreat, before they could totally block his road, to the ancient city called Banaras (Benares), lying on the river Ganges, on the left bank.

Mir Jumlah followed in pursuit, and left him no time to fortify himself there. Thus Shah Shuja' was forced to retreat again, passing by the great city of Patnah, not feeling sufficiently secure there owing to the great open plains of those regions. He took shelter in a little town called Muguer (Munger) that had been founded on the right bank of the river Ganges. It is called by the inhabitants the 'Key of the Kingdom of Bengal,' because it is at the foot of hills, and near it are extensive jungles, called by the dwellers there Burianguel (? Bar Jangal)—that is to say, 'Terrifying Woods,' because in them are many wild beasts, tigers, rhinoceroses, wild buffaloes, and other animals.

At this place (Munger), the best that could be found in those regions, Shah Shuja' fortified himself. For greater security he made [234] a great wall of earth, beginning at the foot of the hill and ending on the bank of the Ganges, a distance, more or less, of half a league. It was made at a distance of twelve leagues from the city of Munger, and its object was to bar the passage to Mir Jumlah. Recognising the great difficulty of making an attack on Shah Shuja', Mir Jumlah began a correspondence with some rajahs dwelling in the wilds referred to, men who also at one time or another had been injured by Shah Shuja'. Valuable presents were forwarded, and they permitted the passage of the army. Thus Mir Jumlah and Sultan Muhammad marched on with the best of their troops, directing their course towards Raiamahal (Rajmahal), the principal residence of Shah Shuja', with the sole object of cutting off his retreat.

Shah Shuja', alarmed at this intelligence, abandoned all his entrenchments, and moving with great rapidity, reached Rajmahal before the arrival of Mir Jumlah, and there he entrenched himself as well as he could. Mir Jumlah failed to get there first, not from want of energy or effort, but by reason of the great forests and many streams on his route. As soon as his men and baggage had come up, Mir Jumlah made an attack upon Shah Shuja', who continued a valiant defence for the space of six days. But finding that the heavy artillery of Mir Jumlah did great damage to the entrenchments, which had been made of earth, gabions (*arca* = boxes), and fascines, he decided to retreat, having no hope of being able to continue his resistance, not only from want of men, but from the near approach of the rainy season.[1] Taking advantage of the darkness of night, he marched away on the road to the city of Daca (Dhakkah), leaving some artillery behind him which he was unable to remove.

He was not pursued by Mir Jumlah, who feared an ambush and suspected the retirement to be a mere stratagem of war. He halted where he was, meaning to begin pursuit the next day; but Shah Shuja''s lucky star favoured him, since during three days there was such heavy rain that Mir Jumlah could not move his army, nor attempt to catch up the fugitive. Shah Shuja' had time [235] to get close to Dhakkah city, and there he entrenched himself on a broad river, and Mir Jumlah was obliged to go into quarters for the rainy season at Rajmahal, for, owing to the rain, the mire, and the full streams, there was no possibility of marching. He occupied the city, and was there four months, from June to September (? 1659). These are the months in which heavy rain falls throughout India, above all in the region of Bengal, and armies cannot march. Thus Shah Shuja' had time to entrench himself anew, making use of the Portuguese, who live in Bengal since they lost their strong places in different parts of India, taken from them by the Dutch, such as the Island of Ceilao (Ceylon) and the Island of Japhonapatao (Jafnapatnam),[2] on the coast of Choramandal. He offered high pay to these men and promised to make them all wealthy, to give full liberty for

1. *Inverno*, literally, 'winter'; it is the word N. M. always uses for the rain season.
2. Colombo in Ceylon was taken from the Portuguese on May 12, 1656, and Jafnapatnam on June 22, 1658 (Dubois, 'Vies des Gouverneurs-Généraux,' p. 187).

their religious orders to raise up churches throughout his realm. It is certain that if fortune had favoured Shah Shuja' he would not have broken his promises, for he was naturally liberal and generous. There were at that period in the whole province of Bengal about eight thousand families of Portuguese, European and Asiatic, the latter popularly called Mestiços (mongrel, or half-castes).

Meanwhile Shah Shuja' entrenched himself near Dhakkah. Sultan Muhammad, his nephew, was angry at his father (Aurangzeb) having placed supreme command in the hands of Mir Jumlah, leaving him to work under his orders without any command. He wanted to have uncontrolled direction of the army, while Mir Jumlah should act under him. To this effect he wrote several times to his father that it did not befit the dignity of a prince, His Majesty's firstborn son, for a subject to command an army while he, though not deficient in military training or power of leading, remained without a command. There were no grounds for His Majesty believing more in Mir Jumlah than in his son. In nothing was he undeserving the post of generalissimo, either by his blood or his known valour. But Aurangzeb paid not the least attention to the request of his son. He was afraid that, should he get hold of an army, [236] he might rebel against him, as is usually the case in this empire of the Moguls, and an ancient habit of theirs.

Finding himself repeatedly rebuffed by his father, Sultan Muhammad gave utterance more than once to words full of wrath and menace depreciatory of Mir Jumlah. He wished to make the troops believe that he (Mir Jumlah) aspired to the crown. All this was known to Mir Jumlah. He dissembled sagaciously, and took no notice of Sultan Muhammad's words. The latter then recollected that his uncle, Shah Shuja', had promised him his daughter in marriage, and he now resolved to rebel against his father and adopt the side of Shah Shuja'. He therefore left the army of Mir Jumlah by boat, accompanied by twenty-five men, without being noticed. Reaching the spot where Shah Shuja' was entrenched, as soon as he saw him he disclosed his purpose and declared his distrust of his father. He offered to serve him and defend him with fidelity, swearing oaths upon the Quran. The only reward he sought was the hand of his daughter, Mahacanom (Mah Khanum), that being the name of Shah Shuja''s daughter.

That prince received Sultan Muhammad with the honours due to him, but did not give him many troops. He dreaded some treachery. He assigned him a lady of the harem as a spouse, deceiving him by the assertion that it was his daughter.

When the rains were over, Mir Jumlah moved in search of Shah Shuja', and then the contests were renewed. Sultan Muhammad at the head of his small force proved his courage, destroying many of the enemy and causing great trouble to Mir Jumlah. When informed of what had happened Aurangzeb ordered Daler Khan, whom he highly esteemed, to proceed against Shah Shuja' with reinforcements. Meanwhile Mir Jumlah employed a stratagem. He prepared a letter to Sultan Muhammad in which he desired him to continue as he was doing, until occasion arose to fulfil his promise to his father. As intended by Mir Jumlah, this letter fell into the hands of Shah Shuja'; and it confirmed him in the distrust he had of Sultan Muhammad. He took away the small body of troops he had assigned him, and forbad him to enter the palace.

When Sultan Muhammad heard [237] of this letter he sent to Shah Shuja' to say that he must not give any heed to Mir Jumlah. The letter was a forgery, meant for nothing but to sow disunion between the two of them; and he ratified afresh the oath to serve him faithfully. But these arguments were not sufficient to secure Shah Shuja's confidence. Unhappy Sultan Muhammad, finding himself out of favour everywhere, and having by this time discovered the deception about his marriage, resolved upon having recourse to his opponent, Mir Jumlah. Abandoning Shah Shuja', he transferred himself to Mir Jumlah's camp, where he was received with due dignity, and a promise was given to write in his favour to Aurangzeb. Mir Jumlah would do all he could to get his father to overlook the past. There are not wanting those who declare that the flight of Sultan Muhammad to Shah Shuja' was planned by Aurangzeb. This is due to what they have experienced of his wiles; but it was not so, because if Shah Shuja' had put faith in Sultan Muhammad, Mir Jumlah and Daler Khan would not have had such an easy victory.

Learning that his son was reconciled with Mir Jumlah, Aurangzeb wrote him a letter full of demonstrations of affection, with an order of recall. Mir Jumlah's orders were to send him back under a good and trustworthy guard, fearing that on the way he might attempt some escapade similar to the last. For this reason he was carried in a palanquin carefully watched. Reflecting on what he had done, and afraid of his father, whose deceitful and vengeful nature he knew, Sultan Muhammad became very anxious, and began to contemplate renewed flight to the mountains of Srinagar. In order to intimidate the guard over him, he jumped frequently out of the palanquin, in the supposition that, either out of fear or respect, he would be allowed to take to flight. But naught availed him, for those in charge of him had received very strict orders. Hearing what was going on during the journey, Aurangzeb sent off the eunuch Danis (Danish), at the head of two thousand cavalry, with the fetters used for Murad Bakhsh. These were [238] at once to be put on him, and he was to be placed on an elephant in a closed howdah. They were to cross the river Ganges, and carry him to the fortress of Gualier (Gwaliyar, Gwalior). There he was detained, and orders were given to ply him continually with the water of *posto* (*post*, opium) until his mind was destroyed.

In that condition the wretched Sultan Muhammad was left, being treated not as a prince, but as a vile slave. By his father's orders all human communication was prohibited; so great was the rigour used that no one could speak in his presence nor answer any question. Such was Aurangzeb's distrust of his son that he did not allow him to have a barber, or a knife to use at his meals. As a trial of his son's resignation, Aurangzeb sent to ask him whether he would like his wife sent to him, the daughter of the King of Gulkandah. In a great rage he replied that he begged to be excused from diversions whilst being treated so tyrannically. The rest of what happened in prison to Sultan Muhammad I will refer to farther on, in its proper place (II. 150).

Mir Jumlah continued vigorously his campaign against Shah Shuja', who on his side responded with such dimished force as he had left. He retreated to the banks of the Ganges river for defence and recovery. But as the results of battles are uncertain, Aurangzeb stood fast with his army on the boundaries of Agrah in order to reinforce Mir Jumlah, if need for help arose. At this time he ordered Murad Bakhsh to be removed from the fortress of Salimgarh, where he was a prisoner, and shut up in close prison at Gwaliyar fortress. His orders were to give him poppy-water to drink, as in the case of Sultan Muhammad; both were treated with the same harshness, nor was the slightest conversation allowed between the two prisoners. Then in the meanwhile, news came to Aurangzeb that Shah Shuja' could still resist for a long time. When assured of this, Aurangzeb retired upon the city of Dihli, and began to issue absolute orders as king; and he caused coin to be struck in his own name, on which [239] were shown these words:

> 'Seca zad der jahan chum badre munir
> Xaa Orangzeb Alamguer '
> (Sikkah zad dar jahan chun badr-i-munir
> Shah Aurangzeb-i-'Alamgir)

—that is to say, 'Struck coin in the world as clear as the sun and moon, I, King Aurangzeb, conqueror of the world.'

While Aurangzeb was at Dihli, Dara marched from Gujarat towards the city of Agrah, at the head of thirty thousand horsemen, relying on the word given him by Rajah Jaswant Singh that he would bring his entire army and incorporate it, so as to make one irresistible army for the destruction of Aurangzeb. The latter, when the report was received, left Dihli to attack Dara wherever encountered. Aware that Jaswant Singh meant to give help to Dara, he directed Rajah Jai Singh to endeavour by letters to persuade the said Jaswant Singh to desist from this purpose. Aurangzeb promised him pardon for his previous rebellion, offered to receive him into favour, make him viceroy of Gujarat, and allow him to retain the treasure plundered during the battle against Shah Shuja'. If he did not refrain from joining Dara there must be much destruction and many deaths on both sides, for he (Jai Singh) would have to seek him (Jaswant Singh) out in the battle-field. As they were both Rajputs, of one nation and religion, the Mahomedans would triumph at seeing them destroyed.[1]

Jaswant Singh was influenced by the letter and promises of Rajah Jai Singh, and decided to break his word, and not move to Dara's assistance according to promise. The latter arrived close

1. Aurangzeb arrived six *kos* from Ajmer on the 26th Jamada II., 1069 H. (March 16, 1659). Jai Singh writes to Jaswant, who returns to Jodhpur; Sipihr Shukoh sent to him there, but without effect. Dara was then entrenched at the village Deorae; Hashim holds up the dead body of Shekh Mir; the battle of two days ended on the last day but one of Jamada II. (March 23, 1659). On the next day Rajah Jai Singh and Bahadur Khan were sent in pursuit. Aurangzeb re-entered palace at Dihli on the last of Sha'ban (May 23, 1659) ('Ma,asiri- 'Alamgi-i,' pp. 18-22).

to the city of Ajmer, near the territories of the said Rajah Jaswant Singh. Finding after a time that he did not come in with his force, Dara wrote to him that it was already time to carry out the word that he had given him, that he was on the spot awaiting him, and he recommended haste, for on him depended whether he succeeded or not. Since Jaswant Singh sent no answer, the afflicted Dara repeated his letter, already dreading that Jaswant Singh would play him false. To compel him to come, he decided to send [240] to him his own son, Super Xaca (Sipihr Shukoh), entreating the rajah not to desert him on this occasion, for on him depended the victory and a decision about the crown. If God willed that he should reach the throne, he would ever recognise the benefit conferred and support given, as would all his descendants. They would be under a perpetual obligation, and would never be backward in due acknowledgments. Let him weigh this; he (Dara) had left the city of Ahmadabad with a small force, because he relied on the promise made to him by the rajah of accompanying him with all his warriors. If the rajah should now fail him, his person and life would be in manifest danger of falling into the hands of Aurangzeb.

All these efforts of Dara were fruitless. For when the rajah heard that the son of Dara was coming to see him, he sent out men upon the road to force him to turn back, proffering a thousand excuses for his non-ability to join, or on this occasion to render aid to, Dara. I leave it to the reader to imagine the affliction of the unfortunate Dara at this disappointment; his hopes were frustrated, and he knew not what course to adopt after this desertion. For to return to Ahmadabad was impossible. The distance was too great, the road lay through sterile country, and it was the commencement of the hot season. Again, if the soldiers found that Dara was in retreat, the greater part would most certainly desert. Thus he held it best to entrench himself among some low hills, the tops of which he occupied with his army, and dug trenches in the valleys, disposing his artillery in the most effective way, under the command of Xanevascan (Shah Nawaz Khan) and Barcandascan (Barqandaz Khan).

Aurangzeb advanced by double marches with Daler Khan, whom he had sent for at this juncture. On arriving within view of Dara's force, he saw that it would be difficult to win a victory, owing to the strength of the position. He forbore a resort to arms, and sought the help of his usual craftiness. He ordered Daler Khan to open a correspondence with Dara, displaying desire to take his part, seeing that Jaswant Singh had broken his promise. The proposal was that on the day of battle he (Daler Khan) should be allowed access to his (Dara's) army, when, incorporating himself with it, they would jointly put Aurangzeb to the rout. He pledged his word with an oath [241] on the Quran to be faithful to him. Dara, in his simplicity, gave easy credit to the false vows of Daler Khan, and ordered his officers on the day of battle not to fight against that general's division. When Aurangzeb learnt of this knavery, he felt already assured of Daler Khan's entry into the army of Dara, and made ready to give battle on the following day.

The day before the battle, which was on the fifteenth of May of one thousand six hundred and fiftyseven (correctly, 1659), an astrologer named Cubatbeg (? Qutb Beg), a Mahomedan of Osbec (*Uzbak*) race, who had studied mathematics under Padre Buzeo, said privately to Aurangzeb that, according to the influences of the stars dominating the next day, there existed danger to the life of him who occupied the chief place in the army. Therefore he besought His Majesty not to occupy the place assigned to a king—that is, upon an elephant and covered by an umbrella, as is the usage in this kingdom of the Mogul. Since this mathematician had a great name, and was revered by everybody as a great astrologer, Aurangzeb took counsel with the leaders of his army. Among them was one called Secmir (Shekh Mir),[1] his tutor, who offered to take the seat on the royal elephant and represent His Majesty's person. He held it to be an honour to give his life to save that of his royal master. Since he had given him his first instruction, he desired now, as a final sacrifice, to lose his life in his service, like a loyal subject. But it was absolutely necessary to keep the matter secret; and it were well that no one within or without the camp got any inkling of it.

Aurangzeb accepted the offer of his tutor, and then directed orders to be issued throughout the camp that on the next day

1. Shekh Mir, Khwafi, a Sayyid by lineage ('Ma,asir-ul-Umara,' ii. 668). According to that work, the man in the *Khawase*, or back seat, was Mir Hashim, Khwafi, not Mir Taql.

at dawn they must be ready to attack the enemy. When the time to move had come, Shekh Mir rode the king's elephant, clad in full regal array, everybody supposing that it was the very Aurangzeb, a deception that was easily believed, as daylight had not yet appeared. The trenches of Dara were attacked with great fury, and he repelled the assailants with still greater vigour, doing great execution with his artillery and musketry. In this first conflict the tutor of Aurangzeb, Shekh Mir, was shot down by a musket-ball, thus gloriously [242] yielding up his life an offering for the safety of his disciple. But the attendant seated behind him on the elephant performed a feat highly thought of at the time. To prevent the army losing heart by supposing that Aurangzeb, whom Shekh Mir represented, had been slain, this man held the body up, and holding its arms, moved them about, encouraging his own side to come on. He ordered the elephant-driver to use his goad to the elephant. His exertions were quite as important as Shekh Mir's resolve, whereby he offered up his life for Aurangzeb. This attendant's name was Mirtaque (Mir Taqi), who gained for Aurangzeb the victory, and as the winner thereof he was rewarded for his great courage and exertions. Aurangzeb at once changed his name of Mir Taqi into that of Fatenuma (Fath-numa)—that is to say, 'Displayer of Victory.' Although I was not in this battle, I have special knowledge of it; for I was intimate for a time with the said Fath-numa and other principal men who were present, and the above facts are notorious throughout the Mogul realm.

Daler Khan, to whom was made over the right attack, signalled to Dara to have the trenches vacated for his passage with his division of twelve thousand horsemen, all Pathans, in order that he might join Dara's army in conformity with the letter he had written. Dara, ignorant of the intended treachery, ordered him to be allowed a passage through the entrenchments without any opposition. In spite of this, a great many of Dara's men declined to let him through, but Daler Khan made his way past them. At that time Dara's army was busy in repulsing the enemy. Daler Khan and his men began at once to fall upon those in advance, putting them to the edge of the sword, and continued to do all the harm they could. Dara's army fell into the greatest confusion, and without making any stand or resistance the whole of them took to flight. Thus, within less than three hours, the time for which the fighting on both sides lasted, the defeat of Dara was accomplished.

If Dara had foreseen the treachery of Daler Khan, and had not allowed himself to be deceived by his pretenses, there cannot be the slightest doubt that he would have [243] given a great deal of trouble to Aurangzeb. For although his numbers were fewer, he had a great advantage from the position he had selected. Thus, during the short time that the contest lasted, the army of Aurangzeb had suffered considerable loss; and, judging from the happy beginning of his defence, Dara could promise himself the victory. In that case he would have had renewed hope of Jaswant Singh's adherence and that of the other rajahs. But just as Fortune inclined benignantly towards Aurangzeb, she equally withdrew from the unlucky Dara. Finding his army defeated and hurriedly taking to flight, he himself also devoid of further hope, he resolved to flee, and retire upon the city of Ahmadabad, whence he had come. This he did with such precipitation that it was impossible to save his baggage, for Daler Khan and his men were already going about the camp destroying everything, and the fallen prince had barely time to carry off his family and the chief valuables lying in his tents. Aurangzeb then ordered Rajah Jai Singh and Bahadur Khan to pursue Dara; their orders were to seize him, dead or alive.

After the flight of Dara, Shah Nawaz Khan was left under the shade of some trees somewhat distant from the battle-field, believing that no one would interfere with him in such a place, where he was quite passive. For he neither wanted to fight nor to defend himself, nor to fly along with Dara. His great reliance was on his being Aurangzeb's father-in-law. For all these reasons he held that he would not be interfered with. But one who did not blush at tyrannizing over his own father, his brothers, and his sons, would hardly forgive his father-in-law for having allowed Dara into Gujarat and having followed him into the field of battle. For this reason Aurangzeb had given express orders to Daler Khan that, wherever he might find the old man, Shah Nawaz Khan, he should take his life without any compunction. Daler Khan learnt that the old man was at the spot mentioned, and went at once with his soldiers, to whom he gave orders not to harm any of those in Shah Nawaz Khan's suite. On beholding the unhappy old man seated upon a carpet spread on the ground [244], he hastened his elephant's pace, and when near enough killed him impiously and cruelly by repeated arrow-shots.

It happened at this time that the victorious soldiers who were pursuing Dara lighted upon a carriage in which was the Dutch factor who had come in Dara's train, hoping that if he took the field he would be rewarded for this extra devotion. He was now retreating on his way to the city of Ahmadabad. The soldiers attacked the carriage on all sides, ordering him to give up his arms and all he had with him. The factor imprudently attempted resistance, and putting hands on his two pistols, made as if he intended to fire, imagining that thereby he would frighten those surrounding him. But at that moment these let fly at him a shower of arrows, and thus he came to lose his life and the goods that he had meant to protect.[1]

During Dara's retreat to Ahmadabad, the fugitives who had caused the rout rejoined him on the road. When he reached the confines of the city he had already a small force. But the hardships suffered by Dara *en route* due to the heated air were increased when, on trying to enter the city, the gates were closed against him by order of the officer in charge. This man had already been gained over by letters written to him by Aurangzeb and by the great promises made to him therein. The soldiers in the poor prince's train, seeing him persecuted on all sides and deserted, resolved to abandon him and thus escape utter ruin. Dara felt acutely being forsaken so ungratefully by even his closest and most familiar friends, such as Barqandaz Khan and the eunuch, Coia Mosqui (Khojah Mushkin). The former plundered him of the few horses of any value [245] he had remaining after the retreat. They were carried off for presentation to Aurangzeb, Barqandaz Khan offering himself to the victor as a follower and servant. The second (Mushkin), of whom Dara thought a great deal, and to whom he had confided his treasure, robbed him of two mules loaded with gold coins, and with these he made off, intending

1. In the Dutch Archives is a letter from Leonard Winninex to the Seventeen, dated from Surat, October 6, 1659, which confirms Manucci. 'Willem Verstegen had gone to seek his fortune with the wandering prince, Dara Shukoh. At the recent great battle, not far from Ajmer, he was shamefully murdered, or lost his life in a shocking way. . . . One of Tombergen's sons also served the royal prince Dara Shukoh, and equally without benefit.'

to offer himself to Aurangzeb. At the outset both were received with a feigned display of favour, but afterwards they received only moderate pay. As a sign of contempt. Barqandaz Khan was made superintendent of the scavengers and of the dogs, one of the lowest offices in the kingdom. This was to show the low esteem Aurangzeb had for one whom Dara had prized so highly. Khojah Mushkin[1] was informed that he would receive a bare daily subsistence, such alms being granted, not because of any personal merit, but in return for the two mules loaded with gold coin. Finding himself despised by the king, from whom he had hoped equal favour, if not greater than Dara had accorded, affronted by everyone, injurious words being continually said to his very face, he planned a disappearance into far-off lands, whence never more was he heard of. These instances, and many more written in our story, may serve to teach favourites with what loyalty they ought to serve their prince equally in prosperity as in adversity.

The unlucky Dara had barely more than two thousand men left in his company, and with these he resumed his flight for the land of Sind, where he was before, traversing once again all those desert lands and plains, in want of water and of food, and suffering from the extreme heat. These hardships made still less bearable the haste with which, day and night, he pressed onwards in his flight before Rajah Jai Singh and Bahadur Khan, who were trying to overtake him. Thus many of the prince's followers, worn out by such continuous marching, fell to the rear in the hope of getting some rest. But they were set upon by robbers, who plundered everyone and killed many.

However much the men of [246] Aurangzeb might follow and press upon Dara, Rajah Jai Singh still so arranged the day's march that there was ever room for the unfortunate and dishonoured prince to escape. Granted that he (Jai Singh) was not well-affected to him, still, he did not intend him to lose his life. It contented him to see Dara expelled into foreign territory, without his falling into the hands of Aurangzeb, when infallibly he would be put an end to, as finally came to pass. Through the scope given him by Jai Singh, Prince Dara, after much exertion, reached

1. The native historians call the eunuch Ma'qul, not Mushkin.

the country of the rajah Cachanagano[1] who received him kindly, furnished him with supplies, many camels, and some horses, these being very plentiful in that country.

Dara would have liked to allow his men a longer rest, but this was impossible, owing to the near approach of the enemy. Nor had the rajah the requisite force to resist the harassing pursuit of Jai Singh and Bahadur Khan. Thus Dara was forced to resume his flight to the river country of Sind, where the inhabitants, directly they heard of his approach, took to flight with their boats, fearing that Dara, after he had used them for crossing, would burn them, as he had done during his earlier flight. Great were the trouble and the danger in which the prince was, being on the one hand pursued by the enemy trying hard to overtake him, and on the other, hindered by the treacherous streams, to pass which there were not enough boats. Therefore he decided to cross the river on rafts, making use of the trees and all the wood from buildings, breaking up the houses for this purpose. Not without great efforts did he succeed in reaching the farther bank of the river, where he found himself with no more than five hundred men; for of the two thousand with which he had left Ahmadabad, the rest had deserted or had been killed.

Having now overcome the obstacle presented by the river, Dara had decided to turn off towards his well-garrisoned fortress of Bhakkar. But he became aware now that the said fortress was invested by Khalilullah Khan with a strong force, and the place was out of his direct road [247]. By this expedient, therefore, he could not escape from the hands of his enemies, seeing that Rajah Jai Singh and Bahadur Khan were at his heels. His next project was to take the road to Persia, which was not far off; also on that road there dwelt Given Can (Jiwan Khian), lord of some territories on the boundaries of the Mogul kingdom and Persia.[2] Formerly Dara

1. Dara, refused entry into Ahmadabad, applied to Kanji, Koli, of Parganah Kari, eight kos distant. Kanji conducted him to the boundary of Kachh, where the rajah received him badly, a great contrast to his former treatment (see the "Alamgirnamah,' p. 411). Thus, Kachh is part of the name, and, following the text on I. 224, the rest of it should read *nagara*, 'a town.'
2. Malik Jiwan, chief of Dadar, afterwards created Bakhtyar Khan (see 'Ma,asir-i-'Alamgiri,' p. 25).

had three times rescued this man from death, when Shahjahan had decreed that for certain offences he should be thrown under the feet of an elephant. He conceived that under compulsion of these repeated favours the man could never refuse at this juncture to make due recognition.

Thus he made up his mind to go to the place where Jiwan Khan dwelt. But among the barbarous and unbelieving Mahomedans, chiefly the Pathan tribes, there is neither former benefit nor obligation that holds good. The ungrateful Jiwan Khan, when Dara arrived in his country flying from his pursuers, resolved on seizing him, in the hope that Aurangzeb would reward him for such a trick, although he thereby committed the greatest treachery and ingratitude that could be done by the whole uncivilized world united. He received Dara in a deceptive manner, with great demonstrations of affection and gratitude. In the interval he collected all his men, with whom he suddenly encircled the wretched prince and all his family, keeping so many men on strict watch that the servants of Dara could find neither opening nor freedom to carry him food and water. To make his deed more assured, Jiwan Khan began with the aforesaid demonstrations, and gave orders that the soldiers of Dara should be invited to various separate places. When this was carried out, he set to work to treat them with cruelty.

The princess, Nomahal Begom (Nurmahal Begam)[1] the first wife of Dara, finding herself in such a difficulty, along with her son, Sipihr Shukoh, and her daughter, Jani Begom (Jain Begam), resolved to take her life with her own hands, so that she might not live to see her sons' and her husband's tragic and lamentable end. Beholding the anguish endured by the afflicted Begam, her favourite house-slave prevented the princess taking [248] the poison, which to this intent she carried in a ring concealed under a precious stone. He said to her that since he owed all he was to the prince, he ought in this great peril to show the fine quality of his attachment by offering his life and person for the ransoming

1. Nadirah Bano Begam was the daughter of Sultan Parwez, son of the Emperor Jahangir. Her mother was Jahan Bano Begam, daughter of Prince Murad Bakht, son of the Emperor Akbar. She died in the country of Sind, in the month of Ramazan, 1069 H. (May-June, 1659) (see the 'Tarikh-i-Muhammadi,' founded on the 'Alamgirnamah'; also 'Ma,asir-i-'Alamgiri,' p. 74, line 5).

of his lord. Let her wait a little, for he had resolved to take the life of the ungrateful Jiwan Khan, although well aware that he could not carry out this design without losing his own. For the execution of the enterprise he begged a pistol from the prince, one given him by the Dutch factor at Ahmadabad as a weapon of value, all inlaid with mother-of-pearl—one that had never been known to miss fire.

Armed with this single weapon hidden in a bag of brocade, he went to the place where Jiwan Khan was sitting. As soon as he got within sight of him the guards stopped the eunuch, and asked why he had come. The courageous Faridum (Farldun)—this being the name of the skilful plotter—replied that he had been sent by his prince to present to Jiwan Khan a jewel contained in the brocade bag. The announcement was made to Jiwan Khan, who, urged by self-interest, ordered the man to be brought forthwith to his presence. Faridun, making with great respect the accustomed bows, came close with the bag laid upon his two hands as if about to present it. On Jiwan Khan extending his hands to take the present, Faridun let off the pistol, which he carried ready cocked. It missed fire! When Fortune takes arms against a man in misfortune, neither apparatus nor plans, however excellent, are anything but mistakes and failures! And of a truth, had this plot of Faridun's taken effect, then, during the confusion that would unfailingly have arisen among Jiwan Khan's men, Prince Dara would have been free to make off into Persian territory as he had intended. The high-minded but unfortunate Faridun was then seized, but they did not slay him, for it was not fair that such a stout and [249] courageous heart should end so inauspiciously.

Finding that Dara had ordered an attempt on his life, Jiwan Khan continued his severities more strictly than ever. He put into prison all the people with Dara, leaving him with none but his family. The afflicted princess, learning that Faridun was taken without effecting his purpose, and already convinced there was not the slightest hope of delivering her beloved prince from the difficulties in which he stood, and aware of the final and crowning disgrace that must inevitably ensue, fell into the deepest desperation. Taking into her hand the poison kept ready for these final and fatal throes, she exclaimed, while sad sighs and torrents of tears interrupted her words: 'O beloved prince! O beloved sons! Now are your misfortunes at their height! Now has the hour come for your lives to end. With your blood the cruelty of Aurangzeb will be assuaged. Would to God that my life could suffice to quench he thirst of this ferret, or that with it I could restore yours, then would not Aurangzeb be so oppressive to you, nor so cruel to me! What could become of me after such a loss? Could I survive without sons, without a husband? Could I endure the deeper disgrace of becoming a concubine to Aurangzeb? God does not delight in this my evil state. But since there is now no other remedy, by taking my life I put an end to all my pains, and this tyrant gathers in by my death a portion of the spoils intended to grace his triumph.'

Speaking thus, she took the poison, which was so potent that as soon as she swallowed it she fell dead. Then her women attendants ran to her, and, seeing their mistress in the last throes of life, they cried aloud. At this outcry everyone ran to see what was the matter. Finding the princess already unconscious, her brilliant colour gone, her eyes suffused with chilly tears, her son and her daughter fell upon her with loud lamentation. At these sounds the unhappy prince Dara arrived and found his princess, Nur Mahal Begam, already cold and quite [250] dead. He was so dejected that he was entirely unable to speak, and quite stunned. He was driven forth by the heartrending weeping of his son and daughter, the despair of the women, and the wailing of the relations.

I wish my readers just to think of the confusion prevailing then in the house of Jiwan Khan. He could not avoid feeling compassion at such an event. For the qualities of Nur Mahal Begam, a princess of the blood royal, were quite exceptional both in body and in mind. If time had allowed, it is possible that he might have taken pity on Dara, and granted him his liberty. But at this time arrived the hurrying Bahadur Khan eager for Dara's blood, and with a great uproar he and his soldiers entered in search of Dara's person. The latter, hearing all the noise, knew it to be the enemy, and tried to get hold of his weapons to end his life fighting, hoping to fall where his cherished companion had expired. But the attempt was frustrated. In a loud voice Bahadur Khan cried: 'Seize the prisoner!' and his luck was such that he could do nothing.

Thus the soldiers rushed at the prince, took him, and separated him from his wives and sons. They behaved with extreme harshness, paying no heed to royal immunities, a prince's privileges, or a master's rights. Without any remorse, chains were put upon his legs and manacles upon his wrists. Then four elephants appeared with howdahs on, and in secrecy they placed the prince on one of them. Each elephant was escorted by three thousand horsemen, armed with swords and spears. There were thus four divisions, and among them were distributed the prince, the sons, and the women, with such secrecy that not a soul knew in what division, or on which elephant, or in which howdah, Dara was. In each howdah was a soldier with drawn sword seated at the back. This was done so that if any outbreak occurred, or any attempted was made to rescue the prince, the assailants should not know in which division he was, and the soldier seated at his back would have time enough to dispatch him according to orders. The march began, Rajah Jai Singh at the head of the vanguard and Bahadur Khan with the rear-guard. They set out [251] for the fortress of Bhakkar.

In that fortress we remained, under continual assaults, defending ourselves boldly. In spite of all their efforts, the enemy were unable by force of arms to overcome us. Therefore, they planned a means of getting the European artillerymen to withdraw from the fortress, and to this end they shot arrows, to which letters were attached. These invited us to abandon the service of Dara and evacuate the place. One of these arrows hit me on the shoulder when I was sitting in my bastion at eight o'clock at night. Withdrawing the arrow, I went with it at once, wounded as I was, to the eunuch. He gave me a robe (*sarapa*) and some bottles of rose-water in recognition of my fidelity.

Since Aurangzeb had strongly enjoined on Khalilullah Khan that he must reduce the place in one way or the other, and he saw that he could not do so by force of arms, he had recourse to many letters containing promises to our eunuch Primavera (Basant), that if he gave over the fortress his demands would be gratified. Enraged at length by the receipt of so many letters, the eunuch wrote to Khalilullah Khan that if he would come in person he would enter into the desired agreement. He meant to surrender the place, as he perceived that Dara's affairs were in a very bad way. Khalilullah Khan received this letter with great delight, fancying he was about to accomplish great things for Aurangzeb, who was so keen on acquiring the place. He started from Lahor with the remainder of his army to bring to a conclusion the anxiously desired surrender. On his arrival a truce was made between the two sides. Khalilullah Khan wrote to the eunuch a letter full of civilities, displaying the great results to be gained by making over the stronghold, whereby he would be taken into favour by Aurangzeb; in fact, in so delivering it, he would find the only way to fortune.

Primavera the eunuch was quite rejoiced at the arrival of Khalilullah Khan, and decided on giving him a reply. With this idea he sent for me, and ordered me to [252] load the cannon nearest to the garden where Khalilullah Khan had encamped with horns and old shoes. It was charged thus up to the very muzzle. The answer was after this wise: 'I hold few words with you, for I am greatly amazed at you, and I hope to supply your want, having been all your life a pimp and used to shoe-beatings from women. Herewith what you deserve;

I offer you a present proportioned to your merits.' The letter went on with more abuse, which I will not insert. Closing it, he ordered it to be handed to Khalilullah Khan. The eunuch watched for the arrival of the boat at the garden, which was not far from the fortress; and when it seemed that Khalilullah Khan must be perusing the letter, he ordered us to fire off the cannon, and we covered Khalilullah Khan's tent with the charge it contained.

The traitor was thereby much shamed and discomfited, not knowing how to hide the affront. The following night, when we were off our guard, he suddenly ordered a discharge of all his artillery and musketry, which was a complete surprise to us, and the shot fell all over the fortress. I assert without exaggeration that a pole on which we had a small flag was pierced by three balls. But our eunuch would not pass over such-like bravado, and the next night he suddenly ordered us to fire all our guns and musketry, and discharge a number of iron bombs, to show that we had ample arms and munitions of war. This took place at eight o'clock. To prove to him still better that we were not afraid, he ordered a number of vessels of artificial fire to be set light to, so that it was clear as day. Thereupon Khalilullah Khan, finding that he could not succeed, turned his face, discomfited, towards Lahor, and left us invested as before.

Forty days after the departure of [253] Khalilullah Khan, we saw one morning a numerous force pass over the river from west to east at some distance from the fortress. Our artillery began to pound them as hard as it could. At this moment a horseman appeared on the river bank with a small white flag displayed. At once the eunuch gave an order for a small boat to fetch the horseman. On his entering the fortress he delivered a letter to the eunuch, and proclaimed loudly thus: 'I demand on behalf of Aurangzeb that you surrender this strong-hold, since we are carrying with us in this army the Prince Dara, whom we have a prisoner.' Hearing this sad and unexpected news, we were all cast down and dropped our arms. The eunuch told the horseman he could not make over the place without the order of his prince, the Lord Dara, from whom he had received charge. The messenger went away with this answer.

Before he had reached the farther bank, we saw coming seven boats full of armed men carrying a number of flags. Their officer was called Chegatcan (? Chaghatae Khan), an Uzbek by race; he was highly elated, as if entering in triumph into his own house. I gave an order to my men to get their guns ready, and some pieces with grape (*varrer*, literally, 'to sweep with a broom'). When they had already got near, we gave them a round from the artillery, which did a good deal of damage, both to the boats and to the men. After that they retreated, while our artillery went on firing.

Seeing how resolute we were, Bahadur Khan repaired to Prince Dara, and requested him to order the eunuch to surrender the stronghold, since, the garrison being firm in their resistance, in all probability the whole of them would come to a miserable end within the fortress. On hearing this Dara had compassion upon his eunuch and upon us, and wrote a note with his own hand, stating: 'Unfortunate is the one for whom you fought, I now request and require you to deliver up the place' [254].

When the eunuch Primavera (Basant) saw the letter, he recognised the writing, and began to weep bitterly. He wrote to Bahadur Khan that we demanded to come out with our baggage, and if he did not consent we would fling the cannon and the treasure into the river, and fight to the death with all desperation. Bahadur Khan sent back an assurance that we could leave with our baggage, but must make over the treasure, the princes, and all the matériel appertaining to the fortress. One condition was imposed: we must cross over to the west of the river, then eight days after he had marched we could take the road for Dihli. He made this condition because he feared we might enter his camp, and do our utmost to rescue Dara. After three days we issued from the fort in which we had endured so much. For, two days before the evacuation I bought two calves for six hundred rupees, and paid one rupee for every ounce of butter. Without exaggerating, I brought one chicken for thirteen rupees.

The army of Bahadur Khan passed out of sight of Bhakkar with their princely prisoner. Then came the order of Aurangzeb, already back in Dihli after the battle of Ajmer, to bring the prince to the presence by forced marches without the least delay. Great caution was enjoined. Bahadur Khan, not to fail in any particular, during every night of the march placed the tent where Dara slept close to his own, and guarded it well by alert sentries. In the very tent was a man shouldering a drawn sword, with orders that if he heard any disturbance or rising in the camp, he should at once cut off Dara's head.

In the space of forty days they arrived near the city of Dihli. When Aurangzeb was informed, he sent off a number of squadrons to meet Bahadur Khan, as an additional precaution. His orders were that Dara should be brought in on an elephant in an uncovered howdah [255], with his son, Sipihr Shukoh, at his side; behind them a man with a drawn sword. In this way they brought the unhappy Dara within the city. Round him were several bodies on horse, all clad in shining steel, with drawn swords in their hands. Bahadur Khan sat alone on his elephant alongside the prince's, while all his cavalry rode with arrows ready in their bows. Thus the afflicted prince rode through the main streets on the twenty-second of October, one thousand six hundred and fifty-seven (correctly, 1659), his feet bound but his hands free, with a dejected face, as if he already saw drawing near his last day of life. When within sight of the fortress a poor *faqir* shouted to him: 'O Dara! when you were master you always gave me alms; to-day I know well thou hast naught to give me.' The prince at once raised his hand to his shoulder, drew off the dark, dingy-coloured shawl that served him as a cloak and threw it to the *faqir*. But Bahadur Khan, who was close by, ordered it to be taken away, saying that a prisoner had no right to bestow anything. Then the irate *faqir* uttered a thousand abusive words against Jiwan Khan, who was present. In this way they arrived opposite the royal palace, where the prince was forced to halt for two hours, made a mark for the eyes of everybody, sitting on a little elephant badly equipped, subject to the heat of the midday sun, and ill-clad —a melancholy spectacle, creating compassion in all those who saw him. For in such brief space was this prince, so mighty, so rich, so famous, so powerful, reduced to the last stages of misery.

There stood the poor prince awaiting the sentence to be passed upon him; and Aurangzeb, to still further affront him, wanted to send an order for him to descend from his elephant and come into the presence on foot, just as he was, in chains. But Shaistah Khan counselled him that it was not wise to act thus, for many reasons. He was carried outside the city to a garden called Gecederabad (Khizrabad), which lies on the bank of the Jamnah. It had been planted by Shahjahan for his repose when he went out to the chase.[1]

A lying order was given that after a few days [256] it was intended to forward him (Dara) to the fortress of Gwaliyar. This was said solely in deference to the grief of the common people. Aurangzeb had recourse to a pretext to discover the wishes of those faithful to Prince Dara. This was by taking the opinions of the principal men. He asked from all of them advice as to what was the best thing, whether to kill Dara or send him to the fortress of Gwaliyar. In his own mind he had firmly resolved to have his prisoner's life taken. As the nobles knew this damnable wish of Aurangzeb, the proposition made being only a feigned deference to them, all of them were of opinion that the unfortunate prince must die, alleging as reason that if he did not die the people would be ever looking for his release. Thus would his majesty never be well served; and, further, his death was required by reason of his being an idolater, without any religion, and an enemy of the Mahomedan faith. Danisbandcan (Danishmand

1. Dara Shukoh was imprisoned in Khawaspurah at Khizrabad (see Khafi Khan, ii. 86, and ' 'Alamgirnamah,' p. 431).

Khan)[1] alone did not share this opinion, although in no way attached to Dara. Those who most insisted that the prince should be put to death were Shaistah Khan, Muhammad Amin Khan, Bahadur Khan, and the physician, Daut (Da,ud).[2] The last named in a short time saw himself in disgrace with Aurangzeb, and died miserably: God's just chatisement being that he who so actively procured another's death to please his master, should by means of the same master come speedily and miserably to his own end. She who more than all the rest clamoured for the death of Dara was Roshan Ara Begam, his sister but his mortal enemy. She died, as I shall relate, by poison administered to her by her well-beloved brother—*i.e.*, Aurangzeb. Aurangzeb, who desired nothing more ardently than the death of Dara, was delighted at the opinion of the nobles. On the twenty-sixt of October (1659) he gave orders to Quelis can (? Khalis Khan)[3] to remove the prince Sipihr Shukoh from his father, Dara's, company, and carry him off to the fortress of Gwaliyar, conceding as a favour that he should not be given opium-water to drink.

Prince Dara, finding his son was sent to Gwaliyar fortress without any mention of himself, recognised that he had only a few days to live. He therefore planned to seek [257] the only true consolation for his soul. To this intent, over and over-again, he entreated with urgence and insistence that the door-keepers should somehow or other seek out and bring to him Father Buzeo, a man well enough known. But on the guards paying no heed to his words, he still more urgently besought them to do him that favour, from which, neither to them nor to Aurangzeb, could any harm arise. Supposing they were unable to bring Father Buzeo, he begged them to produce some European priest or another. Finding himself unable to obtain his wish, he began in loud and heart-rending tones to say these words: 'Mahamed mara micuxet, ebenalla mare ian mi bacxet' (*Muhammad mara, mi-kushad, ibnullah mara jan mi-bakhshad*)—that is to say, 'Muhammad kills me, and the Son of God gives me life.' From these words and

1. This is Bernier's patron and 'Agha' (see 'Travels,' p. 100).
2. Hakim Da,ud, or Taqarrub Khan (see Bernier, 'Travels,' 100, and note 2). He died 1073 H. (1662-63) (see the 'M.-ul-U.,' i. 490, and 'Tarikh-i-Muhammadi,' relying on ' Ma,asir-i-'Alamgiri').
3. This may be meant for Qilich Khan or Mukhlis Khan, but the ' 'Alamgirnamah,' p. 432, states that Saif Khan executed the order.

those he spoke to Father Frei Pedro at the city of Tattah—namely, that if any faith in the world was true, it was that taught by the European priests—and from the pain he endured through not being able to get any priest; further, from information given me by the self-same door-keepers, from whom I made inquiries with great eagerness and minuteness, it is to be inferred that he (Dara) had a great desire to become a Christian.

Before issuing sentence of death against Prince Dara, Aurangzeb sent to ask him, if Fortune had been as favourable to him as it had been adverse, and he had held him (Aurangzeb) a prisoner, what would he have done? Knowing that in no way whatever would Aurangzeb spare his life, and that the question was meant as mere scoffing, Dara replied boldly and resolutely, like a prince and high-hearted leader, that if such had been the case the four principal gates of Dihli would have yielded the answer to his question, where would have been exposed the four quarters of his body.

This answer was conveyed to Aurangzeb, who, furious at such contumacy and license of speech, sent out [258] his sentence of death against the prince, his eldest brother. When he asked who would be so bold as to behead him, the cruel Nasar (Nazar Beg, Chelah) offered himself to do this barbarous harshness and exceedingly hazardous execution. Nazar Beg was one of King Shahjahan's slaves, brought up by him from childhood. When Aurangzeb made his father a prisoner, all the slaves submitted to him (Aurangzeb), who made this man their captain. Nazar Beg had not forgotten how once Dara had abused him for some careless insolence, and to get his revenge offered himself gladly. He took with him the official next in rank to him, one Macbula (Maqbula), and other six of the same sort—namely, Maharam (Mahram), Massura (Mashhur), Asaram (Asarun), Farad (? Furad), Morad (Murad), and Faccibahader (Fath Bahadur). These all set out from the court. After this, to mislead the populace, Aurangzeb ordered out Sefecan (Saif Khan)[1] at the head of four thousand horsemen and some camels laden with kitchen

1. Saif Khan is named on p. 433 of the ' 'Alamgirnamah.' On his return from Gwaliyar he went to Agrah as Governor. He was the son of Tarbiyat Khan, one of Shahjahan's *bakhshih*. He died 1095 H. (1683-84) ('M.-ul-U.' ii. 479).

utensils and the other necessaries for a journey, it being announced that he was about to escort Dara to the fortress of Gwaliyar.[1]

Those executioners of tyranny and barbarity arrived at the garden of Khizrabad at seven o'clock at night. They entered the room where the afflicted prince was walking up and down repeating the words referred to: *Muhammad mara mi-kushad, ibn-ullah mara jan mi-bakshad*. They laid hands upon him, and, showing neither compassion nor respect, flung him to the ground and cut off his head. Leaving the body to welter in its blood, they carried the head with all haste to Aurangzeb's presence. It was then eight o'clock at night, and he was in the garden of the palace. Such was the tragic and lamentable fate meted out to the unhappy prince Dara, first-born and heir to the Mogul empire, loved and cherished by his father, Shahjahan, and respected by the people. Neither his good qualities nor his rank sufficed to deliver him from the evil designs of Aurangzeb, nor from the ill-effects of his own bad qualities.

When Aurangzeb learnt that the head of Dara had arrived, he ordered it to be brought to him in the garden on a dish, with the face cleaned of the blood on the surface and a turban on the head [259]. He called for lights to be brought so that he might see the mark borne by the prince on his forehead, and might make sure that it was the head of Dara, and not that of another person. After he had satisfied himself, he told them to put it on the ground, and gave it three thrusts in the face with the sword he carried by way of staff, saying, 'Behold the face of a would-be king and emperor of all the Mogul realms. Take him out of my sight.'[2]

He gave secret orders to place it in a box, to be sent by runners to the eunuch Atbar can (I'tibar Khan), who had charge of Shahjahan's prison, with orders to deliver it to him (Shahjahan)

1. The procession through Dihli took place on September 8,1659, and the execution in the night between the 21st and 22nd Zi,l Hijjah, 1069 H. (September 10, 1659). Dara was a little under forty-six (lunar) years of age ('Tarlkh-i-Muhammadi, and 'Alamgirnamah,' p. 433). Manucci is in substantial agreement with Muhammad Ma'sum in his 'Fatuhat-i-'Alamgiri' (Ethé, 'Catalogue of India Office Library,' 340, col. 130), chap. lii., as translated in Elliot-Dowson, 'Muhammadan Historians,' vii. 198.
2. In Sloane MS., No. 811, fol. 14*a*, it is said that, on Dara's head being brought to him, Aurangzeb stamped on the face, when 'the head laft a long *ha, ha, ha*! in the hearing of all, I, J. Cambell, present.

when seated at table. It was to be offered in his name as a *plât*. This was planned by Aurangzeb with great glee, to avenge himself for the love lavished on Dara and the little account made of himself. It was as if he said: 'Now has your love come to an end; he that was despised is lord of the empire, and the favourite gone down into death.' After the head had been sent off, Aurangzeb ordered the interment of Prince Dara's body in the sepulchre of the Emperor Humayun. On that night Roshan Ara Begam gave a great feast.

On receipt of Aurangzeb's orders, I'tibar Khan, to comply with them, waited until the hour when Shahjahan had sat down to dinner. When he had begun to eat, I'tibar Khan entered with the box and laid it before the unhappy father, saying: 'King Aurangzeb, your son, sends this *plat* to your majesty, to let him see that he does not forget him.' The old emperor said: 'Blessed be God that my son still remembers me.' The box having been placed upon the table, he ordered it with great eagerness to be opened. Suddenly, on withdrawing the lid, he discovered the face of Prince Dara. Horrified, he uttered one cry and fell on his hands and face upon the table, and, striking against the golden vessels, broke some of his teeth and lay there apparently lifeless. Begam Sahib and the other women present began to wail, beat their breasts, tear their hair, break their ornaments, and rend their garments.

Then I'tibar Khan removed the head. When the old man recovered consciousness he began to pluck out his beard till it was all bleeding, and to beat his face; then, dissolving into a flood of tears, he raised both hands to heaven and said these words [260]: 'Coda teri rasa' (*Khuda! teri riza*)—that is to say, 'My God, Thy will be done.' At this time there came in various women and carried off Begam Sahib, who had swooned. They also removed the aged emperor. I leave out any consideration of the affliction of the father, who loved Dara so tenderly, and of Begam Sahib, who thus saw the lifeless head of the brother she doated upon, for I profess only to write of outward events and not to explain inner feelings.

Following the orders of Aurangzeb, I'tibar Khan then sent the head of Dara to be buried in the sepulchre of Taj Mahal, his mother, which is opposite the palace, as I have said. This (the queen's death) was one of the greatest sorrows endured by the emperor Shahjahan in all his life, as many a time he had declared to the nobles. This is why he built this mausoleum opposite to his palace, thinking by a sight of the tomb to dissipate the pain he felt at the death of his beloved wife, Taj Mahal. But after the head of his beloved son was buried in the same place his sorrows were redoubled, and became so poignant that in a short space his life came to an end. The eunuch I'tibar Khan made a report to King Aurangzeb of what had passed, with all the details, whereby he and Roshan Ara Begam received great delight.

Aurangzeb ordered his men to bring into the palace the lovely Jani Begam, daughter of Dara and of Nur Mahal Begam (who with her own hands took poison, as I have described). When the unfortunate young lady saw the throne of his murderer placed in the palaces where her father had sat, she began to distil from her eyes the tokens of her grief with such deep feeling that her life began to waste away. She was badly treated by Roshan Ara Begam, who incessantly recalled to her the memories of the dead. When Aurangzeb found that the girl was wasting away, he forwarded her to the fortress of Agrah to be made over to King Shahjahan and Begam Sahib. By beholding her the old emperor's sorrows were in part alleviated; Begam Sahib was pleased with Jani Begam's beauty, a reproduction of lost originals; and she herself was delighted at finding herself free from the sight of him who had killed her father, and out of the hands of a cruel enemy, Roshan Ara Begam.

Aurangzeb also sent for the two second wives of Dara—that is to say, the inconstant Udepuri, a Georgian by race, and the faithful Ranadel (Ra'na-dil), a Hindu by birth. Udepuri obeyed and appeared [261] in the presence of Aurangzeb, who made her his wife, and by her he had the prince Kam Bakhsh.[1] But Ra'na-dil—that is to say, 'Clear-heart'—sent to ask the king why he wanted to see her. They answered her that the king wished to take her to wife, since the law thus directed that the wives of a dead elder brother belonged to the living younger brother. On hearing this reply, she sent to inquire with what in her was he enamoured. The king sent word that he had an affection for her lovely hair. Owing to this answer, she cut off

1. Kam Bakhsh, the fifth and youngest son of Aurangzeb, was born on the 10th Ramazan, 1077 H. (March 6,1667). His mother was Bae Udepuri ('Ma,asir- i-'Alamgiri,' p. 538).

her hair and sent it to Aurangzeb, saying that here was the beauty that he longed for, while she wished to live in solitude. But Aurangzeb, who wanted to marry her, sent once more to say that her beauty was great, that he would count her as one of his wives. She ought to assume that he was that same Dara. Not one point should be omitted in the pre-eminence due to a queen, nor in her rights as sovereign lady, being, as she was, wife of his brother.

But the brave Ra'na-dil went into her apartments, and taking a knife, slashed her face all over, and collecting the blood in a cloth, sent it to Aurangzeb, saying that if he sought the beauty of her face it was now undone, and if her blood gratified him he was welcome. Encountering such resolution, Aurangzeb ceased his solicitations, yielding high esteem to her, and treating her with the courtesy deserved by her constancy. This Ra'na-dil was of humble birth, a public dancing-girl belonging to King Shahjahan, with whom Prince Dara fell in love through her exceeding beauty, and wanted to take her to wife. The emperor, his father, was opposed to this, not wishing to give offence to Nur Mahal, the principal wife of Dara. The prince took the matter so much to heart that he began to fade away from this passion, and at last reached almost the last gasp. 'When Shahjahan saw the extremity of the prince, his son, he consented to his taking her as wife. By this she felt she had been so honoured, that on the death of her prince she would accept of no other husband. For the little time afterwards that she lived no one ever saw her in lively spirits or giving any sign of pleasure.

After the death of Prince Dara, the common people composed a song about Fortune and the little durability of its glories, it having placed Aurangzeb on the throne, made Shahjahan a prisoner, and decapitated Prince Dara [262]. It said: 'In turn it changed the *faqir's* (Aurangzeb's) cowl, and beheaded the prince in passing.' When Aurangzeb heard about this ballad, he ordered an announcement to be made that no one should sing it under penalty of losing his tongue. But the song was so pitiful that almost everybody sang it in concealment.

Now I deal with our departure from Bhakkar. After surrendering the fortress, we made over the treasure and the unhappy princes, the little sons of Sulaiman Shukoh, of whom nothing more was ever heard, and it seems as if by order of Aurangzeb they were got rid of within the fortress. After fifteen days the eunuch and all the people in the fort embarked in some boats, and we voyaged by the river to Multan against the stream, but with a favourable wind. In four-and-twenty days we reached the said city, then governed by Lascar Can (Lashkar Khan).[1] He sent an invitation to our eunuch to honour him by dining at his house. But the eunuch replied that he would have liked it much, but the haste he was in did not allow of his accepting. He suspected some treachery, and it seems as if his heart gave him a presage of what was to befall him, as I shall relate.

At this city of Multan we provisioned ourselves for a start by land to the city of Dihli, distant five-and-twenty days' journey. One day a Portuguese, by name Agostinho Dias, begged me to abandon the company of the eunuch, because he knew of a certainty that there existed an order of Aurangzeb for his seizure and execution. We quitted Multan, and in ten days reached the city of Lahor, then governed by Khalilullah Khan. Our eunuch settled himself in a house of his own, which was on the river bank. His men scattered in various directions, there not being enough room in the above house. We Europeans were at a distance of half a mile from Primavera (Basant).

On the third day after our arrival he (Basant) sent for me, but I did not go, as it was already evening. By another messenger he told me to come to him very early in the morning. At daybreak I mounted my horse, and on the road I met a former servant of mine called Delavar (Dilawar), who asked me where I was going. I replied that I was going to the eunuch's house. At this he fell into a fright, and said that for God's sake I must not go. For everybody [263] said that the eunuch would most certainly be killed on that day, and I could easily notice the changes in the city, the soldiers and troopers being posted at so many places. He demanded with much insistence that I should turn back, and reflecting a little, I remembered the advice of Agostinho Dias. In spite of this, the love and the gratitude I felt to the eunuch impelled me to go on to his house without considering the danger.

1. Lashkar Khan (Jan Nisar Khan) was the son of Zabardast Khan. Towards the end of Shahjahan's reign he was Governor of Kashmir, and 'Alamgir, in 1068 H., transferred him to Multan. He was successively Governor of Tattah, Bahar, Multan again, ending as Mir Bakhshi. He died in 1081 H. (1670-71) ('Ma,asir-ul-Umaru,' iii. 168).

Pricking on my steed, I shortly reached the house. Going within, I sat down by Khojah Basant, finding him somewhat perturbed, and a few only in his company. He said to me softly that he had something to say to me. At this moment there appeared in the distance several bodies of horse with banners displayed. All of a sudden there came a horseman to the eunuch, and, addressing him politely, said: 'Khalilullah Khan sends many compliments to your excellency, and intimates that he has received the king's order for your excellency to come forthwith into the city, to a house already prepared for you where you may remain in perfect safety.'

With equal civility the eunuch replied: 'I am only a passerby; I go to the royal presence, nor have I anything to do with the city; I return many thanks for Khalilullah Khan's kindness.' The messenger started off with the reply, and the eunuch, seeing that troops were appearing, became a little bit frightened. He asked me if I could produce my men without delay. I replied that there must be some delay, and that they could not arrive in time, owing to their being so far away. At this point the soldiers present in the room, after whispering into each other's ears, rose one by one and went out. I remained seated along with ten persons, who were house-servants, and, foreseeing the danger, I was anxious to leave, but the pride of a youth devoid of experience hindered me, and I wanted to see the end of it and what would happen.

Then came another message like the first, but more urgent, with this detail; that if he did not give heed to it he ran in danger of his life. But the eunuch gave the same answer, and the infantry and cavalry continued to draw in [264] nearer. During this time the eunuch was looking on calmly at all that was taking place outside, for the place where we were was a little elevated, with a view of the river sands. It had the shade of some great trees, and was enclosed all round with a low wall. On the bank of the river, near the wall and below our position, stood a relation of the eunuch Primavera (Basant) on horseback, lance in rest, waiting to give up his life if need arose.

When the third message came with great urgency, begging the eunuch for God's sake to come into the fort in obedience to the king's order, adding the intimation that it was his last warning, he answered not at all. We saw the messenger start off at a run, and it was no joking matter, for the cavalry continued to advance, and drawing their swords shouted to the messenger, who heard not, through the uproar that had already arisen. The house was encircled by a number of infantry, while on the river sands several squadrons rode from different directions, discharging arrows that fell like rain in the place where we were. The cavalier related to the eunuch, finding that the thing was serious, began to skirmish, pushing his horse at those squadrons, with his lance at the charge, until he got stuck in a marshy place full of mire, where, unable to move, he was killed by the arrows.

The infantry tried to scale the wall, but we defended ourselves and prevented them from climbing over. Among others, we killed the kotwal's son, whereat being enraged they set upon us with still greater fury, and one resolute man leapt over behind the eunuch, and at once cut off his head. Primavera (Basant) had been resisting vigorously on the other side. Many more scrambled over and began to cut down the few of us found here and there. The man that cut off the eunuch's head and some others came against me with great rage, and seeing that our defence was overcome, I went straight to them, and, throwing my sword on the ground, stepped two paces to the front. Placing myself humbly before them, I lowered my head and said: 'Slay me, slay me!' and, shutting my eyes, I awaited the blow. But finding it came not, I lifted my head, and saw a soldier of the same troop of the enemy standing between us two. With hands extended, he was begging on behalf of God that they should not kill me [265]. But the other most angrily, his raised sword dripping with blood, ordered him to get out of the way. He who was pleading for me said: 'First kill me, and spare this other.' My assailant, seeing the determination of his fellow-soldier, went off to find someone else, and left me alone. He who saved me took me by the hand and led me away, saying: 'Come with me; I want to deliver you and place you in safety.' But I, knowing the instability of the Mahomedans, said to him that as he wanted to kill me, he need practise no deception on me, as I was ready for my fate; there was no need to remove me from that place; but if he wanted to kill me, he could do it where we were. Seeing what was in my mind, he sheathed his sword, and gave me his word not to hurt me, but at the cost of his life would prevent others doing so, and take me to a place of safety.

We came forth by a postern-gate, when we saw some thirty men with swords in their hands, who came at me, saying: 'Let us kill him; he, too, is of the eunuch's force.' The man with me then laid one arm upon me, and, waving the other hand, demanded in the king's name that they should not kill me nor lay hands on me. But they were keen to plunder me, and told him he had become my advocate simply to strip me himself; but, grieve him as it might, they meant to kill me and appropriate my clothes. Recognising their purpose and seeing them approach, I took off my turban there and then, and the rest of my vestments, being left with nothing but my under-drawers and my shirt. I threw the clothes to them, and my defender conducted me a little farther; then he said I might go on in security, as I was now out of danger. But just as I imagined I was free there came towards me a soldier, a Hindu rustic, holding a drawn sword, who, with many abusive terms and threats, requested me to make over my shirt to him. Enraged at finding myself amidst so much persecution and so many affronts, I said he might kill me if he liked, but I would never give him the shirt. Overwhelming him with abuse, I provided him with cause for despatching me; but he did not want to damage the shirt, so he allowed me to live. In the end I decided to give up the shirt, so I took it off in a rage, rather than lose my life. With my head sunk, I went on my way, running considerable danger, although stripped naked and full of grief and shame. I sought [266] the house of one of my friends, a professing Mahomedan, whose name was Dulah (? Dulha), a man of learning, from whom I had received much kindness. On my way a woman met me and offered me a sheet with which to cover myself, saying that when I got home I could send it back to her. But, not willing to be indebted to her, I declined, and went on my way in the same pitiable state. When I was only a little distance from my friend's house I saw coming towards me the captain of infantry, whose teeth I had broken with a stone. He recognised me, but took compassion on my plight, and lowering his head, made no attempt to do me harm. Thence in a few more steps I got into the house of my friend Dulha, to whom I recounted all that had happened to me. He welcomed me with great warmth, accorded me full rights of hospitality, and gave me clothes and food. I did not forget to render thanks to God for all His mercies, and for deliverance from so many perils.

This affair happened at eight o'clock in the day, and my servants removed my horse to where my men were, and gave them the melancholy news of my death. All my friends were much afflicted; and they sent off one of their number, called Ignacio Gomens, the one best liked by and the most intimate with me, to the site of the affray to make a search for my body. They instructed him to bring it back, so that they all jointly might inter me in some convenient spot and commend my soul to God, seeing that there was no priest. Thus we were used to do when any of our friends died. All of them said, and were quite certain, that I must be dead. On arriving at the place of death, Ignacio Gomens found eleven dead bodies, with the eunuch's headless trunk. The head had been carried away to lay before Khalilullah Khan, who was eager to satisfy his wrath and avenge himself for the indignity that had been done him. Ignacio Gomens came back and reported what he had seen, and that my body was not forthcoming. My friends supposed that after my death the Mahomedans had, without a doubt, thrown me, a Christian, into the river. So they decided they would all go the next day in search of my body, and give it burial. But I, through God's favour, was still alive.

At six in the evening I left the house of my friend Dulha, and took my road to the place where my followers were with much quietness, rendering thanks to our Lord. On arriving [267] close to them, I knew them all, but they did not recognise me, although they looked at me. Then, all of a sudden, I gave a shout, whereupon they knew my voice and came running with open arms towards me, unable to utter a word by reason of exceeding joy. They all began to weep with content, and after a rest, I related in detail all that had happened to me on that day, and how God, out of His infinite compassion, had been my deliverer.

The following day we received a message from Khalilullah Khan directing us to proceed to court to the king's presence, where we should be well received. By this we were made very contented. With us he sent a captain and thirty troopers; and in their train we reached in eight days the town of Cerend (Sihrind), which means 'Head of India,' as it divides the province of Lahor from Hindustan. Before our entry into the town we saw, in a field a little apart from the gate, some fifteen corpses. Asking whose they were, they replied that they were those of Jiwan Khan, and his relations and servants. After making over to Aurangzeb at Dihli the prince Dara, they had received this reward, That same king gave orders to the governor of the fortress of Sihrind that when Jiwan Khan and his men should arrive on their way to their home, he should have them stoned in this field by all the populace, and thus be both rewarded and slain (a most fitting chastisement for his ingratitude). This gave us all great pleasure, and the Mohamedans themselves uttered a thousand curses over the corpse of Jiwan Khan.

From this town (Sihrind) we went on towards the court, and arrived at Dihli in seven days, where we learnt that the king was much affected by the death of our eunuch, Primavera (Basant), his orders having been to seize, but not to kill him. But Khalilullah Khan excused this excess, writing to the king that his death was necessary, because it was known that he meant to go into Srinagar territory, where Prince Sulaiman Shukoh was, taking with him two thousand fighting men, hardy troops, and the best of the Europeans that Dara had left in the fortress of Bhakkar. Without a doubt, if the eunuch had obtained free passage, we should all have gone to find Prince Sulaiman Shukoh.

After three days [268] we were presented to Aurangzeb. He was very anxious for us to enter his service, recognising the fidelity and valour with which we had served Dara, and that among his own people he could not meet with such fidelity and stubbornness. Therefore, he now fixed four rupees a day for every European, and for me five. My companions accepted his service, but I did not wish to do so, through the antipathy I had to him, and the point of honour I cherished of not serving under the murderer of my master. I communicated to the king my non-acceptance of employment. He caused me to be sent for once more, and asked why I did not accept service with him; did I want higher pay than he offered? I replied to him that I would willingly enter into his employ, but I longed to return to my native land, years having elapsed in absence from it; and thus he allowed me to leave.

Learning that Prince Shah Shuja' had entrenched himself in the province of Bengal, and that to overcome him was most difficult, Aurangzeb, a little time after our arrival in Dihli, ordered Daler Khan to proceed with some fresh troops and cannon, manned by my companions, as a reinforcement to Mir Jumlah in his contest with the above-named prince. At the same time he wrote to the rajahs, or petty kings, and the great governors that all must lend their aid—in men, arms, and money; in short, everything that was necessary to Mir Jumlah. They must so continue to aid him until the prince was taken or expelled from the kingdom. With the reinforcements sent by Aurangzeb, and the assistance given by the petty rajahs and the governors, Mir Jumlah attacked Shah Shuja' with such violence that he was reduced to the last stage of desperation. For poor Shah Shuja', having written letters to many quarters, received no answer to please him. Everyone feared Aurangzeb. Shah Shuja' himself reflected on what his brother had done to their father, Shahjahan, and their two brothers, Dara and Murad Bakhsh, and the victories he had won; and prognosticated similar ill-luck for himself, and saw that, were he to fall into the hands of the 'poor *faqir*,' now become a king, he might count his days as numbered.

He therefore resolved to send his son, Sultan Bang,[1] to the King of Arracao (Arakan) [269], a heathen, otherwise known as Mogo (Magh), beseeching him most earnestly to afford aid in his distress; if he did not agree to that, would he, at the least, consent to receive him and his men within his territory until the season came for a voyage to Persia or to Mouca (? Makkah, Meccah)? When fortune should again be kind to him, he would hereafter recompense him for this favour. The King of Arakan received the prince Sultan Bang with much courtesy and kindness, and after a few days sent him back to his father with a number of boats called *jalias*,[2] which are small galleys commanded by Portuguese subjects of the King of Arakan, inhabitants of Chatigao (Chatganw) on the frontier of that kingdom, where its boundary runs with that of the Moguls. Prince Shah Shuja' was highly satisfied at acquiring so bold a friend, one so powerful as not to be afraid of Aurangzeb, the reason of which we will recount hereafter (I. 270). Finding by this time that he was no longer able to resist Mir Jumlah, and that on every side he was hemmed in, he resolved to quit Bengal, he and his family, with all his treasures.

---

1. *Bang*. Can this be his second son, Sultan Buland Akhtar? The Dutch, in 'Dagh Register, anno 1661,' p. 115, use the form 'Bon Sultan,' and call him the eldest son.
2. For *jalia*, see Yule, second edition, 362, a kind of galley or war-boat.

He took ship at the city of Daca (Dhakah), which is on the boundary of Bengal, on the bank of a very large river. But there was much confusion and great hurry, caused by the necessity under which he lay. For Mir Jumlah did all that was possible to seize him. In these straits the women, who, according to the custom, ought not to allow themselves to be seen in public, so as not to seem immodest or be considered polluted, sat there in the view of everybody. Being a new thing this raised great compassion in the beholders, and caused much sorrow to the prince. In one boat were two hundred and fifty ladies, the most lovely in his harem, mingled with soldiers and boatmen. In desperation he ordered the boat to be sunk, as was done, without reflecting on the people in it, or the treasure loaded in it, or the rich jewels the ladies were wearing.

Another mishap overtook the prince. This was that the boat commanded by Manoel Coelho, containing the larger part and the most exquisite of his treasures, went ashore on the coast of Arakan and became a total loss. Old Manoel Coelho did this on purpose, and thieved everything. After all these afflictions, and various others encountered by this unfortunate prince in his flight, they arrived in the kingdom of Arakan, where they were well received by the Magh king, with many demonstrations of affection. Here Shah Shuja' remained, in expectation of the season for getting to Persia or to Meccah.

The kingdom of Arakan adjoins that of Bengal to the east, and on its border has, as its maritime frontier, Chatganw (Chittagong). Once on a time many Europeans lived there, men of various nations, principally Portuguese [270], and many indigenous to the country, who were all Christians. These inhabitants inflicted great damage on the lands of Bengal, and, penetrating with their boats into all parts of that province, carried off men, women, and children, gold and silver; and when they could get them, they did not hesitate to carry off babes at the breast along with their mothers. When these cried at night, they would, with unheard of cruelty, snatch them from their mothers' arms and throw them into the sea. They lived with such lawlessness that it would take much space if I attempted to record their misdeeds. I say in one word all that need be said; they were unworthy not merely of the name of Christians, but of men. The King of Arakan relied much on this class, and made little account of the kings his neighbours, both from the bravery of the aforesaid men, also from the nature of his country. No one can enter this territory with an army, the ground being marshy, with impenetrable jungles and mighty rivers full of alligators. If this had not been so, the Mogul would have conquered this kingdom and that of Pegu equally with that of Siao (Siam), the which are conterminous with one another on his (the Mogul's) frontiers. Arakan is between them and the Mogul territory. In the kingdoms of Arakan and Pegu there are *macoreos*,[1] thus called, which are sudden floods that at certain seasons overflow the country with great velocity, so that a horse galloping its hardest cannot escape. In less than half an hour more than twenty leagues of ground are flooded. The soil is fertile, yielding abundantly and luxuriantly; but the inhabitants are as barbarous as the tigers, elephants, rhinoceroses, and buffaloes which dwell in its jungles.

PEGU

There remains a little for me to say about the kingdom of Pegu. This kingdom was independent, without any king, till there arose a kind of people called Baramas (Burmans), who go about with half the body painted. These men made themselves masters of the kingdom and of many other petty principalities, subduing and conquering so many territories that they placed one frontier over against China, another at Siam, and another at Arakan. This kingdom is very, rich in rubies, emeralds, gold, *latao* (? tin), copper, lead, iron, lac, honey, wax, sulphur, oil from trees and the earth, and has quantities of ivory. The Burman king takes no tribute from his vassals, and trades by sea with all the nations of Europe. He receives presents, but returns the double of what he receives, which is the object sought by the giver.

In this kingdom the priestly class, like that of Siam, call themselves *Talapoes*,[2] who make profession of three virtues—that is to say, chastity, humility, and poverty. They wear a yellow alb with a stole of the same colour, a scarlet mantle and cap. They

1. *Macareos* (see Yule's 'Glossary,' second edition, 527), a word of doubtful origin, applied to what is now called a *bore*, or tidal wave.
2. *Talapoes* (see Yule's 'Glossary,' second edition, 890, under 'Talapoin'), a word used by Portuguese and other Europeans for Buddhist monks.

are much venerated by everybody, and all that they have they give to the necessitous. The women of the Burmans go almost naked, for [271] they wear no more than a veil of cloth all open in front, and walk with an immodest gait. At marriage the men buy their wives, and can eject the woman from their house whenever they like, and marry another. The wife can do the same. They venerate their king as God. When the nobles have any application to make to him, they speak lying flat with their face on the ground. Should perchance the king order any prince or governor to be lain, a soldier is sent from the royal dwelling, and at a time when the other is seated in audience the soldier appears with a banner and reads the sentence. On beholding the king's signature the condemned man receives the congratulations of his relations and friends, seeing that his sovereign has done him this signal favour of recollecting him. Coming close up to the soldier, he himself bares his throat for the blow.

It is a kingdom governed by the pen, for not a single person can go from one village into another without a paper or writing, whereby the government is made most easy. This Burman king adorns himself with many titles, namely: 'Emperor of Emperors in the East, King of Kings in the West, Perfection of all Justice, First in Glory, Greatness, and Majesty, Noble in Grandeur, Crystalline in Simplicity, Firmament of all the Virtues, a Saturn in elevation, a Jupiter in good fortune, a Mars in valour, a Sun in intelligence, a Mercury in knowledge, a Venus in beauty, a Moon in abundance, Possessor of all others' possessions, Conqueror of all whom he beholds, Dominator of ebb and flood, he who cut off the head of the invincible Viravalamo, Lord of the Golden Hall and of the White Elephant.'

Among all the races of India there is none which has books of laws. But these Burmans keep books of the ordinances, applications, arguments, sentences, and appeals before the king's tribunal. It happened once to a Portuguese that he had bought a ruby of great value. He meant to sell it to the King of Seilao (Ceylon) at a profit. The lapidary on close examination found it had been joined, and with the consent of the Portuguese separated the one piece from the other and then joined them again as before. The Portuguese went off to lodge a complaint before the King of Pegu, without having recourse to the usual tribunal. The king, who was ignorant of the law, asked the Portuguese whether he would take the sentence he should give, without appealing or complaining elsewhere. The Portuguese, assuming the king to be educated and intelligent, said he was content with any finding the king should announce. His order was that he who had sold the stone should be deprived of both eyes as a cheat, and the Portuguese who bought it should lose one eye for being an inefficient trader [272]. Angered at such a judgment, the Portuguese threw down the stone, and coming out, said: 'A barbarous king, a barbarous sentence.' There is much that might be said of this kingdom, but as I am getting very far from my history, I cannot dilate further on it, having, as it is, quite enough to say of the Mogul empire, which is my text.

Some days after the arrival of Prince Shah Shuja' in the kingdom of Arakan, where he had been conducted with much honour, in conformity with the customs of those kings, to a palace outside the city, he was invited by the king to sit with him. But the prince, although a fugitive and in necessity, would not forsake his dignity, holding himself to be a much greater man than the King of Arakan. The latter could not compare in dignity, refinement, or pleasant habits with even a simple captain among the Moguls. Not liking to go and sit with him, Shah Shuja' sent his son, Sultan Bang, with the excuse that he himself was unwell. The Magh was delighted at the coming of Sultan Bang, expecting that he would offer him many jewels, stones of price, and costly pieces of cloth.

When they had taken their seats, there appeared many dishes of food, among them a long basin of raw buffalo blood, a great delicacy with them. At this the prince was much revolted, and held his nostrils. The king had it placed in front of himself, and collected with his hands what was in the basin and ate it with great relish, licking his lips.

The temerity of this king arrived at such a pitch that he asked for a daughter of Shah Shuja' as wife for his own son. The prince Shah Shuja' awaited nothing but the monsoon season to make a start for Persia or Mecca. Its arrival was delayed, and he began to be irritated at the coarseness of the Arakan king, and his overweening conceit in asking for his (Shah Shuja''s) daugher as wife to his son. He was afraid of some act of violence or insolence. His force of armed men was very small, but he found many dwellers in Arakan, Moguls and Pathans, who showed themselves well inclined towards him. He therefore planned an outbreak, intending to slay the king and take the kingdom, and then advance once more to test his fortune in Bengal, having thus previously made sure of a refuge in case of failure.

He confided this design to some of his people, by whom it was approved. But they were not able to carry out the project with the called-for secrecy, and through the delay they made there was time for the King of Arakan to hear of the plot. He planned the assassination of Shah Shuja' and all his adherents, and to this intent called to him his four principal captains, each of whom had three thousand armed men. On these four men he placed great reliance. Each captain with his three thousand men guarded the king for eight consecutive days, and when each had fulfilled his task, it came round to the first one again. To these he issued orders that one morning at daybreak [273] they should all with one accord shout: 'Long live the King of Arakan! Death to Shah Shuja' and all traitors!' Under cover of this they were to kill everyone. The captains carried out the order of their king, killing everybody they encountered. Upon this news reaching the unfortunate prince Shah Shuja', he tried to save his life by getting on his elephant, hoping that he might thereby impose some respect for his person. But it was grievous to see the fury with which the Maghs came on, throwing everything into disorder, with blows and shouts and cries, some saying, 'Death to Prince Shah Shuja'!' others, 'Death to his son, Prince Bang!' others, 'Slay those traitorous Moguls who fled here from Bengal!' Prince Bang was taken prisoner, while Shah Shuja' with a few men fled into the jungle. He made liberal use of his bags of jewels and pearls, which he scattered among these savages, attempting by use of these valuables to mitigate the rage of the soldiers and gain a free passage for his flight. But the Maghs paid no heed to his proffered wealth; they pursued the poor prince like famishing wolves, cutting his body into pieces, stripping it bare, and plundering all his valuables. Such was the lamentable end befalling Prince Shah Shuja', the first who rose against his father, Shahjahan, the first cause of these wars in the Mogul Empire, the occasioner of so many ills, the raiser-up of so many misfortunes. Enamoured of his own opinion and a slave of his own ideas, we see him end thus miserably, his field of battle the swamps of Arakan, and his only sepulchre the bellies of wolves and tigers.

Prince Bang remained for some time a prisoner, but afterwards he regained his liberty. Owing, however, to his attempting once more some treachery, the Magh ordered his head to be cut off with a hatchet. The women and daughters of Shah Shuja' were carried off to the palace of the king. But owing to the distrust aroused there among the other women of the king, he was obliged to expel them, and they moved as castaways from house to house until their miserable lives came to an end.

Rumours of the misfortune and disgrace of these princes reached the Mogul country through the Dutch factors. By this much-desired intelligence Aurangzeb was made very happy, but there being no certain news nor incontestable evidence of the said prince's death, and aware that the populace in Hindustan are incredulous, he did all he could think of to ascertain the truth. For he suspected that under cover of this news there was some plot for a renewed rising in Bengal. On this account he ordered all the factors then in the city of Agrah to be sent for—namely, the English and the Dutch—also several others, private merchants and the priests. All were examined in much detail as to the case [274], and the circumstances of Prince Shah Shuja'. They all replied that Shah Shuja' and his son were dead. For the Dutch factor, called Jantac (Jan Tak)[1] produced a letter from the Dutch factor in Arakan, wherein were minutely set forth the acts, disasters, and attempts of Prince Shah Shuja' up to his lamentable death.[2] This letter was translated into the Persian tongue, for

1. 'Dagh Register, Casteel Batavia, anno 1661' (edition J. A. van der Chijs, the Hague, 1889), pp. 105, 106: 'Meanwhile, the director, on December 21, 1660, sent your letters to the king and the aforesaid Mierarab (? Mir 'Arab) at Dihli, and subsequently, through letters from the merchant, Jan Tak, at Agrah, he learnt that the king and his chancellor Rarogenaet (Rae Raghunath) had for a month been away on a hunting expedition. '
2. There are several notices of Shah Shuja' in the 1661 volume of the Dutch 'Dagh Register': They hear he has fled into Arracan (p. 5, January 5, 1661). Mir Jumlah replaces him in Bengal (p. 6). The date of flight was June 5, and of arrival in Arracan August 26, 1660 (p. 56). They record that on February 7, 1661, after the Prince's house had been surrounded, he set fire to it and escaped with his family and 300 followers, but his eldest and his youngest sons were captured. With his middle son he made for Tipperah (p. 115, May 16). The news of Shah Shuja''s flight was sent to Mir Jumlah,

the greater assurance of King Aurangzeb. When he had finished its perusal, he raised his hands to heaven and recited this verse:

'Tacabar chunanas que aker care pexemanas
Tavasey chisis que derars azisis'
(Takabbur chunan ast, kih akhirkare pashiman ast;
Tawazu' chiz, I, kih dar 'arsh 'aziz,ist

—that is to say, 'Pride is in the end chastised, Humility is prized even in heaven.' He then ordered grand funeral obsequies, and gave alms, principally to those learned in the faith, praying them to supplicate God for that prince dying in the realm of Arakan, within a heathen and idolatrous land. Similar obsequies were ordered to be performed in all the principal cities of the empire. The cunning fellow made these demonstrations of piety, not for his love to the deceased prince, but to make known to all the people that Shah Shuja' was dead. Thus they would, he hoped, accept him (Aurangzeb) as absolute lord of the Mogul Empire. In spite of all these precautions, there subsisted for a long time in the Mogul kingdom grave doubts about the said prince's death, some affirming that he survived and had reached Persia in mendicant's disguise; others asserting they had seen him in the Mogul

---

and he forwarded it to Aurangzeb (p. 319, October 18). On November 29, (pp. 388, 390) they record that the reported death was told by the Dutch at Dhakah to the Governor, who sent on the news to the Court. Finally, on pp. 520, 521 (December 22, 1661), we have the last account that they record: 'As to the Prince Shah Shuja', of whom it was stated in the former Arracan advices of the 22nd Feb. last that he had taken to flight, it was not known if he were alive or dead. The fact is, however, although there can be no certainty, that he was killed in the first outbreak; but his corpse was rendered unrecognisable by the nobles, in order easier to take their own measures with the valuable jewels he possessed. His three sons, together with his women and daughters, have been captured; the women and daughters are placed in the king's palace, while his sons, after a period of imprisonment, have been transferred to a small house. Daily is the gold and silver that the Arracanese have seized being melted down and delivered into the King's treasure-house.' Khan Khanan (Mir Jumlah) had sent letters to the Arrakan King and Voorburg, the Dutch resident, asking for the delivery of the three sons. The letter had been translated out of Persian into Magh; but no audience had been accorded, and the result was not then known. The envoy had brought 12,000 I.°/a (? rupees) to bribe the nobles.

territory itself; and they named this, that, and the other detail, making the matter so certain that over a great part of the kingdom he was held to be alive, and they looked for his yet becoming king. Nor was there wanting a scribe who disguised himself as the prince Shah Shuja', and went off to the Pathans, where he gained over many people, as I shall relate (II. 148). But these uncertainties and expectations came to an end in time through the evidence of many persons coming from Arakan, who had been present at the unhappy prince's death.

The death of two brothers and of so many other people was not enough to assuage Aurangzeb's thirst for the blood of his relations. Learning that Sulaiman Shukoh, son of Dara, was in safety within the lands, and under the protection of the Rajah of Srinagar, he set to work to have him seized in some way or other. But being quite sure that the Rajah would pay no heed either to his promises and presents or to his threats [275], he planned with Rajah Jai Singh that he should be the intermediary for getting the Rajah of Srinagar to abandon Sulaiman Shukoh.

With this purpose in view, Rajah Jai Singh wrote the Srinagar rajah a letter, saying how advisable it was for him to make over Sulaiman Shukoh to Aurangzeb. Thereby he would secure a friend in Aurangzeb, whom he would find of use sooner or later. From Sulaiman Shukoh nothing was to be hoped, a poor prince, whose father had already lost his head, one who had no means of ever prevailing. On the contrary, Aurangzeb was an absolute monarch, victorious and powerful, who was able to confer favours. If he declined to hear the words of a friend, let him not forget that Aurangzeb had generals, soldiers, and treasure wherewith to attain his just demands. He who protected his enemies was also against him. He (Jai Singh) wrote thus with no other object or desire than to secure peace in the rajah's territory, owing to his love for him and his family, they both being of the same religion.

The Rajah of Srinagar replied to Rajah Jai Singh that on no account could he do this harm to his reputation by making over to his enemy anyone who had sought his protection. He was thankful for Jai Singh's friendship; as for Aurangzeb, he heeded neither his promises nor his menaces. He might inform the Mogul that he had no respect for either his power or his victories. He felt no need for his amity. Let him call to mind the occasion when his father, Shahjahan, sent the small army of thirty thousand horse and one hundred thousand foot into the country of Srinagar! Most of these issued from the said mountains without noses, the rest losing their lives. Further, let him know that he who could cut off noses could equally cut off heads. In this matter Aurangzeb might come to any decision he liked, but he would neither make over, nor permit the making over, to him of the fugitive prince.

On being informed of the rajah's decision, Aurangzeb resolved to make use of the rajahs adjoining Srinagar to create a war against it, seeing he was not capable himself of doing it any harm. With this in view, he sent an order to Rajah Jai Singh [276] that by gorgeous presents and large promises, added to persuasive words, he should act on the minds of the said rajahs, so that they might wage war on the Rajah of Srinagar. He (Aurangzeb) said he would give him (Jai Singh) more territory if only he could compel the Rajah of Srinagar to surrender Prince Sulaiman Shukoh.

The Rajah of Srinagar was an old man with a youthful son. The latter, looking forward to a speedy succession, hoped for favours from Aurangzeb, and opened negotiations for the delivery of Sulaiman Shukoh, in opposition to the wish and opinion of his father. His plan was to make his delivery secretly into the hands of Aurangzeb's men, then actually present at the foot of the hills. Prince Sulaiman Shukoh heard of this plot of the rajah's son, and resolved to absent himself from Srinagar. He seized an occasion of going out shooting, as he ordinarily did, with the intention of making off into Tibet, a large province belonging to Great China. He went away with this intention.

When his departure was reported to the rajah's son, he started after him with a sufficient number of men, giving no information of this project to the rajah his father. Overtaking Sulaiman Shukoh, he seized him, put irons on his feet and handcuffs on his wrists, then transferred his captive to the men of Aurangzeb. He sent by them a message that he had done this act of friendship to the Emperor of the Moguls against the wish of his father. If some day he had need himself of aid and favour, he hoped assistance would not be refused.

The poor fugitive was removed a prisoner to Delhi, where they arrived with him at night. Upon receipt of the report, Aurangzeb ordered him to be locked up in the fortress of

Salimgarh. The next day he ordered the fetters to be taken off his legs, and had him brought into his presence, leaving the brass manacles on his wrists, which many imagined to be of gold. His object was to make sure that it was the real son of Dara, also because he had been told that this prince was endowed in every part with the good gifts of Nature. The tyrant gloated over the sight, this being the last thorn that could prick him; all the rest were either already dead or languishing in prison. The unfortunate Sulaiman Shukoh began to weep, beseeching that his life might be spared. Let the king not forget that he was of his blood. But the heart of Aurangzeb was not so compassionate as to be moved by tears. He inquired from the nobles if of a truth this was Sulaiman Shukoh, and all replied that there was not the least doubt. Then he ordered him to be removed to the fortress of Gwaliyar, there to be given opium-water to drink, as had been done to Murad Bakhsh and Sultan Muhammad. One month after his arrival an order was sent to kill him by poison, and he was buried within the said fortress. This poor prince was the eldest son of Prince Dara [277], and endowed with all the gifts of Nature. He was the person who obtained the first victory over Prince Shah Shuja'. But adverse Fate, joined to the plottings and devices of Aurangzeb, forced him to retire into the hills. There he suffered much in wandering amongst those rough, stony, and impassable mountains, travelling on foot or sometimes upon goats (*cabras*)[1] as is the custom there. Many a time he had to traverse dangerous ravines from one hill to another at the risk of his life, in baskets pulled across by ropes. For several days he had to support himself on wild roots and fruits in default of other food. Then when he believed he was in surety, he was uselessly given over to the teeth of that insatiable beast of prey, for such Aurangzeb may be called, which spared neither great nor small.

The aged Rajah of Srinagar felt greatly the vileness of the deed carried out by his only son, and so great was his sorrow that in a short space he ended his days under the disgrace, saying he would sooner have lost his territory and all his wealth than that his son should be guilty of such an act of infamy. This rajah was a great friend of the Jesuit fathers, and had accorded them leave to build churches, and allowed everyone who chose to

1. Presumably the *yak* is intended.

profess the religion of Christ. I knew two Italian priests, great friends of this rajah, Father Etanilao Malpique, and Father Chesco.[1]

Aurangzeb was still in need of confirmation by the chief *qazi,* who is their supreme pontiff, before he could become absolute monarch and judge in all criminal matters, with power of condemning to death or pardoning whomsoever he pleased. The reason was that the chief *qazi,* and the inferior *qazis* objected to his confirmation during the lifetime of the Emperor Shahjahan, and their sorrow still was fresh for the blood of his brothers that he had shed. He, therefore, created another *qazi* named Abdulbahab ('Abd-ul-wahhab),[2] a man of humble origin, who, being under obligation to him for the dignity thus conferred, confirmed his right to the throne. Reasons for consecrating a king can never be wanting to an unjust judge who seeks only his own interests.

Aurangzeb was weighed down by the thought that, however hard he had worked to establish himself in the realm, there was still one difficulty left. Murad Bakhsh yet lived. Many nobles had friendship and affection for him, and wanted him for king, owing to his renown as good soldier and liberal master. Therefore [278] every month he (Aurangzeb) caused the prince's portrait to be taken, to see if the opium-juice produced any change in his natural complexion, and his face gave any sign of approaching death. But finding Murad Bakhsh's natural robustness overcame the poisonous juice, he made a plan to take his life under the forms of justice. By his death the nobles would be deprived

1. About 1648 Father Stanislaus Malpique, or Malpica, a Jesuit, received permission to build a church from the Rajah of Srinagar (Garhwal) (Müllbauer, 'Geschichte,' 284, quoting the Annual Letter of 1953). Malpique was at Agrah in 1656 when Manucci arrived there (I. 153). Father Chesco is probably the Père Anthoine Ceschini, 'thirty years a missionary in the Mogor,' in Kircher's 'China Illustrata,' as quoted on p. 364 of the French edition of Abraham Roger, 'La Porte Ouverte' (Amsterdam, 1670, quarto).
2. See also II, 145 and III 52. 'Abd-ul-wahhab, a Gujarati *bohrah,* was chief qazi before 1079 H. (1668-69) ('Ma,asir-i-'Alamgiri,' p. 78); but the date of his first appointment is not noted. He died in 1086 H. (1675-76). There is a long biography of him in the 'Ma,asir-ul-Umara,' i. 235. His portrait is one of those we give from OD 45 *reserve,* No. 34 of E. Blochet's list.

of any idea of, or hope for, another king, and he then made sure of his own permanent dominance.

I have already told you (I. 165) how, when Murad Bakhsh was governor of Gujarat province, he took the life of his secretary by a stratagem. Aurangzeb thought this homicide gave a good opening for launching his plot without anyone being able to convict him of injustice or cruelty to a prince so valiant in war, so faithful to his word and oath, so ready in counsel. Privily he sent for the relations of the said secretary, inducing them through a third person to require the life of the prisoner in return for that of their dead relation. They were told that without fail justice would be done, and they would be recompensed in money. Their answer was that since the prince was already ruined they had no desire to stir in past matters. This answer did not please Aurangzeb, for it was one not accordant with his designs, but frustrated his intent. Hitting upon another road, he found out that a cousin of the secretary was still alive, a man ambitious but poor. This man was sent for and the same proposal made, coupled with many promises. This miserable creature accepted the scheme, and went off to lodge a complaint for the death of the secretary, his cousin, at the highest tribunal. The *qazi* had already been instructed by Aurangzeb. The petitioner asked for open justice in the sight of all the people, and required the head of Prince Murad Bakhsh in compensation for the death of his cousin. The deceased was a descendant of Muhammad, a Sayyid by birth, against whom Murad Bakhsh's princely privilege could not be pleaded.

The *qazi* passed sentence according to the instructions received, and to execute it the king sent a company of soldiers from his guard with some of his slaves. When they had arrived at Gwaliyar fortress, they cut off Murad Bakhsh's head in the presence of the complainant and other witnesses. He was interred there and then. Thus came to an end the royal blood of the Mogul, leaving none but Sipihr Shukoh, son of Dara, and the son of Murad Bakhsh, of whom I will speak farther on ('Ezad Bakhsh,' II., 144). Aurangzeb remained absolute master of the whole empire. Thus with the blood of his competitors were assuaged the fears which perturbed the Mogul.

Now it remains to state how this king wreaked vengeance on those who laid hands upon those of royal blood. First of all, he who had claimed the head of Murad Bakhsh issued from the fortress to obtain the promised reward, but never again was he heard of. The slaves who first of all cut off Dara's head, and now that of Murad Bakhsh, never left the fortress but met their fate within it that very day. Then there remained Nazar Beg and Maqbula, captains of the slaves, but they did not long survive. One day Aurangzeb sent for Maqbula, the second captain, and in secret said to him: 'What can I do for you, and what do you expect? The command of the slaves belongs to you, and I had meant to give it to you; but this brute of a Nazar Beg, without tact and overbold, leaves me no peace; and for several reasons I cannot take the office from him. If it is your wish, it lies in your hands to become captain by killing him who unjustly holds the place to your detriment. Tomorrow in my presence, while I am giving audience, kill him, and I forthwith declare you captain.'

The ambition [279] of Maqbula induced him to rely on the king's word, never anticipating what was to happen to himself. Going off home he communicated to his wife, in high delight, what the king had said to him. To effect his design, he provided himself with a dagger, and next day at the audience, when in the king's presence, he stabbed Nazar Beg in the breast with such quietness that he fell dead on the spot. Aurangzeb, feigning ignorance in a matter which he had himself directed, gave a signal to the bystanders, who, with their swords, slashed Maqbula into pieces before he could utter a word in his defence. He did this to conceal his tyranny on the pretext that he (Maqbula) had failed in respect by daring to kill his own officer in his king's presence.

After the death of his brother Dara, Aurangzeb ordered them to bring to his presence Acermaad (Sarmad),[1] the atheist, to whom Dara had been devoted (*ante,* I. 153), and asked him where was his devoted prince. He replied that he was then present, 'but you cannot see him, for you tyrannize over those of your own

1. Sarmad is the author of a collection of quatrains which has been lithographed twice; he was put to death in 1071 H. (1660-61) (see Rieu, 'Persian Catalogue,' 370, 547, 10S9). An account of him appears in 'Ma,asir-ul-Umar,' i. 225, under 'I'timad Khan, 'Abd-ul-qavvi.' An anecdote about him is given by Anand Ram, Mukhlis, in a *tazkirah* (see *Indian Magazine,* May, 1903). His tomb is close to the Jami' Masjid at Dihli (Carr-Stephen, 'Archeology,' p. 255; see also Bernier, edition Constable, 317, and Beale, 'Oriental Biography,' 353).

blood; and in order to usurp the kingdom, you took away the life of your brothers, and did other barbarities.' On hearing these words, Aurangzeb ordered his head to be cut off.

Finding there was now nothing else to be seen to, he ordered his chroniclers to write all his battles, and make recital of his glories—how he vanquished such and such powerful adversaries, with all the events, disasters, and encounters up to his ascending the imperial throne. The chroniclers asked how they should record the causes of his father, Shahjahan, being in prison, of the banishment and death of Shah Shuja', and the deceptions practised on the princes Dara and Murad Bakhsh. The king smiled, and displayed his amazement, and said to them: 'Are you so ignorant as not to know the causes of such obvious and well-known events? Cannot you see that the Mogul Empire was in complete anarchy through the bad government of King Shahjahan, my father, and his desire to make over the state to Prince Dara, an enemy of the Mahomedan faith ? It was a just punishment for the son to lose his life, he being an idolater, while the king was dispossessed of the kingdom and placed in confinement for being incapable of rule. As for the prince Shah Shuja', he was deprived of the kingdom because by his ambition he laid claim to the throne which did not belong to him. Then, having sought refuge in the realm of another, he tried ungratefully to rise against his benefactor, and by losing his life received the merited punishment for his revolt. In regard to Prince Murad Bakhsh, a man of good qualities and an excellent soldier, I am innocent of his death. It was due to the demands of justice. Nor was he fit to reign, for he was a heretic, as I have ascertained since his death. If God made me emperor, it was from no other cause than that I had been ever a faithful defender of the Quran. Against my design and my will, which was to live as a poor *faqir*, I was exalted above other men, because that just Lord, who raises the meek and abases the haughty, had so determined.'

I know quite well that some instructed reader will censure this history as not true, if I say to him that Aurangzeb killed the eunuch Shahbaz. I do not condemn the wisdom of a reader who so judges, for there are some historians who assert that the said eunuch continued alive and went to Bengal. Nor can I much blame those writers, for it was the opinion of many that so it was, as they will see in this my short narrative which I insert here, as it has little concern with what follows.

To accomplish his wrongful acts Aurangzeb [280] had recourse to artifice. After he had become absolute, and Shah Shuja' was ruined, he gave certain orders to one of his eunuchs called Faim (Fahim). This man pretended to be Shahbaz, the eunuch of Murad Bakhsh. and went to live in the province of Bengal. Lands were assigned to him which yielded him a sufficient income to support himself in comfort. He ate and drank and amused himself with pastimes. He was fond of the chase and of conversations with Europeans and other foreigners. He always praised the valour of Murad Bakhsh, and claimed to have been faithful to his prince.

Aurangzeb acted thus solely that foreign nations should not speak against him, and say he had killed a eunuch so prudent and so loyal to his master. Be it known to the reader that if the said eunuch was sent to Bengal it was by reason of its being frequented by many traders of various nations. He was not sent to Gujarat or to the Dakhin for fear that he might be recognised, and then no one would give credit to his assertions. He might certainly have been sent to Kabul or Kashmir; but since in those places there were no traders from foreign nations, like there are in Bengal, he was therefore sent to that region, where to this day he lives, and thus gives further support to his words.

The contests between the brothers which disturbed the Mogul Empire began in the year 1655 (correctly 1658), and lasted till the beginning of 1659. By that time Aurangzeb had become undisputed master of the empire, at the cost of so many of his subjects' lives and of the blood of his brothers. Although the empire is one of the most widespread in the world, still he was not satisfied, as I shall relate in the Second Part. For the proverb is true that 'Plus sunt pote, plus sittiuntur,' or, 'The more one drinks, the more one wants to drink for the things of this world can never satisfy human appetites. What happened to Aurangzeb will be shown along with the history of the Mogul kingdom.

END OF PART I.

ADDITIONAL NOTES AND EMENDATIONS

For most of the matter on which the following notes are founded I am indebted to friendly readers of the first three volumes, such as Messrs. H. Beveridge, Dr. O. Codrington, Dr. G. Cóggiola, W. Crooke, A. G. Ellis, D. W. Ferguson, 'W. Foster, Dr. G. A. Grierson, Colonel Love, the Rev. F. Penny, Messrs W. R. Philipps and G. P. Tate. But I have consulted nearly every one of the books quoted before writing my notes.

INTRODUCTION

Page xx-I withdraw the statement that Father Catrou added the latitudes and longitudes; they appear' in Manucci's text. See vol. ii., pp. 424-431.

Page xxxiv, line 7; page xxxvi, note 12.—The letter does not actually say 'on his way home,' and Mr. Ferguson objects to the identification with Galle in Ceylon.

Page xxxiv, line 15: *publication of this little work.*—The care the Senate took to procure a uniform Italian version of the whole manuscript which exists in the shape of Codex XLV points to an intention of publishing the work. Why this inftention remained unexecuted is not known; In 1782 V. Formaleoni (1752-1797) stated that he meant to bring out a complete edition founded on the Venice codices. See 'Compendio della Storia dei Viaggi,' vol. xvi., Appendix to Book V. of Part II.; Venice, 1782. Parts I. to IV. and the two volumes of pictures, all sent by Tiepolo from Paris, were referred by the Senate to the 'Riformatori' for examination and report on July 24, 1706. Their report was submitted on March 23, 1707, proposing to reduce the whole manuscript into one language (Italian), and to seek means of printing it. On March 26 the Senate held it desirable to print the history, provided there was no burden laid upon the public. A translation into Italian was ordered; and a reward for the author was to be considered and recommended. In April, 1707, there was talk of granting Manucci the title of 'Cavaliere,' but there is no evidence that this was actually conferred. Upon March 28, 1708, the translation of the manuscript was confided to the. Public Professor Cardeira in Padua, a native of Portugal. The completed translation up to the end of Part IV. was presented with a report on June 30, 1712. This report says that the head (*Prior*) of the Printer's Guild fixed the cost of production at 14,000 ducats, and no printing house at Venice would undertake the risk. Nor had Venice any artists who could engrave copper plates; and the Senate rejected the proposal to send the original pictures to Rome, Paris, or Holland for that purpose. However, an offer had been received from Antonio Zambelli, advocate in Venice, to print the work in three years, conditional on a grant of a monopoly for twenty-five years for the printing of law forms. On July 23, the Senate decreed the acceptance of Zambelli's offer, subject to the conditions : (I) that the term be reduced to twenty years; (2) that he furnish security for completing his undertaking; and (3) that each year a different printer be employed, there being six or seven firms already engaged in the printing of such forms. Of what happened subsequently I have no information.

Page xxxv, line 23: *falsi* (?).—This doubtful word is due to a misreading; the correct text is, 'and on the other side that of the renowned prince the Dauphin and his three sons.'

Page xxxvii, line 21.—The second Capuchin manifesto of 1707, in Part V., f. 253, says Father Eusebius came from Surat, and in 1704 had been twelve yars in India. He left Pondicherry in February, 1705, as a passenger in the *Saint Louis*, which reached Port Louis near Lorient in October, 1705; Kaepplin, 557, 659.

Page xliv, line 32.—My statement does not give accurately the present condition of Codex XLV. (Zanetti). It is now bound in two volumes; the first containing Cardeira's transcript of the Italian text in Codex XLIV. (Zanetti); the second a copy of the Italian portion of Part III., followed by a translation into Italian of the rest of Part III. and of Parts IV. and V. (Cóggiola, 'Sulla nuova integrale Pubblicazione,' p. 28).

Page xlv, line 25.—Since I wrote my Introduction the original text of Part V. has been found in the San Marco Library at Venice. I have procured a copy, and collated it with my translation from the Italian version. I am indebted to Dr. Cóggiola for the following description of this original MS. It is Italian MS., Class VI., No. 135, 36 centimetres X 23.50 centimetres, a small in-folio of ninety-two folios (four blank). It is bound in brown leather, not corresponding to that of the old collection, and bears an impression of a lion on the outside, such as is the case with MS. No. XLIV. (Zanetti). This binding is probably that in which it came from India, rather common, and more or less damaged. At the beginning is an unnumbered leaf bearing the words, 'Composto por o autor Monsieur Manouchy de naçao Veniziano nesta Fortaleza St. George de Madrasta pattan.' Below this title is affixed the *ex libris* of the library, bearing the name of Girolamo Venier (librarian) and the year '1722.' The first numbered leaf is blank. The text begins on the *recto* of folio 2 with the title, 'Quinte parte do Reconto da Istoria do Mogol nesta present hera de 1705 no mes de Janeiro do ditto anno, pello autor Nicolao Manucchi Veniziano de Naçao.' There are two interruptions in the numbering of the folios—that is, there are no folios 47, 51, or 52. But this is due to oversight, and there is no lacunal in the text. On the *verso* or folio 66 the text changes from the French into the Portuguese language, and it is in a different handwriting. This writing continues up to folio 90. Next come three unnumbered leaves: the first in Portuguese, the next two in French. The handwriting is again different from either of the two preceding ones. The writing of the French text in this codex is the same as that of the French text in

Codex XLIV. (Part IV. of the History); but the Portuguese portion does not correspond to the handwriting of the Portuguese part of that codex (the end of Part III. and end of Part IV.). As a reason for its non-inclusion in the Zanetti catalogue of 1742, Dr. Cóggiola believes that the volume remained in the hands of the Cardeiras, to whom it had been made over in 1712 for the purpose of translation; and it first appears in the manuscript appendix to the catalogue, prepared at the end of the eighteenth century. This theory is confirmed by the fact that Codex XLV. (Cardeira's Italian translation) now consists of much more than the 740 folios catalogued by Zanetti. This increase is due to the inclusion in it, subsequent to 1741, of the fifth part; and as a consequence Codex XLV. (Zanetti) has now been divided into two volumes under the one catalogue number. From a decree of the Venetian Senate, dated January 19, 1712, it appears that the bound volume of Part V. had been delivered by Father Don Girolamo Buzzacarini, a Regular Cleric, together with a letter from the author, dated Pondicherry, February 20 of the previous year (1711), and some other loose leaves. It was ordered that the whole be sent to the 'Riformatori' to be placed with the volumes previously received; further proposals were to be submitted in regard thereto; and injunctions were given them to recover a small box sent to France, which the Padre asserted had been left at Bagiona (? Bayonne).

Page xlix, line 29.—For *grucs* we should probably read *grues—i.e., gurus*. See a letter of the Inquisitor, Antonio Amaral Coutinho, to the King of Portugal, dated January 26, 1731, in J. da Cunha Rivara, 'Ensaio historico da Lingua Concani,' p. 335; 'os Botos, servidores e *Grous* dos Pagodes.'

Page 1, line 24.—Mr. Philipps, as I think rightly, proposes to substitute 'Manaron Sāmi,' 'the Lord Vishnu.' Compare such place-names as Mannār-kovi, Mannār-gudi, and Mannār-kadu.

Page lv, line 18: *his father's Christian name.*—In the Zeno MSS. in the Marciano, Ital. VII., No. 2,321, last document, is a note by Zibaldone, which states that N. M. was born in 1638 of Pasquaglio M. and Rosa [blank], obscure persons of plebeian origin. Some further details are given; but these are disproved by Manucci's narrative, which must be given the preference. See note 2, page 7, of Dr. Cóggiola's 'Sulla nouva Pubblicazione della Storia del Mogol,' 32 pages; Venice, 1908.

Page Ivi (to follow first paragraph).—Mr. H. G. Keene has asked the question whether N. Manucci was or was not a descendant of the celebrated Venetian printers of that name. Dr. Cóggiola has favoured me with the material for the following note: A. A. Renouard, 'Annales de I'Imprimerie des Aldes,' 3 vols., 1834, vol. iii., pp. 208, 209, accepts the theory that N. Manucci might have been descended from the printer family; while Apostolio Zeno, in 'Notizie intorno dei Manuzi stampatori e alla loro Famiglia,' placed as preface to 'Le epistole familiari di Cicerone gia tradotte da Aldo Manutio,' Venice, 1736, says on p. lxxx,.

'there are still some people who claim to be descendants of the Manuzi family of printers.' But Zeno adds' that with the death of Aldo Manuzio in 1597 the direct line of Aldo and Paolo came to an end, and he did not know if the brothers of Paolo left issue. Finally, the learned bibliographer, A. E. Cicogna, in his 'Delle Inscrizioni Veneziane,' Venice, 1830, vol. iii., p. 71, after mentioning the remarks made by Foscarini about N. Manucci, says expressly that the traveller was of a different family from that of the printers. Cicogna promised to prove this assertion at a later stage, but unfortunately his book was never completed; it is to be supposed, however, that he had evidence to prove his case, although the nature of it is not known. Thus the question cannot be determined finally at present.

Page lii (to follow the second paragraph).—Mr. A. Constable refers me to a book in the 'Univers' series, entitled 'Inde,' by A. P. Dubois de Jancigny and L. A. Xavier Raymond (Paris, 1845), for some reproductions of the Manucci paintings. There are eighty-four illustrations in the book referred to. One only is with certainty taken from the volume, O. D. 45, Réserve—*viz.*, No. 56, facing p. 340; a single figure, the portrait of Shivā Ji, from No. 39 in M. Blochet's list. Perhaps the portrait or Mir Jumlah on p. 302 is the central figure from No. 29 (Blochet). One of our illustrations, No. xxxv. (Blochet, No. 39), Rājah Shivā Ji, has been reproduced in full in L. Langlès' 'Monuments Anciens et Modernes' (Paris, 1821), I. 250.

Page lvii, line 23 (1667), line 24 (1667, 1668).—At these places Mr. Ferguson prefers '1666' and '1666, 1667.' I think the difficulties are about equal, whichever of these sets of dates is adopted.

Page lix.—To the personal details in paragraph 1 may be added the curious fact that in 1738 there was a Manrico Manuchy present at Madras. Colonel H. D. Love, R.E., has kindly favoured me with a photograph of a Portuguese auction certificate of November 7, 1738, relating to a small house worth thirty-seven *pagodas*, bought by this man, the vendor being Father Thomas, Capuchin. The document is attested by Francisco Seguiera Peixoto, notary, and two justices, N. Morse and W. Monson. In his will, dated May 18, 1753 (proved November 13, 1753), Francis Conteofre of Madras leaves money for the benefit of the soul of his brother-in-law, Manricio Manuchy, 'as I became his heir by his dying intestate.' 'Wills proved in Mayor's Court. Madras,' Range 288, vol. lx., p. 37. Documents recently traced at Venice show that N. Manucci had a brother, Andrea. On April 7, 1707, this man petitioned for clemency to be extended to his son, Nicolò, who had been condemned to the pillory and the galleys. On April 19, out of consideration for the uncle, the Senate recommended the grant of a pardon, and on the 29th the Council of Ten ordered the young man's release. Again, on March 27, 1708, the 'Riformatori'. support Andrea Manucci's application for 300 ducats to meet the expense of sending a son to India, his own poverty preventing him from meeting the cost.

Apparently this is another son, and not the above-named Nicoló, who was in trouble and had been condemned to the galleys.

Page lxii, line 25: *Ex-Jesuit*.—Mr. Philipps objects to this expression, because bishops taken from the regular clergy did not formally abandon their monastic orders.

Page lxiv, first paragraph: *Manucci's House in Madras*.—On a review of the evidence it would seem that Manucci held two adjoining plots under separate titles. Colonel H. D. Love, R. E., agrees in this; and he tells me that in November, 1696, reference is made to certain 'Parriar Houses . . . next without the mud walls to the eastward of Mr. Manuchy's Garden.' Colonel Love has been so good as to furnish me with the subjoined tracing from a map marked. 'Prospect of Fort St. George and Plan of the City of Madras actually surveyed by order of the late Governor, Thos. Pitt, Esq.' (no date). He considers it was made about 1709; the scale is apparently twenty inches to the mile. The site of Manucci's house is at the south end of the present Popham's Broadway at its junction with the China Bazaar.

Page lxiv, note 23.—On going more minutely into the evidence, Mr. Penny modifies his statement into (line 2) 'up to 1675.' When old Tom Clarke settled at Fort St. George in 1641, he built his house in the north-west corner of the outer enclosure of the Fort, commonly called the White Town. Near by was a gate into the old Black Town, and this acquired the

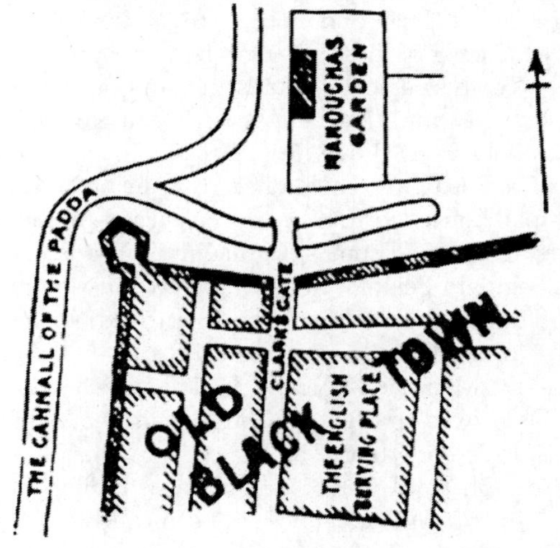

name of 'Tom Clarke's Gate.' In 1675 (owing to the French occupation of San Thome, 1672-1674), a wall and a gate fit for mounting guns were erected. Clarke's house was pulled down. Young Tom Clarke was indemnified, and he bought the lease of some ground just outside the north-west corner of Old Black Town, between his old site and the company's garden in Muttiaipetta. When in

1690-1692 Governor Yale built a wall on the west and north sides of Old Black Town, the name of 'Tom Clarke's Gate' was transferred to a gate in this new wall. Clarke's second house was the one acquired by Manucci on his marriage, and designated by his name in the map of 1709. In May, 1677, Thomas Clarke the younger claimed that his father Thomas was the first settler at Madras (*c.* 1641) (Wheeler, 'Madras,' i. 90, and India Office Factory Records, vol. i.).

Page lxv: *Foscarini's 'Venetian Literature.'*—There is another work on this subject by Gianantonio Moschini, 4 vols., 4to., 1806. In vol. ii., p. 235, he says that as to Manucci he can only echo Zanetti and Foscarini because the work is one of the codices 'which passed into the hands of the French in 1797.' He expresses a hope that as some return the French will make use of this treasure and lay it before the public.

Page lxxvii, add after second paragraph: *Manucci and the French.*—There is possibly an allusion to Manucci in Francois Martin's 'Mimoires' ('Archives Nationales,' Serie T*, 1169), folio 521, *verso.* under date June, 1691: 'We had at that time some letters from Monsieur Deslandes, who dwelt on the difficulty of getting a *farman*. As we had connections with the Mogul court, it was his idea that better success could be obtained there. I wrote about it to a doctor in the prince's service, but without results. We were obliged to resume our efforts with the Sultan (the prince) at Dhaka.'

We have other evidence that Manucci proved of use to the French. In the 'Mémoire sur la Compagnie des Indes' ('Bibliothéque Nationale MS, Français,' No. 6231, f. 30, *verso*), we are' told in January. 1703, the French feared an attack by the Dutch upon Pondicherry. Certain steps were taken, and much of the company's property was placed in charge of the English. Monsieur Martin also set 'Manouchy, surgeon,' in motion at the Nawab's (? Da,ud Khan's) court to make him prevent the Dutch from attacking. The Nawab agreed, and even promised assistance on his being paid Rs. 20,000, if such an attack were made. For further details from the Pondicherry records, see additional note to vol. iii., part iv., note 164.

Page ixxx, paragraph' I: *Family* of *Deslandes.*—A son, François Louis Boureau Deslandes, was born at Chandarnagar on August 17, 1690. He was baptized, September 29, by Père le Duchat, S. J. The godfather was Louis de la Claretie, Chief of Narsingpore, and the godmother was Magdelaine Boureau (the father's sister), represented by Cosmo Gomes, a merchant of the Company. Another child, a daughter was born in 1694. See 'Bib. Nat., Nouvelles Acquisitions françaises.' M.S., No. 9,352, folio 24 (Papiers de P. Margry).

Page lxxxi, paragraph 3: *Deslandes.*—The discrepancy in dates is explained by the fact, only recently learnt by me, that there were two brothers Deslandes in the French Company's service in India. The elder, Joseph, who probably reached India in 1667, was the founder of the Rajapur factory in 1670, returning in 1674 to Surat, where he remained until the arrival of Baron. He was lost In the wreck of the *Solcil d'Orient* in 1681, off the east coast of Madagascar.

The younger brother, Andre Boureau Deslandes, left France in the *Vautour* in January, 1676, and reached Surat on October 16 of the same year. His autograph journal of the voyage out exist in the Archives de la Marine at Paris, No. 1,347, folios 211 to 245. The above information is due to the kindness of M. Paul Kaeppelin, Agrégé d'Histoire, Paris, whose exhaustive work, 'La Compagnie des Indes Orientales et Françōīs Martin, 1664-1719,' is now in the press (January, 1908).

Page lxxxii, line 14; *April* 1688. P. Kaepplin, p. 260, states that Deslandes started on August 30, 1688, on board the *Saint Nicolas*.

TEXT

Page 5, line 6.—The Italian text has '1652.'—Line 10.—The Italian text adds that they left at 3 p.m.

Page 9, line 2.—The Italian text spells the name 'Burza,' so my identification with Brusa is probably correct.

Page 10, line 2: *A. Cheleby*.—The Chevalier Laurent d'Arvieux, who was in Smyrna in 1654, tells us that Cheleby, then forty-six years of age, was a rich Armenian merchant and head of the custom-house, a post obtained through his brother, Hasan Agha, a renegade, who held the same office at Constantinople. When this brother fell from power, Cheleby was sent for by the Grand Turk, and d'Arvieux, who was living few doors off, heard the messengers knocking at Cheleby's door during the night. But their victim escaped by a back-door, took refuge on a French vessel, and put to sea. He landed at Leghorn, and was well received by the Grand Duke, who granted him a site in the main square, where he built a magnificent mansion. He soon tired of it, as it was not on the seashore, and presented it to the Grand Duke. For himself he built another house at the east end of the town, below the hill on which the mill stood. 'II y fit faire des bains & la Turque qui y sont encore.' He died at Leghorn. He had started in life as cook to an Englishman; he knew many languages, English included. See 'Mémoires du Chevalier d'Arvieux' (6 vols., 12mo., Paris, 1735), vol. i., pp. 15, 93, 97. For this reference I am indebted to Père A. Rabbath, S.J., of St. Joseph's University, Beyrout.

Page 14, line 10: *Turks*.—The Italian text reads 'Turkish soldiers.'—Line 10, from foot, *Bottles*.—In the Italian this is utri di pelle, 'leather bags.'

Page 14, line 35, *say*.—This must be meant for *sac*, 'a bag,' meaning the chagal, or leathern bottle used in the East.

Page 19, line 1.—The Italian text says the journey took *fifteen* days.

Page 23, line 14, from foot.—The Italian says 'of various colours.'

Page 23, line 33.—The Italian text adds: 'One Persian will drink as much as four Europebans.'

Page 29, line 23.—After 'ambassador,' the Italian text adds: 'Who took all his retinue and European friends. He was much loved by all there for his good qualities.'

Page 35, line 3: *Jhon*.—The Italian text has 'Young' quite plainly.

Page 37, line 10, and note 4.: *Boas Vuas, Vuas.*—The word vuas is simply *uvas* (grapes), with the two letters transposed. *Boal,* s.m., pl. *Boas,* is a variety of white grape, and very sweet, Roquete, 'Nouveau Dictionnaire Port. Franç.,' Paris, 1841.

Page 38, paragraph 1.—A parallel to this story of self-emasculation may be found in John Stevens' translation of 'P. Teixeira,' p. 349. The hero of it is one Mirza Taki, governor of 'Guilon,' under Shah 'Abbas.

Page 41, paragraph 2.—The Italian text adds that the Persian king was thirty years of age. As to his cruelty when drunk, see Stevens' Teixeira,' pp. 353, 354.

Page 46, line 8.—The Italian text has 'son' instead of 'daughter.'

Page 50, line 16, and note 7, and page 36, paragraph 1.—The Italian text states that when the ambassador was at Shiraz, the English cavalier passed through with Mestre Pit. But at Gombroon, not wanting to wander over the world any more, Pit quitted the cavalier and Entered the English Company's service as a merchant. There had been a William Pitt in the Company's service in Persia at an earlier period, and though there is no record of his return to Persia, this is probably the person met by Manucci at Isfahan, Shiraz, and Gombroon.

Page 53, line 7.—The Italian text has '1653' instead of '1652.'

Page 54, paragraph 1: *Shiraz.*—In the Italian text it is said that Bellomont was visited by a barefooted Carmelite, that order having a small convent there for the benefit of the Armenian Roman Catholics.

Page 54, line 12: *palace of Darius.*—In the Italian Manucci says he visited this 'famous building.'

Page 54, line 17: *Mumiyai.*—There are many notices of this pro duct; for instance, it is mentioned by 'Abd-ul-latif (see the translation by Silvestre de Sacy. 'Relation de I'Egypte,' 4°, Paris, 1810, pp. 200, 201, with learned notes by the editor on pp. 272 and 570). De Sacy combats the notion that the *word* is derived from Coptic, and does not think it originated in Egypt. Mr. A. G. Ellis says the Syriac has a form Mumiayaj, where the final 'j' points to a Pahlavi origin. P. Teixeira (Hakluyet edition, p. 231) says it is found as a liquid issuing from a mountain in 'Sthabanon'; this kind is called Kani (Kan, P., 'a mine'). Baron de Bode, 'Travels in Luristan and Arabistan,' 1845, vol. i., p. 301, saw it flowing from a fissure high up on a mountain-side near the ruins of Arrajan, in Luristan. There it was called *mumiyai-i-Nai,* from the name of the adjoining village. The emperor Jahangir tried its healing virtues on the broken leg of a fowl, but without success. He procured it from Persia direct, and the narrative shows that, as Manucci asserts, it was a royal monopoly ('Tuzuk-i-Jahangiri,' B. M. Add., M.S. No. 26,215, fol. 167a, fifth year). As a rationalistic explanation of its healing qualities, Mr. A. G. Ellis suggests that it probably performed the function now assigned to plaster-of-Paris in modern surgery.

Page 55, line 2: *pauso.*—Mr. Ferguson holds this to be a faulty spelling of poço, 'a well.'

Page 57, paragraph 1: *guinea-worm.*—The Italian text is a little more explicit: 'There is no better remedy for these worms than to apply to the inflamed place some lard, afterwards winding the worm round a small roll of cloth or a thin piece of wood, such as the stem of the marjoram plant, doing very little at a time, and with great care, for fear of breaking the worm.' There is a good account of the disease and its treatment in Hamilton's 'New Account,' i. 42.

Page 57, line 8, and note 7.—*Hide* should be read *hicle* (i.e., *icle*) For explanation see additional note 134, vol. iii., Part iii.

Page 58, line 6.—The Italian has ten instead of *twelve* days.

Page 58, line 19.—The Italian has *tela di bombace—i.e.,* cotton cloth.

Page 59, line 1.—'These friars were Italians, and under the Sacred Congregation "de Propaganda Fide." '

Page 61, line 4.—'Friar Ambrozio Capuchin' is, no doubt, identical with Ambroise do Preuilly. See additional note 221, vol. iii., part iv.

Page 65, line 3.—In the Italian it is '1675' instead of '1676.'

Page 65, line 8 from foot.—Read 'wild goats'; *ores* intended for *orix,* pl. *orixes,* a kind of wild goat.

Page 67, line 2.—*Bundelah,* 'whose country is twenty leagues from Agrah' (Italian Codex).

Page 68, line 20.—For *mountain* the Italian text has *rocca,* 'a rock.'

Page 69, line 26.—The Italian reads: 'The English offered him certain waters to drink, and also a beverage universally in use here among Europeans, which is called *ponce* (? punch), asserting that it affords great relief.'

Page 74, line 37: *Drake's 'Hundred of Blackheath.'*—I am indebted to Mr. Henry Hannen, the Hall, West Farleigh, for pointing out that the work quoted is the first (and only) volume of a new edition of Hasted's 'History of Kent,' edited by H. H. Drake. It appeared in 1886. The Musgraves of Edenhall, descendants of A. Cogan through his daughter Mary, seem to possess two letters of credentials to the rulers of India and China engrossed in gold and colours.

Page 78, line 19.—*Casbegi* was a small Persian coin. F. de la Boullaye le Gouz (1653), p. 509, gives the following values: '2 casbegui=1 bisti; 2 bisti=l schai; 4 schai-1 abbasi; 1 piece de 27 sols de France=1 abbasi and 1 schai; 1 reale d'Empire or 1 reale d'Espagne=3 abbasr, 1 schai; 1 sequin of Venice=6abbasi, 2 schai.' He also gives values for the Mogul territory, for Goa, and for the Bijapur kingdom.

Page 81, line 12: *cemetery.*—There were then *three* cemeteries at Agrah. See 'Transactions of the Agrah Archaeological Society for 1874.'

Page 82, table: *Charles,* 2nd *Viscount Bellomont.*—The correct date of death is June 19, 1667 (see Commander Thomas Southey, 'Chronological History of the West Indies,' vol. ii., p. 76; and his authority, Du Tertre, 'Histoire des Ant-Isles, 1671, vol. iv., pp. 261-274). In the latter, on p. 271, in a list of casualties, we find: 'Le Milord Bellomont, comman dant une compagnie royale (Mort).' C. Dalton, 'English Army Lists and Commission Registers, 1661-1714,' vol. i. (1661-1685), gives on p. 75 the officers of the Barbadoes Regiment raised in England February 11, 1667, and, though the name of Viscount Bellomont does not appear, that of William Stapleton is there; and Du Tertre shows that this officer lost his life while leading the abortive landing at St. Kitts, in which Bellomont also fell. The regiment was turned into a Dragoon one in 1672, and finally disbanded in 1674 (see also Lucas, 'Historical Geography of the Colonies,' vol. ii., p. 141). For the information enabling me to trace out the above facts I am indebted to a note by Mr. George H. King, of St. Kitts, furnished me by the kindness of Mr. F. S. Wigley, Acting Administrator.

Page 84, line 6: *Thomas Roach.*—There is a letter to him from the Surat Council, dated November 24, 1673, where his long experience as a gunner at the Mogul court is mentioned.

Page 84, line 7: *Ruben Smith.*—In the French descriptions of the pictures in O.D. 45. *Réserve*, our author speaks of this man as *Robert Smith*, which is probably correct. There is a Robert Smith named in Sloane MS. No. 811.

Page 87, end of paragraph 1.—The Italian text adds: 'The secretary was never tired of asking me to tell him about various strange things, and to his questions I replied with Italian and Venetian readiness.'

Page 88, line 8.—'Raised his eyes' *half open.*

Page 88, line 19.—'Like a table' *of gold.*

Page 88, line 21.—For 'diameter' the Italian has 'length,' which is more suitable.

Page 88, line 18 from foot.—For 'Turkey' the Italian has 'Asia.'

Page 88, paragraph 3.—Add from the Italian: 'There were also present the agents of all princes in the realm for the purpose of receiving orders.'

Page 94, line 2 from foot.—In place of *thirty* the Italian has *three hundred*; and as to the *sarāpā*, it adds: 'A long and wide cloth with which the head is covered; it forms a hat or turban like those the Armenians wear among us in Europe.'

Page 96, line 10.—The Italian adds that this aged man of letters was a Mogul.

Page 97, end of paragraph 1.—The Italian adds: 'There should be no doubt as to the truth of what I write about the present king, Aurangzeb, because for all I shall say in regard to him I am an eyewitness. *Vivan sani*!'

Page 97, paragraph 3: *miraculous conception by the sun.*—The idea is common in legend, and there are traces of it in marriage customs. See references in Frazer, 'Golden Bough,' second edition, vol. iii., p. 222.

Page 103, paragraph 3: *revenge of the blinded king.*—According to E. Rehatsek, *Indian Antiquary*, 1890, p. 290, a similar story is told in the 'Gulabnamah' by Diwan Kirparam, a modern Persian work published at Srinagar, Kashmir, in 1875. In this version the blinded king is Rai Pitora, and the victim Shahab-ud-din, Ghori.

Page 106, line 15.—The Italian text has 'Passato il pericolo, burlato il santo,' which is the more usual form.

Page 110: *Ranguil Das.*—Dr. Grierson thinks 'Rangila Das' is a possible form for a Hindu name, but the story is a piece of Indian folk-lore, except that in the usual version the king summons *not* the inhabitants of the villages, but the tanks and ponds. It occurs in the 'Mahaummaggajataka' (see V. Fausböll, 'The Jataka,' vol. vi., No. 546, pp. 329-478, quoted by Th. Zachariae, 'Zur Geschichte vom Weisen Haikar,' in *Zeitschrift des Vereins für Volkskund in Berlin*. Heft ii., 1907, p. 176, No. 16). There it is told of King Vedeha of Mithila. We also have a version where Rajah Birbal plays a part. See Munshi Devi Prasad, Kayath, 'Raja Birbar ka jiwan-charitra' (Dilli, S. 1952, A.D. 1895), Story XXVI., on p. 13.

Page 114, note 14: *Faria.*—Probably the passage alluded to is that in Faria y Souza's second volume, Part I., cap. xi., p. 112 in edition of 1674, paragraph 2, copied from Couto, Decada. V., Livro VIII., Capitulo XI. (edition of 1780, vol. ii., p. 258). Couto says the queen was sent on some days ahead, and the child was born at night. Some say that she gave birth to a girl. She knew the Mogul would be very much displeased. She therefore confided in a servant, who secretly changed the female for a male infant of whom the wife of the elephant driver had just been delivered. It was done so quickly that even the mother of the boy was not aware of it. Couto says he got the story from a Pole named Gabriel, who travelled through Muscovy to the Usbeg country, and lived some years at the court of 'Abdullah Khan (1540-1551) of Samarqand. Then he came to the Mogul's court, and was in his household some fifteen years Finally he retired to Goa. When Humayun heard of the birth, he ejaculated, 'Allahu akbar' (God is great), and named the child 'Akbar.' Faria y Souza adds the rumour that Sher Shah, desiring to humiliate Humayun, made over his queen to the elephant-driver, and that the child was his, not Humayun's. He adds that the child was in appearance much more like the elephant-driver than the king, but in character he was great, and is it not true that doves do not engender eagles, nor eagles doves?

Page 116, line 14, and note 17.—Although Manucci attributes it to Shah Dulah, the story is more properly told of Makhdum-ul-Mulk 'Abdullah, Sultanpuri, who died 991 H., 1583-84. See the 'Akbarnamah,' translation i. 612, the 'Ma,asir-ul-umara,' iii. 252-257, and a great deal about him in Budauni, 'Muntakhab-ut-tawarikh.' The story is in Muhammad Husain Azad's 'Darbar-i-Akbari,' p. 311.

Page 120, paragraph 2.—Another instance of a similar opportune fall of rain will be found in the 'Dabistan' (English translation), iii. 120, in regard to the siege of the fort of Imbal in Khwarizm.

Page 125: *Chitor and Padmini.*—There is a long story in Francois Valentyn, vol. iv., pp. 206-212, much on the same line. On page 210 the incident of the empty palanquins is given. But did not Valentyn obtain it from Catrou? See quarto edition, p. 73. I believe the whole story is to be found in Muhammad Jaisi's Hindi poem on Padamawati.

Page 128, line 9.—The suggestion that *sati* was introduced to prevent women from poisoning their husbands is as old as Strabo, xv. 30 (McCrindle, 'Ancient India as described in Classical Literature,' 38), and Diodorus Siculus, xix., 30 (McCrindle, *ibid.*, 202). Alexander Hamilton, 'A New Account of the East Indies,' edition 1744, vol. i., 280, refers to the same belief in Canara; it is also asserted in Ovington, 'Voyage to Suratt' (1696), p. 343.

Page 129: *Akbar and his rebellious son.*—Ed. Terry connects this story with Jahangir and his rebel son, Khusru ('A Voyage . . . ; reprint of 1777, p. 410). This is also the case in the anonymous pamphlet ot 1622, reprinted in 'Harleian Miscellany,' vol. i., pp. 258-262.

Page 129, line 18.—As to the practice in the East of execution by impalement; for Ceylon see an illustration in Baldaeus's 'Ceylon,' Churchill's 'Voyages,' iii., opposite p. 638; and for Achin in Sumatra, see Sir R. C. Temple's 'Thomas Bowrey,' p. 316.

Page 130, line 5: *1563.*—The Italian has, '1566.'

Page 131, paragraph 1.—Mr. Beveridge says this story belongs to the seventh year, and is told with substantial accuracy. The incident occurred in an attack upon an Ahir stronghold on the Isan River, called Paronkh, which is now in the Eta district. See 'Akbarnamah,' ii. 162 (translation, vol. ii., p. 251); also H. Beveridge's article in the *Indian Review* (Madras), vol. vii., 1906, pp. 103-105.

Page 135: *Campaign against Rajah Karan.*—Mr. Beveridge thinks the campaign alluded to must be the affair of Akbar and Sukal Singh, son of Rana Ude Singh, in the twelfth year ('Akbarnamah,' Cawnpore edition, ii. 236, fifth line from foot).

Page 135: *Campaign against Pathans.*—Mr. Beveridge says this seems an exaggerated account of the defeat of Rajah Birbal and Zain Khan by the Yusufzais in the thirty-fourth year, 1586. Manucci would have done better to say '8,000' instead of '80,000' men. See H. Blochmann 'A,in,' i. 404.

Page 136, line 21.—The English were not the first to arrive at Surat the Dutch appeared there in 1602. See J. E. Heeres' 'Corpus Diplomati cum Neerlando-Indicum,' part i. (1596-1650), p. 277.

Page 138, paragraph 1.—Tavernier's account of the paintings at Sikandrah may be compared. See Ball's edition, i. 111.

Page 138, note 27: *Crucifix at Sikandrah.*—I must withdraw the animadversion on Catrou, as the Italian text does not support the Portuguese MS., the former having *sculpite* (carved) and the latter *debuxada* (painted, drawn). This refers to the figures on the sides of the entrance. The angels in the roof or archway vault arc specially noted in the Italian text as paintings.

Page 139, paragraph 1: *the original language.*—There is an account of this experiment in the 'Dabistan' (English translation), iii. 90. When examined after fourteen years the children were found to be entirely dumb.

Page 139-40, paragraph 2, and note 31: *the cow's mouth.*—The 'cow's head' is shown on Baffin's map of India (1619), reproduced in W. Foster's 'Embassy of Sir Thomas Roe.' A modern account of the spot says: '*gau-mukh,* or the cow's mouth, is the name given to the glacier cavern, from which the head waters issue on the melting of the ice and snow.' Tieffentaller is also referred to. The spot is at Gangotri, in *parganah,* Teknaur of Tihri state, a temple on the bank of the Bhagirathi, north lat. 30° 59′ 10″, east long. 78° 59′ 30″ (E. T. Atkinson, 'Himalayan Districts of the North-Western Provinces of India' (3 vols.—x., xi., xii., of the 'Gazetteer of the North-Western Provinces'), ii'i. 237.

Page 146, paragraph 3.—For the story of Akbar's death by poison, somewhat as stated in the text, there is very early authority, of which I was not aware. E. Terry, who visited India with Sir T. Roe about 1618-19, tells it substantially as Manucci does ('A Voyage to East India' —written in 1622, and first published in 1655—reprint of 1777, p. 408, 409). Next we have it in De Laet, 'De Imperio Magni Mogolis. . . . (1631), who relies on a Dutch or Flemish narrative given him by Pieter van den Broecke, Dutch agent at Surat. Broecke was in Asia from 1613 to 1629, and his first, visit to Surat was from August 26 to September 9, 1616. On October 4, 1620, he returned and remained until December 2, 1628. See J. E. Heeres, 'Corpus Diplomaticum Neerlando Indicum, 1596-1650,' pp. 277, 278; and also Valentyn, vol. iv., 220, 224. 'Levens der Groote Mogols,' where the poisoning story is given (p. 216). It is not given in the journal printed in 'Recueil des Voyages. . . .' (12 vols., Rouen, 1725), vol. vii., pp. 380-582. Sir Thomas Herbert, Bart., who was at Surat in 1627, gives almost the same version as De Laet. See 'Some Years' Travels. . . .,' fourth edition, 1677, p. 72 (the book was first published in 1634). In all these versions the noble aimed at was Mirza Ghazi, son of Mirza Jani Beg, Tarkhan, ruler of Sind Among the Rajputs, according to J. Tod, 'Rajasthan,' reprint, i. 325, the intended victim was Rajah Man Singh of Amber. The authorities are collected in R. P. Karkaria's article, 'The Death of Akbar,' *Journal of the Bombay Branch of the Asiatic Society* (1906), vol. xxii., pp. 79 to 208.

Page 149, paragraph 1.—On the caves in Salsette Island, see Couto, 'Da Asia' (Lisbon, 1782). Decada VII., Part I., Livro III., Cap. X., p. 236. On p. 240 he says a Padre with a companion and twenty followers explored the labyrinth for seven days, and the natives declared that you could go by it to Cambay, the Mogul country, and even to Agrah !

Page 150, line 2: *Mahabalipuram.*—Plate XVII. in J. Fergusson, Picturesque Illustrations of Ancient Architecture in Hindustan' (London, 1847), is a view of this temple. Fergusson says it has been described by Bishop Heber, Mrs. Graham, Chambers and Goldingham in the 'Asiatic Researches.' and Babington in the *Transactions* of the Royal Asiatic Society. See also M. W. Carr, 'The Seven Pagodas' (1869).

Page 150, paragraph 2: *China Pagoda.*—Valentyn, 'Choromandel,' Part V., Section 1, p. 6. says this high tower was built by the Chinese; the Dutch flag was hoisted on it, and it served as a beacon for ships. Natives said it had been built by the devil in one night (*ibid.*, p. 3). Mr. Philipps informs me that the brick tower was pulled down in 1869 by order of the Madras Government, as it was in a dangerous state, and threatened to fall on the buildings of the Jesuit College of St. Joseph (now transferred to Trichinopoly). The tower is described by Marco Polo; see Yule, 'Marco Polo,' second edition, i. 319, 320, where there is a sketch of it made in 1846; and articles by Sir Walter Elliot in the 'Indian Antiquary,' vol. vii. (1878), p. 224, and xv. (1886), p. 234. Presumably the natives called it the Jaina Tower, and the Europeans thought they said China Tower.

Page 150, note 40: *Laurens Pit.*—See also Valentyn, 'Choromandel,' pp. 6, 15, 16. Pit was moved to Ncgapatam as Landvogt in 1690, and held the office of Extraordinary Councillor from 1693 to September, 1698.

Page 152, line 22.—The story of the man bitten by bugs appears in Ovington, 'Voyage to Suratt,' p. 301; also see *Bombay Gazetteer*, ii. 328. A long account of these 'pinjrapols' (*panjrapols*) is given in W. Crooke, 'Things Indian,' 371 *ff.*; also see V. A. Smith, 'Early History of India, p. 163, and Duarte Barbosa, 'A Description of (the Coasts of East Africa and Malabar,' edited by Hon. E. J. Stanley (Hakluyt Society), 1866, p. 51.

Page 154, paragraph 2: *Jahangir's Religion.*—In 1648 the Jesuits at Agrah reported that some persons thought Jahangir had been secretly baptized by Father Francesco Corsi, Florentine, who was his intimate friend. The king never clearly confessed it for fear of the prince (Khurram), who had all along shown himself greatly opposed to Christianity. See 'Relation de ce qui s'est passé dans les Indes Orientales. . . .' by Jean Marucci, S.J. (Paris, 1651), p. 21.

Page 154, note 41, line 4.—For 'grandfather' read '*great*-grandfather.'

Page 157, line 3; *Father Joseph da Costa.*—'J. da C., a Piedemontese, died last year (? 1646), aged seventy years, of which thirty-five were passed in the Indian Mission. His services were especially valuable after the sacking of Hugli and the arrival of the prisoners at Agrah' (c. 1631), 'Relation de ce qui s'est passé dans les Indes Orientales ....,' by Jean Marucci, S.J. (Paris, 1651), p. 20. See also 'Agrah Archaeological Society's Transactions for 1876,' p. x. Father da Costa's gravestone bears the date of December, 15, 1646, the place of death being Lahor. Thus his birth would have been in 1576, and his arrival in India in 1611 during Jahangir's reign. A somewhat similar story to that in the text is given by Roe, ii., p. 316 (October, 1616); E. Terry (edition 1777), p. 426, has a version of the story. In both cases Father Corsi is the hero, and not Da Costa.

Page 173, line 8: *Daughters of Prince Khurram.*—The names ought to run: Begam Sahib (*i.e.*, Jahanara Begam), Gonorara Begom (Gauharara Begam), and Roxonara Begom (Roshanara Begam). See further on the correction to i. p. 218. and additional note 100 there.

Page 174, paragraph 3: *Khurram'it stratagem.*—This device for escaping from Bijapur territory, if employed at all. could not have been long persisted in. Jahangir died on his way from Kashmir to Lahor on November 8, 1627. Khurram heard of the event at Juncr on November 28, and the news was known at Surat on December 6; on the 14th Khurram at the head of an army, was close to that town, and had demanded from it a levy of Rs. 10,000. On December 15th the fortress of Surat was delivered to him. There can be no mistake, for P. van den Broecke tells us that he went out and saw the prince, and made him a present ('Recueil des Voyages . . . [1725], vol. vii., p. 571).

Page 176, note 58: *Capture of Hugli.*—There are references to the capture in the Batavia ('Dagh Register' on January 31, March 23, and June 20, 1633. The Dutch heard that 1,560 Portuguese had been killed and 1,500 taken prisoners ('Dagh Register . . . 1631-1634.' ed. Dr. H. T. Colenbrander; Haque, 1898, pp. 145, 159, 195). There is an account of the capture in Faria y Souza, 'Asia Portuguesa,' iii., p. 495.

Page 176, note 59, *Taj Mahal.*—The date is a year out. She died on the 17th, Zu,l Qa'dah, 1040 H. (June 17, 1631, N.S.), at Burhanpur, aged thirty-nine years and four months ('Badshahnamah,' I. 385, and 'Tarikh-i-Muhammadi,' 1140 H).

Page 177, line 17: *Hieronomo Veroneo.*—Sebastian Manrique, p. 352, says that the architect of the Taj was this Venetian, Geronimo Veroneo, who came to India in a Portuguese vessel, and died in Agrah shortly before Manrique's arrival there.

Page 177, line 13 from foot: *decapitated criminals.*—Mr. Crooke writes that this is a good example of the foundation sacrifice. He has given many instances in his 'Popular Religion and Folk-lore,' ii. 173 *ff.* Professor Tylor, 'Primitive Culture,' second edition (1873), ii. 104 *ff.*, regards it as a means of propitiating the earth spirits who have been offended by the digging of the foundations. Grant Allen, 'Evolution of the Idea of God,' p. 249, calls it 'a piece of deliberate god-making.'

Page 182, paragraph 3: The *doorkeepers and the buffoon.*—This story is related of Rajah Birbal. See 'Lata,if-ul-Akbar,' Mahanarayan, editor, Dihli, 1876, p. 7, Story No. 9.

Page 189, last paragraph: T*esting the qualities of women.*—There is another version of this story (not connected with Shahjahan) in Carmichael Smyth, 'Lata,if-i-Hindi,' Story 16, p. 23. The point there is to prove that women from the Purab (east of India or Bengal) are stupid. The indecorous answer was given by the Purbiya woman, and she was ejected as unfit for a court.

Page 190, paragraph 1: *Punishment by snake-bite.*—E. Terry asserts that, among other forms of punishment, malefactors were stung to death by snakes, 'A Voyage to East India,' reprint of 1777, p. 354. He speaks of an actual instance, while he was at Ahmadabad, of this punishment having been inflicted for matricide. Jahangir had been much troubled about 'making the punishment fit the crime,' *ibid.*, p. 362.

Page 197, line 3: Robbery of *Dutch factory at Surat.*—This robbery was committed by 150 well-armed men in the night between April 19 and 20, 1648. The text 'does not tally with the Dutch account, which is given at p. 521 of J. E. Heeres's 'Corpus Diplomaticum Necrlando-Indicum, 1596-1650' (1907), including the resulting events and the heavy demands made and agreed to on September 18, 1649.

Page 198, line 32: *Zaura.*—Dr. A. F. Rudolf Hoemle suggests a possible Hindi word *sauvarna or sauvarnya,* 'a thing made or gold or containing gold.'

Page 200, *Illustration No. XL bis.*—The description placed opposite this picture in the volume O.D. 45, Réserve, says it represents Shahjahan and his four sons, with a shaven Hindu prince named Amar Singh standing in front, and alongside of him, Wazir Khan, then the chief minister. When and how the substitution of this outline drawing of an elephant fight was made I do not know.

Page 202, note 82.—*Jhanwat* is the spelling taken direct from the 'Ma,asir-ul-umara,' with a variant 'Chhanwat,' but the 'imperial Gazetteer of India' (1885), iii 418, spells it 'Chiniot'; Colonel Jarrett, 'A,in,' vol. ii., p. 320, has 'Chaniwat'; and Mr. D. G. Barkley, C.S. (a man with local knowledge), 'Chaniot' or 'Chanyot' (*Journal R.A.S.* for 1899, p. 132). It is in the Jhang district, two miles south of the Chenab, on the road from Jhang to Wazirabad.

Page 203, line 30, of *Canarese race.*—The original word is 'Canarim,' and Mr. Philipps brings abundant evidence to show that I should have used 'Konkani,' or 'native of Goa,' following the Portuguese usage. They speak of the Goa language as the 'lingua canarim,' see Yule 154. J. H. da Cunha Rivara, 'Ensaio Historico da Lingua Concani' (Goa, 1858), p. 4, explains how this came to pass. J. I. Roquete, 'Diet. Portugais-français' (Paris, 1841), has: 'Canarim, s.m., paysan des environs de Goa.

Page 203, lines 30, 31, and note 83: *Dom Matheus.*—Matheus de Castro, a Brahman, was born in 1607 in the island of Divar at Goa. He was never a Christian of St. Thomas. He was educated and ordained priest at Goa, then went to Rome to study at the newly-founded College of the Propaganda, and having taken the degree of Doctor of Theology, returned to India. He became prior of the Collegiate Church of N. S. da Luz, a parish in Old Goa. Returning to Rome, he entered the congregation of the Oratory of St. Philip Neri. In 1637, while still at Rome, he was made bishop of Chrysopolis in *partibus*, and in 1652 went back to India as Vicar Apostolic for the Bijapur and Gulkandah kingdoms. As he had not been approved by the King of Portugal, he took up his residence at Bicholim, not then in Portuguese territory. He is said to have built churches at Bicholim (San Salvador), Banda (St. Felippe Nery), and Vingorla (N. S. da Conceição). He went once more to Rome, and died there in 1679. The family house of Bishop Matheus still exists in Navelim village on the island of Divar. These particulars are from O Anglo-Lusitano' of Bombay, June 2, 1887, founded on eight sources there stated. See also 'Catalogus Vicariorum Apostolicarum ... Bombayensi,' tertii editii (Bombay, 1883), pp. 4, 5; the 'Madras Catholic Directory,' 1878, p. 87; the same for 1907, p. 77; 'Missiones Catholicae ... descriptae, Anno 1901' (Rome, 1901)', p. 194; and Jose Manuel Bras de Sá, 'O Apostolo das Indias, Francisco Xavier' (Goa, 1878), p. 61.

Page 204, line 4: *Parable of the sleeping man.*—The same parable as that used by Dom Matheus is attributed in the 'Dābistān' (English translation), i. 100, 101 (p. 47 in Calcutta Persian text of 1809), to one Azar Kawan, a Parsi sage, who died at Patnah in 1027 H. (1617), aged eighty-two years. Both may have obtained it from a common source, or Dom Matheus may have borrowed it from the Parsi.

Page 205, line 10: *Khan Khanan.*—The person intended is, no doubt, as Mr. Beveridge points out to me, Mahabat Khan, Khan Khanan, Sipahsalar (Zamanah Beg, son of Ghiyur Beg, Kabuli), who died at Burhanpur in 1044 H. (1634-1635), 'M.-ul-U.,' iii. 385, 'Tarikh-i-Muhammadi' (1044 H.). When the ninth year began, 1 Jamada 11, 1045 H., November 1, 1635, Shahjahan was on his march towards Bundelkhand, and reached Datiya on the 18th (November 18), 'Badshahnamah,' i., part ii. pp. 120, 121. This fits in well enough with Manucci's statement.

Page 208, note 87: *Srinagar.*—This campaign of Najabat Khan, in Garhwal, is better told in the 'Badshahnamah,' i., part ii., pp. 90-93.

Page 209, note 89: *Jahanara (Bcgam Sahib).*—For her book Munis-ul-arwah, being a notice of Mu'in-ud-din, Chishti, composed in 1049 H. (1639-40), see Rieu, 'Persian Catalogue,' p. 357*b*; and I have since given to the British Museum what I believe to be a holograph exemplar.

Page 209, line 21: *then sent out of the harem.*—The idea was to transfer the sick man's disease to the slaves, who were then sent out like scapegoats. See many instances in W. Crooke, 'Popular Religion and Folk-Lore,' i., p. 164 *ff*.

Page 213, note 93.: The lines about this paradise on earth are said, in 'Ma,asir-ul-umara,' iii. 464, to be by Mir Khusru, part of a poem on Dihli. I have not succeeded in finding them in his works. Sa'dullah Khan may merely have quoted them.

Page 215, line 10: *Father Malpica.*—By the kindness of Father Van Meurs, S. J., of Baaksem, Limburg, Holland, and Father Alexandre Brou, S. J., of Canterbury, I have obtained further information. Stanilas Malpiqua was born in 1600 at Cantazaro, in the kingdom of Naples. He joined the Society May 29, 1623; and left Lisbon with the same fleet as Father Marcel Mastrilli, S.J. He was Prefect of Studies at Goa, Superior of the Bom Jesus in 1646, made his profession February 2 (? 1646), was provincial in (?) 1661, rector at Rachol 1667, and at the New St., Paul 1673. He died before 1676. According to Jean Marucci, 'Relation ...' (Paris, 1651), p. 16, Father Malpiqua was in Tibet in 1648; he had been a Doctor of Law before he entered the Society of Jesus. He wrote many marvellous things of Tibet and of his perils in crossing rivers. About 1648 he was sent to Srinagar [*i.e.*, Garhwal]. Other details are given. There is a letter from him, dated Rachol, February 5, 1665, to the Portuguese Viceroy of India (see J. H. da Cunha Rivara, 'Ensaio da Lingua Concani,' Nova Goa, 1858, p. 242). He was then provincial of the Jesuits at Goa. Their college at Rachol, in Salsette, 16½ m. south-east of Goa, was established in 1606, and is now the diocesan seminary.

Page 215, line 11: *Father Pedro Juzarte.*—He was born in 1617 at Loures, in the diocese of Lisbon. He entered the society in 1634. Left Lisbon for India 1643; professor of the humanities, of philosophy, and of theology, moral and dogmatic; and rector of the College of the Holy Faith at Goa, 1652; rector at Agrah, 1656-59; subsequently he was at Daman and Macao. He was elected procurator for the province of Japan, and left Goa for Rome in 1667. He became nearly blind, retired to the

Novitiate, and died at Lisbon, 1688. The last statement is furnished to me by Father Hosten, S.J., of St. Mary's, Kurscong, quoting from E. do Guilhermy, 'Ménéloge de la Compagnie de Jésus, Assistance de Portugal,' 1., 198 (February). The rest is obtained from Father Van Meurs.

Page 215, line 12: *Father H. Buzeo, a Fleming.*—There is considerable doubt as to whether this father's real name was (Latin) Busaeus, (French) Busée, (Flemish) Buis, or Hendrick Uwens. Cornelis Hazart, S. J., in his 'Kerekclycke Historic van der geheele Werelt' (4 vols., folio, Antwerp, 1667), Deel I., pp. 245-278, treats of the 'Mogor' mission. He says nothing of Father Busée, but on p. 277, col. 1, has the remark: 'One of the most prominent is Father Henricus Vwens, born at Nimmeghen, who has been now twenty-four years in Agrah, and was long tutor to the princes.' This account of Father Uwens exactly describes Father Busee, of whom there is otherwise no mention. Father Van Meurs has devoted considerable time and research to the question. The result he arrives at is as follows : In 1636 both the names appear in the catalogue of the Flandro-Belgian province—namely, Henri Uwens (*scholasticus*) and Henri Busee (*prétre*). In 1639 Uwens is still given, but Busée has disappeared. In October, 1640 and 1641, it is noted that Uwens had gone to China, and yet he is not to be found in the China catalogues. Father Busfée is recorded as having died in 1638 at Bailleul, and thus he cannot be the person that we find afterwards in India. But at the very moment when the name Uwens disappears from the Belgian lists, we find a Henri Buseus appear in those of Portugal, where he taught mathematics and studied theology. It was not unusual for priests of Teuton origin either to Jake a purely Portuguese name or to modify the sound of their original one. Thus it seems fairly clear that it is Henri Uwens, alias Busee, that we find at Agrah from 1648. He was superior in 1653-56, and then a simple missionary 1656-64. His career may be thus summarized: He was born at Nimeguen April 23, 1618; entered the society October 15, 1634; left for Portugal, on his way to China, 1640; takes the name of Buseus, and from 1641 to 1647 studies in Portugal; leaves Lisbon 1647; is at Agrah 1648; makes his full profession at Lahor February 23, 1653; superior at Agrah 1653-56; missionary at Agrah 1656-64; dies at Dihli on April 6, 1667. The stone over his grave in the Padre Santus chapel at Agrah bears the inscription: | Aqvi Iazo P. Henriqve | Bvses Faleceo em | Delly Aos 6 De Abril | 1667, coloniensis germanvs | (see Father Félix's notes in 'Catholic Directory of Agrah for 1907,' pp. 215 and 220). Jean Marucci, S. J. in 1651 (Relation ...,' p. 21), says Henri Busée, appears to have reached Agrah along with Antonio Ceschi about the year 1648 (see *post*, note to p. 361). He is described as then 'a young man of great ability and with many talents.' He had taught mathematics for four years at Lisbon. On his arrival in Agrah he was sent to live constantly at the Mogul court because the young prince (? Dara Shukoh) was very keen about European sciences, and was very well inclined to them. It was hoped that he would resemble his grandfather, Jahangir, in favouring the Christians.

Page 218, note 100: *the daughters of Shahjahan.*—This note requires revision. The three surviving daughters were (1) Jahanara, or Begam Sahib, b. 1023 H. (1614): (2) Roshan Rae, b. 1026 H. (1617); (3) Gauhar ara, b. 1040 H. (1631) (see 'Badshahnamah,' i. 393. Mumtaz Mahal was the mother of fourteen children, eight sons and ix daughters, dying in childbed when Gauharara was born. Seven children grew up, four sons and three daughters. Suriya Begam, b. 1037 H. (1627-28), lived only seven years (*ibid.*, i 342).

Page 220, last paragraph: *Aurangzeb and the faqirs.*—This story is also found in Ovington, 'Voyage to Suratt' (1696), p. 203, and in Captain Hamilton, 'New Account' (1744), i. 177.

Page 222, paragraph 2 : *Aurangzeb and the dancing-girl.*—The woman's name was Zainabadi. and she was on the establishment of Khan Zaman (Mhd. Khalil), the prince's maternal uncle. The story is told in 'Ma,asir-ul-umara,' i. 790, 791. After pressing the alcohol on the prince, and his consenting to take it, the girl drank it off herself, and said she had only been testing his love for her. Her early death broke off the connection; her tomb is at Aurangabad.

Page 223. note 104.—Dom Francisco Mascarenhas received his letters of appointment in Ceylon December 29, 1644. He left Columbo in January, 1645, but, having been wrecked, did not reach Goa until December. He took charge of his office December 30, 1645.

Page 229, line 2.—Mr. Ferguson points out that there are no diamonds in *Ceylon*.

Page 230, note 118: *Kaliyani.*—As Dr. O. Codrington has pointed out to me, this identification is erroneous. The Kaliyani intended is the one in the Kulbarga district of the Nizam's territories, and once the capital of the Chalukya dynasty. Early in 1657 Prince Aurangzeb left Aurangabad on a campaign against Bijapur, investing Kaliyani and other forts belonging to that kingdom. Kaliyani was surrendered by Dilawar, Habshi, who held it for 'Adil Shah, on 1st Zu,l Qa'dah. 1067 H. (August 12, 1657). Sec Constable, 'Hand Atlas,' Plate XXXI., Dc. (17° 48′ north. 77° 8′ east); Khafi-Khan, i. 754, 755, 756; S. Hossain and Willmott, 'Historical Sketch.' ii. 626.

Page 231. note 122 : *Rotella.*—In his MS. memoirs 'Abd-ul-qadir, Sabit Jang, who served in Ajmer in 1818-19, speaks of a place called Rautalah as then held in appanage under the Kishngadh Raj. Thus. 'Rotella' may be an epithet derived from this place.

Page 237, last paragraph: *Shahjahan's letters to Aurangzeb.*—The real letters will be found in Sadiq Khan's 'Tarikh-i-Shahjahan,' British Museum, Or. No. 174, fol. 200 and following. The prince's first reply was submissive in tone. Shahjahan then sent Fazil Khan back again with friendly messages and presents. Meanwhile intriguers persuaded the prince that Shahjahan's object in pressing him to come was merely to make away with him. Fazil Khan reported the changed attitude, at which Shahjahan was much cast down. Next the author (Sadiq Khan), Khalilullah Khan, and Fazil Khan, were sent together, bearing a letter of which the author gives a copy. On their arrival in the camp, Khalilullah Khan manoeuvred so as to obtain a private audience, at which he put the worst construction on Shahjahan's intentions. Aurangzeb told the other two messengers that not being able to trust his father, he refused to come to court. Shahjahan then bricked up the gates of the fort. As soon as Aurangzeb reached Dara's mansion in the city, desertions to him became incessant, some even jumping down from the fort battlements in their eagerness to get away.

Page 245, line 25: *The traitors ... Khalilullah Khan.*—The passage just quoted from the narrative of Sadiq Khan, an eyewitness and actor in the affair, yields direct corroboration of Manucci's charges against Khalillulah Khan. See *ante*, note to p. 237.

Page 304, line 24: *Lakhi Jan gal.*—That this was once very extensive is shown by the number of parganahs in the *Ain-i-Akbari* which include 'Lakhi' as part of their name. There are thirteen of them. Dr. Grierson writes to me that the tract is now called the 'Jangal' pure and simple. The name is applied to all parts of the region south of the Sutlaj which have not come under cultivation. As cultivation extends the 'Jangal' recedes. A special dielect of Panjabi is called Jangal, but no one admits that he speaks it; it is always 'a fellow a little farther on' who speaks it. See 'Census of India,' 1901, vol. i., p. 250. The country south of the Sutlaj is now called Malwa (quite distinct, of course, from the other Malwa), and the 'Jangal' is now the uncultivated part of the said Malwa.

Page 306, last line: *Zafarabad.*—Mr. Q. P. Tate furnishes me with a reference to W. Barr's 'Kabul and the Punjab in 1839' (London, 1844), pp. 192, 193. This passage shows that there was a fortified *sarae* north of Atak fort, with a ravine between. This *sarae* was very extensive, but is now in ruins, and at present bears the name of 'Begam ki Sarae,' but the remains show that it might belong to Jahangir's time. After exhaustive research on the spot, Mr. G. P. Tate finds Atak now consists of (1) the fort, a purely military post; (2) Mallah-tola, a small village to the south; and (3) Atak town, half a mile to he north-east of the fort; it was founded about sixty years ago, on land given to persons ejected by us from their homes inside the fort. But there were formerly two villages close by, Zafarabad and Banaras, both now destroyed. The site of Zafarabad, 200 yards from the fort, is now occupied by the messhouse, officers' quarters, and other station buildings. This place may well have derived its name from Zafar Khan, son of Zain Khan, Kokah, who was appointed to the charge of Atak in Jahangir's second year (1607). See 'Tuzuk,' p. 53; Blochmann, 'A,in,' i., p. 522 (under Shukrullah). The 'Tuzuk,' p. 343, the last entry of the tenth year, notes the death of Zafar Khan, and India Office MS., No. 181, adds that he died at Ghazni.

Page 312, line 4: *Mirzaiany* (Mirza Jani).—As Allahwirdi Khan was the principal noble with Shah Shujal, it is probable that this Mirza Jani was some relation of his. Can he be the unidentified brother of Allahwirdi Khan, 'Mirza Arjanj,' mentioned in vol. iv., part v., note 69 ?

Page 318, line 32, *Jafnapatam.*—As Mr. Ferguson points out, this town is *not* on the coast of Choromandal.

Page 329, note 190, p. 337, line 4 : *Jiwan Khan.*—I learn from Mr. G. P. Tate that the correct local form of the name is Jiand; he was the eldest son of Ayub, chief of the Barozais, a branch of the Parni (or Panni) Afghans. The Barozais are still settled round Sibi in the Baluchistan Agency. As given in Mr. Tate's local authority, the story is that Jiand undertook to see Dara through the Bolan, but on some pretext quitted him on the way. A younger brother then overpowered Dara and his companions. See also Khafi Khan, ii. 84, and "Alamgirnamah,' 413, 414.

Page 350, line 17 : *Sultan Bang.*—Whatever its origin, and to whichever son it was applied, this name is found in use. See Batavia 'Dagh Register,' 1661, p. 389 (November 29, 1661), and Sir R. C. Temple's 'T. Bowrey,' p. 140, note 2, a quotation from Bernier (Constable's edition), p. 109.

Page 354, line 27: *Use of raw buffalo blood.*—Mr. Taw Sein Ko Government archaeologist in Burma, tells me that raw blood, especially human blood, was looked on as imparting courage. The blood of commanders slain in battle was drunk raw by their enemies and rivals. This barbarous custom has since been much modified by the teachings of Buddhism. Artificial ties of brotherhood were ratified by two men puncturing the arm or finger, and drinking the blood of each other mixed in spirits or water. This is called in Burmese *Thwe-thank* or 'blood-drink.' It has died out in Burma. Dr. John Anderson, 'Mandalay to Momien,' p. 329, describes a solemn sacrifice by the Khakyens at Bhamo in presence of Mr. Sladen. 'With the blood [of the buffalo] a quantity of *shamshu* was mixed, and stirred up with the points of *dahs* and spears; and each chief in turn drank from the bowl, and uttered his vow of fidelity to the common cause.'

Page 356, line 24: *Jan Tak* died at Agrah January 10, 1663. See Batavia 'Dagh Register,' 1663, p. 313.

Page 361, line 2, *Father Chesco.*—Antonio Ceschi di Santa Croce was born at Borgo (Val Sugana), February 9, 1618. and entered the novitiate at Rome in 1633. He left for India November 1, 1643; arrived at Goa August 26, 1645; made his profession at Agrah. 1651: and died at Agrah, June 26, 1656. Extracts from his letters were published at Trent in 1683. and an account of him is given in a Calendario by N. Toneatti, second year, Trent, 1857. See C. Sommervogel, 'Bibliographic de la Soc. de J.,' vol. ix. (supplement). J. Marucci, 'Relation . . .' (Paris, 1651). p. 21, says Father Ceschi had studied theology at the Roman College, and was equally well versed in mathematics. In 1648 he went to Lahor to be confessor and preacher to a governor called Mirza, a Christian high in the king's favour. The date of the Father's death is inscribed on a stone in the mortuary chapel, alias 'Padre Santus,' at Agrah. See 'Transactions of the Agrah Archaeological Society for 1876,' p. x. and 'Catholic Directory for Agra,' 1907, p. 215 (notes by Father F61ix). The inscription runs: 'Aqvi Iazo P. Antonio Ces | Ques Falceo Em Agra Aos 26 D' Ivnho D' 1656 | Borgensis, Germanvs.'

Page 363, last paragraph, *Sarmad.*—The best source for Sarmad's biography is the 'Dabistan' (Oriental Translation Fund, 3 vols., 1843), ii. 294-300. The author knew Sarmad in Sind in 1643, and says he was a Jewish rabbi converted to Mahomedanism, who took the name of Muhammad Sa'id. Sarmad and the author of the 'Dabistan' collaborated in the revision of a Persian version of the first five chapters of Genesis, which had been made by Sarmad's pupil, Abhi Chand.

ERRATA

Page LXXX, line 14, for 'Deslades,' read 'Deslandes.'—Page 38, line 15, for 'pardoned,' read 'spared.'—Page 56, line 2, for 'the river of salt,' read 'Salt River.'—Page 58, note 2, for '*Algofres*,' read '*Aljofres*.'— Page 60, note 7, line 3, for 'Home,' read 'House.'—Page 61, line 3, for 'Freanch,' read 'French.'—Page 61, line 4, for 'Brother,' read 'Frey (Friar).'—Page 62, paragraph 1 at end, insert '[40].'—Page 62, line 16, for 'Paris,' read 'Parsis.'—Page 205, line 10, for 'Khan Khakan,' read 'Khan Khanan.'—Page 211, line 10, for 'rainment,' read 'raiment.'— Page 231, line 31, for 'ew,' read 'few.'—Page 366, under Introduction line 3, for 'pp. 424-431,' read 'pp. 398-405.'